SHATTERED LANDS

Shattered Lands

Five Partitions and the
Making of Modern Asia

SAM DALRYMPLE

WILLIAM
COLLINS

William Collins
An imprint of HarperCollins*Publishers*
1 London Bridge Street
London SE1 9GF

WilliamCollinsBooks.com

HarperCollins*Publishers*
Macken House, 39/40 Mayor Street Upper
Dublin 1, D01 C9W8, Ireland

First published in Great Britain in 2025 by William Collins

3

Copyright © Sam Dalrymple 2025

Sam Dalrymple asserts the moral right to be identified
as the author of this work in accordance with the
Copyright, Designs and Patents Act 1988

A catalogue record for this book is
available from the British Library

HB ISBN 978-0-00-8466817
TPB ISBN 978-0-00-8466824

All rights reserved. No part of this publication may be
reproduced, stored in a retrieval system, or transmitted,
in any form or by any means, electronic, mechanical,
photocopying, recording or otherwise, without the
prior permission of the publishers.

Without limiting the author's and publisher's exclusive
rights, any unauthorised use of this publication to train
generative artificial intelligence (AI) technologies is expressly
prohibited. HarperCollins also exercise their rights under
Article 4(3) of the Digital Single Market Directive 2019/790
and expressly reserve this publication from the text and
data mining exception.

Maps by Martin Brown

Set in Dante MT Std
Printed and bound in the UK using 100%
renewable electricity at CPI Group (UK) Ltd

This book contains FSC™ certified paper and other controlled
sources to ensure responsible forest management.

For more information visit: www.harpercollins.co.uk/green

To Mum and Dad

CONTENTS

	Maps	ix
	Introduction	1
1	The Great Uprising	9
2	The First Partitions of India	33
3	The Drums of War	50
4	The Long March	71
5	War in the Borderlands	98
6	Direct Action Day	130
7	Dividing an Empire	163
8	A Red Dawn	195
9	Into the Abyss	217
10	The Fall of Hyderabad	248
11	Mother Tongues	281
12	The Last Days of the Raj	304
13	Proxy Wars	325
14	Liberation	363
15	The Partition of Pakistan	395
	Epilogue	425
	Appendix: Princely States	431
	Notes	433
	Acknowledgements	487
	List of Illustrations	493
	Index	497

MAPS

The Indian Empire, 1921	x–xi
British India, 1921	xii
The Indian Empire, April 1937	xiii
Southern Asia, 1961	xiv
East Pakistan at the start of 1971	xv
The former Indian Empire	xvi
The Simon Commission's journey, 1928–9	17
Mahatma Gandhi's route, 1929–31	38
The possible borders for Burma	46
The Long March, 1942	81
The Japanese Empire, 1942	100
Imphal and Kohima, 1944	125
Muslim populations in India, 1945	150
India and Pakistan in August 1947, before the accession of the Princely States	205
The Arabian Raj, 1962	284
Greater Nagaland	328
The languages of Bangladesh	412

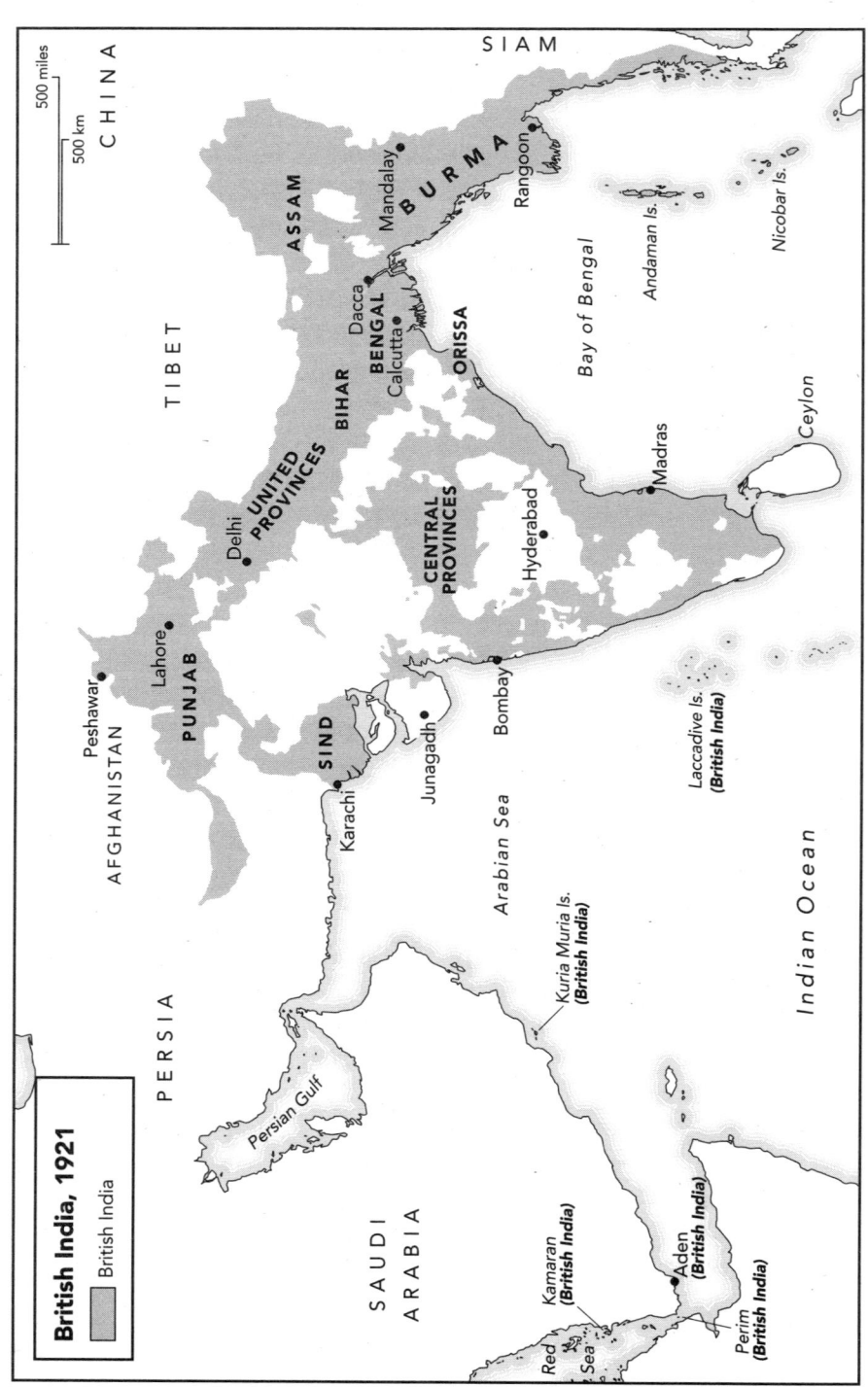

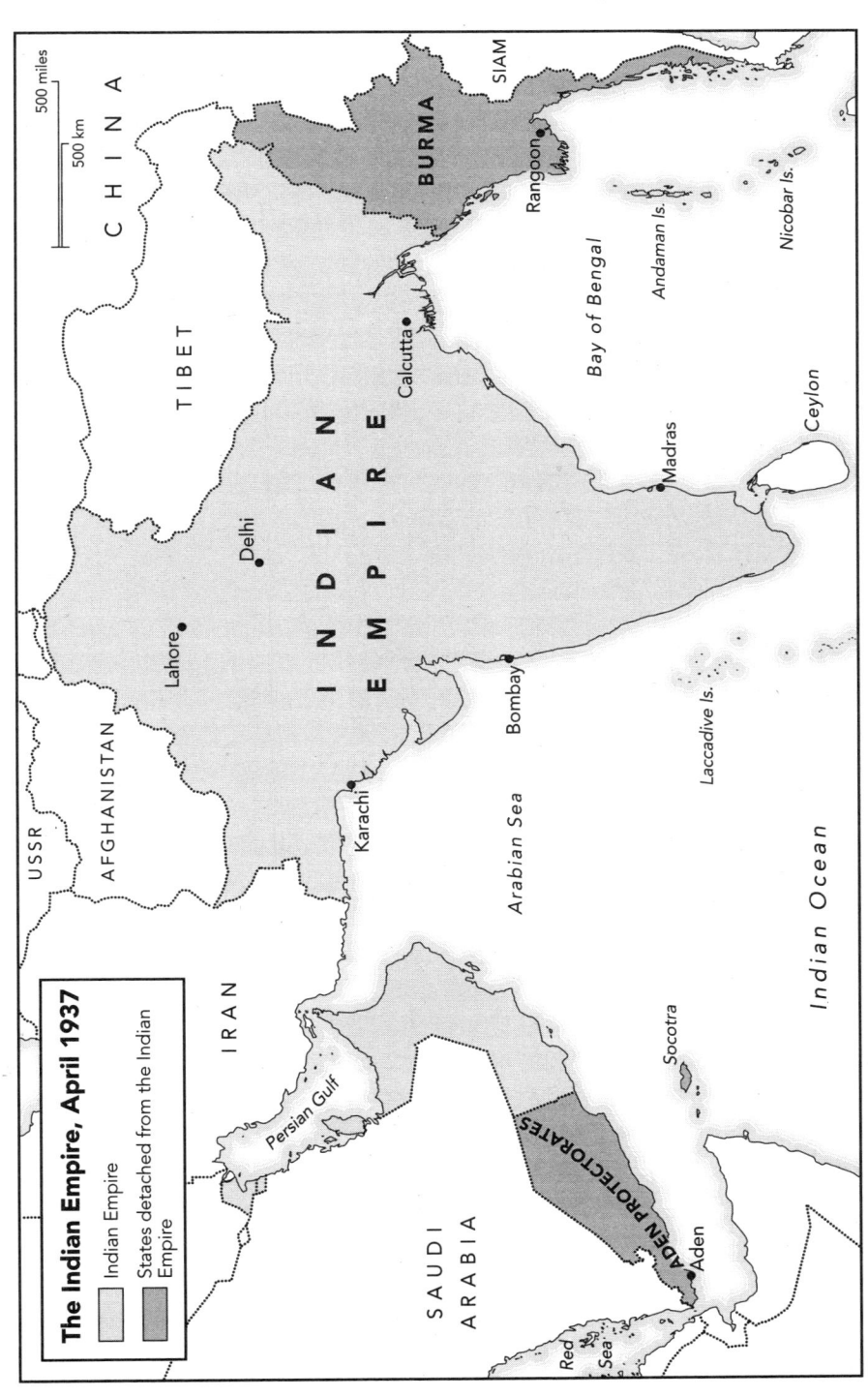

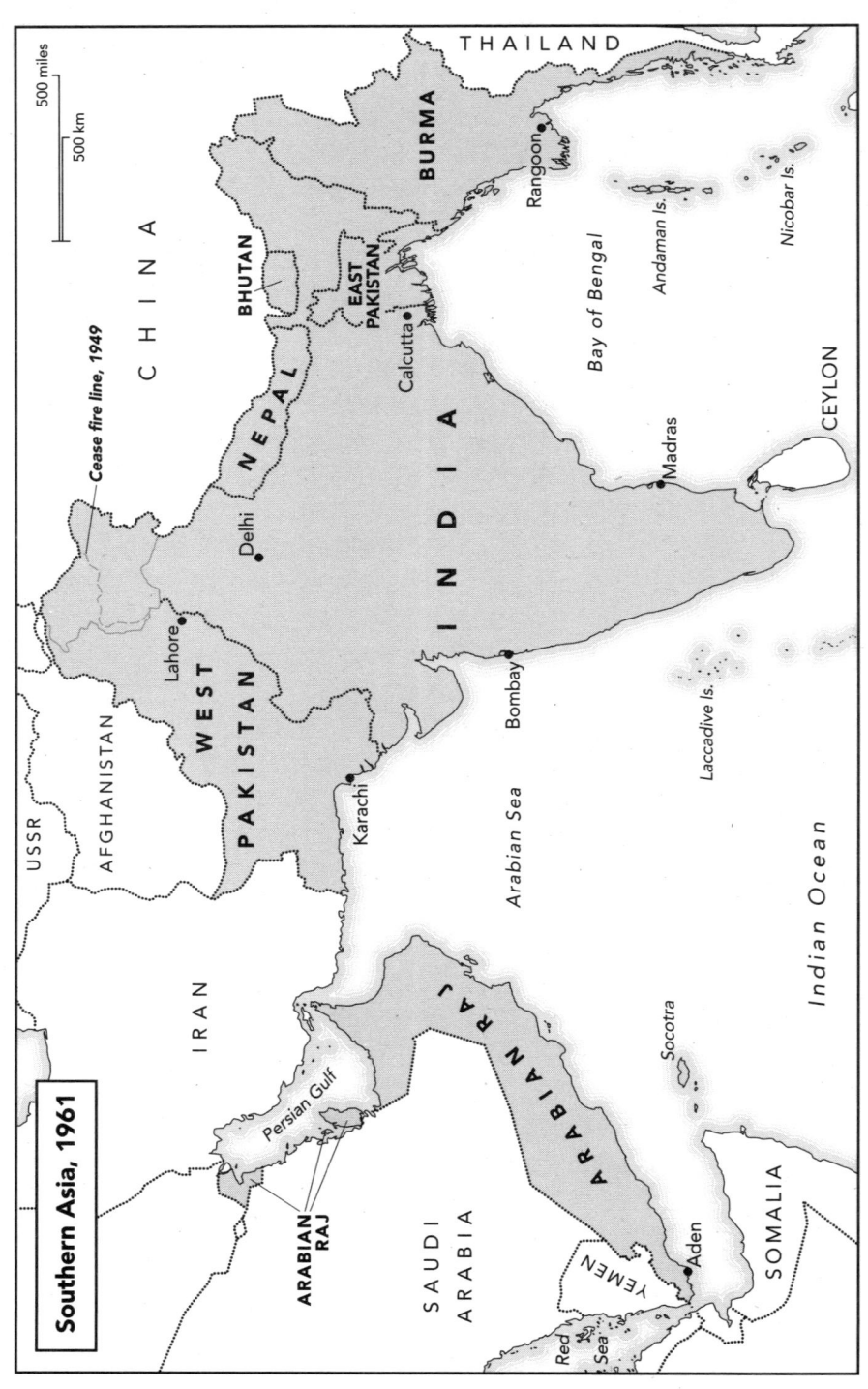

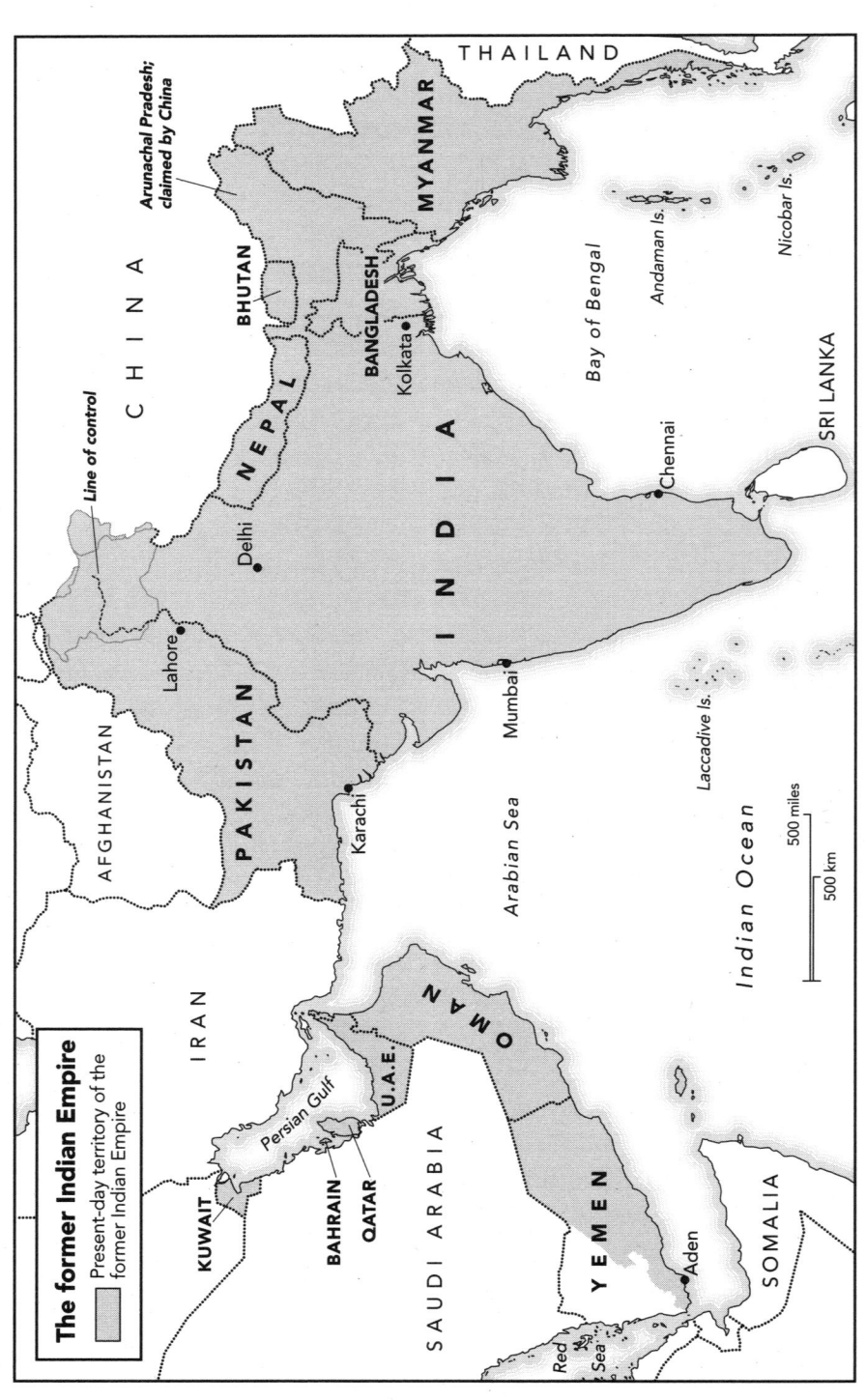

INTRODUCTION

You can't actually see the Great Wall of China from space. It's a myth. Even if you were to squint your eyes while peering down at earth from the International Space Station you would not be able to see it.

But the border wall dividing India from Pakistan is unmistakable.

For more than three thousand kilometres, from the Arabian Sea to the icecaps of Kashmir, a line intended to divide Hindus from Muslims is visibly etched onto the surface of the globe. Three layers of fencing, three and a half metres high, are accompanied by 150,000 floodlights, thermal vision sensors and rows of landmines.[1]

This wall has, for the most part, rendered Indians and Pakistanis completely inaccessible to one another, and until recently one of the only times that they *could* interact without going abroad was to attend a ceremony at the Wagah border post. Here, every evening at sunset, two national flags would be lowered, and the turbaned border security forces of either country proceeded to aggressively goose-step at one another in a jingoistic pantomime that wouldn't be out of place in Monty Python. 'Long Live India,' cried the crowd from one side. 'Long Live Pakistan,' cried the other.

The India–Pakistan border isn't the only heavily armed frontier in the region. Today South Asia is one of the most fortified, fenced and landmined zones on the planet. The barrier dividing Bangladesh from India, for example, is the longest in the world, fitted with thermal-imaging sensors and guarded by drones via a satellite-signal command system. Sixteen hundred kilometres of fencing is currently being built to divide India from Burma.[2]

Yet astonishingly, a century ago none of these borders existed.

As recently as 1928, a vast swathe of Asia – India, Pakistan, Bangladesh, Burma, Nepal, Bhutan, Yemen, Oman, the UAE, Qatar, Bahrain and Kuwait – were bound together under a single imperial banner, an entity known officially as the Indian Empire, or more simply as *the Raj*. It was the British Empire's crown jewel, a vast dominion stretching from the Red Sea to the jungles of Southeast Asia, home to a quarter of the world's population and encompassing the largest Hindu, Muslim, Sikh and Zoroastrian communities on the planet. Its people used the Indian rupee, were issued passports stamped 'Indian Empire', and were guarded by armies garrisoned in forts from the Bab el-Mandeb to the Himalayas.[3]

And then, in the space of just fifty years, the Indian Empire shattered. Five Partitions tore it apart, carving out new nations, redrawing maps, and leaving behind a legacy of war, exile and division.

At the start of 1928, however, few could have imagined how rapidly the Indian Empire would unravel. To most, the Raj still seemed an unshakeable force, its dominion stretching across much of Asia. Indeed on the first day of that year, as snow, sleet and rain showered down onto the streets of London, the British Empire tried for the very first time to contact extraterrestrial life.[4]

It had been a decade since the end of the Great War, and Britain was a country firmly looking towards its future. Aeroplanes were flying over the Atlantic Ocean and there was concern about a new phenomenon called 'traffic'.[5] The British Empire was at its zenith and now it prepared to reach into space as well. Britain's new public radio service, the BBC, had been founded a few years earlier, and as tens of thousands of people tuned in that morning, they could make out the voice of a man with a clipped London drawl. 'Hullo all stars and nebulae,' he began. 'A greeting to all friendly planets circling with us on the everlasting tour.' Have 'our waves' reached you yet?

A pause followed as the broadcaster waited for an answer to arrive from the stars, but none was forthcoming. 'Reply if you please,' he entreated, but again silence ensued. 'London's Message to Mars: No Reply Received' was the main headline on newspaper stands that week.[6]

Instead of speaking to aliens, therefore, the BBC presenter changed tack and turned to address the people of the British Empire, from London to Toronto and from Cape Town to Calcutta. As well as addressing 'the colonies' more generally, a message from King George V was specifically directed to 'the people of India', who represented four-fifths of the British Empire and a quarter of the world's total population. 'I reciprocate your earnest hopes,' the King told his Indian subjects, 'that 1928 may be the dawn of a new era of peace, happiness and prosperity to you all.'[7]

The 'India' he was addressing was almost twice as large as modern India, yet today its scale has been largely forgotten; few books acknowledge its reach into present-day Yemen, Dubai, Burma or Nepal.[8] Even at the time, Britain played down the size of the Indian Empire for diplomatic reasons, and maps depicting it in its entirety were only published in top secrecy.[9] The Viceroy's informal protectorates over Nepal and Oman were never officially recognised as such, and the Himalayan states that bordered China's dependency of Tibet were coloured yellow on Indian Imperial maps for only ten years (1897–1906). Similarly the Arab states bordering the Ottoman Empire were usually left off Imperial maps altogether, to avoid aggravating Constantinople.[10]

Nonetheless, these protectorates were all legally part of 'India' under the Interpretation Act of 1889.* They were run by the Indian Political Service, defended by the Indian Army, and subservient to the Viceroy of India. The standard list of princely states even opened alphabetically with Abu Dhabi (see Appendix), and Viceroy Lord Curzon himself argued that Oman should be considered 'as much a Native State of the Indian Empire as Lus Beyla or Kelat'.[11] The absence of these states from British maps was much remarked upon at the time, and a lecturer to the Royal Asian Society even joked that:

> As a jealous sheikh veils his favourite wife, so the British authorities shroud conditions in the Arab states in such thick mystery that ill-disposed propagandists might almost be excused for thinking that something dreadful is going on there.[12]

---

* This Act defined India as 'any territories of any Native Prince or Chief under the suzerainty of His Majesty, exercised through the Governor General of India or through any Governor or other officer subordinate to the Governor General of India'. This definition even included Nepal and Oman – both informal protectorates that were included in lists of princely states despite never formally being recognised as such. For more, see Willis, J. M. 'Making Yemen Indian: Rewriting the Boundaries of Imperial Arabia' in the *International Journal of Middle East Studies*. 2009. 41 (1): 23–38.

In fact, protectorates such as these constituted almost a third of the Indian Empire: Britain never ruled over all of modern-day India and from Jaipur to Hyderabad, six hundred thousand square miles of the Indian Empire's territory were controlled by monarchs who had given up their foreign policy and defence to the British Viceroy of India but were otherwise independent.[13] These states could vary wildly from minute principalities to considerable countries in their own right: Kashmir was larger than France, Travancore's population was greater than Austria's, and Hyderabad's economy was a similar size to Belgium's.[14]

The Maharajas, Sheikhs and Nizams who ruled these kingdoms were often fabulously wealthy figures. After the death of J. D. Rockefeller in 1937, *Time* magazine named the Nizam of Hyderabad the richest man in the world and the fifth richest in history. British administrators and Indian nationalists frequently dismissed these princes as absurd feudal rulers with an average of '11 titles, 5.8 wives, 12.6 children, 9.2 elephants shot, 2.8 private railway cars, 3.4 Rolls Royce's, and 22.9 tigers killed' between them.[15] Yet the princes were so much more than this. The Maharaja of Mysore was a celebrated philosopher whose state modernised faster than many British-ruled territories, and the Nawab of Rampur built up the most extensive library in Asia. After the fall of the Ottoman Caliphate, the Nizam of Hyderabad was arguably the world's foremost Muslim ruler and his capital the most prominent city of Muslim learning outside the Arab world.

All the lands within the Raj had been connected by trade, marriage and faith long before the British had ever arrived, and until the twentieth century even religious boundaries in the region were fluid. For large swathes of the Indian Empire, devotion to multiple faiths at once was seen as no more contradictory than subscribing to both religion and science. Punjabi Hindu *Khatris* traditionally raised their eldest son as a Sikh, while in Kerala the Virgin Mary was sometimes worshipped as the sister of the Goddess Bhagavati.[16]

Then, with the First World War, everything changed.

By 1919 the war effort had cost the Indian Empire nearly £146.2 million – £14 billion today – and more than a million Indian soldiers had fought overseas, only to return home to find their country unchanged, their rights denied.[17] White-only clubs still dotted the subcontinent, and while incremental reforms granted Indian politicians token positions at the provincial level, true power remained in British hands. The Indian Empire generated vast wealth, yet Indians had little say in how it was spent.

Indian nationalists, emboldened by increasing anti-colonial rhetoric, began to press harder for self-determination. Then, in 1919 British Indian troops under General Dyer marched into a walled garden in Amritsar, blocked the only exit and opened fire on unarmed protesters. Hundreds were killed, perhaps over a thousand. For many Indians, the massacre marked a turning point – proof that the government of British India would never reform itself, only repress.

And so, even as the BBC spoke of Britain reaching the stars, opposition to British rule was hardening on the ground. That very day, as the *Taunton Courier* reported on the empire's attempt to talk to aliens, another story appeared beside a column on the mysterious death of three hundred pigeons. India's largest political party, the Indian National Congress, had recently voted to affirm 'the goal of ... complete national independence'.[18]

The nationalist leader Jawaharlal Nehru had proposed the motion in Madras, the capital of India's humid south.[19] He did this because the British government was planning to write a new constitution for their Indian colony, and the Simon Commission, formed to suggest reforms, had not included even a single Indian on its committee. In fact, most of the Commissioners had never been east of Paris yet they would now be answering the most pressing questions in India's modern history. What was India? Who counted as Indian? And the most important of all – should the Indian Empire be Partitioned?

Demands for 'independence' were widespread, and no one could have suspected that day that the nations of India, Pakistan, Bangladesh, Yemen and Burma would soon emerge from the wreckage of British India. Nor would anyone have imagined that tiny princely states like Bhutan and Dubai would last until the end of the century while massive states like Hyderabad would not. Many of these countries have retrospectively written their histories back into the ancient past. But as late as 1928, not one of the borders that later sliced through South Asia was foreseen.

This book tells, for the first time, one of the great epics of the twentieth century: the extraordinary story of how Five Partitions transformed Britain's Indian Empire into twelve nation states.

The shattering of the Indian Empire began in 1937,* when the first largely forgotten partition carved Burma out from India to fulfil a decades-old demand by the ethnic Bamar community, as well as the desire of Hindu nationalists for 'India' to match the boundaries of the ancient Hindu holy land 'Bharat'. The results would be devastating, triggering famine, a catastrophic migration crisis and laying the seeds for several insurgencies.

A second partition – the Partition of the Arabian Peninsula from India – started the same year with the separation of Aden, and would be completed a decade later with the transfer of the Persian Gulf states in April 1947. Were it not for this separation, most of the Arabian Peninsula except for Saudi Arabia might have become part of India or Pakistan after independence. But instead the states of the Gulf would be the only princely monarchies except for Nepal and Bhutan to survive intact into the twenty-first century.

In 1947 tensions between India's majority Hindu community and the enormous Muslim minority culminated in what might be called the 'Great Partition' of British India,[20] and the creation of Pakistan out of the Muslim majority districts in the east and west of the subcontinent. As the country was torn apart, India descended into violence on an epic scale, precipitating the largest forced migration in human history. Pakistani historian Ayesha Jalal has called it 'the central historical event in twentieth-century South Asia', one that continues to inform how a quarter of the world 'envisage their past, present and future'.[21]

A fourth partition – the Partition of Princely India – occurred the same year. Much of the shape of modern India, Pakistan and Burma was actually determined by the decisions of the Indian princes, rather than British administrators, who chose to 'integrate' their kingdoms with one of the new countries, or become independent. Integration took place mostly along religious lines, with Muslim kingdoms integrating with Pakistan, Buddhist ones with Burma and so on. Yet several large kingdoms broke with this trend, and the massive and overwhelmingly Hindu Jodhpur State very nearly joined Pakistan rather than India. The decisions of these princes would determine over half of the

---

* The much earlier separation of the Straits Settlements in 1867 and the Somaliland Protectorate in 1898 fall outside the remit of this study, which focuses on the period after the introduction of the first Indian Empire passports after the First World War.

India–Pakistan border – more than 80 per cent if we exclude modern Bangladesh.

Finally, twenty-four years later in 1971, the fledgling nation of Pakistan was itself torn apart, this time by civil war, and after a fifth and final partition, East Pakistan gained independence as Bangladesh. South Asia's youngest nation was born and India became the region's undisputed power. The same year, the British abolished their protectorates over the Gulf states: the last of India's princely states to gain complete independence from imperial rule.

Each of these Five Partitions were linked, influencing the next like a set of dominos, and in ways that are often overlooked today. Standard Indian histories often describe 'Undivided India' – roughly modern India, Pakistan and Bangladesh – as a timeless entity, later divided by British policies and Muslim nationalist demands. In reality, this 'Undivided India' was itself a colonial construct, existing only for five months in 1947 following the overlooked partitions of Burma and Arabia. Hindu nationalism was a key driving force in these earlier partitions, envisaging an independent India that resembled the ancient Hindu holy land of Bharat including neither Burma nor Arabia. As we shall see, the Arabian and Burmese frontiers of the Raj were once central to the very idea of India, and several of the founding fathers of Yemen and Burma had even once conceived of themselves as Indian nationalists. As late as the 1920s, the nationalist campaigns of Gandhi and Jinnah had as much of an impact there as anywhere else.

India is not the only country in the region to ignore its complex past. In the decades since 1971, nationalist historians of each of the Raj's successor states have argued that their countries were inevitable. Bangladeshi nationalists, for example, often claim that Bengali Muslims were always fated to form their own nation state and Burmese nationalists often refer to a 'separation' from India, rather than a partition, despite the numerous communities who were divided from one another as a result. Many nationalists from former protectorates of the Indian Empire such as Nepal and the UAE even claim that they were *always* independent, and ignore their former place in the Indian Empire entirely. This book, on the contrary, shows that as late as the 1920s, none of the nation states we see today – from Burma to India to Kuwait – were inevitable.

Even as new borders were being drawn, people assumed that cross-border relationships and trade would continue as before. For more than two millennia, South Asian communities and their cultures had spread out across Asia into China, Afghanistan and Arabia, and from East Africa to Southeast Asia. As European empires were torn apart in the twentieth century, these ancient social and commercial links could have been rekindled. But instead new national identities only hardened. Countless communities found themselves on the wrong side of new borders, leaving a series of suppurating wounds that continue to bleed into the present.

The collapse of the Indian Empire has remarkably never been told as a single story. With every division archives were scattered across twelve nation states – thirteen if we include Britain. Subsequent divisions between the 'Middle East', 'South Asia' and 'Southeast Asia' crystallised after the Second World War. Each Partition is now studied by a different group of scholars and the ties that once linked a quarter of the world lie forgotten. In 2011 Burmese author Thant Myint-U wrote:

> Almost no one I knew in Delhi had ever been to Burma, and ... I was told there are no Burmese-speaking experts in India. Instead, there were hints of a slightly forlorn connection: a relative who had been born in Burma, a recipe that had been kept in the family after a time spent long ago in Rangoon, a sense of old religious or cultural affinity, an interest, but otherwise little knowledge.[22]

Thanks to revolution and social upheaval, the history of the Indian Empire sank into the depths of numerous national archives. In this way, separated by international and academic borders, one incredible tale has itself been partitioned into several very different narratives.

This book, for the first time, presents the whole story of how the Indian Empire was unmade. How a single, sprawling dominion became twelve modern nations. How maps were redrawn in boardrooms and on battlefields, by politicians in London and revolutionaries in Delhi, by kings in remote palaces and soldiers in trenches.

It is a history of ambition and betrayal, of forgotten wars and unlikely alliances, of borders carved with ink and fire. And, above all, it is the story of how the map of modern Asia was made.

1

The Great Uprising

Three weeks after the BBC's ill-fated attempt to contact 'extraterrestrials', the head of the eponymous Simon Commission, Lord John Simon, was preparing to travel to India. 'The sendoff from Victoria was extraordinary,' he wrote to his mother on 20 January 1928.

One of the best-paid barristers of his generation, Simon was a gaunt well-dressed man with wispy silver hair who believed fervently that 'the best families' should make sure to smoke cigarettes rather than cigars. Now, despite having never been to India, he had been placed in charge of suggesting new constitutional reforms for Britain's largest and most lucrative colony. 'We are in for a very difficult time,' he wrote to his ailing mother shortly before departure, and 'can only try'.[1]

Nonetheless, everything got off to a terrific start. The prime minister and a sea of India Office officials had enthusiastically waved them off from the station, and Simon and his six companions crossed the English Channel 'in style'.[2] At Marseilles they boarded the RMS *Mooltan* for India, and here Simon was thrilled to discover his wife's packing had included 'labels on everything, and lists, and medicines all ticketed'. That evening he scribbled another letter to his mother, writing, 'Isn't she a perfect wife!'[3]

In the coming days Simon and his companions cruised past an erupting volcano off the coast of Italy and upon reaching Egypt managed to delay their entire ship to visit the Tutankhamun treasures. It was a 'cheery party,' felt Simon, and although they didn't have as much time for board games as he would have liked, the journey was mesmerising. From Port Said they passed down the desolate limestone crags of the Gulf of Suez and on through the Red Sea to India.[4]

'India' in 1928 began in Aden, the Victorian harbour where the Red Sea opened into the Indian Ocean, and the party reached it on 29 January. Perched in a volcanic crater between enormous fists of igneous stone, Aden was the Indian Empire's westernmost bastion, the largest city in the Arabian Peninsula, and like the rest of Indian Arabia it was governed as part of Bombay Province. 'I had, in fact, a fairly clear picture in my mind of what it would be like,' wrote the literary celebrity Evelyn Waugh who visited Aden around the same time as the Simon Commission: 'A climate notoriously corrosive of all intellect and initiative; a landscape barren of any growing or living thing ... How wrong I was.' Waugh's skin colour had catapulted him into Adeni high society, and in less than a week he had attended 'a dance at the club, a ball at the residency, and a very convivial party given by the sappers'. There were piano recitals of 'God Save the King', followed by a trip to the club 'for beer, oysters and bridge'. Yet venturing away from white society Waugh observed a city racked with division, and in a small club in the ramshackle 'native' part of town a group of Arabs complained to him that they were low on the racial hierarchy in the Indian Empire. The Bank of India would prefer to give loans to Europeans and mainland Indians rather than to Arabs.[5]

Aden would later become the capital of South Yemen, and already the links tying it to India were fraying. But such tensions were completely lost on the Simon Commissioners, who were in a rush to get to Bombay. They merely greeted the military governor, who handed them dispatches from the Viceroy, then hurriedly changed ships onto the SS *Rawalpindi* and set sail for the Indian mainland.

It was only when they entered Bombay harbour that they finally learned the scale of opposition to their arrival. 'The atmosphere was cold and murky,' wrote Simon's companion, the Conservative MP Edward Cadogan, and 'any less ... exhilarating [arrival] ... could not be conceived'.[6] It was pouring with rain, and demonstrators lined the dockyard shouting, 'Simon go back.' Another of Simon's companions, a young Clement Attlee, 'cut a very sorry figure when tackled by the press people' and 'was so hopelessly flabbergasted by the volley of questions that his hand began to shiver as he tried to light his pipe'. Attlee, like the rest of the Simon Commission, had been chosen for the job precisely *because* he 'had a virgin mind' on Indian affairs and had no idea how to respond to the questions being thrown at him.[7] Indeed, other than the 'veritable library of books' on India that he had been supplied with before departure, his only experience of the country had been a stint in a Bombay hospital bed during the Great War. Unbeknown to anyone at the time, this soggy nervous wreck would be the man to grant India her freedom two decades later.[8]

For now the Simon Commissioners hastened into their vehicles and set off to meet the governor. The drive finally afforded an opportunity to admire the city, a maritime London dropped in the tropics and populated by Bohra merchants, Marathi labourers, Parsi industrialists and Gujarati aristocrats. Gothic spires towered over art deco hotels, and they 'drove round the sun-bathed Malabar Point, the sapphire sea on one side and brilliant-hued flowering shrubs on the other'.[9]

At last they reached the elite suburb of Malabar Hill, over which towered Government House. Governor Wilson, a freemason and former marine, was already waiting for them, and after refreshments they gathered in the governor's sitting room to discuss their plans. Wilson was not as enthusiastic about their presence as they had hoped, however. The protests at the harbour had consisted of little more than a hundred people, he told them, but he 'would not have been surprised had there been ten thousand hostile demonstrators'.[10] Moreover, it emerged that a bomb had been prepared for them and they had only escaped due to the bomber dropping it 'from the rack of a railway carriage with unfortunate results for himself'.[11] A little shaken, the Commissioners decided to leave Bombay and set out for Delhi immediately.

What followed was a 'dreary train' journey past 'endless dusty coloured plains, palm trees and mud villages'. After the imperial grandeur of Bombay, Cadogan was taken aback by the 'primitive habitations' he saw out the window, and began to wonder how much British rule was really benefiting the countryside. Things didn't get any better in Delhi, and he writes tellingly, 'Beyond one of our motor-cars running over a child in the native quarter of Delhi, mercifully with no evil consequences, our first days in the capital passed without contretemps.'[12]

The purpose of the commission had been to interview people from all walks of life about how the local government could be improved, but with boycotting protesters filling the streets wherever they went, they struggled to talk to any Indian politicians at all. By mid-February they had only managed to meet Motilal Nehru, a nationalist leader whom Cadogan described as Britain's 'most inveterate foe'.[13] While staying in New Delhi's Connaught Circus, however, the Commissioners finally met another of the great Indian nationalist leaders, the man who was directing the boycott against them and who would soon change the world. His name was Muhammad Ali Jinnah.

When the Simon Commission met Jinnah in the lobby of the Western Hotel in February 1929, everything about him belied the fact that he would soon found the world's first Islamic republic: Pakistan. A reserved Gujarati barrister-turned politician who the *New York Times* described as 'undoubtedly one of the best dressed men in the British Empire', he drank whisky, ate pork and was renowned for chain-smoking cigarettes in his open-top limousine.[14]

The question of how this man evolved into the founder of Pakistan is one that has puzzled historians for close to a century, and that the Simon Commissioners themselves would reflect upon repeatedly in the years to come.

Growing up in Hindu-majority Karachi, Jinnah had originally wanted to be a Shakespearean actor, but he proved unsuccessful and instead enrolled in a law degree, resolving never to fail at anything ever again.[15] By the end of the Great War, he had become one of 'the best-paid lawyers in the country, an elected member of the Viceroy's Imperial Legislative Council; the tallest leader in Muslim politics, and well on his way to becoming the most important Congress leader'.[16] With his meticulous attention to detail, Jinnah could navigate himself precisely where he needed to be, a trait that often made him seem aloof. But those who knew him well found him to be warm and exceptionally intelligent. 'Never was there a nature whose outer qualities provided so complete an antithesis of its inner worth,' wrote Sarojini Naidu, the society hostess and nationalist poet who was a close friend of Jinnah. Jinnah, she believed, should be lauded as India's primary 'ambassador of Hindu-Muslim unity',[17] even if his cold reserve meant you did 'need a fur coat now and then'.[18] She writes,

> His accustomed reserve but masks, for those who know him, a naïve and eager humanity, an intuition as quick and tender as a woman's, a humour gay and winning as a child's. Pre-eminently

rational and practical ... his worldly wisdom effectively disguise[s] a shy and splendid idealism which is the very essence of the man.[19]

Jinnah's rise had seemed unstoppable, but in 1918 he had scandalised Bombay high society by courting Ruttie Petit, the eighteen-year-old daughter of a Parsi baronet and one of the most 'envied debutante[s] of her generation'.[20] The patriarch of the family, Sir Dinshaw Petit, happened to be a vocal supporter of interfaith marriages, believing like many liberals at the time that they would be vital in gluing India into a single nation. When forty-two-year-old Jinnah had asked to marry his teenage daughter, however, Sir Dinshaw was horrified and banned the two from meeting. Jinnah and Ruttie continued their courtship, however, and Ruttie writes that Jinnah burned 'storming passions into the very fibre of her being'. In his presence she appeared utterly radiant: 'like a fairy,' wrote one observer, and two months after her birthday they eloped, with Ruttie converting to Islam the day before the wedding.[21]

'Jinnah has at last plucked the blue flower of his desire,' wrote Sarojini Naidu, who was closely following the scandal along with the rest of Bombay society.

> It was all very sudden and caused terrible agitation and anger among the Parsis: but I think though the child has made far greater sacrifices than she yet realises, Jinnah is worth it all – he loves her: the one really genuine emotion of his reserved and self-centred nature and he will make her happy.[22]

Sarojini's optimism proved misplaced, however. Parsi society ostracised Ruttie, and her father summoned the couple to court, alleging that Jinnah had abducted her. Here Ruttie defiantly stood up and told the judge, 'Mr Jinnah has not abducted me; in fact I have abducted him.'[23] But in the aftermath she was excommunicated from her community, banned from all Parsi social occasions and told she could never return to her childhood home. Having once dreamed a modern India would be able to move past divisions of religion and caste, Jinnah became disillusioned.

For Ruttie, meanwhile, it marked the start of a lonely new life. Her husband revealed himself to be a workaholic with an 'aversion to holidays' and a tendency to forget her birthday. He spent most of his time campaigning for India's nationalist movement, and Ruttie ended up alone for months at a time.[24] Jinnah did love her of course, but as his legal assistant recalled years later:

> They were poles apart ... I remember her walking into Jinnah's chambers whilst we were in the midst of a conference, dressed in a manner which would be called fast even by modern standards, perch herself upon Jinnah's table, dangling her feet, and waiting for Jinnah to finish the conference ... [Meanwhile] Jinnah carried on with his work as if she were not there at all.[25]

The rise of Mohandas Gandhi, who began to overshadow Jinnah as India's leading nationalist politician, only added further difficulties to the Jinnahs' tumultuous marriage. Jinnah was horrified by the way Gandhi brought religion into politics and felt that under Gandhi's leadership the Congress Party was being transformed into 'an instrument for the revival of Hinduism and for the establishment of Hindu Raj [rule]'. He considered Gandhi a diaspora upstart from South Africa who had merely returned to India to cosplay as a sadhu and lecture everyone about how to 'fix' Indian culture.[26] But Gandhi's religious politics proved far more popular than Jinnah's own, and in December 1920 Jinnah was booed off stage for refusing to address Gandhi as the 'Mahatma' or 'Great Soul'. In turn, Jinnah became increasingly convinced that Gandhi was 'a fake and a demagogue',[27] and when Gandhi proposed a political boycott of British government institutions, he protested that such a move would only end up closing government schools and courts. He tried to rally nationalist leaders against Gandhi, but after months of despair, he finally announced that he was leaving the Congress altogether. 'I will have nothing to do with this pseudo religious approach to politics,' Jinnah wearily announced.[28]

Outside of Congress, however, Jinnah's political career began to decline and his relationship with Ruttie deteriorated. Depressed and alone, Ruttie sought solace in Bombay's jazz clubs while Jinnah focused on building a political base in the Muslim League – a rival political party to the Congress. But his growing emphasis on his Muslim identity only alienated Ruttie more, and one day, when she drove to meet him at the town hall, he screamed at her for packing ham sandwiches.

'What have you done!' he exclaimed. 'If my voters were to learn that I am going to eat ham sandwiches for lunch, do you think I have a ghost of a chance of being elected?'[29] Ruttie distanced herself from her husband after that, and instead started experimenting with drugs and spirit communication, leading friends to worry about the number of morphine needles she left scattered around her room.

With their marriage falling apart, both Jinnah and Ruttie neglected their newborn daughter, who would remain nameless for almost six years. The 'little baby is one of the most pathetic, heart-breaking things I have ever seen,' wrote Sarojini's daughter Padmaja Naidu to her sister in 1921. 'I simply cannot understand Ruttie's attitude – I do not blame her as most people here seem to do, but whenever I remember the dazed, scared child, like some mortally hurt animal, I come near hating Ruttie in spite of my great affection for her.' Three years later Padmaja's sister also met the child, and described her as 'the one dark shadow (an exquisite little shadow) ... [an] unnamed and unloved little baby, [who] clung to me and begged me "not to go" when I was leaving her nursery'.[30]

Jinnah, meanwhile, poured his energy into the question of Muslim representation in a future Indian parliament. Although Muslims made up a third of India's population, they were thinly spread across the country and in any new democratic system would almost always find themselves at the whims of the Hindu majority. Months before the Simon Commission's arrival, Jinnah put forward a 'bold set of proposals' for Muslim representation, which he hoped might resolve the matter.[31] Sarojini Naidu, who had recently been elected the first woman Congress president, bought him a gold casket to mark the occasion, engraved with the inscription:

To Mohammed Ali Jinnah, Ambassador of Unity. From his loyal friend and follower, Bombay, May 1927, Sarojini Naidu.[32]

It was around this time that Jinnah learned that no Indians would be included on the Simon Commission. He was quickly recognised as a leader of the anti-Simon Commission boycott, and wrote to a Labour politician: 'The exclusion of Indians from the Commission is fundamentally wrong ... [and] is calculated to humiliate and wound the self-respect of the people of India.'[33] His career was taking off again, but on 4 January 1928, three weeks before the commission's arrival, Ruttie announced she was leaving him. Afterwards they sat for hours in a train carriage, before parting ways at Bombay's Victoria station. Jinnah was 'too proud and hurt to stop her'.[34]

A month later, when the Simon Commission encountered Jinnah in the lobby of Delhi's Western Hotel, they found him 'immaculately ... attired in European dress', but a shell of his former self. Accompanying him was fellow nationalist Lajpat Rai, who immediately told Cadogan that 'he had no inclination for social interaction with any member of the Commission'. Cadogan could see that Jinnah was 'struggling to maintain' his role as an ambassador of Hindu–Muslim unity, however.[35] Cadogan would never meet Jinnah again, but another of the Simon Commissioners would, under very different circumstances. Twenty years later Clement Attlee would speak to Jinnah as the prime minister of Great Britain, while Jinnah was the founder of Pakistan, the world's first Islamic republic.

In the months following their meeting with Jinnah, the Simon Commission zigzagged their way across the Indian Empire, from the grand palaces of the Punjab to the remote tea estates of Assam. As they moved eastward, they encountered a rapidly modernising subcontinent. In the giant metropolises of Bombay, Madras, Rangoon and Calcutta, 'talkies' packed out cinemas, and across the Punjab Muslim women increasingly discarded their full-body burqas for fashionable synthetic saris. Roads and railways linked previously isolated regions to the outside world and a flood of affordable Japanese-manufactured bicycles gave labourers access to a social life far beyond their farms and villages.[36]

'Simon's Seven Dwarfs' (as they were labelled in the press) attended balls and garden parties, dined with Indian royalty and soon got into a rhythm. 'I eat and sleep well,' wrote Simon to his mother that October, 'and usually either ride a horse before breakfast or play tennis.'[37] At the same time the sheer size and diversity of India began to play on their minds. 'It seems ridiculous to treat this part of the world as the same country as Madras or Bengal,' wrote Simon on arrival in Baluchistan, the desert wastes in the western borderlands of the Indian Empire.[38] How would they write a single constitution for a landmass larger and more diverse than Europe?

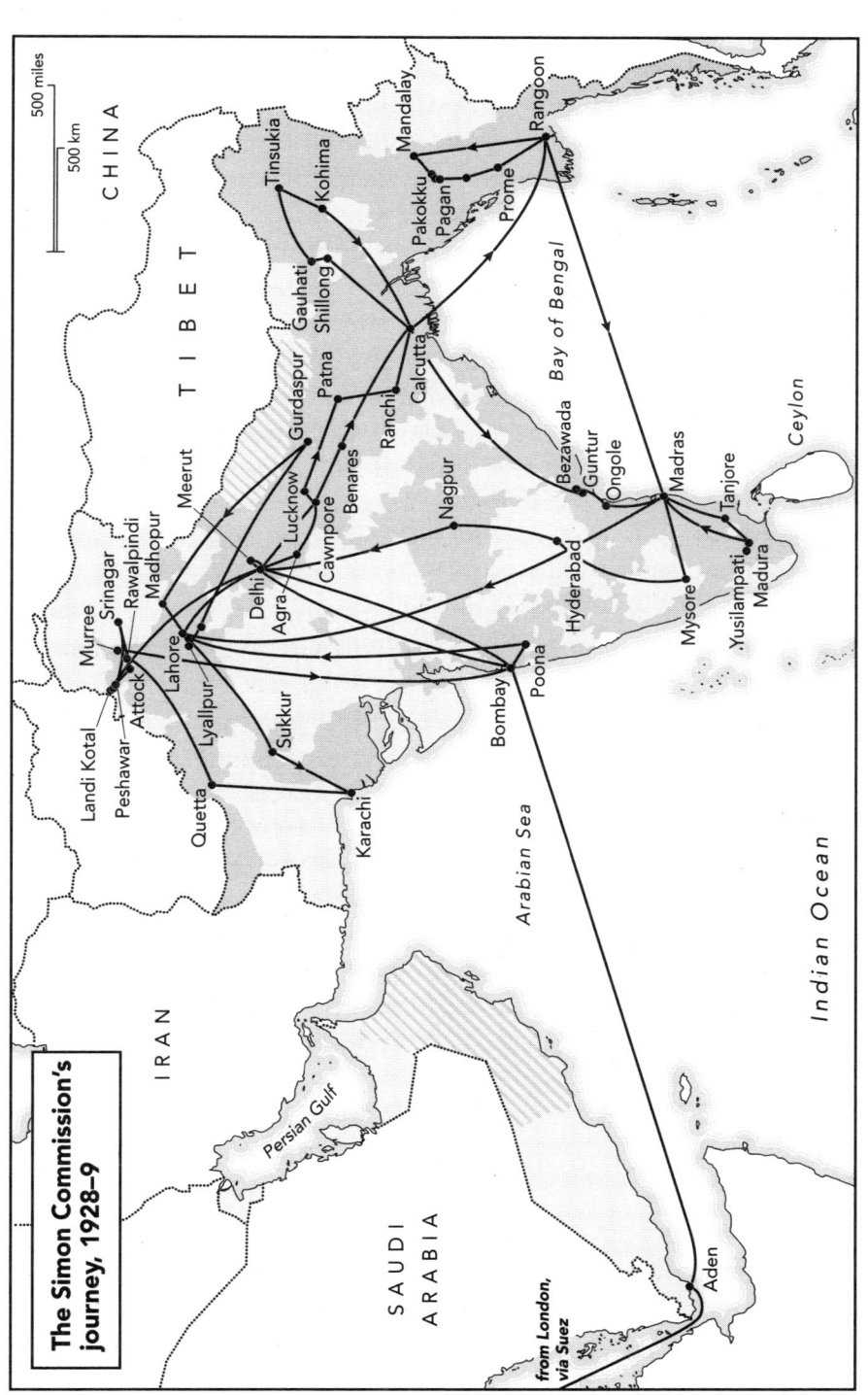

Finally, at 5 p.m. on 29 January 1929, after a year of travel, the motley crew of men arrived in India's easternmost province of Burma aboard the SS *Tairea*, berthing opposite the Sule Pagoda in downtown Rangoon as a stream of young men in black morning coats and white topees lined up on the wharf to greet them.[39] Rangoon is 'a fine city,' Attlee wrote to his brother Tom, and its grand pagodas were 'rather jolly, being all gilded'. The Commissioners refused to visit any of these pagodas, however, due to 'sundry quarrels about removing shoes'.[40]

In recent years Rangoon had transformed from the old teak port into an imperial metropolis of classical pediments and Victorian boulevards, with gardens that 'bloomed with tropical profusion – bougainvillea, poinsettias, laburnum and tall delphiniums of piercing blue'.[41] The economy was booming, attracting Armenian, Tamil, Bengali, Chinese and Japanese traders, and in the 1920s more migrant workers set sail for Burma than across the Atlantic Ocean. The Burmese Dream was rapidly outpacing the American one and as one British labour official wrote shortly after the Simon Commission's visit:

> [Rangoon] was till recently second only to New York in importance as an immigration port. It now occupies pride of place as the first immigration and emigration port of the world.[42]

Yet not all Rangoon's residents welcomed this influx of immigrants. Indigenous Burmese communities found themselves increasingly pushed out of work, and Burma – despite being the largest and richest province in the Raj – was routinely sidelined in Indian politics. It was called the Cinderella Province, 'beautiful and ignored compared to its sisters, Madras, Bengal and Bombay, a Cinderella perhaps, for whom the shoe never fitted'.[43] What's more, Indian elites frequently treated the Burmese 'as a heretic hill-tribe',[44] and when the Nobel laureate Rabindranath Tagore visited, he had felt that the Burmese were suffering from 'double colonialism'.[45] Much like Aden, the first city the commission had visited in the Indian Empire, therefore, Rangoon was thus now questioning its connection with India. Unlike in Aden, however, the Simon Commission were explicitly asked to consider whether Burma should be separated from India and made into a distinct colony.

A century later the border between India and Burma is often treated as unremarkable; a natural border that always existed. But this was certainly not the case when the Simon Commission arrived in the province. Indeed at the time there was a huge amount of opposition to even separating Burma at all. Many Burmese worried that separation would eviscerate their thriving economy, and Burma's most prominent politician at the time, U Ottama, argued that Burma was an integral part of the Indian nation. A short Buddhist monk with large ears and a scar on his forehead, Ottama had joined the Indian National Congress at a young age, and brought Gandhi's non-violent campaigns to Burma. So closely was he identified with the Mahatma that upon him being arrested by the British authorities, eight thousand people gathered at the Shwedagon Pagoda in protest, christening him 'Mahatma Ottama'. The unfortunate magistrate who convicted Ottama later had his sister's funeral boycotted.[46]

By the time the Simon Commision arrived, therefore, the separation of Burma was not yet a given, and it is fully possible to imagine a world in which Burma had remained a part of independent India as its easternmost province. But the Simon Commission had made up their minds before they even arrived and shortly before sailing into Rangoon harbour, Simon had written to his mother, 'Burma is not really India at all.' There was a sense among many British officers that its people were racially distinct from the rest of India, and since no railways crossed the Patkai Hills that divided Burma from Bengal and Assam, most Brits had never been there.[47] Even the letters of Attlee – a liberal and anti-colonial member of the Labour Party – were dominated by casual racism and racial stereotypes. 'The Burmans are very cheery looking folk – rather Japanese ... [but with] an unfortunate propensity to murder,' he wrote to his brother after a few days in Rangoon.[48]

To make matters worse, Burma's Anti-Separation League boycotted the Simon Commission, and as a result, the Commissioners met only those who supported separation. On their second day in the city, a wealthy Indian merchant and his English wife held a garden party to introduce the commission to local socialites. It was a picturesque scene, with tea tables arranged by a lake and a young Burmese girl dressed in the old costume of the Mandalay court dancing for the guests. A cool wind fluttered through the tablecloths and the commission got to work, chatting away with senior officials about whether or not Burma should be separated from India. Yet district magistrate Maurice Collis noticed that the Burmese themselves 'were not much in evidence' and that the local British governors the commission had interviewed seemed to have decided on separation already.[49] 'We had a most interesting visit to Burma,' wrote Attlee later, 'and speedily arrived at the conclusion that its inclusion in the Indian Empire was a mistake.'[50]

By the time they left Burma, the Simon Commissioners were convinced that support for separation was near-total. The resulting controversy was plastered over every newspaper in India. 'This attitude towards the "separation" question is, indeed, one which strikes deep into the very existence of India,' wrote the correspondent of the *Scotsman*.

> If one province breaks loose, no reason can be shown why similar claims by others should not be granted.[51]

Over the course of their trip from Aden to Rangoon, the Simon Commission had conspicuously failed to meet one Indian in particular, someone who, along with Muhammad Ali Jinnah, would change the face of Asia forever. Soon after the Commissioners returned to London, however, Mahatma Gandhi set sail for Rangoon himself.

Gandhi had recently finished writing his autobiography, and over the next year and a half he would be one of the last people to traverse the vast territory of the Indian Empire, from Rangoon to Aden, while it was all still a part of India.[52] His story was already famous: the son of Porbandar State's chief minister, Gandhi had grown up in a Gujarati-speaking family on the coast of the Arabian Sea. At the age of thirteen he was married to the fourteen-year-old Kasturba, and after the birth of their first child he had sailed to London to study as a lawyer. Here he had passed the bar at the Inner Temple, taking classes in ballroom dancing and dressing 'like a Wildean dandy' complete with 'silk top hat, starched collar, rainbow-coloured tie … and a silver mounted stick'.[53] Gandhi had been an avowed imperialist at the time, a very different man from the one who would later gain international fame, but when he moved to South Africa to open a legal practice his views began to change. Here, despite his valid first-class ticket, he was thrown off a train at Pietermaritzburg because of the colour of his skin. Horrified by the discrimination, Gandhi started protesting racial injustices and, over the course of several decades, emerged as the most prominent civil rights leader in the world.[54]

In 1915, a year after the outbreak of the Great War, Gandhi returned to India and took over the Indian National Congress, transforming it from an elite institution into a grassroots national movement. He didn't initially call for political independence, however, and his early campaigns had more to do with spiritual liberation. Indeed Gandhi viewed the political and the spiritual as inseparable, and he ran his campaigns from a simple ashram on the banks of the Sabarmati river. Colonial officials found him completely perplexing, and one governor described him as being 'cunning as a cartload of monkeys'.[55] Nonetheless, Gandhi's message of non-violent struggle transformed him into a pan-Indian figurehead, and perhaps the single most famous person in the world.[56] 'You have not heard about him?' Nobel laureate Romain Rolland once asked the British naval commander-in-chief's daughter. 'He is another Christ!'[57]

The morning that Gandhi's ship pulled into Rangoon on 7 March 1929, the sea was calm and the deck resounded with recitations of Tulsidas' poetic epic 'The Ramayana'. With the rising dawn, Gandhi could see the distant smoke billowing from the city's factories, mills and oil refineries, and soon he made out a 'monster cosmopolitan gathering' of people from across the Raj jostling on the extensive waterfront jetties to greet him.[58] 'The crowd cried out, "Long live Mahatma Gandhi!"' recalled a Burmese writer who was present, and 'a young boy watching up a palm tree clapped his hands with glee, and fell down'.[59] As the gangway was lowered, and before Gandhi could even step onto dry land, a mob of journalists charged aboard to bombard him with questions. Why had he come to Rangoon at such a critical moment? they asked. Had he 'come to advise and influence the Burmese on the burning question of the hour ... separation?'[60]

In fact, Gandhi had come to visit his law-school friend Pranjivan Mehta, scion of a Rangoon jewellery firm who had founded the Burmese wing of the Congress and now bankrolled Gandhi's non-violent *satyagraha* campaigns. But the Mahatma's attitude towards separation was already well known. Two years earlier he had come out as the most high-profile proponent for Burma's separation from the Indian Empire, writing: 'I have no doubt in my mind that Burma cannot form part of India under *Swaraj* [Self-rule].'[61]

Like many Hindus, Gandhi identified India with Bharat – the holy land of the ancient *Mahabharata* Hindu epic. Neither Burma nor Arabia featured in the epic, and thus many Hindu nationalists felt that these regions should be separated off from India. Gandhi's support for this stance had caused a rift with his Burmese acolyte Ottama, who tried to publish a rebuttal in Gandhi's magazine.[62] But Gandhi refused to publish the article, writing, 'The Burmese should certainly have my sympathy if they wished to secede.' Indeed, when he visited Burma that spring, he declined to meet Ottama at all, telling him, 'I am sorry indeed that anybody should have mentioned anything to you about my proposed visit to Burma.'[63]

When Mahatma Gandhi arrived in Rangoon, therefore, Mahatma Ottama was conspicuously absent.

Gandhi went swiftly on a 'procession through the streets', then set off on a series of rallies.[64] When his hosts tried to take him to a theatre one evening, he startled them by declaring theatres 'satanic' and refusing to go. His speeches nonetheless attracted thousands and at a meeting with Rangoon's Gujarati community, he addressed the question of separation, declaring that Burma was 'not what we call Bharatvarsha [the land of Bharat]'[65] – not a part of ancient India's Hindu geography – and that Indians should act like guests in a foreign country there. A few days later he expanded upon his thoughts, explaining that it would only

> be worth the while of Burma to remain part of India if it means a partnership at will on a basis of equality with full freedom for either party to secede whenever it should wish. The main thing is that Burma should have an absolute right to shape her destiny as she likes.[66]

To his surprise, crowds muttered in disapproval, and the protests only got louder as he headed into the surrounding towns, snaking his way down the coastline by train to the Eurasian colony of Moulmein, then turning north to Prome, Paungde and the old capital of Mandalay. 'At all places, the Burmese leaders uttered a note of protest against the talk of separation from India',[67] and the extent of the anti-separation feeling astonished Gandhi, who was not so sure by the end of his trip that separation was as obvious a suggestion as he had previously thought. 'The cry for separation of Burma has created a gulf between the Burmese and the Indians,' he admitted as he prepared to leave. The solution, he felt, was to 'Let the Burmans decide the question for themselves.'[68]

In hindsight, Gandhi's visit would be a crucial moment in Burma's gradual march to separation from India. Yet the controversy over separation was only a footnote in his political agenda at the time, much as it had been for the Simon Commission. Gandhi's real aim was to draft a better constitution for India than the one proposed by the commission.

It was an opportunity for Gandhi, Jinnah and the other leading nationalists of the day to put aside their differences and forge a new path for India's future, and a set of all-party meetings was hastily arranged. Jinnah, however, was delayed by personal tragedy. Days before the conference, he learned that his estranged wife Ruttie had been found in a drug-induced coma in Paris and had to rush to her side. Some leaders suggested postponing the meetings until his return, but Motilal Nehru's son Jawaharlal, who had long detested Jinnah, insisted they go ahead. Ruttie eventually recovered, but by the time Jinnah returned to India, a new 'Nehru Report' had done away with separate electorates for Muslims and reduced their reserved seats in parliament. Moreover, Gandhi had thrown his weight behind the report, proposing a new campaign of non-violent resistance to British rule unless it was accepted.

Jinnah was deeply worried by this. 'We are sons of the land, we have to live together,' he cried. 'I believe there is no progress for India until Muslims and Hindus are united.'[69] He appealed to his opponents, 'not as a Mussalman [Muslim] but as an Indian', and argued for a secular India where Hindus and Muslims could live together. The key, Jinnah argued, was to give Muslims adequate representation in parliament: ideally a third of all seats. Yet these proposals were attacked by other Congressmen, who labelled him a 'spoiled child' and a 'naughty boy'.[70] Jinnah left the conference early and the next day, at the train station, his friend Jamshed found him in tears. He 'was standing at the door of his first-class coupe compartment, and he took my hand,' recalled Jamshed years later. 'He had tears in his eyes as he said "Jamshed, this is the parting of the ways."'[71] It was the first time Jamshed had seen Jinnah cry.

Back in Bombay, Jinnah now began dropping in on his estranged wife, who had moved into a separate house. But on her twenty-ninth birthday Ruttie decided to kill herself. According to her closest friend Kanji, 'she chose to die on her birthday'.[72] Her last letter to her husband read:

> Try and remember me, beloved, as the flower you plucked and not the flower you tread upon … Darling I love you – I love you – and had I loved you just a little less I might have remained with you … The higher you set your ideal the lower it falls. I have loved you my darling.[73]

Ruttie's suicide would be hidden for many years and only those in the Jinnahs' inner circle were told the truth. Yet as Sarojini Naidu wrote to her daughter Padmaja:

> Poor little Ruttie had taken an overdraught of veronal … But, darling you realize of course that this is not the official version … Poor mad little suffering child. Maybe [now] she'll find the peace that she was denied – or denied herself on earth.[74]

Jinnah's friend Dwarkadas sat next to him at Ruttie's funeral, and he later described the scene.

> Never have I found a man so sad and bitter. He screamed his heart out … Something I saw had snapped in him. The death of his wife was not just a sad event, nor just something to be grieved over, but he took it, this act of God, as a failure and a personal defeat in his life.[75]

With Ruttie gone, Jinnah found solace in his still-nameless daughter, who soon took the name Dina. As a single father, he made her his primary project, moving to London and enrolling her at a new school in Sussex. By the time he returned to India, he would be a changed man.

* * *

By early 1929, with Jinnah living in Europe, Gandhi once again assumed supreme leadership of Indian politics. Looking to find a way to unite everyone, Hindu or Muslim, Bengali or Burmese, behind a single cause, he announced his intention to stage a national protest against the British Salt Act which gave the British government a monopoly on the manufacture and distribution of Indian salt.[76] Of all the things to protest about British rule, the Salt Act was an unexpected one, raising eyebrows even among Gandhi's most devoted followers. But it proved to be an act of political genius and one of the last major political movements to unite Burmese and Indian nationalists.

Gandhi made sure his protest was an international spectacle. Clad in white home-spun cloth, with a walking stick in one hand, he led thousands of protesters through some of the poorest districts in Gujarat, exposing the media to the gruelling poverty that existed under supposedly enlightened British rule. After twenty-four days, the crowds reached the small fishing village of Dandi on the coast of the Arabian Sea. Following a prayer and an oily massage, Gandhi clasped a lump of salty mud from the ground and boiled it, announcing to rapt crowds, 'With this I am shaking the foundations of the British Empire.'[77] 'Hail, Deliverer,' cried Sarojini Naidu from within the crowd.

In the aftermath, millions of men and women followed Gandhi's lead, peacefully breaking the law and making their own salt. Women publicly joined the freedom struggle en masse for the first time, and one participant recalls:

> Even our old aunts and great-aunts and grandmothers used to bring pitchers of salt water to their houses and manufacture illegal salt. And then they would shout at the top of their voices: 'We have broken the salt law!'[78]

The brutality of the British response, beating protesters, was recorded in full in the international press, just as Gandhi had hoped, and further waves of resistance to British authority washed across the length and breadth of the subcontinent, from Madras to Rangoon.[79] To Gandhi's dismay, however, many of the protesters saw violence as a better route to independence than non-violence, and at 10 p.m. on Good Friday, a group of Sinn Féin enthusiasts calling themselves the IRA – the Indian Republican Army – attempted an 'Easter Rising' in

Chittagong, the main port in the Bengal-Burmese borderlands. In a matter of hours, revolutionaries seized control of an armoury, severed phone lines and hoisted an Indian national flag above the city, before fleeing into the surrounding hill tracts. It became clear that the IRA had smuggled arms up to Chittagong through the Burmese underground, where Bengali revolutionary societies were known to proliferate under the guise of men's fitness clubs.[80] IRA flyers began to appear on school walls across Rangoon encouraging students to take up arms against their foreign oppressors.[81]

Elite Rangoon society tried to act as if everything was normal, and a wealthy property tycoon threw a lavish garden party for eight hundred Punjabis, Bengalis, Burmese and Europeans – handing out gold sovereigns to all the guests.[82] But this twilight world of cosmopolitan excess was not long for Burma. A great crescent of land, from Bengal through the Patkai Hills of Assam and down the Burmese coastline, would soon descend into armed struggle.

The year 1929 changed everything for the Indian Empire, setting it on the road to Partition. First came the US stock market crash of October 1929 that kickstarted the Great Depression, decimating the colonial economy. In a matter of months, the global cost of rice dropped 40 per cent and hundreds of thousands of Burmese agriculturalists defaulted on their loans. Many Burmese farmers had relied on cheap credit from a group of Tamils from the southern tip of the Indian peninsula – the Chettiars – who had sailed across the sea for generations, bringing with them their distinctive cuisine, gods and subprime mortgage loans. Unable to recover their loans, the Chettiars began seizing vast amounts of Burmese farming land as collateral. 'Chettiar banks are fiery dragons that parch every land that has the misfortune of coming under their wicked creeping,' reads one testimony.[83] The rhetoric of separatists had revolved around fears of Indian immigrants stealing honest Burmese jobs and Chettiar land seizures seemed a damning proof of the point.

The second spark was a 7.3-Richter earthquake, which hit Rangoon the same day that news reached the city that Gandhi and his Congressmen had been arrested for their salt protest. The earthquake toppled the golden spire of Rangoon's sacred Shwedagon Pagoda and 'in the ensuing panic,' wrote a British observer, 'a crowd of Indians ran through the streets crying "Victory to the Holy Gandhi"'.[84] A group of South Indian labourers went on strike to protest Gandhi's arrest, but they quickly got into a fight with Burmese labourers who their employers brought in to replace them. Rumours subsequently spread that the Indian labourers had mutilated a young Burmese girl's breast and armed Burmese men set out for an Indian neighbourhood to take revenge. What followed was Rangoon's first major pogrom.

By the time British officials persuaded some of these angry gangs to lay down their weapons, the Indian neighbourhoods had also armed themselves. Violent fights broke out across the city, and seven thousand targeted Indians took shelter in the Rangoon Lunatic Asylum.[85] When the army eventually showed up, an estimated 300–500 people had been killed and a thousand injured. District magistrate Collis reported that 'the condition of the tenements proved there had been savage play ... The very walls dripped blood.'[86]

As tensions between Burma's communities reached fever pitch, the Simon Commission finally released their report. Simon, Attlee and the other Commissioners had ultimately rejected any ideas of Indian independence and instead suggested a representative government should be established in each of India's provinces, with a British Viceroy maintaining order from the top. Hindus and Muslims would be given separate electorates so long as communal tensions continued and a set of Round Table Conferences would also be organised, where Indians themselves could debate finer constitutional details. Most notable of all was the Simon Commission's decision on Burma:

> There is ... one province, today an integral part of British India, which should, we think, be definitely excluded from the new polity, and that is Burma. As the Montagu-Chelmsford Report pointed out, 'Burma is not India.' Its inclusion in India is an historical accident.[87]

The report would prove a turning point. A few months later, amid mass debate over the future of the Indian Union, economic collapse and the largest display of civil disobedience the Raj had ever seen, a rebellion broke out in central Burma.

★ ★ ★

Three days before Christmas, the police in Burma's Tharrawaddy district received an anonymous tip-off that 'trouble was brewing' in the region.[88] Wedged between the Irrawaddy river and the Pegu hills, the alluvial Tharrawaddy plains north of Rangoon were a beautiful if rather uneventful place to be posted. If you were lucky, you could still spot the odd leopard or rhinoceros wandering through the forests, but wilderness was rapidly giving way to rice paddy and the wild beasts were not as common as they had once been. Tharrawaddy had been one of the worst-hit areas by the Great Depression, and a popular petition had been drawn up to demand a temporary reprieve on taxes. Sir J. A. Maung Gyi – recently made the first ethnic Burmese governor – had brashly rejected the idea, however, and outrage was simmering.

When the police received the tip-off, therefore, they immediately began to investigate. It had been an unusually stormy December, and as two officers set off around the district, the undergrowth shone an emerald green.[89] Roads were still waterlogged, but the atmosphere was calm, and when they returned to the police station a few hours later they were happy to report that nothing seemed amiss.

That very night, however, a mysterious group of rebels murdered two headmen and a deputy forest ranger. The next night, 'a Chinaman and two Indian shopkeepers' were killed as well.[90]

News of the attacks reached Rangoon in the form of whispered rumours. Amid Christmas preparations, there was talk of Indian troops being picked off in the Burmese jungle one by one. 'For the first hectic weeks of the outbreak,' recalled a Rangoon-based British lawyer,

> the white community in the country wondered just how serious matters were, and if we were to be faced with a general rising. With the usual British disregard for grim possibilities, we carried on with a seeming contempt for events happening within fifty miles or so of the capital. Police officers would possibly identify a score of dead rebels one morning, then dash into Rangoon to back their fancies on the race-course that same afternoon.[91]

Soon complacency was no longer an option. Unrest erupted across the Irrawaddy basin and within days the Indian Army was sent in to quell the rebellion. Yet the revolt only grew, and reports took on ever more fantastical tones. Mr Fields-Clarke of the Imperial Forest Service was said to have been murdered 'so that his spirit would fight ... against his former employers',[92] and one report claimed the rebels' tattoos 'make them invulnerable'.[93]

All the while the cause of the rebellion baffled officials.[94] The Saya San rebellion remains one of the most fascinating and overlooked events in the history of the Raj and its origins are obscure even to this day, but traditionally the insurrection began at the Pagoda of the Emerald Green Mountain.[95]

Wearing gem-studded slippers and surrounded by an entourage carrying white umbrellas, a Buddhist monk named Saya San is said to have crowned himself king at precisely 11.33 p.m. on 28 October 1930. Seventeen days later, so the story goes, he imbibed a series of invincibility potions made of oil, lime and betel nuts, and then, entering a bamboo 'palace' on a hill near Tharrawaddy township, he had settled down for a royal breakfast with his five queens and four new ministers. Seated upon a lion throne carved from banyan wood, with ruby eyes, Saya San had announced, 'I, Thupannaka Galon Raja, declare war on the heathen British who have enslaved us.'[96]

'Information was obtained of a mysterious leader called Saya San,' read one report, 'and of a headquarters, considered by the rebels as their king's palace, in the forests ten or fifteen miles east of Tharrawaddy.'[97] The Indian Army moved quickly, and on Christmas Eve raided Saya San's 'palace' and burned it to the ground. Nonetheless, Saya San remained at large, and descriptions of him continued to vary wildly. *The Times* said he was an 'eccentric' middle-aged man of forty-three with a large scar carved into his forehead, whereas the *New York Times* reported a 'tall, muscular blond body, tattooed head to foot', 'duplicating the tactics of Lawrence of Arabia'.[98] A premature obituary announcing the death of 'King Golden Crow' only contributed to his mythology, and soon the British press had labelled Saya San an alchemist and practitioner of black magic.[99]

Today the Saya San rebellion has largely been forgotten outside Burma yet in the following months his rebellion would evolve into the biggest and most sustained revolt in the history of the post-1857 British Raj. Almost half the districts in Burma took up arms, and Bengali, Shan and Naga revolutionaries fought alongside Burmese. Almost seven thousand Indian Army troops would be deployed to suppress it.[100]

As the colonial government scrambled to understand what was going on, it became clear that Indians were being targeted as well as the British. Attacks on Bengali and Tamil shops and houses were reported across Lower Burma and one British administrator wrote to Rangoon that 'it is very difficult to prevent villagers from going out at night, one or two at a time, and setting fire to isolated huts where Indians are living alone in the fields'.[101] Many of the rebels had recently had their land seized by the Chettiar bankers and were out for revenge.[102]

The uprising reached its bloody climax as the searing heat of summer gave way to monsoon rains. In the district of Prome, the Burma Frontier Force and the 2/15th Punjab Regiment arrived in Paukkaung to stake out some rebels, only to find the town empty. Then five hundred knife-wielding men charged out of the jungle, attacking British and Indian soldiers before fleeing back into the undergrowth. Colonial forces responded by decapitating sixteen enemy corpses, wrapping their heads in 'cotton blankets taken from the rebels' and forcing three prisoners to carry them to Prome police station for identification. Durga, an amateur photographer from the city, published a photograph of the scene in the *Thuriya* newspaper and overnight sparked outrage across the country and caused nationalist politician U Saw to write a horrified letter to the British secretary of state.[103]

In the wake of the beheadings, over a thousand rebels surrendered in Prome alone and shortly afterwards Saya San's men betrayed him on the edge of the Nawngkwan jungle. After a year of fighting, Saya San was put on trial. To everyone's great surprise he looked nothing like the scarred 'blond body' reported in the newspapers, and instead was merely 'a thin, small man of medium size' with a 'strong determined face' and 'glowing eyes'. Nonetheless, his trial was a sensation. Saya San's prosecution demanded 'that all those who were tattooed were rebels and should therefore be convicted', despite there being no evidence against them. Tattoo artistry was a deep-rooted cultural obligation for many in Burma, and the decision might have gone in the prosecution's favour if it wasn't for the fact that one of the Burmese judges was himself covered in tattoos.[104]

U Saw, the nationalist who had protested the Prome beheadings, leaped to San's defence as a lawyer, publishing a pamphlet exposing

British war crimes entitled: 'Not Plaster Dolls – But Human Heads'.[105] However, he would be outshone by another defence lawyer: the sophisticated Ba Maw who would himself soon lead Burma to war against the British during the Second World War. In the coming years, these two men would evolve into Burma's most prominent politicians, with devastating consequences for the Indian population.

Until this point, colonial officials were still utterly bewildered by Saya San's motivations. But now, to everyone's surprise, it emerged that the fight *against* separation from India had been one of his primary concerns. As his junior counsel later revealed:

> Saya San ... formed those secret associations in order to oppose the forcible separation of Burma ... That was one of his grounds, My Lord, for his taking up arms against the Government ... set out clearly in his written statement filed before the special tribunal.[106]

A month later Saya San was condemned to death, going up the scaffold 'with his head erect,' wrote one of the judges later. 'Saya San, U Aung Hla and other rebel leaders were hanged, but the nationalism that they had helped to further refused to be buried with their bodies.'[107]

In the aftermath the surviving rebels went underground, shifting their target from colonial officers to the 'Indians' who collaborated with them. Already shaken by the riots earlier that year, many Burmese surmised that the Chettiars weren't their only enemies: the Indian soldiers putting down the rebellion were too.[108]

Rural Chettiar properties became particular targets and telegrams reached Gandhi reporting that: 'Lives, properties of innumerable innocent Indians in Burma are still in great danger. Massacres [are] reported daily. Pray persuade authorities take immediate necessary steps to restore peace and harmony.'[109] Police-administered camps had to be set up in Rangoon to look after besieged Indian labourers and it was only when two prominent Chettiars in Madras demanded police protection for the community's 'life and property' that attacks on Indians started to slow.[110]

Indians were coming to be seen as foreign to Burma. Yet the concepts 'Indian' and 'Burmese' still meant different things to different people. When nineteen-year-old Lu Gyi, a Burmese rebel, decided to attack Indian goat herders – supposedly as revenge against atrocities by the Indian Army – he tried to separate the Indian herders from the Burman ones. But this proved difficult and among the goat herders he killed for being 'Indian' was a man with the Burmese name On Thu, while among those he freed for being Burmese was a man with the Indian-sounding name of Ismail.

Indeed as a subject of the Indian Empire, Lu Gyi himself was still technically Indian himself.[111]

2

The First Partitions of India

Lord Irwin, later known as the 'Old Fox' Halifax, had always excelled at charades, and over the course of that week, the crowning achievement of his tenure as Viceroy of India, he beat everyone.

It had been a dark and cold month in the city of New Delhi, unusually rainy and thick with fog, and the opening hockey match of the celebrations had been played under 'ominous black clouds'.[1] But on 10 February 1931, as the Viceroy's guests gathered along the grand Kingsway to celebrate the new capital's inauguration, the clouds lifted and revealed bright blue skies. The starch-collared members of his privy council arrived at 10:30 a.m. sharp, followed by a handful of bejewelled princes, and then, half an hour later, a thirty-one-gun salute and a fanfare of trumpets announced the arrival of the Viceregal couple themselves.[2]

The next week was an endless flurry of events. There was a polo tournament, a prince's banquet, an air display and even a 'Hog Hunter's Ball'. A new war memorial called India Gate was opened, and a garden party was held on Raisina Hill. In the Mughal Red Fort, amid jewel-encrusted pavilions, guests were treated to wrestling and tent-pegging shows, a 'pageant of Indian transport' and even an operatic performance of *Madame Butterfly*. Outside the fortress walls, elephants and dancing bears were provided to entertain those not fortunate enough to be invited.[3]

Finally, on 12 February, Viceroy Irwin celebrated the opening of his brand-new palace. Designed by Edwin Lutyens, a celebrated architect of British country houses, it was larger than Versailles and its basement required a fleet of bicycles to get from one side to the other.[4] Hindu *chattris*, Mughal gardens and a Buddhist stupa-like dome represented the diversity of the Indian Empire in stone, and as far as most people were concerned, it was a masterpiece. 'I can't describe to you how beautiful it is,' the travel writer Robert Byron wrote to his mother when he first laid eyes on the place.

> The Viceroy's House is the first real vindication of modern architecture. People simply don't realise what has been done, how stupendous it is. It is so unlike the English – one would never have thought them capable of it.[5]

By February 1931 the construction of New Delhi was considered perhaps the most impressive and ambitious architectural feat constructed anywhere in the British Empire. It had been intended, 'like Rome', to 'be built for eternity'[6] and Lutyens had overseen everything, from the shape of the door knobs to the plan of the new city itself. He had hired twenty-nine thousand labourers, uprooted whole villages and even diverted the sacred Yamuna river for the project.

It had been built to overlook one of the most historic cities in the world. For Hindus, Delhi was the site of the legendary city Indraprastha; for Muslims it was the seat of thirty-two sacred Sufi shrines; and for Sikhs it was the site of their Gurus' martyrdom. Now, along the breezy boulevards connecting the ruins of former empires, rows of neem, jamun and arjun trees shaded whitewashed bungalows and art deco embassies.

But not everyone was charmed, and when the novelist Aldous Huxley arrived during a meeting of the Chamber of Princes, he felt that the new capital 'pullulated with despots'. 'At the Viceroy's evening parties,' Huxley wrote, 'the diamonds were so large that they looked like stage gems; it was impossible to believe that the pearls in the million-pound necklaces were the genuine excrement of oysters.' With the rebellion in Burma only just dying down, racial tension was all-pervasive, and Huxley felt that

> the comedy of Delhi and the new India, however exquisitely diverting, is full of tragic implications ... The dispute of races, the reciprocal hatred of colours, the subjection of one people to another – these things lie behind its snobberies, conventions and deceits.[7]

Nineteen years earlier, when the city had been commissioned, Britain had appeared invincible. Like the *Titanic*, launched the same year, it had seemed impossible that Britain's Indian Empire could ever sink beneath the waves. Now, however, no one was quite as sure. Saya San's rebellion in Burma had deeply shaken colonial officialdom, as had Gandhi's spectacular Salt March. Iris Portal, a British woman brought up in Delhi, recalls her father and uncle worrying about a prophecy at the time. 'If anyone ever raised the subject of New Delhi my father would always quote the Persian couplet in a most gloomy voice,' she remembered. 'Whoever has built a new city in Delhi has always lost it: the Pandava brethren, Prithviraj Chauhan, Feroz Shah Tughluk, Shah Jehan ... They all built new cities and they all lost them. We were no exception.'[8]

As Viceroy Irwin's week of celebrations concluded, therefore, no one was quite sure what to make of the whole inauguration. The absence of most of India's political leaders that week certainly boded badly for the future. Most Congressmen who weren't still in prison for their role in the salt protests had gathered in Allahabad instead, to mourn the passing of Congress president Motilal Nehru. Here Motilal's son Jawaharlal derided Viceroy Irwin's celebrations as 'vulgar ostentation and wasteful extravagance'.[9]

Most ominous of all was the talk of breaking up the Indian Empire. A conference had recently been concluded in London, and among the topics discussed was whether India should be partitioned. As the celebrations of that week came to an end, one journalist described it as 'the funeral of our Indian Empire'.[10]

The first Round Table Conference held in London had brought together British and Indian leaders to debate the future of the Raj. The discussions were fraught, the questions existential: Could India remain united? Would the British relinquish control? And who, in the end, had the right to speak for India? Briefly returning from his self-imposed political exile, Jinnah made the prime minister promise not to carry out any form of partition without first understanding the will of the people – this was precisely what the British were now attempting to find out.[11]

'I scarcely think I exaggerate,' the Viceroy Lord Irwin said, 'when I say that history, a hundred years hence ... will find in [the Round

Table Conferences] the turning point of the constitutional history of India.'[12]

A first round had been attempted without Gandhi's participation, but everyone agreed that this had had an 'air of unreality'.[13] As a result, the Viceroy released Gandhi from prison, and two days after the celebrations of Delhi's inauguration had finished, at 2.20 p.m. on the dot, the Mahatma entered the halls of Viceroy's House for the first time. He wore a woollen shawl and loin cloth, and in England the rowdy young Winston Churchill deplored the scene.

> It is alarming and also nauseating to see Mr Gandhi, a seditious Middle Temple lawyer, now posing as a fakir of a type well-known in the East, striding half-naked up the steps of the Viceregal palace, while he is still organizing and conducting a defiant campaign of civil disobedience, to parley on equal terms with the representative of the King-Emperor.[14]

Nonetheless, on 5 March Gandhi and Viceroy Irwin signed a pact. The Mahatma would suspend his civil disobedience movement, and attend the Round Table Conferences, and in exchange the British government would release political prisoners. 'If the pact was a victory,' Gandhi said, it belonged to both sides. He had negotiated with the Viceroy as an equal, 'as no Indian had done before.'[15]

Gandhi set off for the conferences in London soon after, and along the way he stopped for a few nights in Aden.[16] The dry moonscape presented an utterly different world from the lush scenery he had visited a year before in Burma, but his reception was much the same. 'Literally the whole population was out,' wrote Sarojini Naidu, who was accompanying the Mahatma to London.

> [There were] Arab women draped in black veils standing about in huddled groups and the Jewish women from Yemen leaning out of their windows with picturesque kerchiefs knotted round their handsome, provocative faces.[17]

As in Burma, hundreds of people descended on the pier to greet Gandhi, and a young journalist called Muhammad Ali Luqman jumped onto the gangway before the Mahatma could even step onto dry land.

'I stood silently in front of a man who has been sent by god to change the face of Asia,' Luqman recalled years later. 'He wore nothing on his body, with the exemption of his meticulously clean white loin-cloth, a pair of Indian chappals, his silver-white nickel glasses and his silver pocket watch attached at the waist.'[18]

Like Rangoon, Aden was rife with talk of a potential partition from India. The man at the heart of the controversy was the Aden resident Bernard Reilly, an old-school colonialist who pined for the days of Lord Curzon while wandering around in the sweltering heat in a cream-coloured suit. The administrator saw Arabs as fundamentally different from Indians and felt that much-needed reforms were always bogged down by the vast Indian bureaucracy. Separating Aden and the Arab protectorates from India, Reilly thought, would improve efficiency, so he had started encouraging 'the growth of self-conscious, anti-Indian sentiments among the Arabs of Aden'.[19]

Aden's Gujarati and Parsi residents protested the city was an integral part of the Indian nation. But many Arab residents opposed this, and one Muhammad Mackawwi argued:

We will never submit to Indian domination ... What has India done for us? Nothing. We are backward, very backward and the fault is entirely with India ... Where are the Arab teachers? ... One of my sons, who is in Edinburgh, has just failed an examination and of all things he has failed in Arabic. It is a disgrace and for that disgrace we have India to thank.[20]

Gandhi was largely unaware of these fault lines, but the young journalist Luqman, who appointed himself the Mahatma's Gujarati-Arabic translator for the day, embodied the tensions.[21] Like many Arabs in Aden, Luqman had spent much of his life as an Indian nationalist. He saw the connection with India as organic, and on a road trip across India with the Dalit* leader B. R. Ambedkar had been inspired 'with new ideas of patriotism'. 'For many years afterwards,' he wrote, 'I eulogized the aims of the Indian Congress.' But by 1931 anti-Arab sentiment had begun to change his mind. 'I started propagating Arab Solidarity and disseminating Arab aspirations,' he noted years later.[22]

---

* Communities formally referred to as 'untouchables'.

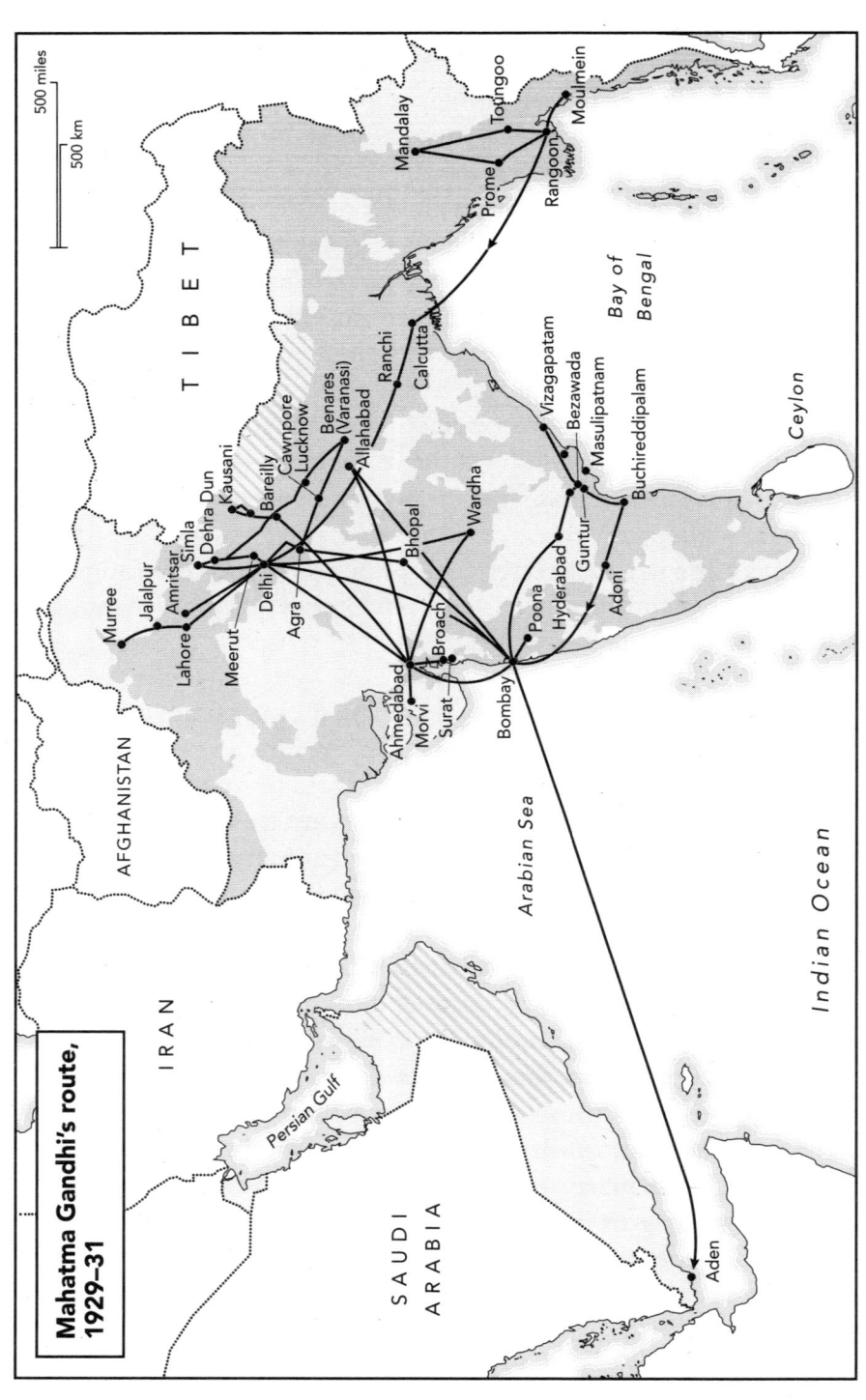

Nonetheless, Luqman was awed by Gandhi's arrival and together in a tent under the glaring sunshine they unfurled the Indian national flag to 'mad cheers by all those present'.[23] Gandhi spoke about independence for all colonised peoples (whether from Britain or India was left unclear) and triumphantly announced that in London he would not settle for anything short of independence.[24]

During his travels from Rangoon to Aden, Gandhi had still not left the borders of the Indian Empire. But now, as he stepped back onto the London-bound SS *Rajputana*, he finally departed its shores.

By the time Gandhi arrived at the Round Table Conference in September 1931, Sarojini Naidu was fed up with him. 'I am really bored to tears by the caprices and vagaries, vacillation and vanities of the little man,' she wrote to her daughters on 23 September 1931.

> He does not know his own mind for three minutes consecutively!! With great difficulty I have found and officially established him in a beautiful house overlooking Hyde Park where he can see people, but some kink in his brain makes him cling to the East End to the utter weariness and rebellion of all his staff.[25]

The Round Table Conference that Gandhi had come to participate in proved equally frustrating and his relationship with India's Muslim leaders crashed to new lows that week. The Aga Khan, leader of a prominent Muslim sect, had organised a midnight meeting between Gandhi, Naidu and major Muslim leaders including Jinnah in the Ritz Hotel. He hoped it would be the beginning of a new political alliance, proving that Hindus and Muslims could fight alongside one another. But in the course of the gathering, Gandhi successfully alienated all of the Muslims present, telling them:

> I cannot in truth say ... that I have any paternal love for Muslims. But if you put the matter on grounds of political necessity, I am ready to discuss it in a co-operative spirit.[26]

The 'chilly effect' of Gandhi's comments 'persisted throughout the Round Table Conference' and for Jinnah it only confirmed his distrust of the Mahatma.* Henceforth, whenever Gandhi met the Muslim leadership in London, they would bring up a new and unexpected set of questions: Was India one nation or two? 'Was Islam merely a religious minority, or were Muslims [a nation unto themselves?]'[27]

Sarojini Naidu had been chosen as one of only three women representatives at the Round Table Conferences, and she found the whole drama bitterly dissatisfying. 'I have never attended anything more disappointing and dull in every way,' she wrote to her daughters. 'It is almost worse than the endless Unity and All-Party Conferences we have had ad nauseum in India!' When Gandhi 'discusses the second chamber, finance and franchise, he is less than convincing,' she wrote. Indeed, for Sarojini, the only fun to be had was a rogue encounter with Charlie Chaplin, who she found to be 'shy and quite charming' and who, much to her amusement, Gandhi had 'never heard of'.[28]

Things got more interesting on 27 November 1931, when the special Round Table Conference on Burma opened at the Palace of Westminster. 'All the Cabinet was there,' Sarojini wrote to her daughters, and 'old John Simon came up to me as if he loved me and shook my hand'. She delighted in the 'Mona Lisa smiles' and was thrilled by the colourful costumes of the delegates, the 'pinks, primrose yellows, forget-me-not blues and glowing plums and petunias'.[29] Indeed the 'clothes were the best part of the show,' she felt, for once the talk began it was the normal 'Blah Blah speeches of gratitude' that so bored her.

A few days later the conference addressed the issue of Burma's separation. A pamphlet written by Mahatma Ottama, entitled 'The Case Against the Separation of Burma from India', was hastily distributed among the invitees, envisaging a future for India in which Burma remained an integral part.[30] 'The Simon Report Survey is trying to fix the wedge between two sister-peoples,' wrote Ottama. 'Burma's demand is for her rightful place as an honoured and equal partner in the coming All-India Federation.'[31]

But to the Burmese delegates' surprise, they found that British officials had already accepted 'the principle of separation'.[32] Rather than

---

* Gandhi would later claim his comments had been misconstrued and that although he did not have any *paternal* love for Muslims, he did have a *fraternal* sort of love for them.

debating the question of partition, they were to assume it would go ahead and instead they were asked 'to discuss lines of a constitution for a separated' Burmese colony.

To many of those present, the situation reeked of foul play. The anti-separation delegate Ba Maw described the talks as 'formal, frigid, unyielding and even hostile beneath the surface' and the whole exercise as 'completely cynical, because everyone knew that the most important decisions were already made, or would be made regardless of anything the Burmese had to say'.[33] There is little evidence that separation was a conspiracy to minimise a future independent India's sphere of influence, as some nationalists later claimed. Yet in the words of Ba Maw:

> Separation was rejected, but the British forced it upon us; the proposed constitution also was rejected, but the British forced this too upon us; and so ended all illusions ever entertained by the Burmese regarding the British in Burma.[34]

So it was that the decision was taken. On 12 January 1932, thirty-three delegates made their way through the Tudor gates of St James's Palace. Edward VIII, the Prince of Wales, presided over the meeting, and delegates tentatively set a date for the formal separation of India and Burma: 1 April 1937. A few days later the British government agreed that Aden and the neighbouring protectorates would be removed from Bombay's oversight and discussions soon began about separating Arabia entirely from the Raj so that Indians would 'not be allowed to run the Persian Gulf' in the event of independence.[35]

The first Partitions of the Indian Empire were becoming a reality.

As late as 1930 it had still been possible for anti-colonial activists in Aden, Rangoon, Lahore and Dacca to conceive of themselves as part of a future Indian nation. Ottama, Luqman and Jinnah had all certainly done so. Yet in the wake of the Round Table Conferences this would no longer be the case.

For the first time in history, 'India' would extend from the Khyber Pass and Baluchistan in the west to Assam and the Naga Hills in the east, Kashmir in the north to Kanyakumari in the south. This new image of India matched the boundaries of the imagined 'Bharat' of

Hindu nationalist imagination and would henceforth become eulogised as 'Undivided India'. People too often overlook the fact that this 'Undivided India' was only created by explicitly dividing the Indian Empire.

Of course not everyone was happy to accept this new reality. Bombay protested that Aden was an 'integral part of India', while in Burma anti-separationists won a landslide election in the Legislative Assembly.[36] Most intriguing of all, in a final attempt to forge a 'greater India', Mahatma Ottama thrust himself into an unlikely alliance with the Hindu Mahasabha, a Hindu nationalist pressure group, to oppose separation.[37] By mid-1935 he had been elected its president, the only time a Buddhist ever held the position, and at his inauguration he announced that 'the proposed separation of Burma from India ... [is] a deliberate step towards the dismemberment of the great Hindu nation'. The solution, Ottama proclaimed, was 'an intensive campaign in both countries on the lines of the anti-Partition agitation in Bengal a quarter of a century ago'.[38]

Ottama's gambit failed, however, and few Hindus wanted to listen to the Buddhist monk. In Rawalpindi nationalists shouted him off stage with cries of 'Shame'.[39] When Ottama returned to Burma, declaring that he came 'not as a Burmese leader but as an Indian leader',[40] here too he found himself increasingly out of touch with nationalist opinion.[41]

In 1933 a short and stocky Bengali cyclist called Ramnath Biswas began frantically biking his way across Burma with a small triangular sign reading: 'Round-the-World Hindoo Traveller'.[42]

Born in a strict Brahmin household in a village in the Assam-Burma borderlands, Ramnath had yearned to travel the world since he was a child. Joining the army, he went to Afghanistan, Persia and Malaya, but in 1931 his connections to the radical Bengali revolutionary group Anushilan Samiti lost him his job. Destitute, he made the unusual decision to go round the world by bicycle instead.

Ramnath crossed into Burma through Thailand in 1933 and was immediately enchanted by the region, writing of the tall bamboo 'leaning over the road from both sides' and the 'ample' papayas he was fed in roadside villages.[43] Dense forest flanked deep black water and he watched in delight as a family of elephants passed by. But the rural idyll stood in complete opposition to the vicious politics gripping the towns and cities. Racial tensions were evident from Ramnath's first destination, the southern bazaar town of Margui, as a Burmese headmaster complained to him about the town's Indians:

> The Indians have taken away all government jobs from us ... The Chettis are buying our land and houses, the Bengali Muslims have occupied all navigational jobs. The foreigners are now everywhere in our country and we are now fast becoming extinct. I am scared of foreigners. We are now trying to take Brahmadesh [Burma] out of India, and we will definitely be successful.[44]

Meanwhile, a sense of hopelessness had come upon the Indians in Margui. Two Bengali policemen helped Ramnath find shelter with a rich Indian man, but Ramnath was taken aback when his host started interrogating him about whether he was a thief. The next morning, after Ramnath decided to find lodging elsewhere, the man apologised and explained:

> This country is very much like our own country. I do not dislike you, but I remain always anxious because I know the future of my countrymen here. I do not feel the urge to go back to my country either. Perhaps, I will have to go to England; else, I'll never be at peace anywhere.[45]

As he cycled north on bumpy hilly roads skirting the Burmese coastline, Ramnath became aware that he was witnessing history unfold. In a village inhabited by the Kachin community, who considered themselves neither Indian nor Burmese, villagers terrified by the 1930 Indo-Burmese riots remained convinced 'that the Burmese would also attack them'. Yet they were also 'baffled by the exploitative policies of the British and the Indians'. A British rubber plantation nearby only employed economic migrants from across the Bay of Bengal, thus 'depriving the Kachin people of this job opportunity'. Ramnath concluded that: 'One day, these Kachin people [too] would become anti-Indian.'[46]

Ramnath felt the system of Indian labour in Burma to be the root of the problem, for it meant people had 'started to believe that the Indians were exploiting them everywhere', when in fact Indians were only working on 'the orders of the British'. When he confronted some young Indian men about their treatment of the Burmese, however, telling them it would only lead to Indians being forced out of the region, they 'readily rationalized such exploitations with the Darwinian phrase "survival of the fittest"'. A shocked Ramnath wrote: 'The arrogance of all these Bengali *baboos* in Burma was surprising as if they had gone there to rule the country. They never considered that they too were nothing but slaves to the British.'

Ramnath reached Rangoon utterly depressed about the future and decided to visit the places where the 'Burmese killed the Indians' in the riots of 1930. When a journalist from the *Thuriya* newspaper interviewed Ramnath on his travels, Ramnath blasted the reporter about *Thuriya*'s silence on the Rangoon riots. 'If you want to separate your country from ours, then do it,' he cried, 'but was it right to kill illiterate Indian labourers and their hapless families and children?' The reporter was unfazed. 'There was a large political conspiracy behind this riot,' he told Ramnath. 'The people of Burma have realized that the rich Indian businessmen are our real enemy.'[47]

Around this time Victor 'Hopie' Hope of Hopetoun House, better known as Marquess Linlithgow, arrived in Bombay. As the new Viceroy he was given responsibility for implementing the Partition of the Indian Empire.

Linlithgow had grown up in one of Scotland's grandest country houses, described by the *Sunday Express* as 'quiet, shy, tall, with a willowy figure ... Born an aristocrat, he is in character and temperament a democrat.'[48] He knew India well from his time as chairman of its Royal Commission of Agriculture and his papers show an obsession with health and improving sanitation. 'Making Delhi Healthier' reads one headline, proudly pasted in his journal.[49] In addition to the separation of India, Burma and Southwestern Arabia, Linlithgow aimed to bring political franchise to roughly 40 per cent of the adult male population, and merge the six hundred-odd princely states with British India into a united federation.[50]

So it was that Linlithgow's administrators set about the task of dividing the Indian Empire. There were discussions on what separation would mean for Burma's banking system, and what it would mean for Aden's opium supply. Yet one topic was curiously absent from the discussions. Drawing borders is a fraught process at the best of times, and the people living on either side of a border will always have more in common with one another than with the politicians of their respective capitals. But the creation of the India–Burma border was particularly strange, for everyone involved seemed remarkably unfussed about where the border should actually be.

The precise demarcation between Burma and Assam had always been 'fuzzy'.[51] In the Patkai Hills, the mountainous new frontier, British rule amounted to little more than the occasional outpost, beyond which the land was terra incognita to the central government. This became particularly clear when a speaker at the Royal Geographical Society excitedly told a rapt crowd how he had explored 'one of the few un-surveyed areas of India ... a country of densely wooded hills ... inhabited by the Naga tribes'. The speaker briefly noted the existence of 'other Naga tribes also on the Burma side' of the Patkai but admitted that 'little is known of them'.[52] Ironically, the un-surveyed – and largely unadministered – areas he had visited were precisely where the new border was about to fall.

For most of the past century, Naga communities had been largely isolated from national political currents. 'We were like frogs in a well,' was how one chief put it. 'We barely knew there were other frogs in other wells – except for our immediate neighbours and they were all our enemies.'[53] But Nagas did not sit back as new borders threatened to slice their homeland in two.

Angami Zapu Phizo, a Bible salesman and insurance broker from one of these 'Naga tribes', would eventually launch the biggest movement against the India–Burma Partition.[54] His father was a worldly man who had travelled across the Indian Empire as a trader, and Phizo himself had spent many years working at the 'Naga Club' in Kohima where the first embers of Naga nationalism were sparking. Kohima was perched precariously on the tip of a hill, overlooking misty bamboo forests flecked with French marigold and broad-leafed rhododendron, and when the separation debates had filtered through town, Phizo and his colleagues had felt that they were neither Indians nor Burmese, but another nation entirely. They had thus petitioned the Simon Commission to give Nagas their very own colony, separate from both India and Burma. But to their dismay they never heard a response.[55] Over the subsequent few years, it became clear that Burma would indeed be separated from India, but until the last moment it

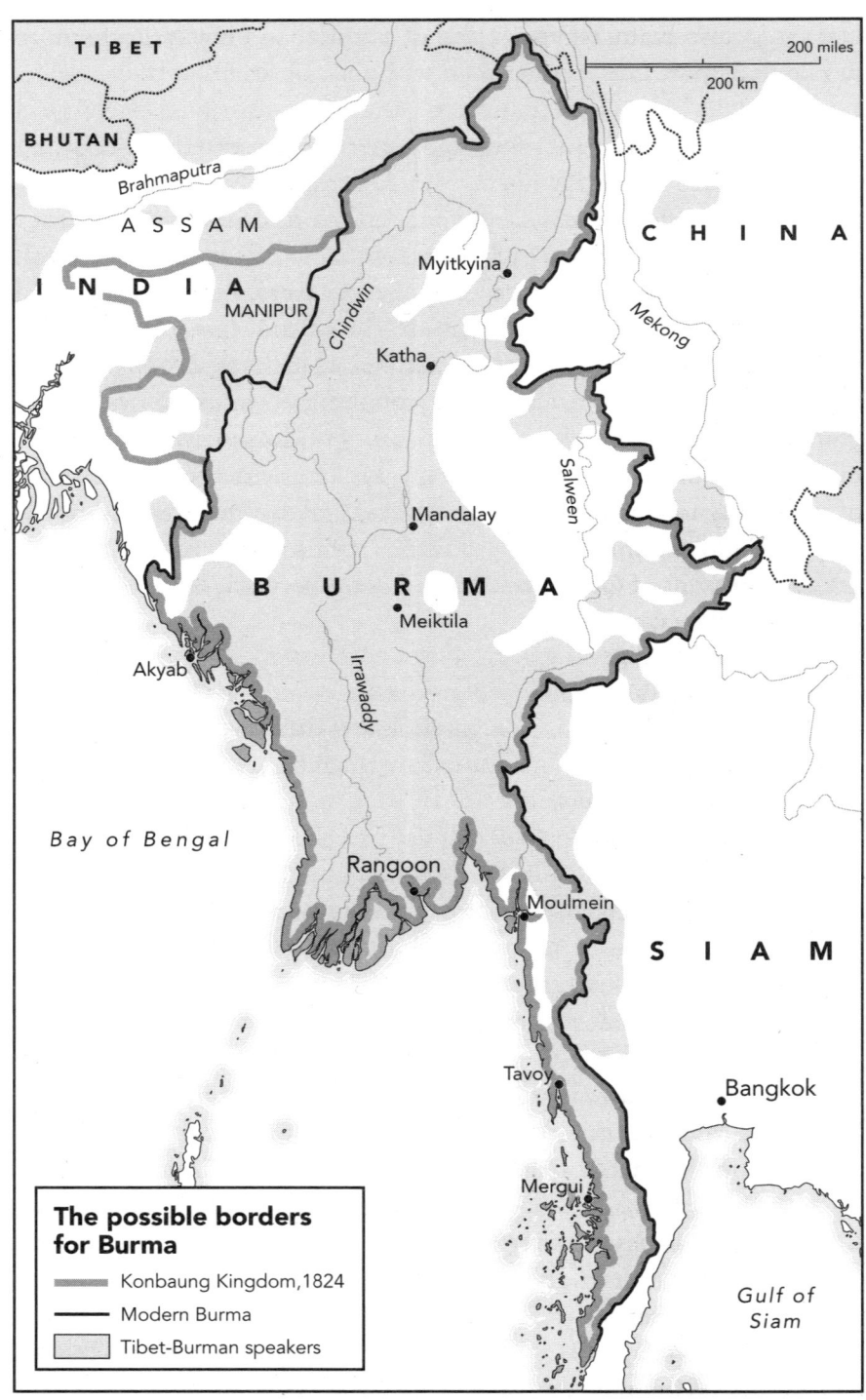

remained uncertain which of the two colonies Phizo's hometown would end up in.

The First Partitions separating the eastern and western ends of the Indian Empire came into effect on 1 April 1937.[56] 'His Majesty's Government chose to make this epochal change on April Fools' Day,' read an article in *Time* magazine. 'Millions of the Indian people rose that morning ... to don black armbands and break out black flags and bunting.'[57]

Burma's inauguration ceremony took place in the newly constructed Rangoon City Hall, a monumental fusion of neoclassical architecture with multi-tiered Burmese *pyatthat* roofs. A new governor of Burma took an oath and then the Viceroy ceremonially handed a silver mace to the newly independent Burma Senate. In Aden meanwhile, where there was no suitable hall, the ceremony was held outside the royal crescent in front of Queen Victoria's statue. Bernard Reilly arrived by car, escorted by camel troops, and a seventeen-gun salute was fired by the Royal Artillery.

King George VI did not make either inauguration ceremony, but he sent short telegrams to be read out under a fluttering Union Jack:

> Aden has been an integral part of British Indian administration for nearly 100 years. That political association with my Indian Empire will now be broken, and Aden will take its place in my Colonial Empire.[58]

A similar king's speech was read out in Rangoon:

> Today Burma ceases to form part of the Indian Empire ... It had become clear that the welfare of the country will be better served if henceforth she follows a course independent of India.[59]

In the coming days, news of the Partition of the Indian Empire was plastered across every newspaper in the country. A set of new stamps were released, showing a fissure dividing the Taj Mahal from Rangoon's Shwedagon Pagoda.[60] It would be a prescient image for the cultural alienation that was soon to follow.

'Burma Divorces India,' announced one newspaper headline. The article described the union of India and Burma as based merely 'upon convenience in governing and historical accident' – and concluded that 'there will be some readjustment for the 1,000,000 Indians who are in Burma as government servants, traders and merchants, or labourers'.[61]

Brand-new questions gripped the newly fragmented Indian Empire. Who now had the right to live where? What would happen to Indians in Burma, the Burmese in Aden and the Arabs in India?[62]

The Partition also had important consequences for India's demographic make-up. By separating the largely non-Hindu parts of the Indian Empire and at the same time making India resemble the 'Bharat' of Hindu legend, the British had given credence to the Hindu nationalist claim that India belonged primarily to Hindus. Although Indian nationalists have been more successful than any of their counterparts in South Asia at projecting a sense of long-term continuity onto their modern nation state, the creation of Bharat in 1937 is as central an event in South Asian history as the separation of Burma and the later creation of Pakistan. Britain's 'Indian Empire' may have included all the bits of South Asia that Hindu nationalists dreamed of unifying – including Kashmir, Sindh, Bengal and Tamil Nadu – but until this point it had always previously included further-flung regions like Burma, Dubai and Aden.

Bharat, much like 'Christendom', was an idea that stretched back millennia, but one that had never referred to a unified political unit. By conflating India and Bharat, however, Indian nationalism would henceforth take on a particularly Hindu flavour, which would alienate many Muslims and be an important trigger for the creation of Pakistan. The same year as the separation of Burma and Aden, the Congress adopted 'Vande Mataram' as the national song of India. It identified the holy motherland of Bharat with the Hindu goddess Durga, which raised mass protests among Muslims. Notable among these Muslim leaders was Muhammad Ali Jinnah, who increasingly saw Congress as a vehicle for exclusive Hindu nationalism. The stage was being set for further partitions.

When Burma achieved separation from India, roughly a fifth of the Naga population had ended up on the Burmese side of the border, and the other four-fifths in India.[63] Phizo's hometown Khonoma had become part of the Indian 'excluded areas', which were under the direct control of Assam's governor and thus denied the right to vote in the upcoming elections. Ominously, the hallowed monolith of mankind at Meikhel, from where all Nagas traced their origins, toppled over later that year.[64]

Ottama's battle against Burma's separation from India was lost and in the Hindu Mahasabha he was replaced by a young radical called Vinayak Savarkar. Savarkar had recently formulated a Hindu nationalist political ideology called 'Hindutva' which sought to establish Hindu hegemony across India, and at the time of writing this is the state ideology of India's ruling party. Savarkar declared his commitment to Hindutva from his opening speech, in which he declared his belief that 'there are two antagonistic nations living side by side in India ... the Hindus and the Muslims'.[65] Even within Burma, Ottama's star was being eclipsed by new political groups, whose ideas of self-determination were centred around slogans like 'Burma for the Burmans'.[66] In 'the last days of U Ottama,' wrote the historian Maung Maung years later,

> the public ... no longer cared enough to make sure he had food in his *thabeik* ... I had seen him with his bowl walking past along Phayre Street in front of the *Rangoon Daily Mail* ... Nobody bothered to call him in and talk to him ... He died of gangrene developed from a sore in the foot because he was suffering from diabetes, an easily controllable disease. He had few friends left who would take him in to their house for a meal, but even they had ceased to care.[67]

3

The Drums of War

In the wake of separation, racial relations in Burma would worsen beyond anyone's imagination. The man at the centre of this change was U Saw, one of Saya San's former lawyers, who would transform anti-Indian xenophobia into a political ideology.*

A squat, loud man with little formal schooling, U Saw struck his contemporaries as 'a jovial but sinister scoundrel'.[1] On a personal level, he could be charming and had a way of wrapping officials around his finger, despite frequent boasts about his nine maternal uncles having each, quite literally, got away with murder. But in the years before Burma's separation, Saw had gained recognition for his anti-immigration columns in the *Thuriya* newspaper, which lauded Hitler's treatment of the Jews as a role model for what to do with immigrants. Saw directed particular ire at the Chettiar Tamil community that, by 1938, had seized an astonishing quarter of Burmese agricultural land – up from 6 per cent in 1930.[2]

Saw's life had taken a dramatic new path three years earlier after members of the secretive Black Dragon Society approached him on a visit to Japan.[3] Founded by a pan-Asianist judo master years earlier, the Black Dragons played a central role in Japan's transformation into an imperial power, encouraging the annexation of Korea in 1910 as well as

---

* British imperial historian Matthew Bowser has recently brought to light just how much influence U Saw had in the division of Indians and Burmese in the late colonial period in his extraordinary thesis *Misdirected Rage*, by far the best work so far available on the Partition of India and Burma. Much of this chapter draws directly from his pathbreaking work, published as Bowser, M., *Containing Decolonisation: British Imperialism and the Politics of Race in Late Colonial Burma* (Manchester: Manchester University Press, 2025).

the encroachment of Chinese territory in the early 1930s.⁴ The details of Saw's meetings with the Black Dragons were never written down, but he returned to Burma extraordinarily rich, with enough money to buy a majority stake in the *Thuriya*. He subsequently turned it into a pro-Japanese mouthpiece and exclaimed in its pages that the Japanese 'were the only Asiatic people to become a great world power'.⁵ A few months later the Japanese consulate rewarded him with a car.

Awash with money, Saw took to hosting massive parties, renowned for limitless alcohol and beautiful women, and founded a political party called 'Myochit' – literally the 'Love of Race' Party.⁶ All the while he was covertly recruiting unemployed young men into a private paramilitary group called the Galon Tat, modelled on Mussolini's brownshirts.⁷ With *Thuriya* as his personal voicebox, and the Galon Tat his personal militia, Saw set out to rid Burma of Indian immigrants, who he perceived to be at the root of all its problems. Contemporaries would term his movement 'Galon – or Garuda – Fascism'.⁸

At the time both fascism and communism were making inroads across South Asia: in Calcutta primary schools offered *Mein Kampf* as a prize for Class VIII students, and it was not uncommon to hear North Indians speak proudly of their 'Aryan' ancestry. Private paramilitary outfits were far from uncommon and militant youths marched in khaki uniforms in a number of political organisations, including the RSS, the Muslim League National Guards and the Congress Youth Wings. Nonetheless, Saw's movement would have an utterly radicalising effect on Burma, for his party was founded at precisely the moment that a limited form of democracy was introduced to South Asia.

While neither Burma nor India were yet independent, as part of the new reforms their politicians were now allowed to stand for elections and take over certain government portfolios. The man elected as Burma's first premier was Ba Maw, the lawyer who had overshadowed U Saw at Saya San's trial and who would later lead Burma to war against the British in the Second World War. As one of Burma's most prominent anti-separation leaders, he represented everything that Saw despised.⁹ He was a man 'with bright roguish eyes', whose stutter disguised a great 'capacity for mischief' and an 'almost professional skill' at draughts.¹⁰ Unlike Saw, who had never completed his education, Ba Maw had also studied in Bordeaux, writing a PhD in French on

Buddhist and animist syncretism, and his mixed-race heritage meant he shunned Saw's racial nationalism.

Saw conspired to take down Maw's ministry from day one, breaking the rules in Burma's House of Representatives by speaking in Burmese, and whenever he was asked to speak in English protesting that Ba Maw cared only about foreigners. The premier quickly took a dislike to Saw, describing him as a man 'corrupted by a demon-like personal ambition uncurbed by either a clear political faith or a conscience'.[11] But British officials did little to oppose Saw, distracted by visiting celebrities like the aeronaut Amelia Earhart who was attempting to circumnavigate the world by plane, and an ex-railway engineer called Major Hart who was travelling up the Irrawaddy in a collapsible canoe.[12] So Saw went on, joking that Ba Maw was really an 'Indian Premier',[13] targeting Buddhist fears of being overwhelmed by immigrants, and demonising inter-faith marriages.

In January 1938, as Burma Oil workers staged mass strikes, U Saw spotted his moment to humiliate Ba Maw's government once and for all.

The strikes were led by Aung San, a student activist from a small-town family who would later be regarded as the founding father of independent Burma. He was 'awkward and angular in behaviour,' recalls one friend, 'slight of build, square-jawed and square-shouldered ... [and spoke] loudly, in short stilted sentences'.[14] He was renowned for eccentricities and was frequently found wandering off into bushes and practising political speeches in the shrubbery. Aung San 'helped himself freely to our clothes ... [and] would not take [them] off for days,' recounted another university friend. 'We would literally have to force him to take a bath when he started to smell.'[15] Nonetheless Aung San was a commanding orator with a strange charisma, and in January 1938, he led a surge of protesters from across the country in support of the workers at the Chauk oilfields.[16]

U Saw saw an opportunity. With cold calculation, he circulated an inflammatory pamphlet called *Abode of the Nat* to every newspaper and Buddhist monastery in and around Rangoon. It depicted a Muslim claiming Islam's superiority to Buddhism, a crude piece of provocation but devastatingly effective. U Saw used it to generate an entirely manufactured national outrage, effectively redirecting the protests for his own means, and to stoke further outrage he plastered the following words on the headline of *Thuriya*:

BUDDHISM HAS BEEN INSULTED. TAKE IMMEDIATE STEPS[17]

Saw then announced that a meeting would be held on 26 July to resolve the insult to Buddhism. The events that followed have been labelled by one scholar as the 'Burmese Kristallnacht'.[18]

When the day finally arrived, ten thousand Buddhists gathered in the shadow of the Shwedagon Pagoda. Outraged monks gave anti-Muslim speeches, and a speaker called for protesters to march on the Sortee Bara Bazaar 'to show the real blood of the Burmese people'. A torrent of yellow robes descended the pagoda hill shouting 'Burma for the Burmans' and '*Kala-Kala-Yaik-Yaik* [Assault the Foreigners]',[19] and upon reaching the bazaar, began smashing up Indian shops.

The mostly Indian police tried to disperse the mob, but the protests instead turned into street battles. The morning after the brawl, U Saw's newspaper printed images of Indian police officers attacking yellow-robed Buddhist monks, and in retaliation Indian men were murdered across the city. It was a repeat of the 1930 Rangoon riots, but more organised.

The ensuing pogroms were the largest in Burma's recorded history, engulfing every major city, killing hundreds of people, injuring thousands and damaging 204 million rupees' worth of property.[20] A speaker in the Indian Legislative Assembly was not alone in wondering 'why, if a Burmese Muslim was responsible for the book, Indians got into trouble'. But Indians and Muslims would increasingly be treated as interchangeable and the word '*kala*' or 'foreigner' soon applied to both.

The correspondent for the *Civil & Military Gazette* was horrified by 'the mounting list of deaths and injuries' and noted that nearly all Indian shops were shuttered.[21] Authorities were forced to ban public gatherings of more than five people and soon armed escorts were evacuating Indian families from Burmese-majority neighbourhoods, effectively ghettoising them in temporary shelters. The killings continued until September when administrators locked down the whole of Rangoon. Colonial officials noted that religious and racial riots seemed to erupt in the countryside wherever issues of U Saw's *Thuriya* newspaper were distributed.[22]

A Tamil shopkeeper called M. P. Mariappan remembers how 'relations with the Burmese people began to suffer'.[23] Mariappan had been born into a Dalit family treated as untouchable back in Southern India and his family had migrated to Burma to escape the stigma of their caste. They kept a small shop and Mariappan had taken on the name Maung Chit Pyon and learned Burmese. 'I lived as a Burmese man with other Burmese,' he recalls.[24]

But one day Mariappan watched as fifty Burmese villagers approached his village carrying 'sickles, staffs, and other weapons' and shouting slogans. He was terrified that they would attack his shop, until a group of Burmese policemen lined up to protect the town, warning the mob that if they stepped any closer, they would shoot. When the mob refused to listen, the sub inspector gave orders to fire and a volley of bullets rang out. Four men crumpled to the ground dead and the rest ran away. The police had stopped the riots, but thereafter the atmosphere in the village had changed.

> Some Burmese even called me a *kala* now and then. I don't remember exactly how this happened, but whenever I heard such a thing, I would turn around and head in some other direction ... if I said anything they beat me up. Sometimes, they would come to the shop drunk and ask for something. I had to give them what they wanted, or they would start a fight ... When they began to call us *kalas*, we no longer got the respect that we deserved.[25]

Before long Mariappan decided it was best that he close his shop and relocate to a nearby town, where a larger Indian presence might protect him from Burmese mobs in the future. Across the country, thousands of Indians were doing the same.

Although officially termed 'riots', the violence unleashed on Indians in Burma could better be described as ethnic cleansing. It had been only two years since the separation from India, and the country was already on the road to becoming an ethno-nationalist state – something that it still struggles with today.

The British government seems to have been aware that U Saw was behind the riots, as the inquiry report refers to 'the irresponsible politician' who riled up the nationalist press.[26] But when Saw was hauled in front of a district magistrate in August 1938 he was swiftly acquitted of any wrongdoing. Meanwhile, the anti-Indian violence had become so overwhelming that Indian politicians suggested threatening war on the newly separated Burma unless it could stem the violence. On Christmas Day, Jinnah's Muslim League passed a formal resolution condemning the slaughter. His argument that South Asia's Muslims needed legal safeguards was looking increasingly prescient.[27]

Ba Maw, the Burmese premier, loudly denounced the violence. But it made no difference and in early 1939 U Saw ousted him in a no-confidence motion. A new premier called U Pu was brought in to replace him, with U Saw becoming minister of agriculture and forests. Saw's star was rising, and U Pu would last even less time than had Ba Maw. As the year came to an end, the official Nazi Party newspaper in Germany, *Völkischer Beobachter*, gave a 'seal of approval' to U Saw's Myochit Party.[28]

From this moment on, Burmese politics took a darker turn. The government started defining who counted as truly Burmese and who did not, and Indians meanwhile found themselves systematically boycotted and harassed. In Mandalay the Indian government's agent reported 'organised persecution' with Indian businesses 'boycotted, their shops picketed'.[29] The children of interracial marriages were particularly targeted, and in March 1939 the *Rangoon Gazette* published an anonymous letter stating:

> Neither the Burmans nor the Indians will accept us for one of them. The Indians call us Burmans and will have nothing to do with us. The Burmans call us Indians (Kalas) and denounce us as their enemies. We do not know what to do, or where to go, for we have no place to go.[30]

Almost unnoticed, a trickle of Indians started to leave Burma, sailing across the Bay of Bengal to restart their lives in India. Among them was the future Nobel laureate Amartya Sen, whose father had moved to Mandalay as a visiting fellow in Mandalay University. Amartya's childhood had been typical of Bengali children in Burma at the time. Growing up on the eastern edge of Mandalay, he had learned some Burmese from his nanny and enjoyed spotting leopards in the countryside outside the old capital, paying homage to the tomb of Bahadur Shah Zafar in Rangoon and travelling to Maymyo where many other Bengalis lived. 'The fact is, I could not have been happier,' he wrote years later.³¹ But in 1939 his parents decided to move back to his hometown of Dacca in India. Many others followed suit.

The India into which these refugees entered was rapidly changing too. Like in Burma, a limited form of democracy had arrived. As the country prepared for elections, Gandhi was notably absent, for the Mahatma's behaviour had become increasingly erratic.

In 1932 the Mahatma had undertaken a fast unto death in protest against the British government's Communal Award, which granted separate electorates to marginalised communities including the so-called 'untouchables' (now known as Dalits). Gandhi saw his protest as a way to prevent the division of Hindu society, but his stance was widely criticised, particularly by Dalit leader Dr B. R. Ambedkar, who had fought for political safeguards to uplift his community from centuries of oppression. By the time that his fast was called off, therefore, Gandhi's saint-like image had been heavily tarnished.

His star plummeted further in 1934 when he told the victims of an earthquake their misfortune was 'a chastisement for your sins'.³² Then, when the Mahatma's eldest son converted to Islam, Gandhi had suffered a nervous breakdown, moving to central India to live in seclusion. '[His] mind has ceased to work with directness,' wrote a concerned Sarojini Naidu to her daughter Padmaja, and 'he grows more and more fanatical in his arguments'.³³

It was therefore not Gandhi but his acolyte Jawaharlal Nehru who led the Indian National Congress into the elections. A socialist aristocrat brought up in Allahabad's grandest mansion, Nehru was a Kashmiri Brahmin descended from a long line of Mughal courtiers, who had spent his childhood being driven around by an English chauffeur.³⁴ After schooling abroad at Harrow and Cambridge, and law training at London's Inner Temple, he returned to India. 'I was a bit of a prig with little to commend me,' he later mused with characteristic self-awareness.³⁵ Nehru was more confident in English than other languages and found that his western education had alienated him from India. In England he had become enchanted with ideas of liberty and civil rights, but like so many others he quickly learned that back in his own land he didn't have any.

For much of his life, Jawaharlal Nehru had been more of a champagne socialist than a revolutionary, but in 1919, on a visit to the Sikh holy city of Amritsar, his life had changed forever. He was taking the train back to Delhi, when the British general Reginald Dyer got into a nearby bunk. Days earlier Dyer had ordered the massacre of hundreds of civilians for breaking a curfew, and from his bunk Nehru overheard the general boast that 'he had felt like reducing the rebellious city [of Amritsar] to a heap of ashes, but he took pity on it and refrained'. Nehru watched in horror as Dyer 'descended at Delhi Station in pyjamas with bright pink stripes, and a dressing gown'.[36] The military man had been born in Punjab and his callous disregard for Indian lives seemed to embody everything that was wrong with British imperialism. Nehru subsequently dived headfirst into Gandhi's *satyagraha* movement, and despite their striking ideological differences the two men developed a deep relationship. 'His smile is delightful, his laughter infectious,' Nehru wrote of his guru, 'and he radiates light heartedness. There is something childlike about him which is full of charm.'[37] With Gandhi's backing, Jawaharlal Nehru had shot to the top of the Congress Party, and was finally elected its president in 1936, shortly before the national elections.

Nehru's passion for politics left him little time for family life, and he cut a distant and cold figure to his wife Kamala and daughter Indira. Months before the election, Kamala died of tuberculosis, and he entered the contest devastated by the loss of a woman who he had never spent enough time with. Nonetheless, for three months, forty-seven-year-old Nehru charmed his way across India by train, car, bullock cart and even canoe.

Nehru found himself unable to comprehend the size of the crowds who attended his speeches. 'Why does this happen?' he wrote to Padmaja Naidu, Sarojini's daughter. 'I can't make it out and all my vanity does not help me to understand.' His palms swelled from shaking so many hands, and his voice grew hoarse from countless speeches. After the loss of his wife, he began confiding in Padmaja, and as the two got closer his letters filled with yearning. 'My dear how you fill my mind,' he wrote. 'When I ought to be thinking of something else, your image creeps in unawares through some window and upsets the train of my thought.' On a visit to the old Mughal capital of Agra, Padmaja's image 'got rather mixed up with the moonlight and the Taj', and by April Nehru was signing his letters 'my love to you, *carissima*'.[38] It was an unlikely time for romance, but then Nehru had a tendency to find love in the strangest places.

Nehru's chief rival in the elections, Muhammad Ali Jinnah, had fundamentally changed since his meeting with the Simon Commission years earlier. He had left politics after the death of his wife, the only exception being a brief foray into the Round Table Conferences, which he had walked out of midway through because of 'a distinct feeling that unity was hopeless, that Gandhi did not want it'.[39] That might have been the end of Jinnah's political career but for his rivalry with Jawaharlal Nehru, whose 'atheistic socialism' he despised. When a friend told Jinnah at a dinner party in London that Nehru regarded him as 'finished', Jinnah decided to return to India to 'show Nehru', accepting an invitation to lead the Muslim League in the upcoming elections against Nehru's Congress.[40]

Jinnah knew the Muslim League could not rival the popularity of the Congress, but by claiming to be the undisputed 'sole spokesman' of India's Muslims, he hoped to enter a coalition government and ensure that India's Muslim population – the largest in the world – had a voice in the new parliament and would not be dominated by the Hindu majority.

However, when the election results were announced in February 1937, Congress had managed to take power in seven of eleven provinces, while Jinnah's Muslim League had been decimated, failing to gain a majority in a single province. In Muslim-majority Punjab – today Pakistan's most populous province – the League did not win even a single seat. 'I shall never come back to Punjab,' announced Jinnah. 'It is such a hopeless place.'[41]

Writing Jinnah off as a has-been, Nehru refused a coalition between their two parties. Indeed, rather than meet Jinnah, he chose to visit Burma with his daughter.[42] It was a 'fatal error,' wrote the civil servant Penderel Moon later, and was, according to him, 'the prime cause of the creation of Pakistan'.[43]

Since the Round Table Conferences, many of India's princely states had made it clear they were willing to join an Indian federation in exchange for certain privileges. Linlithgow spent much of his first years as Viceroy trying to negotiate with the princes to enter the federation. One of his more intriguing attempts was to organise a week-long princely sports day where the maharajas and nawabs could play each other at squash and cricket. Yet this ended in disaster when the prince of Garauli 'tried to relive his youth with a sprinting and extra-long run-up to bowl – and suffered a heart attack in the process. No one wanted to discuss tiresome subjects like the abridgement of princely powers, grouping protocols and the consequences of democracy.' Nonetheless, by 1939 almost three-quarters of the states required to create the federation had accepted the Viceroy's terms.[44] Then, quite suddenly, everything had to be put on hold.

On 1 September 1939 Adolf Hitler invaded Poland. Two days later the United Kingdom declared war on Germany and without the consultation of any of the recently elected politicians, India and Burma were pulled into war as well. Plans to merge British India and the princely states into a federation were instead put into 'cold storage'.*

News of the conflict – a Second World War – rattled through the airwaves. It was slower to reach the smaller towns, and in the monsoon-soaked coastal city of Calicut the news arrived only 'along with the morning eggs'.[45] By midday, however, most people knew their lives had irrevocably changed. 'Everyone is buying or if they can hiring radio sets,' Sydney Ralli wrote in Karachi.

> Every single person walks around with a gas mask ... All the shops are practically empty, most of them closed at 5 o'clock. Everyone is doing some sort of national service. Sandbags everywhere. Everything is pitch black at night and no one is advised to be out after dark as it is dangerous.[46]

Even in India, the story of the Second World War is still usually told as a story centred on Europe. But the war would be the 'most general conflict' in Asian history since the Mongol Conquest. In a matter of months, conflict would sweep across the continent from eastern China all the way to India, and in the following years war would claim almost thirty million lives.[47]

Amartya Sen, whose family had just left Mandalay, remembers being 'dimly aware that even though all the adults in my family seemed very opposed to Nazi Germany, they thought that India should not be brought into the fight without first consulting Indians'.[48] Nehru, with

---

* This would be crucial to the endgame of empire, for India would finish the war with no constitutional link between British India and the princely states.

particular prescience, joked that the Viceroy's callous decision not to consult any elected Indian and Burmese politicians before dragging them to war would make the British Empire 'go to pieces and not all the king's horses and all the king's men will be able to put it together again'.[49] Linlithgow, he mused, was 'heavy of body and slow of mind, solid as a rock and with almost a rock's lack of awareness'.[50]

Over the next six years India and Burma would undergo militarisation on an enormous scale. When the war began the Indian Army consisted of 205,000 soldiers from British India and another 84,700 hailing from the princely states. By the end of the conflict India had deployed the largest 'volunteer' army in history: 2.5 million men, out of whom 90,000 would be killed or maimed.[51] In the words of historian Yasmin Khan, 'Britain did not fight the Second World War, the British Empire did.'[52]

These soldiers were supported by a vast network of cleaners, drivers, engineers, cooks, intelligence agents, sweepers, propaganda writers and barbers. Women who had been in purdah only a generation earlier now joined as nurses or as part of the Women's Auxiliary Force, and children found themselves facing an onslaught of war propaganda. During a fair at the British Residency in Mount Abu, for example, children were invited to throw tennis balls at cardboard figures of Hitler, Himmler, Goering and Goebbels, and whoever managed to knock over Hitler won a prize.[53]

Not everywhere would be affected equally. British administrators had labelled certain communities as 'martial races', and racial pseudo-science continued to loom large in the psyche of the British Indian Army – 'martial' communities would bear the brunt of the war effort. Almost two-thirds of the army came from the Punjab alone, in effect militarising the province and playing a large role in the scale of bloodletting there two years after the war's climax.[54]

The British recruitment drive also brought to the fore unresolved questions about nationality in the Indo-Burmese borderlands. In 1939 the border between Burma and India in the Patkai Hills was still not precisely demarcated and the governments in Assam and Burma were only just expanding their respective administrations over the Naga region of the Patkai.[55] This created very real problems for Major Sample of the Rangoon Recruitment Office when Angami Zapu Phizo, the homesick Naga Bible salesman, walked into his office and asked to join the Royal Artillery for 'King and Empire'. Phizo was offered a role in the Corps of Royal Engineers, but Sample explained that to fight, Phizo would have to choose between Indian or Burmese nationality. Phizo's response was uncompromising: 'I am a Naga first, a Naga second, and a Naga last.' When Major Sample protested, Phizo replied, 'If you tell me to go, I will go, but for my part I have offered my services.'[56] After Sample insisted there was no way for him to join without taking either Indian or Burmese nationality, Phizo stormed out of the office.

War eventually hit the former Indian Empire* in 1940, when Mussolini's Italian forces launched air raids on Aden. Punjabi battalions were sent to guard the city, while anxious Adeni Arabs had to be reassured that: 'British South Arabia would not, at any point in the future, become re-colonized as an Indian South Arabia.'[57] The anxiety was short-lived, however, and after Aden saw a surge of support for the war effort, the Colonial Office wrote approvingly that the 'nationalist bug' had not yet infected the city.

This was not the case in India and Burma. Britain was the largest imperial power on the planet, whose institutional racism was woven into the fabric of life in the Raj. Hitler himself had used the British autobiography *The Lives of a Bengal Lancer* to teach the SS 'how a tiny elite could subjugate an inferior race',[58] and as Ba Maw later reflected, 'For us in Asia and Africa there was as little difference between the two policies [of Nazism and imperialism] as there was between the devil and the deep sea.'[59] To make things even more morally ambiguous, two of the Axis powers – the USSR and the Japanese Empire – had long been idolised by many liberal Indians, including Nehru, as a communist utopia and an Asian liberating power respectively. Indeed, Ba Maw found it rather trite that the British were so concerned with Germany's invasion of Poland when Britain had been invading other countries for years. 'We concluded that the British were making a basic distinction between ... the white and other races,' he wrote. 'The Burmese were Asians and were conquered by the British, whereas the Poles were European and conquered by the Germans.'[60]

---

* I use the phrase 'former Indian Empire' to refer to the whole region that had been part of the Indian Empire in the 1920s.

Nehru by contrast recognised the dangers of Nazism, and swiftly declared that if Britain was truly fighting for democracy, it should set India free so that they could fight together on an equal footing. When the Viceroy refused to accede to the demands, however, Nehru's Congress ministries resigned, something that Jinnah celebrated as a 'Day of Deliverance'.

Viceroy Linlithgow needed a way to challenge the power of the Congress and he asked Jinnah to come up with a 'constructive policy' to contest its claim to speak on behalf of all Indians. This was to be a request with world-changing consequences.

Although many Pakistani nationalists have since projected their nation state into the distant past, the idea of creating a new country for India's Muslims was a remarkably recent one. Indeed, until the start of the Second World War, the idea of Pakistan was still largely unheard of.

There were precedents of course. In 1930 the poet Allama Iqbal had suggested the Muslim-majority regions of Northwest India be amalgamated into a single province. Three years later the term 'Pakistan' or 'Land of the Pure' was coined by Cambridge student Rahmat Ali Choudhary as an anagram for Northwest India's Muslim majority provinces: P for Punjab, A for Afghanistan, K for Kashmir, S for Sindh, and TAN for Baluchistan. Indeed, inspired by the separation of Burma, Rahmat Ali imagined his 'Pakistan' severing its ties with 'Hindu India' entirely, writing:

> While Burma is being separated from Hindoostan, it remains a mystery to us why Pakistan ... is to be forced into the Indian Federation.[61]

Rahmat Ali's ideas were widely dismissed, however, and as late as 1940 Tamil separatism in South India was a far bigger political issue than Pakistani separatism. Even Jinnah himself rejected the idea of Pakistan as 'some sort of Walt Disney dreamland, if not a Wellsian nightmare'.[62]

By the time war started, however, Jinnah had come round to the idea, writing in January 1940 that there were 'in India two nations who both must share the governance of their common motherland'.[63] And when, on that fateful day, Viceroy Linlithgow asked him to come up with a 'constructive policy' to challenge Congress' dominance, Jinnah made him a proposition.

Congress, he told the Viceroy, would not cooperate with the war effort unless India was granted immediate independence. But if Muslims were considered a nation unto themselves, with Jinnah as their 'sole spokesman', Congress would be unable to claim to speak on behalf of all of India. Jinnah could then help persuade Muslims to the British war effort.

Jinnah announced the idea to the public two weeks later at the Muslim League session in Lahore. A colossal marquee was erected in Minto Park, surrounded by white tents and green bunting, with the Mughal Badshahi Mosque and Fort looming over them. Discarding his monocle and silken suits, Jinnah arrived dressed in the sombre *churidars* and a black *achkan* of Northwest India's Muslim community – a costume notably alien from his own Gujarati community. After a welcome address, he ascended the podium flanked by men dressed in khaki and held the stage for a hundred minutes, bellowing in English – a language unintelligible to many of the hundred thousand people in the crowd – that India's Muslims were 'not a minority' but a nation unto themselves and should have equal bargaining power over a future constitution.[64] India, Jinnah argued, was an artificial construct forged by the British and should be divided into 'independent states'.

Jinnah's bombshell announcement would quickly become known as the Pakistan Resolution, but in his speech he never used that word. In fact, Jinnah was remarkably vague as to what he was advocating for, allowing him to skate over the diverse demands of the Muslim population across the subcontinent.[65] Jinnah likened politics to a game of chess – slow, methodical and pragmatic – and at this stage he probably saw his autonomous Muslim state as existing within an all-India federation. Yet his demand would soon take on a life of its own, beyond anything even he could imagine or control. Pandora's box had been opened.

Almost immediately, Jinnah's speech incited outrage across the political spectrum, including among Muslims. Sir Sikander Hyat Khan argued that instead of 'a Muslim Raj here and a Hindu Raj elsewhere', politicians should look for one system that would work for everyone,[66] while Hindu organisations condemned the idea for shattering the Hindu holy land of 'Bharat' that had so recently been achieved. Only the Dalit leader B. R. Ambedkar commented on the irony that the same people who had argued Burma should be separated to establish 'Bharat' were now crying that the 'unity of India' was being broken. 'What is the unity the Hindu sees between Pakistan and Hindustan?' Ambedkar wrote.

> The unity between India and Burma was not less fundamental ... if the Hindus did not object to the severance of Burma from India it is difficult to understand how the Hindus can object to the severance of an area like Pakistan.[67]

Congress, meanwhile, went on the defensive, nominating Maulana Al-Hussaini Azad as its new president. Azad spoke Arabic as his first language and belonged to a Muslim family from Delhi that had emigrated to Mecca shortly before the fall of the Mughal dynasty. His father was a Sufi pir, and as a teenager Azad had reacted by turning away from mysticism towards rationalism and science. 'It is one of the greatest frauds on the people,' he declared in response to Jinnah's declaration, 'to suggest that religious affinity can unite areas which are geographically, economically, linguistically, and culturally different ... We are an indivisible nation.'[68] Jinnah, however, accused Azad of being a sellout, telling him:

> I refuse to discuss with you by correspondence or otherwise as you have completely forfeited the confidence of Muslim India ... Cannot you realise that you are made a Muslim Show Boy Congress President ... The Congress is a Hindu body. If you have self-respect resign at once.[69]

Jinnah, the former ambassador of Hindu–Muslim unity, was now challenging the very idea that Hindus and Muslims could form a single nation.

Things were equally fractious back in Burma and to help get Britain through the war, the hapless new governor Reginald Dorman-Smith increasingly threw his support behind U Saw. An Anglo-Irish diplomat with a receding hairline and a pencil moustache, Dorman-Smith was an odd, lonely, but erudite man whose strong views against 'scientific farming' once led him into a zealous crusade against pasteurised milk. His ancestry made him sympathetic to Burmese anti-colonialism, yet he also thoroughly underestimated U Saw, whom he considered 'a true patriot' and a 'loveable rogue'.[70] Unbeknown to Dorman-Smith, Saw had recently made overtures to Japanese secret agent Keiji Suzuki for military aid to help overthrow the British. 'U Saw asked me if Japan would be prepared to give military aid in Burma's struggle for freedom,' Suzuki later revealed.

> He mentioned ... arms, aeroplanes, money, and I made a quick calculation in my mind, and found the figures fantastic. I told U Saw that I was only a newspaper reporter, and he should discuss the matter at higher levels, perhaps with the Japanese Consul.[71]

Saw's meeting went undetected by British surveillance, yet the British director of the Burma Defence Bureau was nonetheless deeply suspicious of him and warned Dorman-Smith that he was a known admirer of Hitler's *Mein Kampf* who aimed to bring 'Burma within the economic orbit of Japan ... and driving out all foreigners':

> He has consistently followed ... the Hitlerian method of advancing to power ... All my informants agree, independently, that U Saw wishes to become the first Dictator of Burma if and when British rule comes to an end.[72]

Despite the warnings, Saw's rise continued unabated, and on 7 September 1940 he helped topple U Pu's ministry. Two days later Dorman-Smith swore in U Saw as the new premier of Burma and a somewhat naïve justification found in a secret British file to Churchill reveals that Europeans in Burma regarded Saw 'as being a great power for good as well as for evil' and simply preferred 'to see him as Premier of Burma than in any other capacity'.[73]

After he was elected, Saw declared it his government's 'sacred duty' to promote Buddhism's proper practice, while asking non-Buddhist 'minorities, especially ... Anglo-Burmans and Burma-Muslims, to throw their lot in with the indigenous people of the country'.[74] The implication here was, of course, that Saw didn't consider these communities indigenous. He set about passing bills that were prejudiced against Indians, including making visas to Burma too expensive for most Indians and making it an official requirement to seek government permission for a marriage between an Indian man and a Buddhist Burmese woman. Back in India, Gandhi condemned the 'wretched agreement' and despite having originally supported Burma's separation, he derided the results of the recent Partition.[75] 'The Indo-Burma Immigration Agreement ... has caused me deep pain,' Gandhi said.

> The burden of proving the right to remain in Burma has in every case been thrown on the Indian resident ... The whole thing appears still more hideous when we recall the fact that only a few years ago Burma was an integral part of India. Does the partition make India a leper country the presence of whose inhabitants must carry heavy penalties?[76]

Soon even the Viceroy's executive council demanded the agreement be scrapped. Yet Saw's entire political platform was based on the idea that Burmese women were under threat from foreigners, and he flatly refused to remove the clause.

It would be Saw's new census, however, that would have the most enduring consequences. The premier ensured a subtle change was made in counting the population of Arakan, the diverse and densely forested region that bordered the Indian coastline. Historically, it had been an independent kingdom wedged between separate Burmese and Bengali kingdoms, resulting in an ethnic melting pot of Arakanese Buddhists, Bengali poets, Portuguese pirates, Afghan archers and even renegade ronin samurai from Nagasaki.[77] Now Saw instituted rules to reclassify certain Muslim communities as Indian foreigners, including a group calling themselves the Rohingya. Decades later the Burmese military would use this as proof the Rohingya were not indigenous to Burma and justify a genocide of the population.*

---

* Distinguishing between the Rohingya and Bengali Muslims remains controversial in Burma. A small Muslim presence in the region dates back to the ninth century with the arrival of Arab traders, and increased during the kingdom of the Mrauk U, when the Muslim-dominated port of Chittagong was annexed to Arakan and when the region became the centre of the slave trade across the Bay of Bengal. Nonetheless, the Muslim presence vastly increased in the colonial period, when Bengali Muslims began to settle in the region. Many Burmese claim the Rohingya arrived with the British, whereas the Rohingya themselves trace their origins to the earlier waves of Muslim migration in the region. See Myint-U, T., *The Hidden History of Burma* and Bowser, M. J., *Misdirected Rage*.

By September 1941 Saw's actions were making Viceroy Linlithgow anxious. He began sending a stream of letters to Secretary of State Leo Amery warning that Saw had 'organized anti-Indian feeling in the past and will do so again ... [the] parallel with Nazi tactics is exact ... [and] the new Governor [Dorman-Smith], I fear, is already in danger of succumbing'. With Amery's help, Linlithgow managed to persuade Dorman-Smith to bypass Saw and get the marriage clause of the immigration bill scrapped, but it wasn't easy. An ominous telegram indicated how 'the shadow of Saw ... looms and the Ministers are scared'.[78] The premier was already rounding up dissenting groups, including Aung San's Thakins, and as the monsoon of 1941 subsided even Saw's former mentor U Ba Pe had been arrested for treason. Dorman-Smith's secretary later chillingly recalled:

> When I once twitted him after he became a Minister on his unforgivable action in stirring up communal trouble in the riots of 1938–39 [U Saw] replied with a smile that, if one was in opposition, anything that would embarrass Government was justifiable, but if his political opponents thought they could do the same to him, they would find themselves in jail. This prophecy seems to have been fulfilled![79]

In late 1941 the wars in Europe and China still seemed distant to most people in India and Burma. The Viceroy's aide-de-camp had enough free time to go for picnics in Delhi's Red Fort,[80] while a civil servant in Moradabad wrote that the lack of knowledge of the war was 'appalling ... I asked one chap if he had ever heard of Hitler *Budmash* [hooligan] and he said he supposed it must be the new *Patwari* [village accountant].'[81] But Dorman-Smith was increasingly worried that war might soon come to Burma.

The signs were everywhere. Neighbouring French-Indochina had already been partially occupied by the Japanese and the 'Burma Road' connecting Burma with China had become the last remaining artery through which supplies reached the Chinese nationalist resistance to Japan's invasion. Dorman-Smith thought a Japanese strike on Burma to control this road increasingly likely and he began giving advice in case of 'War with Japan'.

Few people listened to him, and the sluggish complacency of British officers was matched only by Premier U Saw, who appeared more interested in arresting his opponents. After all, Burma was protected by vast forests, and intelligence reports noted how difficult it would be to invade the country through Thailand. Only a few shrewd civil servants pointed out that 'Burmese elephant thieves drove stolen animals into Thailand this way on a regular basis'.[82]

Attention in Burma instead fixed on the appointment of Winston Churchill as Britain's prime minister. The Churchill name was already famous, for it was Churchill's father who had ordered the conquest of Upper Burma and Mandalay in the first place. To Burmese dismay, Winston proved just as imperialist as his father and soon after signing the Atlantic Charter, recognising the 'right of all peoples to choose the form of government under which they will live', the prime minister admitted he hadn't meant for it to apply to colonial subjects.[83] George Orwell, the Bihar-born anti-colonial essayist provided a sharp retort: 'The unspoken clause is always: not counting niggers.'[84] With the Burmese press outraged by Churchill's words, in late 1941 U Saw decided to petition the British PM personally to grant Burmese independence, smugly telling a reporter he 'was not going to London simply to kiss Mr Churchill'.[85] Then Saw climbed into a private plane, sailed into the sky and circled the Shwedagon Pagoda nine times for good luck before heading off west.

Upon arriving in London, U Saw presented a bamboo and silken sunshade to the Queen, and set off to meet Churchill.[86] But with London decimated by the Blitz, Churchill bluntly told him that now was not the time to discuss such matters, so U Saw left the capital early, bitterly broadcasting on the radio that 'the British government is apparently more interested in obtaining the freedom of countries under the Axis than of countries under the British Commonwealth of Nations'.[87] He flew on to Washington where he hoped to put pressure on the Roosevelt administration, but their meeting was similarly disappointing.[88] Finally admitting defeat, Saw boarded a plane for Burma, stopping overnight in Honolulu on 6 December 1941.

The next morning as Japanese planes swooped overhead and bombed the naval base in Pearl Harbor, Saw personally witnessed the devastation: in front of his eyes, the world seemed to change. An Asian power had crippled America.

Blocked from continuing across the Pacific, Saw flew home via Portugal, sneaking into the Japanese embassy in Lisbon to offer his services. Then he set off east, intending to continue on to Bangkok to help a pro-Japanese 'Free Burma Government'. Unbeknown to him, however, the British had decoded Japanese cyphers and had a full transcript of everything that transpired.[89] When Saw stopped to refuel in Palestine, a mysterious man diverted him to a room in a small building and locked the door behind them. An inspector began searching Saw, taking 'special interest ... in the heels of his shoes', and eventually, after a short interrogation, Burma's premier was flown to Uganda and imprisoned in 'a small house enclosed by a wire fence', where he was to remain for the next five years, forbidden from having his hair cut out of fear that he might 'attempt to transmit some message' to the barber.[90] Soon after, British officials started asking 'why we allowed a man like U Saw to be in charge of the administration of Burma' at all.[91]

The morning after the bombing of Pearl Harbor, Rangoon's leading officials woke up with terrible hangovers following a night of drinking at the Governor's Horse Racing Cup.

Spectators had been asked not to wear their top hats to the horse race, 'in deference to wartime austerity',[92] but afterwards Rangoon society attended a dazzling ball at the Strand Hotel where 'a stout lady, popular with local audiences ... sang a comic song, concluding it by throwing up her skirt'.[93] Now, however, the hungover officials learned that Japanese troops had simultaneously attacked American positions in the Philippines and British positions in Hong Kong and Malaya, cycling through the supposedly impenetrable Malayan forests using a form of 'bicycle blitzkrieg'.[94] Another division had landed at Burma's southernmost tip, Victoria Point, and was advancing up the isthmus. The British Empire's war with Japan had begun.

The war escalated fast. On 11 December 1941, Hitler and Mussolini declared war on the United States. The fighting in Europe and Asia suddenly became one and the same conflict, and Roosevelt wrote to Churchill:

Thank the lord you have HE-SAW, WE-SAW, YOU-SAW under lock and key. I have never liked Burma or the Burmese and you people must have had a terrible time with them for the last fifty years ... I wish you could put the whole bunch of them into a frying pan with a wall around it and let them stew in their own juice.[95]

But although U Saw was under lock and key, the impact of his premiership would be felt for decades to come. Burma's Indian communities wondered if their days in the country were now limited, and an employee of Tata Oil Mills, Nadir Tyabji, recorded the sense of terror:

I got the feeling that the Burmese were just waiting for an opportunity to drive the Indians out and take their place in the scheme of things ... [The Indian population] has begun to get restive and from odd bits of gossip which I picked up, it became evident that any Japanese advance from the south would result in a massive movement of Indians.[96]

Burma's Indian population was preparing to flee.

4

The Long March

It was a Tuesday when the first Japanese bombs fell on Rangoon.

The morning sun shone hot and bright, and with only two days until Christmas of 1941 most of Rangoon's Goan community were more concerned with shopping for presents than preparing for the coming war. There was excited chatter about the new Bob Hope and Bing Crosby film *Road to Zanzibar*, which was about to open at the New Excelsior Cinema,[1] and Isabelle Vaz remembers that her grandmother 'was busy making special plum cakes and roasting stuffed ducks which she supplied annually at Christmas'. Among Isabelle's Goan neighbours, 'No one really took heed of the Japanese when they announced over the radio ... that they would soon be showering Rangoon with "Christmas toys".'[2] Schools had closed after the bombing of Pearl Harbor, and the rich had begun evacuating to smaller towns, but war still felt like a distant mirage. 'We were always being told that Japan was going to attack,' recalls Eric Menezes, a family friend of Isabelle's who was eight years old at the time,

> but ... the only reminder of an expected war was the digging of an L-shaped trench in the garden ... for use in case of an air raid ... We felt no anxiety. The government communiques were guarded but not alarming, and people were advised not to keep too much cash at home to avoid robberies. So life went on as normal, a little subdued perhaps, but there were no shortages of food or any other essential supplies.[3]

An air-raid siren went off at half past nine, but Donald Menezes recalled that 'after the initial panic, people relaxed and began moving in the streets, as in the usual practice alerts'.[4] Forty-five minutes later, fifty-four Japanese bomber planes appeared in the sky over downtown Rangoon. The lookout at Monkey Point had mistaken them for Allied planes and failed to give another alert. It was the noise that struck Donald first:

> First the vroom-vroom-vroom of de-synchronized aircraft engines, then the howl and scream of diving planes. This was followed by the crump and explosion of light bombs and murderous chatter of machine guns ... We could hear our faithful [servant] Yeriah running about closing doors and windows ... I ran up to the house again yelling in Hindustani 'Yeriah you fool come down!' ... As I ran towards the trenches, I looked up at the sky. Just beyond the overhang of the upper verandah, I saw four black puffs of smoke ... [and] a Japanese plane disintegrate in the smoke. Our Anglo-Indian ack-ack gunners of the Burma Auxiliary Force had brought down their first Japanese plane.[5]

Not everyone made it to an air-raid shelter in time. Eric remembers 'people who were standing in the street and watching the planes, being machine-gunned or blown to bits along with buildings. Whole lines of shops in the Surtee Bazaar were strafed by Japanese fighters, leaving hundreds dead', and Eric himself only got into his trench once the bombing was over. 'It may seem stupid,' he later observed, 'but we were all standing in the garden, mesmerized, stomachs churning, frozen with fright, watching Rangoon burn in the distance and feeling the shock waves of bursting bombs.'[6] Indeed, many who witnessed the destruction that day record a similar morbid fascination with watching their city burn.

It lasted just over half an hour, but Donald hid in his trench with his family and servants for what seemed like an eternity. Only when he heard the marshals calling that everyone should evacuate did he get out and look around at the devastation. Bodies lined the streets and 'great holes were gouged in the roads, with water spewing out of burst water mains'. A home for European sailors at the end of his street had 'collapsed like a pack of cards' and 'the phosphorous pellets emitted from the bombs had ignited fires. Two trees in the compound were ablaze, and the fire had spread to the adjacent house.' Donald helped put out the flames, then heard his friend crying out, 'Eddie is dead! Eddie is dead.' Eddie was Donald's uncle, and a bomb had torn a hole in the front porch of his home. 'As Arnold and I entered Uncle's house, we were met by a scene of horror and death,' he later told oral historian Yvonne Vaz Ezdani:

> Aunt Connie's body had fallen forward from the piano stool in a semi-upright position. Her head, bashed in by the bomb blast, rested face down on the radio set. She had delivered her baby, due that day. It lay dead on the floor. Blood, bones, brains and limbs lay scattered around. There were no recognizable bodies. However, three others had died in that bomb blast; a five-year-old child, Winsome, her Burmese nanny, and Connie's mother, Mrs Marshner.[7]

In the aftermath, Isabelle's family moved temporarily into the Menezes house on the outskirts of the city away from the centre of the bombing. Other Goans did the same, and soon the Menezes had eighteen guests living with them. 'The spare bedrooms were allocated,' remembered Eric, 'and all was cosy with a sense of safety that comes with numbers.'[8] As they made up their minds about how to respond, everyone frantically tried to keep up the festive spirit. On Christmas Eve Eric accompanied his parents into town to pick up a Christmas cake. But it was a mournful sight, and the streets were empty except for howling street dogs and Lady Dorman-Smith, the governor's wife, who was charging around trying to raise morale. Even she headed home distraught, however, after learning that most of the doctors at the city hospital had simply run away.[9]

The next morning, Christmas Day, the Japanese bombed Rangoon again. This time the Goan families ran at once to the nearest trench to hide. No one was hurt, but everyone was shaken. '[After that] the city of Rangoon emptied,' recalls Donald Menezes. Many Burmese made for the teak monasteries on the outskirts of the cities, while 'a mass of fleeing Indians were reported at Prome, nearly two hundred miles north of Rangoon', escaping by 'bus, truck, train, bullock cart, pushcart and bicycle, and on foot, anything that moved, carrying their few belongings'.[10]

In the four years since Burma's separation from India, Indians had been systematically excluded from life in the colony. Fearing what ethnic Burmans might do to them if the British evacuated from the area, half of the entire Indian community had decided to flee en masse. Yet officials demanded proof of vaccination and inoculation in order to depart for India. As a result, a throng of twenty thousand Indians haphazardly bedded down outside the city of Prome and cholera quickly took hold.[11]

The Menezes' two South Indian servants were among the first to flee, announcing on Christmas evening that they were leaving. 'There was nothing else to do but give them some rice, sugar, a little oil and two hundred rupees to meet their expenses on the way,' remembers Eric.

> We never saw them again ... [Then] our landlords the Gardners, themselves decided to leave, and offered to sell the entire bungalow to Daddy for a throwaway price of only five thousand rupees, which Dad had to decline as we did not know our own future. Apart from a few slices, the Christmas cake was uneaten and nobody had any inclination to enjoy the small Christmas lunch.[12]

With the servants gone, the women took over the work of the household, while the men went out to scavenge for supplies. 'All of us went for Mass, Confession and Holy Communion at the nearby church, so as to be prepared for death,' remembers Isabelle. Along with the rest of Rangoon's Indian population, they feared for their safety, deeply aware that the Burmese had brutally attacked their community twice in the last decade and 'their memories of the violence of the 1930s now swollen by rumours of Japanese atrocities to come'.[13] The family set about covering windows and lamps around the house with brown paper so that no one could tell people were living there, and then they began to debate their future.[14]

★ ★ ★

The speed of the Japanese advance towards Rangoon was astonishing. Within a month of bombing Pearl Harbor, they had captured half of Burma's southern isthmus and the large city of Tavoy. Their success was partly thanks to Burmese allies: thirty young men later known as the Thirty Comrades, the founding fathers of Burmese Independence. The leader of this unlikely militia was Aung San, the oddball student activist who had undergone one of the most extraordinary transformations of the war.

Six days after Ba Maw's arrest the previous year, Aung San had been horrified to learn the British had put a reward on his head of five rupees, 'about the price of a fair-sized chicken'.[15] So he smuggled himself onto a Norwegian cargo steamer delivering rice to China, suffering seasickness en route and falling unconscious in a heap of coconuts, only to wake up in Amoy in Southeastern China.[16] Here he waited for weeks trying to contact Chinese communists, until one day in November he received word from Colonel Keiji Suzuki, a 'slim man with refined, sharp Japanese features' who 'had a habit of scurrying around town as if in a perpetual hurry with his fingers anxiously twisting the right tip of moustache'.[17] It was the same agent that U Saw had contacted months earlier.

Aung San was subsequently flown to Japan, and he met Suzuki on the runway of Tokyo's Haneda Airport on 12 November 1940. While Aung San was a socialist at heart, disliking the Japanese monarchy and finding certain Japanese ideas barbaric, he agreed to work with Imperial Japan to further Burmese independence. Indeed the excitement of being in Imperial Japan briefly went to his head. 'What we want is a strong state,' Aung San wrote in a new manifesto in early 1941. 'There shall be no parliamentary opposition, no nonsense of individualism. Everyone must submit to the state which is supreme over the individual.'[18]

Eventually, disguised with a set of false teeth that made him look a bit like a chipmunk, he snuck back into Rangoon and smuggled thirty other Thakins off to Suzuki's training camp.[19] Soon the thirty young men were undergoing six months of gruelling Japanese military training and then each took a new codename. Aung San chose Bo Teza, 'Officer Fire', while Shu Maung, the future dictator of Burma, adopted the moniker Bo Ne Win, 'Officer Radiant Sun'. Suzuki, ever the romantic, chose the name Bo Mogyo, 'Officer Thunderbolt', in homage to an age-old Burmese prophecy that British rule would be ended by a thunderbolt. Then, on 31 December 1941, in a rundown house near Bangkok's Khao San Road, they formed the core of a new 'Burmese Independence Army' (BIA).[20] The young men slit their fingers and mixed their blood with liquor in a silver bowl. Then they took a sip and recited an ancient warrior's oath: 'To be indissolubly bound together by this bond of blood when fighting the [British] enemy.'[21]

Days later they were marching alongside an army of Japanese soldiers on the way to liberate their homeland from British rule. The group's numbers swelled as they went north, often through areas that had risen up during Saya San's rebellion, so that by the end of the year the ragtag BIA numbered around eighteen thousand recruits.

The old Burmese capital of Moulmein fell to the advancing armies on the last day of January and two weeks later news filtered in that Britain's primary base in the Indian Ocean, Singapore, had also fallen to the Japanese. Eighty five thousand Indian Army soldiers had surrendered, in addition to twenty thousand British and Australian, in the worst British military defeat since the first Afghan War a century earlier. Within days, on 20 February 1942, the Burmese government ordered the evacuation of civilians from Rangoon itself.

The evacuation would unveil the deeply entrenched racial and class hierarchies of colonial society for all to see. Aeroplanes were suddenly reserved for Europeans and Anglo-Indians only, and spaces on passenger ships were rationed along racial lines so that on one ship almost a third of deck berths were given to Anglo-Indians, despite their tiny relative population. Goans like the Menezes were another privileged community, and when Eric and Isabelle's families decided to leave, their Christian names and European dress ensured easy access to ships.

Most Indians were not so fortunate and a clerk called H. K. Mukherji complained the 'big merchants, chettis [and) gujarati banias' who waxed lyrical about 'independence' and 'brotherhood' now 'paid huge bribes to get themselves onto steamships'.[22] Many Indians were stopped from escaping by inane political rivalry between the government of India and the government of Burma. When India suggested that those without money should be evacuated for free, Burmese ministers refused to spend money on non-indigenous 'foreigners'. The political impasse was only resolved weeks later but by then it was too little too late.[23] Burma's government had become so concerned about the exodus of essential workers that it banned the sale of deck-class boat tickets to Indian men unless they were accompanied by at least five women. To circumvent the new rules, some terrified families even subtly changed their names to pose as Anglo-Indians so that 'Ramasamy became Ramsay ... Lakshmi became Lucy'.[24]

The evacuation also divided families. Gurusamy, the brother of M. P. Mariappan – the Nadar Tamil who had witnessed the 1938 riots – had long been anxious about the Japanese invasion, telling Mariappan that unless they left now, 'We may not be able to go back to India.' But twenty-two-year-old Mariappan didn't care, at least not yet. In his mind, Burma was home. 'Why would I go to India?' he remembers thinking. And so Gurusamy and his wife left on the last ship to India, sailing back to their dusty ancestral village of Pudur while Mariappan stayed in Burma with another brother, Mutharasu. Between December 1941 and March 1942 an estimated seventy thousand Indian civilians were evacuated across the Bay of Bengal by sea.[25]

As Rangoon emptied, crucial jobs went unfilled. The city's sewage works had been staffed by low-caste Indians and after they fled, a putrid stench filled the air. Meanwhile, inmates walked out of prisons and 'lunatics' were reported leaving asylums. Rumour had it that 'chimps, lions, a fierce black panther and ... the most deadly snakes' had escaped from the city zoo. On one occasion a mob of yellow-clad Buddhist monks was spotted looting a bazaar, seizing felt hats and 'huge piles of women's underwear'. Governor Dorman-Smith blamed the panic on war correspondents, who he labelled sensationalist 'vultures',[26] but it was undeniable that a sense of hopelessness had descended upon Rangoon. On 21 February a report read:

> Apart from our small party, I do not think that there was a single sober man anywhere. The crews of the boats alongside the troops had looted liquor and were rolling around the place in the last stages of drunkenness.[27]

As civic authority in Burma collapsed, so did its military. Much of the Indian Army was fighting Nazi Germany in the Middle East and an official report later admitted that 'despite the breathing space of six weeks between the outbreak of War and the start of the Japanese drive into southern Burma ... Burma still remained practically defenceless'.[28] Just one and a half divisions of the British Indian and Burmese armies were now pitched against four divisions of Japan's Fifteenth Army and although their valiant defence of Rangoon was initially compared to the Battle of Britain, any such analogies soon gave way to a sense of imminent defeat.

Evacuation camps were underfunded and understaffed and the only Burmese radar units were sent to guard the frontiers of India. Troops remaining in Burma began to desert, fearing themselves hopelessly outnumbered. Elsewhere, a scorched earth policy was enacted to deny infrastructure to the Japanese, pre-emptively destroying boats along the Indian and Burmese border. 'To deprive the people in East Bengal of their boats is like cutting off a vital limb,' cried Gandhi in protest.[29] It was to prove a prescient comment when Bengal descended into famine a few months later.

At the end of the month, as the sky glowed red from fires across the city, Governor Dorman-Smith announced that his government would evacuate. Abandoning his treasured collection of top hats, the governor and his aide-de-camp set about destroying essential items to prevent them falling to the Japanese, an act that apparently included throwing billiard balls through all the portraits hanging in Government House. Then, before dawn on 1 March, Dorman-Smith fled Rangoon for the Burmese hills.

When the British left, extreme Burmese nationalists and bandits 'ruthlessly murdered the Indians' who remained in the city. The precise chronology of events is unclear as is the death toll, for few people had time to write anything down during the chaos, and much of what we know comes from a single account by a Rangoon-based doctor. Nonetheless, it is evident the anti-Indian bloodshed was only stopped when the Japanese arrived two weeks later, erecting severed heads at the four corners of the Surtee Bazaar.[30] British prestige had been eviscerated, and the British, Jawaharlal Nehru wrote, were 'already a second-class power'.[31]

With the Japanese advancing north at extraordinary speed, and British protection from Burmese mob violence absent, hundreds of thousands of Indian civilians began a 'Long March' over the Patkai Hills to India, in one of the largest refugee crises that South Asia had yet known.[32]

This astonishing migration features remarkably little in the national imaginations of any of the countries involved. There is no memorial for the dead in India, Burma or Bangladesh. Memories of the Long March have been eclipsed by other, more traumatic events, from the Bengal famine and the 1947 Partition to the Burmese civil war and Bangladeshi independence. Few of the survivors ever committed their experiences to paper and only in recent years have a few testimonies come to light.[33] Nonetheless, an estimated six hundred thousand Indian civilians fled Burma for India in 1942 and upwards of eighty thousand would never make it. Many of the women had never been out of purdah before.[34] At the time, the Long March was the largest mass migration ever recorded.[35]

The refugees were amazingly diverse and the official 'Register of Evacuees' lists nurses and firemen, sweepers and servants, cowherds and mining engineers, religious leaders and lighthouse keepers.[36] The family of Anglo-Burmese photographer Richard Bartholomew fled since their Christian names marked them as enemies in the eyes of the Japanese. The Indo-Burmese family of Helen Richardson, later one of Bollywood's biggest stars, left for similar reasons. Nonetheless, an astonishing 96 per cent of the refugees who fled Burma in 1942 were Indians and in the words of the scholar Matthew Bowser, 'The Long March should not be viewed as a spontaneous decision to "return home" by itinerant Indian migrants, but rather the violent culmination of a First Partition of India.'[37]

Burma had descended into brutal ethnic violence, but beneath the racial animosity thousands of real friendships were being torn apart. 'There was one friend I trusted more than anyone else,' recalls M. P. Mariappan, who had finally decided to escape Burma with his elder brother Mutharasu after the fall of Rangoon:

> Ko Chet Pon was his name. Everyone called him *makkambuwe* which meant 'moustache-man' in Burmese ... it was in his hands that I put the shop, the keys, all my things, before I left for India ... 'Give it back to me when I come back, if we manage to find each other once more,' I said to him. And then we left.[38]

Mariappan and Mutharasu slipped out of the town with seven others and jumped on a train to Prome in central Burma. Despite the conflict between Indians and Burmese elsewhere, hundreds of Burmese civilians volunteered in its refugee camp to feed the Indian refugees – a sight that made one bureaucrat write how 'in their heart of hearts they were brothers and fellow creatures'.[39] Here Mariappan and Mutharasu learned that around five hundred others were preparing to walk through the lower Patkai Hills to Akyab, from where boats were still leaving to the Indian port of Chittagong. The road would put them near the front line of the Japanese advance, but with the alternative of walking the deadly mountain trails of the northern Patkai, the brothers thought they would try their luck. In 1942 only three dusty tracks crossed the Patkai. Mariappan and Mutharasu bought two bullocks and a cart, and began their march through 'endless thickets of bamboo'.[40] Poisonous plants grew in the streams and Mariappan recalls that:

> People would scoop up water from a stream to drink. They would then get diarrhea and struggle for their lives. This was what happened to a quarter or maybe half of those who came walking that way. Many of them, close to death, crowded on both sides of the path, with containers in their hands. 'Ayya, water … Ayya, water,' they would beg those of us who were passing along that way on carts. No one would do anything to help them.[41]

The brothers were just two among the 150,000 refugees to walk the 110 miles over the Taungup Pass. Since most colonial officers had evacuated by this point, when Mariappan and Mutharasu arrived there was only a single brave British officer from the Forest Service who had stayed to help out. After just a few days the path was lined with bodies, its refugee columns stalked by vultures.[42] 'We had to cook and eat right beside them,' remembered Mariappan.

> There were bodies lying right along the path and the bullock carts were driven right over them. I remember how the feet of the bulls and the wheels of the cart would grind into those bodies as we passed … the government did nothing for us there.[43]

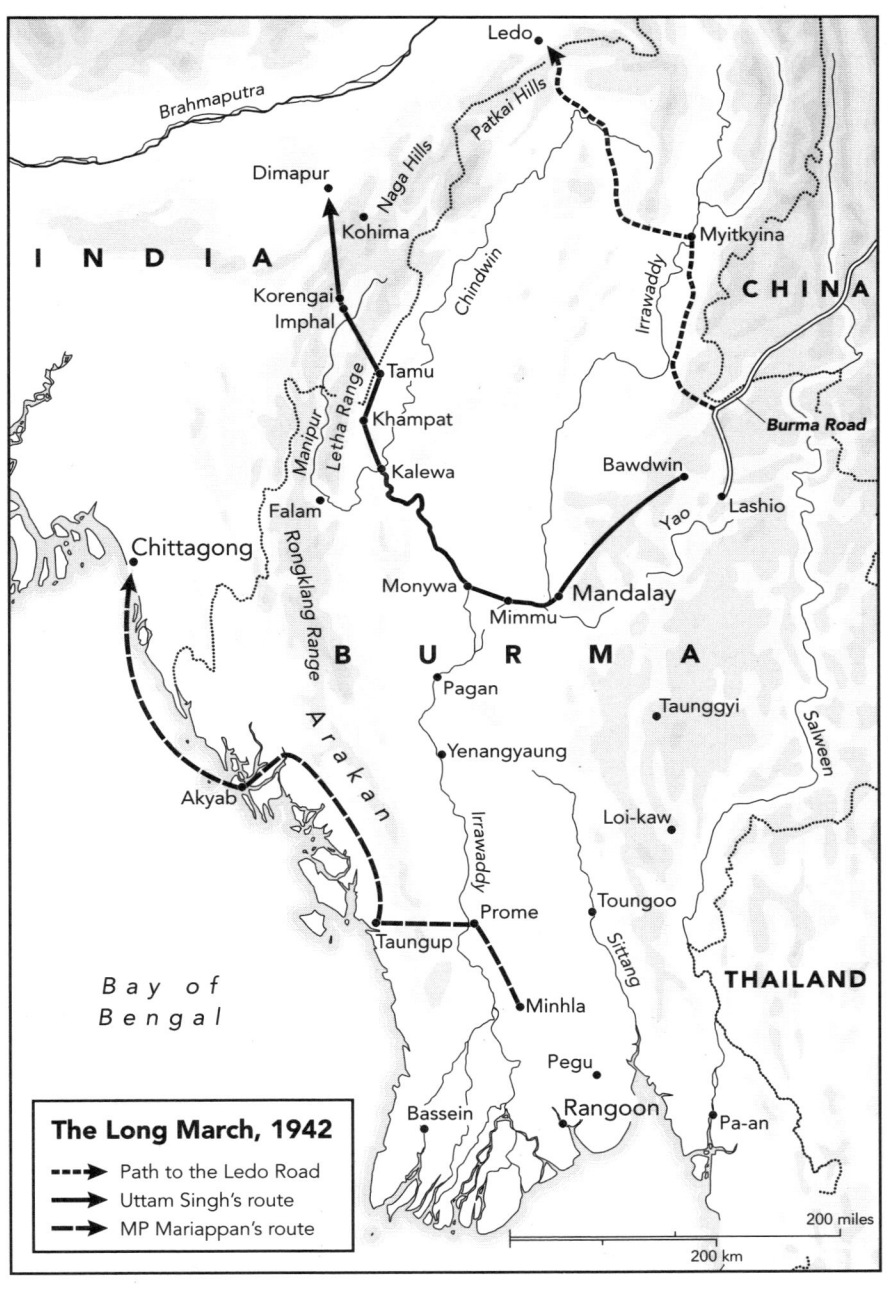

As they went, the refugees were forced to make horrible decisions: save a friend or save yourself. Halfway across the mountains, a man from near Mariappan's hometown succumbed to diarrhoea.

> We were afraid that if we carried him along with us, none of us might make it to India ourselves. And so we left him there, sitting up against a tree.[44]

The group began the descent down to the Arakan plains soon after, but arrived in a city dangerously low on water. As local officers tried to take charge, touring local springs and organising local supplies, the number of refugees arriving simply overwhelmed them. With no government evacuation camps available, most people simply slept on the Akyab jetty, yet amid the chaos Mariappan and his brother managed to squeeze onto a boat to Chittagong.[45] From there the brothers transferred onto a train to their ancestral hometown and reconnected with their younger brother Gurusamy, but also found themselves face to face with the family of the man they had left behind.

> 'Just tell us whether he's alive or dead,' they begged us ... but what could we say ... Imagine how it must have been, to leave that life to struggle for survival without doing anything to save him. I was distressed by this for a long time to come ... his memory will not leave me.[46]

The stigma attached to Mariappan's caste in Pudur had been one of the primary reasons for his family's migration to Burma in the first place, for Burma had no caste system. Now Mariappan was forced back into the caste-ridden society of his birth, and once again became untouchable. A decade after leaving Pudur, he was back where he started, with little money or wealth to show for himself; only a sense of trauma and loss, which would never leave him.

Situated on the Indo-Burmese border, the district of Arakan had seen growing tensions between its religious communities ever since U Saw had reclassified the Muslim Rohingya population as Indians a year earlier. Now things devolved even further into chaos. Forty-eight hours after Mariappan had squeezed onto a boat in Arakan's capital, the British commissioner abandoned the district. The deputy commissioner U Kyaw Khine worked frantically to ease hostility between Buddhists and Muslims, while continuing to evacuate Indians – in the following weeks an estimated thirty-five thousand men, women and children would be safely shipped off the Arakan coast to India.[47] His attempts at calming communal tensions, however, proved less successful. It remains contested as to who precisely started the violence. Buddhist sources blame Muslims and Muslim sources blame Buddhists. Whatever the case, all sources agree that on 28 March 1942 Arakanese Buddhists attacked a group of Indians and Muslims in central Arakan and in retaliation Muslims set Arakanese Buddhist villages and monasteries aflame, and even murdered U Kyaw Khine himself.[48] Attacks provoked other attacks, and as racial anxieties unleashed by U Saw and the separation debates transformed into violent ethnic cleansing, the diverse borderland began to fragment into a Muslim north and a Buddhist south.

A month later Aung San's Burmese Independence Army, swollen with new recruits, marched into the chaos of Arakan, led by two Japanese officers. Some might have hoped the BIA would calm the violence, for Aung San had been outspoken in his aim of unifying Burma's ethnic groups in opposition to the British. But he had already lost control of his ragtag army. The first thousand men had been Burman convicts from Thai prisons, given an ultimatum by the BIA to 'stay in jail or go and fight'.[49] These had later been joined by thousands of students – as well as gang members – associated with the Thakins. As the army marched north, its members had begun settling old scores against ethnic minorities, such as against the Karen community, who many Burmans distrusted for their Christian faith and outsized position in the British Indian Army. After Karen villages surrendered their weapons to the BIA, their homes had been ransacked, with soldiers taking part in the plunder, sparking a terrible conflict that would last for months.

This scene now repeated itself in Arakan, as the Indo-Burmese borderland became the front line of the Second World War and, for the first time, Indians and Burmese faced one another on a battlefield. One Dr Kyaw Zan, an Arakanese surgeon 'of a bold and cheerful disposition', tried to save the lives of several Indians in Arakan, negotiating on their behalf with the Japanese, but when he himself fled the state at the end of 1942 'most of the remaining Indians were killed'.[50]

War on the front line was brutal. Soldiers on both sides tried to dehumanise their adversaries, but despite these efforts the enemy's humanity was occasionally made very clear. Lieutenant M. A. Gilani found a letter on a dead Japanese soldier reading:

> I show[ed] your photograph to our son and he has started recognising you. I am sending a few leaves of your favourite flower. All are fine here. I get your letters very late. When are you coming on leave? I miss you a lot ... Look after yourself.[51]

All the while the Rohingya community were caught in the crossfire. Somewhere between twenty thousand to a hundred thousand Muslims were displaced during the violence, while ten thousand to fifty thousand Buddhists were driven south, creating tensions that continue to this day.[52] When, in the summer of 1942, the Japanese tried to negotiate peace between the communities, they offered Arakan's Muslims 'arms, money, food, and the establishment of Pakistan'. The promises never amounted to anything but four years later would help fire a conflict between the Rohingya and the Burmese government, leaving them caught not just between India and Burma, but between India and Pakistan as well.[53]

With Arakan under Japanese control, the last sea route from Burma to India was closed and the remaining evacuees set out for the Assamese mountains further north instead. 'The butterflies in Assam that year were the most beautiful on record ... [and] added to the sense of the macabre as they flitted amongst the corpses.'[54]

One of the most fascinating accounts to survive from this time comes from a Sikh mining engineer called Uttam Singh. He and his brother Narayan were the second generation of their family to live in Burma after their father had moved there from Punjab in 1890, and for forty years they had worked for a British mining company in the princely state of Tawngpeng.[55] Polite, hardworking, and gregarious, Uttam was a machine shop foreman and gurudwara secretary. Both were fluent in Burmese, and had long considered Burma home, but when the bombs began dropping overhead, Uttam knew he had to get his children to the safety of India. His brother decided to stay behind. It would be several decades before they saw each other again.[56]

Uttam would write in his diary every evening as the sun went down, and eight decades on it remains one of his son's most prized possessions, and a rare glimpse into those disturbing months of war. The first entry, written the day Uttam and his family left Bawdwin and after one last photo had been taken of the Sikh community there, records the anguish he felt for 'countless loved Sikhs and friends who were left behind'.

> At dawn on 12 March 1942, we took a shower and went to the Gurdwara ... Then, at 6 a.m., my family, friends and I got onto a lorry and with teary eyes looked at our Gurdwara, located on a hill, for the last time. After bowing at it from a distance, we left.[57]

Uttam would never return to Bawdwin, yet he and his family were lucky, for his employers were the rare sort who had a plan to evacuate the families of their employees. After surveying three land routes to India, the mining company recommended travelling via Tamu and attached a list of important contacts and a map to its report. For a time the plan worked perfectly. The Bawdwin Sikhs caught a train via Kambo to Mandalay, where another Sikh, Sardar Tek Singh of Khighola, fed the group and invited them to shower at his house. However, in Mandalay they encountered their first issue: their luggage had gone missing, and when they eventually found it in the hands of the station attendants, the men demanded bribes for handing it over. The same day the family learned that the fall of Rangoon had rendered the railway route advised by the mining company impossible.

By now Uttam's group had swollen to eighty people and together they decided to go by river instead. Uttam paid sixty-four rupees to rent a boat upstream to Mimmu, and after prayer, supplication and group chanting of the Sikh holy book the Guru Granth Sahib, they shouted, '*Sat Sri Akal*' and left the riverbank. Sailing north up the Irrawaddy, Uttam was enchanted by the 'numerous residences of Burmese sadhus and ... the beautiful pointed pagodas' that lined the surrounding hills, but became infuriated with the 'corrupt policemen

[who] had already posted themselves at different locations and were asking travellers for money for any travel clearance', encountering them again on the Magawi Bridge and in Channgoo, where the police were organising onward transport for refugees in exchange for money. 'The ones who couldn't afford the bribe and the high cost of lorry travel would be stuck in Channgoo for days,' wrote Uttam, increasingly disheartened.[58] Nonetheless, after extensive haggling, the group paid a reduced bribe, and finally reached Monywa at dawn.

For most refugees taking the Manipur route, Monywa was the last major city before the Indian border, an arid market town on the banks of the Chindwin river lined with neem and tamarind trees. It was dotted with derelict pagodas and refugee tents, and there were no good roads beyond. Uttam wanted to explore its two impressive gurudwaras, famous among Burma's Sikh community, but before he could get off his bullock cart, the Burmese police once again approached the group for bribes. When the refugees protested, a fight broke out. 'Some men were lathi-charged while others were attacked with hunters,' wrote Uttam in his diary.

> When the [district commissioner] came, he did not investigate the police brutality and said that the population of the city, usually about 14,000 people, was skyrocketing to about 22,000 currently. He further stated that there is a fear of a plague outbreak, and that is why travellers are currently stopped from entering the city.[59]

From Monywa, it took the group ten days to sail north to Kalewa, the next inhabited town up the Chindwin. They began to get into a daily schedule:

> We woke up in the morning, made tea and then after shouting the *jaikara*, we would bring the boat back into the river and proceed. In the afternoon, we would find a better spot, dock the boat, and we made lunch and ate. And then, when it was nearly dusk, we would find a clean spot, dock the boat, make dinner and sleep the night.[60]

Upriver, human settlements became smaller and further apart, and raging currents presented a greater danger than the corrupt policemen of the Burmese plains. The eighty Sikhs, huddled on bamboo rafts, paddled their way through an unknown jungle echoing with the howls of wild animals, sleeping each evening on the riverbank. 'Snakes were going here and there but nobody bothered,' recalls Uttam's son Avtar. On one occasion a member of their party fell in the river and vanished in the current but luckily washed up on the stony riverbank alive. Another day the sun came out and the group took the opportunity to wash themselves and their clothes, but Uttam's youngest son Iqbal fell into the river. 'By the grace of the Tenth Guru who wears a Kalgi, he was held by someone and was saved,' Uttam wrote. Soon it started to rain heavily. 'We saw two or three corpses floating in the river today,' he recorded. 'The riverbanks were stinking and the water ... looked infected. No one dared to drink from that stretch of the river. Wherever we got off to eat, we would dig deep into the ground for water.'[61]

Finally on 1 April they reached the settlement of Kalewa at the confluence of two rivers. Two weeks had passed since leaving Bawdwin, and for the first time in ten days the group slept with a roof over their heads. Kalewa was little more than a village of thatched huts, but there were doctors and government of India officials there to oversee the refugees. From this point they made safe but slow progress, and Uttam stayed for almost two weeks waiting for the undermanned officials to allot him a small boat to the base of the Patkai, from where he would make the final hike west across the hills into Manipur and India. 'You could see people selling their personal items as it was hard for them to transport all their goods further,' he wrote. 'You could get a typewriter for 30 rupees and a sewing machine for 20 rupees.' Eventually some of the Bawdwin Sikhs were assigned boats, and the group that had been together through a treacherous couple of weeks splintered.

For Uttam and his family, celebrating the Punjabi harvest festival of Baisakhi in Kalewa stands out as a moment of happiness and community that pierced the otherwise depressed mood of the evacuation. 'The sky was pure and clear,' he wrote that evening. 'Everyone woke up before dawn and took a bath. Then we placed the Guru Granth Sahib on a pedestal and decorated the place. We sang *Asa di Waar* only using the tabla.' By good fortune, his family was offered a boat that afternoon and by noon the next day they reached a small refugee campsite.

While waiting for a bullock cart with which to face the final eight-day trek into India, Uttam worked in the camps, performing Sikh devotional songs with a harmonium and a tabla to lift the mood. 'This would have been the first time that Sikh cries would have roared inside that jungle,' he wrote proudly. He stayed in the camp for another two weeks, tending to the sick, until only four of the Sikh families remained. Then his turn to leave came.

Uttam had not travelled light. 'My father had this library with him, about twelve boxes,' remembers his son Avtar.

> We had the Guru Granth Sahib and all these very old religious books which we had planned to take to our ancestral village in Punjab. He realised there was nobody to pick up our luggage and two to three miles into the walk he started burning all his books to reduce the weight. But when it came to the Guru Granth Sahib he said no, I can't leave this one here, so we still took that one with us.[62]

The image of the fire lingers in Avtar's mind eighty years on. The family burned all the papers and old photographs that they could not carry, and the fire blazed until 4 a.m. 'It rained that night,' wrote Uttam. 'We couldn't find any shelter and so we had to make tiny camps and tents using the bedding we had in hand.' The next morning a man appeared from over the hills and said that seven jeeps had made it across the hills with space to carry the suitcases, women and children up to Tamu on the Indian border. They needn't have burned anything at all.

Putting his family safely onto a jeep, Uttam and the few men left set off for the ninety-six miles to Tamu on foot. There were moments of pure serendipity during the trek. In a small settlement called Khampat, Uttam unexpectedly ran into an old friend. But the monsoon rains shattered the earlier idyll of the forest. Flies, mosquitoes and leeches became endemic, and refugees succumbed to new airborne diseases that ravaged their already weakened bodies. Amid the downpour, the road turned even more treacherous, and they struggled to keep their footing. When the skies cleared, the sun was piercingly hot, making it difficult to walk. Uttam and his companions forged ahead into the Burmese Naga Hills, their bodies caked in mud, on a slippery footpath strewn with bodies:

> By 2 a.m. later that night, we reached the settlement of Yedok. There was no shelter there. We tried to look into the houses of a few Nagas who lived there, but even those were filled with refugees. As a result, we had to cover the top of the bullock carts with clothes, and spent our night under it. On the wet earth, we put some grass and hay and slept. Since food could not be made that night, we had to sleep on an empty stomach.[63]

After reuniting with his family in Tamu, by then nicknamed 'city of the dead' for the number of corpses littered around it, Uttam crossed into India.[64] But their traumas didn't end. From here colonial officials distinguished between a better-supplied 'white route' for European refugees and a longer and more treacherous 'black route' for Indians. What's more, the Indian princely state into which they entered – Manipur – was itself on the verge of crisis. The Maharaja had fled and approximately three thousand refugees were being registered there every day.[65] Indeed the government of India was even less prepared for war than the Burmese one: the only organisation that had moved into action was the Assam Tea Planters' Association, which had erected makeshift camps across the hills. Sanitation levels were low and there were severe shortages of basic supplies.

'The camp was so bad,' recalls Uttam's son Avtar. 'There was disease, and when Japanese bombs began to fall in the night, my mother and another lady decided that we couldn't stay here.' The group – now reduced to fifteen – hitched a lift on an army truck towards the railhead at Dimapur. After the three months they had spent on the road, arriving at Dimapur gave them a shock. The army had camps and food was readily available for refugees. 'They were making a full aloo, vegetable and puri for people who had not eaten properly for three months – people were eating so much,' remembers Avtar. From Dimapur the Sikhs took a train to Lucknow, and from there to their ancestral village of Dhaheru in Punjab, where relatives lived. Yet more tragedy was in store. As Uttam wrote to the colonial authorities soon afterwards:

We all fell sick. One of my relatives who came with me from Burma expired on the 20th June, my eldest son expired on the 9th August, my mother expired on the 4th October, my brother's wife expired on the 12th December and my nephew on 1st February 1943. All these deaths occurred one after another, and all of them were Burma evacuees.[66]

Like most of those who left Burma in 1942, Uttam never went back. The Long March marked the brutal end to his Burmese days.

The Japanese had now all but conquered Burma and almost all of its Indians had fled. Only the town of Myitkyina still held out, where Governor Dorman-Smith and around twenty other evacuees were taking refuge, struggling to understand what was happening to the country. With food running low and accusations raging over the government's mishandling of the evacuation, a guilt-racked Dorman-Smith promised 'to stay on long enough in Burma to get all the hapless Indian refugees out'.[67] Yet as April turned to May, and the Japanese approached his final holdout, his superiors ordered him out. On 4 May 1942, the first anniversary of his arrival, Dorman-Smith climbed into a plane with his wife and his pet monkey Miss Gibbs, clasping 'a few official papers and a tiny bundle of personal belongings', then slumped in his seat 'lost in thought' as he watched Burma slip past below.[68] The Japanese marched in two days later. Burma had fallen.

Within days the monsoon rains reached the parched Patkai Hills, transforming them into rivers of mud, halting the Japanese advance at the border. 'India becomes for the time being the centre of the war,' noted George Orwell from London. 'One might say the centre of the world.'[69]

Dorman-Smith would quickly find that he was not particularly welcome back in India. In the recently inaugurated capital of New Delhi, Viceroy Linlithgow's aide-de-camp wrote in his diary that amid the 'unpleasantness of the heat':

Our first visitor is the refugee Governor of Burma, whose daughters had already stayed at Viceroy's House two months ago. He obviously regards charm as one of his few remaining assets, and in consequence uses it rather too lavishly. He annoys

Lady Linlithgow by referring to his wife as 'Her Ex[cellency]', a designation to which she is not entitled in India certainly, and it's more than doubtful if she has it in Burma.[70]

But Dorman-Smith was doing better than most refugees. By May around three hundred thousand of them had been registered in Bengal, from where they spread out across the country, from Madras to Gorakhpur.[71] 'They were arriving diseased,' a British officer stationed in Bengal wrote:

Bringing in a particularly virulent type of malaria, and bringing in hair-raising stories of atrocities and suffering ... The natural effect of that on the people of Bengal ... was to feel that times were extremely uncertain and that terrible things might happen.[72]

Once-grand families moved into refugee shelters, and among those arriving in Calcutta was Mirza Mohammad Bedar Bakht, the half-Burmese descendant of the last Mughal Emperor, who had been exiled to Rangoon in 1858. Bakht was to remain a refugee all his life, working 'in a bread factory and dying in poverty' in 1980. Afterwards his widow was left to sell 'tea on the pavement at Calcutta's Howrah station'.[73]

These 'Burma refugees' had a profound impact on India. In the foothills of the Indian Patkai, discontented communities feared they would be overwhelmed by them and found a voice in a magnetic tribal ascetic called Ratanmoli Noatia who raised his flag in revolt.[74] In India's metropolitan cities, meanwhile, the refugees had a remarkable effect on India's culinary taste. Burmese khow suey began appearing on restaurant menus across North India, while in Lucknow a refugee called Mohammad Rafique started making Rangoon-style biscuits under the brand name Burma Biscuits Co.[75] Chinese merchants who had previously sold Burmese goods in Madras opened restaurants instead, leading to the growth of Chinese restaurants across South India, while Bangalore's Mavalli Tiffin Room took to replacing rice with semolina when making *idlis*, to deal with the loss of Burmese rice supplies. The result was the rava idli, a breakfast dish that continues to be popular across India to this day.[76]

As well as facing the ire of their Indian brothers and sisters, refugees from Burma quickly learned that they were still not entirely safe.

Japanese troops marched into India's Andaman Islands in the Bay of Bengal in March 1942 and Japanese forces bombed the Indian port of Vizag in April that year. An invasion seemed imminent in Bengal too, and Gandhi was not alone in his inclination 'that the Allies could not win the war'.[77] Some princely rulers even started preparing for the British Empire's collapse and the Maharaja of Patiala hatched secret plans to annex British Punjab and rebuild the Kingdom of Lahore. The Maharaja of Indore even announced that his capital would be an 'open city' to all invading armies – a suggestion that drew British accusations of betrayal.[78]

'We passed full days and some anxious nights when scares of invasions called us from our beds,' wrote General Bill Slim from Calcutta. The son of a Bristol ironmonger, Slim was a down-to-earth soldier who respected his men and was respected by them in turn. He had been given charge of the Burma Corps in the midst of the army's withdrawal from the country and on getting his troops back to India, he wrote proudly, 'They might look like scarecrows, but they looked like soldiers too.'[79] Slim was appalled by the racist treatment of his half-starved troops when they reached India and travelled on to hospitals in Bihar and Ranchi to oversee their care. In the months to come he would prove himself one of the war's greatest generals, but in those days he was trying desperately to unite his Indian and British troops into a coherent force. 'We know now that the Japanese never seriously contemplated a seaborne invasion,' he wrote later, 'but at the time it loomed constantly over us.'[80]

With the Japanese on the India border, tens of thousands of wealthy Bengalis fled into the countryside. Just as novels like *The Lion, the Witch and the Wardrobe* memorialise the experiences of British evacuee children during the London Blitz, numerous Bengali novels, memoirs and poems (written mostly by the landowning *bhadralok*) memorialise the flight from cities in 1942.[81] Amartya Sen, the boy who had left Mandalay for Dacca just three years earlier, was sent off to Shantiniketan to live with his grandparents and the partition of India and Pakistan only five years later would render a return to Dacca impossible. 'There was no electricity,' he writes:

But I got used to living in the light of kerosene lamps – and doing my studies in it as well ... My grandfather would wake every day at around 4 a.m. when it was quite dark and, after getting ready, would go out for a long walk. On mornings when I was up too ... he would try and make me familiar with the stars ... he knew all of them by their Sanskrit names and some by their English names too. I loved accompanying him as the dawn broke ... but most importantly it gave me the wonderful opportunity to bombard him with questions.[82]

For wealthy evacuee children, the war felt far away and it was easy to forget the turmoil facing the rest of the country. Amartya loved the freedom of Shantiniketan, and like many children who found themselves in the countryside during the war, he made a new connection to nature. But the war was getting nearer, as he found out on a visit to Calcutta.

My father was right about the possibility of Japanese attacks ... On one occasion, when I was staying in Calcutta with some family friends for a short holiday, the Japanese bombed the dock area five times during one week.[83]

All the while national politics was a powder keg waiting to blow. In March 1942 Churchill had sent the Labour politician Sir Stafford Cripps to Delhi to solve the deadlock between Nehru and Jinnah, and negotiate Indian political support for the war. Cripps offered 'unambiguous assurance of independence after the war, not hedged around with qualifications about minorities'.[84] Yet his mission was doomed to failure. Gandhi rejected his call to war on the basis of non-violence, while Nehru spurned the offer as it allowed provinces to leave the Indian Union if they wished. Jinnah supported the war but rejected the constitutional settlement for not creating 'Pakistan'.

As the political stalemate continued, news of Britain's preferential treatment for European and Anglo-Indian refugees plunged its reputation to new lows. A damning Congress report on the government's evacuation alleged that Indians had been sent on a different route to Europeans and that evacuees had received sexual harassment from officers posted to help them. The government responded by claiming that the black and white routes only referred to paths stocked with curries and sandwiches respectively.[85] When the Muslim League – which unlike Congress supported the war effort – decried the 'shameful discrimination against Indian nationals', even Viceroy Linlithgow could tell Britain's days in the subcontinent were numbered.[86] 'We are not going to remain in India,' he admitted to an American journalist soon after. 'Of course, the Congress does not believe this. But we will not stay here. We are preparing for our departure.'[87]

Congress was, of course, increasingly desperate to hurry the Viceroy on his way. In an interview, an outraged Gandhi attacked Britain's response to the refugee crisis:

> Hundreds if not thousands, on their way from Burma perished without food and drink, and the wretched discrimination stared even these miserable people in the face. One route for the whites, another for the Blacks! And discrimination even on their arrival in India ... India is being ground down to dust and humiliated ... one fine morning I came to the decision to make this honest demand: For heaven's sake leave India alone.[88]

On 7 August, at Bombay's Gowalia Tank Maidan, Gandhi announced that Britain should immediately 'Quit India'. 'Here is a mantra, a short one, that I give you,' the Mahatma cried. 'The mantra is: "Do or Die". We shall either free India or die in the attempt; we shall not live to see the perpetuation of our slavery.'[89]

Linlithgow responded by simply arresting the entire Congress leadership. This mass incarceration was remarkably civil, with Congressmen driven to Bombay's towering Victoria Terminus and packed onto a train. Congress president Maulana Azad was put in the same compartment as Jawaharlal Nehru and Sardar Vallabhbhai Patel, and later recalled the surreal train journey in his memoirs:

> Each ordered what he desired, some had eggs, poached, fried or boiled; some had toast with coffee and tea, but the majority had only fruits and milk. As we passed station after station, we found the platforms guarded by the police, with not even railway staff or porters on the platform.[90]

Eventually, the Congressmen were marched into the medieval Ahmadnagar fortress, the awe-inspiring citadel where the Mughal Emperor Aurangzeb had died two and a half centuries earlier and where they would remain for three years, until the end of the war. Nehru set about writing a history of the Indian subcontinent entitled 'The Discovery of India', while Maulana Azad spent his time composing Persian and Arabic couplets on the origin of music. Gandhi, however, was kept separate from the others and, after a brief plan to incarcerate him with U Saw in Uganda, was interned in the Aga Khan's palace in Poona, along with his wife and secretary.[91]

It was to be a time of emotional turmoil for the Mahatma. Soon after his imprisonment, the seventy-two-year-old suffered a seizure and while recovering, his wife Kasturba contracted bronchitis and pneumonia. Gandhi had long opposed 'western' medicine and told his wife, 'I would like you to give up using medicine now.' Their son Devdas had pleaded with Gandhi to let his mother use penicillin, but the Mahatma stubbornly refused and asked his family simply to place their trust in God. A few days later Kasturba died. On the evening of her funeral, Gandhi's disciple Miraben caught the Mahatma weeping.[92]

The 'Quit India' movement that erupted in the aftermath of the arrests was a decentralised, unorganised, popular campaign that cut across class lines. It wasn't so much a single uprising as a series of different rebellions, each run by different communities for different reasons. One of its most mythologised participants was Aruna Asaf Ali, daughter of a Punjabi restaurant owner whose husband was incarcerated with Nehru. Aruna joined a protest against the arrest of the elected Congress leadership and was horrified when the police lathi-charged the demonstration, throwing tear gas into the crowd. In Bombay alone, police brutality killed thirty-three people within just three hours of the Congress arrests. Aruna took it upon herself to raise the Congress flag over the Gowalia Tank Maidan where Gandhi had given his speech the previous day, and then went underground to organise further resistance to British rule.[93]

Protests, strikes and acts of civil disobedience broke out across the country. Great swathes of India became ungovernable and whole villages rose up in rebellion. 'The civil disobedience campaign causes a good deal of excitement,' noted Linlithgow's aide-de-camp in August:

40 people killed in Old Delhi, British officers chased by the mob in Connaught Place, to which we are forbidden to go. Armoured carriers & troops patrol the streets night & day. 'Quit India' is the slogan.[94]

The Viceroy's response betrayed how weak his authority in India had become, for on 15 August Linlithgow legalised 'machine gunning from the air' to quell extreme rebellion, after which crowds in parts of Eastern India were gunned down by Royal Air Force planes. A British official in the central provinces allegedly 'boasted at the club in the evening that he had jolly good fun having shot down twenty-four niggers himself'.[95] In Bengal's Tamluk subdivision, rebels established an entire parallel government – a predecessor of the later Naxalite movement. As Raghu Karnad put it in his family memoir, 'The Japanese had not come, but it was like war all the same.'[96]

The Indians who had fled Burma were now divided about whether to help Britain fight the Japanese or to oppose them. In Madras 'Burma refugees' sabotaged railway lines and cut telegraph wires as part of the Quit India movement, taking revenge on the colonial masters who had abandoned them.[97] But other Burma evacuees felt that without the return of British rule it was unlikely they would ever be able to return home to Burma. Some even argued for a halfway house where Burma was reattached to an independent Indian Empire as part of a 'triune commonwealth' comprising Hindustan, Pakistan and Burma, independent of any direct British control.[98]

Britain's political allies in India were suddenly few and far between, but the arrest of the Congress leadership also allowed for new political forces to grow. Several mullahs in the North-West Frontier Province helpfully declared a jihad against the invading Japanese, while the Dalit leader Ambedkar derided the timing of the Quit India movement, with Imperial Japan on the Raj's doorstep, as 'irresponsible and insane'.[99] Burmese communist leader Thein Pe crossed into India and began giving lectures to 'get Indians to see the truth and not to romanticise the Japanese'[100] and Ottama's successor at the Hindu Mahasabha, Vinayak Savarkar, called for his constituents to 'stick to their posts' and help the British.[101] Some maharajas also gave their support, shaken by the fact that unlike previous Gandhian campaigns, the Quit India movement had penetrated deep into princely India.[102]

The person who gained most from the situation, however, was Muhammad Ali Jinnah, who advocated for the British to remain in India indefinitely until safeguards were put in place to protect India's Muslims from its Hindu majority. With Congress leaders in prison, his Muslim League would skyrocket in popularity and by late 1943 coalitions with the League were formed in five out of eleven Indian provinces. All the while Jinnah pushed for the establishment of Pakistan, using the separation of Burma as precedent for another partition of India. 'Where was the blue-print, when the question of Burma's separation was decided at the Round Table Conference?' he proclaimed to one writer. 'It didn't need to exist ... [Once] the principle of separation was accepted; the rest followed.'[103]

But on the ground the Pakistan demand was having increasingly nasty consequences, leading playwright Saadat Hasan Manto to pen an essay, 'Save India from Leaders'.[104] Manto was baffled by the way that religion was being politicised and ever more concerned by Jinnah's Pakistan demand. He took to carrying two caps with him whenever he left his house – a Hindu one and a Muslim one – which he would switch as he drove through different areas of the city. 'Previously religion used to be in one's heart,' he wrote. Now it was all about performance. In response to the slogans 'Long Live India' and 'Long Live Pakistan', Manto quipped his own: 'Long Live Caps'.[105]

In a single year the subcontinent's political chessboard had changed beyond recognition. Most of Burma's Indian population had fled and the border between two British colonies had transformed into an international boundary. When the Japanese started issuing their own 'Japanese Government Rupees', even the currencies of India and Burma were decoupled at last. It had taken an occupation by a different colonial force, but the Partition of India and Burma was finally complete.

5

War in the Borderlands

When the rains petered out in late 1942, the Japanese Empire had conquered almost all of Southeast Asia. Japan now ruled over approximately 20 per cent of the world's population and had overtaken the British Empire as the most populous power on the planet.[1] Meanwhile, British India was in full-scale revolt and battling one of the largest refugee crises in its history. Its military establishment was terrified of a renewed Japanese onslaught. But the assault never came.

Three events changed the direction of the Second World War in quick succession. First, in June 1942, the US won a decisive victory over the Japanese at the Battle of Midway. The Japanese had overstretched themselves and as their troops were sent east to fight in the Pacific, Japan's invasion of India was postponed. A few months later at El Alamein in Egypt, the British and Indian armies scored their first major victory against the Nazis in over a year, providing a much-needed morale boost to Allied troops. Finally, towards the end of the year, the Soviet Union began to emerge victorious from the single deadliest battle of the war – the Battle of Stalingrad – pushing Nazi Germany onto the defensive for the first time. Alan Brooke, Chief of Britain's Imperial General Staff, was amazed at the way the tide had turned so quickly on the Axis powers. 'We started 1943 under conditions I never would have dared to hope,' he wrote in his diary. For the first time since 1939, it felt like Britain was 'beginning to stop losing this war'.[2]

For the former Indian Empire, 1943 was a time for regrouping, political change and shifting alliances, a brief pause before the chaos of total war returned. To the east of the Patkai Hills, Japan set about solidifying its gains in Burma, building a new administration and creating separate

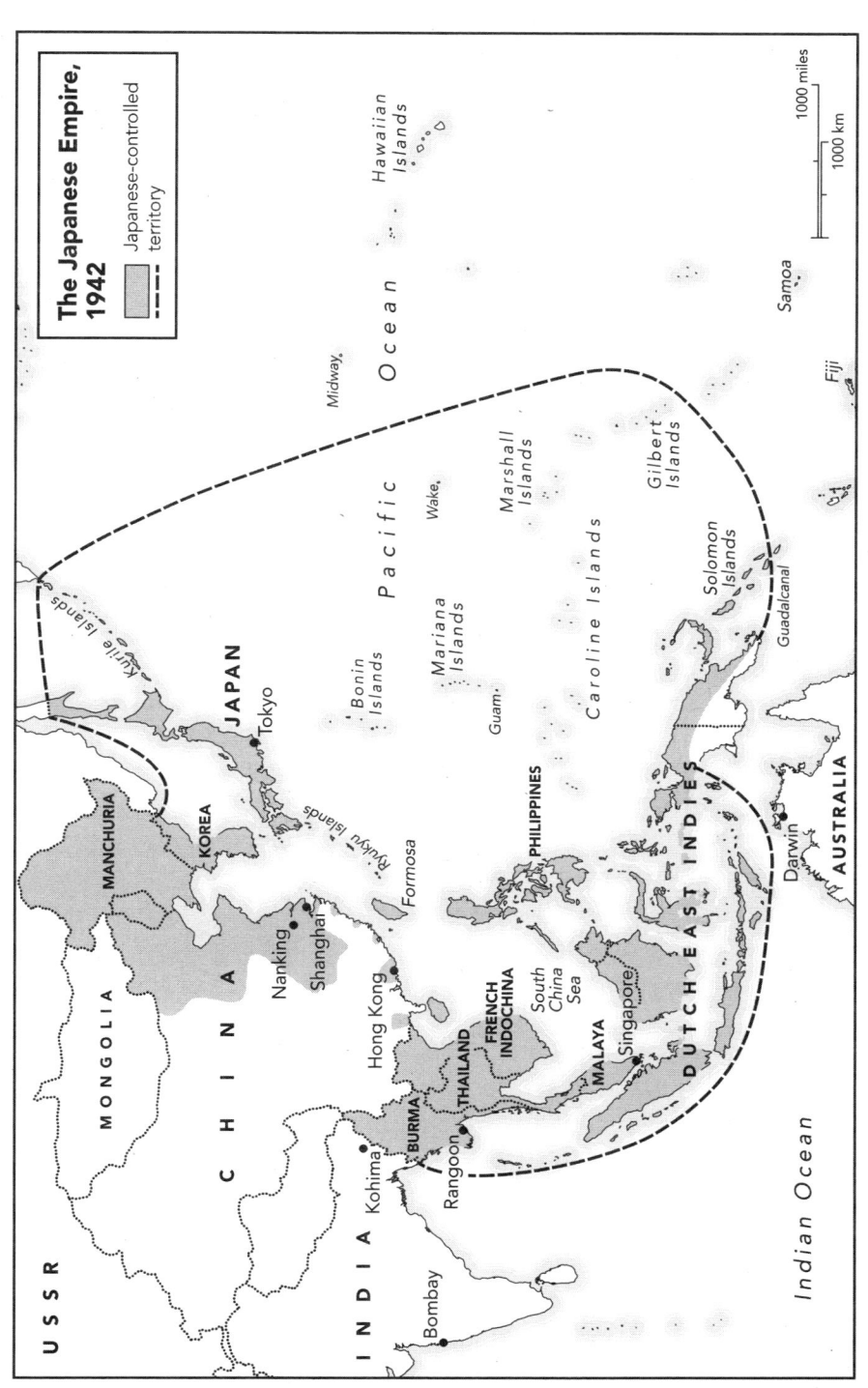

Indian and Burmese puppet states, each with their own national armies. To the west, the British established a new 'South East Asian Command' to oversee Britain's reconquest of Burma, cementing the idea that it belonged to a separate 'Southeast Asia' rather than the Indian world. All the while the economic fallout of Burma's severance from India would become apparent, as the Bay of Bengal descended into famine.

In mid-April, as the future of the subcontinent hung in the balance, Daw Kinmama devised a plan to break her husband out of prison. Kinmama was a fiercely intelligent woman with a 'quick cat-like mind'. Educated by Catholic nuns, and obsessed with etiquette, she had spent most of the last few years lovingly caring for her six children. But war has a way of changing people and on 13 April Kinmama disguised herself as a Shan noblewoman, tied a cotton longyi 'with a traditional zigzag pattern' around her waist and drove to the top of a small hill near Mogok in central Burma, 'one of the sweetest and most salubrious [towns] ... to be found anywhere'. With the engine still running, she unfolded a second disguise reserved for her jailed husband: the pre-war premier of Burma, Ba Maw.[3]

Ba Maw had been languishing in his British prison cell for almost two years, endlessly re-reading John Steinbeck's *The Grapes of Wrath* and learning the names of Mogok's local trees – silver pine, eucalyptus and wild cherry, and so on. Occasionally newspapers arrived to inform him of the surreal events taking place in the outside world, but these were few and far between so he had little idea of the immense changes happening outside his cell. Indeed so far the local administration in Mogok had been unaffected by the Japanese conquest of Burma. Then one day Kinmama arrived to pay Ba Maw a visit. With the help of two conspirators – a medic and a sympathetic jailor – she sneaked her husband a key and a pouch of Naga ghost chillies, acquired from an Arakanese shop, thick 'with fragrant steam from black pepper soup'.[4] Ba Maw raised an eyebrow. 'Are we cooking something?' he asked. Kinmama explained her plan.

The 13th was the second day of the Burmese new year festival, Thingyan, and the streets filled with people throwing water on one another in celebration. Thein Pe and U Myint set about persuading guards to go out and attend the festival, while Ba Maw himself requested the prison cook roast the chillies for a special Thingyan dish. The cook was a 'slight, translucent skinned Shan man from a neighbouring village' and he had no idea that he was holding one of the deadliest chillies in the world, which would release a distressingly spicy smell when roasted. Ba Maw waited in his cell until, as expected, a 'noxious cloud of pepper smoke' began spreading across the prison, incapacitating a group of prisoners queueing by the kitchen.[5] 'The stench it gave out was devastating.' Ba Maw called out to the warder that the smoke was making his rheumatism worse and pleaded to sit in the garden. The warder obliged.

> With all the appearance of being badly shaken ... I limped out into the garden carrying a book in my hand to convince the warders around that I intended to rest outside for some time reading undisturbed and alone. I strolled about until I succeeded in getting close to a small wicket opening into the main road. There I lay down on a grass plot nearby ... hidden behind a clump of trees.

Ba Maw waited until the warders were tending to the other prisoners, then moved into action.

> As soon as I felt it safe to do so I walked to the wicket, unlocked it with a key I had been given beforehand, and walked out calmly.[6]

Running up the street, he was noticed by 'the fat warden' who went 'tumbling after him' but ran out of breath halfway up the hill.[7] At the top, Kinmama emerged from a bush.

> I wrapped the Shan turban round my head, she had the shawl thrown over hers, and within a few minutes we were headed to the next state ... I was free again.[8]

The euphoric couple weren't safe yet. 'I was a hunted man trying to hide right in the middle of a sprawling battle-zone,' Ba Maw recalled later. From Mogok they drove to the eastern princely state of Mainglon, before embarking on a long, dangerous trek across the front line to a Japanese outpost in the Shan Hills. Here, unshaven and unwashed, the ex-premier gave himself up to a Japanese colonel, using a photo from a political calendar to prove his identity. The soldier simply replied, 'Very glad, very glad', and sent Ba Maw and Kinmama off to Mandalay.[9]

In the coming months Ba Maw would emerge as the head of Japan's puppet Burmese government, but after being locked away in prison for two years, he had a lot of catching up to do. 'A good part of the city had been wantonly bombed and burnt and sacked,' he wrote in shock after he entered the charred remains of Burma's historic capital.

> The old Burmese palace with its priceless treasures and memories was nearly gone; most of the landmarks had similarly disappeared, and whole areas within the city were now a mass of charred posts and ruins. As for the people, they looked plainly bewildered by the events which had overtaken them.[10]

War had devastated the country, the great Chauk oilfields were aflame, and innumerable towns across the land had simply ceased to exist. Moreover, politics had evolved beyond Ba Maw's comprehension. He had imagined the Japanese and Burmese Independence Army heroically liberating Burma side by side but instead found that Mandalay 'was tense with the wildest rumours and alarm ... chiefly with all sorts of stories about the tension between the two armies'.[11] Eventually a shaven-headed Aung San brought him up to speed. Their relationship had always been complex, for as a student activist Aung San had once helped bring down Ba Maw's government. Ba Maw's daughter recalled how Aung San used to accuse her 'father of surrounding himself with sycophants' while Ba Maw 'lashed out at Aung San for having a rose-tinted view of the world'.[12] Now, after a gap of two years, Aung San was no longer a student activist playing at politics. He was the '*Bogyoke*', the general who had expelled the British from Burma, and was even married, having fallen in love with a nurse called Ma Khin Kyi. He described the events of the last few months to a bewildered Ba Maw.

The BIA had proven more popular than anyone had expected, Aung San revealed, ballooning into a force almost as large as the Japanese invasion force itself,[13] but as a result it was 'hardly more than an armed, vaguely revolutionary mob which had been collected at random with very little training or equipment or arms'.[14] Rogue BIA cadres had started looting the Burmese countryside, a bad precedent for military rule, and Burmese journalists wrote of 'pongyis [monks] being slapped, of monasteries being defiled, of sacred palms bearing inscriptions of the scriptures desecrated, [and] of the shooting out of hand by the BIA of bad hats'.[15] With the BIA out of control, the Japanese took to arresting them.

The fallout became clearer to Ba Maw over the coming days. As one man explained to him, 'When the Burmese terror was checked ... the Japanese terror began.'[16] Although the Japanese had initially pushed for pan-Asian brotherhood, many of their soldiers carried a racial superiority complex as ingrained as their British predecessors', and their habit of slapping subordinates outraged Burmese villagers. Japanese prostitution rackets had sprouted across the country, and in Maymyo the Fifteenth Japanese Army had set up 'The Inn of Brightness', a geisha house that served sake, sex and imported sushi to officers. Burmese girls seem to have been among the hundreds of thousands of 'comfort women' who served in these brothels in a form of imperially sanctioned sexual slavery and anyone accused of collaboration with the British was simply beheaded. Those who did not comply were often hauled off to brutal prisoner of war camps and a few unfortunate victims were even taken to the infamous UNIT 731 for human experiments or to be dissected alive.[17]

The Japanese also temporarily went back on their promises of granting Burma independence. Keiji Suzuki, the man who had first recruited Aung San, genuinely believed in Burmese aspirations and had tried to establish a BIA administration after the conquest of Moulmein. But Suzuki's superiors had other plans. Japan's South Area Army issued a new policy to grant Burmese independence only 'after the Greater East Asian War', and when the two armies had marched into Rangoon, the Japanese rather than the BIA occupied Government House. Suzuki, meanwhile, was transferred back to Japan.[18]

By the time he met with Ba Maw, Aung San was thus deeply wary of his new masters. 'I went to Japan to save my people who were struggling like bullocks under the British,' he complained, 'but now we are treated like dogs.'[19] With the Japanese firmly in charge, however, he had no choice but to work with them. So Aung San and Ba Maw went to meet the Japanese high command and, in Ba Maw's words, they 'started ... to organise the apocalypse'.[20]

In the weeks that followed, the two men helped build up a semblance of administration in Burma. Ba Maw became a figurehead for a new government, while Aung San became his number two, reorganising the Burmese Independence Army to dispose of 'bad hats', and eventually abolishing it altogether, with a new smaller, more organised force taking its place.[21] The Japanese were still really in charge, though, and Aung San was begrudgingly forced to remove the word 'Independence' from its name so that the Burmese Independence Army became the Burma Defence Army and later the Burmese National Army. Nonetheless, a strange sense of normality emerged in towns across lower Burma and the new administration even managed to ease racial tensions so that Indians, Karens and other minority ethnic groups began to filter back into Rangoon.[22]

On 26 April 1943, a Nazi U-boat and Japanese I-29 submarine surfaced off the stormy coast of southeast Madagascar. The German sub lowered a rubber dinghy into the choppy waters and two men – Subhas Chandra Bose and his right-hand man Abid Hasan – climbed inside. The Indians waved goodbye to their Nazi companions, with whom they had shared a cramped submarine interior for over two months, and then with some difficulty paddled their way across to the Japanese sub, getting drenched in sea water in the process. Just a few years earlier Bose had been the president of the Indian National Congress. Now he was on his way to Tokyo to plan the Axis' invasion of the British Raj.[23]

Subhas Chandra Bose remains one of the most polarising figures in Indian history, revered as a secular liberator by some and reviled as a Nazi collaborator by others. Born into a wealthy Bengali family, and graduating from Cambridge University, Bose had turned down a career in the Indian Civil Service in order to join Gandhi's growing anti-colonial movement, yet he opposed the Mahatma's commitment to non-violence, and admired the muscular nationalism of Nazi Germany and Fascist Italy. In 1940, when the Nazis marched into Paris, the British had placed Bose under house arrest in Calcutta where he would remain for half a year. Then, on 16 January 1941, he had slipped out of the gates in the dead of night disguised as an Afghan. With the help of his nephew and the Abwehr's military intelligence, Bose had driven across Northern India, through the Khyber Pass into Afghanistan and made for the Soviet Union. Under the alias of an Italian count called Orlando Mazzotta, he had flown into Germany and moved in with his estranged wife, a Viennese stenographer called Emilie Schenkl who he hadn't seen in almost four years.

Bose and Emilie lived together in the Third Reich for the next two years, based in a 'luxurious residence' in Berlin provided by the Nazi Foreign Office. Complete with 'a butler, cook, gardener, and SS-chauffeured car', it was a comfortable place to spend the war and Bose's attitude towards the Nazis during this time was ambivalent.[24] 'Germany may be a fascist or an imperialist, ruthless or cruel,' he once said, 'but one cannot help admiring these qualities of hers ... Could not these qualities be utilized for a nobler cause?'[25] On another occasion he candidly told an Indian prisoner in Germany's Colditz prison, 'I am not in full agreement with the Nazi philosophy, but I hope to gain India's independence through Nazi help.' This he did with great fervour, swiftly setting up a radio service called Azad Hind Radio and organising the creation of a militia known as the 'Tiger Legion', named after Britain's fiercest eighteenth-century opponent, the Muslim Indian ruler Tipu Sultan. This unlikely regiment of the German Army, which would later merge with the Waffen-SS, was made up entirely of Indian prisoners of war who were willing to fight against their former British paymasters. By 1942 over a thousand Indians had joined the Tiger Legion, pledging their allegiance to both Subhas Chandra Bose and Adolf Hitler.[26]

That same year, Emilie gave birth to a daughter, Anita, but Bose proved a neglectful father, too focused on securing Indian independence. However, after a face-to-face meeting with Hitler in May, he concluded the Nazi leader was completely insane. Moreover, thanks to Germany's ill-fated invasion of the Soviet Union, the Führer was also less willing to march on India than Bose had hoped. Just four months after his daughter's birth, Bose abandoned his new family and set off for Japan aboard a German submarine. The trip took place in such secrecy that Bose's right-hand man, Abid Hasan, initially thought they were going to Greece and took a Greek grammar book with him. It was a long and claustrophobic journey, but after two months they were transferred onto the Japanese submarine where the food, unlike on the German sub, was sublime. Three weeks later they walked on dry land in the Japanese-controlled East Indies, from where they flew on to Japan.[27]

The Japanese proved much more eager to help Bose destroy the British Raj than the Germans had been. After meeting with the Japanese high command, he was handed leadership of an 'Indian National Army', a counterpart to Aung San's BNA.[28] The INA was of a different order of scale from the Tiger Legion, and with Japan on India's doorstep, actual combat appeared an imminent possibility.

The Tokyo-born teenager Asha Sahay encountered Bose at Tokyo's Teikoku Hotel and captured the awe with which he was regarded. 'He is like the heroes we read about in books,' she wrote in her diary that evening, 'a divine spectre who brings clarity and consciousness on sight.' As well as attracting Indian civilians like Asha, the INA also drew on Indian prisoners of war, just as the Tiger Legion had, and units were named after Gandhi, Nehru and Azad. Asha wrote excitedly in June 1943 about how Japan was freeing Indian soldiers 'under the condition that they join the INA',[29] but this stipulation was far from insignificant. Forced labour awaited those who refused to fight alongside Bose, a fate that would kill more than 150,000 Tamils alone. Thirty-five-year-old Khair Mohammad, a Punjabi soldier from Rawalpindi, would later recall only joining the INA 'to escape torture of concentration camp and avoid starvation'.[30] Although the Indian state today reveres the forty thousand Indians who enlisted in Bose's army, almost four times that number died refusing to join him. These men and women have largely been forgotten.[31]

Nevertheless, Bose's INA was a diverse and inclusive organisation, attracting Indians from various class and racial backgrounds. Muslims and Sikhs were prominent as well as Hindus, and there was a conscious effort to break from the colonial theory of martial races that still governed British Indian Army recruitment. Asha joined the all-women Rani of Jhansi Regiment and her experience at the training camps near the Burma–Thailand border was typical. 'Life here is rustic,' she scribbled in her diary. 'Cows, goats, chickens and so on are all members of the family … There is no bed here. We place a sheet on a mattress and sleep. After all this is military life.'[32] She was anxious to get to the front line, and jotted down haikus to while away the hours, a practice she had cultivated during her childhood in Tokyo. Other activities included learning to use a bayonet and stabbing effigies of Churchill and Roosevelt made of sacks. 'We take ten steps forward, and on the eleventh step we shout "Jai Hind" and pierce the effigy,' the seventeen-year-old wrote.

> I firmly believe I can now kill the enemy without hesitation ... I wish there were some *goras* [white people] here itself, so that I could pierce their necks with the tip of my bayonet.

Amid all the trained aggression, in moments of introspection Asha pondered on what her life might be after the war. That night the women dressed up in sarongs and taught each other dance moves. She spent the time chatting with her fellow soldier Shanti by a lake.

> The evening passes by us, a cool breeze blowing from the south ... [Shanti is] talking about her fiancé – how they will meet in India, how they will live in Calcutta ... I wonder – will the same thing happen to me at some point? Will someone use the words 'let's meet in Free India' with me?[33]

Asha went to sleep early that night. The next morning she woke at dawn to learn how to fire a machine gun.

A substantial part of the INA was made up of diaspora troops like Asha, and it offered Hindi classes as part of their training. Indeed, Bose's companion Abid Hasan later recalled a conversation outside Rangoon with Captain Janaki, second in command of Asha's regiment. 'We went to a hillock and sat there looking at the ground around us. "Doesn't the countryside remind you of home?" I enquired, adding "It looks so typically Indian."' To his surprise she simply replied, 'I do not know ... I have never been to India.' Janaki had grown up in Malaya, but new Malay nationalism had eroded her sense of belonging, just as Burmese nationalism had done to the Indians in Burma. The power of nationalism was so great that much of the army marching to liberate India was made up of soldiers who had never actually been there.[34]

Ba Maw and Bose finally met each other at Singapore Airport in July 1943 and hit it off instantly. Bose was 'a man you could not forget once you knew him,' wrote Ba Maw, and he seemed to agree with Ba Maw on 'all the fundamental questions'. As a former anti-separationist who had 'always believed that the struggle for liberation in India and Burma was one and indivisible', Ba Maw found Bose's shift away from Gandhian non-violence 'a very exciting change'.[35]

In 1943, as India continued to deal with the massive influx of exiles from Burma, a new wave arrived from across the ocean: Allied civilians from Greece, Persia, Somalia, Aden and even Canada, fleeing war. Polish refugees alone numbered ten thousand.[36]

As people flowed into India, cultural misunderstandings were common. Indians grew anxious about the growth of brothels selling sex with Indian women to British, American and African soldiers, while the new arrivals expressed concerns about the open display of swastikas on shops across the country. On more than one occasion British troops ransacked Indian shops on the assumption that the shopkeepers were Nazi sympathisers, and General and Air HQ India eventually found the need to circulate pamphlets explaining that the swastika was in fact an ancient Indian symbol of good luck, and that its presence there had preceded its use by the Nazi Party by several thousand years.[37]

Despite these growing pains, the Indian economy was at last transforming into a war economy, employing millions of men and women. Aerodromes sprouted from the North Indian plains and Spitfires were soon shooting over the swamps of Arakan, attempting to push back the Japanese lines. Factory employment increased by a third, and in the gem bazaars of Jaipur, cutters of semi-precious stones found new careers in making scope lenses for snipers. The troops descending on the country also had to be housed and fed, and an up-and-coming hotelier called Mohan Singh Oberoi spotted a business opportunity. He leased and later bought Calcutta's Grand Hotel, offering cheap accommodation to British troops, for which he was later given the title Rai Bahadur by the British government. By the time the war ended, Oberoi Hotels would be sprouting across India, from Peshawar to Delhi.[38]

Money was particularly funnelled into upgrading the infrastructure across the Patkai Hills, until this point the least developed part of India, creating a whole new middle class in the region. Mohammad Abdul Barik Khan, commonly known as Gedu Mian, had grown up in Tripura on the banks of the Haora river in a family of hereditary elephant *mahouts* (drivers), and he had found work as a small-time contractor. But in 1942 Gedu Mian unexpectedly bagged a contract to build Tripura's first ever airport so that by the end of the war the former mahout was the wealthiest non-royal in Tripura, living in a mansion resembling the palace of the Maharaja himself.[39]

Just five years earlier, when the new Indo-Burmese border had first carved through the Patkai, few outsiders had ever been there. Now the region came under a sudden and intense scrutiny. Roads penetrated deep into the hills, and in the process officials began to realise how 'very silly' the Indo-Burma border was, cutting through tightly knit communities for 'administrative convenience'.[40] Buoyed by a sense that the war was starting to tip in Britain's favour, British officials wondered if the border should be redrawn after their reconquest of Burma was complete. The governor of Assam, a prolific writer called Robert Reid, took the lead, insisting the people of the hills were fundamentally different from those of the plains:[41]

> We have no right to allow this great body of non-Indian Animists and Christians to be drawn into the struggle between Hindu and Muslim, which is now … with ever increasing intensity, the dominating feature of politics in India proper … Palpably outrageous though they are, the claims of Congress to include the hills of Assam in a Hindu Raj and of the Muslim League to make them part of Pakisthan are seriously meant.[42]

Reid lobbied to unite the Patkai peoples on both sides of the border in a completely separate crown colony, under the thumb of neither Rangoon nor New Delhi.[43] The Viceroy and Indian secretary of state were both impressed by Reid's idea, and they started secretly debating the possibility of another partition after the war with the Burmese government-in-exile, now living in Simla alongside the government of India.[44] Burma's exiled governor Dorman-Smith, who had arrived in Simla with his wife and pet monkey some months earlier, was among those who supported another partition, but his subordinates argued the proposal had come too late and that 'Opinion against [another] partition would be bound to reveal … objections which it would be futile to ignore.'[45] The plan was thus abandoned, even though both the Indian and Burmese governments remained open to moving the border after the war. In the words of the chief secretary to the governor of Assam, the 'old fortuitous division ought not to be restored'.[46]

While Britain's ruling class obsessed over post-war plans, they fatally ignored a looming crisis on their eastern front, where severed economic ties between India and Burma led to catastrophe. Fifteen per cent of India's rice had come from Burma, and this supply had been abruptly cut off by the Japanese advance.[47] In the Chettinad region of Madras, where incomes had relied on the Chettiar merchants' trade with Burma, one resident wrote how starving men and women 'are coming day by day in overwhelming numbers begging for alms. They present a pathetic sight. All of them have got no flesh on their bodies, in fact they can be called living skeletons. They want only food.'[48] Scarcity also hit the Aden Protectorates in Southwestern Arabia, which had been reliant on trade with areas now under the Japanese Empire. Rangoon Radio was prompted to broadcast a message about the 'nutritional value of grass' and how it 'could be eaten in difficult times such as the present'. But despite scarcity across the Indian Ocean, Bengal was hit the hardest.[49]

In the spring of 1943, nine-year-old Amartya Sen was playing at school in the Bengali town of Shantiniketan when a younger student told him that two class bullies were teasing a 'man with evident mental derangement' near the school's cricket ground. Together with a group of other children, Amartya confronted the bullies, who fled. He tried to speak with the victim, but the man was 'barely coherent,' remembers Sen.

> But we gathered that he had not eaten anything for nearly a month ... That was my first direct contact with a famine victim. But soon there were others who came into our neighbourhood in the hope of escaping starvation. Their numbers grew as the classes stopped in May for the summer vacation ... [and] by the time the school reassembled in July, the trickle had grown into a torrent of miserable humanity. They were looking for anything whatever that they could eat. Most of them were on their way to Calcutta, nearly a hundred miles away, having heard rumours of arrangements there for the feeding of destitutes.

In fact, the government wasn't providing any relief. A few private charities tried to help but it wasn't enough. By September Amartya Sen estimated that a hundred thousand starving people had passed through Shantiniketan on their way to the non-existent relief camps in Calcutta.

> The continuous cries for help – from children and women and men – ring in my ears even today, seventy-seven years later. My grandmother allowed me to give a cigarette tin full of rice to anyone who begged for food, but she explained, 'even if it breaks your heart, you cannot give more than one tin-can of rice to anyone, since we have to help as many people as we can'.

The famine that struck Bengal during the summer of 1943 remains one of the greatest tragedies in the history of the British Raj. As refugees had arrived from Burma in vast numbers, a devastating cyclone hit the Bay of Bengal, overwhelming numerous rice farms. At the same time crucial links in the economy began to vanish one by one. In big cities like Calcutta and Dacca, many shopkeepers had evacuated to the countryside, while on the Arakan frontier in East Bengal boats had been torched to deny them to the Japanese, meaning rice farmers simply couldn't get their rice to market. Although there was still enough rice to go around, hoarding and skyrocketing prices ensured that Bengali labourers were increasingly unable to afford to feed themselves.[50] Amartya was just about to turn ten years old and was bewildered as to what was going on.

> I listened to the anxious discussions on the possibility of impending doom ... My parents and grandparents, my uncles and aunts all had views on why prices were rising and how if it continued and intensified there would be widespread starvation ... Listening to these family conversations on tragedy and doom was a sobering way of growing up fast.[51]

As the death toll grew, the streets filled with corpses. In Calcutta Amartya was horrified to see 'famished, destitute people' in long lines outside the few food kitchens that operated in the city. 'All of them opened at the same moment so that no one could go and eat at more than one [and] the starving fought with each other to get a place in the queue before the cut-off number was reached.'⁵²

A nasty gendered edge also emerged. The trucks deployed to pick corpses off Calcutta's streets, 'like the plague carts of seventeenth century England',⁵³ found the bodies were overwhelmingly those of women and children, who hungry Bengali families had neglected to feed in favour of their working men. All the while Calcutta's Bengal Club continued serving its members five-course meals.

Over Radio Syonan, Subhas Chandra Bose placed the blame unequivocally on the British government and offered to ship a hundred thousand tons of Burmese rice across the front line to save the people of Bengal. The British refused even to acknowledge the offer.⁵⁴ Bengali newspapers were heavily censored in 1943, but cultural magazines weren't, and an article in *Desh* sarcastically compared 'The Glory of the Churchill government' with the glory of the Roman emperor Nero, playing the violin as his capital descended into flames. To this day, millions of South Asians hold Churchill directly responsible for the calamity.

Elected Bengalis had been in control of the Bengal government since 1937, and a significant portion of responsibility can be attributed to them. Provinces like Madras had faced similar conditions, but public food kitchens helped alleviate the situation. The government of Bengal, on the other hand, refused to officially acknowledge a state of famine and instead complicated aid efforts with unnecessary bureaucratic obstacles.

Nonetheless, Churchill played a central role in the tragedy. In a callous example of colonial apathy, his War Cabinet had continued shipping Bengali rice overseas well into August, even after Viceroy Linlithgow and the Indian secretary of state Amery had demanded they release it to the Bengali public. At least part of this was due to Churchill's racism towards Indians. 'I hate Indians,' he had proclaimed to a rather shocked Amery, and sending them relief was unlikely to help, he felt, because they kept 'breeding like rabbits'. Although Churchill had declared a war on fascism, he remained an imperialist and had long predicted that losing India would mark the beginning of the end of the British Empire. 'I do not admit that a wrong has been done to the Red Indians of America or the black people of Australia,' Churchill had said a few years earlier. 'I do not admit that a wrong has been done to these people by the fact that a stronger race, a higher-grade race, a more worldly-wise race ... has come in and taken their place.'⁵⁵ Amery later admitted to his diary, 'On the subject of India, Winston is not quite sane ... I didn't see much difference between his outlook and Hitler's.'⁵⁶

Things would only start to change when, in September 1943, the brilliant one-eyed commander Archibald Wavell was brought in to replace the exhausted Linlithgow as Viceroy of India. Strikingly different from his predecessor, Wavell had a fondness for literature and one of his first acts as Viceroy was to send Nehru a copy of his recently published poetry anthology *Other Men's Flowers*.⁵⁷ Arriving in India, Wavell flew immediately to Calcutta to set up a food ration scheme and described the famine as 'one of the worst disasters that has befallen any people under British rule'.⁵⁸ Like Amery, he was shocked by Churchill's refusal to help. 'Winston sent me a peevish telegram to ask why Gandhi hadn't died yet!' the Viceroy scribbled in his diary in July. 'He has never answered my telegram about food.'⁵⁹ That autumn food stockpiles in the United Kingdom had swelled to 18.5 million tonnes.

Amartya Sen would later become the great expert on the Bengal famine, winning a Nobel Prize in Economics for his writing on how famines work. He has argued that although Churchill should certainly be condemned for his racist rhetoric, it would have made little difference had he stopped the export of Bengali rice, for there was never any overall decline in the availability of food in Bengal. 'The British government was claiming that there was so much food in Bengal that there couldn't be a famine,' he writes. But 'people can't live on the knowledge – no matter how secure – that there is a lot of food around. They have to rely on their ability to buy the food.'⁶⁰ The real problem, he asserts, was that a decline in wages coincided with massive amounts of people and money flowing into Bengal, leading to skyrocketing inflation. Bengal's peasantry was unable *to afford* rice. The Madras government's setting up of public kitchens and famine camps had supported 180,000 starving people in Bellary district alone. Yet because there was still technically a surplus of food in Bengal, the Bengali administration threw up its hands and did nothing.

Another crucial issue was Britain's wartime censorship of the press. It was only in October 1943 that Ian Stephens – editor of Calcutta's English language newspaper the *Statesman* – revolted against the information blackout, publicly exposing the scale of the starvation for the first time. 'News of the famine was carefully kept away from the British public until then,' recalls Sen. 'This was critically important for even though India had an autarkic imperial rule, the governance was controlled by a functioning democracy in Britain.'[61] Within a month of the *Statesman*'s articles, the British Parliament had discussed the famine and military aid began to arrive. By then the catastrophe had killed over a million people, so that ironically in a year of the least fighting the highest civilian death toll was recorded. By the time the famine concluded at the end of the war, three million Bengalis would be dead – a death toll roughly comparable to the total number of casualties in the Vietnam War.[62]

As well as destroying public trust in the British government, the famine deepened Bengal's religious divide. It had long been one of the most religiously syncretic regions in India, and it was often difficult to differentiate between Hindus and Muslims there at all. Devotees of the two faiths spoke the same language, shared the same script, ate the same food and in many cases even worshipped the same gods. The very first Bengali-language biography on the life of the Prophet Muhammad, for example, described Muhammad as an avatar of Niranjana, the immaculate one who had previously come down to earth as the Hindu deity Rama.[63] Well into the twentieth century, despite sporadic communal violence between Hindus and Muslims, many rural Bengali Muslims continued to worship Allah alongside supernatural beings like Bonbibi, a 'Muslim' forest goddess (regarded as Hindu by Bengali Hindus), who protected travellers in the marshy Sundarban jungle.[64]

Now, however, Vinayak Savarkar of the Hindu Mahasabha aggravated the crisis by demanding Hindus boycott government efforts to buy up their rice. The Muslim League government in Bengal was untrustworthy, he argued, and Savarkar called for 'every Hindu' to 'send all help, to rescue, clothe and shelter Hindu sufferers alone'. Most of Bengal's rural poor – the people actually suffering from the famine – happened to be Muslim and so Savarkar's boycott condemned millions of Bengalis to starvation. In the process, Savarkar helped make 'Muslim freedom from Hindu economic domination' an attractive idea to Bengali Muslims for the first time.[65]

★ ★ ★

Even as British India reached its lowest point, General Slim's efforts to reform the Indian Army were finally paying off. With an attitude towards Indians that was about as far from Churchill's as possible, Slim fought tirelessly for 'no distinction between races or castes in treatment', preaching that 'the wants and needs of the Indian, African and Gurkha soldier had to be looked after as keenly as those of his British comrade'.[66] Slim recognised the importance of keeping his men both mentally and physically healthy, and sought to tackle the prevalent malaria in the Patkai, after seeing his men struck down even if they survived the onslaught of the front line. Anti-malarial medication was distributed widely and its consumption strictly enforced so that between 1942 and 1944 hospital admissions almost halved. Psychiatrists were also appointed to every military division in India, and a psychiatric clinic was erected just sixteen miles from the front line.

Slim also began to better adapt the Indian Army for jungle warfare, bringing in Jim Corbett, legendary author, conservationist and hunter of man-eating tigers, to teach soldiers how to live in the wild, and also employing the help of animals.[67] The Burma campaign would be the last in Asian history to use elephants in war, with 'Elephant Bill' recruited as 'Elephant Advisor' to Slim's Fourteenth Army.[68] Another animal in demand was the humble mule, whose transport to the front line created an entire private industry, with at least 650 animals shipped all the way from Bolivia. Upon arrival the mules were smothered with chloroform rags and had their vocal cords cut out, enabling a group of long-range troops, nicknamed the 'Chindits', to wreak havoc behind enemy lines.[69] Although the Chindits' effectiveness has been questioned, particularly given the extraordinary fatality rate of those involved, the image of British and Indian troops crossing into Japanese territory proved a propaganda coup. Not only did it convince many people that Britain still had fighting spirit, it also terrified the Japanese.

All the while news filtered in about Subhas Chandra Bose's Indian National Army. '[Churchill] accused me of creating a Frankenstein by putting modern weapons in the hands of sepoys,' wrote Wavell. 'He spoke of 1857, and was really childish about it. I tried to reassure him, both verbally and by a written note, but he has a curious complex about India and is always loath to hear good of it and apt to believe the worst.' In fact, many sepoys who had fought against the Japanese found Bose's call for brotherhood with them unconvincing. 'He promised to liberate India,' said Gian Singh, a sepoy in the 7th Indian Division, 'and said the Japanese were the friends of India. Not many truly believed him. Least of all us who saw the Japanese in their true colours. Much as we felt sorry for our brothers [in the INA] ... we often gave them no mercy.'[70]

Contrary to the many nationalist myths that have been propagated since Indian independence, the number of Indian soldiers who defected to the INA was actually quite limited and fifty times as many fought for the British Indian Army. Numbering more than two million soldiers, that force remains the largest non-conscripted force in history.[71]

By August 1943, a general reorganisation of the army was rolled out and military command over the former Indian Empire had been divided into three: Middle East Command, India Command and South East Asia Command. The names South East Asia and Middle East had never been popularly used before this moment but would become increasingly popular geographical terms throughout the Cold War up to the present day, reinforcing the mental partition of these previously united regions.[72]

To head South East Asian Command (SEAC), Churchill appointed a famously charming naval officer whose penchant for pomp and ceremony would loom large over the subcontinent in years to come. Lord Louis 'Dickie' Mountbatten was a cousin of the king and a relative of virtually every royal in Europe. Four years later he would oversee another, even greater Partition of India, on the basis of religion rather than race.

It was not Mountbatten's first trip to the subcontinent. In 1921–2 he had accompanied the Prince of Wales on a four-month tour, beginning in Aden where a huge banner greeted them with the words 'Tell Daddy We Are All Happy Under British Rule' – an amiable start to a rather tense trip. Gandhi had announced mass protests to the royal visit, and Mountbatten was fated to travel across a riot-stricken landscape. 'I need you so badly,' wrote the lovesick lord to his girlfriend Edwina as he toured across India, and so she decided to join him. She was one of London's wealthiest women, descended from both the British prime minister Palmerston and Pocahontas, yet her youth had been an unhappy one, complete with a wicked stepmother and boarding school bullies who ridiculed her for her Jewish German heritage.[73]

India provided Edwina with an escape beyond her wildest imagination and she fell in love with it instantly. She met up with Mountbatten shortly before the Valentine's Day dance at the Viceregal Lodge. 'I danced 1 and 2 with Edwina,' he wrote in his diary. 'She had 3 and 4 with David, and the 5th dance we sat out in her sitting-room, when I asked if she would marry me and she said she would.'[74]

The glamorous socialites returned to the UK the next month and were married in St Margaret's Church, Westminster. On their honeymoon they were hosted by Charlie Chaplin in Hollywood but nonetheless their marital bliss was short-lived. Edwina came to detest Mountbatten's long absences in the navy and embarked on a long series of affairs, while he grew deeply jealous of her infidelities, particularly when they crossed the racial line. When she started sleeping with the black cabaret star Leslie Hutchinson, band member Alfred Van Straten recalls Mountbatten approaching him in a drunken stupor and mumbling, 'I am lonely and drunk and sad.' Pulling out a seat opposite, he spat, 'That n*gger Hutch has a prick like a tree trunk and he's fucking my wife right now.'[75]

By the end of the decade, the marriage had effectively become an open relationship, and he had started an affair of his own with the French socialite Yola Letellier (and possibly a slew of men as well). 'Edwina and I spent all our lives getting into other people's beds,' Mountbatten later recalled.[76] But unlike Edwina's short-lived affairs, his continued over many years, greatly upsetting her. 'It was all right for her to have her own boyfriend, but she wasn't so keen on my father having a girlfriend,' remembered their daughter Patricia. 'She suffered from this dreadful jealousy all her life and even when she didn't want him herself, she still hated the thought of him with anyone else.'[77]

The Mountbattens' turbulent marriage began to flounder and by the late 1930s Edwina was spending most of her time partying, while Mountbatten was inventing strange contraptions including elasticated shoes and a 'simplex' shirt 'that he could slide into like a stretch suit'.[78] One of the only things they still had in common was their enthusiasm for collecting exotic pets, from chameleons to a Malayan honey bear nicknamed Rastus.[79] The arrival of war thus provided the couple with a much-needed sense of purpose.[80] Edwina volunteered at air-raid shelters while Mountbatten lived out his fantasies of wartime derring-do.

He wasn't very good at it, but he did discover a fabulous talent for PR. After sinking his ship, the *Kelly*, he managed to transform his defeat into a story of such valour that the British government financed an entire film about it. The Ministry of Information briefly protested that a film about sinking a British ship would damage wartime morale but was forced to renew its support after Mountbatten personally petitioned his cousin, the king. A young Richard Attenborough was cast to debut in the film, entitled *In Which We Serve*, and the fraught production ended up being nominated for Best Picture at the Oscars, only losing to *Casablanca*.

Still, when Churchill and Roosevelt appointed Mountbatten as Supreme Allied Commander of South East Asian Command (SEAC), the military regarded him more or less as a joke. 'Seldom has a Supreme Commander been more deficient of the main attributes of a Supreme Commander than Dickie Mountbatten,' concluded the head of the British Army.[81] US general Joseph Stilwell agreed, describing Mountbatten as nothing but a 'glamour boy' with 'nice eyelashes',[82] while his soldiers joked that SEAC stood for 'Save England's Asian Colonies' or 'Supreme Example of Allied Confusion'.[83] However, Mountbatten himself was thrilled with his new appointment in India, and thought it might even help his ailing marriage. 'I really don't know how I will be able to do this job without you,' he wrote to Edwina. 'Wouldn't it be romantic to live together in the place we got engaged in.'[84] But she was engrossed in an affair with a British officer, Bunny Phillips, and declined her husband's offer. Mountbatten worried he might have to file for divorce, and set off for Delhi alone.

Once in India, he initially did little to dispel his 'glamour boy' image. In a mirroring of Dorman-Smith fleeing Burma with his pet monkey, Mountbatten arrived on the front line trailed by a personal barber and his pet mongoose Rikki Tikki. Misfortune awaited the poor animal: the morning before a visit to the 4th West Kent Regiment, Mountbatten's steward accidentally stepped on Rikki Tikki, killing her. 'Poor Moore was quite white from the shock of having been the cause of her death,' wrote Mountbatten. But despite the 'terrible tragedy', the new commander utterly inspired the West Kents. One lance corporal noted with amazement how this polished aristocrat who 'looked like a movie star' was in fact very down to earth, and another jotted in the regiment war diary that 'morale was raised as if by magic'.[85]

Soon after, Mountbatten moved SEAC headquarters to the Kandy botanical gardens in Ceylon. He designed his new organisation a logo and set up his own radio station, Radio SEAC, which beamed news of the war to soldiers from Aden to Japan. Then he began preparations to turn the tide of war against the Japanese.[86]

On 1 August 1943, Ba Maw invited Subhas Chandra Bose as his personal guest to witness Japan finally grant Burma its 'independence'.

Ruling Burma was proving unmanageable for the Japanese war machine, and as a result the Japanese government had conceded the idea of handing the Burmese a form of independence two months earlier. This 'Free Burma' would not include the Shan Hills, since the Japanese recognised the separate sovereignty of the Shan princely states, but Ba Maw decided to accept the offer anyway.[87] The 1st of August was 'a fine bright day with a slight rain falling at times' and he arrived dressed in a black silken shirt, a red waistcoat and velvet slippers.[88] From the dwarf herald to the rituals carried out by Manipuri Brahmins, everything about the ceremony was designed to echo the courtly culture of precolonial Mandalay. At 11.20 that morning Japan declared Burma an independent state and Ba Maw its *Adipadi* – a Sanskrit title popularly translated as 'dictator'.[89] Aung San was appointed his minister of defence and lastly, with Churchillian zeal, Bose stood up and gave a speech:

> From 1925 to 1927, I used to gaze from the veranda of my cell in Mandalay Prison in the palace of the last independent King of Burma and I used to wonder when Burma would be free once again. Today, Burma is an independent state and I am breathing the atmosphere of that liberated country ... Nothing on earth can keep India enslaved any longer and just as the peacock emblem now flies over the Government House in Rangoon – so will the tricolour soon fly over the Red Fort of Delhi.[90]

Afterwards he and Ba Maw drove to downtown Rangoon to pay homage to the tomb of Bahadur Shah Zafar, the last Mughal Emperor whose descendants had just fled Burma in the Long March.

Two months later, in October, Bose announced his own provisional government for Azad Hind, or 'Free India'. A stage was 'set up in front of the steps of the Japanese Parliament building with large chairs festooned in red, yellow and gold colours',[91] and Ba Maw and Bose were invited to represent their 'free' countries at Tokyo's Greater East Asia Conference, alongside other Axis countries. Here Japan's prime minister handed Bose the Andaman and Nicobar Islands as the first part of Free India, and formally recognised his government. Then Nazi Germany, Thailand and the government of Ireland followed suit.[92]

Aung San quietly thought the whole thing a sham. 'Free' Burma and 'Free' India were both still part of Japan's 'Greater East Asia Co-Prosperity Sphere', which basically amounted to indirect Japanese rule. Without fanfare he began to make new plans for his future, and a month later, in early November, a British major stationed in the Patkai Hills noted in his diary that he had received word from 'a certain Aung San of the Burma Defence Army' who 'was planning to turn his forces against the Japanese when the opportunity presented itself'.[93]

In late 1943 Bengal was starving and Britain's Indian Empire seemed weak. Moreover, the success of the British Chindits in getting a military force through the Patkai showed the Japanese that they could get their soldiers through as well. After being weighed against gold to raise money for the INA 'much against his wishes', Bose convinced Japanese high command that an INA advance towards the Indian plains would cause an uprising in India and destroy the British Raj.[94] Japan seized its chance to knock Britain out of Asia once and for all.[95]

Both armies stepped up their propaganda, with the Japanese giving lectures about British atrocities and the British publishing articles on Japanese crimes.* To bring the Nagas on side, the British enlisted the help of a debutante from Kensington called Ursula Graham Bower who had spent years living with remote Naga communities as an amateur anthropologist. Ursula would unexpectedly transform into the first female guerrilla commander in British history, mobilising hundreds of Nagas to fight against – and spy on – the Japanese. The

---

* P. N. Oak, who would later become notorious for setting up the 'Institute for Rewriting Indian History' and writing a number of 'Hindutva histories', may have been among the propagandists in INA ranks. His claims included the idea that the Taj Mahal was actually a Hindu temple called the Tejo Mahalaya and that Christianity was actually a form of Hinduism known as Krishna Neeti. Roy, K., *The Indian Army in the Two World Wars* (Leiden: Brill, 2011) pp508–11.

intelligence they gleaned proved decisive in the upcoming battles, even if not all of it was reliable. One Naga is reported to have told the British that a Japanese commander was 'living with two wives and a maid ... having two monkeys with him trained to hurl grenades'.[96]

Similarly, the Japanese were trying to get the Nagas on side. Thanks to his ethnically ambiguous looks, Angami Zapu Phizo had stayed on in Rangoon when most Indians fled, settling into Japanese rule as a wholesaler. One day a Japanese car drove up to Phizo's front door. 'My brother and I were asked by the Japanese to assist them,' he wrote some years later and in response he agreed to help 'Japanese patrols into and beyond the unadministered area of Nagaland'[97] on the condition they annul the British border through the Patkai and establish a third 'Free' state called Nagaland.* 'They promised to recognise Nagaland as an independent sovereign state,' writes Phizo, and in exchange, 'We rendered whatever service we could towards what seemed to us to be the liberation of our country.'[98]

Despite Japanese assurances, no Naga National Army was ever created and Phizo had to be 'virtually admitted into the ranks' of the INA[99] – a big slap in the face to a man who had refused to join the army for having to choose between Indian or Burmese citizenship.[100] Bose's 'arrival caused problems,' Phizo explained to his biographer years later, and despite their 'polite' relationship,[101] the INA leader seems to have been opposed to Phizo's idea of further partitioning India.[102] Although Phizo's brother spent much of 1943–4 guiding Japanese troops through the Naga Hills, Phizo had already become disillusioned. Neither of them were ever allowed on the front line – proof in his eyes the Japanese had never truly intended to create an independent, united Nagaland. Yet Phizo's dream of erasing the border of 1937 didn't die there, as the governments of both India and Burma would learn soon after the war.

In 1944 the two largest empires of the twentieth century prepared to clash once more in the Patkai Hills. A Japanese attack in the Arakan lured British and Indian troops to the Indo-Burmese coastline in February. Then, on 6 March, Japan's U-Go offensive launched: three divisions of the Fifteenth Army crossed the Chindwin – tens of thou-

---

* This is arguably the first time 'Nagaland' was used to refer to a sovereign Naga state.

sands of men, accompanied by '12,000 horses and mules, 30,000 oxen and more than 1,000 elephants'[103] – and marched on the Patkai, while two divisions headed for the Manipuri capital of Imphal, and another contingent of fifteen thousand Japanese troops proceeded further north to the Naga town of Kohima to try and cut off the road. It was an awe-inspiring sight.

The twin battles of Imphal and Kohima have been variously called 'one of the greatest Allied victories of the war', the 'greatest Japanese military disaster of all time' and 'one of the four greatest turning-point battles of the Second World War'.[104] And yet Slim's army were already calling themselves the 'Forgotten Army' – neglected by the press compared to the great armies and battles in Europe and the Pacific.

The Japanese reached Manipur first, the princely state on the Indo-Burma frontier and the 'only considerable oasis of flat ground in the great sweep of mountains between India and Burma'.[105]

Dotted with medieval temples and centred around the moated Kangla Fort, Manipur's capital Imphal had been a picturesque town before the war. But by 1944 over two hundred thousand refugees had marched through – including Uttam Singh's family – and camps had spread across the countryside. Meanwhile, 120,000 Allied troops poured into the area from the other direction as Slim prepared to engage the Japanese in the Manipur valley itself, where Japan's supply lines extended over the Patkai. One affluent young Meitei woman recalled the sense of panic when the people of Manipur realised war was coming to their doorstep.

> Prophecies from the Purans began floating freely, with nobody actually knowing how they originated. The one that caught the people's paranoid imagination most was that the flight of 18 white egrets across the Manipur sky would signal the beginning of the war. When the phenomenon was sighted, the advice was to flee and take shelter at places with names beginning with the consonant 'K'. Everybody watched the skies day after day for the white birds with anxious expectation and apprehension.

The Imphal valley, previously a backwater of the Raj, turned into a microcosm of the British Empire. Gurkhas and Punjabis prepared to fight alongside Burmese, Nagas and Scots, and Manipuri women sang and danced for South African soldiers. 'Some of us became very close to the Africans,' recalls Naorem Kalimohon. 'Sometimes after dinner, they took us to Laithemfam ... to watch movies and other performances.'[106]

Many of the military generals later to rule Pakistan, like Ayub Khan, were stationed here alongside soldiers like Sam Manekshaw, subsequently the Chief of Indian Army Staff. In December 1944, when Wavell knighted General Slim in the city of Imphal, a young Manekshaw would be one of two Indian officers decorated at the ceremony. The other was Lieutenant Niazi, the future Pakistani commander who would surrender East Pakistan to Manekshaw's Indian Army.[107]

As the battle for Imphal loomed, Mountbatten was notably absent, On 7 March a bamboo stump struck his eye while he was driving in an open jeep, rendering him completely immobile for five crucial days and reinforcing his critics' view of him as a mere 'Glamour Boy'.[108] The very next day on 8 March 1944, Japanese troops entered the valley, and Bose and the INA finally stepped onto Indian soil.[109]

Elsewhere, the third Japanese contingent was advancing further north towards Kohima – where Phizo had once been a janitor – to cut the Imphal–Kohima road, and 1,500 British and Indian troops waited, scanning the treeline for movement. On 30 March the defenders accidentally shot a cow, thinking it a member of the Japanese Army. Confusion filled the ranks and one cavalry officer noted that everyone was at 'panic stations'.[110] But all they could do was stretch themselves out along the Kohima ridge and wait for the enemy to attack. Then, around three in the morning on 3 April, the first shot was fired over the Patkai. Immediately there was shouting and Lieutenant Hayllar began to recite Psalm 23:

Even though I walk
Through the valley of the shadow of death
I will fear no evil
For you are with me[111]

Several troops were killed but then, as quickly as they had appeared, the Japanese ambushers receded into the forest again. By dawn all was quiet once more.

No one could sleep that night and every noise had soldiers unloading bullets into the undergrowth. 'Almost every LMG [light machine gun] and rifle in the position opened up and fired wildly in every direction for about an hour,' wrote the commander of the British 1st Assam Regiment. '[There was a] complete lack of fire control and discipline and troops obviously were shaken.'[112] At 4 p.m. the next day, Japanese troops opened fire on the ridge. Gunfire was sporadic but what scared the British officers most was the voice of INA soldiers in the enemy ranks shouting across the battlefield. Lieutenant Hayllar, who understood Hindustani, found it terrifying.

> Sometimes they would shout to our soldiers, 'Kill your officers.' If it was your own men you could be sure of them. But I was put in charge of people I had never seen before ... It was a horrible situation.[113]

That night the first group of Indian troops slunk off across the front line to the Japanese side.

On 5 April Radio Tokyo announced that Kohima had fallen. It hadn't, of course, but the British and Japanese armies were now a stone's throw away from each other, and each side dug into trenches, reminiscent of the First World War. 'It was awful in the trench,' recorded Private Tom Greatly, an eighteen-year-old who had lied about his age to get himself into the army. 'We never ate a cooked meal and we all ended up with beards and long hair.' On the Japanese side things were no better and with supply lines dangerously extended, many contracted dysentery. In the words of Lieutenant Yamagami, 'The battle of Kohima, life in a trench for forty days, had begun.'[114]

The Battle of Kohima would be one of attrition – a grenade thrown here, a mortar there. Both armies were largely cut off from their command centres and by the start of April men began dying of hunger and disease. 'For the most part,' writes one chronicler of the battle, 'men rotted where they had been killed. Anybody going out to collect the bodies was a target for snipers.'[115]

In the British ranks, it soon became clear that anyone who was going to defect to the INA already had and lying together in their trenches, the Indian, Burmese, African and British troops bonded. 'We felt close

WAR IN THE BORDERLANDS

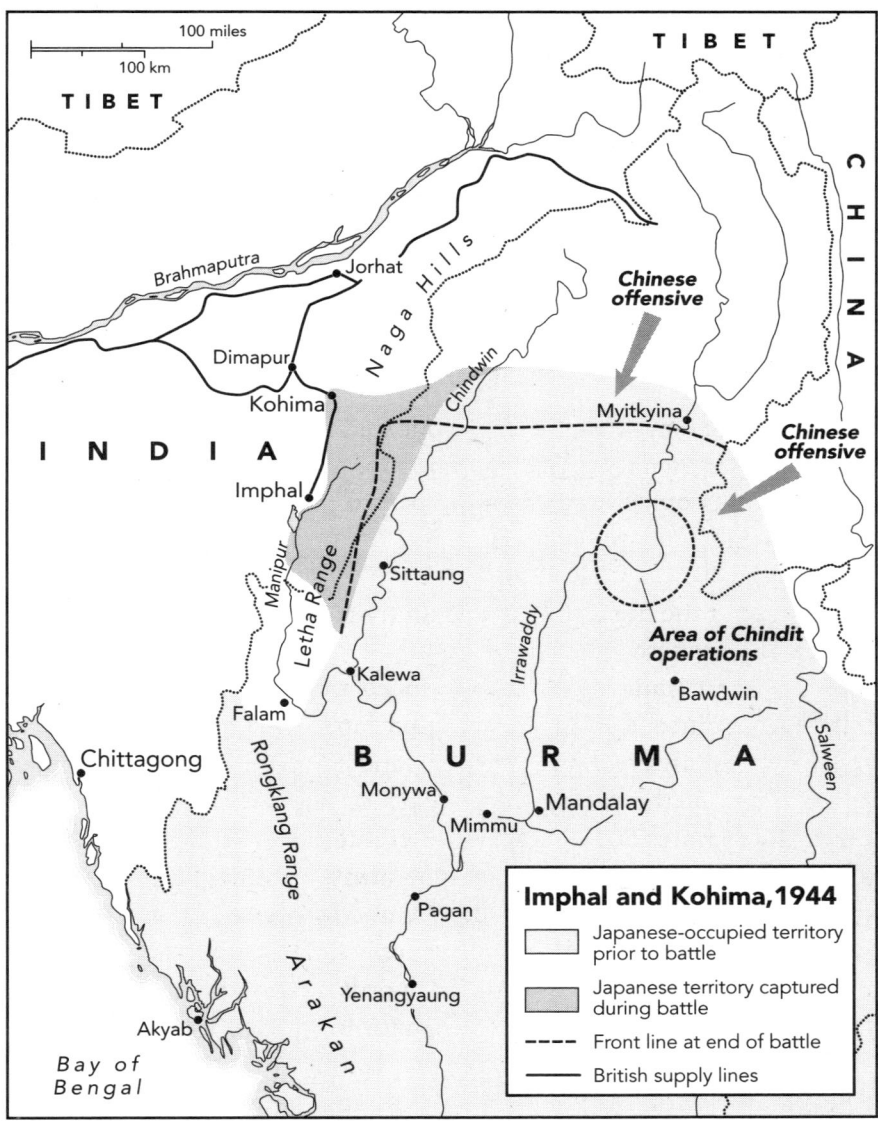

to each other,' recalled Lieutenant Hayllar. 'Whether you were Christian or a Muslim or anything we used to pray together and help each other. It didn't matter what you were.' And meanwhile, British governor Charles Pawsey toured the trenches 'in a trilby hat with an umbrella and two Naga spearmen as his escorts'.[116]

In mid-April the Japanese managed to skirt around the front line and advance towards Pawsey's bungalow. Within hours the governor's tennis court had become the battleground, and Japanese snipers took up positions in the governor's cherry trees. At such close contact, the fighting frequently devolved into hand-to-hand combat, and when one apprentice plumber-turned soldier saw his friend bayonetted, he grabbed a spade and hacked his assailant to death.

The 'Battle of the Tennis Courts' would subsequently become the most famous battle of the conflict, subject of numerous memoirs from those who fought in it – ranging from standard regimental military histories to the rather intriguing account of infantry commander Miyazaki, who wrote a narrative of the battle from the perspective of his pet monkey Chibi, who sat on his shoulder throughout the fighting. Volleys of bullets and grenades, rather than tennis balls, shot across the court, and on 17 April the Japanese captured Pawsey's bungalow, restricting the Anglo-Indian troops to Garrison Hill beyond. It looked like the invaders would finish the battle off, but at dawn the next morning British reinforcements arrived.[117]

The relief of the siege of Kohima turned the tide. The British managed to recapture Kohima ridge and, in early June, the monsoon rains arrived. Overnight the Patkai turned to mud and Japanese supply lines through the jungle frontier collapsed. Their soldiers were forced to retreat. Kh Nasii, a Duonamai Naga, recalls British, Indian and Japanese forces holding peace talks in his village. Japanese leaders took over a man called Dahrii's house while British and Indian forces requisitioned a man called Chozii's house and all the while Kh Nasii and his friends watched in bewilderment. 'I wasn't aware that the Japanese were retreating after being defeated at Kohima,' he observes. The peace talks went nowhere, however, and Japanese soldiers were forced to continue their retreat along what would become known as 'the Road of Bones'.[118]

It would be the biggest land defeat in the history of the Japanese Empire and in the following months some 30,000–50,000 Japanese died, by far the majority from malnutrition and disease. As they fled, the invaders enacted their own scorched earth policy – a mirror of Britain's two years earlier – further obliterating a Burma that had already been burned to the ground.[119]

'By the middle of 1944 we no longer believed in the possibility of an Axis victory,' Ba Maw admitted years later. 'Their defeats were too decisive and uninterrupted.'[120] But he stayed loyal to the Japanese, trying to persuade young Burmese men to join suicide kamikaze squads. Aung San was not so dependable. With his wife pregnant, he had become more direct in his opposition to the Japanese, publicly deriding the fake independence at the anniversary of Free Burma's Independence Day. 'We are supposed to be free now, but who can enjoy this freedom?' he boomed.[121] By August he had secretly garnered Burmese communist and Karen support for a rebellion, and when Ba Maw returned from a tour of Japan, he found Aung San even more vocally anti-Japanese than ever. Burma's head of state tried to keep Aung San under control, even attempting to remove him from his position in the BNA, but Ba Maw's authority was waning. Aung San was infinitely more popular, and songs were already being written about his valour.

Throughout these final months of war, Aung San had been in secret contact with Mountbatten, who was working doggedly to get him recognised as a British ally. Unlike most of the British high command, Mountbatten was sympathetic to Indian and Burmese nationalists, partially thanks to the influence of Edwina, with whom he had recently been reunited. Bunny Phillips had left her for another woman, and Mountbatten had written her a compassionate letter about his 'genuine love and affection' for her, enabling the estranged couple to reconnect after many years. 'Nobody gave me an idea of the strength of the nationalist movements,' he later admitted. 'Edwina was the first person to give me an inkling of what was going on.'[122] Dorman-Smith objected that 'it would be a disaster to give even a semblance of recognition to Aung San ... while legitimate Government still exists',[123] but he was overruled and Mountbatten covertly began to distribute thousands of weapons to the BNA.

Aung San made his gambit in mid-March 1945. After a parade across Rangoon, he drove out of the city with the BNA and headed for the front line, allegedly to fight against the Allied advance. Then he drew up a letter for Ba Maw and handed it to a courier:

My Dear Adipadigyi
I am sorry that I was unable to meet you before I came out here ... Conditions were such that I had to do things in a hurry ... I shall be coming back to Rangoon &, if conditions do not worsen so unexpectedly, I hope to meet you again ... The struggle for our

national independence must go on till it ends in victory. And I will do my best. You might misunderstand me now perhaps …

Aung San[124]

Five days later Aung San ordered his troops to turn on the Japanese and in turn Mountbatten formally recognised the BNA – renamed the Patriotic Burmese Forces – as an Allied force. The question now, as Slim observed, was 'How to treat the Burmese National Army?' The British commander finally met Aung San a few weeks later, when the young general arrived at Slim's office in full Japanese military garb, complete with a sword at his belt. 'The greatest impression he made on me was one of honesty,' wrote Slim. 'He was not free with glib assurances and he hesitated to commit himself, but I had the idea that if he agreed to do something he would keep his word.' Slim asked why he had come when he knew the risks. 'Because you are a British officer,' Aung San replied, winning Slim over, and he began to negotiate for the BNA to form part of Burma's military after the war.[125]

All the while Bose's INA continued their dogged resistance to the Allied advance.[126] Japanese troops fled Rangoon, but five thousand INA soldiers remained in the capital, and it was they who eventually surrendered the city to the Allied army. Aung San and the BNA goose-stepped into its charred remains alongside Slim's forces, only to discover that Mountbatten had flown ahead of them in a seaplane and already taken the best suites in the Strand Hotel. Four days later Aung San's wife gave birth to their baby daughter, Aung San Suu Kyi.

With Rangoon reconquered, the remnants of the INA and the Free Burma government scattered. Ba Maw's daughter Tinsa was heavily pregnant and her waters broke during the retreat. They reached the town of Kyaikto just in time for the delivery but had to plough onwards within days. It would be the last time Bose and Ba Maw saw each other. When Ba Maw reached Tokyo a couple of months later, he learned that Bose had died in a plane crash. 'Numbed by the crisis I had been passing through for days and nights … my mind did not take in fully what the officer had told me,' he wrote in his autobiography.[127] A few months later he gave himself up to Allied forces.

★ ★ ★

The India–Pakistan border as seen from space

The Indian Empire passport, once issued as far west as Aden and as far east as Rangoon

Indian banknote featuring Burmese script but not the Devanagari Hindi script

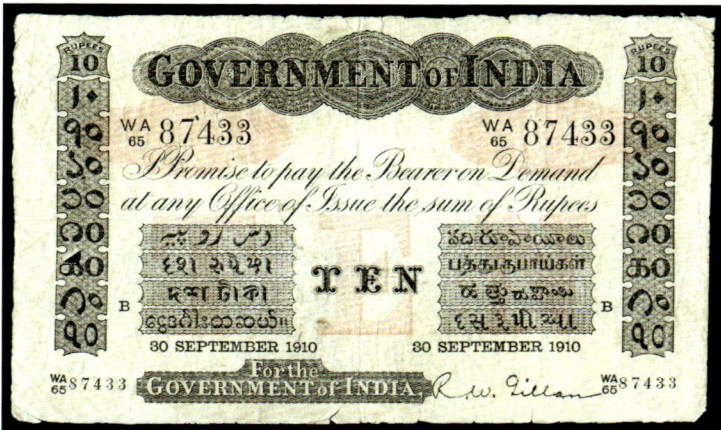

The Ruling Princes of India

Aden, still India's westernmost city, celebrates the 1921 visit of the Prince of Wales and Lord Mountbatten with a banner reading: 'Tell Daddy we are all happy under British rule'

'The Viceroy's House is the first real vindication of modern architecture … It is so unlike the English – one would never have thought them capable of it' – Robert Byron

Ruttie Jinnah

A young Muhammad Ali Jinnah

The British government's decision to exclude Indians from the Simon Commission – set up to draft a new constitution – sparked widespread protests across India

Saya San, accused of leading the largest rebellion against British rule since 1857, is sentenced to death

Throughout the 1920s, Burma was central to Indian nationalist political campaigns. Here, Gandhi addresses the Indian National Congress in Rangoon

Burmese lacquer bowl of Gandhi designed after his 1930 visit

Mahatma U Ottama, Burma's most prominent politician and one-time president of the Hindu Mahasabha, consistently argued that Burma was an integral part of the Indian nation

Sarojini Naidu and Gandhi attend the Round Table Conferences

A Saopha Prince from the Shan States arrives at the Burma Round Table Conference in London

The Round Table Conferences brought together British and Indian leaders to debate the future of the Raj, and whether it should be partitioned

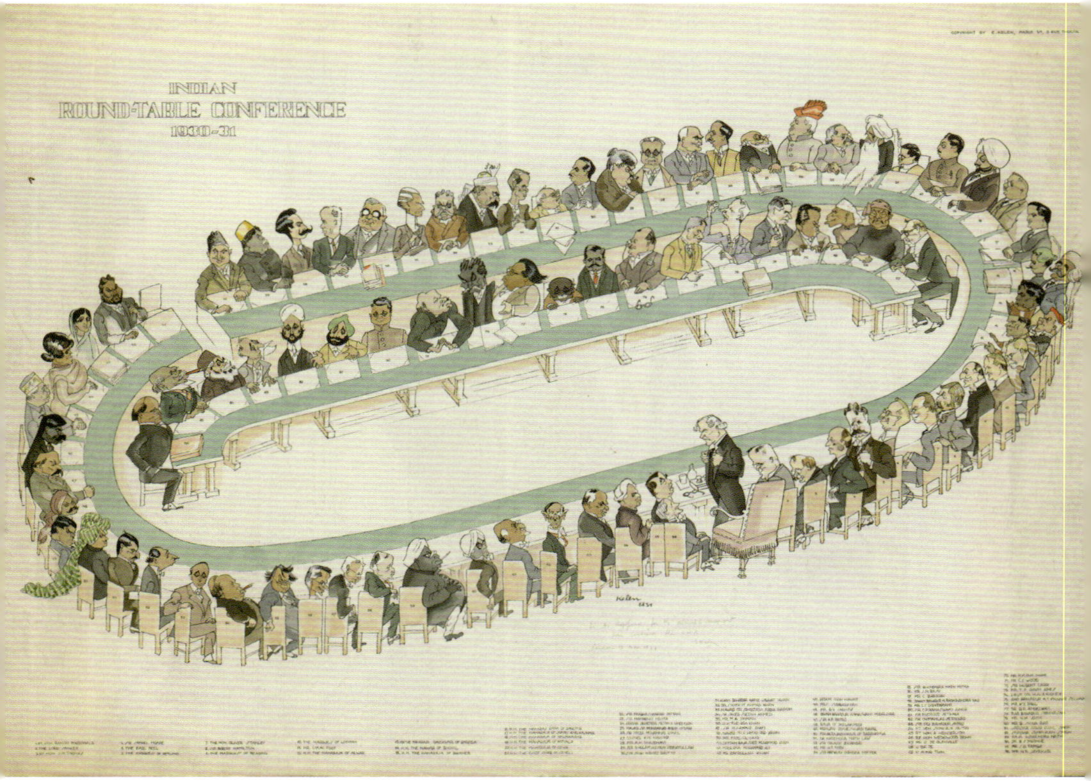

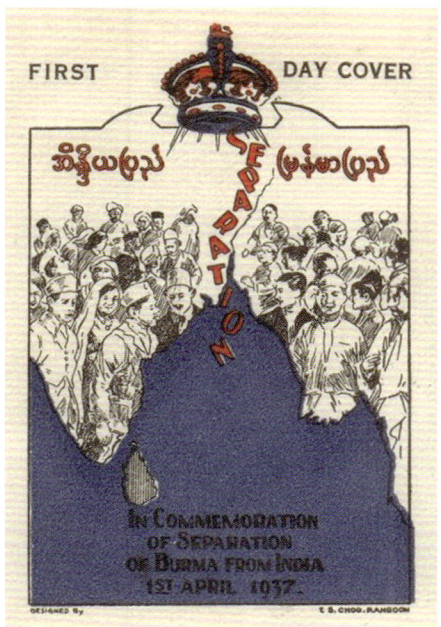

Stamps issued to celebrate the separation of Burma from India

U Saw: Burma's 'Galon fascist' leader who led the anti-Indian lobby

A new recruit to the Indian Army. When the war began the Indian Army had around 300,000 soldiers. By the end of the conflict, India had deployed the largest non-conscripted army in history: 2.5 million men, out of whom 90,000 would be killed or maimed

Parsi women training for air raids. World War Two affected everyone in the subcontinent, and soldiers were supported by a vast network of cleaners, drivers, engineers, cooks, intelligence agents, sweepers, propaganda writers and barbers

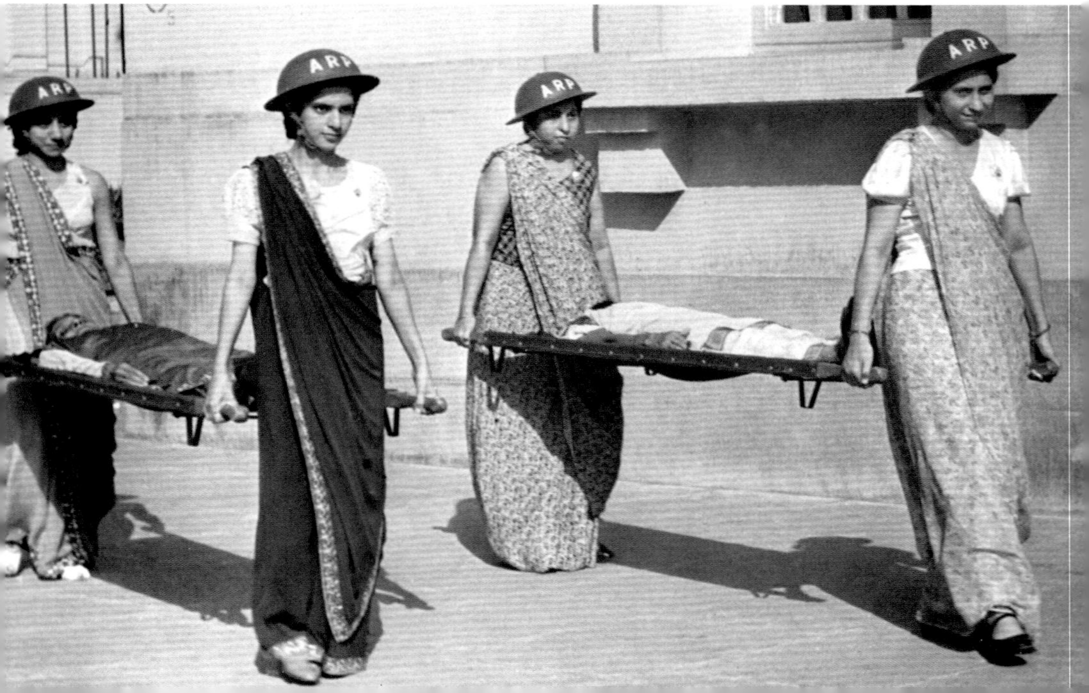

By the spring of 1945, the war against Japan was ending. The British Indian Army had reconquered Burma, temporarily undoing the partition that had divided India and Burma for almost a decade. On 30 April 1945 Adolf Hitler committed suicide in a bunker in Berlin and shortly afterwards the war in Europe came to an end. War lingered on in Asia, but on 6 August an American Boeing B-29 dropped an atomic bomb on the Japanese city of Hiroshima. None of the survivors can recall hearing the bomb, but everyone saw it – a terrifying flash of white light that cut across the sky, from the city centre out towards the hills. In a city of 245,000, the bomb incinerated a hundred thousand people in an instant. A hundred thousand more were left injured, including the majority of doctors. As they dragged themselves and their loved ones through the smoke towards the Red Cross Hospital, one of the few surviving buildings in the city, 'droplets of water the size of marbles' began to fall onto the smoking streets.[128] Three days later a second atomic bomb was dropped over the Japanese naval city of Nagasaki, turning it silent: 'Not a sound. No birds, not even a lizard. Just brown, treeless soil like cocoa, no grass, and twisted girderwork.'[129] Japan surrendered. Just like that the war was over.

Across the world, people struggled to articulate the news. J. Robert Oppenheimer, the man who had built the bomb, described his feelings in an interview:

We knew the world would not be the same.
    A few people laughed. A few people cried. Most people were silent.
    I remembered the line from the Hindu scripture, the Bhagavad Gita. Vishnu is trying to persuade the prince that he should do his duty, and to impress him takes on his multi-armed form, and says: 'Now I am become Death, the Destroyer of Worlds.'
    I suppose we all thought that.
    One way or another.[130]

6

Direct Action Day

As news of Japan's surrender spread, South Asia erupted in collective celebration. It was a moment of unbridled optimism and people everywhere looked forward to a future without rations or air raids. 'One by one, the finer things of life return,' read a cigarette advert in Lahore's *Civil & Military Gazette*.[1] 'Will the Atomic Bomb Abolish War?' asked another, even more hopeful article in the same paper.[2]

Fireworks burst over Aden, while adobe rooftops across the Arabian desert glimmered with blazing celebratory bonfires. In Lahore, green boulevards were 'transformed into veritable fairylands with hundreds of electric bulbs, profusely decorated with flags and bunting', and further to the east, crowds thronged the Taj Mahal for a triumphant picnic. Across the corpse-strewn Patkai Hills, it dawned on the soldiers of the Indian Army that they had actually survived the war.[3] Major-General Kartar Singh later recalled,

> While all of us were sleeping in our tents, one British officer … heard on the radio that the Japanese had surrendered. He got quite wild about it and went straight to the tent of the CO and brought him out of bed in his night suit. And when they heard that news, they sent the *subehdar* and ordered all officers to come to the mess as they were … some were dressed in their *lungis*, some in their pyjamas, and they kept on celebrating and drinking for a long time that we have survived.[4]

This post-war euphoria did not last, though, as apprehension about the future set in. Many Japanese soldiers refused to believe that their emperor had surrendered and kept on fighting, pointlessly wasting more young lives. Meanwhile, newspapers placed pictures from Nazi concentration camps in eerie juxtaposition with discussions on the recently published findings of the Famine Inquiry Commission, and reports from Hiroshima and Nagasaki.[5] 'I did not know what an atom bomb was,' wrote Balwant Singh, a Sikh civil servant in Burma, 'but the press's description of its power and of the devastation it caused was stunning ... Offices were closed in celebration and a victory parade was organized [but] personally, I found it difficult to cheer.'[6]

When wartime defence laws were relaxed and the leaders of the Indian National Congress finally walked free from jail, they were confronted by a vastly changed country. The population had been radicalised by famine and war, and formerly non-violent Gandhians preached new militant forms of nationalism. Most important of all, Jinnah's 'Pakistan demand' of four years earlier was now furiously debated in households across India, just as the Burma separation had been a decade before. The Muslim League had exploded in size and popularity, with Jinnah himself noting that, for him at least, 'the war which nobody welcomed proved to be a blessing in disguise'.[7] And yet, having spent the war in prison, the Congress leaders completely underestimated how much Jinnah's star had risen. Woodrow Wyatt, a Labour MP, later recalled Nehru's insistence that the Muslim League's popularity was 'just a myth ... just in the imagination of the British'. It took Wyatt four hours to persuade Nehru otherwise. 'He had been in jail so often,' remarked the MP, '[that] he hadn't realised the enormous pressures that had been building up.'[8]

Meanwhile, something extraordinary had happened to Britain. It was estimated the country had lost a quarter of its total wealth since the start of the war – GDP had contracted, reserves were empty, infrastructure had been destroyed and vast loans needed to be repaid. The war had thus not only left Britain broke but actually in debt to Government of India,* and the poet Sarojini Naidu felt the Raj now

---

* During the Second World War, Britain funded its military operations in India by accumulating sterling balances – essentially an IOU – rather than paying in cash, leaving it in debt to the government of India by about £1.3 billion. However, India couldn't freely access this money as it was held in London, and Britain, facing its own post-war crisis, restricted withdrawals to protect its economy. After independence, India negotiated partial repayments, but much of the debt was never fully settled, making the ironic reality that a colonised India had effectively financed its coloniser's survival.

shone with 'the iridescence of decay'.[9] When Churchill held post-war elections in July 1945, he was, to his great surprise, voted out, ushering in an anti-colonial Labour government under former Simon Commissioner Clement Attlee. The same day as Emperor Hirohito declared Japan's surrender, 15 August, King George proclaimed in the British Parliament his intention to grant 'the early realisation of full self-government in India'.[10] A similar policy was decreed for Burma so that, of the former Indian Empire, only the states of the Arabian Peninsula now figured in Britain's long-term plans. The question was, when would the transfer of power happen, and who would the British hand over power to?

After decades of struggle, Indian and Burmese independence appeared imminent. Yet, in the words of historian Patrick French, the years following would prove 'an unexpected tale of confusion, human frailty and neglect ... Many of the key events of the 1940s were the result of chance, or even of error, and some of the most important decisions of the period were made on an almost random basis ... Yet few moments in modern ... history have had a more lasting impact on so many people.'[11]

Who would run British India without the British? Gandhi, the Congress' greatest asset, had grown more erratic and emotionally unstable since his wife's death, and when the ailing and grief-stricken Mahatma approached Jinnah to negotiate a power-sharing agreement for India's future, their meeting only reinforced Jinnah's power by convincing the press that they were political equals. Just as Gandhi was often referred to by the epithet Mahatma, or 'Great Soul', so Jinnah was now called 'Quaid-i-Azam' or 'Great Leader'.

Gandhi took the failure personally, and resolved to mentally challenge his willpower. Over the coming years, he began his controversial 'brahmacharya' experiments, sleeping next to naked women, including his sixteen-year-old grand-niece Abha, to test his vow of celibacy. Although there is no indication that Gandhi ever made any sexual advances on these women, the conduct caused them deep emotional turmoil. 'I don't remember whether he had any clothes on or not,' Abha later recalled. 'I don't like to think about it.' Many of the Mahatma's staff resigned over the experiments but Gandhi stayed firm. 'If I can master this,' he apparently said, 'I can still beat Jinnah.'[12]

By the time the Congressmen met Jinnah again in Simla, few considered a settlement likely. 'Gandhi and Jinnah are behaving like very temperamental prima donnas,' wrote Wavell in frustration.[13] India's freedom struggle thus entered a strange new phase during which Britain had at last agreed to leave but India's leading politicians, having spent decades campaigning for precisely this moment, stalled for time as they fought over who would take the reins of power.

All the while Hindu–Muslim riots became more and more frequent. A year after Amartya Sen witnessed the Bengal famine, a Muslim labourer called Kader Mia stumbled through the gate of Amartya's family home in Dacca, 'screaming pitifully and bleeding profusely' after being stabbed in the street by a Hindu nationalist. As Amartya's father drove him to hospital, Kader Mia rambled about how 'his wife had told him not to go into a hostile area during the riots. But he had to go out in search of work and earning because his family had nothing to eat.'[14] The Bengal famine, it seemed, was not entirely over, and scarcity was continuing to fuel a growing religious divide.

Amartya was puzzled by how quickly communities who had lived side by side for generations now turned on one another. 'How much of India's rich history is missed,' he wrote years later, 'if the great religions of India are perceived as isolated islands surrounded by unnavigable waters or – worse – as islands of belligerent foes dedicated to attacking one another.'[15] Bengal was Muslim majority, and indeed Bengali Muslims were the second largest Muslim ethnic group in the world after Arabs, but for Amartya this disguised a pluralistic, not a monolithic society. Nonetheless, Amartya's family saw the writing on the wall. Soon after Kader Mia's stabbing, they decided to leave Muslim-majority Dacca for Bengal's Hindu-majority capital Calcutta, their second migration in five years. Accompanying them were several other Hindu members of Dacca University's faculty, including the brilliant quantum physicist Satyendra Nath Bose whose work with Einstein had given rise to Bose-Einstein statistics, and whose name was immortalised in the subatomic particle, the 'Boson'.[16] They would be among the first of millions to make such a migration.

For the time being, however, it was migration between India and Burma – and the question of whether Indian evacuees should be allowed to return to Burma – that monopolised the news. In the event, no policy whatsoever was enforced and when the Indian Army marched into Burma, many Indian evacuees followed in their wake. Doris D'Mello, a Goan who had fled during the Long March, remembers her emotional return to the southern Burmese town of Thaton.

> It was really sad to see all the shops razed to the ground. Everything, even our homes had disappeared. All that was left was rubble. But would you believe it? Our dog came running out from somewhere and jumped on my mother, and then greeted all of us.[17]

Burma evacuees had spent three years in India building a new life for themselves, and M. P. Mariappan, the Tamil Dalit who witnessed the 1938 pogroms, was one of those who decided to remain there. Soon the only evidence of his Burmese youth was his lack of moustache, which he continued to pluck in the Burmese manner using a pair of quarter anna coins.[18] But Mariappan's brother did go back and was delighted to find their old shop still standing, looked after by their old friend, the 'moustache man' Ko Chet Pon.

Civil servant Balwant Singh, meanwhile, moved into the house of an 'absentee Indian' and was assigned a bulldozer to help demolish the ruins of blitzed buildings across his city. 'I had never seen one before,' he writes, and 'wondered how this would affect the future role of the elephant'. Yet as the influx of Indian returnees increased, debates over the role of Indians in Burmese society reignited, particularly as U Saw was returning to Burma. 'Large numbers of armaments remained,' writes Balwant, 'and new fires of rebellion were igniting.' In India and Burma, the war had strained community tensions. 'Were we seeing the last stages of World War II,' he wondered, 'or was this the beginning of a new conflict?'[19]

For many Indian troops, the Japanese surrender did not mean an end to fighting. It just meant turning their guns on new opponents. As part of the post-war Allied agreement for dealing with the rump of the Japanese Empire, Mountbatten's SEAC had been ordered to pacify the surrendered Japanese across Southeast Asia.[20] Ninety per cent of SEAC land forces came from the Indian Army, so it was largely Indian troops who were now ordered to hand Southeast Asia back to its erstwhile colonial masters. The whole charade was a recipe for disaster.

In the Dutch East Indies,* where the nationalist leader Sukarno had declared the independence of a new sovereign country called Indonesia, British Indian troops were suddenly deployed to help reimpose Dutch colonial rule. In Indochina, meanwhile, a similar charade was unfolding.† Scottish major-general Douglas Gracey had been charged with disarming the Japanese, restoring order and handing the erstwhile colony back to the French government. But in the power vacuum between the Japanese surrender and Gracey's arrival, a Vietnamese revolutionary called Ho Chi Minh had hastily declared eastern Indochina's independence as the Democratic Republic of Vietnam.[21] When the twenty-six thousand troops under Gracey's command marched into Saigon, the major-general ordered the Indian Army to expel Ho Chi Minh's men from Governor's House. In his own words:

> I was welcomed on arrival by the Vietminh who said 'Welcome' and all that sort of thing. It was a very unpleasant situation, and I promptly kicked them out.[22]

When Ho Chi Minh's party, the Viet Minh, responded with a strike, Gracey declared them a 'threat to law and order' and instigated martial law across southern Indochina.[23] Then, while entertaining Edwina Mountbatten at Governor's House, he started arming French nationals to overthrow the Viet Minh altogether. Ho Chi Minh subsequently launched a rebellion, which Gracey sent the Indian Army to suppress. Through a mix of incompetence and disobedience, Gracey's army of Punjabis and Gurkhas had unknowingly fired the opening shots of the Vietnam War.[24]

The 'liberation' of Southeast Asia would be the last time the British Empire was able to deploy Indian soldiers in battle.[25] Mountbatten himself was rather alarmed at the way the simple mission of rounding up the Japanese accidentally pitched the Indian Army against nascent Southeast Asian nationalist groups. It would be a 'grave mistake,' he wrote to the chiefs of staff, to assume that British and Indian soldiers

---

* Modern Indonesia.

† Indochina was a French colony comprising present-day Vietnam, Cambodia and Laos. For most of the war it continued to be governed by Vichy France officials in collaboration with the Japanese.

were 'about to get involved in putting down local independence movements on behalf of other governments in countries they are liberating'.[26] Back in India, Nehru was already busy comparing Britain's involvement in Indochina to Nazi involvement in the Spanish Civil War, demanding the Indian troops in Southeast Asia be sent home.[27] Ultimately SEAC was forced to replace its Indian troops with surrendered Japanese soldiers, leading to some very awkward questions in the House of Commons about 'why British and Japanese troops were apparently engaged in joint military operations against independence movements in the colonies of two foreign powers'. These Japanese soldiers – nicknamed 'Mountbatten's Samurai' – would continue to be used as a replacement for Indian soldiers in Southeast Asia for 'peacekeeping' purposes until late 1947.[28]

Mountbatten himself flew from Kandy to Rangoon in late August 1945, riding aboard a 'comfortable white-leather padded Dakota' aeroplane.[29] Accompanying him was Tom Driberg, a journalist and possible Soviet spy whose capacity to flaunt his homosexuality without arrest baffled his friends.[30] The plan was to go and check up on politics in the Burmese capital, before driving south down the Malay Peninsula so that Mountbatten could formally accept the Japanese surrender in Singapore, and from their very first meeting aboard the plane, Mountbatten struck Driberg as a perfectionist. 'He tends to become obsessed with detail and therefore, perhaps, not to delegate sufficiently,' wrote the journalist. 'On this journey something was wrong with the lock of the lavatory door: the ADC heard about little else till we arrived at our first stop.'[31] Emerging from the plane in Rangoon a few hours later, Driberg found the great city had been replaced by a makeshift morass of half-destroyed slums. Rangoon had lost decades of development and most of its boats, cars, bridges, roads, and its proud rows of neoclassical buildings were in ruins. Eighty per cent of the city would have to be rebuilt. To make matters worse, the Allies had declared Japanese currency worthless, so wiping out almost everyone's savings. The only people exempt were those who escaped back to India on the Long March – and they had already lost everything anyway.[32]

Mountbatten and Driberg set off south, joined by Edwina who was visiting liberated prisoner of war camps and had apparently been 'hobnobbing with some Communist republicans', making Mountbatten 'exceedingly angry'.[33] The two, wrote Driberg, were an unusual and interesting couple. Both were extremely good at their jobs – so much so that there was almost a kind of competition between them. At breakfast they would compare the total numbers of British prisoners in the camps whom each of them had spoken to and shaken hands with ... Edwina was the more left-wing of the two: she showed an instant strong sympathy with any Asian nationalist.[34]

The couple worked in synch. At each PoW camp, they would jump onto a truck – Mountbatten first, followed swiftly by Edwina – and order the liberated soldiers to break ranks and listen to 'the latest news of war and peace'.[35] In private, meanwhile, they revealed a sense of childish privilege and on one occasion in Penang, when Mountbatten's batman misplaced the military decorations for his evening dress, an RAF aircraft was commandeered to fly them in from Kandy in Ceylon* before dinner. Nonetheless, by the time the Mountbattens arrived in Singapore, Driberg was decidedly taken by the prince-commander and his wife. On 12 September at 11.10 a.m., he watched on proudly as Mountbatten accepted the Japanese surrender at Singapore's Municipal Building, formally ending Japan's occupation of Southeast Asia.

A few weeks later Driberg returned to Rangoon and met up with Mountbatten who had now fallen out with Burma's governor Dorman-Smith.[36] The two men may have been united in their love for exotic pets, but a rift had developed between them over how to treat thirty-year-old Aung San, who had stepped down from the army and announced his entry into civilian politics, unifying the BNA, the Communist Party of Burma and several older politicians in the catchily named Anti-Fascist People's Freedom League (AFPFL). Driberg writes of Aung San as 'a slight, boyish figure with a surprisingly strong, deep voice; physically and mentally agile, with an irrepressible sense of humour'.[37] His speeches could be long and rambling, but also electric, and each was translated into Burmese, Tamil and Urdu, as well as English. Aung San was already publicly denouncing British plans to keep Burma's frontier regions under British rule after independence. As one nationalist put it, 'Independence without the Frontier Areas would be meaningless: a partition of Burma.'[38]

---

* Modern Sri Lanka.

Mountbatten wanted Aung San to be treated as a leader-in-waiting, but Dorman-Smith insisted Burma's pre-war politicians such as U Saw should be part of any future government and refused to let Aung San send a delegation to the UK. Driberg describes Dorman-Smith as 'a blimp of the old school, bitterly mistrustful of Aung San and out of sympathy with Mountbatten's progressive ideas'. Having spent much of the war walking his dogs in Simla, the governor didn't seem to grasp the changes that had overcome Burma. One memorable evening, Driberg sat silently in a private hotel room as Mountbatten and Dorman-Smith argued with each other about Burma's future. He writes that, 'Each time one of them went out of the room to pee, the other would say to me, "Take no notice of what he's saying – he's just a hopeless reactionary."'[39]

It all came to a head during a dinner at Rangoon's Orient Club as a group of stuffy imperial statesmen with 'dainty pink or mauve headdresses' looked on at Mountbatten's parley with the young Burmese leader with disgust. 'They had been crass enough to put Aung San at a lower table at the far end of the room,' writes Driberg, and:

> His name was not in the printed toast-list on the menu. Mountbatten insisted that Aung San should be called on to speak, even threatening that if Aung San did not speak, he, Mountbatten, would not speak either. Aung San's was the speech of the evening.[40]

Mountbatten had won the day, and Aung San was now increasingly seen as Burma's prime minister-in-waiting.

Around this time the Indian Army started to demobilise. Soldiers returned from the front, some with new Burmese brides, and long-separated family members saw one another again.[41] 'What a reunion it was,' wrote Ramesh Benegal on returning to Poona.

> After a dinner that I don't remember eating, I passed into a deep sleep. I heard that my mother sat beside me all night, and touched me now and again to make sure that she wasn't dreaming, and that this was really her son, come back to life.[42]

It was an emotional moment but fraught with problems for the imperial government. Two million men came home with no guarantee of employment and demanding radical change, trained in arms and accustomed to violence. Veterans were horrified by the conditions they went back to, and among them was a sailor called B. C. Dutt:

> I was 22. I had come through war unscathed – a war fought to end Nazi domination. I began to ask myself questions. What right had the British to rule over our country? Nationalist India had asked the British to leave Indian affairs in Indian hands. The British always proved intransigent. To Nationalist India we were mere mercenaries. It was up to us, I felt, to prove this was not so. Without quite realising it, I had become a conspirator.[43]

Anti-British sentiment spread across the subcontinent. Shortly before the Nuremberg trials, Viceroy Wavell made the spectacularly ill-advised decision to publicly try three officers of the INA for war crimes – one Hindu, one Muslim, one Sikh – within the sandstone walls of Delhi's Red Fort. Thanks to wartime censorship, many Indians had been entirely unaware of the INA, but the high-profile trials proved a better promoter of the INA than anything Bose had done in his lifetime.* The public hung on every word and one court transcript even remarked: 'This trial is far more sensational than the trial of Jesus Christ.'[44]

Amid this atmosphere, Indian political parties of all persuasions campaigned for a new round of elections – the first since 1937. Even though the voting franchise was still limited to a fraction of the Indian population, it was nonetheless an exciting moment. When the election results were announced, Congress won a landslide, with 58 per cent of all votes. The Communist Party of India also received 2.5 per cent, having been legalised during Britain's wartime alliance with the USSR, and having helped tremendously with famine relief. However, most surprisingly, Jinnah's Muslim League won 27 per cent, including a staggering 87 per cent of the Muslim vote. His Pakistan demand had transformed his party into a force to be reckoned with and as the British administrator Penderel Moon wrote, 'It is now abundantly clear

---

* The INA's continuing popularity in India largely originates from these trials.

that the Pakistan issue has got to be faced fairly and squarely. There is no longer the slightest chance of dodging it.'[45]

Pakistani narratives often portray the 1946 election as the moment the Muslims of India finally united and put forth their demand for Pakistan. But the Pakistan that people were voting for was by no means the Pakistan that we are familiar with today. At this remarkably late juncture, it remained unclear what Pakistan actually meant, an idea still 'dangerously fluid, a ghostlike garment that would fit anyone who cared to dream of it'.[46] Just as the British Raj was divided between two types of rule – British India and princely states – many people imagined a federal India divided between Muslim rule and Hindu rule, ultimately forming one cohesive whole.

Intriguingly, the most fervent support for Pakistan had come from Muslims in Hindu-majority provinces – precisely the people who could never have ended up in a Pakistani state – and one Muslim leader later admitted how 'the Frontiers of Pakistan had not been defined and it never entered our heads that Delhi would not be within it'.[47] The essential error in Jinnah's thinking, argued the Kashmiri politician Sheikh Abdullah, was that even if Pakistan were established, many millions 'of Muslims living in Hindu majority provinces of UP, CP, Bihar and Madras could not be forced to migrate to Pakistan'.[48] Indeed, there was little support for the movement in many Muslim-dominated cities on the North-West Frontier so that as late as early 1946 the Hindu owners of Gulab Rai and Sons Wine and General Merchants were investing in opening bacon and alcohol shops across Peshawar to cater to non-Muslims.[49] The only province where the Muslim League received an unequivocal majority was Bengal – later the only province to successfully secede from Pakistan.*

★ ★ ★

---

* The establishment of Bangladesh just two decades later has meant the fact of Bengal's central role in the creation of Pakistan tends to be forgotten. But as Anam Zakaria writes, the Muslim League was founded in Bengal, 'enjoyed popularity in the region ... this support played an instrumental role in the creation of Pakistan, [but] the Muslim League's relationship with East Bengal after Partition had turned people against the party. Today, the League is remembered as an antihero that deprived East Pakistan of their rights. The fact that the same party had enjoyed such backing only seven decades ago is a difficult truth to negotiate with.' Zakaria, A., 1971: *A People's History from Bangladesh, Pakistan and India* (Penguin Vintage, 2019) p48.

Despite all this, the 1946 elections firmly put the question of Hindu and Muslim political control on the Indian political agenda. If you lived in a Congress constituency, it was now a Congressman who ran your public affairs and controlled your access to justice. If you lived in a Muslim League province, the Muslim League oversaw your bureaucracy, your police and your postal system. As more power was devolved to Indians, soon only five hundred British civil servants and five hundred British policemen remained in employment across the whole of India. Having essentially lost all sway in the nation's politics except at the top, the British government became reluctant to invest in India any further and cut funding to police departments.[50]

India was home to more than just two faiths, of course, and other religious communities now began to question their own futures too. The Christian-majority Nagas felt particularly betrayed.[51] They had been essential to Britain's victory in the battles of Kohima and Imphal and had hoped for some acknowledgement of their defence of India, yet they seemed to have become disposable in national politics. The Naga Hills divided between Burma and India's Assam province were claimed as part of India by Nehru, while Jinnah claimed them as part of Pakistan. Few seemed interested in what the Nagas themselves thought.

Angami Zapu Phizo had just spent seven months in a Burmese prison for his collaboration with the INA, during which time an untreated bacterial infection had rendered the right side of his face almost entirely paralysed. Released shortly after the INA trials, he had been inspired by the way that Burma's Karen community were 'organizing a mass movement for independence for themselves, outside of any proposed Union of Burma' and decided to hurry back to the Naga Hills to try and help Nagas gain a stake in their own future.[52] 'What I found on my return to Nagaland was nothing,' he later said to his biographer. 'No unity, no ideas. Everybody waited to hear first what the District Commissioner wanted … [but] I had seen nationalists at work in Burma. I had witnessed what patriotism could achieve.'[53] Phizo cut a spellbinding figure, and his nephew Niketu recalls village elders transfixed by his words, his frozen face morphing in the flicker of kerosene lamps. 'My uncle had a twisted mouth,' Niketu remembers, 'so he would push it [up] when he wanted to say something, speaking to our people with total attention.'[54]

Phizo subsequently spent months travelling across both sides of the Patkai, promoting the idea of independence.[55] 'We wish to remain within the fold of Christian nations and the Commonwealth,' he would tell his followers, warning them not to be complacent and to quickly declare their independence from India and Burma.[56]

The Nagas were not alone in asserting claims to nationhood. Sikh leaders called for a homeland named 'Sikhistan' or 'Khalistan' to be established; Bengalis began to speak of a separate 'Bangalistan'; and Pashtuns talked of a separate 'Pakhtunistan'; there was even a demand for a homeland for India's lower castes to be called 'Achchutistan'.[57] Many of the larger princely states also planned to reassert their independence after the British departed, and the Nizam of Hyderabad was so confident about his political prospects he started making serious overtures to Portugal for the lease of a Goan free port for his state, and set aside 250 million rupees to dam the Godavari river.[58] A fear of the Raj's imminent Balkanisation pervaded political meetings and one Saumya Gupta noted:

> Giving in to the Pakistan demand would only lead to endless partitions ... all minorities would ask for the right to self determination. How would we stop them? Even women ... would one day demand a separate Jananistan [Land of Women]![59]

As late as 1946, therefore, Pakistan was far from the only country that could have been carved out of British India.

In January 1946 a group of British RAF servicemen who 'resented being made tools of imperialism' in Vietnam and Indonesia went on strike, and within days fifty thousand airmen from Karachi to Singapore had mutinied. They were threatened with firing squads before being controversially sentenced to up to a decade in prison.[60] Just three weeks later Indian sailors aboard HMS *Talwar* rebelled, pulling down the Union Jack and flying 'three entwined flags: the tricolour of the Congress, the Green of the Muslim League and the Red of the Communist Party'.[61] Twenty thousand sailors mutinied over five days aboard seventy-eight ships across the Indian Ocean. The naval ratings were eventually persuaded to stand down, but by then the insurrection had done its work. A Hindi leaflet found in

Bombay's Victoria train station recorded the revolutionary mood of the moment:

> Kill every white man ... take his weapons and his life ... there is no power on earth that will stop us.[62]

Anyone who worked with the British was branded a 'collaborator', and Indians like the Bengali author Nirad Chaudhuri who lauded the synthesis of Indian and British cultures under the Raj found their lives increasingly difficult:

> On Burn Bastion Road ... a man came up to me and ordered me to take off my tie and hat, these being regarded as the outward signs of an inward loyalty to British rule. I did not obey him of course, but I did not try to pass through the city. I had acted prudently ... men in European dress were set upon ... in New Delhi the military procession was jeered at, and ... two field marshals, who had fought the Germans victoriously, went home, admitting defeat at the hands of an Indian rabble.[63]

This new sentiment was not limited to British India. In the northernmost state of Jammu and Kashmir, around three hundred people were arrested for demanding the Maharaja 'Quit Kashmir', and in Hyderabad State a colossal armed struggle led by the Communist Party sought to overthrow feudal landlords. Like Bengal, Hyderabad had been reliant on Burmese rice and after supply vanished during the war, landlords pressed tenants to produce more food.[64] But Chityala Ailamma, a washerwoman, refused to hand her hard-earned produce to her landlord and called locals to protect her fields. Resistance to paying tax spread rapidly following Ailamma's protest, and police raids of villages turned violent.[65]

The spirit of rebellion spread to the Indians in Malaya who had supported the INA, leading Viceroy Wavell to request Nehru travel to Southeast Asia to calm the situation. It was in Singapore, on 18 March 1946, that Nehru met the Mountbattens for the first time. As with Aung San, Mountbatten treated the Indian politician as a leader-in-waiting, dropping formalities and offering Nehru his own car.[66] At one point, while attending a rally, Edwina was knocked over in a rush of people, and Nehru and Mountbatten linked arms to push through the crowd and rescue her. Afterwards the three dined together. 'We talked about everything under the sun,' Mountbatten later recalled. 'And that is where our friendship started.'[67] The relationship forged on that day would be crucial to the endgame of empire. Mountbatten would shortly be nominated to be India's last Viceroy, and the dominoes were already beginning to fall.

After their meeting, Nehru continued on through Southeast Asia. Aung San hoped to meet him, but Governor Dorman-Smith had forbidden the Congressman from coming to Rangoon.[68] Nonetheless, while Dorman-Smith was away, Nehru's plane made an unexpected landing at the city's Mingaladon Airport, allegedly because of 'engine trouble'. After rushing to the airport, Aung San drove Nehru to the Strand Hotel, where they planned an Asian 'Potsdam Conference' for the leaders of Asian 'subject nations',[69] getting on so well that Nehru's 'hearty laugh' could be heard outside. Dorman-Smith was furious, but with Britain no longer able to call in the Indian Army, real power had already passed out of British hands.

The relationship between Nehru and Aung San boded well for the future of India and Burma, but Aung San was not the only Burmese politician in the picture. U Saw – the man most responsible for souring Indo-Burmese relations – had recently returned from East Africa, 'thinner ... and less gross-looking' in the words of one Mr Hughes.[70]

Saw was on a campaign to rehabilitate his tainted image and he attempted to court Nehru, so as to position himself as the rightful leader of Burma and undermine Aung San.[71] Saw took to hosting lavish parties for Rangoon society, and from his house on Victoria Lake he started rebuilding his pre-war political party. 'He was forever surrounded by pretty women,' writes one author,

> and, above all, he was nothing like the ice-cold intellectuals of Indian politics ... [He had returned from Uganda] with a brand-new German 'wife' who was very much the talk of the town ... [and] the British seemed prepared to forget, or at least forgive, U Saw's overtures to the Japanese.[72]

The British colonel Emile Foucar was one such Brit, who later recalled meeting Saw at a cocktail party. Foucar had heard for months about the 'secret comings and goings' at Saw's lakeside house, 'often by boat across the water', and now he found Saw as 'exuberant as ever'. Wearing a well-cut dinner jacket and sipping whisky and soda, Saw had 'a broad grin upon his round, bucolic face' and was holding forth on his political rival. 'Aung San!' he cried.

> He won't last long. You see sir, the people know me ... These boys, what do they understand of political matters. Nothing at all ... I am waiting for the right moment. Very soon, sir, I shall be in office.[73]

U Saw was quite open about his aim 'to crush Aung San'.[74] Yet he was also scared of his rival's newfound power. Friends had warned him 'to be careful regarding going about in the country in case the gangs of Aung San might get you'.[75]

It was the start of a dangerous new rivalry. An intelligence report notes that Aung San was 'severely terrified of U Saw' and his 'criminal gangsters',[76] and on one occasion confided in the Burmese governor about his growing anxieties. But 'you are the people's idol?' responded Dorman-Smith, somewhat taken aback by Aung San's vulnerability. 'I did not seek to be that,' revealed Aung San. 'Only to free my country. But now it is so lonely.' With tears in his eyes, he whispered, 'How long do national heroes last? Not long in this country; they have too many enemies ... I do not give myself more than another eighteen months of life.'[77]

Soon afterwards a rival politician accused Aung San of murdering a headman during the war. Whitehall initially ordered Dorman-Smith to go ahead and arrest him, but the order was rescinded a few hours later. Aung San had won the battle of wills. Meanwhile, under pressure from Mountbatten, prime minister Clement Attlee was growing increasingly concerned about Dorman-Smith's handling of the situation, and the inconsistency of his messages. Dorman-Smith was made to resign soon after and Mountbatten's old deputy Hubert Rance took over as Burma's new governor.

Rance faced a wave of strikes and unrest, and was immediately struck by the oratory of Aung San and U Saw. At one point Aung San gave a speech lasting over five and a half hours, but 'U Saw was not impressed, as his record is twelve hours'.[78] Nonetheless, Rance backed Aung San and a few weeks later announced that he would become deputy chairman of a new executive council, effectively becoming Burma's de facto prime minister. Elections would be held the next April to confirm if this was truly the will of the people.

The morning that Aung San was to be sworn in, his newborn daughter – his fourth child – passed away. After the ceremony, he whispered to a colleague:

> In our five years of married life, we have had four children. That's perhaps too many, but to bring forth an innocent child that she may die after a few days is so sad and futile.[79]

In the *Evening Express*, U Saw was reported as calling it 'beneath his dignity to attend the Executive Council meetings in which a youth like Bogyoke Aung San is a Vice-Chairman',[80] and as the mutual antipathy between the two reached fever pitch an army jeep pulled up alongside U Saw's car at a roundabout and four men fired at him before speeding away. The bullets missed their mark, but a shard of glass embedded itself in Saw's eye, causing the eye to weep continuously for the rest of his life. Disfigured and embittered, Saw took to wearing dark sunglasses, even indoors, growing convinced Aung San was responsible for the attempt on his life. Henceforth he became 'obsessed with the two main ideas: of getting himself made Premier again, and of taking revenge against Aung San'.[81] According to Ba Maw's daughter, who was back in Rangoon, 'U Saw ... wore his crocodile smile proudly like a military star, his intentions so obvious that I almost came to respect his blunt honesty.'[82]

The question of who would lead Burma after the British left had now more or less been decided. But in India it was still uncertain. In March 1946 the British made another attempt to persuade the Muslim League and the Congress to form a political settlement and get on with ruling the country. This time around three members of the cabinet, nicknamed 'the Magi' by Wavell, threw their hats into the ring.

One of the things the Cabinet Mission was tasked with deciding was the future of the princely states. In May 1946 the Maharaja of Sikkim and the prime minister of Bhutan began lobbying the Mission, arguing that as border states whose Buddhist population[83] was of 'Mongolian stock', their states should not be considered 'Indian'. Even Nehru proved sympathetic and a few months later, he recognised the 'special problems of Bhutan and Sikkim'.

Likewise, to argue for Nepal's continued independence, Nepali diplomats used a 1923 treaty between Britain and Nepal that had formally recognised Nepal as a sovereign nation, even if informally it still fell under the Viceroy's jurisdiction.[84] In this remarkably haphazard and random way, the rights of Nepal, Bhutan and Sikkim to remain independent after the end of British rule were secured.

Even more important for the Cabinet Mission, however, was the Pakistan controversy. After months of torturous negotiations, they proposed an ingenious solution to India's political deadlock, one that is still beguiling seventy-five years later because of how close it came to stopping the Great Partition of India.

It was a scheme designed to bridge the unbridgeable, to keep India whole while still granting Pakistan to the Muslim League. Pakistan, in this vision, would exist – yet not as a fully separate nation but as part of a loose Indian federation, much as Scotland and Wales were bound to the United Kingdom. It was an elegant compromise that might have averted the bloodbath to come.

And then, astonishingly, Muhammad Ali Jinnah accepted it.

On 6 June 1946 the man who had built his political career on the unyielding demand for a separate Muslim homeland agreed to a united India. He would take Pakistan in name, but within the framework of an undivided country. The dream of a single, independent India had been salvaged at the last possible moment.

But just as suddenly, this dream was shattered. Nehru and Gandhi insisted that the Congress-dominated North-West Frontier Province should be excluded from any Pakistan region within the federation – a seemingly trivial amendment, yet one with catastrophic consequences.

For Jinnah, who had finally yielded to their demand for India to remain united, this spat of betrayal. If the Congress would not honour this agreement now, how could he trust them to honour it once they controlled the government? Furious, he rescinded his acceptance, and the carefully constructed Cabinet Mission plan collapsed. The British Viceroy, exhausted and exasperated, threw up his hands and told

Nehru to form an interim government – without the Muslim League, if necessary.

The last chance to avert Partition had been squandered and soon after, Jinnah announced:

> One India is [now] an impossible realisation ... it will inevitably mean that the Muslim will be transferred from the domination of the British to the caste Hindu rule ... Freedom must mean freedom ... Hundreds of millions of Muslims will never agree merely to a change of masters.[85]

He called for Muslims everywhere to observe 'Direct Action Day' on 16 August. It's aim, he said, was to establish 'either a divided India or a destroyed India'.[86]

In the course of this day, the political tug of war between India's Muslims and Hindus – 'until then waged around negotiating tables and in debate halls – turned violent'.[87] Not that anyone could have foreseen the chaos. With the prospect of a 'second famine' in Bengal occupying most people's thoughts, Direct Action Day appeared low on the news agenda. The Muslim League's upcoming protest barely made it onto page five of the *Civil & Military Gazette*, whereas a hopeful article on the import of rice from Java held the front page.[88] A similar report on the need to 'Grow More Food'[89] appeared as the *Calcutta Municipal Gazette*'s main story, while the *Statesman* ran the ominous headline 'Millions to Die of Starvation'.[90] There was, nonetheless, a sense that the debates over Pakistan were coming to a head at last. Jinnah's paper *Dawn* resounded with hyperbole about the imminent 'rape of the Muslim Nation',[91] while Hindu nationalist papers published columns on medieval Muslim temple desecration to convince Hindus to oppose 'Muslim rule'. Some members of the Hindu Mahasabha had even begun calling for another partition of Bengal along religious lines, arguing that in a United Bengal Hindus would always be subject to the whims of the province's Muslim majority.[92]

At the time the Muslim League National Guards – a paramilitary force formed to help establish a Muslim nation – spent the same days training Muslim youths in self-defence.[93] The future Indian prime minister Atal Bihari Vajpayee, meanwhile, spent his time working for the Rashtriya Swayamsevak Sangh (RSS), a Hindu nationalist paramilitary organisation that continues to wield enormous influence over Indian politics to this day. Part boy scouts, part militia, it remains the largest volunteer organisation in the world, founded with the goal of transforming India into a *Hindu Rashtra* – a Hindu nation. Inspired by the RSS's call to 'awaken and unite the Hindus', Vajpayee spent the days before Direct Action Day moving through the volatile neighbourhoods of Kanpur, 'teach[ing] the Hindus how to prepare themselves to resist a possible attack ... [and] patrol[ling] the sensitive areas'.[94]

As the only province in which the Muslim League had an unequivocal majority, Bengal was the most tense before Direct Action Day. Its new Muslim League premier, Huseyn Suhrawardy, had been the minister of civil supply during the famine, and his appointment horrified Hindus.[95] A large aristocrat with pursed lips, silk pyjamas and a fondness for loud jazz, Suhrawardy was described by acquaintances as 'totally unscrupulous, but not communal or religious. He ate ham and drank Scotch and married a Russian actress'.[96] Long before he became a politician, Suhrawardy had been known as an expert lawyer who jumped at the opportunity to represent those who needed him, but he also did little to deny alleged links with the criminal underworld.

True to his nickname the 'king of the *goondas* [thugs]',[97] Suhrawardy had recently written ominously in the *Statesman* that 'bloodshed and disorder are not necessarily evil in themselves, if resorted to for a noble cause'.[98] He subsequently formed 'an almost purely Muslim ministry ... with an almost purely Hindu opposition',[99] and when he announced that Direct Action Day would be celebrated as a public holiday across Bengal, Hindus everywhere felt their worst fears becoming reality.

Around this time a strange schism emerged within the Muslim League itself over differing interpretations of what 'Pakistan' would actually look like, foreshadowing the creation of Bangladesh two and a half decades later. To several Bengali and Assamese Muslim Leaguers, including Suhrawardy, Jinnah's reference to 'Muslim States' had implied the possibility of entirely separate Muslim states in East and West India. But in April 1946 Jinnah had made clear that the plural 's' in 'states' had been merely a 'printing mistake', and pushed through a new resolution to establish a single 'independent sovereign state' made up of two 'zones'.[100] The change seems to have come as a genuine shock to Suhrawardy, who had been hoping to rule over an independent Muslim-majority Bengal – a sort of proto-Bangladesh – and he

sought to organise Calcutta's Direct Action Day on a far bigger scale than elsewhere to demonstrate his political strength to both Congress and Jinnah.

Suhrawardy's acolyte Mujibur Rahman, better known as Mujib, was studying liberal arts at Calcutta's Islamia University. Mujib would one day fight feverishly to break up Pakistan and establish the nation of Bangladesh, but at the time he was fiercely devoted to the Muslim League. He spent the day before Direct Action Day attaching loudspeakers to cars to blare out the League's demands across the streets.

The next morning the air was thick and heavy, as if a storm were about to break. Mujib and his friend Nuruddin rode their bicycles through Calcutta's streets at 7 a.m. to raise the Muslim League flag above Islamia University. 'Nobody opposed us,' he recalls. 'But we came to know later that as soon as we had left, the flag was lowered and shredded to pieces.'[101] At this early hour things were already swinging into action. A British report notes how 'Hindus [had] started putting up barricades at Tala Bridge and Belgachia Bridge ... to prevent Muslim processions coming into the town, and Muslim goondas ... [forced] Hindus to close their shops.'[102] Mujib had planned for unpleasant confrontations, but he wasn't ready for what greeted him back at his university hostel: a group of students covered in blood, suffering from stab wounds. When he learned that they had been attacked by a Hindu mob, he resolved to accompany some other boys and confront those responsible. Student activists like Mujib would be instrumental in the start of Direct Action Day's violence. Mujib himself writes how he came across a maulvi

> chased by a group of men armed with sticks and swords ... A few of us immediately cried out, 'Pakistan Zindabad' ... We picked up whatever bricks or stones we could find and started to attack them.[103]

The students were only scattered when the police started throwing tear gas at them.

A few hours after the scuffle outside his university, Mujib and his friends joined a hundred thousand other Muslims at the Ochterlony Monument in Calcutta's Maidan Park to witness Premier Suhrawardy's speech. Precisely what Suhrawardy said remains highly contested: many Muslims would claim he told them to go home and celebrate Ramadan, while many Hindus would assert he subtly hinted to the crowd that they were free to enact violence as they pleased.[104] Whatever the case, Calcutta was a tinderbox waiting to blow. Taking advantage of the political scuffles diverting policemen, looters began raiding shops to stock up before the feared 'second famine'. Religious paramilitary groups had spent weeks preparing for attacks, and with their shops and houses being looted, they prepared to go on the offensive.[105] Within hours of Suhrawardy's speech, scenes of looting and violence were widespread across Calcutta.

The police were largely able to break up any fighting that afternoon, and when a thunderstorm started at dusk, the streets emptied. Army chief Roy Bucher, who had briefly considered sending in the military, decided the police would be able to handle the situation themselves and refrained from taking any action. But that evening, soon after midnight, armed gangs re-emerged into the flooded streets, hunting down men and women of the other religion. Calcutta gangsters took a leading part in the violence, as did freed INA soldiers armed with weapons left over from the war. Most chilling of all was the way that everyday people simply turned on one another. An intelligence report writes how 'Men, women and children were slaughtered by both sides indiscriminately ... When Mullick Bazaar was burnt, three Hindu children were thrown into the flames.'[106] In north Calcutta, 'the severed heads of Muslims impaled on spikes were paraded through the streets'.[107]

In a single night the fight over resources transformed into full-on ethnic cleansing. Nirad Chaudhuri writes with horror about a local fruit seller who was set upon by his regular customers, and how 'soldiers discovered a man tied to the electrical connector box of the tramlines, with a hole made in his skull so that he might die slowly by bleeding'. On another occasion a mob stripped a fourteen-year-old boy to check if he was circumcised, and when they confirmed that he was Muslim, the boy 'was thrown into a pond nearby and kept under water by bamboo poles, with a Bengali engineer educated in England noting the time he took to die on his Rolex wristwatch'.[108]

Many people tried to save their friends of other religions. From the Muslim League youth office, Mujib would later recall that:

Of the many calls we had received ... many were from Hindus. They had stowed away their Muslim friends and acquaintances and had called for them to be rescued.[109]

This gave a strange intimacy to some of the violence. Narayan Chandra Pal was studying at the National Medical College, and when the fighting erupted, he hid on the top floor of his hostel along with his Hindu friends. For people like Narayan, locked away in their rooms, it is the *sound* of the pogroms that they remember decades later – the choruses of 'Pakistan Zindabad' and 'Vande Mataram', and the screams of children emanating from the streets outside. Narayan stayed there for a week, fed by Muslim neighbours who brought the boys food and biscuits. One day the same Muslim neighbours 'murdered an innocent passer-by in broad daylight'. When Narayan 'asked why they weren't killing him, since he was also a Hindu ... they all simply said that they knew him, so it was different'.[110]

It took a full week for soldiers to arrive and evacuate them from the area and several more days before the violence had been completely suppressed. Counterinsurgency tactics were employed on the streets of the Raj's former capital, and Mujib writes how:

> Anyone seen in the streets after dusk would be shot at sight. The army usually would leave the person they had shot on the streets. They would aim their guns at every open window. In the morning we would see many dead people on the road.[111]

The events following Direct Action Day would soon become known as the 'Week of the Long Knives' or the 'Great Calcutta Killings'. Four thousand people were confirmed dead, but this is considered an underestimate because of just how many bodies had been burned or stuffed in sewage pipes. Margaret Bourke-White, arriving after reporting on the Holocaust, described Calcutta as 'a scene that looked like Buchenwald'.[112] The killings fractured the relationship of the Congress and the Muslim League beyond the point of repair, and a few days later, when Wavell invited Jinnah's old friend Sarojini Naidu to dinner, she spoke of Jinnah 'rather as of Lucifer ... a fallen angel, one who had once promised to be a great leader of Indian freedom, but who had cast himself out of the Congress heaven'. Later, when Wavell approached Nehru and Gandhi themselves to reconcile with Jinnah or face a potential civil war, Gandhi slammed his fist on the table and cried out, 'If India wants her bloodbath, she shall have it!'[113]

As with many events to follow, Direct Action Day remains mired in controversy. Indian narratives tend to blame the Muslim League for staging the riots in order to demonstrate that Hindus and Muslims could no longer live together in harmony. Meanwhile, Pakistan and Bangladesh argue that Congress-sponsored thugs descended on peacefully demonstrating Muslims to teach them a lesson. In the words of Nisid Hajari, it is a question freighted with immense meaning: the guilty party is, by extension, held to be responsible for the hundreds of thousands of deaths to come ... [But] ultimately it is not possible to assign blame entirely to one side or the other. What exploded so violently in Calcutta in August 1946 were the pent-up fears of communities convinced they faced imminent subjugation by the other.[114]

Ten per cent of Calcutta fled the Raj's erstwhile capital in its wake, spreading stories of sectarian violence across Bengal. Many villages in East Bengal saw a pre-emptive wave of retaliatory ethnic cleansing, with Muslims forcibly converting Hindu families to Islam under the threat of death. This violence almost always had a political dimension, however, and in Noakhali district, east of Calcutta, it was organised by a mobster who had lost the recent election, and directed at his political opponents. In some cases elected politicians themselves were at the heart of the violence. Sultan Ahmed, a Muslim Congressman in Bihar, complained that other politicians of his own party did little to investigate the murder and robbery of his community. In reality, few massacres were properly investigated for fear of further inflaming the situation, and government reports merely tallied rival columns of Hindu versus Muslim deaths. News fractured along communal lines so that Muslims heard of atrocities against Muslims while Hindus heard of atrocities against Hindus. Violence spread westwards up the Ganges and soon Hindus were murdering Muslims in Bihar and the United Provinces in retaliation.[115]

Hindu paramilitary groups ballooned in size and gradually took the lead in the violence. In the town of Garhmukteshwar, two hours east of Delhi, a Congressman described the Hindu nationalist RSS carefully marking 'all Muslim shops, which after dusk were burnt according to a plan without doing the least injury to the neighbouring Hindu shops'.[116] Meanwhile in Lahore, the organisation trained young men 'in bombs and pistols' on the banks of the Ravi river.[117]

In turn Jinnah assigned the 'shadowy' former railway guard Khurshid Anwar to expand the Muslim League National Guards a hundred-fold and drill them in armed combat. 'Instruction is being given in the art of knife and acid throwing, and in the use of fire-arms,' read one ominous intelligence report.[118]

By November it was estimated that five thousand people had died as a result of the Hindu–Muslim riots following Direct Action Day, and an army memo records:

Calcutta was revenged in Noakhali, Noakhali in Bihar, Bihar in Garhmukteshwar, Garhmukteshwar in ????[119]

When Nehru visited Calcutta with his sister soon after the killings, she recorded that 'many of these people who came to us seemed utterly bewildered ... even those who had taken part in the killings seemed not to know why. Often, they said to Bhai [brother], "We don't know. It's you politicians who have done this, because we have lived in peace for years."'[120] Nehru himself was horrified by what he experienced. 'Murder stalks the street and the most amazing cruelties are indulged in by both the individuals and the mob,' he wrote.

Riot is not the word for it – it is just the sadistic desire to kill.[121]

On 2 September, two weeks after Direct Action Day, Nehru's new interim government was inaugurated. Initially, the Muslim League declined to join, but later Jinnah appointed Liaquat Ali Khan as minister of finance and, surprisingly, Bengal's Dalit leader Jogendra Nath Mandal as minister of law.[122] The most extraordinary new role, however, was that of the Congress strongman Sardar Vallabhbhai Patel.

Patel, a stocky man with a bald head and perpetually furrowed brow, had long been Congress' most competent enforcer. He was a man who could get things done, and his flexible views on morality enabled him to act with a firmness Nehru could only dream of. If Nehru hesitated over principles, Patel dismissed them as obstacles, and now he was placed in charge of the most powerful ministry in the government – the Ministry of Home Affairs. With it came the secret intelligence machinery of the entire Indian Empire.

Patel wasted no time in consolidating power. He swiftly blocked the Viceroy's access to the director of intelligence and stopped the flow of information to senior Muslim League officials.[123] But Patel's control would have dramatic consequences. Two months after the appointment, the Intelligence Bureau chief suggested Patel ban paramilitary groups like the RSS and the Muslim League National Guards, who had been found to have engineered many of the communal pogroms sweeping India. Patel ignored the advice and, worried about alienating Hindu nationalists, he actively leaned on the RSS for support instead. These organisations' role in fomenting the violence would be kept hidden even from Nehru for many months.[124] As the fateful year of 1947 began, therefore, the government administration was divided between Congress and the Muslim League, neither of whom would speak to the other.

These disagreements were vividly demonstrated when Aung San arrived in India on 2 January 1947 and was forced to see Nehru and Jinnah separately. Aung San and Nehru got on just as well as they had in Rangoon, and Aung San's announcement that Burma would provide India with a hundred thousand tons of surplus rice helped ease the relationship further.[125] The two men's lives were running in a strange parallel, as they each attempted to bring order to their respective countries, integrate their princely states, stop their nations from Balkanising and take over the reins from the British. Nehru even organised for a tailor to design Aung San a suit, calling him an 'old friend and comrade in common understanding'.[126]

Days later Aung San flew on to Karachi to see Jinnah, who had recently moved there. Yet Aung San quickly found himself in a predicament. At the airport both Congress and the Muslim League representatives tried to get him to stay with them, and in order not to offend anyone, Aung San was forced to divide his luggage between the cars, asking his staff 'to go in the Congress Party car while he himself rode in the car belonging to the Muslim League'.[127] Eventually he booked himself an entirely separate hotel, and that evening he was able to meet with Jinnah and discuss the 'Rohingya problem':[128] the continued demands among Muslim leaders from Arakan for their land to merge with the future nation of Pakistan.

Finally, on 8 January, Aung San set off for London to negotiate a deal with British prime minister Clement Attlee. 'He was depressed,' wrote Tom Driberg, who met up with him in the British capital, 'and seemed full of foreboding – undefined, though he saw clearly the difficulties ahead.'[129] Aung San was also worried that if Attlee refused his demands, he would have to lead Burma into rebellion, bringing war back to an already ransacked country. He had by now planned the details of such a rebellion, just in case, and a British civil servant called Nick Larmour was later shocked to learn from a Burmese friend:

> The plan was to murder as many as possible of British officers and their wives. And this friend of mine told me with gusts of laughter, 'I was to kill you and Nancy'! Well, that took me somewhat aback but he seemed to think it was a joke, so I thought to treat it as a joke too. Still, I never felt quite the same about him.[130]

In the event, Aung San's deadly precautions were never put into effect. He made speedy progress in his talks with Attlee, and his deputy Tin Tut recalled:

> It was snowing hard outside on that winter's day ... but the Cabinet room at number 10 Downing Street was pleasantly warm ... Our final meeting on Monday afternoon was formal ... There was tense silence as Mr Attlee and U Aung San inscribed their signatures with firm hands to both copies [of the agreement].[131]

The Aung San–Attlee agreement was poised to set a united Burma on the path to independence. In a last-minute attempt to disrupt the process, U Saw and Ba Sein refused to sign, but the new Burmese governor disregarded their objections.[132] Aung San now had to persuade the leaders of Burma's ethnic minorities to accept the agreement, emphasising that narrow nationalisms could only lead to chaos.[133] Thus, in February 1947, in the small Shan town of Panglong, Burma's new leaders convened a conference, one that would later be celebrated as the cornerstone of the Burmese state and ensure the accession of the forty-odd Shan princely states into Burma.

The princess of Yawnghwe State, Sao Sanda, accompanied her father Sao Shwe Thaike and her stepmother the Mahadevi to the Panglong Conference. 'There was a festive feeling and I had to serve hundreds of cups of tea,' she remembers. As well as political discussion, there were also *pwe* performances, cattle shows, screenings of *The Battle of Britain* and even gambling tables.[134] 'All in all, there was a carnival atmosphere ... [and] many of the Burmans were surprised that the Shans were not so backward and were amazed there was a working local press.'[135] Sao

Sanda's father arrived at the conference bitterly opposed to integrating the Shan states into Burma. Nonetheless, Aung San's conciliatory attitude convinced him and he and several other Shan representatives ultimately agreed to be part of the Union of Burma as long as certain conditions were met.[136] On the penultimate day, Aung San gave a speech:

> In the past we shouted slogans: 'Our race, our religion, our language!' Those slogans have gone obsolete now. What is race after all ... During the war, when I served as war minister, I had dinner at a Karen battalion. A Karen soldier, speaking on unity, quipped that we were all the same, Burmese and Karen, the only noticeable difference being that the Burmese liked to play cards while the Karen enjoy fishing in the woods.[137]

On 12 February a historic agreement was sealed at Panglong, guaranteeing the participation of the nation's diverse ethnic minority groups in the governance of a post-independence Burma. Notable signatories included leaders from the Kachin and Chin communities, as well as both princely and anti-feudal representatives from the Shan states, which became the first princely states in the former Indian Empire to relinquish their sovereignty and merge with another dominion.[138]

Nevertheless, the Panglong Conference and the subsequent formation of the new cabinet in Burma left certain ethnic groups noticeably absent. The Nagas, for example, had insultingly been refused an invitation to Panglong on account of the 'primitive nature of their culture'.[139] Even more ominous was the absence of any Karenni leaders, despite the Panglong Conference pledging to amalgamate the five Karenni princely states into the Burmese Union. Arakanese separatists clamoured for a separate country of their own, while the Rohingya continued to harbour hopes of aligning with Pakistan. Little did these groups know how rattled Clement Attlee's Labour government had been by the massacres of Direct Action Day, and that British politicians had already quietly resolved to grant Burma independence as a unified entity.[140] Before long these unresolved tensions would culminate in what remains the longest ongoing civil war in the world.

★ ★ ★

Back in India, Gandhi was trying to calm the spread of chaos. For four months the seventy-seven-year-old marched across the countryside, staying in Muslim houses and holding interfaith prayer meetings; one journalist described the 'astonishing sight':

> With a staff in one hand and the other on his granddaughter's shoulder, the old man briskly takes the lead as the sun breaks over the horizon ... As the sun begins to climb, villagers from places along the way join the trek. They come by twos and fours or by dozens and scores, swelling the crowd as the snows swell India's rivers in spring ... Here, if I ever saw one, is a pilgrimage.[141]

Mujibur Rahman, the college student who had taken part in the riots of Direct Action Day, was amazed how in Gandhi's presence, 'the whole atmosphere changed' and described the man as 'a magician'.[142]

But just as the violence in Bengal began to calm, another wave of unrest swept the Punjab in India's northwest. When Sikh leader Master Tara Singh proclaimed that, 'Our motherland is calling for blood ... Finish the Muslim League',[143] Muslim mobs responded by decimating Sikh villages around Rawalpindi. Four per cent of the army's strength during the war – some one hundred thousand men – had come from this solitary district, which was now awash with guns and men who knew how to use them.[144] In the words of one Congress Party report, the pogroms that overwhelmed Rawalpindi 'were not riots but deliberately organized military campaigns ... The armed crowd which attacked ... were led by ex-military men on horseback, armed with Tommy guns, pistols, rifles, hand-grenades, hatchets, petrol tins and some even carried field glasses.'[145]

Everywhere there was physical violence, there was also sexual violence. In the village of Thoa Khalsa, at least ninety women jumped in a well to escape being raped. Basant Kaur was one of the only women to survive and decades later she described her survival as:

> like when you put rotis in a tandoor and it's too full, the ones near the top, they don't cook ... So the well filled up, and we could not drown ... Those who died, died, and those who were alive, they pulled out.[146]

Kaur would later learn that her own husband had 'martyred' her daughter to defend the girl's 'honour'. Her son 'had watched his father kill his sister' and 'described the incident with pride in his voice, pride at his sister's courage and her "martyrdom" for she could now be placed alongside other martyrs of the Sikh religion'.[147]

In the wake of the Rawalpindi massacres, the Congress Working Committee passed a resolution calling for a division of Punjab into two provinces on the basis of religion. Yet the political debates that had engulfed the subcontinent were still far away for many Punjabis. 'We only realised later that Hindustan was to become Pakistan,' explains Ishar Dar Arora.

Ishar grew up in Bela, a small Punjabi village of mudbrick houses perched on a tributary of the Indus, walking four kilometres each day to his primary school in the neighbouring village of Ziarat, to read and write in Urdu. After school he played gulli-danda, kabaddi and marbles with the other children, regardless of age or religion. Across the river was a special echoing hill which the children would shout at, jumping up and down with excitement when they heard their voice echoed back at them. Until 1947, Ishar explains, there was little religious animosity in the village. Ishar's father Nanak Chand sold fruits and nuts on his porch, while Ishar's mother tended to household chores and made *choori* sweets for the village Muslims after their Friday prayers. His ostensibly Hindu family embodied the fluid religious identities of the region, 'donating' their eldest son to the Sikh faith, while themselves observing Hindu rituals,* and referring to their Muslim neighbour Muhammad Khan as 'another son'. 'People lived with love and there was no hatred,' recalls Ishar. 'But later, when the riots started, friends became enemies.'

Ishar was playing with his friends when the commotion started in the village and he heard someone angrily demanding supplies from the

---

* Among many Hindus of Punjab, a syncretic culture of reverence of the Sikh gurus had existed since the earliest days of Sikhism. These Hindu followers of Guru Nanak were called Sehajdharis, or the slow-believers, and they both observed Hindu rituals and read the Guru Granth Sahib. It was common for people to raise one child as a Sikh, but in spite of this he remained within the Hindu fold, as Sikhs were considered Hindus by them. The son would marry a Hindu bride, matched by his family, and although his children would be Sikh, it was not uncommon for daughters to be married to Hindu men of the same *baradari* [clan]. Sehajdhari Sikhs include Master Tara Singh and Udham Singh.

shop. Bewildered as to what was happening, he remembers his parents telling Muhammad Khan to shut up the store. 'We have to leave from here,' Ishar's father said. 'There is something wrong in the village.'

It was the women who took charge. As night fell, Ishar's mother and aunt dragged him and his brothers into a shed behind the house where they kept fodder for the animals. 'Mother shut the door ... and put me in a basket, and made father hide in a certain spot,' he remembers. 'My father would cough a lot, but that night, by the grace of god, he didn't.' In the dark of the shed, Ishar couldn't see anything, but he could hear it: 'People wreaking havoc outside, chaos in all directions.' His mother was perched by the entrance, using a gap in the door to peek outside.

Seventy-five years later, Ishar still has nightmares about that night. He explains how Muhammad Khan arrived shortly before midnight, full of foreboding, to ask the family, 'What do I do? How do I save you?' Ishar's mother told him to join the looters 'so that people don't become suspicious that you are with us', but to let the *numberdaar*, or village headman, know where they were. Muhammad protested, but eventually he left to join the mob looting other Hindu houses, while Ishar and his family 'spent the night in terror'.

After what seemed like an eternity, two men arrived outside the family's hiding place. 'They were holding axes and their faces were very scary,' remembers Ishar. They had come to sneak Ishar and his family out of the cowshed and into the numberdaar's haveli. Sitting on the man's shoulders, Ishar could see Hindu houses ablaze across the village. When they reached the numberdaar's house, they saw Sher Khan, his son, on the rooftop, holding a gun. The terrified family were smuggled into a small room at the back, given some food and then Sher Khan locked them in, telling them, 'Nobody can touch you as long as I am alive.' Ishar piped up: 'Uncle, my school books are with your son, please give them to me.' It broke the tense atmosphere and Sher Khan burst into laughter. Seventy-five years later, Ishar giggles at his own words: 'At a time like that, when fighting was going on and this man didn't know if we would live, I was worried about my books!'

Ishar never did get his books. Instead Sher Khan went back to the roof with his rifle, and after a while a mob arrived at the gate. Ishar could hear Sher Khan's voice booming down to them: 'I have no Hindus with me ... [but] you can't enter my house unless you kill me.'

Ishar's Hindu and Sikh family had been saved by two Muslims, Muhammad Khan and Sher Khan.

The next morning the military arrived in Bela and helped Ishar's family evacuate to East Punjab and finally to Delhi. 'What happened after that night,' laments Ishar, 'is the story of Hindustan and Pakistan.'[148]

7

Dividing an Empire

In the spring of 1947, Britain's 'retreat from empire began to resemble a rout'.[1] Faced with repaying its war debts, the government shut off the nation's electricity for five hours a day, and over the course of a single week Whitehall announced that it could no longer afford to fight communist guerrillas in Greece, that it would start to pull out of its mandate for Palestine and that it would withdraw from India by the end of June 1948. 'This announcement meant Partition,' remembered the political officer Penderel Moon, 'and Partition within the next seventeen months.'[2]

The man who was assigned to carry out this Partition was Lord Louis Mountbatten. Since leaving SEAC several months earlier, he had returned to England and spent his time lobbying for the marriage of his nephew Philip to the young Princess Elizabeth. He had almost pulled it off when, on 18 December 1946, Clement Attlee lost faith in Wavell and offered Mountbatten the Viceroyalty instead. The mission, the prime minister explained, was simple: get Britain out of India, whether India was ready for it or not. More power would be granted to Mountbatten than to any other Viceroy in history, but he was still reluctant to take up the offer. 'I don't want to go,' he told his aide-de-camp as he set off for India again. 'We'll probably come home with bullets in our backs.'[3]

Having recently undergone a hysterectomy, Edwina was even more reluctant to leave.[4] But the moment their plane taxied to a stop on 22 March 1947 and the customary thirty-one-gun salute was fired from Delhi's Palam Airport, both Mountbattens were on best behaviour. At 3.45 p.m., Louis and Edwina Mountbatten rode through the gates of Viceroy's House in an open landau carriage, as Wavell stood waiting on the steps, next to a group of Scottish bagpipers and scarlet-clad Sikh bodyguards.[5] Dismounting from the carriage, the Mountbattens bowed and curtseyed to the incumbent Viceroy and lingered on the red-carpeted flight of steps 'long enough for the ubiquitous camera-men to take some pleasant shots of them'.[6] Then they went inside to talk business.

As with his appointment to SEAC, many of Mountbatten's compatriots thought he didn't deserve the job. New nicknames included 'Pretty Dickie' and 'Trickie Dickie',[7] and the conference secretary protested to Mountbatten's ever-present press attaché, Alan Campbell-Johnson, that Mountbatten 'knows nothing about India' and 'is bringing a staff who know nothing about India ... He is a playboy ... [and] there is no good reason for his [Wavell's] removal.'[8] Home minister Sardar Patel likewise considered Mountbatten little more than 'a toy for Jawaharlalji to play with'[9] and the only people who seemed unanimously positive about the appointment were the princes, who felt that India's aristocracy would be safe in the hands of the king's cousin.[10] Their enthusiasm, however, would be misplaced. The journalist Leonard Mosley learned that Mountbatten 'regarded [the princes] as semi-enlightened autocrats at their best and squalid degenerates at their worst. He called them "a bunch of nitwits" for not democratising their administration when they saw the power of the Congress rising, and for not joining the Indian Federation when they had the opportunity in 1935.'[11] Indeed, Mountbatten would very soon oversee their downfall.

The evening of Mountbatten's arrival, Wavell handed him a file entitled 'Operation Madhouse', telling him, 'Alas, I can see no other way out.'[12] The Viceroy's plan involved the British gradually devolving more power to India's provinces and then exiting the scene before they could be embroiled in the civil war that had in some sense already arrived. That very morning the religious violence that had been spreading across the countryside had reached Delhi, and a communal riot left two people dead and six injured, just a few miles from the Viceroy's House.[13] A curfew was subsequently put in place and the press suppressed so that, in the words of the chief commissioner, nights in the capital 'passed quietly except for a certain amount of shooting'.[14]

Despite the urgency of the task ahead of him, however, Mountbatten did not initially seem to grasp the scale of the issues at hand. After waving off Wavell the next day, he spent the morning dressed in underpants and vest, discussing with his press attaché how his swearing-in ceremony might be filmed.[15] Finally, on 24 March, Mountbatten was sworn in as India's last Viceroy. With trumpets blowing from the roof of Viceroy's House, the Mountbattens entered the Durbar Hall, surrounded by a dazzling array of glittering princes, starchy officers, trimmed diplomats and dhoti-clad ex-revolutionaries. 'Arc lights played down upon the scene,' wrote Mountbatten's press attaché, as

> the Lord Chief Justice of India administered the oath and Mountbatten repeated it after him, never faltering with his formidable string of Christian names ... Film cameras whirred and the flash bulbs went off for the first time in the confines of the Durbar Hall ... the acoustics were abominable; even quite near to him it was difficult to catch what he was saying ... [but] I noticed both Nehru and Liaquat Ali Khan listened with the utmost attention to the speech.[16]

When the oath was completed, a guard of honour burst into a rendition of the national anthem.[17] Fifteen minutes later the ceremony was over. Only then did it seem to dawn on Mountbatten what he'd got himself into. 'I realised that I had been made into the most powerful man on earth,' he later admitted. 'One fifth of humanity I held in my hand. A power of life and death.'[18]

Beyond the confines of Viceroy's House, the streets were filled with protest. 'Riots Break Out in Gurgaon Area', read one headline. '1,000 People Killed in Pindi Alone', reported another. Even those not caught up in the violent communal riots could see India's future was teetering on a precipice. Police were mutinying in Bengal, the threat of famine continued to loom, and Liaquat Ali Khan's budget for the interim government had sent the economy plummeting. A much-anticipated hockey tournament was cancelled in Jhelum, and the Confectioners Federation of Lahore were out on the streets, protesting after their quota of sugar had been diverted to refugee camps.[19] The *Daily Herald* noted that while the politicians continued their game of brinkmanship, ordinary people suffered. Communalism had 'plunged the fertile Punjab into bloody, burning chaos', and the only question now was whether with 'Lord Mountbatten's arrival, the clear decision of the British Government to leave, and the urgency of the situation', would bring India's leaders 'at last to respond?'[20]

As the new Viceroy and Vicereine, the Mountbattens had to try and acquaint themselves with these leaders. The next few weeks would be a flurry of meetings, dinners and social occasions. Every week the Mountbattens would host 'two garden parties, three or four luncheons for 30, and two or three larger dinner parties, each comprised of at least 50 per cent Indians, with their dietary preferences indicated by a different coloured ribbon on the back of their chair'.[21] By the end of day one, Mountbatten was already so exhausted he felt like a 'boiled egg'.[22]

It helped that much of India's political leadership happened to be in town that week. Just down the road from Viceroy's House, the Asian Relations Conference that Nehru had planned with Aung San had begun and in the cool heat of the spring sun ten thousand delegates from twenty-eight Asian countries entered Delhi's Purana Qila, literally 'Old Fort', through a towering sandstone gateway. The fort had been built by Sher Shah Suri, the man who had briefly overturned the Mughal Empire, and Nehru now hoped to overturn that empire's successor. Delegates were housed in the Lutyens-designed palaces, chauffeured around in maharajas' private cars and treated to a ballet adaptation of Nehru's *Discovery of India* with music performed by the young sitar player Ravi Shankar.[23] It was a dazzlingly grand affair, with many of the delegates having travelled for weeks to reach New Delhi,[24] yet some felt Nehru could not have chosen a worse time. Shahid Hamid, private secretary to the Indian Army's commander-in-chief, felt he was playing the 'fiddle while India burnt', and scribbled in his diary, 'No wonder that he is called "Nero".'[25]

Nonetheless, most people considered the conference a grand success. Perhaps most important of all were the discussions on 'Racial Problems and Inter-Asian Migration', where 'it was generally agreed ... [that] at any one time a person can have only one nationality'. This would have wide-ranging implications across post-colonial Asia, particularly for the families that had been displaced by indentured labour and the trading diasporas that had thrived under imperialism. What would happen to the Gujaratis of East Africa or the Tamils of

Ceylon? One delegate protested that 'India did not have space' to 'take back' Ceylon's Tamil population, many of whom had never been to India.[26] These were crucially important questions, but ones that were never truly resolved.

Even as these dramatic debates were taking place, Mountbatten sat down with two of his 'oldest personal friends in India'[27] – Maharaja Sadul Singh of Bikaner and Nawab Hamidullah Khan of Bhopal – and discovered quite how divided Indian politics had become. Both friends had been mysteriously absent from his swearing-in ceremony, and when they came to explain their absence, it emerged that in the course of a year they had become bitter political rivals. Bikaner was lobbying for the princes to join the Constituent Assembly and help draw up a new constitution for India,[28] but Bhopal wanted the princes to remain outside the Constituent Assembly, and instead suggested unifying the princely states into a third dominion called 'Rajastan', on a par with India and Pakistan.[29] 'I am unhappy about everything in this country,' he had written to Mountbatten's political adviser a short while earlier.

> The States, the Moslems, and the entire mass of people who relied on British justice, and their sense of fair play, suddenly find themselves totally helpless, unorganised and unsupported ... I have no hope of any support for the States from the British and without this support the Princes cannot survive.[30]

Bhopal was not the only prince to feel this way. Ever since the British had announced their departure, several of them had started 'to luxuriate in wild dreams of independent power in an India of many partitions'.[31] As far-fetched as it might seem today, the princely states – from Hyderabad to Dubai – still had no constitutional link with British India, and at this late stage there was nothing to stop them from asserting independence after the British had left. Indeed, only a few years earlier Churchill had talked of dividing India into 'Pakistan, Hindustan and Princestan'.[32] The morning of Mountbatten's swearing-in, therefore, the *Daily Herald* had named Bhopal one of the five most consequential politicians in India, whose success or failure would determine the future of 40 per cent of the Indian landmass. As one historian noted:

> The practicability of Pakistan must be admitted, but the more the separation of the States from British India is considered, the more impracticable it seems. India could live if its Moslem limbs in the North-West and North-East were amputated, but could it live without its heart?[33]

The meeting with the rulers of Bikaner and Bhopal revealed to Mountbatten 'the full scale of the split amongst the princes',[34] but despite the urgency it would be some time before he devoted his attention to the future of princely India. Nonetheless, during his first few days as Viceroy one of the most important events in the princely endgame of the Indian Empire occurred: the transfer of the Persian Gulf Residency.

Remarkably, as late as March 1947, the states of the Persian Gulf were still administered by the Indian Political Service. But a decade earlier during the Aden separation debates it had been decided that India would 'not be allowed to run the Persian Gulf' after independence[35] and a member of the British legation in Tehran even wrote of his surprise at the 'apparent unanimity' of 'officials in Delhi ... that the Persian Gulf was of little interest to the Government of India'.[36] In hindsight the negotiations read like India's greatest lost opportunity, willingly giving up the combined oil wealth of Kuwait, Qatar, Bahrain and the UAE. However, in the early 1930s the oil industry was still in its infancy and the Sheikhs were some of the poorest rulers in the Indian Empire, not even worthy of a gun salute.[37]

As Gulf resident William Hay put it, 'When the British decided to transfer power in India it would clearly have been inappropriate to hand over responsibility for dealing with the Gulf Arabs to Indians or Pakistanis.'[38] So it was that on 1 April 1947, exactly a decade after the separation of Aden, the Persian Gulf Residency was finally separated from India. The Indian Political Service, 'which had put tremendous emphasis on ceremonious arrivals and departures, hastily packed its bags and unceremoniously disappeared'.[39] Yet even as Indian soldiers quietly disappeared from the Gulf, they were quickly replaced by British ones.[40] When Attlee proposed a British withdrawal from the Arabian territories at the same time as the withdrawal from India, he had been shouted down, and as a result the British would remain in the region for another two decades.[41]

Nonetheless, just a few months later, when Indian and Pakistani officials set about integrating the hundreds of princely states into the new nations, the Arab states of the Persian Gulf such as Dubai, Qatar, Kuwait and Abu Dhabi would be missing from the ledger. Few batted an eyelid, and seventy-five years on the importance of what had just happened is still not fully understood in either India or the Gulf. Without this minor administrative transfer, it is likely that the states of the Persian Gulf Residency would have become part of either India or Pakistan after independence, as happened to every other princely state in the subcontinent.

Whatever the case, the second partition – the Partition of the Arabian Peninsula from India – was now complete.

Back in New Delhi, Mountbatten was aware of Nehru's influence over Britain's Labour government and he placed extra importance on this relationship, seeking out the Congressman the very same day as his audience with Bikaner and Bhopal. 'In Mountbatten's view Nehru was extremely frank and fair,' recorded Campbell-Johnson.

> At the end of the interview, as Nehru was about to take his leave, Mountbatten said to him, 'Mr Nehru, I want you to regard me not as the last Viceroy winding up the British Raj, but as the first to lead the way to the new India.' Nehru turned, looked intensely moved, smiled and then said, 'Now I know what they mean when they speak of your charm being so dangerous.'[42]

The Mountbattens saw a lot of Nehru in the coming days, and they soon picked up their close relationship from where they had left it in Singapore. Edwina grew particularly close to him, and when the Mountbattens held a garden party for the delegates of the Asian Relations Conference, Nehru was photographed sitting cross-legged by her feet. That evening 'Edwina accompanied Jawahar back to his house on York Road for a night cap – with her daughter, but without her husband.'[43] Ten days after the Mountbattens' arrival, Shahid Hamid noted that 'Nehru's relationship with Lady Mountbatten is sufficiently close to have raised many eyebrows.'[44]

The Mountbattens' relationship with other political leaders would not be so smooth. When Edwina invited Aruna Asaf Ali into Viceroy's

House, the legendary hero of the Quit India movement came out dejected. 'It's a transfer of power,' she spat. 'Not a revolutionary transformation at all.'[45] Meanwhile, when Gandhi was invited for high tea, he 'did not touch either the cakes or the sandwiches, but chose to eat a bowl of goat's curd which he had brought with him'.[46] In the course of the meeting Gandhi suggested India's unity might be saved if Jinnah were made prime minister of India and India's cabinet was made exclusively Muslim. Mountbatten, taken slightly aback, politely told the Mahatma he would think about it, knowing full well that he wouldn't.

The other important relationship established in that first week was between the Mountbattens and the gruff home minister Sardar Patel who would control the Viceroy's access to secret intelligence throughout his tenure. Mountbatten had been 'somewhat apprehensive' about meeting Patel, and both he and Edwina were rather shocked when Patel suggested using the army to 'get rid of the Moslem League'. In the event, the encounter went better than expected and Mountbatten 'detected a twinkle in Sardar's eye'.[47] But soon afterwards Patel revealed his political edge by sacking the head of India's Intelligence Bureau, replacing him with a Congressman and forbidding Mountbatten from meeting him. The fact that a Congressman had controlled the intelligence services months before independence would be kept secret for years afterwards, and the official Transfer of Power documents would falsely claim that its previous director Norman Smith had continued to serve in his role until independence.[48] The embarrassing truth, however, is that the entire Partition of 1947 took place when Patel, rather than his British superiors, controlled the intelligence services.

Edwina later told Isobel Cripps that:

Both Dickie and I like Vallabhbhai Patel very much indeed, although we quite realise the dominant attitude he adopts and his rather dictatorial manner. He and Dickie, however, are getting on very well indeed and when he behaves like a bit of a gangster, Dickie, as you well imagine, does not lag behind.[49]

Although Mountbatten's relationship with Patel would be rocky, he had reserved his most difficult meeting for last. On 5 April, two whole weeks after his arrival in Delhi, Mountbatten finally met Jinnah. The leader of the Muslim League proved 'formal and reserved', and began his conversation by giving the Viceroy a list of demands. But Mountbatten shot him down at once, saying, 'Mr Jinnah, I am not prepared to discuss conditions or, indeed the present situation until I have had the chance of making your acquaintance and knowing more about yourself.' Jinnah was 'completely taken aback' and 'for some while did not respond, remaining reserved, haughty and aloof. But in the end his mood softened and he duly succumbed to Mountbatten's desire to hear him recount the story of the Moslem League's rise to power in terms of his own career.'[50] Later Mountbatten suggested that if India was to be divided, then so should religiously mixed provinces like Punjab and Bengal. The suggestion horrified Jinnah. 'Pakistan without Calcutta,' he had long maintained, 'would be like asking a man to live without his heart.'[51] The two men left the meeting with a bitter taste in their mouths. When Jinnah was gone, Mountbatten turned to Campbell-Johnson and said, 'My God, he was cold. It took most of the interview to unfreeze him.'[52]

It was the start of a difficult relationship that even Edwina couldn't crack. After a 'frigid afternoon tea' with Jinnah's sister Fatima, Edwina described her as 'almost fanatical at times in her attitude'.[53] In a letter to Isobel Cripps she admitted that both she and Dickie had found the Jinnahs 'most difficult', even though they sympathised 'so much with their fears and apprehensions'.[54]

The warm relationship established with Nehru, the tense but functional relationships with Gandhi and Patel, and the actively hostile relationship with Jinnah foreshadowed just how different the new Viceroy would be from his predecessors. Whereas Linlithgow had been partisan towards the Muslim League and Wavell had straddled some sort of middle ground, it soon emerged that Mountbatten's Viceroyalty would be decidedly pro-Congress.

In late April Mountbatten wrote to Whitehall, explaining that the only solution he could see to Punjab's violent demonstrations was to divide India from Pakistan, and partition the province between the two.[55] Patel had recently convinced the Congress Working Committee that Pakistan should be accepted on the condition that Punjab be divided between Pakistan and India.[56] Although Jinnah publicly rejected the partition of Punjab, even advocating for a land bridge connecting the

Muslim-majority areas in India's east and west, Campbell-Johnson felt he too 'seemed to be resigned to the partition of Punjab and Bengal'.[57] Of all the national leaders, only Gandhi continued to resist the option of Partition.

Other plans continued to float around, of course. Secret telegrams briefly proposed forging an entirely separate 'Calcutta Free City', a city state along the lines of what would later happen in Singapore.[58] This would allow East and West Bengal to maintain an economic relationship with the capital and give Pakistan's eastern half – which would be separated from the rest of the country by almost two thousand kilometres – a chance at survival. Two days later, however, Mountbatten shot the idea down and wrote a revealing secret telegram to the governor of Bengal on 28 April 1947:

> It is not for me to make Pakistan into a sensible scheme. I want it to be seen for what it is, while giving Muslims everything to which they are entitled, and every chance to work out their own salvation ... Do not forget that my scheme leaves the door open to a united but independent Bengal belonging neither to Pakistan nor Hindustan. Jinnah would raise no objection to this. Do you think Suhrawardy could bring this off?[59]

Suhrawardy certainly tried his best and made an impassioned plea for an 'independent, undivided, and sovereign Bengal',[60] eliciting support from Subhas Chandra Bose's brother, the Dalit leader Jogendra Nath Mandal, and even Jinnah. It was, however, not to be.

Despite objections from India's commander-in-chief, many nationalist leaders were convinced that the quicker British troops left India, the sooner peace would be restored.[61] Mountbatten agreed, and by April 1947 the number of British troops in the country was wound down to 11,400 despite the escalating violence. On 15 April Jinnah and Gandhi issued a joint statement condemning the violence but this 'proved only that Jinnah had as little control over Muslim India as Gandhi had over the Hindus'.[62] Moreover, despite the statement, the two men were still refusing to speak. It was only two weeks later that Mountbatten double-booked his meetings and, by complete accident, succeeded in getting Gandhi and Jinnah to sit in the same room as each other for the first time in three years. They sat at opposite ends of

Mountbatten's office, 'like two old conspirators engaged in a long-distance dumbshow',[63] so that the Viceroy could barely hear what they were saying. Nonetheless it felt like progress, and the two men agreed to meet at Jinnah's house for another discussion in the near future.

In early May the Mountbattens travelled north to Simla, the Himalayan summer capital of the Raj. The city was 'as remote as it was precarious – an avalanche of villas – faintly reminiscent of Tunbridge Wells, poised to cascade off its ridge',[64] and it was here that the fate of India would be sealed. 'Viceregal Lodge Hideous'[65] was Edwina's assessment the morning she arrived, but she cheered up two days later when Jawaharlal Nehru joined the couple. 'We sat and talked with him in the garden,' she wrote in her diary, then 'sunbathed in the flowers'.[66] The cool mountain air was wonderful after the increasingly oppressive heat of Delhi, the atmosphere friendly and informal, and by the end of the week the Mountbattens were referring to Nehru as 'Jawa'. 'During our walk up and down the orchard terraces,' writes Campbell-Johnson, 'Nehru ... gave us a demonstration of a new technique by walking uphill backward. This, he said, made breathing easier, and rested the calf muscles.'[67] Nehru's agility would become a theme of the week, and one morning the Mountbattens' daughter Pamela 'opened a door and found the acting Prime Minister standing on his head, a daily yoga ritual. She was taken aback when he cheerfully carried on a conversation from that position.'[68]

Two days into his stay, Mountbatten received word from London that his solution for the transfer of power had been approved. Although he was meant to present it to the Muslim League and Congress together, in his excitement he broke with convention and showed Nehru the plan early. Rather than mirroring Mountbatten's enthusiasm, however, the Congress leader turned 'white with rage'. The proposal – unencouragingly named 'Plan Balkan' – transferred power separately to each of India's provincial governments, and allowed each one to subsequently choose whether to federate with other provinces or not. Nehru 'took a long while to control himself,' recalled Mountbatten,[69] and so Plan Balkan went the way of the Cripps plan, the Wavell plan, the Cabinet Mission plan and the many others that had been put forward before. Fretting that the only solution was 'to take away the option for independence either for Bengal or for any other Province',[70] Mountbatten turned to V. P. Menon, the most competent civil servant on his staff, and 'gave him a single night to devise an alternative, coherent and workable plan for independence'.[71]

Although Mountbatten would later take all the credit, over the next twenty-four hours Menon would create history. The chain-smoking Malayali had grown up in the Malabar Hills, but after burning down his school, and running away from home, he spent five years as an indentured gold miner with a steel ring fastened around his arm. It was an unconventional background for a civil servant, yet after finding basic employment in Simla, Menon had remarkably worked his way up to the top of the government bureaucracy. By the 1930s he had become a close friend of Jinnah's, and the two men had travelled to the Round Table Conferences together, shopping for fresh dates at Suez and discussing history over glasses of wine. But they had lost touch and when they met again years later, Menon found that

> I could not get in a word. His whole talk was one long tirade against the Congress ... I will not attempt to explain it. But the change in that man's mind between 1930 and 1946 is one of the greatest tragedies of Indian History.[72]

Now Menon locked himself in his room to make his estranged friend's dream of a Muslim homeland a reality, a tumbler of whisky in hand and a lit cigarette in his mouth, turning Mountbatten's notes into a detailed plan for partitioning India into two independent dominions.

Reeking of smoke, Menon handed a completed manuscript to Mountbatten three hours later.[73] Nehru gave his approval and not long afterwards the British cabinet did the same. Soon even Gandhi had begrudgingly acquiesced, and on the evening of 2 June 1947, Mountbatten accompanied his chief of staff Lord Ismay to 'go and wrestle with Jinnah', the final piece of the puzzle. Ismay writes that: 'He was in one of his difficult moods ... describing the plan as scandalous' but 'after a good deal of "horse trading"', the Viceroy received 'an admission that Mr Attlee might safely ... go ahead with his announcement about the plan to the House of Commons the next day'.[74] A letter later that night confirmed that important Sikh representatives had accepted the proposal as well. For the very first time the only major leader who raised an objection to a plan for the transfer of power was the ex-Congress president Azad, who felt that Partition would 'spell disaster for the Mussalmans'. Yet Azad was quickly sidelined and told to 'make way for a younger man'.[75] A telegram was sent to Rangoon to brief Aung San on the fact that India would indeed be Partitioned, and preparations were set in motion to formally broadcast the plan on All-India Radio.[76]

Seventy-five years on it is common to think of the Great Partition of India and Pakistan as causing the mass violence that would become associated with its name. But in June 1947, Partition was seen as a way to stop the violence. 'We were tired men and we were getting on in years,' Nehru later admitted. 'The plan for Partition offered a way out and we took it.'[77]

News leaked out quickly that India's politicians had finally come to an agreement, but for the next twenty-four hours details were vague and unsubstantiated. Workers in Madras and Hyderabad went on strike, while in Delhi saffron-clad sadhus lined the banks of the Jumna river in protest at the expected announcement.[78] A short investment boom hit the stock market[79] and the correspondent for the *Civil & Military Gazette* noted that 'Cryptic messages recording the order of arrival and departure of India's leaders at the Viceroy's House ... comprise all the "news" at the moment on the most momentous conference in India's history.'[80]

Every newspaper was plastered with speculation so that the rather extraordinary news that evacuees would be formally permitted to return to Burma was considered a minor story by comparison.[81] 'The atmosphere in Karachi was one of suppressed excitement,' an American vice-consul noted. 'Thousands of persons from all classes of society had assembled in the streets and public parks to hear the broadcast, while radio shops and stores put on loud-speakers to give passers-by an opportunity to hear the announcement.'[82] Wireless radios from the Thar Desert to the Patkai Hills tuned in to All-India Radio, and then at 7 p.m. on 3 June four voices rang out over the airwaves. As Mountbatten explained:

> There can be no question of coercing any large areas in which one community had a majority to live against their will under a government in which another community has a majority – and the only alternative to coercion is partition.[83]

They then gave the details of their plan. Unlike the separations of Burma and Aden in 1937, the Great Partition of 1947 would see provinces themselves being divided between India and Pakistan. Elected politicians in Punjab and Bengal would be allowed to vote on whether their provinces should be partitioned while North-West Frontier Province and Sylhet in Assam would hold referendums to decide which country they would join. 'It is with no joy in my heart that I commend these proposals to you,' admitted Nehru on the radio,

> though I have no doubt in my mind that this is the right course ... Let us bury that past in so far as it is dead and forget all bitterness and recrimination. Let there be moderation in speech and writing ... There has been violence – shameful degrading violence – in various parts of the country. This must end.[84]

Balwant Singh expressed regret that the Sikhs would not receive a land of their own, and Jinnah ended his speech with the words 'Pakistan Zindabad [Long Live Pakistan]', spoken with such a posh English drawl that many listeners were convinced he had said 'Pakistan's in the Bag'.[85]

When the speech was over, Mountbatten set off back to Viceroy's House for some 'well-earned whiskeys-and-sodas',[86] and the next morning, feeling triumphant, he delivered a second surprise. In a short announcement to the press, he explained that the deadline for the transfer of power would be moved forward almost a year to 15 August 1947. 'The date I chose came out of the blue,' Mountbatten later recalled. 'Why? Because it was the second anniversary of Japan's surrender!'[87]

'It was a bombshell!' wrote the commander-in-chief's private secretary Shahid Hamid in his diary that afternoon. 'Two states will be born 77 days from now. There is no parallel in history!'[88] Precisely why Mountbatten rushed the transfer of power remains highly debated. The most persuasive answer is that, with Sardar Patel blocking his access to the intelligence services, he felt burdened by the responsibility over millions of lives and had no knowledge of what was actually going on, or power to change it. Whatever the case, Mountbatten's Viceroyalty would be remarkable for its brevity. After decades of procrastinating over minute constitutional details, suddenly every question had to be resolved in under three months. Mountbatten went on to describe his thinking over a dinner at Viceroy's House:

> You give your staff a plan, and ask how long they need to put the plan into operation. Let us say they estimate four weeks. Then you tell them, 'Do it in two!' Everyone is shocked into action and you surprise your enemy.

The response to his statement was silence, however. Then, after a few seconds, a civil servant sitting nearby raised his voice and asked:

And who is your enemy, sir?[89]

Within twenty-four hours the division of India was being compared to the splitting of the atom and the creation of the atom bomb.[90] No one could have known it would be bloodier.

For the many British men and women who had lived their whole lives in India, the sudden race towards independence came as a shock, and for a time no one knew if Indian-born Brits would become Indian or British.[91] Indian Political Service officer Reginald Michael Hadow, for example, had grown up on a tea estate in Shillong and speaking Khasi rather than English as his first language. His friend Tarlok Singh had recently persuaded him to stay on in India after independence, but after personally petitioning the Congress, he had

> a rather awkward interview with Nehru ... at which he informed me that, much as he liked me, my face was the wrong colour to be acceptable in the new Indian Foreign Service. He wished me well in the UK Foreign Service, which he advised me to join.[92]

This sense of uncertainty was infinitely greater among the Indian population, particularly those in the Punjab and Bengal who were left completely in the dark as to which country they would soon belong to. Where exactly would India and Pakistan be? Would the army also be divided? What would be the role of religion in the new states? And most important of all, who would qualify as Indian and who as Pakistani?

The official secrecy that surrounded the border negotiations only made life more precarious for the farmers, fishermen and factory workers who lived there. Would Muslims living in India count as Indians or as stranded Pakistanis? And what would be expected of the subcontinent's other religious communities – the Sikhs, Christians, Buddhists, Jains, Parsis, Jews, Sanamahis, Bahais, Bons, atheists and agnostics? Even the basic question of who counted as Hindu and Muslim had yet to be worked out. The Ahmadiyya community, for example, identified as Muslims but were not considered so by many other Muslims because they believed Muhammad was not the last prophet of Islam.* Likewise, although many Hindus claimed the Dalit community as their own, many Dalits themselves denied that they were Hindus. Given that districts would now be divided along religious lines, it was of the utmost importance to understand who counted as what.[93]

Demonstrative of the scale of confusion, there was even disagreement over whose responsibility the partition actually was. Muslim Leaguers argued the British should oversee the process, while Congress claimed the Congress-dominated interim government should be the one to decide. Once again Mountbatten fell on the side of Congress, so giving the 'nascent government of free India a quite unjustifiable advantage over its rival'.[94]

Horror, bewilderment and confusion were common emotions across India in the hot summer months of June and July 1947. For Hindus who worshipped the subcontinent's sacred landscape, the Great Partition was nothing less than the dismemberment of a goddess. 'The British have saved their worst injury for the end – the amputation of our Mother India,' scribbled Asha Sahay, the ex-INA recruit.

Many senior Muslim Leaguers were equally horrified by the plan to partition India and a group called the 'Pakistan National Movement' derided it as Jinnah's 'greatest betrayal'.[95] Another Muslim Leaguer with a sense of betrayal was Hasrat Mohani, the revolutionary maulana who had co-founded the Communist Party of

---

* Ironically, given the persecution they face in Pakistan today, Ahmadis were at the forefront of supporting the creation of Pakistan. Zafarullah Khan, who was an Ahmadi, was involved with the drafting of the Lahore Resolution and served as Pakistan's first foreign minister.

India and coined the popular phrase 'Inquilab Zindabad' – 'Long Live the Revolution'. Following a long tradition in the Gangetic plains, Mohani considered the Hindu god Krishna to be a 'manifestation of god – in the same manner as any pre-eminent Sufi master', and he frequently made pilgrimages to the city of Krishna's birth, composing poetry in Krishna's name. These beliefs had coexisted with a strong support for the Pakistan movement, yet he had always conceived of Pakistan as a separate federal unit within a unified India, on the model of the socialist republics within the Soviet Union.[96] When he learned that Pakistan would be an entirely separate country, therefore, he resigned from the Muslim League and cried out from the benches of the Legislative Assembly, 'Down with Jawaharlal and Down with Jinnah!'[97]

It took only six days from the announcement for the first attempt on Jinnah's life. He was in Delhi addressing the All-India Muslim League Council at Delhi's art deco Imperial Hotel when the attack began. A group of Muslim Khaksars erupted into 'the garden at the side of the hotel, and startled peaceful residents during tea by rushing through the lounge brandishing *belchas*, or sharpened spades ... shouting "Get Jinnah!"' Crockery went flying, chairs were overturned, and the Muslim League National Guards attempted to push them back using gardening tools. Eventually police arrived armed with tear gas, and the attackers were forced back onto the street.[98] The Khaksars, noted Alan Campbell-Johnson in his diary, felt that by creating Pakistan Jinnah had betrayed Indian Muslims.

> A party from Viceroy's House going along later in the evening for dinner found the place in the utmost disorder. The large grill-room was a shambles. Its air-coolers were smashed and its furniture broken up. The forces of fanaticism and revolution are on the move, and this incident confirms that the crust upholding order from the depths of chaos is dangerously thin.[99]

The Partitions of Burma and Arabia had been planned meticulously over years. The Great Partition of 1947 by contrast would be put together haphazardly over just ten weeks. Civil servants and military officers raced to figure out not only which areas would belong to Pakistan, but how the military, the civil service, the banking and educational systems would be divided. 'Everything is moving so fast that it is difficult to keep track of things,' wrote Shahid Hamid. 'Everyone is in a spin. There is no time to relax.'[100]

It was a mad rush between the Congress and Muslim League to get as much as they could. In the coming weeks the people of each Muslim-majority province were asked to cast their vote on Pakistan. Muslim League National Guards and RSS cadres marched across the landscape, campaigning and intimidating voters from the back of boats, bicycles, trucks and camels. Bribery and political intimidation were endemic, and a soldier posted in Sylhet noted that: 'Pressure is already being brought to bear on Hindu voters in villages that they should cast their votes for Pakistan if they want to live in peace.'[101]

Voters didn't divide along communal lines as much as one might have expected. Muslim preachers of the Jamiat-ul Ulama-i-Hind campaigned on behalf of Congress,[102] while the Dalit leader Jogendra Nath Mandal continued to campaign on behalf of the Muslim League. In the Andaman Islands, some 850 miles east of the Indian mainland, inhabited by neither Hindus nor Muslims, decisions were made by Delhi politicians who had little familiarity with the region. Congress wanted them to become part of India; the Muslim League lobbied for them to be made a refuelling point between East and West Pakistan; the British Navy suggested they remain British; and a group of Anglo-Indians even proposed they become a homeland for their community.

In the end, Sindh and Baluchistan voted to join Pakistan while Bengal and Punjab voted on partitioning their provinces between the two dominions. Partition committees proliferated, staffed by equal numbers of Muslim and non-Muslim bureaucrats to divide the country, an exercise 'tedious in its detail and terrifying in its scope'.[103] Their job included dividing everything from rivers to stationery sets, and on 3 July Alan Campbell-Johnson noted in his diary that, 'We considered whether a partitioned India meant also a partitioned Kennel Club.'[104] The solutions to these problems were slapdash so that on one occasion, 'The Encyclopaedia Britannica was divided up, with alternate volumes given to each country; dictionaries were ripped in half – A to K going to one country and L to Z to the other.'[105] Meanwhile, the Indus, from which the words 'India' and 'Hindu' were derived, was given to Pakistan. A few days later the Partition councils would turn their focus to the famed Mohenjo Daro necklace, an ancient artefact of jade and agate, threaded on a golden string 4,500 years earlier when the Indus valley civilisation was trading with Ancient Egypt and Mesopotamia. Here the solution was to cut the necklace in half so that an equal number of beads could be sent to India and to Pakistan. Even history, it seemed, would be divided.

The question remained, however, who would oversee the division of land? It was Jinnah who finally proposed Cyril Radcliffe, a lawyer and ex-director general of Britain's Ministry of Information who was said to be of 'great legal abilities, right personality, and wide administrative experience'.[106] The fact that Radcliffe had never been east of Paris and knew nothing of India was considered to be evidence of his potential as an unbiased mediator. Yet tasking a man who knew nothing of the subcontinent with determining its fate would yield deadly results. Radcliffe was given just a matter of weeks to mark out 'contiguous areas of Muslims and non-Muslims' while taking into account 'other factors' such as the flow of rivers and the placement of holy shrines. 'I was so rushed that I had not time to go into the details,' he later admitted. 'What could I do in one and a half months?'[107] Soon even Mountbatten was beginning to realise what he had done by rushing independence, writing to his daughter Patricia:

> I've made a mess of things through over-confidence and overtiredness. I'm just whacked and worn out and would really like to go. I'm so depressed darling, because until this stupid mishandling of the Jinnah situation I'd done so well.[108]

As lawyers and bureaucrats divided up the country, princes and politicians, journalists and bureaucrats, representatives and refugees streamed into Delhi. People arrived from all corners of the subcontinent, including a group of Nagas led by Angami Zapu Phizo who turned up at Gandhi's residence to explain their plans for Naga independence. 'We felt somewhat disappointed when we saw Gandhiji first,' wrote one of the Naga delegates. 'He was teethless, bald headed and ugly. We entered the room and we were asked to sit on the mats on the floor.' But after a few minutes of complete silence, Gandhi suddenly 'looked beautiful. All the ugliness we saw at first disappeared.'[109] The Nagas left convinced the Mahatma supported their bid for independence, although this was actually a misunderstanding.*

In late June Nehru accepted Mountbatten's suggestion that he stay on as joint governor-general of both India and Pakistan for a few months after independence, but Jinnah, despite having earlier suggested some sort of 'Supreme Arbitrator' over Indian and Pakistani affairs, abruptly rejected him and refused to budge. Throughout the spring Nehru's relationship with the Viceroy's wife had raised more and more eyebrows among Jinnah's close associates, one of whom even claimed Nehru 'was having a roaring love affair with Lady Mountbatten ... with the tacit approval of Mountbatten'. He was far from the only one who thought this and references to their intimate relationship abound in the memoirs and diaries of the Viceroy's inner circle. Padmaja Naidu, who a decade earlier Nehru had referred to as his 'carissima', even 'threatened to commit suicide' over his relationship with Edwina.[110] 'There are all sorts of conjectures about their relationship,' wrote Shahid Hamid in May:

> Nehru is in and out of the Viceroy's House to meet Edwina. She has hypnotized and captivated him. Krishna Menon says it is more than that. God knows! ... Edwina often says that Nehru is a lonely man and needs a woman in his life. I suppose she has decided to be the one. It is said that she writes adolescent and

---

* When Phizo's delegation told Gandhi they were planning to declare themselves independent on 15 August 1947, Gandhi replied with the words, 'You can be independent ... if you have non-violence ... I will come to Kohima and ask them [the Government] to shoot me before they shoot one Naga.' This line would later be interpreted by generations of Naga nationalists to argue that Gandhi supported Nagaland's independence from India. But what Gandhi meant by 'independence' has since been questioned. He may well have been talking about economic or spiritual independence and would go on to tell the delegation, 'You cannot be in complete isolation ... I will teach you the art of spinning and weaving. You grow cotton and yet you import cloth. Learn all the handicrafts. That is the way to peaceful independence.' Whatever the Mahatma's intention, however, Phizo and his delegates left the meeting with a newfound resolve, and what they interpreted as Gandhi's full support to declare their independence from India on the same date as Pakistan. This would presage disaster, but for the time being all remained calm. For quotes see Gandhi, M. K., *The Collected Works of Mahatma Gandhi LXXXVIII (May–July 1947)* (New Delhi: Publications Division, Ministry of Information and Broadcasting, Govt of India, 1970) p373. For further discussion see Lintner, B., *Great Game East: India, China and the Struggle for Asia's Most Volatile Frontier* (Noida: HarperCollins India, 2016).

juvenile letters to Nehru and he does like-wise ... Her relationship with Nehru has been of immense help to the Congress.[111]

Perhaps the most electrifying claim of all came from S. S. Pirzada, later the foreign minister of Pakistan, who alleged Jinnah intercepted intimate letters between Nehru and Edwina. One read: 'I have fond memories of Simla – riding and your touch', while another said: 'You forgot your handkerchief and before Dickie could spot it I covered it up.' A third included the line: 'Dickie will be out tonight – come after 10.00 o'clock.'[112]

Under previous Viceroys Nehru had spent much of his time in prison, but under Mountbatten he seemed to be passing his evenings in the Viceregal bedchamber. Whether their relationship turned sexual remains contested,[113] but there is no doubt that in an extraordinary bookend to two hundred years of British rule, India's prime-minister-in-waiting and the wife of the last Viceroy did fall deeply in love. By the end of June, therefore, it was clear to Jinnah he could no longer rely on Mountbatten to be an impartial arbitrator. 'Mountbatten ... was honestly pro-Hindu and the Mahomedans felt that,' recalls Paddy Massey, commander of the Mountbattens' Bodyguard.

> [When Lord] and Lady Mountbatten were being seen off at Delhi airport by Nehru, Nehru kissed ... Lady Mountbatten in the European fashion, and a fizzle of horror went through Mahomedan India. After that Mountbatten hadn't a hope of becoming Governor General of Pakistan and I believe he never realised why.[114]

So it was that as a result of the suspected relationship between Nehru and Edwina, there would be no one left to arbitrate a conflict between the fledgling countries of India and Pakistan after independence.

Even as the Great Partition of British India was beginning, it was still unclear precisely what would happen after independence to the 40 per cent of the subcontinent under princely rule. To many nationalists in both the Congress and the Muslim League, the basic assumption had been that the 565 princely states would be partitioned along religious lines with British India, but it quickly emerged that these would be entirely separate processes. The fate of Princely India would be left to the whims of royal families, who had the option to 'integrate' their kingdoms with one of the new countries or to remain independent. Muslim-majority Kashmir's future would instead be left to the decision of its Hindu Maharaja, while the future of Hindu-majority Hyderabad would be handed to the Muslim Nizam.

The map of South Asia would look very different if it were not for the decisions of these princes. Indeed, contrary to popular perception, less than half of the modern India–Pakistan border would be drawn by Cyril Radcliffe. Instead, roughly 81 per cent of India's border with West Pakistan would be determined by the decisions of seven princes and 36 per cent of the border with East Pakistan by another ten.[115] Only Hindu Bikaner was unequivocally eager to join the dominion that aligned with its ruler's religion. For all other states, it was a matter of pragmatism. Which state could offer the best deal? The borders of South Asia – usually understood as a legacy of the British – are as much the legacy of India's princes.

Many more states made a bid for independence than is traditionally acknowledged, and within weeks of the 3 June announcement, states from Bilaspur to Bhopal and from Kashmir to Kalat had all announced plans to remain outside of either India or Pakistan. France and the United States were rumoured to be considering a recognition of Hyderabadi independence.[116] Bhutan even demanded the return of territory conquered by the British. 'If Great Britain is parting with Indian territory in general to Indians,' Bhutan's representatives argued, 'so logically Great Britain ought to part with this small piece of territory, which is not Indian at all, to the Bhutanese.'[117] But political officer Arthur J. Hopkinson drew the line at returning ceded territory. 'Were the case otherwise,' he mused:

> Britain would not bequeath 'independence' on India. Instead, it would restore Bombay to the Portuguese from whom she received the sovereignty over Bombay, and Lucknow to the eldest surviving descendant of King Wajid Ali Shah of Oudh, likewise Delhi to the eldest surviving Mogul (still living there), with some Mahratta in hot dispute: and this would of course solve all our problems, for large chunks of potential Pakistan

would be restored to some Sikh ruling in Lahore on the gaddi of the Lion of the Punjab. Chunks of Behar would go to Nepal, and Mahrattas would come up near Calcutta.[118]

Prior to Partition, Jinnah recognised the legal right of the princes to pursue independence and was always quick to argue that Pakistan's creation had to be settled before the issue of the princely states. Unlike the Muslim League, however, the Congress never recognised the princely states as having any right to independence – with the sole exceptions of Nepal, Bhutan and Sikkim. Instead, they felt the Balkanisation of India had begun and the man Nehru deemed responsible was Mountbatten's political adviser Conrad Corfield. With an air of quiet authority, Corfield had set about burning documents that could be used to blackmail the princes and had secretly procured arms for the Nizam of Hyderabad. Whether he was using the threat of princely independence as a bargaining chip to ensure a better deal for the princes is uncertain, but to Congress at least Corfield was the man who stood in the way of integrating the princely states.[119]

It was only on 13 June that Mountbatten finally held a meeting to address the situation. Nehru, Jinnah, Patel and Liaquat Ali Khan were all present, as was Corfield, against whom Nehru launched an immediate attack. Instead of offering a defence, the Viceroy stayed silent and it was Jinnah rather than Mountbatten who eventually came to Corfield's aid, arguing that 'every Indian State was a sovereign State' and 'free to do as they liked'.[120] The intervention curtailed Nehru's diatribe, but the way the Viceroy had undermined his political adviser was visible to all. Mountbatten then proceeded to undermine Corfield further, announcing that he would be setting up a new States Department, to take over the issue.

As far as Corfield was concerned, Mountbatten was betraying Britain's age-old allies in favour of the very politicians responsible for the ending of British rule. The Viceroy 'had been authorised by the Prime Minister to negotiate with individual states for adjusting their relations with the Crown,' he wrote, 'not with successor governments.'[121] Mountbatten's actions were nothing less than treason. When he asked Corfield to organise a meeting of the Chamber of Princes, at which he would pressure them to abandon dreams of independence, it was the final straw. Corfield obliged but handed in his letter of resignation and left India three days before the meeting took place. A friend later described him as 'a dispirited and broken man'.[122]

Just as the Partition Council was in charge of the Great Partition of British India, the new States Department would be in charge of the Partition of Princely India, corralling the 565 princely states into either the Indian or the Pakistani union. Patel and the chain-smoking child labourer-turned civil servant V. P. Menon would mix 'fury with charm and persuasion with coercion' to ensure that in a matter of months over 550 sovereign states vanished from the map.[123]

Menon took the lead, warning London that if they recognised princely states as independent, Britain's legacy in the subcontinent would be destroyed.[124] Next he set about drafting two documents which, when signed, would leave states in a similar position to their status under the Raj. Any who resisted could be treated as hostile states. Finally, with both carrot and stick to hand, Menon started getting Mountbatten to take personal responsibility for the accession of the states. Observing that the Viceroy's Achilles heel was concern over his legacy, Menon decided the best approach was to stroke the Englishman's ego. He later wrote how Mountbatten

> was deeply touched by my remark that the wounds of partition might to some extent be healed by the States entering into a relationship with the Government of India and that he would be earning the gratitude of generations of Indians if he could assist in achieving the basic unity of the country.[125]

Menon's plan worked, so much so that once again Mountbatten subsequently tried to take credit for coming up with the whole idea in the first place. Soon afterwards he took it to Patel, who told him, 'I'll buy a basket with 565 apples' – the computed number of states – 'but if there are even two or three apples missing the deal is off.' 'This,' said the Viceroy, 'I cannot completely accept, but I will do my best. If I give you a basket with, say, 560 apples, will you buy it?' 'Well I might,' replied Patel.[126]

On 25 July, in the heat of the summer, almost a hundred princes bedecked in jewels gathered in a circular room in the heart of the city. 'It was stifling hot,' writes Campbell-Johnson, 'and the portly Jam Sahib of Nawanagar stood directly under the one fan, complaining that it moved far too slowly.'¹²⁷ Some of these princes ruled over minute principalities of less than a square mile of land; others ruled an area larger than Korea. All of them had been Britain's closest allies for over a hundred years and now the British were leaving India, many looked forward to regaining their states' independence. Yet on that fateful day, as Viceroy Mountbatten swaggered through the heat in an ivory-white robe, anxious murmurs rippled through the crowd.¹²⁸ Over the next hour he made it clear that if the princes refused to accede to either India or Pakistan, Britain would not come to their aid and possibly even hit them with sanctions.¹²⁹ The princes, meanwhile, sat there, 'like plump, velvet cattle, their large, sad, calm brown eyes fixed trustingly on their herdsman – who was about to tell them the best way to the abattoir'.¹³⁰ At one point the prime minister of Cutch pointed out that because his state was on the border, he would need to ask his prince which dominion he wanted to join.

> Mountbatten thereupon picked up a large round glass paperweight ... 'I will look into my crystal', he said, 'and give you an answer.' There followed ten seconds of dramatic pause when you could have heard a princely pin drop. 'His Highness,' Mountbatten solemnly announced, 'asks you to sign the Instrument of Accession.'¹³¹

The room erupted into laughter, a jolly way to end the meeting. Yet the more politically astute princes realised the earth had shifted under their feet. The Instrument of Accession forced them to give up their communications, defence and foreign policy to the new government. They retained control over internal autonomy, although as they would soon find out, even these guarantees would be quickly discarded by the newly independent governments of India and Pakistan. The very same evening Mountbatten held a party for fifty princes, and Menon writes that

> those of the rulers who had not yet signified their intention of acceding were taken by the [aides-de-camp], one by one, for a friendly talk with Mountbatten ... When he had finished with them, he passed them to me in full view of the company, and I in my turn, conducted them across the room to Sardar.¹³²

Within six days, the first twenty-five states had signed India's Accession.

Mountbatten was no republican, yet he had just set in motion one of the great revolutions in world history. From this moment on Menon and Patel would use faith, fortune and occasionally force to corral over 550 states into relinquishing their sovereignty. A contemporary journalist would dub Patel 'a Hindu Cromwell, courteously decapitating hundreds of little King Charleses'.[133] Mountbatten himself noted the irony that India's politicians, renowned for 'non-violence', had taken to using threats of violence against the princes: 'You always talk about wooing people, and yet in the case of the States, you threaten,' he joked to Gandhi. 'Would you woo a girl you wanted to marry with a stick and expect her to accept?'[134]

As well as the intrigues of Patel, Menon and Mountbatten, the growing threat of communist revolution played an important role in ultimately convincing rulers to give up their independence. Soon after the end of the Second World War, the author George Orwell noted in an article that a state of 'cold war' was beginning to develop between the Soviet Union and its wartime allies Britain and the United States. Communist governments were starting to appear across Eastern Europe, and north of the Himalayan mountain range, the bitter civil war between China's nationalist government and its Communist Party had resumed.

Communism, with its promises of equality and the eradication of feudalism, struck a particular chord in India's princely states, which by definition were ruled by feudal aristocracies. An uprising in the Telugu regions of Hyderabad against exorbitant taxation and bonded labour was gradually evolving into a fully fledged communist rebellion against their princely overlords, while in Kashmir communists had infiltrated deep into the leading National Conference Party. Communist opposition to princely rule was also observed in Tripura, Manipur and the hills of Travancore, and many princely rulers knew the British Indian Army was all that stood between them and violent overthrow. 'I tell you straight,' wrote the Nawab of Bhopal to Mountbatten in late July, 'that unless you and His Majesty's Government support the states and prevent them from disappearing from the Indian political map, you will very shortly have an India dominated by Communists.'[135]

The threat from communism became particularly clear after events in Travancore. Nestled on the southwestern tip of the Indian subcontinent, between the verdant western ghats and the azure expanse of Arabian sea, Travancore was one of the great maritime kingdoms of the Indian subcontinent, a magnet for traders from Aden and Dubai. It was a kingdom founded on the pepper trade, and officially ruled not by the Maharaja but by his patron deity Padmanabhaswamy, whose closed-off temple vaults remain to this day the richest place of worship in the world. One estimate of the value of treasure contained within these vaults is $22 billion – several thousand times more than those of the Vatican. At the time of writing, the inventory is under a court seal, but if opened it would likely be the single most important archaeological treasure trove since the uncovering of Tutankhamun.*

In 1947, however, it was another Travancore treasure trove that caught the world's attention. The state had the second largest quantity ever discovered of monazite: a rare mineral crucial to creating fuel for nuclear reactors. After signing an agreement with the British government to supply the material for Britain's nuclear ambitions, the Diwan, or prime minister, announced that from 15 August that year, 'Travancore will become an independent country.'[136] With one of India's most literate populations and a lengthy coastline connecting the state to the sea, he added, Travancore would be in 'no worse position than Denmark, Switzerland and Siam'.[137]

Support for Travancore's independence came from unexpected quarters, including both Jinnah and the British minister of supply. Even the Mahasabha leader Vinayak Savarkar celebrated the state's 'courageous and far-sighted determination' to stay out of the Indian Union.[138] Nehru and Patel, by contrast, threatened an economic blockade and the use of air power if Travancore refused to accede. But the state responded by negotiating shipments of rice from Sindh and Burma and banning the Congress Party within its borders.

Patel took to threatening the Diwan, telling him he had secured funding to create trouble in the state and that the Diwan's very 'life

---

* In 2011, a Supreme Court-appointed team catalogued that in one room alone, hidden under a granite slab, were some '100,000 historic gold coins, weighing 700kg–800kg in total, including from the Napoleonic, Mogul and British periods ... more than 100 heavy gold chains studded with precious gemstones such as emeralds and sapphires, rings, a crown, anklets and other traditional Indian jewellery'. on.ft.com/3P11NVi

could be in danger'. But the Diwan simply replied, 'You can have me assassinated but then there will be no one left to fight Communism.' A few days later, however, an activist from Kerala's Socialist Party stabbed the Diwan in the street as he walked out of a music concert. He survived but the attack proved a turning point and on 30 July the Maharaja sent a signed instrument of accession to New Delhi. The accession 'of Travancore after all [Diwan] C. P.'s declarations of independence has had a profound effect on all the other States,' wrote Mountbatten, 'and is sure to shake the Nizam [of Hyderabad].'[139]

By the end of July 1947, outright independence was looking less appetising to all but the largest and most sophisticated states. There was still, however, one more option: acceding to another country.

Throughout the summer the Khan of Dir mulled over acceding to Afghanistan, while Manipur considered merging with Burma.[140] Some of the Khasi states near Shillong tried to join Pakistan, but with the Muslim League in a perpetual state of chaos, it seems their officials simply lost the papers or forgot to reply. Similarly, the Hindu Maharaja of Cooch Behar approached the premier of Bengal – Huseyn Suhrawardy – no fewer than three times for advice on whether to join Pakistan.[141] As with the Khasi states' accession, he never heard back. Along the western border, 'League Agents' offered Hindu and Sikh states 'all manner of inducements'[142] and soon Patel began to worry about an unbroken chain of contiguous Pakistani land reaching right through to Bhopal, a 'dagger into the very heart of India'.[143]

Given that a state could only join a dominion it bordered, the solution for Menon and Patel was to ensure a wall of states from Punjab in the north down to Gujarat in the south acceded to India before Independence Day on 15 August. This would be ensured most effectively if they could bring round just four states: Bikaner, Jodhpur, Jaisalmer and Cutch.

On 7 August the ever-loyal Maharaja of Bikaner signed the Instrument of Accession,[144] becoming the first border state in western India to do so. At the same time, however, the rulers of Jodhpur and Jaisalmer met with Jinnah.

Tourist guides in modern India are often oblivious that some of the country's most celebrated tourist destinations – from the blue city of

Jodhpur to the golden dunes of Jaisalmer – very nearly became part of Pakistan. Indeed Jinnah's offer to the Maharajas of Jodhpur and Jaisalmer was tempting. 'Your Highness,' he said, 'I sign on the dotted line, and you fill in the conditions.'[145] Signing the paper with a fountain pen, Jinnah handed it to the twenty-four-year-old Maharaja of Jodhpur, who nervously turned to the much younger ruler of Jaisalmer for advice. Jaisalmer responded that he would sign on one condition: 'If there was any trouble between the Hindus and Muslims, he would not side with the Muslims against the Hindus.'[146] Jodhpur paused, and quickly his aide-de-camp, Colonel Thakur Kesari Singh, whispered into his ear the words, 'Your Highness, before you sign, you must ask your mother.'[147]

Singh's appeal to matriarchal authority saved the day for the Indian government. The Maharaja postponed signing away his future and returned to the blue city of Jodhpur where his mother and his guru both pressed him not to join Pakistan. Three days later he returned to Delhi still anxious and conflicted, but when Mountbatten also pleaded for him to join India, he was convinced. That afternoon, on 11 August, Jodhpur signed India's Instrument of Accession rather than Pakistan's.[148] The moment Lord Mountbatten went out of the room, however, Menon writes that:

> The Maharajah [of Jodhpur] whipped out a revolver, levelled it at me and said: 'I refuse to accept your dictation.' I told him that he was making a very serious mistake if he thought that by killing me, or threatening to kill me, he could get the accession abrogated. 'Don't indulge in juvenile theatricals,' I admonished him.[149]

Menon's 'near-death experience' would become the stuff of national myth in decades to come. Only later did it emerge that he had exaggerated the incident and that the 'revolver' was in fact a magic prop.*

Jodhpur's decision was a turning point and within a day both Cutch and Jaisalmer had also thrown their lot in with India.[150] A wall of states along India's western flank from Punjab to Gujarat had now cut off

---

* Years later, the same prop would be used by Mountbatten to gain entry into an elite society of magicians (Basu, *V. P. Menon*, p320).

most of the princely states from Pakistan; with the stroke of a pen, the possibility of a vastly larger Pakistan had been averted.[151]

Throughout the summer of 1947, politicians in Burma looked at news from India with terror. Possibly because of the religious polarisation being seen in India, Aung San had declared that his country would not have an official religion, horrifying some of his Buddhist colleagues. Soon afterwards his new interim government passed an emergency immigration bill, putting a sudden stop to the influx of Indians from neighbouring Bengal. In the weeks before independence, therefore, Indo-Burmese relations plummeted once again, with Nehru condemning the act's effects on the three hundred thousand Indians still residing in Burma.[152]

That July, as relentless monsoon rains slashed down on Rangoon, Aung San sat positive in the knowledge that the Shan states' accession to the Union of Burma had been secured at the Panglong Conference.[153] Of course, there was still work to do. The Karenni states announced that they would only join a Burmese Union when the Burmans 'proved that they are loyal and faithful to their words', and the Wa states refused to give any kind of commitment.[154]

Around this time, a stash of weapons and ammunition went unexpectedly missing and a man called Daine reported to Britain's chief intelligence officer how 'at a drinks party in Rangoon, U Saw had boasted that he was collecting arms and sinking them in the Victoria Lake'. The officer never acted on the information and would later tell an inquiry: 'I was more concerned with the impropriety of Daine's consorting with drunken Burmese than with the possibility that the boast might be true.'[155]

Nonetheless, Aung San was warned his life was in danger, and in late July he told the deputy inspector general of Rangoon Police an assassination attempt was possible.[156] The next rain-drenched morning, Burma's new executive council gathered in the council chamber of Rangoon's red-brick Secretariat Building to discuss the mysterious theft of two hundred Bren guns from the city's ordnance depot. Aung San, dressed in a silken jacket and chequered longyi tied around his waist, sat at the centre of the room, with his new ministers gathered around a large semi-circular table. At 10.30 a.m. an army jeep with a false licence plate was waved through the entrance of the Secretariat by unsuspecting policemen. Five men in emerald-green army fatigues got out and ran up the stairs towards the council chamber, while one stayed with the jeep. A guard by the doorway tried to stop them but he was shot. At 10.37 the men burst through the doorway of the chamber and pulling out automatic Sten guns shouted, 'Don't run away!'

Aung San stood up in shock, then the assassins opened fire, killing him and sending a spray of automatic bullets around the room, slaughtering everyone on one side of the table and wounding most of those on the other side, who had managed to duck under it in time to save their lives. The assassins turned and fled, shooting a bodyguard on their way out and leaving in their wake 'the smell of carbide, blood-stained floors, spent cartridge cases, and the bodies of the father of Burmese independence and some of his closest associates'.[157] Only three of the ten ministers survived.

The attack caused panic. Mountbatten was 'inexpressibly shocked' when he heard the news,[158] and Gandhi held a prayer meeting in Hindi mourning the fallen 'warrior' alongside the victims of communal violence in India.[159] Burmese officials speculated that the assassins were communists, but police soon traced them to U Saw's lakeside residence in northern Rangoon, finding a jeep still wet with a fresh coat of paint sitting on the driveway. Officers burst through the door and found the assassins gathered around U Saw, who was drinking whisky from the barrel of the gun that had killed his nemesis. Officer Carlyle Seppings recalled:

> U Saw was sitting down in a chair in a vest and a lungyi and he was drinking something which turned out to be whiskey. And as I went in there with my pistol ... he said, 'What the hell are you doing here!' And I said, 'We are raiding your house.'[160]

A ballistics expert matched the bullets used at the Secretariat with the guns from Saw's mansion and he and the assassins were swiftly taken to Insein prison.[161] Meanwhile, Governor Hubert Rance was left frantically searching for someone to take over from Aung San. Months from the transfer of power, Burma's whole executive council had been either killed, wounded or arrested.

Eventually Rance landed on U Nu, an author and a playwright who had been Aung San's best friend at university. Nu was not an obvious choice for Burma's new prime minister-in-waiting. Described as 'Gandhi without Gandhi's predilection for politics', he had long yearned to retire to a monastery.[162] But he was popular, and U Thant, the future general secretary of the United Nations, described him as 'the sort of person you wanted to go on an adventure with because you knew it would be fun'.[163] As one of the few living politicians who both the British and the Burmese could get behind, U Nu was swiftly sworn in to lead Burma to independence.

All the while the investigation into Aung San's assassination continued and a group of divers discovered a petrol drum at the bottom of U Saw's lake filled with automatic weapons.[164] Saw denied any knowledge of it and Dorman-Smith even tried to intervene on his behalf. But the ex-governor could not save his friend. On 30 December 1947 U Saw was found guilty of masterminding the assassination and the next day condemned to death. 'Why should I be handcuffed!' he shouted in the courtroom before marching out.[165] U Saw's sentence would be delayed until after independence, but on 8 May 1948 he was hanged.

Questions remained, however. Soon after Saw's arrest, detectives discovered that the weapons in the lake had been sold to him by two British officers: Captain David Vivian and Major Henry Young. Rumours spread rapidly that the British had conspired to murder Aung San, with communist groups claiming he had been killed for trying to bring them back into the fold.[166] Many Burmese continue to believe that British intelligence were the real masterminds behind the assassination to this day.

8

A Red Dawn

'Last evening, a bomb exploded in a cinema hall at Bhati gate,' wrote Fikr Taunsvi from the Punjabi capital of Lahore on 9 August 1947, five days before the transfer of power. 'All those who died were Muslims.'[1] In retaliation, a mob set about murdering over a hundred Hindus and Sikhs.

The diary of satirist Fikr Taunsvi remains one of the most powerful and visceral Partition memoirs to have ever been published. A Hindu with a Muslim-sounding name, Taunsvi identified strongly with a composite Punjabi identity that transcended religious boundaries.[2] In the event he would become one of the greatest biographers of how his beloved city was torn between the two.

Hours after the explosion, the army was deployed onto city streets. Markets shut down and for over twenty-four hours Taunsvi was locked in his house, unable to get to work. He set about trying to soothe his anxious mind by listening to his favourite records on the radio, but eventually he was distracted by a commotion below his balcony. 'The washerman who lived on the ground floor ... had become the father of a tiny baby at three in the morning,' Taunsvi noted in his diary, and 'was worried that the bazaars were shut. The sweet-seller who sold milk had locked his shop from inside and was hiding there. He had received no supply today because all milk-vendors are Muslim, and this being a Hindu locality, they couldn't step into it. Hospitals were not functioning, neither were doctors, nurses and medicines, and both the mother and the infant were crying.' The scene made Taunsvi wish he could put Nehru and Jinnah in the skin of the washerman and his daughter. 'Then demand Pakistan and Hindustan,' he wrote with anger.[3]

Two days later the curfew was lifted and Taunsvi set out for work. Walking the streets, he 'felt as if everyone on the road were carrying a bomb or a knife ... All men kept turning around ... Hundreds of scared and hesitant enemies had stepped out of their homes.' His route took him through a Muslim-majority area and he went cautiously, only to see the building abutting his office in flames and a 'curious mass' of Hindus and Muslims who had gathered to put the blaze out. The building had been owned by a Hindu who sold Muslim Qurans, and 'the fire', he noted with irony, 'had united two cultures, two religions'.[4]

Eventually Taunsvi located his friend Arif and, a bit shaken, they went to get some food. Upon sitting down at Islami Hotel, near the medieval gates of Old Lahore, they overheard a group of Muslims exclaiming about taking revenge on Hindus and Sikhs for the condition of the Muslim refugees who had arrived in the city that morning. Taunsvi and Arif decided to eat somewhere else. Later they stumbled upon a group of old friends, and here Taunsvi was in for another shock. Four of his Hindu friends – Mittal, Jagdish, Kapoor and Rehbar – had concluded that Lahore would soon form part of Pakistan and had decided to leave the city. 'My head was exploding,' writes Taunsvi. 'It felt as if hammers were being struck on my head ... Jagdish ... this fan of Iqbal, who is in love with Islam, this poet of Urdu, is leaving.'[5]

Already almost half of Lahore's Hindu population had fled and Taunsvi spent the next morning failing to persuade Jagdish to stay. Eventually he gave up and headed back home, past lines of refugees. At one point he came across 'a group of Hindu boys who had broken into a Muslim vegetable vendor's shop, and were picking up bananas, guavas and oranges, and were throwing them in the drain'. Intimidated, Taunsvi closed his eyes as he passed, trying to avoid eye contact. When a bus pulled up at the side of the road, he jumped in and sat down deflated, uncertain of where it would take him.

By early August a great migration had begun. Government workers were the first to move, with many Muslim officials choosing to work in Pakistan after independence. The second-in-command in India's Intelligence Bureau, for example, migrated to become Pakistan's first spy chief.[6] And with Muslim soldiers leaving India en masse, many Muslim civilians fled as well, fearing they would be left to the whims of a purely Hindu army and bureaucracy.

In Punjab the violence had spiralled so out of control that Mountbatten had assigned around twenty thousand soldiers to a Punjab Boundary Force, meant to keep the peace. Woefully undermanned in a province of fifteen million people, the soldiers were soon calling themselves the 'Poor Bloody Fools'. Many of them had expected to face minor criminals but instead found themselves confronted with well-trained militias. Sikh maharajas armed *jathas* with rifles and grenades while Muslim aristocrats like the Khan of Mamdot smuggled war-grade munitions to private mercenary squads.

Paramilitary groups such as the RSS and Muslim League National Guards were at the forefront of the violence, as were land grabbers, who took advantage of the law and order situation to loot rich people's houses. For most, however, the brutality was simply inexplicable. 'I cannot explain it,' a Sikh called Harjit later recalled, 'but one day our entire village took off to a nearby Muslim village on a killing spree. We simply went mad. And it has cost me fifty years of remorse, of sleepless nights – I cannot forget the faces of those we killed.'[7]

To escape the PBF, these groups merely needed to retreat into princely territory where the soldiers had no jurisdiction.[8] The letters of one of its members, an Irish brigadier called John Keenan, give a revealing glimpse into the peacekeeping efforts during those terrifying months. 'Panic reigns everywhere,' he wrote to his wife Maisie.

> Muslims and Sikhs are killing each other like flies. Being a woman or child does not save you. Of course, Lahore and Amritsar are far and away the worst, but it's pretty widespread … We are all longing for the boundary award to be announced and get it over.[9]

Born in Bangalore and having grown up in Rangoon, Keenan belonged to a family of Irish Catholics who had migrated to India five generations earlier. The family felt it ironic that 'colonised Irishmen became part of the colonisation of India',[10] continuing to serve with the British government even after the founding of the Irish Republic. Keenan himself excelled in bayonet fencing, gymnastics and 'Roman Urdu', all apparently crucial for a job in the army. Working under the command of Major-General Rees and two advisers (one of whom, Ayub Khan, would later stage the first military coup in Pakistan's history), he was put in charge of keeping the peace in three heavily disputed districts – Montgomery, Ferozepore and Lahore.

This, he soon learned, was easier said than done. Sikhs refused to give up their *kirpan* knives for religious reasons, and in response many Muslims insisted on keeping knives themselves. 'I have never felt the animosity between Muslims and Sikhs more in all my service in India,' Keenan wrote to his wife Maisie just a few days after his appointment.

> In Lahore, despite the presence of about six [Battalions] ... tanks, thousands of sappers and what not, the Muslims are slowly but steadily killing all Hindus and Sikhs who take their toll of Muslims. You see men dressed in green and white, trained Muslim Leaguers and 'soldiers' of Pakistan, waging war against the Sikhs, burning and looting day and night. Two hundred dead Sikhs were found on Lahore station platform night before last. They say – and I believe it – Muslim police did this ... Exactly the opposite is happening in Amritsar where the Sikhs are more numerous and have the upper hand. They are butchering every Muslim they can.[11]

Amid all of this, Nehru's home minister Sardar Patel was convinced 'the only way to re-establish a decent relationship between the Muslims and non-Muslim communities was to remove Hindus and Sikhs from Pakistan and drive out the Muslims of the East Punjab'.[12] Patel continued to monitor the situation through the Intelligence Bureau and in mid-August he was reported saying that 'Hindustan could quickly make an end of its Muslim inhabitants if Pakistan did not behave'.[13] Jinnah, certainly, was convinced Patel's grip on the intelligence services was total, and that provocative anti-Muslim leaders were only out of jail thanks to him.

As far as Keenan was concerned, however, it was Mountbatten, 'the Fairy Prince', who was most responsible for the chaos. 'I have no great admiration of LL Mountbatten,' he wrote to Maisie after a meeting with the Viceroy.

> He bitched this show with his acceleration and I am told he did it deliberately. Wavell, the honest, God-fearing soldier, said he wanted two years, but Nehru, scared stiff that Labour would be

defeated and Churchill come back, urged immediate action which Mountbatten implemented. Now everyone curses Mountbatten for all this chaos, including the Indian politicians.[14]

Little did Keenan know that Mountbatten was about to cause even more chaos. On 12 August Radcliffe finally finished drawing his line and in the hours that followed he burned all his papers, refused his fee of forty thousand rupees and fled the subcontinent, writing:[15] 'Nobody in India will love me for the award about the Punjab and Bengal, and there will be roughly 80 million people with a grievance who will begin looking for me. I do not want them to find me.'[16] Now, in yet another callous decision, Mountbatten ordered the borderline's announcement be released a few days *after* independence, in order to 'divert odium from the British'.[17] So it was that on the stroke of the midnight hour on 14–15 August 1947, Indian and Pakistani independence arrived before anyone knew where the border between the two actually lay.

A day before independence, the Mountbattens flew south to the seaside city of Karachi, which had been chosen as Pakistan's new capital – partly because no one knew which others would be included in the new nation. Muslims from across the subcontinent had gathered there to celebrate the country's independence and Governor's House had been 'decked up to look just like a Hollywood film-set' for the occasion.[18] A monocled Jinnah awaited the Viceregal couple at the entrance, standing cheerily beside his sister Fatima, but without his daughter Dina, who had decided to remain in India with her Parsi husband after Partition.

Remarkably, the province of Sindh where Karachi was located had seen none of the violence that was tearing North India apart. There were, of course, tensions between locals and North Indian migrants, but virtually the entire minority populations were still in situ. Indeed Jinnah had set the tone two days earlier with a surprising speech by announcing to Karachi's minorities:

> You are free to go to your temples, you are free to go to your mosques or to any other place of worship in Pakistan. You may belong to any religion or caste or creed – that has nothing to do with the business of the state.

It remains contested whether the speech proves that Jinnah wanted Pakistan to be a secular country or whether he just meant to persuade the Indian government to ensure the welfare of Indian Muslims, but whatever the case the atmosphere in Karachi when Mountbatten arrived was one of expectant optimism.[19] Hopeful speeches about the future were made at a banquet that evening, and afterwards 'a band of bearded warriors in kilts' played 'sweet music' to the gathered dignitaries. Only Alan Campbell-Johnson noticed Jinnah, dressed in a pearl white *ashkan*, cutting a 'lonely figure', 'towering above his guests, and talking to very few' of them. 'I had never dreamt,' Campbell-Johnson later wrote, 'that the creator of a nation at the moment of reaching the promised land could, when surrounded by his devoted followers, be at such a distance from them.'[20]

Jinnah's attitude may have been affected by his daughter Dina's refusal to migrate to Pakistan. He had last seen her a year earlier and although neither knew it, they would never meet again.[21] Like so many families, the Jinnahs would be divided by Partition. With Dina absent from his celebration party, Jinnah's only commiseration was the following letter:

My darling Papa,
First of all I must congratulate you – you got Pakistan ... how hard you have worked for it ... I do hope you are keeping well – I get lots of news of you from the local newspapers in Bombay ... Are you coming back here? ... Take care of yourself Papa darling.
  Lots of love & kisses,
  Dina[22]

The next day, 14 August, Karachi prepared for the birth of Pakistan – despite the new government having yet to secure the accession of even a single princely state and still unaware of which parts of Punjab or Bengal would become part of the new nation.* On the very morning before independence, Pakistani officials therefore had no idea

---

* Of course, Pakistan's leaders had not been pushing the matter. Several princes had reached out to discuss their accession in the summer prior to Partition, but had been ordered to stop by Jinnah. Several princes, particularly the princely states on the North-West Frontier, had already indicated their intention to join Pakistan.

where their new country's borders would be, or which countries they would border.[23] Nonetheless, every inch of the shell-shaped Legislative Assembly was soon occupied, and after a rousing speech from Jinnah, Campbell-Johnson noticed 'Lady Mountbatten press Miss [Fatima] Jinnah's hand affectionately'. Ignoring warnings of an assassination attempt, the Mountbattens and the Jinnahs went in an open car through the city, and after greeting 'lorry-loads' of ecstatic sailors from the new Pakistani Navy, the quartet reached Governor's House in one piece. 'Thank God I have brought you back alive,' laughed an unusually jovial Jinnah.[24]

That evening Anglo-Indian swing artist Ken Mac performed for delegates of the Karachi Club, while the Mountbattens said their goodbyes.[25] Campbell-Johnson accompanied the family back to Delhi, and while flying over Punjab, he spotted 'several large fires' from the window, 'beacons of ill-omen dominating the landscape for miles around'. But the day's busy schedule didn't allow him to dwell on the matter too much, because from the moment the plane touched down in Delhi he had to organise a press release. 'The Viceregal machine in the task of dismantling itself was at full pitch to the end,' he wrote proudly in his memoir.[26]

Mountbatten, by contrast, had a more relaxed evening, settling down in his sandstone palace with Edwina to watch the new Bob Hope movie, *My Favourite Brunette*. After congratulating himself for having wrapped up centuries of British imperialism in less than seventy-five days, he paced around his office trying to decide how to use his last few moments as 'the most powerful man on earth'.[27] Finally, at 11.58 p.m., he decided to grant the title 'her highness' to the Nawab of Palampur's Australian wife. It would be his final act as Viceroy.

A short distance away in India's new Constituent Assembly, Nehru was already rising to his feet to make a speech. 'Long years ago, we made a tryst with destiny,' he exclaimed.

> And now the time comes when we shall redeem our pledge, not wholly or in full measure, but very substantially. At the stroke of the midnight hour, when the world sleeps, India will awake to life and freedom. A moment comes, which comes but rarely in history, when we step out from the old to the new, when an age ends, and when the soul of a nation, long suppressed, finds utterance.[28]

Moments later the British Empire had lost four-fifths of its population, and India and Pakistan were free.

Minutes after independence, Nehru and Rajendra Prasad, the president of the Constituent Assembly, arrived at the former Viceroy's office and invited Mountbatten to be the country's first governor general. He duly accepted. Across the new but still undefined border, however, it was Jinnah who became Pakistan's first governor general. So it was that Mountbatten's partiality towards India finally became a point of state duty.

The next day Delhi was filled with rejoicing. Nehru and the Mountbattens distributed sweets in Roshanara Park, and over a banquet that evening Nehru gave a toast to the king he had just secured independence from.[29] Schools across the country held sports days and in Shantiniketan Amartya Sen won a sack race – the height of his sporting career.[30] 'In city after city,' wrote one observer,

> lusty crowds have burst the bottled-up frustrations of many years in an emotional mass jag. Mob sprees have rolled from mill districts to gold coasts and back again ... [T]he happy, infectious celebrations blossomed in forgetfulness of the decades of sullen resentment against all that was symbolized by a sahib's sun-topi.[31]

Celebrations were even held in places no longer attached to the Indian Empire. In Aden an Indian tricolour flag was unfurled in the compound Gandhi had visited sixteen years earlier, while in Kuwait the flags of both India and Pakistan were raised above the Persian Gulf agency.[32]

Not everyone was celebrating, however. In the Patkai Hills, Angami Zapu Phizo spent the day drafting letters to foreign diplomatic missions requesting recognition of Nagaland's independence.[33] Gandhi, meanwhile, was fasting with Suhrawardy in Calcutta, appealing for an end to Partition's bloodshed. 'Do you wish to hold a celebration in the midst of this devastation?' he spat.[34]

Although often forgotten, several hundred princely states also celebrated their own, completely separate, independence. Only a hundred and thirty-six of them had signed an instrument of accession by Independence Day, so those that had not thus technically became independent. Although none had gained international recognition, the 15th of August saw the birth of over three hundred new countries from the wreckage of the Indian Empire, not just India and Pakistan. Their newfound freedom proved a bureaucratic nightmare, however, and in Orissa the 150-mile journey from Cuttack to Sambalpur suddenly required permits for three separate countries.[35] Moreover, it meant that even two months later there was still 'no map in existence of the whole of the subcontinent as divided between India and Pakistan', because displaying the princely states as separate would be to recognise their independence as legitimate.[36]

There were thus numerous different ways that independence was experienced, and not just the images of cheering nationalist crowds that we often imagine. Indeed, many people didn't even realise that British rule had ended. M. P. Mariappan, the man who had walked from Burma to India, recalled that:

> When India got its independence one day in 1947, I didn't know this had happened ... I wasn't reading the papers at the time, and no one told me anything about this event ... That day, like every other day, I spent doing business.[37]

Those living in the borderlands could not afford such a luxury. Although it was presumed that Lahore would become part of Pakistan, no one actually knew for certain, and Fikr Taunsvi found himself roaming the city's streets in a strange frenzy. Eventually he met up with his friend Mumtaz and, sitting together on a *charpoy* smoking cigarettes, all he could think about was how all the 'gods were running away':[38] idols were being taken to safety by their devotees in case the city ended up in Pakistan. The process was being repeated across the country: a Digambar idol from Multan was taken to Delhi's Lal Mandir for safety; a Gopinath idol from Dera Ghazi Khan was removed to Vrindavan; and Dacca's 'Dhakeshwari' idol was spirited off to Calcutta. The largest migration in human history had begun and even the gods were on the move.

Partitioning India's fluid religious landscape on the basis of religion would lead to violence on an epic scale, as unexpected as it was brutal. As Punjab descended into a mutual genocide, in the coming months tens of millions of people would be displaced across religious lines, creating ripples of mass sectarian violence and an overwhelming refugee crisis. Between one million and three million people would perish in the process, and many more would be subject to massacres, forced conversions and sexual violence. Pakistan emptied of Hindus and Sikhs, while the enormous Muslim community that remained in India were turned into political pariahs, their loyalty forever questioned. The Great Partition of British India would be the single most important 'historical event in twentieth-century South Asia', one that continues to inform how a quarter of the world 'envisage their past, present and future'.[39]

Two days after independence, as the first British troops sailed away from India, Taunsvi and Mumtaz huddled around a radio to listen to the broadcast of the Radcliffe Line. When it was revealed that Lahore had become part of Pakistan after all, they went outside to see 'crescent flags of freedom' waving all down the street.[40] Mumtaz bought a map from the market and together the two friends drew out the new borderline on it, trying to visualise what it actually meant. After a few seconds Mumtaz realised his hometown Batala had become part of India rather than Pakistan. 'It was as if a great wave of tears had risen in Mumtaz's throat,' recalled Taunsvi in his diary that evening. 'He was shouting himself hoarse ... wondering how Batala, with a population of 80 per cent Muslims, could go to India.'[41] And all the while Taunsvi wondered how Nankana Sahib, the birthplace of Sikhism, had ended up in Pakistan.

Similar scenes repeated themselves across the borderlands. In the Bengali city of Murshidabad, where Muslims, Hindus and Jains had raised the Pakistani flag on the city gates, Indian forces arrived to replace it with an Indian one instead.[42] Along the Burmese border, the Buddhist-majority population of the Chittagong Hill Tracts were shocked to learn that their land had become part of Pakistan, despite a meagre 2 per cent of its population being Muslim. Indeed, Radcliffe's border left a remarkable 42 per cent of Bengal's non-Muslims in Pakistan, ensuring, in the words of one historian, 'that the political fiasco that had prompted Partition in the first place – the inability to overcome communalist politics – was set to carry on'.[43]

The new border forged its way through rivers, mountains and jungles where no one had any idea about the fraught politics of

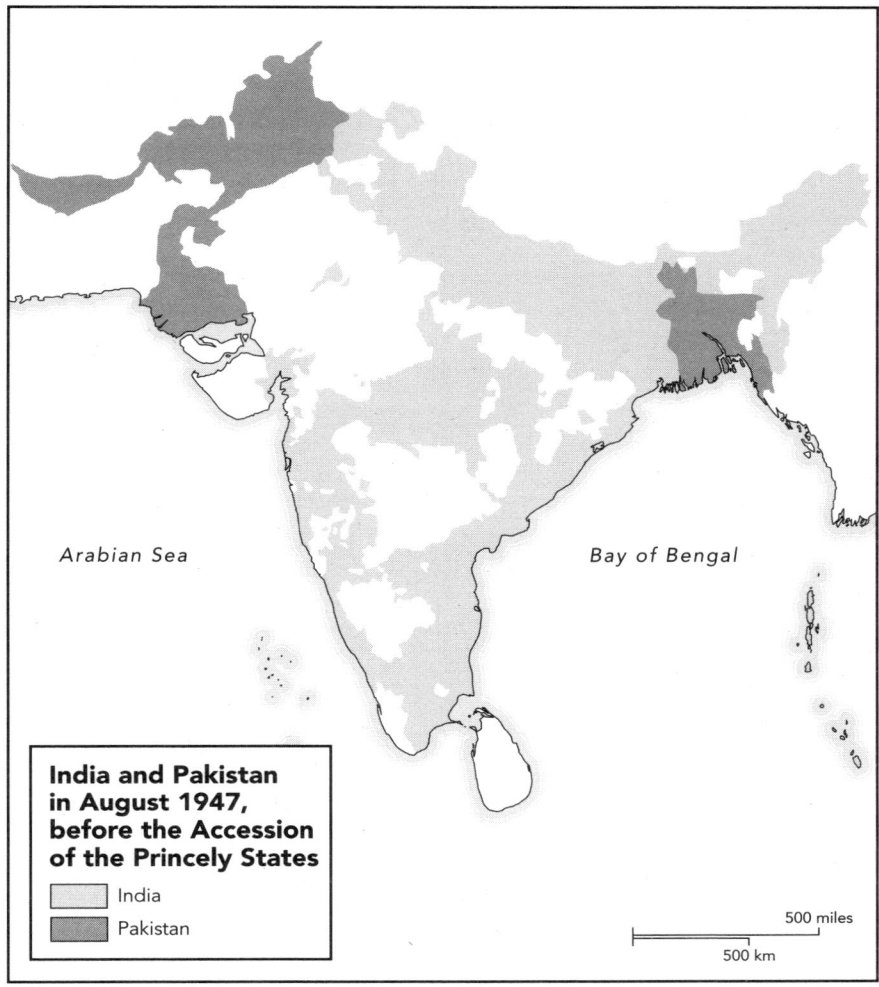

India and Pakistan in August 1947, before the Accession of the Princely States
India
Pakistan

Partition. Amid bucolic mango groves, scarlet *krishnachura* blossom and ponds of clustered water lilies, the line sliced in half the medieval city of Gaur, where Bengali identity had first crystallised centuries earlier. Around 1500, Gaur had been the fifth most populous city on the planet, and throughout the colonial period it had been one of the most iconic and popular tourist sites in India.[44] After 1947, however, Gaur would simply fall off the map. It being evenly divided between Hindus and Muslims, Radcliffe's Bengal Boundary Commission had decided to make the sloping terracotta ramparts of the Kotwali Gate into the border of India and East Pakistan, so that the royal inner city fell in India and the suburbs landed in Pakistan. The greatest city of medieval

Bengal – a central symbol of Bengali identity – had itself been partitioned.

The new geography of the subcontinent was bizarre, and overnight India's Northeast was transformed into a uniquely tenuous geographical oddity, only connected to the rest of the country by a ten-kilometre strip of land that would become known as 'the chicken's neck'. Pakistan appeared even stranger, with the eastern and western halves separated by over a thousand miles of hostile Indian territory. In the words of Salman Rushdie, the newly born nation was a 'fantastic bird of a place, two wings without a body, sundered by the land-mass of its greatest foe, joined by nothing but God'.[45]

Paranoia was rife. Delhi politicians voiced concerns about the 'Rangoon Precedent' of political assassination, and many leaders were worried the partitioned Indian military – still led by British officers – could easily overthrow the new Indian or Pakistani governments.[46] All the while the police and the Indian Army were still in the process of being divided, and one soldier would claim he had 'a bigger fight getting through Pakistan' than he 'ever had in the war fighting the Germans'.[47] This ensured that apart from the Punjab Boundary Force and a few Nepali Gurkhas who were seen as neutral, there were few men available to keep the peace. John Keenan wrote to his wife:

> Firing a village is a normal occurrence like having breakfast, murder is like having a cigarette, and on the long trails to the main roads, you see everything from headless corpses and maimed women and butchered children to smouldering bullock carts and other property, marking the way ... I tell you, darling, it is sheer hell, and I have never conceived of such sufferings as I have witnessed ... I don't think there is a parallel in history of two communities as numerous as these two (Hindus and Muslims) just going at each other with hammer and tongs ... The misery just makes one feel devastated and one's thoughts are of God and one's prayers are for mercy to suffering mankind.[48]

As clumsily improvised borders were hastily branded onto the landscape with little preparation, both Congress and the Muslim League issued plea after plea for people to stay put. Instead millions began to flee their homes. The Ministry of Rehabilitation soon estimated that a million people had migrated across the Radcliffe Line and by the end of the year the number was closer to twenty million – more than the combined populations of Ireland, Greece, Iraq and Afghanistan. Refugee caravans called *kafilas* stretched for fifty miles across Punjab, the longest consisting of forty thousand people and taking eight days to pass a single point.[49] No other migration in human history comes close.

The great migration was visible in every corner of the subcontinent. Sylheti Hindus migrated en masse to Shillong and Tripura, while Bihari and Bengali Muslims descended on the riverine fields of East Bengal. Gujarati Muslims sailed for Sindh, and Sindhi Hindus fled for Bombay. Decisions to migrate were never simple, nor did they necessarily fall neatly down the religious divide. Sometimes the choice was driven by ethnic cleansing while at others by a millenarian desire for a religious homeland. For many Dalits, migration offered a liberating change of status, and some Muslims, like the grandfather of Bollywood star Shah Rukh Khan, migrated to India out of the desire to live in a secular state. Whatever their reasons, by train, plane, bus, boat, steamer, camel, bicycle and bullock cart, millions of people fled their homes, and as one woman observed:

> The strangest thing was that we never realised … when India ended and Pakistan began. There were no obvious differences between one land and its conjoined neighbour, and so I suspect that we gained our new citizenship in a moment curiously lost on us. Tucked away in a corner of an overcrowded train, we had quietly become Pakistani.[50]

South Asia's religious, ethnic and linguistic make-up irrevocably changed. Punjabi banks and law firms had tended to be run by Hindus while Punjabi mechanics and railway engineers tended to be Muslim, and with the exodus of these communities, entire professions disappeared from cities. In Delhi the same medieval fortress that had so recently hosted the Asian Relations Conference was transformed into a refugee camp for fifty thousand of the city's Muslims, awaiting transfer to Pakistan.[51] The Delhi novelist Ahmed Ali would later lament how his city's language shrank after Partition. 'All that made Delhi special has been uprooted and dispersed,' he said. 'So many words are lost.'[52]

If the refugee crisis was staggering in size, so were the attempts to rehabilitate the refugees. In some cases these were small family-led initiatives. Uttam Singh, the Sikh miner from Bawdwin, witnessed the great migration from his ancestral village, and his son took to smuggling medicine and supplies to Muslim children hiding in the sugarcane fields behind his house.[53] On other occasions organisations like the RSS, the Jamat-i-Islami and the Communist Party of India took the lead in distributing aid. Nonetheless, lacking any coordination, these efforts were often unable to help those who needed it most. 'Rescue vans would come and go and we wouldn't even get to know,' recalls Musarrat Abrar, a teenage girl from Gurdaspur who had migrated to Pakistan. 'People from the surrounding areas would come and distribute food to us, but that too stopped eventually.'[54]

In Punjab many refugee trains were attacked on route so that they crossed the new border dripping with blood and packed with corpses. Such was the scale of the violence there that within just two days of independence the new prime ministers of India and Pakistan were forced to agree to a wholesale exchange of populations in Punjab.[55] Yet so overwhelming was the refugee crisis that within a month Pakistani prime minister Liaquat Ali Khan began to protest that Pakistan simply did not have the space for all South Asian Muslims. 'While Pakistan is willing to provide refuge to Muslims,' he declared, 'it does not want that Muslims from regions other than East Punjab leave their *watan* [homeland] and property and come to Pakistan ... The Partition of the country was done on the principle that minorities would remain in their regions.'[56]

This was a dramatic volte-face for the leader of a self-proclaimed homeland of Indian Muslims. But times were desperate and Pakistan was born into a state of emergency facing the worst refugee crisis in history. The boundary commission had awarded it few major cities, not a single currency mint and only a fraction of the Raj's bureaucratic machinery. Much of the administration functioned from shipping containers, and East Pakistan had received only one Bengali member of the former Indian Civil Service. Perhaps the most remarkable thing about the new nation of Pakistan was that it survived at all.[57]

Even in the far south of the subcontinent, the violent convulsions of Partition often felt scarily close to home. With the railways incapacitated, letters frequently arrived weeks late, leaving millions of divided families waiting anxiously for news of their loved ones' safety. When news did come, it often left a deep impact. Brigid Keenan, John's eight-year-old daughter, was staying with her mother in the Nilgiri Hills, and vividly remembers a letter from her father describing how all the refugees carried

> light quilts known as razais in India – which they let fall when attacked or collapsing from hunger, exhaustion or illness, so that in places the whole landscape was patterned with these colourful cotton bedcovers trodden into the dust, or later the mud. Of all the horrors Dad describes, somehow the image of those thousands of abandoned quilts – and what they represent – is the one that I cannot shake from my mind.[58]

'In this land once called India,' wrote the acclaimed Urdu writer Saadat Hasan Manto,

> such rivers of blood have flowed over the past few months that even the heavens are bewildered ... Before our eyes lie dried tracks of blood, cut up human parts, charred faces, mangled necks, terrified people, looted houses, burned fields, mountains of rubble, and overflowing hospitals. We are free. Hindustan is free. Pakistan is free, and we are walking the desolate streets naked without any possessions in utter distress.[59]

A Kashmiri living in Bombay, Manto had grown up in the revolutionary heartlands of Punjab and spent his schooldays flying kites and playing practical jokes. He was a member of Amritsar's 'Free Thinkers' circle, a group who were required to 'make a fool of someone once a month',[60] and as a teenager he had got into a bar fight after trying to persuade a photographer that the Lahore traffic police wore coats made of ice. Nonetheless, it was through this association that he developed relationships on Punjab's literary circuit and imbibed a fascination for the absurd contradictions of everyday life. At university he began translating Russian and French novels into Urdu, obsessing over Chekhov, Oscar Wilde and Mirza Ghalib, and had eventually made a name for himself by exposing the dark hypocrisies of Indian society in his stories.

One day, as his wife travelled to Lahore in order to prepare for a family wedding, Manto found himself gripped by anxiety about her safety. The atmosphere of thick communal suspicion had reached Bombay itself, and Manto was horrified by his work colleagues' sudden change in attitude. 'If communal hatreds were poisoning even this haven of sophisticates, breaking up old collaborators because of religions that they barely practised, perhaps, he felt, the Bombay he loved was over.'[61]

Like many of those who eventually made their way across the new border, Manto had never intended to migrate to Pakistan. 'Despite trying, I could not separate India from Pakistan, and Pakistan from India,' he wrote. 'When I think of the recovered women, I think only of their bloated bellies – what will happen to those bellies?' Will they 'belong to Pakistan or Hindustan?'[62]

Manto's closest friends were Hindus, yet such friendships proved increasingly difficult. One day, while he was travelling with his Hindu friend Ashok, a Muslim wedding procession surrounded his car. Manto had a panic attack. On another occasion his friend Shyam told him that 'were it not for the fact they were friends, he would have killed Manto. The next day Manto packed his bags.'[63] Shyam tried to apologise and brought out a bottle of brandy. But instead they merely had a final emotional drink. His granddaughter writes:

> Shyam threw his arms around him and said, 'Swine'. Holding back his tears, Manto replied, 'Pakistani swine'. Shyam shouted back in earnest, 'Zindabad Pakistan'. 'Zindabad Bharat,' Manto retorted before leaving for the port to board the ship taking him to Karachi. Shyam came with him all the way to the ship's deck, telling him funny stories, as was his wont. When the gong sounded announcing the ship's departure, he ... stepped down the gangway, and walked away.[64]

'Bengal's culture, art, dance and music were divided,' wrote Fikr Taunsvi a few days after the Radcliffe Line's announcement. 'Punjab's ploughs, farming, songs and romance had been carved up.' And most curious of all, 'both Hindus and Muslims were dissatisfied'. Taunsvi's neighbourhood, Sant Nagar, was now 'adorned with big locks', put there by Hindu families who had fled their homes, and he had grown numb with the endless stories of dead, wounded and missing friends and relatives. 'Only this much?' he writes. 'Tell me some bigger news. Tell me that today there is not a single human left in the Punjab!'[65]

Monsoon downpours only added to the chaos, and when Lahore's streets flooded, cutting off the city's electricity, rumours spread that 'the Sikhs had demolished the big dam ... and had stopped the power supply'. That evening Taunsvi couldn't sleep, as shouts and screams echoed outside his window. 'Tonight, there was to be no end to the destruction of Lahore,' he scribbled in his diary. But it was all rumour. 'Neither was a dam demolished, nor had the electricity been cut. No band of Sikhs ever attacked.'[66] It was simply a monsoon flood.

Taunsvi's thoughts shifted to the refugees migrating on foot, for whom the rain would make their journeys even more perilous. Xenophobia against incomers had become common, and one day his friend Mumtaz started raving that Indian Muslims should not be allowed to 'set foot in Pakistan' because 'this is our country, not theirs'.[67] Such were the unresolved questions of Partition, that even after Pakistan had been created, many remained puzzled over who exactly it had been created for? Were the intended beneficiaries the Muslims in the Hindu-majority provinces, or the Muslims who lived in what was now Pakistan? In a strange turn of events, Taunsvi, a Hindu, found himself defending the right of Muslims to come to Pakistan, while Mumtaz, a Muslim, tried to persuade him that Punjab did not have space for all the Muslims in the world. When Mumtaz told Taunsvi that as a Hindu he shouldn't speak to him on the issue, the comment stung. Even his best friend was now speaking in terms of Hindus and Muslims.

Soon afterwards devastating news arrived that Mumtaz's son Achha had been killed by a mob of Sikhs in Batala. In shock, Taunsvi set off back to his own village to be with his wife, Kailash, and their two daughters. However, further tragedy awaited. Shortly after he arrived home, Taunsvi's neighbour Ali Mohammad Butt appeared at his door, carrying the body of Taunsvi's dead daughter. 'Forgive me, my friend,' wept Ali Mohammad. 'I did not break this branch. A harsh and rapid gust came, and she broke with a snap.'[68] Taunsvi's neighbour had killed his daughter.

His eyes wet with tears, Ali Mohammad desperately pushed his own son Rashid towards Taunsvi, crying out, 'Fling him, Fikr bhai, dash him hard on the ground, such that my sins may be forgiven! My heart may come to rest and I stand punished. Dash him, dash him, my friend!' Instead Taunsvi ended up 'comforting the killer of his own child', hugging 'the little rose-like Rashid' and urging Ali Mohammad to get treated for mental illness.[69]

For women like Taunsvi's wife Kailash and surviving daughter Rali, the breakdown of law and order was infinitely more threatening than for the men. When Taunsvi was forced to return to work in Lahore, Rali and Kailash stayed with family parents in Taunsa. But he soon began to fear for them, and sent two of his Muslim friends, Qateel and Rahi, to bring them to Lahore. Qateel and Rahi's trip across the plains was treacherous, and the ticket collector on their train checked the passengers 'not for tickets but for *kaffirs* [unbelievers]'. When they arrived in Taunsa, however, Rali and Kailash refused to go with them. 'My in-laws were amazed,' writes Taunsvi after the two men returned empty-handed. 'Qateel and Rahi were Muslims, how could I expect Rali and Kailash to be sent with them?'[70]

As the threat of abduction and sexual violence loomed, migration became a thankless task. In the coming months some seventy-five thousand women are estimated to have been abducted and subjected to sexual violence.[71]

As Punjab descended into a living hell, Bengal remained curiously calm. On 2 September, Gandhi had announced a fast to the death unless violence across Calcutta ceased. After two days without food, the violence began to ebb and Gandhi broke his fast with a glass of orange juice. Mountbatten wrote in awe, 'In the Punjab we have 55,000 soldiers and large-scale rioting on our hands ... In Bengal our forces consist of one man, and there is no rioting.'[72]

The princely states played an oft-forgotten role in curbing the migration or acting as places of refuge. Bahawalpur's administration persuaded much of the Hindu population to stay, and Jaipur's state army chief convinced its Muslim population to do the same. Most incredible of all, in Muslim-ruled Malerkotla the government – uniquely in Punjab – prevented a single communal incident taking place in the state throughout 1947.[73]

Elsewhere, however, princely administrations helped to foment violence rather than calm it. In Hyderabad State, the Nizam increasingly leaned on a Muslim paramilitary group called the Razakars to suppress pro-India agitations, while in Gwalior the Maharaja's patronage of the RSS ensured that 'hundreds of Muslims were stripped naked, identified, killed and thrown out of the trains'.[74] In Patiala the Maharaja's soldiers even threatened to 'disgrace' Muslim women if their families didn't leave.[75]

In Faridkot, where John Keenan had been charged with evacuating its sixty thousand Muslim subjects, rumours circulated that the Maharaja was distributing explosives to Sikh militias.[76] Keenan met him but afterwards wrote to his wife with disgust: 'He giggles, talks about going to England for a few days, and about his armoured cars.' Keenan tried to persuade the Maharaja to look after the Muslims for ten days until he was certain the roads and railways would 'not be molested', but a week later he came across a vast, eight-mile-long refugee Muslim *kafila* fleeing the state. It had been attacked by a mob hiding in the elephant grass, and vultures were swarming overhead, devouring the bodies of the dead. Keenan 'drove straight to Faridkot and stormed into the rajah's palace with his revolver in hand, intending to shoot him. But the rajah pleaded for his life and said he had only allowed his people to attack the refugees because they thought he was pro-Muslim and he had to prove he wasn't.'[77]

Perhaps the most controversial princely led ethnic cleansing took place in Alwar and Bharatpur, two Hindu-ruled states on the edge of Rajputana where Meo Muslims made up a quarter of the populations. Meos were officially Muslims but were frequently rejected as such by other Muslims because of their devotion to gods like Ram and Krishna. Only a few months earlier the Maharaja of Alwar had been considering accession to Pakistan, but after a Hindu nationalist was appointed prime minister of Alwar and informal adviser of Bharatpur, the two states' armies began to 'cleanse' their lands of Muslims. They started to force Meo Muslims to eat pork and leave Islam if they wanted to live, leading to around twenty thousand forced conversions and the death of some thirty thousand Muslims.[78] When a British traveller tried to give some water to a dying Muslim woman on a train platform in Alwar State, an unshaven Hindu told him, '"Don't do that, Sahib!", forced a bottle of petrol into the girl's mouth and set her alight.'[79]

According to Alwar's former army captain, an important and largely forgotten role here was played by Indian home minister Sardar Patel who gave the order to 'clear the state of Muslims' so that 'the killings of Hindus at Noakhali and Punjab' could 'be avenged'.[80] The truth of these allegations remains uncertain, but the bloodletting of Partition had certainly changed Patel, hardening him, and by late 1947 he had come to see India's Muslims as a seditious fifth column. He compared Partition to the amputation of a 'diseased limb'[81] and had become outspoken in his belief that most Muslims were 'not loyal to India' and should 'go to Pakistan'.[82]

Moreover, Patel subsequently took a central role in keeping Hindu RSS cadres out of prison. Around this time, the head of the RSS was found congratulating Hindus in areas of Delhi where the most Muslims had been massacred, while local RSS cadres were arrested for posters encouraging the massacre of 'all remaining Muslims in Delhi'. An order from Patel's office, however, swiftly ensured that all the accused were out of jail within half an hour.[83]

A month later, an intelligence report revealed an RSS plan for the 'total extermination' of Delhi's Muslims. 'According to the Sangh volunteers,' it read, 'the Muslims would quit India only when another movement for their total extermination similar to the one which was started in Delhi some time back would take place.' In the words of the diplomat Rajeshwar Dayal, the UP police chief B. B. L. Jaitley subsequently brought to light 'incontrovertible evidence of a dastardly conspiracy to create a communal holocaust throughout the western districts' of the United Provinces, collected after raids on the RSS premises. Instead of punishing the RSS, however, Patel protested to Jaitley 'that the Muslims were already against them and he did not want the Hindu public also to go against them'. He feared Nehru's cabinet included many who were sympathetic to the RSS, and alienating them risked pulling the Congress apart. Rather than ban the movement, therefore, Patel sought to divert 'the enthusiasm' of its young men 'into constructive channels'. Indeed he subsequently entrusted the RSS with managing refugee rehabilitation in Punjab, and nominated an RSS chief as the province's acting governor.[84]

To Patel the RSS were 'patriots who love their country'. To Nehru, however, they were dangerous extremists and he increasingly held them responsible for 'disturbances not only in Delhi but elsewhere'.[85] He declared that India would not become a 'Hindu Pakistan' and argued that the 'idea of a theocratic state is not only medieval but also stupid'.⁸⁶ By late September he was even lambasting Patel for placing RSS cadres in key government positions when their 'connection with disturbances' had become 'fairly well known'.⁸⁷ 'We have a great deal of evidence,' Nehru wrote:

> To show that the R.S.S. is an organisation which is of the nature of a private army and which is definitely proceeding on the strictest Nazi lines, even following the technique of organising ... It is not our desire to interfere with civil liberties. But training in arms of large numbers of persons with the obvious intention of using them is not something that can be encouraged.⁸⁸

Patel responded by attacking Nehru's conciliatory approach towards Muslim aggressors. It was the beginning of a dramatic rift between the two Congressmen.

As the chaos of Partition spread, Fikr Taunsvi finally decided to leave Lahore. News had stopped arriving from his family's village in mid-October, and one day he was nearly killed by a Muslim gangster. 'What torment, what agony is this,' Taunsvi wrote that evening. 'Am I a foreigner now? ... The mind refuses to accept that at a distance of 20 miles begins a foreign nation, an alien culture.'

Taunsvi wept with his friends the next day, and one of them, Sahir Ludhianvi, suggested one day in the future their whole group 'should meet at the Wagah border, and exchange each other's flags'. Taunsvi was taken by the romance of the idea, as were several other writers in the room. 'A storm of love had been triggered,' he felt. But on 7 November, and with still no word from his family, Taunsvi admitted himself to a refugee camp, from where the army was taking Hindu and Sikh refugees to India. Five Muslim friends came to see him off: Sahir, Arif, Rahi, Chaudhuri and Rabi. 'Comrade Fikr!' Sahir said as they reached the camp, 'I apologize on behalf of all Islam, for you could not live here.' Touched, Taunsvi threw aside his luggage and sat with his friends one last time. They talked with one another for over an hour, as the increasingly frustrated Gurkha and 'other Hindus of the camp' glared at them, 'rubbing their eyes and wondering how this newly admitted Hindu had developed such trust with these Muslims'. Eventually, the Gurkha told Taunsvi to get on his way and so he was forced to cross a line beyond which his Muslim friends were not allowed to step.[89]

The refugee camp thronged with people, and an old woman was crying, 'I don't want to go to young India! Bring me my little one! My babe!'[90] Four soldiers were carrying corpses on a stretcher, and another was having a fight with the camp barber for trimming his moustache in the wrong way. And in the middle of it all, Taunsvi sat in bewilderment, preparing to leave the land of his youth for one just twenty miles away. The next morning a truck evacuated Fikr Taunsvi to Amritsar, where he was allotted a tent in Khalsa College Camp.

Around him everyone was hanging up lights to celebrate Diwali and by chance he came across a cousin who told him his wife and daughter had also safely crossed to a refugee camp in Ambala a few days earlier. That evening 'the camp was glittering with the light of lamps' and Taunsvi's mind turned to the future. 'Where will we go now?' he wondered silently.[91]

9

Into the Abyss

The relationship between India and Pakistan was, from the moment of their birth, a difficult one. By the end of the Indian Empire's third partition, the Great Partition of India and Pakistan, their leaders resented one another, and their civilians were murdering one another. However, by the end of the Indian Empire's fourth partition, the Partition of Princely India, the two countries would finally go to war.

By late September numerous princely states had acceded to India but not a single one had successfully joined Pakistan. Indeed, since India had secured the accessions of Bikaner, Jodhpur and Cutch, a lack of contiguity had made accession to Pakistan impossible for most, a fact made brutally clear when the tiny state of Dujana outside Delhi became the only princely state to be rejected by Pakistan. Punjab's smallest princely state, Dujana was a collection of thirty villages, a small walled town and a hundred square miles of mustard fields and eucalyptus trees. It had seen little communal violence and the boundaries between its religious communities were remarkably blurred. But when nearby Gurgaon descended into fully fledged ethnic cleansing, a mob crossed into the state to attack the town's Muslims.

The violence that accompanied Partition is often described as 'medieval', and in Dujana it literally took the form of a siege. A mob attempted to break down the gate, but a local soldier called Halvidar Singh climbed onto the old battlements and fired the great medieval cannons at them. The attackers scattered and in the aftermath Dujana's Muslim community fled to Lahore in the Nawab's personal train.[1] While in Pakistan he offered his accession to Pakistan, but as the secretary of Pakistan's Princely State Department would later write, 'His accession could not be accepted ... We could not possibly accept the accession of a state next door to the capital of India.'[2] Rejected, the Nawab of Dujana was forced to join India instead.[3]

Ironically, however, Jinnah would accept his first accession from another non-contiguous state only a few days later on 15 September 1947. Like Dujana, Junagadh State was surrounded by Indian territory. But unlike Dujana, Junagadh was on the Gujarati coastline. Welcoming this state would nearly send him to war with India.

Junagadh was not a famous princely state. It had neither the romance of Kashmir, nor the opulent wealth of Hyderabad, yet it was close to the ancestral homes of Gandhi, Jinnah and Patel, and so loomed large in the imaginations of all three. The fourth largest Muslim-ruled state in the Raj, it lay in a fertile alluvial landscape of cashew, tobacco and castor farms on the edge of the Arabian Sea on India's west coast, and had strong maritime ties with both Aden and Rangoon.[4] One of the Nawab of Junagadh's vassals – the ruler of Mangrol – was even an Arab Sheikh.

The region was mostly flat but at its centre lay Girnar, an extinct volcano and ancient Jain pilgrimage site, at the base of which, through a faux-Mughal gateway, stood Junagadh city, a Gujarati-speaking town of French Gothic and Mughal baroque, with pointed arches and clustered columns that wouldn't feel out of place in Chartres. Here one of the great spectacles of twentieth-century South Asian history was about to play out, laying the groundwork for the Kashmir dispute, the annexation of Hyderabad and the ongoing insurgency in Baluchistan.[5]

The life of the last Nawab, Mahabat Khanji III, has been clouded by seventy-five years of mythmaking aimed at ridiculing the ruler and undermining his hugely consequential decision. Today he is remembered in India mostly as 'a vaguely ridiculous character',[6] whose eight hundred pedigree dogs each had a private servant. Every time one of the dogs died, so the story goes, Junagadh State went into mourning, playing Chopin's Funeral March in the streets. Moreover he is said to have drained the state's entire treasury in 'marriage parties' for his precious pooches, one of which cost £60,000 and was attended by fifty thousand people 'not counting the dogs'.[7] The most lavish of these apparently saw his favourite dog Roshana 'scented and jewelled in an ornate coat' and carried on a silver palanquin to marry a British Labrador called Bobby, who was wearing 'gold bracelets, gold necklace, and embroidered silk cummerbund'. The two dogs were wed atop elephants in a ceremony conducted by Hindu priests.[8]

Recent scholarship, however, has revealed much of this wonderful story to be exaggerated. The Nawab was certainly obsessed with dogs – his whippet kennels and dog racetrack both survive, and a portrait of him sitting beside a bejewelled hound hangs in Junagadh's museum to this day. Yet the story of Bobby and Roshana is entirely fictional, and probably originates from a local tradition of marrying two dogs before a royal wedding to remove unwanted *nazar* [evil eye]. The elephants, the number of guests and the cost of the wedding all appear to be apocryphal.*

Indeed, the Nawab was a more fascinating figure than he is often given credit for. His dynasty was responsible for saving the Asiatic lion from extinction, and at the time he was regarded as one of the region's more progressive rulers. He established a multi-faith court, a semi-welfare state and free primary education for all. He banned the slaughter of cows, pioneered animal conservation, and his ancestral hunting grounds are today the only place outside of Africa where lions roam free in the wild.[9] Yet his final act as ruler, to try and merge his Hindu-majority state with Pakistan, would overshadow all these achievements.

There is evidence he initially intended to join India, but he began to change his mind when his Diwan (prime minister) convinced him 'the Congress would kill off his beloved dogs ... curb his passion for cruel

---

* Remarkably few authors writing on the downfall of princely India appear to have ever visited Junagadh. Its archives await proper study and even brilliant and thorough scholars like Ramachandra Guha and Srinath Raghavan have uncritically parroted the claims about the Nawab of Junagadh's dogs. Reference to the story can first be found in Menon's autobiography and appears to have been embroidered over the years until it reached its final form in the account of Diwan Jermani Dass, a man who may have never actually been to Junagadh. Rather than an oriental character from the annals of Victorian make-believe, Junagadhi scholar Praduman Khachar argues, Mahabat Khanji III should instead be understood as a belligerent Europhile obsessed with whippet racing. A similar conclusion was reached by author Divyabhanusinh after interviewing many residents of Junagadh. See Khachar, P., *Sorath Sarkar: Nawab Mahabatkhanji* (2012) and Divyabhanusinh, *The Story of Asia's Lions* (Navi Mumbai: Marg Publications, 2008).

sports, ration his concubines and rationalize the Gir lions'.[10] The final decision came when his Diwan was replaced by Shahnawaz Bhutto, a knighted Sindhi aristocrat who strutted around in western suits. Bhutto 'loved the women and he loved drink,' recalled one retired police inspector years later. 'He had the money and he spent it.'[11] With Jinnah's personal reassurance that 'Pakistan [would] not allow Junagadh to be stormed and tyrannised', Bhutto convinced the Nawab to accede to Pakistan instead of India.[12] This political coup would change the face of the subcontinent and help transform the Bhutto family into Pakistan's most prominent political dynasty.[13]

Had the Nawab of Junagadh succeeded in joining Pakistan, almost 5 per cent of modern Gujarat would today be Pakistani territory. But from the outset the Indian government was eager to prevent this from happening. They first learned of Junagadh's accession to Pakistan in the newspapers, and their outrage was palpable. Junagadh was 82 per cent Hindu, surrounded by India on three sides, and contained two of Hinduisms most sacred pilgrimage sites – Somnath and Dwarka. Indeed, Bhutto himself noted that 'in the estimation of our non-Muslim people, Junagadh is considered the most sacred place after Kashi [Varanasi]'.[14] As far as India's leaders were concerned, Junagadh belonged firmly 'inside Indian territory'.[15]

The essential question, of course, was whether the Muslim ruler of Junagadh had the right to make his Hindu-majority state a part of Pakistan. And if so, what did that mean for other states with rulers of a different religion to their subjects? Kashmir State, for example, was 77 per cent Muslim but had a Hindu Maharaja, while Hyderabad State was overwhelmingly Hindu but with a Muslim Nizam. Until this point everyone had generally assumed that states would join the country of their majority religion. But if the Nawab of Junagadh was allowed to join Pakistan, anything was possible.

India responded with aggression. Within two days India's home minister Sardar Patel had sent a 'Kathiawar Defence Force' to surround Junagadh and maintain 'law and order'.[16] He swiftly enforced a blockade, stopped coal or petrol from entering state borders and ordered his Communications Department 'to tap all trunk calls and telegraphic messages from Junagadh to outside'.[17] The state's economy shattered, and when riots broke out across its cities, many Hindus began leaving. At precisely the same time, Muslims from elsewhere in Gujarat started crossing into Junagadh to seek shelter within its borders, while Bhutto wired increasingly distressed messages to Jinnah about Indian subterfuge 'both inside [the state] and out'. Jinnah, in turn, warned Mountbatten that 'any encroachment of Junagadh's sovereignty' would be considered 'a hostile act' against his country.[18] The stage was set for a confrontation.

To try to defuse the situation, India's indentured labourer-turned civil servant V. P. Menon 'started by car for Junagadh on 19 September'. He records in his memoir:

> As we proceeded on our way, I could feel the interlacing of jurisdiction which made Kathiawar such a veritable jigsaw puzzle. For a few miles, because we were in the territory of some progressive ruler like Gondal, who kept his state roads in good condition, it would be a comfortable ride, but then the car would plough through bumpy stretches and one gathered at once that this must be the territory of some other ruler who had neglected his roads. Every few miles I would see carters, who were carrying goods to the ports, paying tolls and customs duties, and who were being harassed by State officials all along the route.[19]

Pulling into Junagadh palace, Menon was greeted by Shahnawaz Bhutto. But Bhutto regretted to inform him that the Nawab was ill so could not possibly meet him. When Menon asked to see the crown prince, Bhutto snubbed him again, saying that 'the prince was very busy with a cricket match'.[20]

Menon was forced to leave empty-handed, but he had a plan up his sleeve. Junagadh had four vassal states whose status had never quite been worked out; 'ridiculous little principalities', in the words of Mountbatten's chief of staff, 'with a total annual revenue about large enough to keep a sparrow'.[21] Menon now decided to use the confusion over the vassals' status to his advantage.

His first step was to bribe one of them, Mangrol, into acceding to India. In exchange Menon offered the Mangrol Sheikh recognition that his state was independent of Junagadh. The ruler accepted, but within two hours tried to retract the accession. Menon and the Indian government, however, regarded the deed as done. The increasingly paranoid

Nawab of Junagadh then sent troops into another vassal state, Babariawad, to stop its ruler doing the same, while simultaneously yet another vassal state, Manavadar, attempted to accede to Pakistan as well, independently of the Nawab.[22] By the last week of September no one was quite sure what was going on and which parts of the state belonged to who.

Outside the state, meanwhile, Gandhi's cousin Shyamaldas established a rogue new 'government-in-exile', and after meeting with Menon began receiving funds through the Congress Party of Bombay. A few days later his men broke into the Nawab of Junagadh's palace in Rajkot and after 'a couple dozen of the Nawab's mystified servants were taken into custody', they erected the Indian flag on the rooftop.[23] Soon Shyamaldas' provisional government had made contact with student activist groups across the state. 'Our sabotage consisted of spreading false rumours to cause panic, and supplying information back to the provisional government,' remembers Krishnakant Vakharia, who was a student at the time.[24] Even younger students got involved, and Dhirubhai Ambani – later to become the richest man in Asia – remembers being 'carried away by the fervour of student activists around him' and selling *bhajiyas* at school to raise funds for the provisional government.

All the while disagreements between the Nawab and Bhutto escalated.[25] Shyamaldas' provisional government started to 'capture' villages, and a political group called the Rajkot Hindu Sabha took to making provocative speeches in 'liberated' villages.[26] The Indian government itself was divided over what to do with regard to these 'unauthorized captures' and Muslim refugees flooded into Junagadh city from outlying villages.[27]

The Nawab seems to have realised around this time that Pakistan was not coming to his aid. Finally, on 24 October 1947, he decided to speak to Jinnah, and after ordering Bhutto to use 'judicious discretion ... to avoid bloodshed of my beloved subjects',[28] he climbed aboard his private Dakota aeroplane and flew away from Junagadh for the last time. Before boarding, the Nawab had looked tearfully towards Girnar mountain and muttered, 'Who will protect my lions now?'[29] He had dedicated much of his reign to preserving the animals, but in his absence rival princelings from neighbouring states would set out to try their luck in hunting the famed beasts. A wholescale killing of the big cats ensued, just a month before an ancient depiction of the lions was made into the national emblem of the Republic of India.*

Over the years the Nawab's departure has generated many rumours, and most accounts have him abandoning one of his wives so that her seat on the plane could be taken by one of his beloved canines. According to Mahabat Khanji's grandson, however, his only companions that day were his greyhound Crystal and his Goan cook Eugene Fernandes. Mahabat Khanji had not meant to flee but to garner support from Jinnah, and it was only when it became clear that Pakistan was refusing to provide military support that he organised for his family to join him in secret. His son and heir Dilawar was abruptly woken by state officials a few days later and flown to join the Nawab in Karachi.[30] Bhutto, meanwhile, was left in charge.

When news got out that even the Nawab's family had left, however, Hindus seized the opportunity to take revenge, massacring Muslim communities who had earlier threatened them.[31] Junagadh's ruling class scattered.

Until this point Shakira Afzal remembers being largely oblivious to events going on around her. Her memories of the turbulent months of independence mainly revolved around going to primary school and picnicking on the ramparts of Uparkot Fort. It's her mother's singing that comes to mind, the sweet mangoes of the monsoon months, and raising the Pakistani flag on 14 August 1947. The second of seven children, she had, however, noticed that her father was increasingly absent at mealtimes and no longer had the time to read them bedtime stories. Her father was the great scholar Qazi Junagadhi, one of the Nawab's closest confidants and a polyglot, fluent in French, Hindi, Urdu, Gujarati, Persian, Arabic, Sanskrit, German and English. Qazi was more interested in his studies than his official duties.[32] Nonetheless, he had become one of the most influential men in the state, at various points the mayor of Junagadh, head of the state archaeological department and president of the Jameet-ul-Musalmeen – a political

---

* Similar big cat massacres occurred after the accessions of Durgarpur and Cutch, where tigers and leopards were driven to extinction. These states had seen the two earliest successful reintroductions of large carnivores in the world. Divyabhanusinh, *The Story of Asia's Lions*, and Divyabhanusinh, 'Junagadh State and its Lions: Conservation in Princely India, 1879–1947', *Conservation & Society* 4:4 (December 2006).

organisation with ties to the Muslim League. In 1947 he had become one of the signatories on the Nawab's document of accession. 'After Nawab fled, Father came and told us that we had to leave for an unknown period,' Shakira remembers.

> Mother packed our clothes and utensils and then we drove across Junagadh: me, my father, two mothers, three siblings and one cousin. I was told we were going to the Portuguese colony of Diu, close to the southern tip of Junagadh state, rather than directly to Pakistan, because a bounty recently placed on Father's head meant that travelling overland to Karachi would be dangerous. We spent the night at Father's friends house in Kacch Mandavi, then in the early morning took a boat to Diu and sought political asylum.[33]

Qazi and his family stayed in Diu for several months, uncertain of their future, until a friend managed to organise their travel on to Karachi in a ramshackle motorboat. There they met one of the Nawab's wives who had not made it onto the plane with the rest of the family and had travelled to Karachi with her three sons on a vegetable boat stacked with potatoes and onions.[34] 'When we came to Pakistan, I finally realised that we would never go back home,' Shakira remembers seventy-five years later.[35]

By the last week of October, Bhutto admitted that the 'Muslims of Kathiawar seem to have lost all enthusiasm for Pakistan'.[36] The Indian Army marched into Mangrol and Babariawad, and civilians in Junagadh city prepared themselves for a final showdown. However, on 9 November Bhutto invited the government of India to take over the state's administration. He had just one condition: that a plebiscite be held on which country Junagadh would join.[37] Patel accepted, and days later walked triumphantly through Junagadh's Lord Ray Gate, announcing his intention to rebuild the temple of Somnath, which had been sacked by Islamic rulers centuries earlier. His message was obvious: Hindu rule had returned to Junagadh.

In the plebiscite, held a few months later, the state voted overwhelmingly to join India. The Nawab, meanwhile, began making desperate overtures to the Indian high commissioner to return to

Indian infantrymen train for war

Aung San (right) and two of his Thirty Comrades wearing Japanese kimonos

The Japanese conquest of Rangoon eviscerated British prestige and made Jawaharlal Nehru conclude that Britain was 'already a second-class power'

Uttam Singh (far left) and Sikhs of Bawdwin before they set off on the Long March

An estimated 600,000 Indian civilians fled Burma for India in 1942. At the time, it was the largest mass migration ever recorded

Ba Maw (far left) and Subhas Chandra Bose (far right) represent 'Free Burma' and 'Free India' at Japan's Greater East Asia Conference in Tokyo, 1943, alongside other Axis countries

Subhas Chandra Bose tries to get support for Indian independence from Adolf Hitler

Muhammad Ali Jinnah, standing between his sister Fatima and his daughter Dina

West African troops arriving in India for the Burma Front, 1944

The tennis court of Kohima, briefly the front line between the British and Japanese empires

A map of the Bengal Famine, where each dot equals 100 deaths

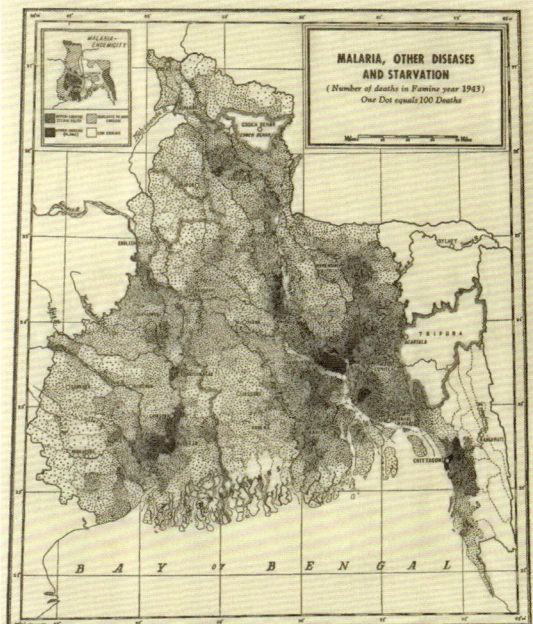

Japanese and British propaganda during WW2

Lahore Fort, where Jinnah and the Muslim League announced the Lahore Resolution

Gandhi and Jinnah laughing during their talks in Bombay, 1944. This meeting reinforced Jinnah's power, convincing the press that they were political equals

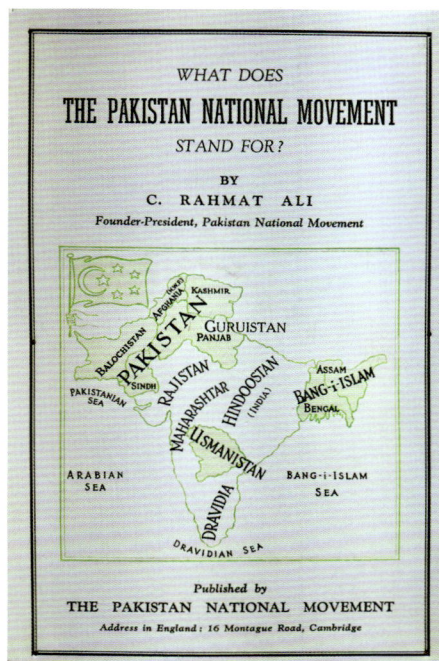

Rahmat Ali Choudhary's vision of Pakistan

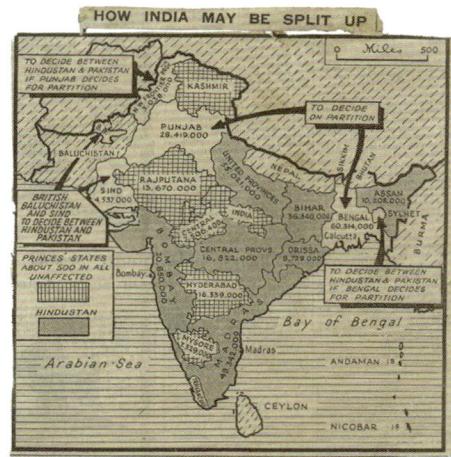

As late as June 1947, no one knew where Pakistan would actually be. This map, published by the *Daily Herald* that month, demonstrates the scale of confusion

Communist delegates marching in Punjab, 1945. Legalised during Britain's wartime alliance with the USSR, the Communist Party would play a major role in famine relief and post-Partition refugee rehabilitation efforts

The Indian interim government, with Nehru one from the right. In the centre stands Patel, the Congress home Minister who would control the intelligence services throughout the final year of the British Raj, with fatal effect

A statue of Sardar Patel is now the world's tallest statue, towering twice the height of the Statue of Liberty

Louis and Edwina Mountbatten are sworn in as the last Viceregal couple

Junagadh in exchange for a full accession to India and the introduction of democracy. But it was too little too late. 'Steps were taken to dispose of the dogs which the Nawab had left behind,' noted V. P. Menon in his autobiography. 'Their maintenance alone was costing Rs 16,000 a month.'[38] Many of the Nawab's relatives stayed in India, however, including Vali Mohammad Khan Babi, whose daughter Parveen Babi would become a Bollywood sensation. Another was the infant ruler of Balasinor, a rival princely state that was under a regency council at the time of accession. The Nawab's granddaughter Aaliya Babi – a self-taught palaeontologist known as the 'Dinosaur Princess' – claims that he also made overtures to her grandmother to come to Pakistan with him but was turned down.[39]

Soon after Patel's arrival, the government of India brought in a new law to reallocate abandoned properties. Some of the most unassuming victims of this proved to be the Muslims who were working in Aden or Burma, who suddenly found their land seized by India's new 'Evacuee Property Ordinances', despite having never travelled to Pakistan.[40] Yunus Hajee Shakoor, a Rangoon-based partner of Maiman Row & Company travelled home only to discover that petty officials had claimed his house. When he showed a reference from the government of Burma to the evacuee officer in charge, the man replied that he couldn't do anything and turned him away.[41]

India's ambassador to Burma, M. A. Rauf, was soon swamped by Junagadhi Muslims working in Burma who, amid continuing anti-Indian rhetoric where they were living, learned their property back in Junagadh had been sold off. When Rauf petitioned India's Ministry of External Affairs to help these men and women, the ministry's responses betrayed a naked suspicion of Muslims: 'I presume that these Memons, unlike some Muslims from other parts of India residing abroad, are not indulging in pro-Pakistan activities in Burma,' the ministry's Mr Dutt wrote back. 'As you know we take a serious view of the activities of such persons who behave virtually as Pakistan nationals while continuing to retain their interests in India.'[42]

Seventy-five years later, Pakistan continues to claim Junagadh and its vassals as an integral part of the nation and includes them on its survey maps. Even at the time, however, many Pakistani leaders were actually pleased a plebiscite had been held in Junagadh, since it set a precedent for another to be held in a state infinitely larger and more important to the Pakistani government: Jammu and Kashmir.[43]

In many ways Kashmir faced the opposite situation to Junagadh in 1947.* Where Junagadh's Muslim Nawab had ruled over a predominantly Hindu population, Kashmir's Hindu Maharaja led a predominantly Muslim one. Yet Kashmir was far more diverse than Junagadh: its Muslim majority followed a wide variety of sects, and across the state were large pockets of Hindus, Sikhs and Tibetan Buddhists. Indeed, Kashmir was larger than either France or Britain, with the second largest population of any princely state and stretched from the plains of Punjab to K2, the second highest peak in the world. At its heart was the eponymous Kashmir Valley itself, an emerald vale fringed by snowy peaks that had been a favourite summer retreat for both the Mughal emperors and their British successors.

Ever since 1947 Kashmir has been the cause of numerous wars and military skirmishes between India and Pakistan, who both claim the state in its entirety. Conflict around the issue would lead to South Asia's nuclear proliferation and transform Kashmir into one of the most militarised regions in the world.[44] Yet the state's history remains deeply contested. It's a fascinating story, and crucial to understanding the modern world's most volatile nuclear hotspot.

Like Junagadh, the essential question revolves around the issue of whether a state's ruler or a people had the right to choose which of the two new dominions to accede to – India or Pakistan.

The ruler of Kashmir in 1947 was Maharaja Hari Singh, an imperious soldier who held a world record for duck shooting, and the fourth Maharaja of the Dogra dynasty to sit on the throne, yet he was deeply unpopular. Valley Kashmiris had long regarded his family as outsiders – they came from the Jammu valley in the far south of the state, his great grandfather having bought the right to rule Kashmir for 7.5 million rupees from the East India Company. Indeed under Dogra rule, Kashmir had become one of the most economically disadvantaged regions in South Asia so that in 1901 only 2 per cent of the capital Srinagar's residents were literate. Nonetheless, the public had initially regarded Hari Singh himself with tentative hopefulness. Opinion of

---

* Henceforth I will be using 'Kashmir' as shorthand for the entire state of Jammu and Kashmir.

him soured only after he got caught up in an international sex scandal, and when three of his wives died mysteriously in quick succession.[45]

Anti-Maharaja protests subsequently catapulted an idealistic politician called Sheikh Mohammad Abdullah to national fame. The son of a shawl weaver with an endearing smile and a large mole above his right cheek, Abdullah was deeply inspired by the politics of the Soviet Union, just sixteen kilometres north of Kashmir. He promised to redistribute Kashmiri land to the people and in 1946 he had formally called for the Maharaja to 'Quit Kashmir'. Hari Singh responded by imprisoning Abdullah and his party but, as Krishna Mishra recalls, 'when [the] male leadership was put behind bars or driven underground, the women leaders took charge and gave a new direction to the struggle'. Abdullah's wife Begum Akbar Jehan led the political underground, and Freda Bedi, the British wife of a Punjabi activist, began to organise an 'underground messenger service', disguising herself in a burqa. A British communist noted with wonder that 'the people's movement of Kashmir is the strongest and most militant of any Indian State'.[46]

This was the situation facing Kashmir in 1947, when suddenly it was asked to choose whether to join India or Pakistan. With a Muslim-majority population in all three of the state's provinces and almost all exports going through Pakistani territory, it might have been expected that most people would want to join Pakistan. After all, the 'K' in Pakistan stood for Kashmir, and even several Hindus supported accession to Pakistan, from *Kashmir Times* editor G. K. Reddy to the state prime minister Ram Chandra Kak.[47] But opinion within the state was divided. Kashmir had for centuries been the epicentre of Hindu learning and was central to the idea of the Hindu holy land Bharat. Abdullah's communist leanings made him wary of the elitist Muslim League, and his National Conference Party fluctuated between demanding independence and accession to India. Meanwhile, its rival party the Muslim Conference also refused to declare in favour of Pakistan, despite strong sympathies. The opinions of people from the frontier districts were never even recorded.[48]

Mountbatten himself had travelled to the Kashmiri capital to persuade Hari Singh to make a decision one way or the other the previous June. But the ruler had procrastinated, sending the Viceroy off on a fishing trip. Mountbatten eventually managed to corner him over dinner towards the end of his trip but before they could speak the

Englishman accidentally hit a switch and triggered 'an elaborate electric bell system', which the Maharaja had set up to tell the state band when to play 'God Save the King'. The band started up, 'all the guests had to rise awkwardly to their feet during the soup course',[49] and Mountbatten's attempts to pin down his companion were thwarted once again. The Viceroy only got a word in at the very end, urging Singh to 'consult the will of the people and do what the majority thought best for the state'.[50]

The Maharaja ignored the advice, however, and resisted holding any sort of plebiscite. Both Gandhi and Jinnah subsequently urged him to let Kashmiris determine their own future. Indeed scholars have noted that although Jinnah frequently claimed that 'Kashmir will fall into our lap like a ripe fruit', he did remarkably 'little prior to independence to engineer that eventuality'. This attitude was in striking contrast to Nehru, who likely interfered with Cyril Radcliffe's line-drawing to ensure India had a road link to Kashmir.[51] 'Kashmir affects me in a peculiar way,' Nehru would confide to Edwina one morning. 'It is a kind of mild intoxication – like music sometimes or the company of a beloved person.'[52]

Perhaps inspired by Nepal, Bhutan and Sikkim, which had been allowed to retain their independence as 'Himalayan states', Maharaja Hari Singh eventually decided to keep Kashmir independent and transform it into a neutral 'Switzerland of the East'.[53] 'It has always seemed to me tragic that a man as intelligent as my father ... [should have] so grievously misjudged the political situation,' wrote his son Karan four decades later.

> In retrospect the only rational solution would appear to have been ... a peaceful partition of his State between the two new nations. But that would have needed clear political vision and careful planning over many years. As it turned out, the State was, in fact, partitioned, but in a manner that caused untold suffering and bloodshed, poisoning relations between India and Pakistan right down to the present day.[54]

It was the Punjab pogroms that changed everything. Punjab shared a porous northern border with Kashmir and soon after independence, Hindu mobs crossed to massacre the state's Muslims in Jammu. Ian

Stephens, the *Statesman* editor who had leaked the Bengal famine, wrote:

> In the Jammu province ... within a period of about eleven weeks ... systematic savageries ... practically eliminated the entire Muslim element in the population, amounting to 500,000 people. About 200,000 just disappeared, remaining untraceable, having presumably been butchered, or died from epidemics. The rest fled destitute to West Punjab.*

Maharaja Hari Singh blamed Pakistan for the anti-Muslim violence and absolved his own regime of any wrongdoing.[55] But in the hills of Poonch, a region in western Jammu known for its pro-Pakistan and anti-Maharaja sentiments, such excuses were not easily accepted. The tipping point came when thousands of mostly Muslim Poonchi protesters, upset over perceived preferential treatment for Hindus and Sikhs, clashed with state forces, resulting in casualties and sparking an anti-Maharaja uprising among the Muslims of Poonch. Desperate telegrams from Jammu now began to reach Jinnah's office, one reading: 'Public being looted and shooted at random ... Kindly intervene.'[56]

Much of the controversy over Kashmir revolves around this moment. At what point *did* Pakistan intervene? An Indian officer, Major O. S. Kalkat, would claim it had drawn up plans to invade Kashmir as early as 20 August 1947,[57] but most others put the start of the intervention in early September, when the director of weapons and equipment at the Pakistani Army HQ, Brigadier Akbar Khan, was introduced to a young rebel from western Jammu called Sardar Ibrahim Khan.

The scion of a wealthy Poonchi family, Ibrahim Khan had graduated from Lincoln's Inn and become one of the first Muslim barristers in all of Kashmir. In early 1947 he had entered politics and been voted the chief whip of Kashmir's second-most popular political party, coming out in favour of Kashmir's accession to Pakistan.[58] He 'was not promi-

---

* There were certainly awful massacres in which the Maharajah's forces seem to have been complicit, but it is also very difficult to distinguish between Jammu Muslims who were killed or who fled west to Sialkot and elsewhere. Malhotra, A., *In the Language of Remembering: The Inheritance of Partition* (Gurugram: HarperCollins India, 2022) p465.

nent enough to be known in Pakistan,' noted Akbar Khan in his memoir, yet he seemed 'passionately stirred',[59] and had apparently gained the support of the Muslim Conference as well as 'progressives among the non-Muslim Communities'.[60]

Just as the Junagadh crisis had been heating up, the young rebel had persuaded Brigadier Khan to support the Poonch rebels, and by 12 September Pakistani prime minister Liaquat Ali Khan had given the plan an informal go-ahead, while stopping short of involving the Pakistani Army. Instead the driving force would be the Muslim League National Guards, Jinnah's answer to the RSS, run by the shadowy former railway guard Khurshid Anwar.[61]

'We fixed a day in September as the "D" Day' for supporting the rebellion against Kashmir's Maharaja, wrote one of the conspirators, but on the chosen day Anwar went 'missing', having recently got married and 'disappeared on his honeymoon'. Pakistan's intervention in Kashmir was thus delayed until his return.[62]

Remarkably, it seems Jinnah was entirely oblivious to the plan. He kept his focus squarely on securing the peaceful accession of Bahawalpur and Khairpur, the two prosperous states across the Thar Desert from Rajputana. On 3 October the two signed accessions finally arrived on Jinnah's desk and a quarter of the modern Indo-Pakistani border – today erroneously known in its entirety as Radcliffe's Line – was formed. The Nawab of Bahawalpur would save Pakistan's economy from the brink, personally footing six months' worth of Pakistani government salaries from his state's treasury.[63]

Jinnah may have been unaware of events in Kashmir but thanks to India's aggression in Junagadh, he was increasingly paranoid. When Alan Campbell-Johnson visited Karachi the next day he noted that:

> Jinnah ... is utterly convinced that the Indian leaders' real aim is to strangle Pakistan at birth, that Gandhi ... is all the time spreading 'Hindu poison', and that Nehru in spite of the appearance of moderation, is not really the master in his own house. He regards Patel as the real dictator, who, he alleges, has entered into an unholy alliance with the Hindu Mahasabha and would be quite ready to overthrow the Congress if it failed to serve as an appropriate instrument for his anti-Muslim designs.[64]

That same day, with support from the Pakistani government, the Kashmiri rebel leader Sardar Ibrahim Khan formed a 'revolutionary government on the Junagadh model' called 'Azad [Free] Kashmir'.[65] When Jinnah learned about his government's involvement some days later, his response was characteristically terse. 'Don't tell me anything about it,' he said. 'My conscience must be clear.'[66] In the words of Faiz Ahmed Faiz, the communist poet and editor of the *Pakistan Times*, 'There ended the opportunity of Kashmir's accession to Pakistan … The rest is history.'[67]

That October, the shadowy former railway guard Khurshid Anwar at last returned from his honeymoon and his men began to move into action. British officer Frank Leeson* was airlifting Hindu and Sikh refugees out of the North-West Frontier when he noticed hundreds of 'tribesmen' driving towards the Kashmir border in buses 'covered in graffiti'.[68] They wore 'baggy trousers,' he noted later, 'roughly tied turbans' and had 'shirts hanging outside with waistcoats.

> They streamed down in busloads; Mohmands and Mahsuds, Afridis and Afghans, from Buner and Bajaur, Swat and South Waziristan, Khyber and Khost; the light of battle in their eyes, half forgotten war cries on their lips.[69]

Leeson wasn't the only one to notice them. Governor George Cunningham also observed the sudden movement of tribes rallying 'for jehad' in Kashmir.[70] Suspicious, he called up Frank Messervy, the British commander-in-chief of Pakistan's Army, who revealed he had just been ordered to return to England. Messervy's aide-de-camp, Hew Hamilton-Dalrymple, had likewise been sent duck shooting with the Wali of Swat. Messervy contacted Liaquat Ali Khan that Sunday, but Pakistan's prime minister told him to ignore the matter.[71] Cunningham would later theorise that all British officers in Pakistan had deliberately been sent away to stop them from intervening.[72]

A few days later Brigadier Akbar Khan drove towards the border and

---

* Leeson was one of numerous British officers who had chosen to stay in the subcontinent after Partition. He was far from unusual in this respect, and indeed the army commander-in-chiefs of both India and Pakistan that October were still Brits.

saw lorries 'full to the brim, carrying forty, fifty and some as many as seventy. Men were packed inside, lying on the roofs, sitting on the engines and hanging on to the mudguards. They were men of all ages from grey beards to teenagers. Few were well-dressed – many had torn clothes, and some were even without shoes. But they were good to look at – handsome – and awe-inspiring.'[73] The motivations of this 'lashkar [tribal army]', as they came to be known, were as diverse as their backgrounds. If some sought to liberate Kashmir from feudal rule, others wanted retribution against non-Muslims, the opportunity to loot, or a mix of all three.[74] The Pirs of Wana and Manki Sharif seem to have been central in recruiting the tribesmen, but most important of all was Khurshid Anwar. Secret British files theorise that Anwar had been a member of Subhas Chandra Bose's INA during the war, and in early 1947 he had linked up with the tribesmen of the North-West Frontier to create a counterbalance to the pro-Congress redshirts along the frontier. 'I am told that the man is a complete adventurer,' wrote the British high commissioner's deputy in Peshawar.

> He is said to have got away with a good deal of loot during the brief disturbances in Peshawar city last September, and to have sent several lorry-loads home for himself in Kashmir ... He is reputed to have worked on the tribesmen's feelings, already aroused by tales of the suffering of Muslims, and then to have proposed to the Mahsuds first an expedition to help the oppressed Muslims of Kashmir.[75]

Before dawn on 22 October, Khurshid Anwar and his men crossed into Kashmir State and headed for the city of Muzaffarabad, on the confluence of the Jhelum and Kishanganga rivers. It had rained the previous night and the early morning air bore a bracing chill, a reminder of the impending winter. Orchards brimmed with ripe apples, saffron crocuses unfurled in regal shades of deep purple, and the chinar trees, once adorned in golden yellow, now blazed in hues of crimson. At five that morning, the lashkar's gunfire began reverberating around the valley. 'It was part of their agreement with Major Khurshid Anwar of the Muslim National Guards ... that they would loot non-Muslims,' revealed Brigadier Khan of the Pakistani Army some years afterward. 'They had no other renumeration.'[76]

Moments later, Muzaffarabad was in chaos and chants of 'Loot the wealth of the Hindus, behead the Sikhs' were echoing through the streets.[77] Sikhs were more easily identifiable than Hindus thanks to their turbans, and by the afternoon the raiders had rounded up three hundred of them at the old Dumel bridge. 'We'll let you go; we're just collecting you in one place,' the Sikhs were told. 'No harm will come your way.' But when they were gathered together, the raiders opened fire on the crowd. A few men and women survived by jumping off the bridge into the river but most were murdered on the spot and their corpses piled up on the sacred Hindu ghats.[78]

Inder Kaur, a mother of three, was separated from her two sons in the frenzy, and 'not knowing what to do ... [she] went hiding with her infant'. Her nephew Amarinder Singh recalls how, with 'no food, no water and being famished herself, she had no milk in her to feed the child who kept crying out of hunger. The wails were so loud that everyone around her, people who were also in hiding, told her the baby would give them away, so that the raiders would find them and kill all of them.' To save everyone, Inder did the unthinkable and threw her baby in the river.[79]

In the wake of the attack on Muzaffarabad, a long caravan of Hindus and Sikhs fled for the Kashmiri capital of Srinagar, avoiding the main road and taking paths across high meadows, relying on the kindness of strangers for food and warmth.[80] Meanwhile, Anwar's lashkar advanced down the Jhelum Road towards Srinagar, joined by discontented Muslims from the Kashmir State Forces and, most importantly, ex-INA soldiers. In the decades since, Indian nationalists lauding the INA have often ignored its soldiers' prominent role in trying to secure Kashmir for Pakistan. After they overwhelmed the Maharaja's beleaguered forces with ease, people began to talk of the lashkar reaching Srinagar for the festival of Eid a few days away.[81]

For days most people in the capital didn't really understand what was going on. In the palace, Maharaja Hari Singh himself finally decided to offer accession to India on the condition that his terms were the same as those of the Nizam of Hyderabad, who was said to be nearing a deal with the Indian government. At half past nine in the evening, the raiders reached the Mahoora power station.[82] Karan Singh, the crown prince, was sitting injured in a wheelchair in Srinagar's Durbar Hall at the time, staring at the 'richly decorated papier-mâché ceiling',[83] when he was 'plunged into darkness'. He would later recall:

> Suddenly this terrible cacophony of jackals starting howling in the darkness. It was really a very eerie, sort of weird moment ... One had heard that there was trouble brewing, but it was at that moment that one realised an invasion was underway.[84]

'Dusk was beginning to settle down over the Vale,' recorded Father George Shanks from the orchard in Baramulla's convent the evening before the raiders arrived, and 'the last rays of the sun still fell on the summits of the Pir Panjal, bathing their snows in that incredible fiery pink'. How hard it was, he thought, to reconcile 'Kashmir in late autumn ... with stories of rape'.

Perched at the mouth of the Kashmir Valley, on the southern bank of the Jhelum, Baramulla had once been one of Kashmir's great river ports. Father Shanks was the senior priest of the city's Catholic missionary convent, and that morning he saw St Joseph's Hospital in a frenzy as they tried to flee the approaching lashkar. 'Women half-dead with T. B. or cancer' and 'young mothers with their few days' old babies' were 'hurried off their sick-beds by fearful husbands' and taken off to Srinagar on tonga carts. The road was jammed with fleeing buses, trailers and bullock carts, and in a matter of hours prices for a ride increased fifty-fold. Soon only a handful of patients remained at the hospital.[85]

Remarkably, almost no Europeans had been killed in the Partition violence sweeping the subcontinent that year, and as a result Father Shanks was unfazed by the incoming marauders.

> We did not think there would be any bodily danger for us, so we decided that our best policy, would be to carry on as if nothing special was happening. The Sisters were going about their morning rounds of the Hospital ... so we fell back on the Englishman's remedy for lack of work and ordered tea. Firing started at 10.30 promptly ... [and] from a vantage point on the terrace in front of the Presbytery, we watched the progress of the party with detached interest.[86]

But Shanks' complacency was misplaced. Within hours the raiders had clambered up the convent walls and smashed through the doors with their axes. He found himself surrounded by 'fifteen of the most unpleasant hoodlums' he had ever seen, 'armed to the teeth' with rifles and daggers. 'Money, watches, keys, were taken away from us,' he writes, and then: 'Father Mallett and I were half dragged, half pushed into my two roomed house … [where] locks were burst open with axe blows, drawers were pulled out and emptied, furniture overturned and ripped open.'[87] The nuns in the next-door hospital had pushed a cupboard in front of the door, and the attackers were thrashing at the door to force it open. One of them wrested a crucifix from one of the friars, and another tried to pull out Sister Celeste's gold tooth. Then came a shot and Mother Teresalina's body fell to the floor.[88] Minutes later five others had been killed: Mrs Motia Devi Kapoor, Jose Baretto, Philomena the nursing assistant, and Tom and Biddy Dykes.[89] It was only the arrival of a Pakistani officer on a motorbike, Major Hyat Khan, that brought the violence to a stop. Hyat Khan was wearing civilian clothes and so the survivors were never sure whether he was there on the orders of the Pakistani military.[90]

Baramulla was just an hour from the capital's airport, and had the raiders continued on to Srinagar that day it is likely they would have captured the Kashmiri capital there and then. If that had happened, it is possible all of Kashmir would today be under a Pakistani administration. Instead the attackers remained in Baramulla for three days of looting and pillaging. Several accounts mention that the local cinema, which had initially been earmarked as a refuge for minority women, was soon transformed into a 'sort of restricted brothel'. 'It was a stunning blow to those who had welcomed them with open arms as liberators,' writes Muhammad Yusuf Saraf, a politician from Baramulla who later became the chief justice of Azad Kashmir.[91]

The question of why the lashkar stopped so long in Baramulla still puzzles scholars. Indian narratives tend to assume the raiders' lust for pillage simply got the better of them, while Brigadier Akbar Khan claims Khurshid Anwar halted the lashkar to secure 'his own position in the future Government of Kashmir'.[92] More persuasive, however, is the account of a British official in Peshawar who was told that the hold-up occurred after Anwar 'asked all the tribal leaders to sign an undertaking on behalf of their men to abstain from looting, to respect Government property, protect treasuries and so on', and that 'two valuable days were wasted in tribal discussion and arguments'.[93] Whatever the case, it was enough time for everything to change.

As news of the lashkar's actions in Baramulla reached Delhi, V. P. Menon flew into Srinagar to take stock of the situation. The Kashmiri palace had descended into chaos. 'Servants [were] frantically running around with petromax lamps,' writes Karan Singh, and his father the Maharaja was 'ashen-faced and grim'.[94] In the bitter cold of that early morning, they decided to flee the Kashmir Valley for Jammu.

> All through that dreadful night we drove, slowly, haltingly, as if reluctant to leave the beautiful valley that our ancestors had ruled for generations. Our convoy crawled over the 9,000 ft Banihal Pass just as first light was beginning to break ... [and] my father spoke not a word as he drove. When the next evening he finally reached Jammu and pulled up at the palace he uttered but one sentence – 'We have lost Kashmir.'[95]

Hours later Menon, the Kashmiri prime minister Mehr Chand Mahajan and a commanding officer in the Gorkha Rifles called Sam Manekshaw flew to Delhi. A tense emergency meeting convened at Nehru's house on York Road.[96] 'Give us the military force we need,' Mahajan pleaded with India's prime minister. 'The army must fly to save Srinagar this evening or else I will go to Lahore and negotiate terms with Mr Jinnah.'[97]

Interpreting this as a threat, Nehru turned visibly angry, shouting at Mahajan, but Patel intervened. 'Of course, Mahajan, you are not going to Pakistan,' he said, before an aide walked into the room and handed Nehru a slip of paper. It turned out that Sheikh Abdullah had also arrived in Delhi and been listening in from the adjacent room and he agreed with Mahajan. 'The Prime Minister's attitude changed on reading this slip,' writes Mahajan.[98] Patel turned to Nehru. 'Jawaharlal, do you want Kashmir, or do you want to give it away?'

'Of course, I want Kashmir,' Nehru snapped back. Before he could say anything else, Patel turned to Manekshaw and said, 'You have got your orders.'[99]

After the meeting Menon set off to get the Maharaja's signature on the instrument of accession, while Manekshaw and the army prepared to fly into Kashmir and face the lashkar. The question of whether Indian troops reached Kashmir before or after the accession was signed remains controversial to this day.[100] India continues to insist the Maharaja signed before the troops landed, and that they were thus merely sending troops into their own territory. Pakistan, meanwhile, argues the Indian troops arrived before the document was signed, and was thus the primary aggressor.[101]

In fact, the Maharaja's accession to India 'was almost certainly signed on 27 October 1947 – not the 26th as claimed by India'.[102] Indeed that is what Nehru's correspondence written on that day says, implying that India sent troops into Kashmir *before* its accession.[103]

Ultimately a more important question is, given the lack of support for the Maharaja's rule, and the fact that he had already fled his capital, to what extent did the Maharaja of Kashmir's accession carry legitimacy? After all, he was only in control of a portion of his state at the time even before the tribal lashkar had crossed the boundary.[104]

The next morning the airlift of Indian troops from Delhi's Palam Airport to Srinagar began, and a few days later India installed Sheikh Abdullah as the head of Kashmir's emergency administration, promising to hold a plebiscite as soon as the raiders were pushed out of the state.

Abdullah's party would prove crucial to the Indian Army's success in the valley, canvassing support for the new arrivals and providing them with intelligence from two hundred National Conference spies.[105] He set about organising the people of Srinagar into a popular militia, and the city's communist intelligentsia signed up in droves. Young children marched around city streets in caps bearing the National Conference's Soviet-inspired logo and hundreds of unveiled women – Muslims, Sikhs and Hindus – stalked the Kashmiri capital in a women's militia, rifles slung over their shoulders.[106] 'The army gave us training … and we were given very heavy guns,' recalls Usha Khanna. 'Muslims protected Hindus, Hindus protected [Muslims]: we were side by side.'[107]

The morning of the Indian airlift, the Indian Army's commander-in-chief Sir Claude Auchinleck received a frantic phone call from General

Douglas Gracey who had been appointed acting commander-in-chief of the Pakistani Army. Gracey recounted how a furious Jinnah had ordered him to march the Pakistani Army into Kashmir. Gracey had refused, becoming the first Pakistani general to question the orders of his civilian government, and he urged Auchinleck to help him stop the two countries from going to war. 'Jinnah withdrew orders but is very angry and disturbed,' Auchinleck wrote later that day. 'Situation remains explosive and highly dangerous.'[108]

All-out war between India and Pakistan had been averted, but for how long? Two days later events spiralled even further out of control after a coup in the arid moonscapes of Gilgit, in the far north of Kashmir. The Maharaja of Kashmir had leased the area to the British years earlier, and the 'Gilgit Agency' established there subsequently became responsible for British relations with two entirely different princely states: Hunza and Nagar. In addition to having a rather vaguely defined territory, in 1936 the *Kashmir Times* noted that Hunza confusingly paid 'tribute to four governments – British, Chinese, Russian and Kashmiri'.[109] Just two weeks before independence, the agency had been transferred back to the Maharaja resulting in widespread anger, particularly among the Gilgit Scouts regiment.

Eventually twenty-four-year-old Scottish officer William Brown decided to take matters into his own hands.[110] 'I considered that the whole of Kashmir, including the Gilgit Province, belonged indubitably to Pakistan in view of the fact that the population was predominantly Muslim,' Brown wrote years later, and 'therefore felt it was my duty, as the only Britisher left, to follow a course which would prevent [Gilgit becoming part of India]'. According to Brown's memoir, his planned coup was formulated with his friend Captain Jock Mathieson over a bottle of gin. 'Jockie boy, we are going to get blind drunk for the last time until the Gilgit Province has become a part of Pakistan,' laughed Brown before downing his glass.[111] 'Neither of us have a very clear recollection of what happened after that,' he writes.

> But as far as I can gather, we became uncontrollably hilarious, created a terrific disturbance by singing every song we could think of … [and] must have wakened the Governor over the way. With three bottles of gin inside us … we weaved an unsteady way

to bed ... That was the last time we touched a minimum of alcohol until our mission had been fulfilled.[112]

As it turned out, many of Brown's officers had been planning something similar, and on 31 October 'Operation Datta Khel' was put into action.[113] '[A] bright moon lit up the parade ground with a pale ghostly effect,' wrote Brown, and the Gilgit Scouts platoons 'moved out from the barracks rooms in single file'.[114] They fanned out across the city, taking the post office first, then the bridge, and by morning had surrounded the Gilgit Residency and taken the Dogra colonel into custody.[115] Outmanoeuvring a group who wanted to declare the independence of 'the United States of Gilgit' rather than join Pakistan,[116] Brown raised the Pakistani flag over the city and invited its government to take charge of the region. 'I had contracted to serve the Maharaja faithfully,' he admitted.

> I had drawn his generous pay for three months. Now I had deserted. I had mutinied ... My actions appeared to possess all the ingredients of high treason. Yet I knew in my own mind that I had done what was right.[117]

Shortly afterwards Brown accepted signed Pakistani instruments of accession from the Mirs of Hunza and Nagar and sent them off to Jinnah. Yet Jinnah delayed accepting them, fearful that recognising Hunza and Nagar as independent would weaken his hand in the dispute over Jammu and Kashmir as a whole.* According to a telegram sent from the UK high commissioner in Karachi,

> Liaquat stalled and sent an official to contact them. On 22 February he received a telegram to say they were disappointed not to have received an official answer from Pakistan and that if their accession were not accepted, they would accede to Russia.[118]

---

* Both India and Pakistan regard them as a part of the disputed Jammu and Kashmir State to this day. China dropped its claims to Hunza in the 1960s. Seventy-five years later, the two states remain 'administered by Pakistan' while legally falling outside the country's constitution. See Bangash, 'Three Disputed Accessions: Gilgit, Hunza and Nagar', *Journal of Imperial and Commonwealth History*.

Indian officials would interpret Brown's actions as incontrovertible evidence that Britain had been partisan to Pakistan, but in Britain's Commonwealth Relations Office at least, Brown's exploits took everyone by surprise. 'The fate of Gilgit appears to rest with Major William Brown,' noted one British official. 'Who *is* Major William Brown?'[119] Whatever the case, the entry of the Gilgit Scouts into the Kashmir conflict was a game changer. Unlike the lashkar wreaking havoc in the south of the state, the Scouts were trained professionals. When Pakistani authorities finally arrived to take over Gilgit from Brown two weeks later, they were amazed to find that little looting or murder had taken place in the town, and indeed most of Gilgit's Hindus and Sikhs were still plying their trades as usual. 'I arrived here expecting to find a war-torn ravaged country,' a Pakistani official admitted, 'and instead of that it seems as though nothing had happened at all!'[120]

Indian troops had now arrived in the Kashmiri capital, while Pakistani troops had taken over Gilgit to the north. All the while Khurshid Anwar's tribal lashkar continued to cause mayhem across the state. India and Pakistan were still not at war with each other, but they were close.

On 1 November Mountbatten made Jinnah a proposal: if he persuaded the tribal lashkar to withdraw, they could jointly hold a Junagadh-esque plebiscite in Kashmir, along with *all* other states where the ruler was of a different religion to their subjects. These plebiscites would be held under UN auspices and joint supervision of Indian and Pakistani forces.[121] Had Jinnah accepted, the Kashmir conflict might have ended there and then. As Sardar Patel later admitted, 'We would agree to Kashmir if they agree to Hyderabad.'[122] Instead Jinnah rejected the offer over a technicality. Mountbatten was incredulous. 'Can you imagine the Pakistanis being so stupid as not to withdraw the tribesmen?' he later raged. 'I told Liaquat, "All you've got to do is pull out. Have the plebiscite, and you'll win. You'll get in again."'[123] But Jinnah had lost all trust in Mountbatten, and although his earlier involvement in the conflict is uncertain, Jinnah now formally ordered that Pakistan maintain at least five thousand tribesmen in Kashmir at all times.[124]

Across the front line, Khurshid Anwar's lashkar had advanced to within four miles of the Kashmiri capital of Srinagar, in 'sight of its twinkling lights'.[125] But hemmed in on the main road thanks to the lakes that surrounded the capital, the raiders suddenly found themselves facing machine-gun fire from not merely Kashmir State forces but the Indian Army. It was a strange sort of battle, and in between bouts of gunfire Akbar Khan remembers birds twittering among the trees and groups of wild duck and geese flying past in formation, 'line after line, their colourful wings flashing when caught by the suns' rays'.[126] Then Indian fighter planes began dropping bombs on the lashkar.

Khan set off back up the Jhelum to Rawalpindi to urge the Pakistani generals to provide the lashkar with armoured cars. Pakistan was already so heavily implicated, he argued. 'Would a couple of armoured cars make ... [India's] accusation any worse?'[127] But brigadiers Sher Khan and Raja Ghazanfar Ali Khan rejected the idea, worried that sending in actual Pakistani troops would precipitate all-out war. And so, lacking crucial military support, the tribal lashkar was pushed back. Both Akbar Khan and Khurshid Anwar would complain bitterly of the lack of support from Pakistan, and according to Governor Cunningham even Jinnah was 'conscious of having made a blunder, having assumed that tribal intervention would not at once – as seemed obvious to me – throw Kashmir into the arms of India'.[128]

As the raiders were driven back from Srinagar, they turned south to Mirpur, where once again non-Muslims were rounded up and imprisoned in a gurudwara. 'The women collected firewood to make a fire to kill themselves,' remembers one survivor, 'but never did.'[129] All the while Sardar Ibrahim Khan and the Poonch rebels were left bewildered at the events that had overtaken their rebellion against the Maharaja. As one Reuters correspondent noted, 'The Poonchis did not much care for the tribesmen' who had usurped their liberation movement.[130]

In late November Liaquat Ali Khan agreed to his first meeting with Nehru since the tribal lashkar had first crossed into Kashmir over a month earlier. As expected, the talks began in a stormy fashion. Auchinleck suggested they 'partition the state, giving the Muslim portions, namely Kashmir, Mirpur [and] Poonch to Pakistan and the Hindu parts such as Jammu to India'.[131] But the government of Pakistan pointed out that in the census of 1941 Jammu province had been 61 per cent Muslim while Ladakh, which Indian propaganda characterised as a Buddhist region, had been over 80 per cent Muslim. If either region were no longer Muslim-majority, it was only because mobs had forced all the Muslims out. Moreover India's acceptance of Kashmir's accession, argued Pakistan's leaders, was a 'repudiation of the very principles on which [India] ... had only one month before opposed Junagadh's accession to Pakistan'.[132]

Nonetheless, in the next few days, a potential deal emerged, and Alan Campbell-Johnson wrote hopefully: 'The storms which have threatened to overwhelm the sub-continent following the transfer of power may at last be subsiding.'[133] Despite disagreements the two countries approached a deal about how to divide the Raj's money and debt, and came within a hair's breadth of resolving the Kashmir dispute.

India would withdraw most of its forces, Pakistan would 'persuade the rebel "Azad Kashmir" forces to cease fighting'[134] and the United Nations would send a commission to Kashmir to make recommendations on the best way to go ahead with a plebiscite. But in mid-November news reached Nehru that the RSS had crossed into the state en masse 'with Patel's connivance' and were undermining Abdullah's attempts at keeping order in the valley.[135] Possibly because of this, Liaquat started encouraging additional fighters to pour into Kashmir from Pakistan. The peace that had come so close fell from their grasp.

Rather than calming the situation, the proxy war between India and Pakistan threatened to escalate elsewhere along the Indo-Pakistan border, particularly in Tripura.[136] On Christmas Day Nehru summoned Major-General K. S. Thimayya and told him the Indian Army should cross into Pakistani Punjab and 'obliterate' the 'bases and nerve centres' that kept the war going.[137] The assault, however, never came. Instead, as the winter snows arrived, the Kashmir conflict entered a winter lull and on New Year's Day 1948, Nehru referred the dispute to the United Nations. A resolution to the fighting was now in the hands of the world's statesmen.

As 1948 got underway, the former Indian Empire was in a dire state. Two new dominions – India and Pakistan – were on the precipice of all-out-war, 'with British generals commanding armies, on both sides ... and British diplomats taking up cudgels on behalf of the hostile governments they were accredited to'.[138] That February Pakistan assigned three-quarters of its total budget to its military, a move that ensured the prevalence of its armed forces in decades to come.[139] The British government was itself divided about how to handle the situation, with Prime Minister Attlee sympathetic to Pakistan and a group led by Stafford Cripps sympathetic to India.[140]

The situation was so terrible that many people had entirely forgotten about U Nu's Burmese government. Nonetheless, Burmese independence finally occurred on 4 January at 4.20 a.m., a time thought to be auspicious by leading astrologers. Celebrations were a subdued affair compared to the pomp that India and Pakistan had witnessed. Balwant Singh, the Sikh civil servant, took part in a ceremony in a small town in the Shan Hills:

> On 4 January we were up at 3 a.m. ... at 4.19 the Union Jack was hauled down; at 4.20 the flag of independent Burma went up ... yet somehow our ceremony seemed mundane and the newly liberated citizens unconcerned ... Soon the ceremony was over. We returned home, shivering in the cold, no longer an occupied country but a free people. I did not feel any great sense of change.[141]

In Delhi Mountbatten and his staff celebrated the day at the house of the Burmese ambassador. 'Most of the time was given over to Burmese music and Sidaw dancing,' noted Campbell-Johnson, and the Viceroy presented the ambassador with a historic Burmese *taktaposh* and carpet. That evening the Burmese dancer Po Sein danced for select delegates at the Imperial Hotel.[142]

In Rangoon the Congress president Dr Rajendra Prasad gifted the fledgling nation a sapling of the Bodhi tree, under which Buddha had gained enlightenment two and a half millennia before, and the *New Times of Burma* noted how the gift 'struck the imagination of Buddhist Burma'.[143] Prasad also urged the seven hundred thousand Indians still residing in Burma to 'get assimilated' and become Burmese nationals.[144] When John Furnival arrived in Rangoon, which he had not visited since Burma's separation from India, he was amazed by the change that had come over the capital, noting with surprise: 'Rangoon is no longer an Indian city.'[145]

★ ★ ★

All the while the UN began debating the crisis in Kashmir. Pakistan's delegate was the eloquent Zafrullah Khan, who accused India of organising a genocide of Muslims in Punjab. In response India sent in Sheikh Abdullah himself to argue that India could not remove troops until Pakistan withdrew the lashkar.

On 12 January 1948, Gandhi, now seventy-eight years old, decided to intervene and announced another fast, refusing to eat until peace returned to Hindus, Muslims and Sikhs. Unlike previous fasts, however, this one was partly directed at Patel, who was refusing to send Pakistan 550 million rupees the Indian government owed it as part of their Partition asset exchange. 'You are not the Sardar I once knew,' Gandhi supposedly told him upon starting the fast.[146] Two days later they had a massive fight, with Gandhi ending up in tears. Punjabi refugees gathered outside the gates of Birla House cursing Gandhi for aiding Pakistan, but the next day a striking letter from Patel arrived on the Mahatma's doorstep. 'The sight of your anguish yesterday has made me disconsolate,' he wrote.

> It has set me furiously thinking. The burden of work has become so heavy that I feel crushed under it. Jawaharlal is even more burdened than I. His heart is heavy with grief. Maybe I have deteriorated with age and am no good anymore as a comrade to stand by him and lighten his burden ... It will perhaps be good for me and the country if you now let me go. I can only act in my way. And if thereby I become burdensome to my lifelong colleagues and a source of distress to you, and still I stick to my office, it would mean that I allowed the lust for power to blind my eyes.[147]

Gandhi continued his fast and his voice became feeble, his body frail. Visitors started arriving one after the other, to attend to the Mahatma, and news came that Mountbatten had cancelled a state banquet in honour of his fast. By the 17th, Muslims in Karachi were writing to Gandhi to ask about when they might be able to return to Delhi. A fruit seller promised to start offering fruits to Muslims once again, and across the city Muslims were distributing sweets in Hindu neighbourhoods.[148] The transformation was nothing less than extraordinary. Not everyone had a change of heart, though, and according to Gandhi's niece Manu, 'One party shouted "bhai-bhai" [we're all brothers] and the other, "Stab! Kill!"'[149] A group of Sikhs chanted, 'Let Gandhi Die'.[150] Nonetheless, visitors to his bedside soon included Sikh leaders, members of the RSS and the high commissioner of Pakistan. The Indian government conceded to pay the money it owed Pakistan, and leaders from a range of militant organisations signed an agreement to restore order to Delhi. So, at 12.25 on the 18th, following Hindu, Buddhist, Muslim and Zoroastrian prayers, Gandhi at last broke his fast with a sip of lime juice mixed with glucose.

The next twelve days saw a remarkable peace return to Delhi. Yet all was not resolved, and just two days later an assailant lobbed an explosive at the Mahatma. He missed but it was a dire warning of what was to come. On 30 January Gandhi awoke in a somewhat dejected mood, and while brushing his teeth lamented to his niece Manu that 'my influence is waning even on those who stay close to me'.[151] He spent the day reading newspapers and trying to learn some Bengali, and when his two nieces hurried him across the lawn of Birla House to a prayer meeting, a young man dressed in khaki pushed his way through the crowd with arms folded, as if to pay his respects to the Mahatma.

Then, at seventeen minutes past five, the man fired three shots at Gandhi's chest point blank. Gandhi cried out the words 'Hey Rama' and crumpled to the floor.

'The smoke was very thick,' writes Manu, and as the crowd surged forward she noticed that 'streams of blood' had 'stained our white clothes all over'.[152] An official from the US embassy who had come for the prayer meeting wrestled the assassin to the ground, then the gardener charged up and hit him on the head with a shovel. Moments later a policeman took the bloodied man into custody and Gandhi was pronounced dead.[153] That afternoon Nehru exclaimed:

> The light has gone out of our lives, and there is darkness everywhere, and I do not quite know what to tell you or how to say it. Our beloved leader, Bapu as we called him, the father of the nation, is no more. Perhaps I am wrong to say that; nevertheless, we will not see him again, as we have seen him for these many years, we will not run to him for advice or seek solace from him, and that is a terrible blow, not only for me, but for millions and millions in this country.[154]

The response came at once. 'Business houses, shops, restaurants and cinema houses were immediately closed,' wrote the *Civil & Military Gazette*. 'A marriage procession proceeding along Connaught Place halted and whispered silently. Traffic in the city came to a standstill. Men, women and children who were on their evening walks in Connaught Circus were visibly moved and many of them broke into tears.'[155] In Lahore prayers were held for the Mahatma on the banks of the River Ravi and in Varanasi the Burmese author Baragu heard 'the cries of students and faculty, through his hostel in the ensuing days of mourning'.[156] There was also anxiety about the identity of the killer. Muslims worried they would be targeted if the killer was Muslim, and John Keenan feared that 'if Gandhi has been killed by a Britisher, we will all be dead by suppertime'.[157]

In fact the assassin was revealed to be a Hindu Agatha Christie enthusiast called Nathuram Godse. He had been obsessed with proving his masculine virility, partly the result of his parents having brought him up as a girl for the first decade of his life to appease their family deities. Godse had joined first the RSS and then the Hindu Mahasabha, and had been plotting the assassination for weeks. He felt the Mahatma's commitment to religious tolerance and non-violence – especially his fasts and calls to placate Pakistan – was responsible for the suffering of Hindus, and the partition of India's sacred geography. Eight others were soon arrested as part of the plot thanks to Godse's careless covering of his tracks.[158] One of them was the Hindu Mahasabha leader Vinayak Savarkar. Although his role in Gandhi's murder would never be firmly established and he would later be released, his association with Godse would taint the organisation for years to come.

Within days, Nehru decided to patch things up with Patel. 'With Bapu's death, everything is changed and we have to face a different and more difficult world,' he wrote to the home minister. 'The old controversies have ceased to have much significance and it seems to me that the urgent need of the hour is for all of us to function as closely and cooperatively as possible.' Patel reciprocated Nehru's sentiments, and the two men put aside their differences.[159] The home minister banned all communal organisations in India, including the Muslim League National Guards and the RSS, a prohibition that would remain in place until 1949. The ban coincided with a remarkable calming of Partition violence across the country, as religious violence somehow became discredited overnight.

In many accounts, people refer to the assassination as having finally shocked the two nations to their senses.

At Gandhi's funeral the day after the assassination, the crowds were like nothing anyone had ever seen. His body was 'placed, inappropriately enough, on a gun carriage'[160] and carried in a long procession to Raj Ghat on the banks of the Yamuna, where his funeral pyre awaited. Alan Campbell-Johnson sat cross-legged before the fire with some of the Mahatma's closest companions who were 'threading small garlands of white flowers' when 'seven hundred thousand' others 'restlessly converged on the sacred spot' and together the crowd watched as 'the flames and smoke of the pyre billowed upwards'.[161] It was a moment of collective mourning for the former Indian Empire. In Dubai and Muscat, shops were shuttered while Burma closed all public institutions, including schools.[162] Gandhi's ashes were taken to be scattered in all the rivers of the subcontinent, including the Ganges, the Krishna, the Indus and even the Irrawaddy. It was a last breath of unity in a now shattered land.

10

The Fall of Hyderabad

On 28 February 1948, a month after Gandhi's death, the last British unit in the subcontinent finally set sail from Bombay. Indian guards of honour gave a royal salute to the sound of 'God Save the King', and the departing troops of the 1st Battalion of the Somerset Light Infantry responded with a royal salute to the nationalist anthem 'Vande Mataram'.[1] John Keenan was present at the ceremony with his daughter Brigid. 'Though I was only eight years old,' she recalls,

> I was aware that we were watching history, and that everyone around me was feeling emotional. We saw the last British soldiers march off the parade ground, through the Gateway of India, and straight onto the launches that took them to their ship.

It was a 'potent, visible end to the British Raj'. But that didn't stop Brigid from eating the rice grains that had been stuck on her forehead, and everyone else's, 'as a ceremonial gesture on arrival, and getting into trouble with dad for disrespect'.[2]

That afternoon, as the sun dipped below the horizon, the remaining British men and women in the subcontinent sensed their time in the land rapidly slipping away. They weren't alone and many Anglo-Indian, Armenian, Chinese, Jewish, Irish and Burmese communities who had flourished in India under colonial rule were also leaving. 'It seems so tempting to stay on,' wrote Keenan.

One is only 45 and there may be many years to come. However, for better or for worse, for richer or for poorer, I have decided not to serve on with India or Pakistan. We must think of our home in some very nice place in England and make a quick break with the East ... India is no place for us now.[3]

There was an overwhelming feeling of futility and bitterness as the final *firangis* left India. Some 'returned' to the shores of distant and unfamiliar Britain, while others, driven by a lingering attachment to the colonial way of life, sought new beginnings in Nigeria, Canada, Kenya and Australia.[4] Leaving was a long-drawn-out process and ships were fully booked for months, so many families moved into a set of 'transit camps' set up in Bombay's Colaba district.[5] A full year after independence the Keenans, too, set foot aboard the SS *Franconia* from Bombay to Liverpool. As Brigid later wrote:

On board were more than 1,000 people from families exactly like ours ... a whole cross-section of those who had made their lives in India: missionaries, office workers, tea planters, dressmakers, telephonists, typists, engineers and nurses ... Many lifetimes of experiences and possessions, acquired over the decades by our forebears, were left behind ... [and] when we arrived in cold, grey, post-war, not-very-friendly Britain, what we missed and cried for was warmth – the warmth of the sun and, above all, the warmth of the people.[6]

Bengal had fallen under the sway of the British East India Company two hundred years earlier, just fifty years after the Union between England and Scotland, and nearly fifty years *before* the Act of Union with Ireland. The British Association for Cemeteries in South Asia recorded two million British graves in India. Now Britain and the subcontinent had been pulled asunder, and the sense of estrangement recorded by Calcutta-born writer Lee Langley, standing 'newly arrived on a Cornish hillside, desperately shouting Hindi words', was not uncommon.[7] Brigid herself only knew Hindustani nursery rhymes and she later wrote: 'The pain and the loss and the homesickness of leaving India ... [was] a feeling which has niggled away somewhere deep down all my life.' She had been to Britain only once before – her family was of Irish origin after all – and after generations of living in India, they had no other real home. 'Socially, the returnees were faintly despised,' she would write in a memoir.

> The feeling seemed to be that they had lived high on the hog, they hadn't suffered the Blitz or rationing or cold winters and so what could they expect now? My uncle had been killed in Burma, but somehow the suffering of the war in the East, so far away, didn't seem to count in the same way as the war in the West. The returnees, bereft in many different ways, didn't get any sympathy – nor did they really expect any.[8]

The aide-de-camp to Pakistan's Army commander-in-chief found work in an Edinburgh brewery, while the Keenans moved to a farm in Hampshire to work with cows. John Keenan's admiral friend found work cleaning toilets in Waterloo Station, and gradually memory of the Raj receded into the annals of history.

The same month that the Somerset Light Infantry sailed from Bombay, a Soviet-sponsored coup d'état overthrew the Czechoslovak government in Europe. It would mark a turning point in the growing Cold War, and Soviet spokesman Andrei Zhdanov urged a more confrontational approach between 'people's democracies' and 'imperialist' nations.[9] International observers increasingly perceived world conflicts through the lens of the burgeoning USA–USSR rivalry, and when the UN delegation arrived in Kashmir that spring, one delegate worried the region was 'on the road to a radical left-wing totalitarian dictatorship' and 'might eventually become a hub of Communist activities in Southern Asia'.[10]

Fears in Kashmir were probably overblown, but there is no doubt the Communist Party was rapidly gaining ground across South Asia. On 28 February the second congress of the Indian Communist Party opened in Calcutta and a microcosm of pre-Partition India descended upon the former capital with delegates from India, Pakistan, Nepal and Burma (including one of Aung San's wartime Thirty Comrades). Although the new borders imposed by Britain were rejected as a 'sham independence',[11] a new Communist Party of Pakistan was formed at the meeting. More importantly, a new confrontational stance was adopted in the face of 'the reactionary forces of Congress and Muslim League'. Moni Singh, later head of the Communist Party of East Pakistan, recalls 'a very rousing speech' by Than Tun of Burma, and soon the anti-feudal revolution in Hyderabad was chosen as a model for uprisings elsewhere.[12]

'Just after the Calcutta Congress,' writes Moni Singh, 'the governments of both India and Pakistan started mass arrests and repression of Communist Party leaders.'[13] Similar steps were taken in Burma when intelligence agencies learned that a Burma-resident Bengali communist called Hari Narayan Goshal was planning the seizure of Rangoon via revolutionary means later that year. In the coming months armed communist insurrection would be reported from Tripura to Travancore, and from Bengal to Burma.[14]

Louis and Edwina Mountbatten were in Burma shortly before the first shots of insurgency were fired. Upon their arrival the couple attended a tea party with Aung San's widow and daughters at Government House and then gave a tribute to Burma's assassinated cabinet members, still lying in state in glass coffins, their 'mouths gaping wide', eight months after their assassination.[15] With the flags of Britain, Burma and India strung up everywhere, Mountbatten gave a speech about the 'shocking loss' of Aung San and Mahatma Gandhi. Then he pulled a cord, 'dropping a vast red curtain to reveal the magnificent gold-lacquered throne dulled with age'.[16] The enormous thirty-foot throne of the last Burmese king had been sitting in Calcutta Museum since Burma's annexation to India a century earlier and was so big it had to be broken up into 460 separate pieces to be transported to Burma. Its return symbolised that British – and Indian – hegemony over the nation had at last come to an end. After the ceremony was over, Mountbatten took Prime Minister Nu aside to address the growing communist threat. 'There are deep fissures [here],' noted Campbell-Johnson, 'between Burmans and Karens, between Aung San's Anti Fascist people's Freedom League and the Communists, and between the Communists themselves. There are the symptoms here of complete political disintegration.'[17]

By the time Mountbatten arrived back in Delhi a few days later, the endgame of the partition of the princes was underway, with both India and Pakistan beginning to use their militaries to secure the accessions of the final independent princely dominions: Kalat, Hyderabad and the Khasi states.

Renowned as the wettest place on earth, the Khasi Hills around the city of Shillong were studded with mountains, glittering lakes and standing stones, erected in honour of the deceased. Having flirted with joining Pakistan, most of the twenty-five states there had acceded to India the previous December, but the two tiny states of Nongstoin and Rambrai still resisted.[18] Shortly before Mountbatten's return, the Assam Rifles had been used to pressure the ruling *Syiems* into signing the accession. Nongstoin's ruler subsequently asked the UN Security Council 'to direct the Indian Government to withdraw its troops from his territory', but his appeals went unheeded.[19] Instead Khasi farmers found themselves unable to sell their products to markets in East Pakistan and, as the modern border between India and East Pakistan came into being, the pungent scent of rotting orange orchards floated through the hills.[20]

At precisely the same time Pakistan was using military intimidation to secure the accession of the far-western state of Kalat, a move that would trigger decades of conflict in Baluchistan. Nestled in its rugged expanse, Kalat had been the third largest state in the Raj, set apart by its remarkable geography and unusual political structure. Unlike the absolute monarchies of other princely states, Kalat was essentially a confederation of disparate tribes and chieftains, a set-up described by one British governor as 'not unlike that of the Arab Sheikhdoms'.[21] Having recently introduced two elected houses of parliament to his state, the Khan put the question of accession before his newly elected politicians. They rejected the idea and Baluchi politician Ghaus Bakhsh Bizinjo argued:

> We have a distinct civilization ... We are Muslims but it is not necessary that by virtue of our being Muslims we should lose our freedom and merge with others. If the mere fact that we are Muslims requires us to join Pakistan, then Afghanistan and Iran, both Muslim countries, should also amalgamate with Pakistan.[22]

In the run-up to independence, Jinnah had actually recognised Kalat's right to independence. But in October 1947 he changed his tune and started pressuring Kalat to merge with Pakistan, employing the same technique that India had used in Junagadh. He approached Kalat's vassal states – Kharan, Las Bela and Makran – and offered them recognition as independent states. On 17 March 1948 Jinnah recognised them as independent, essentially severing Kalat from half its territory, resources and coastline.[23]

In a mirror of Indian actions in the Khasi Hills the same week, Pakistan then swiftly dispatched its military into the Baluchi vassals and according to the Khan, began gearing up for a 'police action' against the rump of Kalat State. Tensions mounted, and rumours suggested that the Khan of Kalat had secretly reached out to both Afghanistan and India for assistance. On 27 March the airwaves crackled with a startling announcement. All-India Radio reported that Kalat had tried to accede to India. The story was subsequently denied by the Indian and Kalat governments, but by then it had unleashed a wave of anger among Kalat's population. Precisely why All-India Radio made this ostensibly false announcement remains unclear, but it clearly forced the Khan's hand. 'It had never been my intention to accede to India,' he pleaded afterwards, and that same afternoon he finally did what he had been resisting for seven months, and acceded to Pakistan.[24]

The Khan's parliament had not been consulted, however, and refused to accept the accession. The Khan's brother, Abdul Karim, fled to Afghanistan with several hundred others, and started a rebellion against the Pakistani state.[25] Decades of insurgency in Baluchistan had begun.

By the end of March 1948 the vast and landlocked state of Hyderabad was the only princely state of any importance whose future relationship with India and Pakistan remained unresolved.

Established by the old Mughal *subehdars* of the Deccan, Hyderabad State was essentially a fragment of the Mughal Empire that had survived into the twentieth century, and its opulence was unparalleled. The eponymous capital was praised by poets as the 'bride among cities',[26] with palaces built on hilltops, on lakes and even overlooking the city's famed racecourse. The Nizams had long been Britain's closest allies in the subcontinent, and the city's architecture fused Mughal and British aesthetics in unlikely ways. Ayman Garh and Hill Fort Palace were built as mock-Gothic castles while Falaknuma Palace combined a Palladian façade with a Scots baronial interior, and a ceiling brimming with Islamicate *muqarnas*. Most extraordinary of all, however, was the palace of minister Salar Jung, the greatest art collector in India, whose teak *baradaris* were embellished with thousands of rare Chinese porcelains, renaissance Italian sculptures and Mughlai miniature paintings that made contemporary collections in Europe look provincial by comparison.[27]

Here more than any other state, the British had found the orientalist fever dream they yearned for, where *shirwani*-clad noblemen 'kept as pets tigers, ostriches and panthers',[28] and could occasionally be spotted hunting rare beasts across boulder-strewn landscapes. 'The city of Hyderabad seems to have been dropped to earth from an Oriental Dream,' wrote the author Elizabeth Cooper in her book *The Harim and the Purdah*. 'It is the most Eastern city in this most Eastern land and you are filled with a sense that it is not all real, but especially staged and set up for your amusement, and when you leave it will all disappear.'[29]

Ruling over all this was the Nizam himself, whose etiquette was as baroque as his formal name: General His Exalted Highness Rustam-i-Dauran, Arustu-i-Zaman, Wal Mamaluk, Asaf Jah VII, Muzaffar ul-Mamaluk, Nizam ul-Mulk, Nizam ud-Daula, Nawab Mir Sir Osman Ali Khan Siddqi Bahadur, Sipah Salar, Fath Jang, Faithful Ally of the British Government, Nizam of Hyderabad and Berar, GCSI, GBE.

Despite his grand title, Nizam Osman Ali Khan was a man of unassuming demeanour, of short frame, his face adorned with a bushy moustache and 'eyes that could pierce you ... like steel'.[30] He had been installed on Hyderabad's *gaddi* aged twenty-four after his charismatic father's death – allegedly from alcohol poisoning – and his coronation had involved the sacrifice of a cock, the release of eighteen prisoners and a glorious durbar at the Chowmahalla Palace.[31] As well as penning thousands of 'perfumed ghazals', the Nizam gradually amassed one of the greatest collections of medieval literature in the subcontinent. His harem was equally large, and according to his grandson, each evening he would enter 'the garden outside the *zenana* quarters where the wives would gather' and place a 'white handkerchief' on one of his wives' shoulders. 'That way,' his son later recalled, 'she would know she had to report to his bedroom at nine o'clock.'[32]

The British had hoped the poet Nizam would be a malleable leader, but they quickly found he was more politically inclined than they had bargained for. He lobbied for Britain to return ceded land and transformed Hyderabad into a modern nation with its own passport, currency, bank and airline. The state's public works outdid those in British India, and Osmania University was the Raj's first college to teach in a non-English vernacular (Urdu). After the death of J. D. Rockefeller, the Nizam was crowned the world's richest man, and the fifth richest in history.[33]

Over time the Nizam transformed Hyderabad into an extraordinary seat of empire in its own right, employing the Sultans of Qu'aiti state (in modern Yemen) as Jemadars in his Irregular Arab Forces. The Sultans would reside in Hyderabad years after Arabia's separation from the Indian Empire, and their government would become an 'Arab-Indian hybrid'.[34] These Arabian vassals allowed the Nizam to argue that Hyderabad was no ordinary princely state. With a third of people living under princely rule and an income and expenditure rivalling 'those of Belgium and exceed[ing] ... those of twenty members of the United Nations', Hyderabad, the Nizam argued, was not just a princely state it was a country in its own right.[35]

However, the Nizam's greatest idea was still to come. He planned to transform Hyderabad into the seat of the global Islamic Caliphate, with his dynasty becoming the leaders of Sunni Islam across the globe. First, in 1931, he married his sons to the daughters of the deposed Ottoman Caliph Abdulmecid II. A week later he purportedly secured a deed from the last Caliph, nominating their joint grandchildren as the next Caliphs of Islam.* To signify the revival of the Caliphate in Hyderabad, he began construction of a grand Ottoman tomb for Abdulmecid II in the sacred Hyderabadi town of Khuldabad, a short distance from the Ellora Caves. Although Abdulmecid would never actually be laid to rest there, Hyderabad came to be regarded as 'the most prominent Muslim city outside of the Holy Land', its name uttered in the same breath as Mecca and Jerusalem.[36]

If Hyderabad's central place in the Islamic world has today been forgotten, it is only because of the events that were to follow. Hyderabad State remained majority Hindu, with a tenth of its land

---

* This deed – discovered by the brilliant researcher Imran Mulla – is controversial, and there have been allegations that it is a forgery. However, as noted by Mulla, it 'would actually be fascinating if it turned out to be a forgery, because the question then becomes who forged it and why'. For more, read Mulla, I., *The Indian Caliphate: Exiled Ottomans and the Billionaire Prince* (Hurst, Forthcoming).

ruled by fourteen Hindu vassals called the Samasthans.[37] The Nizam considered Hindus and Muslims to be the two eyes of his state and he endowed Hindu temples just as lavishly as he did Muslim mosques, funding the creation of the *Mahabharata*'s critical edition and even restoring the ancient Buddhist murals of Ajanta.[38] But with the Hindu–Muslim divide growing and the Pakistan demand gaining steam, the Nizam's leaning into Islamic identity gained him enemies – particularly among Hindu nationalist groups.

At the same time many started to regard the Nizam as an anachronistic and feudal aristocrat who did little to address the vast poverty in his domains. Much of the state's wealth was derived from heavy taxes and *vetti* bonded labour, which to many observers was little different from slavery. Urdu was promoted as the state language, but at the expense of the more widely spoken Telugu, Marathi and Kannada languages. 'My mother tongue ... had no proper place in the school curriculum,' wrote one critic years later. 'I had to sing every morning prayers wishing continuance of Nizam's rule forever' while 'my father was undergoing a prison sentence ... for agitating against the despotic and feudal rule'.[39] It was a sentiment that would crop up more and more as the 1940s progressed, and Iris Portal, a British writer and friend of the Nizam's daughter-in-law, paints a picture of a state on the edge of collapse.

> [The Nizam] was mad as a coot and his [chief] wife was raving. It was like living in France on the eve of the revolution. All the power was in the hands of the Muslim nobility. They spent money like water, and were terrible, irresponsible landlords, but they could be very charming and sophisticated as well. Many had English nannies, and had been to English schools or universities. They would take us shooting – snipes and partridges – talking all the while about their trips to England or to Cannes and Paris, although in many ways Hyderabad was still in the Moghul Middle Ages, and the villages we would pass through were often desperately poor. You couldn't help feeling that the whole great baroque structure could come crashing down at any minute.[40]

Like the Maharaja of Kashmir, the Nizam had decided not to accede to either India or Pakistan. He received support from not only Muslims, but also Hindu elites like the Samasthans as well as the two major Dalit organisations in the state – the Independent Scheduled Caste Federation and the Depressed Classes Association.⁴¹ Nusratullah Shah recalls that at Nizam College, where he was studying, 'there were strong Muslim factions rallying for Hyderabad Deccan to be acceded to Pakistan' but most students 'favoured it to be an independent state'.⁴² Elsewhere, however, particularly in the outlying districts, there was a strong desire for merging with the Union of India.

India perceived Hyderabadi nationalism through a simplistic lens of Muslim separatism, and the Nizam's claims to independence garnered significantly more outrage than similar claims in Kashmir, Kalat, Bhutan and Sikkim. The situation 'did not fluster Hyderabad's nobility', however, who 'carried on as if nothing was about to change'. The Nizam's 'personal 60-piece string orchestra, conducted by an Anglo-Indian named Henry Luschwitz, played waltzes and foxtrots at garden parties', and like Iris Portal, civil servant Philip Mason retrospectively observed that living in the city felt 'like the spring of 1789 at Versailles':

> At the buffet suppers that the grandees of Hyderabad enjoyed so much, the men were elegant in black sherwanis or gorgeous in gold brocade, the ladies wore saris of sapphire or starlit blue ... [and] the plates were covered with Persian pilaus, Mughal kebabs, Indian curries, French salads – dishes to suit every taste.⁴³

On 8 August the Nizam offered India a 'treaty of association',⁴⁴ but India rejected the idea, wanting full accession on its own terms. Patel and Menon argued that as Hyderabad was surrounded on all sides by Indian territory, it could not be given the same option of independence as Kashmir. For the Nizam, this slapdash claim merely masked the basic difference that he was a Muslim ruler while Kashmir's was a Hindu.⁴⁵

For his part, Jinnah warned Mountbatten that if Congress 'attempted to exert any pressure on Hyderabad, every Muslim throughout the whole of India ... would rise as one man to defend the oldest Muslim dynasty in India'.⁴⁶ But Jinnah's relationship with the Nizam was just as tortured as Nehru's and although many 'regarded Hyderabad as an independent Muslim state in South India, the corollary of Pakistan in the north',[47] Jinnah had previously been banned from even entering Hyderabad. During a rare meeting with the Nizam in 1946, he had spread his legs and lit a cigar, causing the Nizam to shout, 'Is this the way you behave towards the Nizam of Hyderabad?'[48] Jinnah apologised but their relationship would never quite recover.

Hyderabad's independence was greeted with a range of emotions. Members of the Razakar paramilitary group celebrated openly. Congressmen and union workers tried to hoist an Indian flag rather than a Hyderabad one, but were arrested.[49] In Secunderabad, state troops opened fire on a mob. It was a foreboding start for Hyderabad's independence, and the Nizam's establishment of an interim government with equal numbers of Hindus and Muslims was derided by many as an 'eye wash'.[50]

Home Minister Patel initially offered the Nizam a plebiscite on the matter of independence, but the ruler only consented to a standstill agreement.[51] Both India and Hyderabad, however, quickly convinced themselves the other was violating their agreement. The Indian Army, which had commandeered Hyderabad's military equipment during the war, refused to send the weapons back and enforced an informal blockade on the state. Congressmen were frequently found disrupting its institutions and by early 1948 more than seven thousand people had been arrested.[52] Meanwhile, the Indian government complained of the way that Hyderabad had banned Indian currency and given Pakistan a loan of two hundred million rupees.

To make things worse, they caught Hyderabadi General El Edroos trying to source weapons from abroad. The suave military commander had travelled to London, where intelligence agent Dennis Conan Doyle, son of the Sherlock Holmes author, had introduced him to 'an adventurer who was prepared to get involved in rackets'.[53] Before the two men could organise anything of substance, El Edroos ran into Mountbatten, who was celebrating his nephew Philip's marriage to Princess Elizabeth. India's outgoing Viceroy asked El Edroos what he was doing in London, and the general said he was in the city for 'the treatment of my eyes'. Mountbatten replied with a wink, before ordering the Hyderabad government to recall Edroos immediately.[54]

El Edroos found it impossible to send weapons to Hyderabad without any recognition of it as an independent country, but no third party was willing to do this for fear of angering India. Hyderabad was thus forced to rely on an elaborate bluff to keep law and order. State propaganda began maintaining that a 'Peacock Division' stationed in its Arabian vassal had 'a hundred bombers ... ready to bomb Bombay' and was sending 'arms and ammunition' to the Nizam's capital.[55] But the Indian blockade had made any movement of tribesmen from Arabia to Hyderabad impossible, as demonstrated on 8 April, when sixty-four Qu'aiti subjects attempted to join Hyderabad's state forces. 'On our arrival at Bombay, the police authorities took us to jail and detained us in custody for one month,' read a statement from the sixty-four men. After the Bombay police compelled them to board a dhow back to Arabia, they were dropped off at an Omani port, rather than in Qu'aiti State, where they remained stranded for months with 'no one over there to tell us what to do'.[56]

Hyderabad's fortunes were about to change, however, with the unexpected arrival of a daring Australian pilot called Sydney Cotton. He was 'in his middle 40s,' writes El Edroos, 'tall and well built', with an air of smug confidence.[57] Born on a cattle station in Queensland, Australia, Cotton had learned to fly in the First World War, and subsequently helped to pioneer the idea of air mail. In 1938 he joined the British intelligence services to photograph German bases as an aerial reconnaissance pilot but had eventually been kicked out. By 1948 Cotton had become something of a travelling rogue.

Thunder clouds swirled around Cotton's plane throughout his journey to Hyderabad, but as the palatial capital came into view, the sky cleared and 'three brightly tinted rainbows' arched overhead. 'I had heard many stories of the fabulous wealth of the Nizam,' Cotton remembered, 'and I could not help recalling the fairy-tale about gold at the end of the rainbow.'[58] He had come to buy his friend Miranda some groundnuts, which the blockade had made impossible to source elsewhere, but found himself enthralled by the state's fraught politics. 'The citizens of Hyderabad, it seemed to me, very much wanted to keep their independence,' he writes. 'The Moslems because they did not want to be absorbed by India, and the Hindus because many of them were "untouchables" who expected to suffer from absorption into the Indian Union.'[59]

Sympathising with Hyderabad's plight, and seeing the potential of working for the world's richest man, Cotton organised a meeting with the Hyderabadi leadership and suggested 'it would be quite simple' to airlift vital supplies in from Karachi. Given the go-ahead, he flew to Karachi and met the Pakistani defence secretary, who agreed to seek Jinnah's approval for the operation.[60]

That week, Pakistan's governor general happened to be visiting the province of East Bengal – the waterlogged eastern wing of his new nation – for the very first time. A motion in Pakistan's Legislative Assembly to make Bengali a state language had recently been rejected, despite its speakers making up some 55 per cent of Pakistan's population. The result was mass protest and Jinnah's presence would only make the situation worse. Mujibur Rahman, the Muslim League student activist who had partaken in the Direct Action Day riots, remembers his excitement at the prospect of Jinnah's visit to Dacca. 'We had all got drenched in the rain,' he writes in his memoir, 'and yet we waited to greet him in our wet clothes.' But when Jinnah arrived at the rally, he told the gathering that 'Urdu, and no other language' would be the state language of Pakistan and that 'Anyone who tries to mislead you is really the enemy of Pakistan.'[61] Mujib and his friends were livid, raising up their hands in protest and shouting, 'No, no.'[62] Other meetings proceeded along similar lines and Jinnah left East Pakistan soon after, never to return.

The chasm of difference between Pakistan's east and west would lead to the Partition of Pakistan itself two and a half decades later, with East Bengal becoming Bangladesh. In the meantime, Jinnah returned to Karachi hardened by the experience and convinced Indian fifth-columnists were everywhere. The episode in Dacca led him to make 'two fateful decisions': first to approve Sydney Cotton's airlift of weapons and supplies to Hyderabad and second to formally order the Pakistani Army into Kashmir.[63]

No longer would Pakistan be fighting in the princely state through proxies. India and Pakistan, just seven months earlier a single country, were now, formally, at war.[64]

The same month that Jinnah ordered the Pakistani Army into Kashmir, Sardar Patel had a heart attack.

He had been working around the clock for months, promising the princes they only had to give up their defence, foreign policy and communications.[65] Yet he had recently begun pressuring them to merge their state administrations with India entirely, and had started seizing princely property for the Indian state. The Nawab of Pataudi – captain of the Indian cricket team – had discovered that half of his cricket ground had been taken by Patel's states ministry.[66] By May 1948 only twenty-five princely states retained their original borders and administrations – a traumatic rupture for many princely subjects.* In this feverish atmosphere, and beset by grief over Gandhi's death, Patel succumbed to a heart attack. When he came to afterwards, his first words were, 'I had to go with Bapu. He has gone alone.'[67]

Although most militias had been banned after Gandhi's assassination, in the same period they increased massively in Hyderabad. Communists used burra katha, a musical folk tradition, to spread anti-Nizam sentiment, and in response their performances were outlawed altogether.[68] However, the communists were just the tip of the iceberg. Sardar Patel's strategy to ensure the state's accession had been 'to manufacture border incidents and instability … to justify military intervention',[69] and on his orders 1,600 men were mobilised and armed, as weapons were confiscated from Muslims in the same area. Patel kept channels with RSS leaders open even after the organisation was banned for involvement in Gandhi's murder, and when RSS-associated Congressmen offered to send several thousand men into Hyderabad, he told them to 'keep your boys ready'.[70] In one chilling instance, an 'armed mob' of more than sixty individuals descended on the Muslims and government workers of Bhanasgaon village, setting their homes alight. On another occasion raiders staged a full-blown bank robbery, stealing two hundred thousand rupees and killing two bank employees.[71]

In the border region of Osmanabad, Hyderabadi district collector Mohammad Hyder witnessed the state's slow descent into chaos first

---

* Historian Manu Pillai has noted that although it 'may be awkward to register today', the end of the princely states was considered a great tragedy by many of their residents. The integration of Baroda into the new state of Gujarat caused 'a feeling of depression and sorrow' and Patel's men recorded numerous protests against integrating the state of Pudukkottai into Madras. 'The local legislature – and many states had legislative councils – went so far as to demand a plebiscite, insisting that Pudukkottai continue as Pudukkottai in independent India, because that identity and its physical bounds meant something. The ruling family here, ironically, had not been terribly popular and could claim its fair share of scandal and ignominy; yet, evidently, their subjects identified with the principality.' Pillai, M. S., *False Allies* (2021) p11.

hand. Here in the Marathi-speaking west, near the basalt bastions of Naldurg Fort, with enclaves of Indian territory dotting the district, self-appointed Indian freedom fighters frequently made raids from across the border; and by the time Hyder was employed, sixty-one attacks had been reported in the district.[72]

'It was clear almost immediately that the raids were a cause of concern among the inhabitants,' he wrote years later. 'Corruption was rampant ... [and] life was becoming intolerable for the majority of people ... A sense of ceaseless menace pervaded the atmosphere.' The district magistrate of Sholapur across the border fervently denied the existence of border camps within his jurisdiction, but when Hyder 'offered to go with him and identify the camps', the magistrate rejected the offer. In response Hyder started training up locals to protect themselves and announced that anyone involved with the cross-border raids would have their property confiscated. But he grew frustrated with his government's lack of concern for the borderlands and at a conference in the capital he found 'there was no recognition of the untenable border situation, no clarification of the government's plans to defend our frontiers, or guidance on how to meet an incursion there'.[73]

Gradually the Nizam fell back on the militant Razakars for support. The paramilitary group had emerged from the state's pre-eminent Muslim political party, the Majlis-e-Ittehad, and by 1947 had fallen under the sway of the militant lawyer Kasim Razvi. Mohammad Hyder met Razvi in November that year and describes him as 'a small man, short and very thin with sharp Arab features ... a man of iron will, and a very dangerous enemy ... [with] bright, piercing eyes'. Razvi chewed paan, chain-smoked cigarettes and occasionally fidgeted with his beard in an 'absurd and frightening' manner, and when Hyder asked why the Muslim minority should continue ruling over a Hindu majority, Razvi told him: 'We Muslims rule because we are more fit to rule!' Hyder noted that Razvi 'could not quite mask his fear of the Nizam', and privately seemed unsure of how far he could push his own power. Publicly he spoke of magnanimously planting the Asaf Jahi flag on the gates of Delhi's Red Fort. 'India is a geographical notion,' Razvi told Hyder that evening, but 'Hyderabad is a political reality. Are we prepared to sacrifice the reality of Hyderabad for the idea of India?'[74]

Razvi's threatening anti-Hindu rhetoric would cast fear into the hearts of many Hindu Hyderabadis, tearing apart the state's religiously plural ethos. The poet Samala Sadasiva later remarked how:

> Every day, Deccan Radio would broadcast the emotion-packed hate speeches by Qasim Razvi. There were loudspeakers throughout the city and the speeches were audible everywhere. Listening to these speeches, we would walk in the city with fear. In the evenings, both Muslim and Hindu teachers gathered in two opposing sides and there was an intense fear among us all. That fear was totally new; it was something that we had never experienced before. However, the Muslim educators in the institute ... always would say: 'Qasim Razvi is just a day dreamer' ... Their words gave us lots of relief and they were totally critical about the new developments in Hyderabad.[75]

By November it was unclear to many in New Delhi whether the Nizam retained control over his state, or whether Razvi really held the reins of power. In a letter to Mountbatten, the Nizam had called the lawyer a 'somewhat demented' and 'stupid person who is a man of low station'. But after Razvi led tens of thousands of protesters to intimidate the government that October, the Nizam had begun to bend to his demands. Over the following nine days, more than a hundred thousand Hindus fled the state.[76]

Throughout 1947 South India had been remarkably bereft of violence and migration, but in the summer of 1948, as itinerant militias roamed the state, an astonishing 1.2 million people would be displaced across the borders of Hyderabad, almost double those displaced in the Palestinian Nakba the same year. Some 750,000 Muslims entered the state, fleeing Partition violence in North India, while another 400,000 people – mostly Hindu, but also some Muslims – went in the other direction. The modern Indian state of Telangana may not usually be associated with Partition, but in 1948 the scale of movement to and from the region was comparable to that in Bengal and Punjab.[77]

Razvi's Razakars were primarily pitted against the Telangana communists and border raiders, but over time they started extracting bribes from blameless villagers. Where there was resistance, 'arson, murder, desecration of temples and even rape and abduction of women followed'.⁷⁸ At the time Champabai Dattambhat Purohit was living in Afzalpur, near the old capital of Gulbarga, and was pregnant with her first child. She remembers how 'in many homes, belongings were stored underground so as to escape the looting' and how the local revenue collector desperately tried and failed to keep the roaming militias under control. Gradually her relatives fled across the border into India, and although her father was the village's Hindu priest, Champabai decided to pray to the Sufi saint of Gali Saheb for protection. 'I prayed that if I am unharmed by the Razakars, I would come to the dargah every year,' she recalls. Luckily she 'remained unharmed during the massacre' that followed and safely crossed into India to deliver her baby. Seven decades later she still keeps her promise to the saint, returning to the shrine each year.⁷⁹

Precisely how strong the Razakars actually were is still controversial, with Razvi claiming more than two hundred thousand volunteers and a BBC correspondent maintaining there were no more than thirty thousand. 'Razvi organized a Razakar parade for me in Hyderabad city and told me it would be a big show,' the correspondent wrote. 'I had expected at least three thousand Razakars ... [but] I counted fewer than four hundred of whom twenty or thirty were children under ten years of age.'⁸⁰ In fact, as Mohammad Hyder noted, 'The Razakars and the marauding freedom fighters existed in a state of adverbial symbiosis, each entity conjured up to fight the other, and likely to lose its reason for being if the other disappeared. Both were a threat to law and order.'⁸¹

Over time individual families found themselves torn between rival political factions. Mrs Awadhi Shirani Bawa recalls her grandfather working with the Paigah nobles and loving the Nizam's regime, while her cousin was a founding member of Hyderabad's Communist Party and actively worked for the Nizam's downfall. A family friend joined the Razakars. Bawa found it hard to demonise any group completely – even this paramilitary group, who she found were often just as scared themselves – but she sympathised most with her communist cousin, and eventually began learning Russian, on top of speaking Urdu, Hindi, Marathi, Telugu and English.⁸²

All this generated an unprecedented atmosphere of fear and constant suspicion and one civil servant observed that 'the majority of the population had resigned themselves to being alternatively beaten up by the

Police, by the Army, or by the Communists'.[83] Yezdyar Kaoosji, a Hyderabadi Parsi, likewise recalls having to cover his 'house's windows for the sake of safety'.[84] By early summer even loyal allies of the ruling establishment worried it was time to leave. In May the Sultan of Qu'aiti State and his family tried to board a ship to flee, but his wife's blood relationship with the Nizam was discovered by Indian authorities and her application to leave – and that of her infant son – was rejected. The family briefly moved into Bombay's Taj Mahal Hotel but negotiations failed and Nazirunissa and Ghalib were ultimately forced back to Hyderabad, where they would remain for years to come. Sultan Awadh, meanwhile, set off back to Arabia without them, accompanied by two rabbits smuggled across the Arabian Sea in the deep pockets of his sherwani robe.[85]

As the administration in Hyderabad broke down and another great migration was set in motion, Indian reports on anti-Hindu violence in the state grew ever more exaggerated. They claimed, for example, that Hyderabad's forces were arming and training the Razakars despite the state's army having virtually no weapons to give them in the first place. In fact, Hyderabad's General El Edroos had tried to persuade the Nizam to ban the Razakars and claims to have slapped Kasim Razvi on one occasion.[86] But 'exaggerated reports of chaos in Hyderabad' and of attacks against Hindus were circulated by India's agent general in the state who was a virulent supporter of the RSS and Mahasabha, believing that only Indian military intervention could overthrow the Nizam's regime.[87]

In fact the conflict was more complicated than many Indians realised, particularly given the strong pro-Nizam stance among Hyderabadi Dalits, many thousands of whom joined the Razakars.[88] At the heart of this unlikely political alliance were the magnetic orators B. S. Venkatrao and Shyam Sunder, renowned for their 'lofty thoughts ... polished manners and delicious humour'. The two began speaking at Razakar rallies, calling upon Dalits to 'revolt against caste Hindus' to ensure that Muslims rather than Brahmins remained in power. The alliance paid dividends, as the Dalit community were granted massive amounts of land in return.[89]

But Indian politicians remained convinced Hyderabadi Hindus were in imminent danger, and soon after Mountbatten's return from Burma he learned the Indian government had drawn up plans for a military intervention. It was nicknamed Operation Polo, and Nehru emphasised it was only a contingency plan, prepared 'wholly and solely against the extreme emergency of Razvi carrying out his threat of murdering all the Hindus with his Razakar'. Even India's prime minister was unaware, however, that Patel had already fixed a date for the invasion should negotiations for Hyderabad's accession fail: 13 September.[90]

As negotiations with Hyderabad stalled, Edwina and Nehru grew ever closer, with Edwina now keeping an 'informal snap shot' of India's PM on her desk and signing her letters to him 'Love ever, Edwina'.[91] A few weeks after the Mountbattens' return to Delhi, Nehru joined the couple on a hill retreat and when he left, Edwina wrote, 'I hated seeing you drive away this morning ... You have left me with a sense of peace and happiness. Perhaps I have brought you the same?' He agreed, and years later he would confide that 'some uncontrollable force, of which I was only dimly aware, drew us to one another. We talked more intimately, as if some veil had been removed, and we could look into each other's eyes without fear or embarrassment.'[92]

While Nehru and Edwina were busy gazing into each other's eyes, it was dawning on Mountbatten that he had just a single month left in India before his tenure as governor general came to an end. Ever obsessed with his legacy, he began to pour all of his efforts into the intractable Kashmir and Hyderabad problems. As the summer heat set in, he dispatched his press attaché Alan Campbell-Johnson to Hyderabad to try to resume the negotiations.

Campbell-Johnson arrived in the state just before lunch on 15 May, and gained an audience with the Nizam that evening, in a palace 'cluttered high with Victorian bric-a-brac'.[93] 'H.E.H. was dressed most shabbily,' he wrote, with a brown fez balanced precariously on his head, and

> what looked like a thin white cotton dressing gown and white trousers with light brown cotton socks lying loosely about his ankles, and caramel-coloured slippers ... He is a small man with a pronounced stoop; his mouth is loose and his teeth are in a deplorable condition ... But his whole personality is held together

by the intensity of his expression and the vehemence of his high-pitched voice. Although he may be physically decrepit, he is obviously mentally alert.[94]

Campbell-Johnson told the Nizam that Mountbatten would remain India's governor general for only another month and that it would be better to strike a deal while he was still acting in that capacity, rather than negotiating with his Congress successor. 'What could he hope to do in a month?' replied the Nizam. India already had his terms and 'he had nothing more to say to any other party, even on a private basis'. The Nizam then changed the topic, subjecting Campbell-Johnson to a lecture on the importance of celebrating Muharram, and another on why constitutional monarchy 'may be all very well in Europe' but it 'had no meaning in the East'. The press secretary left thoroughly puzzled by the whole experience and reported back to Delhi that: 'The interview left me with the impression that I had been spoken to by an eccentric Professor on his special subject.'[95]

Shortly before he left, Campbell-Johnson attended a buffet dinner held in his honour at Shah Manzil, a Mughal-modernist pile of crenulated arches and cement *jaalis* overlooking the great Golconda Fort. It was, he said, 'a glittering social occasion' and he was surprised to see 'Hindu and Moslem mixing freely' with 'no sense of imminent crisis'. Although this cross-section of society merely represented the aristocracy, it struck him that 'for all the feverish propaganda', Hyderabadis seemed 'stirred with less passionate ferocity than their compatriots in the stern and stormy regions of the north'.[96]

Back in Delhi, however, the attitude couldn't have been more different. When Campbell-Johnson returned north in late May, he found that V. P. Menon's general opinion of Hyderabad 'had hardened'[97] and that Nehru was now dismissing the state's history as an inglorious series of capitulations to other powers. Patel called Hyderabad an 'ulcer in the heart of India'.[98] Mountbatten, meanwhile, wished he had sent Campbell-Johnson sooner. The time for a resolution, it seemed, was slipping away.

The days that followed were punctuated by lengthy negotiations. Menon proposed a vote for Hyderabadi independence, just as had been held in Junagadh. But when Hyderabad's prime minister Laik Ali agreed, Sardar Patel withdrew the offer.[99] Negotiations broke down again, and on 17 June, a week before Mountbatten left India, the Nizam's adviser sent a telegram with one word: 'LOST'.[100]

With Mountbatten's plans to resolve the conflict over Hyderabad in tatters, he made one last effort to resolve the Kashmir crisis, suggesting a partition on religious lines. Maps were 'marked up and discussed … but the Pakistanis refused'.[101] The outgoing Viceroy thus gave up. He would depart India leaving both Kashmir and Hyderabad as open sores.

'We dined with Jawaha and his family,' wrote Edwina a few days before leaving, '[and] sat in the garden with full moon. Sadder and Sadder.'[102] When their final day in India arrived, the Mountbattens drove through Chandni Chowk, Old Delhi's main thoroughfare, and attended a farewell party at Viceroy's House, to which all two thousand staff were invited.[103] Nehru gave a speech and turning to Dickie, he said:

> Maybe we have made many mistakes, you and we. Historians a generation or two hence will perhaps be able to judge what we have done right and what we have done wrong … We did try to do right and I am convinced that you tried to do the right thing by India and therefore many of our sins will be forgiven.[104]

After a deafening pause, Nehru turned to a tearful Edwina:

> To you madam … the gods or some good fairy gave … beauty and high intelligence, and grace and charm and vitality … and they gave you something which was even rarer than those gifts, the human touch, the love of humanity, the urge to serve those who suffer and who are in distress. And this amazing mixture of qualities results in a radiant personality and in the healer's touch. Wherever you have gone, you have brought solace.[105]

The next day, 21 June 1948, Edwina and Dickie boarded a plane for England and Edwina burst into tears. She took off her St Christopher necklace and asked an assistant to deliver it to Nehru. They passed the long flight home in 'sombre silence'.[106]

★ ★ ★

In the wake of the Mountbattens' departure, the Pakistani government finally admitted having sent troops into Kashmir. 'We are thus in open, though formally undeclared, war with Pakistan,' Nehru wrote to Mountbatten on 1 August.[107] Both armies raced to control the high passes of Ladakh, the high-altitude plateau in the east of Jammu and Kashmir where the Buddhist and Islamic worlds collided on the edge of Tibet.[108] It would be relatively easy for Pakistani troops to make it, but the Indians had to cross the high-altitude Zoji-La Pass, which was under thirty foot of snow. For three days and nights, the Indian Army beat great drums to trigger avalanches, before a column of troops made their ascent.[109] On entering Ladakh, both armies clashed at 11,500 feet. The Pakistanis dug in around a town called Kargil, and in response India began airlifting tanks onto the plateau, an area that had previously not even seen bicycles.[110] Soldiers who had fought alongside one another in Burma found themselves facing each other on a high-altitude battlefield, and some even smuggled cigarettes and letters across the front line to old friends.[111] 'Those relationships are very difficult to explain,' recalled Lieutenant-General S. N. Sharma years later. 'It was power. Not religion. The hunger for power and authority is what drove us to madness.'[112]

Elsewhere the relationship between India and Hyderabad had plummeted further. By now the torturous negotiations had tried everyone's patience and on 24 July after a spat with some Pathans and Razakar militias, the Indian Army took over a Hyderabadi village called Nanaj. In response Hyderabad's army did nothing. 'Not until after Nanaj did I fully realise how weak our own army was,' writes Mohammad Hyder. He travelled back to the capital to meet the Nizam's cabinet, but once again the politicians barely acknowledged his requests for help. Hyder discovered that Pathan irregulars had established protection rackets and he 'began wondering if they had been behaving like this all over Osmanabad'. He wanted to ban them from the area, but without help from the state's army, he found himself leaning on these same Pathans to guard the border.[113]

In the last week of August, after the Razakars murdered Shoebullah Khan, the editor of Hyderabadi newspaper *Imroze*, Nehru sent a message to his high commissioner in the UK, Krishna Menon. 'Situation inside state is getting intolerable,' the Indian prime minister wrote:

Razakars stopped train the other day and attacked and looted passengers ... If unchecked, [the Razakars might] create state of lawlessness throughout Hyderabad State and neighbourhood. As we have already told you this we cannot allow to happen. Police action against Razakars and their sympathisers in Hyderabad cannot, therefore, be postponed much longer.[114]

Nehru had lost patience with the Nizam, and having long resisted Patel's calls for military intervention, he began to take a more confrontational tone. Indeed, it was no longer just the Razakars who worried him. In some areas the communists now virtually conducted a parallel administration, with four thousand villages run by 'village soviets'. Telangana was spoken of as the launchpad of a pan-Indian revolution,[115] and communists as far south as Malabar had been reported using slogans like 'Telangana Way, Our Way' and 'Land to the Tiller, Power to the People'. On one occasion the Indian Army had even had to be called in to 'quell' a rebellion.[116] Speaking to the American embassy about the situation in early September, V. P. Menon argued it was now 'necessary for the Indian Government to march into Hyderabad ... to put down the Communists, who were completely out of control'.[117]

As things seemed to be approaching a final showdown, Laik Ali suggested to Nehru they refer their dispute to the United Nations. The Indian PM rejected the offer, so Laik Ali secretly climbed aboard Sydney Cotton's aeroplane and flew to Karachi to seek Jinnah's assistance. Upon landing, he learned that Pakistan's governor general was gravely ill, so had to travel to the Baluchi hill station of Ziarat where Jinnah was recovering. But the Pakistani leader's health was much worse than he had expected. 'I could see anxiety on everyone's face when I reached ... [Jinnah's] residence,' Laik Ali writes.

> There were two or three doctors in the consultation. I was told that an hour ago some injection had been administered which had caused a very severe reaction, and at the moment he was in great agony and in a state of semi-consciousness ... [Jinnah's sister Fatima] kept frequently going into his room and returned disappointed each time ... [Jinnah], she told me, only with great difficulty, waved his fingers indicating that his agony was too

great. Around three o'clock in the afternoon I gave up all hopes of meeting Jinnah.[118]

Laik Ali returned to Hyderabad empty-handed and events began to move quickly. On 10 September Nehru issued Hyderabad an ultimatum to let Indian troops re-establish themselves in the state, and the British government started an evacuation of its civilians, ordering 'all British officers to resign from the Hyderabad Army, on the basis that they could not be asked to take up arms against one of His Majesty's Dominions'.[119] As the monsoon rains subsided, news trickled in that prominent Muslim politicians in Bombay and Madras had been rounded up by the Indian police and temporarily detained.[120]

While India and Pakistan faced off in Kashmir, and India and Hyderabad geared up for war, Jinnah was flown back to Karachi after developing a case of pneumonia. His personal physician later wrote of how 'the withdrawing monsoon' made the skies turbulent that day and the frail Jinnah had to be given oxygen during the flight. Upon landing, the governor general was whisked away in an ambulance, but on the way to the hospital it broke down. His clothes were now 'wet with perspiration', and 'for an hour he lay dying, parked on the roadside'.[121] Eventually a replacement ambulance arrived to take Pakistan's founder to Government House, but there, at 10.20 p.m. on 11 September, Muhammad Ali Jinnah finally died.

As news of his death leaked, people rushed to get a glimpse of his body. 'There was a very eerie silence all around,' recalls one witness. 'Just a stunned silence because I think most people didn't expect ... that he was about to die.' The following day the body was taken from Karachi's Government House to the site of an unbuilt mosque to be buried in a funeral for which a million people gathered, the silence of the previous twenty-four hours replaced by 'a sea of humanity sobbing and wailing' as Jinnah was lowered into the grave.[122] It was later revealed he had been battling tuberculosis and acute lung cancer for years and Mountbatten lamented that 'if he had known the seriousness of ... [Jinnah's] illness, he might have delayed independence, and there may have been no partition'.[123]

'How shall we judge him?' wondered Nehru that afternoon.

I have been very angry with him often during these past years. But now there is no bitterness in my thought of him, only a great sadness for all that has been ... He succeeded in his quest and gained his objective but at what a cost and with what a difference from what he had imagined. What must he have thought of all this. Did he feel sorry or regret?[124]

An era had come to an end and within a year of the British departure, the architects of Burmese, Indian and Pakistani independence were all dead. Aung San's legacy had been extraordinary, Gandhi's even more so, but of the three men it was arguably Jinnah's legacy that would be the most enduring of all. As his biographer Stanley Wolpert later put it:

Few individuals significantly alter the course of history. Fewer still modify the map of the world. Hardly anyone can be credited with creating a nation state. Mohammad Ali Jinnah did all three.[125]

The next morning, as Pakistan shuddered with grief for its founding father, Nehru approved Operation Polo and the Indian Army began its march on Hyderabad.[126] Officially the Indian government referred to the advance as a 'Police Action' to restore law and order. But with Indian tanks rumbling over the border and Indian fighter planes swooping overhead, there was little to distinguish it from a military invasion. Mohammad Hyder writes:

That day, Major Mohsin found himself sinking into a state of absolute helplessness. The men under his command were no better equipped than civil defence forces. Major Mohsin kept himself busy burning papers, hurrying to receive army messages and making last ditch efforts to keep up the morale of his men. He went about his business like a man under sentence of death. One of the earliest casualties in Osmanabad town was the jail sentry ... hit as he stood at his post in front of the jail gates. As he fell, our advance unit (sent out to resist the tanks) came running back, thoroughly frightened and panting for breath. Major Mohsin now informed me that he had no means of resisting the advance of the tanks. His men were armed with .303 rifles and hopelessly short of ammunition. What was Hyderabad importing all these days, I wondered? What were those legendary feats of gun-running?[127]

Despite Sydney Cotton's exploits, Hyderabad's army remained wildly under-equipped, with 'dummy aeroplanes of bamboos and gunny bags' placed in airports to convince the Indians they had an air force.[128] The Indian Air Force quickly established supremacy of the skies and the solitary anti-aircraft gun in Hyderabad was not even unwrapped from its packaging. By the end of day one, seven Indians had been killed, compared with 632 Hyderabadis.

Realising the game was up, Mohammad Hyder fled Osmanabad for the capital. Driving by jeep over a waterlogged landscape, he found the authorities in a state of utter confusion in every town he passed through. In Murud the state forces told him they had been given no instructions and in Bidar forces didn't even seem to know where the Indian Army was. Arriving in Hyderabad on the night of 15 September, Hyder discovered that his feet 'had swollen from staying upright for too long, and my shoes could only be removed by cutting the laces'. A further shock was in store for him. Although schools were closed, none of the city's politicians 'seemed concerned about the possibility of bloodshed in the city'. Prime minister Laik Ali blindly asserted that everything was going according to plan and that the state forces were preparing for a final showdown outside Hyderabad; only Kasim Razvi seemed to take the threat of open warfare seriously. On learning that Razvi was planning to order his Razakars to massacre all Hindus in the city, Hyder spent the next day trying to persuade him out of it.[129]

By this point El Edroos had secretly instructed his troops not to resist the advance of the Indian Army, but Deccan Radio and All-India Radio were blasting out completely contradictory news of the war, so that for the most part the population had no idea what was going on.[130] Hyderabad Radio promised civilians that Pakistan was on its way and even that King Farouk of Egypt had promised full support 'for a struggle against the Indian government'.[131] Yet neither Egypt nor Pakistan, nor Qu'aiti State, sent any help.

Over the next few days the Nizam fell into an ever-deeper gloom. By the morning of the 16th, Laik Ali observed that he was 'far from his usual self', 'non-communicative' and 'unusually absent-minded'.¹³² The two men now considered a hasty resolution by the UN Security Council their only hope and the same afternoon the UN met in Paris to discuss the situation in Hyderabad. But talks moved far too slowly, and after hearing the cases of both India and Hyderabad, the Security Council fixed a second hearing for four days' time. By then Hyderabad would cease to exist.¹³³ Mir Moazam, a district collector, recalls:

> As head of the district, I was sitting with the Brigadier in the staff car, trying to decide what to do, when the Indian Air Force started strafing us from the air. Our car windows exploded ... In the end the Brigadier and I took refuge under an arch of the bridge we had been supposed to blow up. The rest of our troops tried to find cover behind clumps of trees along the river. The Brigadier and I managed to escape under intense firing and strafing, and after that we just retreated and retreated ... When the Emperor Aurangzeb invaded Golconda [in 1687], the Hyderabad troops managed to keep the Moghuls at bay for seven or eight months. In our case we only held them up for four days. It was a total collapse.¹³⁴

On the afternoon of 17 September, General El Edroos set out to surrender to the Indian Army, accompanied by his aide-de-camp and his chauffeur. The Indian column arrived at the proposed meeting point at 4 p.m., led by Major-General Chaudhuri, and after the two men saluted each other, Chaudhuri offered El Edroos a cigarette which El Edroos accepted. A ceasefire was then agreed and a formal surrender occurred the next day: 'In total, the Indian government counted 42 Indian soldiers, 490 soldiers of the Hyderabad army, and 2,727 Razakars killed in the fighting.'¹³⁵

Syed Moazzam Ali Taufeeq, the seven-year-old grandson of an advocate at Hyderabad's High Court, was playing at his Hindu friends' house at Troop Bazaar when the surrender was announced. 'The radio was on and, all of a sudden, words like "Fall of Hyderabad" caught my ears,' he recalls. 'We were utterly confused about the meaning of "Fall of Hyderabad" and ... when I returned home, I saw the women of our house weeping and mourning. They told me to sit down, and had all the doors of the house locked from the inside' for fear of violence.¹³⁶ Civilians took shelter in schools while pro-Nizam militias like the Razakars started frantically burning their uniforms and burying weapons in holes in the ground.¹³⁷ Begum Khurshid Abdul Hafiz was one of the first two women parliamentarians in Hyderabad's state assembly, the author of a book on women's rights, and having taken a prominent role in training the Women's National Guards, she now worried about all the weapons she had stored in her house. As her son Khalid recalls:

> I saw my mother dumping all the rifles in the backyard of our house and setting them on fire ... and watched them burn. All the wooden butts had been burnt down and I learnt from my sister later that the metal barrels were dumped into the river that night.¹³⁸

Indian troops entered Hyderabad city, but for several hours no one really knew what was going on and rumours were rampant. Arun Kumar Chatterjee remembers hearing wild claims that Indian soldiers were looting the Nizam's palace and torturing the women of the harem. 'The palace gates used to shine with lights and jewels,' Chatterjee says, 'but from that time onwards, they never shined the same way again.'¹³⁹

In the next few days the Indian Army banned the Razakars and began putting down the communist armed struggle, a fight that would continue until 1951. Enemies of the Hyderabadi regime took advantage of the chaos, acting as informants against their political rivals and in a matter of days thirteen thousand of the Nizam's Muslim subjects had been rounded up and arrested, including both Laik Ali and Razvi. Eighty-five per cent of arrested Muslims would be released within half a year for lack of evidence that they had committed any crimes.¹⁴⁰ With the Indian Army arresting and deporting many of those who had been loyal to the Nizam, many Muslims decided to flee.* Both Laik Ali and Razvi later escaped prison and fled to Karachi, Laik Ali doing so disguised in a burqa. But Mohammad Hyder was unlucky: arrested by

---

* So many Hyderabadis reached Karachi in the following days that a residential neighbourhood called Hyderabad Colony was eventually established in the city.

a Congressman whose property he had confiscated in Osmanabad, and imprisoned for three years.[141]

As well as imprisonment, Hyderabad's new military government also set about deporting 'outsiders', invariably Muslims. After 750,000 North Indian Muslims were sent 'home',[142] the new Indian government also resolved to 'get rid of the Pathan and Arab outsiders in Hyderabad as quickly as possible'.[143]

Hyderabad had always been close to the Arab states of the former Indian Empire – as well as having an Arab vassal state in southern Arabia, it had one of the largest Arab populations in the subcontinent. But now tens of thousands of Arabs were rounded up and readied for deportation,[144] sparking strong protest, particularly in Aden where the newspaper *Al Nahda* warned of the 'brutal action ... against the Arabs of Hyderabad' and demanded those in the state be allowed to live 'in the same way as the Hindus do in Aden'.[145] Yet a decade after the separation of Aden and a year since the separation of the Gulf, the idea that 'Arab' could be an Indian ethnicity like Bengali or Punjabi – one that had been common for centuries – had finally died.

It was the Hyderabadi general El Edroos who saved the day. An Arab from Southern Arabia himself, he managed to convince India's military leadership not to deport his kinsmen en masse. A deal was struck to reduce the number of Arab deportees from twenty-five thousand to seven thousand.[146] The Indian government would only actually pay for two thousand of them to leave, while another 'several hundred Arabs made their way from Hyderabad to Aden on their own initiative, often by hitching a ride in boats used for the import of dates'.[147] Those who remained moved to the Arab-dominated ghetto of Barkas, but, traumatised by the ordeal, most would migrate to the Persian Gulf a few years later.[148] Meanwhile, the Qu'aiti family, who for generations had ruled their Sultanate in South Arabia from Hyderabad, ended their association with the state and 'sought the liquidation' of their property and assets in India.[149]

All the while the Nizam himself was left to ponder his future. The government of India chose not to depose him, and he remained in his grand palace of King Kothi as a figurehead for the new military government. Intriguingly he was never forced to sign any papers of accession to India. Only a year later would he issue a *farman*, ordering that 'the Constitution of India should be the Constitution of the State of

Hyderabad'.¹⁵⁰ With that, all of his dreams of becoming an independent sovereign vanished into thin air.

India's military annexation of Hyderabad terrified Pakistan's leadership, convincing many that it had similar designs for Pakistan. On 8 October, only a fortnight later, Liaquat Ali Khan made an announcement that would loom large over the young country's future. 'The defence of the State is our foremost consideration,' declared Pakistan's prime minister. 'It dominates all other government activities. We will not grudge any amount on the defence of our country.'¹⁵¹ Before long an extraordinary 70 per cent of its annual budget would be spent on defence. Within a matter of years, the military dominated Pakistan economically and even politically.

India's leadership, on the other hand, considered Operation Polo a remarkable success. *Time* magazine described the brief war as 'one of the shortest, happiest wars ever seen' with 'no terrible outbreaks of violence'.¹⁵² Only a few weeks later reports of anti-Muslim violence started leaking out. 'Large numbers of Moslems who were trying to get out of the country were hauled off trains,' wrote Sydney Cotton, 'accused of being Razakars and killed on the spot.'¹⁵³ Dalits were also targeted, thanks to their leader's proximity to the Razakars,¹⁵⁴ and in the Marathi-speaking parts of the state Hindu Congressmen were reported trying to 'snatch back' land from Dalits and attack those 'who resisted'.¹⁵⁵ Nehru and his cabinet initially ignored such reports as hyperbole, but when the PM's spurned former lover Padmaja Naidu brought him similar news, he could ignore it no longer.¹⁵⁶ In November Nehru wrote frantically to Sardar Patel's office that:

> The figures of killings mentioned are so big as to stagger the imagination ... If there is even a fraction of truth in these reports, then the situation in Hyderabad was much worse than we had been led to believe. It is important that the exact facts should be placed before us.¹⁵⁷

Nehru appointed a committee to investigate, which arrived in Hyderabad on 29 November and over the next month travelled to nine of the state's districts. The men, known as the Sunderlal Committee, were horrified by what they discovered and wrote back to Nehru:

> In many places we were shown wells or *bawaries* still full of corpses that were rotting. In one such we counted 11 bodies which included that of a woman with a small child sticking to her breast ... Many [other] women were forcibly taken from their homes, kept for a number of days and then sent back to their homes ... Adult males of a locality had been killed [and] the women and children were generally 'persuaded' to adopt the Hindu faith. We came across hundreds of Muslim women who had been forcibly tattooed on the forehead right in the orthodox Hindu style as a mark of their conversion. Some even had their new Hindu names tattooed on their forearms. We saw children whose ears had been freshly bored in the Hindu style ... At some places we were informed that the victims were removed to some adjoining temple and then finished off in the sacred precincts.[158]

Hyderabad had essentially been left without a functional administration for several weeks, as the Indian Army had taken time to set up its own control.[159]

Much of the violence was retaliatory, in revenge for earlier Razakar atrocities, and in Kasim Razvi's hometown of Latur, 'the killing continued for over twenty days. Out of a population of about ten thousand Muslims there we found barely three thousand still in the town,' wrote the Sunderlal Committee. Nonetheless, they also noted that 'these atrocities were not limited to those who had suffered at the hands of Razakars'. A 'large mix of trained and armed men from a well-known Hindu communal organization' had 'filtered into the state along with the Indian Army from Sholapur'[160] and they had looted the Muslims of Hyderabad State at random.

Even more concerning was the complicity of members of the Indian Army and the police. The Sunderlal Committee described India's General Chaudhuri as 'a man without any tinge of communal prejudice' and his officers as being of a 'high standard of discipline'. Yet they also found 'unimpeachable evidence' that junior soldiers and policemen had 'encouraged, persuaded and in a few cases even compelled the Hindu mob to loot Muslim shops and houses'. The committee eventually suggested that by 'a very conservative estimate', between twenty-seven thousand and forty thousand Muslims had been killed during and after the 'Police Action'.[161] Other scholars would later suggest numbers as high as two hundred thousand.[162]

The findings of the Sunderlal Committee would be suppressed for half a century and only declassified in 2012. Sardar Patel was particularly contemptuous of its conclusions, lambasting the committee members that 'your appreciation of the position lack[s] balance and proportion'.[163] Ignoring the report, Patel would order Major-General Chaudhuri to give a secret amnesty to all 'Hindus involved in retaliatory action just after the Police Action';[164] while tens of thousands of Muslims languished in prisons since the Indian invasion, Hindus were soon allowed to go free. The new administration avoided investigating the conversion of Muslim holy sites into temples, claiming that the several hundred attacks were merely the 're-conversion of what were originally temples, but were converted into mosques, into temples again'.[165] At the same time Chaudhuri set about dismantling the Nizam's state, replacing Muslims with Hindus in the administration to make it more evenly weighted, and removing state patronage from a host of institutions. In his memoirs Chaudhuri notes that:

> The Nizam maintained even a string orchestra and whenever I wanted to hear some light music, I used to invite the orchestra to the Guest House where I was staying and they would present a programme which was absolutely delightful. Unfortunately, once Hyderabad was merged, the string orchestra had to be disbanded. The bandmaster went to Australia where I understand he found a good job.[166]

On New Year's Day 1949, Pakistan's commander-in-chief Douglas Gracey and India's commander-in-chief Roy Butcher negotiated a ceasefire between the two countries to stop the war in Kashmir extending to Punjab and Sindh. Over the next six months, a 'ceasefire line' would be drawn, informally partitioning Kashmir between India and Pakistan. Although still not accepted as a border by either country, it has evolved into one of the most fortified borders in the world.

In little over a year since the departure of the British, over 550 states had vanished from the map. Burma had increased in size by a third, India by almost two-thirds and Pakistan's landmass had doubled. There is arguably no other revolution in world history that ended so many monarchies in so short a span of time. V. P. Menon later reflected on his accomplishment: 'For the first time India has become an integrated whole in the real sense of the term.'[167]

Of course, obliterating hundreds of separate states did not happen without huge economic and cultural loss. While the 'civilising' mission of the British stamped out many of India's traditions elsewhere, India's princely states had continued patronising age-old traditions of music, dance, art and crafts. When all these royal families were paid off by 'privy purses' and abolished, thousands of bards, artists, courtesans, camel trainers and courtly cooks found themselves unemployed. Hundreds of ancient art forms vanished. In Janjira, south of Bombay, it spelled the end for the only kingdom in the world where a Muslim Nawab descended from Abyssinian pirates ruled through a Jewish prime minister. The Partition of Princely India was now complete.

There is an irony here that at precisely the moment of decolonisation, British ideas of sovereignty, government, race and religion were extended to a population several times larger than that which the British had ever forced them on. And yet the merger of the states also created the world's largest democracy – one in which many of the princes would themselves take part. When Soviet premier Nikita Khrushchev found out what had happened, he looked on in disbelief. How had India managed 'to liquidate the princely states,' he asked, 'without liquidating the princes?'[168]

11

Mother Tongues

In 1950 a conflict in Bengal finally brought the vast migrations of the Great Partition to a close. It began with a Pakistani crackdown on (mostly Hindu) communists in the East Bengali town of Khulna.[1] Nehru described the situation to Mountbatten in a letter:

> Somehow, we cannot put an end to all the terrible consequences of Partition ... Kashmir today is almost of secondary importance because of the Bengal situation. Practically every Hindu in East Bengal is clamouring for evacuation ... There are 12 million Hindus in East Bengal and so you can understand the nature of the problem.[2]

East Bengal's Dalits were particularly targeted, despite their conscious choice to become Pakistanis rather than Indians, and many in Nehru's own cabinet, including Sardar Patel, called for all-out war with Pakistan.[3] But Nehru was convinced that war would only hurt the future prospects of India and Pakistan's remaining minorities, and that if a population exchange could be averted there was still a chance of 'East Bengal joining West Bengal at some future date'.[4]

In April Liaquat Ali Khan flew to Delhi and together with Nehru embarked on a remarkable attempt to stop further displacement.[5] The statesmen established a pact that made both India and Pakistan legally responsible for their minorities, subsequently hailed as the 'Magna Carta of Minorities Rights'.[6]

An unprecedented stabilisation of the refugee crisis followed. By May an Indian official was even speaking of 'the very friendly relations between the two governments brought about by the Nehru–Liaquat Pact'.⁷ The same month a joint press conference brought journalists from India and Pakistan together for the first time in three years, and correspondents burst into tears upon seeing their old co-workers again.

> [They] spent hours talking, trying to get to the bottom of what was happening across the border and learning about life in a place which had now become mysterious and inaccessible. A Pakistani journalist admitted that he was relieved to find that the reports he had seen in Pakistan of gangs massacring Muslims [in India] had been exaggerated ... Nehru reflected that the two states had to find a way to get their people to meet as often as possible.⁸

Together Liaquat and Nehru had brought about the impossible. Peace and hope had returned to the subcontinent.

In the wake of the pact, there was a palpable sense that the worst had passed and, for the first time in almost a decade, people were able to begin moving on with their lives. A new journal called *Nai Zindagi* (New Life) was published in Karachi to help local Sindhis and migrants from India better understand each other, and across the border in India a 'Marriage Bureau' started putting 'displaced men and women in touch'.⁹ Richard Bartholomew, an Anglo-Burmese boy who had fled Burma during the Long March, fell in love with Rati Batra, a Bengali girl whose life had been uprooted during 1947, and their partnership exemplified the hopes and dreams of the early 1950s when the shackles of the old world seemed to have given way to a strange new order of limitless possibility.¹⁰ Even the markets were at last recovering from the aftermath of Partition, and the *Indian Express* correspondent reported that 'after three years of uncertainty ... the year has closed on an unmistakable note of confidence'.¹¹

The orphans of empire set about navigating their changed circumstances. The impact of ending princely rule was now becoming clear, as artists across the subcontinent adapted to new mediums like radio and film. The sitar player Ravi Shankar, who had performed at the Asian Relations Conference and studied Indian classical music in

Maihar State, was forced to find work at All-India Radio by the collapse of royal patronage. Mehdi Hasan, the great ghazal singer from Rajasthan, was likewise compelled to abandon music after 1947 and work in a Lahori bicycle shop until a lucky break with Radio Pakistan revived his music career. The sheer number of dispossessed musicians and dancers moving into the film and radio industry in the 1950s may account for the prevalence of song and dance in South Asian cinema, and with the Indian film *Awaara* in 1951 Bollywood went global for the first time. The film became Chairman Mao's favourite and Soviet statesman Nikolai Bulganin would on one occasion perform an a cappella rendition of the titular song for Nehru. By some metrics, *Awaara* remains the most globally successful film of all time.[12]

Within South Asia, the 1950s are often treated as the end of history and the beginning of modernity, an era of centralisation, five-year plans and independent nation-building.[13] But contrary to popular perceptions, not all of Britain's former Indian Empire had even gained independence yet. As India, Pakistan and Burma looked back on their first years of freedom, the great crescent of Arabia – from Aden to oil-rich Kuwait – remained under the British thumb, with an 'Arabian Raj' now reporting to Whitehall rather than to the Viceroy of India.* In the words of Gulf scholar Paul Rich, this was 'the Indian Empire's last redoubt, just as Goa was Portuguese India's last solitary vestige, or Pondicherry was the tag-end of French India'.[14] The official currency was still the Indian rupee, the easiest mode of transport was still the 'British India Line' and the thirty Arabian princely states were still governed by 'British residents' who had made their careers in the Indian Political Service. Indeed, the Persian Gulf Residency, situated in

---

* For the term 'the Arabian Raj' I am indebted to Kristopher Radford's work on the Gulf's role under Viceroy Curzon. See Radford, K., *An Arabian Raj: The Indian Empire and the Persian Gulf States, 1899–1905* (Master's Thesis, University of Calgary). By 1950 the Arabian Raj was no longer under a single government as it had been in the Bombay Presidency. It was a confusing set of colonial territories, and the British public was largely oblivious of its existence. The Gulf states were governed by the Foreign Office, as was Oman despite British insistence that the state was entirely independent. Meanwhile, the states of Southern Arabia were given the vague title of 'Protectorates' – despite the fact that Britain had never done anything much to 'protect' them. Only in the city of Aden itself did the British own up to their presence. Nonetheless, the region was treated as a single unit – both by the British and by the revolutionaries who sought to tear it down.

Bahrain, was still populated entirely by Goanese servants, and the resident's sedan chair was the very same one used to carry Lord Curzon ashore during his visit to Bahrain in 1903.[15]

'The Raj maintains here a slightly phantasmal sway,' wrote *The Times* correspondent David Holden, 'a situation rich in anomaly and anachronism.' After a regrettable stint as a geography teacher, Holden had been excited about his Arabian posting, but he hadn't expected to be attending a garden durbar at the Residency in honour of 'Queen Victoria, Empress of India'. His memoir is a remarkable testament to the ways in which the Raj lingered in the Arabian Peninsula in the 1950s: 'The servants are all *bearers*, the laundryman a *dhobi*, and the watchman a *chowkidar*,' he wrote, 'and on Sundays the guests are confronted with the ancient, and agreeable, Anglo-Indian ritual of a mountainous curry lunch.'[16] In Hyderabad's erstwhile vassal of Qu'aiti State, the military still marched around in now-defunct Hyderabadi army uniforms, and the list of Hyderabadi exiles included the royal rabbits.[17] In the words of the governor of Aden himself:

> One had an extraordinarily powerful impression that all the clocks here had stopped seventy years ago; that the Raj was at its height, Victoria on the throne, Gilbert and Sullivan a fresh and revolutionary phenomenon, and Kipling a dangerous debunker, so strong was the link from Delhi via Hyderabad to the South Arabian shore.[18]

Despite these lingering ties, however, the world in which Gandhi had travelled from Rangoon to Aden, without leaving the Indian Empire, was now the distant past. Three Partitions had separated Burma, Arabia and Pakistan from India, and a fourth had divided over five hundred princely states between these new nations. Excluding Kashmir, whose status remained disputed, 562 states had joined India, 12 had joined Pakistan and 52 had joined Burma.* Only the Himalayan and Arabian states remained intact within their old borders.

The new map of South Asia would have baffled anyone from twenty years earlier. But there was a fifth and final Partition still to come. In the fateful year of 1971, a civil war in Pakistan would bring the Cold War powers to the brink of nuclear annihilation and carve a final Partition through the former lands of the Indian Empire. After nine

---

* Numbers relating to the princely states must be treated as rough estimates, as they change dramatically depending on how you count them. Take for example, the number of states that acceded to Pakistan. If we count the number of rulers who successfully acceded to modern Pakistan, we find twelve states: Bahawalpur, Khairpur, Chitral, Swat, Hunza, Nagar, Phulra, Dir, Las Bela, Kharan, Makran and Kalat. Several others, however, attempted and failed to accede to Pakistan, such as Junagadh, Manavadar, Dujana and even some of the Khasi states. Junagadh's accession to Pakistan was even formally recognised by Jinnah. And what of Kashmir, whose ruler never acceded to Pakistan, yet half of whose territory is today administered by Pakistan? To make things even more complicated, several of these states were vassals of other states. Phulra, for example, was a vassal of Amb.

brutal months, South Asia's youngest nation – Bangladesh – would be born and India would be transformed into the undisputed power in the region. The same month India would formally abolish the several hundred monarchies it had absorbed two decades earlier, and the British would abolish their protectorates over the Arab Gulf states: the last of the Indian Empire's princely states to gain complete independence from imperial rule. 1971, not 1947, would be the year that modern South Asia was born.

As the 1950s began, the battles that had plagued the subcontinent were by no means over, and religious, communist and ethnic militias still roamed the countryside. The separatist movement led by the Khan of Kalat's brother in Baluchistan continued to bubble away and in 1953 Nehru imprisoned his old Kashmiri ally Abdullah for speaking of Kashmiri independence from both India and Pakistan. Nowhere would see more separatist sentiment, however, than the Patkai Hills, where the borders of India, Pakistan and Burma all met.

After independence the citizens of the Patkai found themselves ignored by national elites in all three countries. The new borders that had ruptured their land were treated as unproblematic, and national representation of the region was limited to images of 'a faraway Shangri La of green hills, bamboo groves and quaintly dressed innocent exotics who danced a lot'.[19] The fact that a Naga led the Indian football team into the Olympics didn't seem to help and even Nehru admitted:

> I knew nothing of the place and it all seemed so strange, all these little groups wanting their own states and countries. I decided I wasn't going to have anything to do with these demands.[20]

In both India and Pakistan, the Patkai inhabitants were legally termed 'tribals', and despite their literacy rates being significantly higher than elsewhere in South Asia, they were portrayed as 'backward' and 'primitive'. When Mizo dancers were invited to India's new Independence Day parade, they were told their suits and sarongs were not exotic enough and local art competitions were hastily organised to design entirely new 'tribal' costumes.[21] The same invented costumes are still pulled out every Republic Day in India seventy-five years later to display 'traditional' Mizo culture, despite the fact that there is absolutely nothing traditional about them.[22]

The Muslim Rohingya were the first Patkai peoples to challenge the borders of Partition through armed insurgency. Having feverishly campaigned for Pakistan, they found themselves part of Burma and organised a militant group called the Arakan Mujahed Party to fight against the Burmese state and 'join up with East Pakistan'. Burmese prime minister U Nu's government sent 'planes to bomb the insurgents',[23] but the sudden appearance of armed militias burning Burmese villages while bearing the Pakistani flag created a diplomatic spat between the two countries and Pakistan had to emphasise that it had no territorial ambitions in Burma.[24] Burmese counterinsurgency tactics triggered a 'massive refugee exodus' to East Pakistan.[25] The Burmese state would henceforth always view the Rohingya as foreigners who rightly belonged in Bengal. The real problem, of course, was the border, but opportunities to shift it had gone. For better or worse, it was now fixed.

It would be the first of numerous insurgencies in Burma. Chairman Mao's communist victory in China the same year saw Burma's low-level communist insurgency intensify, and it was quickly followed by mutinies in both the Karen and Kachin divisions of the Burmese Army. Mandalay fell, and within weeks the anti-state militias had dug in on the outskirts of Rangoon itself. U Nu's government looked to be going the way of Aung San's – under a hail of enemy bullets.

Nehru was still struggling to suppress the communist revolt in the Hyderabadi countryside, and he became convinced the fall of Nu's government to communists would invite revolution in India itself. Pakistan had closed its frontier with China after communists were apprehended entering the country, and Indian spies learned from 'secret and reliable' sources that two Burmese Indians – a 'Madrasi' called Krishna Reddi and a Bengali called M. I. Majumdar – had already 'infiltrated' the refugee camps of Chittagong and planned to 'start secret work in Assam'. Indian intelligence even briefly detained Naga leader Angami Zapu Phizo on the suspicion that he was a communist, although he was later released.[26] Convinced that communist revolution was imminent, Indian intelligence began to work closely with Pakistan and Britain to prevent the fall of Rangoon.[27]

It was the start of a decade of remarkable collaboration between the three primary heirs to the Indian Empire.* Newly armed with both Indian and Pakistani supplies as well as British intelligence, a Burmese general and old companion of Aung San called Ne Win went on the offensive. Described as a 'playboy, tyrant, numerologist and onetime post office clerk', he managed to push the Karen rebels back and turn the tide. By 1951 it was safe enough for travel writer Norman Lewis to journey through the interior.[28] Yet Burma would never be quite the same. In the 1930s it had been the richest part of India, but now it was 'the poorest sizable country in Asia, with a per capita income of less than $50 a year'.[29] Its rice and teak industries had been decimated and oil exports were less than half what they were before the war. The military had become the glue that held the country together; its gradual slide into decades of martial rule had begun.

In 1951 Burma was considered the country in South Asia most likely to break up. But twenty years later it was Pakistan, not Burma, that would fall apart. Pakistan, envisaged as a Muslim utopia, was certainly unstable from the start, and could never have lived up to all the hopes and dreams associated with it. Slogans like *'Pakistan ka matlab kyaa? La Ilaha ila'allah'* [What does Pakistan mean? There is no God but Allah] certainly 'rallied the pious' but as one historian has recently joked, it 'had all the specificity of "Brexit means Brexit".'[30] Pakistan was not a ship without a rudder after Jinnah's death as some historians have suggested, however. Liaquat Ali Khan took the helm with astonishing alacrity, and while continuing many of his predecessor's policies, he worked hard to try to induct as many Bengalis – severely underrepresented in the state services – as possible into government jobs.[31]

---

* As the Cold War deepened, the US would also take an increasing role in South Asia, signing a military alliance with Pakistan in 1954. India remained formally non-aligned in the Cold War, but privately Nehru told British and US officials that he would side with them in the case of a global conflict. As a result the US provided both countries with an astonishing $12 billion to fight off communism. Nonetheless, India would not completely shun the USSR and between 1955 and 1957, Indian exports to the Soviet Union rose sevenfold. See McGarr, P. M., *The Cold War in South Asia: Britain, the United States and the Indian Subcontinent, 1945–1965* (Cambridge: Cambridge University Press, 2013) and Sherman, T., *Nehru's India: A History in Seven Myths* (Oxford: Princeton University Press, 2022) Chapter 2.

Aung San, wearing Nehru's jacket, meets Clement Attlee in London to discuss a path to Burmese independence. U Saw stands behind him, wearing sunglasses to conceal his one weeping eye

Ten days after the Mountbattens' arrival in Delhi, the commander-in-chief's secretary wrote that 'Nehru's relationship with Lady Mountbatten is sufficiently close to have raised many eyebrows'

Nehru and Edwina in Simla, May 1947. 'We sat and talked … in the garden,' Edwina wrote in her diary, then 'sunbathed in the flowers'

Direct Action Day in Calcutta saw the first Partition violence. Margaret Bourke-White, arriving after reporting on the Holocaust, subsequently described Calcutta as 'a scene that looked like Buchenwald'

An exhausted and defeated Nehru votes for Partition

Nehru, Aung San and Jinnah on the eve of founding new nation states

Gandhi leads a peace march of both Congressmen and Muslim Leaguers after the massacres in Noakhali, December 1946

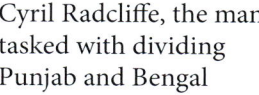

Cyril Radcliffe, the man tasked with dividing Punjab and Bengal

The Kotwali Gate of Gaur, which the Radcliffe Line transformed into the border between India and East Pakistan. Once a tourist destination, Gaur subsequently fell off the map

The Great Partition in 1947 triggered the largest forced migration in human history. Tens of millions of people would be displaced across religious lines, creating an overwhelming refugee crisis. Between one million and three million people would perish in the process

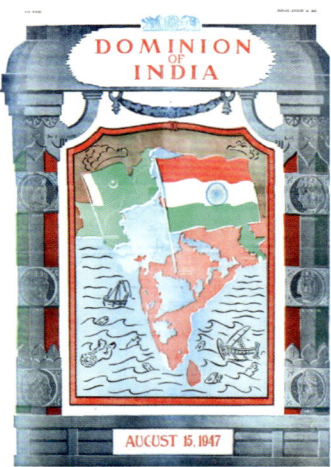

On 15 August 1947, over three hundred princely states gained independence alongside India and Pakistan. The map of India published by *The Hindu* on Independence Day thus doesn't include any of the princely states as part of India

Crowds celebrate Indian independence on 15 August 1947

The Wali of Swat signs the Instrument of Accession to Pakistan

The accession of Junagadh, a Gothic town of Gujarati-Mughal baroque, would almost send India to war against Pakistan for the first time

The Nawab of Junagadh is remembered in India today mostly as 'a vaguely ridiculous character', whose eight hundred pedigree dogs each had a private servant

The Women's Militia of Srinagar, preparing to fight the Pakistani-sponsored Lashkar

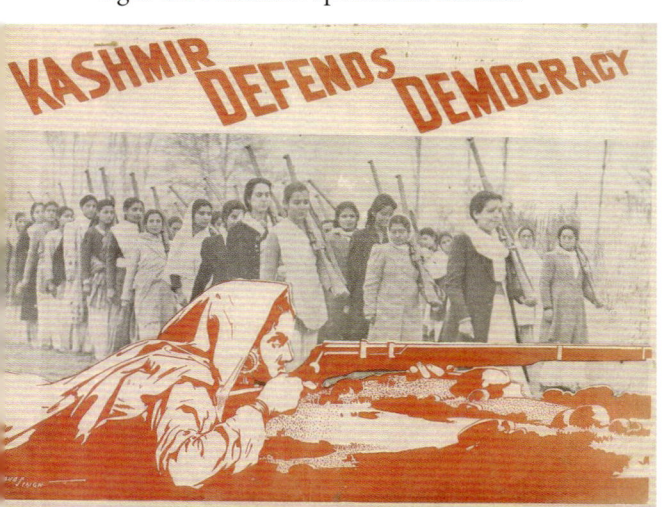

The Nizam of Hyderabad, the richest man in the world and the fifth richest in history

Egyptian president Gamal Abdel Nasser returns to cheering crowds in Cairo after announcing the nationalisation of the Suez Canal Company, August 1956

Just a few years after its separation from India, the Gulf's oil economy had skyrocketed to rival that of the USA

The Sultans of Qu'aiti State – today part of Yemen – once saw themselves as 'jagirdars' or vassals of the Nizam of Hyderabad

Sultan Ghalib Al-Qu'aiti, great-nephew of the Nizam of Hyderabad and the last Sultan of Qu'aiti State

The first hoisting of the United Arab Emirates flag by the rulers of the emirates in Dubai, 2 December 1971

Things started to change in March 1951, when Liaquat's cabinet was shaken by an attempted coup. Discontented officers in the Pakistani military, including the architect of the Kashmir struggle Akbar Khan, had formed an unlikely alliance with the Pakistani Communist Party and Marxist poet Faiz Ahmed Faiz, embittered at what they perceived as a betrayal of the Kashmiri cause.[32] Their coup was thwarted but just months later, in October, Liaquat Ali Khan was shot dead in a park in Rawalpindi. Still unsolved, his murder 'deprived Pakistan of shrewd and experienced leadership at a time when it was most needed'.[33]

The killing would seriously destabilise Pakistan, orphaned for the second time in quick succession and with many questions about its future still unanswered. Unlike India, which had implemented a constitution in January 1950, Pakistani leaders had yet to agree on how their state would be run and power be shared between its varied communities. Discontent simmered in East Bengal where, in 1954, the collapse of the region's jute economy – a result of the Radcliffe Line dividing the plantations in East Bengal from the production mills in West Bengal – triggered the feared 'second Bengal famine' in Khulna district.

It is often assumed that famines in South Asia ended after independence in 1947, but they afflicted the Bengal delta and the surrounding hills well into the 1970s, exacerbated by sluggish bureaucracies and the recruitment of civil servants alien to the region.[34] This first post-colonial famine – the 1954 Khulna famine – killed around twenty thousand East Pakistanis and played a major role in the province's growing disillusionment with its government.[35] The governor took to blaming Hindu zamindars but minister Huseyn Suhrawardy – under whose government Direct Action Day had occurred – began to openly criticise the Pakistani leadership for 'incompetence, oppression and nepotism'. The newspaper *Pakistan Observer* accused the central government of spending twice as much money on roads around Karachi than 'the starving people of Khulna' and Bengalis were horrified when a Karachi crossword puzzle paired the clue 'Plentiful in East Pakistan' with the answer 'Lice'.[36]

In the wake of famine, tensions over access to food emerged between urban Bengalis and the Urdu-speaking refugees who thronged the major cities. Despite their minority status, Urdu-speakers found it easier to get government jobs and often looked down on their Bengali neighbours as culturally inferior. When a Dacca college principal ordered that Bengali-language dramas could only be performed with the 'written consent of the majority of the Urdu-speaking students',[37] many Bengalis felt this was deliberately discriminatory, particularly given that Urdu-speakers made up less than a tenth of all students. Proposals to get rid of the Bengali script only furthered the Bengali sense of alienation in their own land. Pakistan 'was contrary to the Pakistan I had dreamed of,' wrote Bengali political activist Mujibur Rahman in his diary. 'The country had become independent: why wasn't anything being done to alleviate [our suffering].'[38]

In early 1952 Pakistan's first Bengali prime minister, Khawaja Nazimuddin, flew into Dacca to try and resolve matters. The rotund Nazimuddin couldn't have been more different from his predecessor Liaquat Ali Khan, and just six months before Partition he had admitted to a British governor that he didn't really know what Pakistan actually meant.[39] A feature in *Vogue* magazine showed him sitting regally alongside his brother-in-law, the Nawab of Dacca, amid elephant skulls and prints of Napoleon, and a caption described him as a man of 'enormous power and straightforward charm' who had been educated at Cambridge University and thus 'put mostly Oxford and Cambridge men into his cabinet'.[40] Instead of responding to Suhrawardy's economic and political criticisms, however, Nazimuddin criticised him for being too 'ready to play with the Hindus' and reiterated Jinnah's words that 'Urdu, and no other language' would be Pakistan's state language. It caused uproar.[41]

In Dacca a massive procession marched against Nazimuddin's speech and simultaneously all schools and colleges went on strike. Another strike was planned for 21 February, but the day before it was due to take place the Pakistani government banned all processions or mass gatherings in Dacca. Despite this, five thousand Hindu and Muslim students assembled the next morning at Dacca University, a short walk from where the Muslim League had been founded nearly five decades earlier. The government responded with lathi charges and tear gas, and when the students fought back the police opened fire, killing one and injuring seventeen more. Chief minister Nurul Amin, himself a Bengali, refused to visit the injured students in hospital, triggering a walk-out of politicians from the assembly. The next day an even larger group of students gathered to protest the killing, this time joined by shopkeepers and rickshaw-wallahs. More students were killed that afternoon, and the office of the *Morning News*, which tried to place the blame for the deaths on 'Indian Agents', was burned to the ground.[42] Folk musicians composed songs 'about the growing disparity between the two wings of Pakistan', and across rural Bengal there was a sense the government 'was trying to snatch away their language from them'.[43]

The twenty-first of February would retrospectively be considered the foundational moment of Bangladeshi nationalism and is hailed as International Mother Language Day; proof that Pakistan was doomed from the start. Those slain in 'the Dhaka killings', 'a phrase denied to the earlier slaughter of Hindus and reserved exclusively for this comparatively modest affair',[44] were hailed as 'language martyrs'. As one Bangladeshi told oral historian Anam Zakaria, '1952 is far more important to us than 1947.'[45]

There was a darker side to the movement, however. As Bengali politics coalesced around language, Urdu-speaking refugees were pejoratively labelled 'Bihari' and became unwitting symbols of 'Pakistan's "internal colonialism" over Bengalis'.[46] The fact that the governor general (Nazimuddin), chief minister (Nurul Amin) and the man who proposed replacing the Bengali script (Fazlur Rahman) were all Bengali themselves was forgotten.

The Language Movement sowed the seeds of Bangladeshi nationalism, yet it did not make Bangladesh inevitable.[47] Indeed, in a remarkable symmetry, a similar movement racked India at precisely the same time. Throughout 1952 speakers of Telugu – India's fourth most spoken language – had been pushing for a Telugu-speaking homeland to be carved out from Madras and Hyderabad states and a man called Potti Sriramulu even embarked on a Gandhian hunger strike for the cause. On 15 December that year he died of starvation, triggering disorder across South India. Indian police opened fire on demonstrating crowds, just as Pakistani police had in Dacca.[48] In 1952 Bangladesh was no more inevitable than an independent Telugu-speaking state.

Indian elites were just as deeply apprehensive about giving in to these demands of Telugu statehood, as those in Pakistan were wary of giving in to Bengali demands. 'Any attempt at redrawing the map of India on a linguistic basis,' wrote the *Times of India*, 'will lay an axe at the very root of India's integrity.'[49] But Nehru conceded to the demands for a Telugu-speaking state called Andhra Pradesh and within a year had even set up a commission to reorganise the rest of the country along linguistic lines. Indian provinces like Madras, Bombay and Mysore were replaced by new provinces like Tamil Nadu, Karnataka and Gujarat.

Apprehensive as many were at the time, linguistic reorganisation has, in hindsight, only strengthened India's unity. As historian Ramachandra Guha has noted, 'It has proved quite feasible to be peaceably Kannadiga – or Tamil, or Oriya – as well as contentedly Indian.'[50] By contrast Pakistan's refusal to give in to linguistic demands would dangerously destabilise the young country. As a result the Muslim League was routed from the East Bengal Assembly and on 19 April 1954 forced to concede the idea of Bengali as a national language.[51] After the election a new provincial administration was established in East Bengal led by Fazlul Huq, the Bengali leader who had first presented the Lahore Resolution for the creation of Pakistan. But riots in the Adamjee Jute Mills of Dacca between Bengali and Bihari migrants weeks later showed the direction things were going. Around the same time Huq told two foreign correspondents that he regretted Partition and wished Bengal could be independent.[52] Karachi panicked, and within days Huq had been arrested, his ministry replaced by governor's rule and Pakistani Air Force planes were dropping leaflets over Bengali villages denouncing the deposed chief minister as a 'traitor to Pakistan'.[53] The new military governor, Iskander Mirza, was also a Bengali, but this did little to sway Bengalis who had just had their democratic rights trampled on. Discontent only grew when Prime Minister Bogra – yet another Bengali, and the third Pakistani prime minister in just five years – announced:

> There will be no Bengalis, no Punjabis, no Sindhis, no Pathans, no Baluchis, no Bahawalpuris, no Khairpuris. The disappearance of these groups will strengthen the integrity of Pakistan.[54]

Bogra subsequently dissolved all Pakistani provinces and replaced them with two new provinces: East Pakistan and West Pakistan. Instead of strengthening the integrity of Pakistan, however, the attempt to crush regional identities only galvanised them. Across the border Nehru protested that 'East Bengal is being treated like a colony of Western Pakistan and a colony under military domination.'[55]

The break-up of Pakistan was still not a given though, and even Bangladesh's founding father, Mujibur Rahman, remained a staunch Pakistani nationalist. 'There was nothing wrong with the concept of Pakistan,' he wrote around this time. 'But those who had been left in charge of the nation were more interested in their own fortunes than those of the people.'[56] Indeed East Bengal remained central to the very idea of Pakistan, with its inhabitants making up a majority of the nation's inhabitants. Bengalis would continue to dominate Pakistan politically for much of the 1950s, producing four of its first eight prime ministers.

Nowhere is this early Bengali dominance clearer that in Jinnah's tomb, a Mughal-modernist masterpiece of marble and concrete, the construction of which began in 1960. With four pointed arches and sixty-one acres of gardens, it was meant to reflect both Pakistan's past and future. The architect was an Indian from Bombay – demonstrative of the fact that in the first decade of independence, Indians and Pakistanis were still able to cross the border for work with relative ease – and, surprisingly, Jinnah's gravestone is written in both Urdu and Bengali.

Jinnah had once imagined a 'Pakistan without Calcutta' being like 'a man ... without his heart'.[57] A Pakistan without Bengal at all was still unthinkable.

At precisely the same moment as language movements galvanised protesters across India and Pakistan, a similar movement was sweeping the Arabic-speaking world. At its heart was the new president of Egypt, Gamal Abdel Nasser, who would transform pan-Arab sentiment into a weapon against the British and overthrow their 'collaborators' in the Arabian Raj. His rise was meteoric. The son of an Egyptian postal worker, he despised the wealthy elites who he felt had sold out his country and was a fiercely political teenager. He fought during the 1948 Arab–Israeli war and was radicalised by the Arab defeat, becoming convinced that all his country's woes lay in the dual evils of feudalism and colonialism. Together with the 'Free Officers Movement', he overthrew King Farouk of Egypt on 23 July 1952. Like Jinnah, he was addicted to Craven A cigarettes and in a charismatic and dictatorial way he fought for social justice while also brutally quashing dissent.[58] On 20 April 1954 – the same day as the Muslim League conceded to giving Bengali national status in Pakistan – Nasser became Egypt's president.[59]

Nasser's radio programme *Sawt Al-Arab* [Voice of the Arabs] brought him popularity across the Arabic-speaking world, and in the minds of many he became the living, breathing embodiment of Arab nationalism. 'He simply bestrode the Arab World,' remembers Britain's political agent in Bahrain at the time.

> His top political priority was to rid the Arab World of the relics of British domination and his voice carried [via radio], literally and metaphorically, to the furthest peasant hut and Bedouin tent.[60]

Aden's British colonial officers confined themselves to their grand Victorian edifices, convinced their great crescent of Arabia stood outside the nationalist currents that had forced them from the Indian subcontinent. But under Nasser's influence, new national and racial identities were crystallising.

At the same time the Arabian Raj was hurtling into a new and unexpected future thanks to the discovery of a putrid, viscous, sticky liquid: oil. When Arabia had been separated from the Indian Empire a few years earlier, the oil industry had still been rather small. But when Iran nationalised the Anglo-Iranian oil company and cut Britain and the US off from its supplies, prospectors started boosting production along the Arabian coastline.[61] Extraordinarily, just a few years after its separation from India, the oil economy of the Gulf region had skyrocketed to rival that of the USA.[62] Old earthen townhouses were pulled down as architects experimented with new styles such as 'Doha Deco' in their place.[63] 'Once gatekeepers to the Indian jewel, [the Arabian princes were] now guardians of the Gulf's black gold.'[64] An oil refinery soon dominated both Aden's landscape and economy, accounting for a staggering 90 per cent of the city's industrial gross output. It pumped life into Aden's veins, contributing 10 per cent to its GDP and a staggering 75 per cent to its export earnings.[65]

Awash with oil, Aden transformed in a matter of years from a peripheral and neglected corner of the former Indian Empire into the second port in the world – more important to global trade than Bombay, Madras or Rangoon. It was a vibrant city of businessmen and dreamers where cruise ships jostled alongside the old Arabian dhows and Yemeni Jews mingled with Gujarati Hindus and Somali Muslims. Two hundred thousand passengers disembarked at Aden every year, seeking out the best duty-free bargains in Asia and maybe taking a camel desert tour while they were at it. What Dubai was to the early years of the twentieth century, Aden was to the 1950s. But the British were unwittingly laying the groundwork for their own demise. As the refinery thrived, the surge of migrant workers deepened racial fault lines. Aden's population increased five-fold within fifteen years and the gap between rich and poor widened into a gaping chasm.[66] But the British Colonial Office brushed the issue aside, noting that: 'We were not in the habit of housing all of Calcutta.'[67] This disenfranchised community would be the vanguard of Aden's Arab nationalist movement.

One of those to experience this boom was Dhirubhai Ambani, the young student activist from Junagadh who had protested against the state's dog-obsessed Nawab, and who had recently set sail for Aden's shores. Indians still didn't need visas to work there, but Muhammad Ali Luqman, Gandhi's old Arabic translator and now 'the premier intellectual voice' in the city, was lobbying for new laws to restrict immigration.[68] Seventeen-year-old Dhirubhai had thus quickly found passage aboard an Italian cargo freighter called the *Caboto*.[69] Disembarking in the searing heat of early June, Dhirubhai drove through the narrow rocky pass to the ramshackle slopes of Crater, where the Indian community lived in the bed of an extinct volcano. He checked into a bachelor's hostel with twenty-five other Gujarati boys and was given an identity card recording his 'race' as 'Hindu'.[70] Crater would be his home for the next turbulent decade of his life.

Dhirubhai's boss at A. Besse & Co. put him in charge of refuelling the vast ships that docked at the harbour, a lucrative job, and with his newfound wealth he briefly returned to Gujarat to marry. His new wife Kokilaben had never left the state, but thanks to the networks that still tied Aden to Gujarat, she bumped into a distant relative on arrival in Aden.

In the face of mass immigration, Aden's citizens started to raise profound questions about what it meant to be Adeni.[71] Did Indian residents really have more of a claim to the city than Yemeni migrant labourers? Adeni opinion had already grown suspicious of Indians after the attempted deportation of Arabs from Hyderabad after the 'Police

Action', and the commissioner in Aden had to warn the Indian government of the 'heavy propaganda against Indians' in the city.[72] Now the debate was starting to take on the language of Arab nationalism. One of the most influential voices was Luqman himself, who had distanced himself from his Indian roots. Alongside newspaper columns on 'the wonders of plastic surgery',[73] his papers provided an outlet for Yemeni nationalists who spoke of a 'Greater Yemen' uniting the Kingdom of Yemen to the north with the ex-Indian territories of South Arabia.

Amid this racial tension, in 1956 Nasser nationalised the Suez Canal, a trade artery connecting the Mediterranean Sea to the Indian Ocean that had been controlled by France and Britain since the days of high imperialism. In response, Israel, France and Britain formed a secret alliance to reclaim control and remove Nasser from power. Their military operation commenced in late October that year, but the United States and the Soviet Union, both wary of the escalating conflict, pressured them to withdraw.

At the time David Holden had been settling into his new role as Arabian correspondent for the *Sunday Times*, beginning a passionate romantic affair with ex-communist and spy Leo Silberman, the subject of a classified CIA file.* After all, he wrote to his brother, in such a conservative environment, 'What is a fellow to do except turn queer?'[74] Holden later wrote that

> the Suez campaign revealed the futility of Britain's imperial posture in a post-imperial world. The Canal was blocked, the trans-desert pipelines from Iraq to the Mediterranean were blown up, Saudi Arabia refused to pump oil for British (or French) tankers, and there were riots in Bahrain and explosions in Kuwait. For months Britain was forced to endure petrol rationing and the flight from sterling approached the level of a national disaster. When the final cost was reckoned, it included the destruction of nearly all remaining trust between Britain and the Arab world.[75]

Holden correctly understood that the Suez crisis marked a paradigm shift, a change in Britain's role in the world.

---

* Holden's murky connections to several rival spy agencies would ultimately lead to his mysterious assassination, execution-style, in Cairo twenty years later.

Staying in the British area of Steamer Point in Aden, however, he was surprised to find elite British society living life as usual: 'The sun-bleached daughters of bank managers and Air Commodores were properly squired by bronzed young subalterns to black tie dances on the roof of the Crescent Hotel,' he wrote. 'The privates cut loose in women-less drinking in the bars around the corner. The servants called their mistresses "memsahib" and passed the cucumber sandwiches at afternoon parties.'[76] At noon Holden headed up to the bar of the Crescent, and over pink gins recorded vivid snippets of the pompous British expatriate community in denial: 'Mustn't take too much notice of Nasser, old chap,' one man laughed. 'Flash in the pan, that's all.' His companion agreed: 'Pity we didn't finish the job at Suez – could've done except for those bloody Yanks … They don't understand the wogs like we do.'[77]

Holden felt they were like 'voices from beyond the grave pleading causes that were already dead … they spoke as if the appeal of Nasser … was somehow created by propaganda, bribery and intimidation alone'.[78] The journalist was shocked at the extent to which British legislators dismissed every demonstration for workers' rights in Aden as the result of bribery. 'Had any of them made an effort to talk, or listen, to the leaders of the demonstrators, they might have been less complacent,' he wrote. 'Blinded by the mists of colonial narcissism they scarcely noticed how warped and shabby were the buildings of the Aden Government.'[79]

The situation could not have been more different in Aden's crowded old city of Crater, where workers like Ambani lived. 'The thrill of an Arab victory ran like an orgasm through the back streets of Aden,' wrote Holden. 'In room after dark room, in shop after cramped shop, the familiar face of President Nasser gleaming from the walls … The Indians and Pakistanis, fearful of their minority standing, might not like the new mood of nationalist politics; the Somalis, preoccupied with their own independence efforts in Africa, across the water, might not care. But the Arabs were plainly conscious that they had found a leader, a new Saladin as their press and radio had christened him, and they were jubilant.'[80]

The rise of Nasser's Arab nationalism was felt across the peninsula. In quick succession states all over the Arabian Raj formally tied citizenship to 'a fair knowledge of Arabic' and being 'Arabs belonging to an

Arab Country'. In the process the once cosmopolitan Indian Ocean society would gradually be replaced by arbitrary new national identities such as 'Kuwaiti', a term that had never been used in local sources until the oil boom.[81] Residents who couldn't prove they fitted the new citizenship requirements of these new legal identities were excluded from trade unions, banned from political activity and deported with little notice. The exact details varied from state to state, but in nearly every case South Asian families found themselves on the wrong side of the citizenship line and were forced to sell their properties.[82] The partition of Arabia from India was crystallising further.

In the wake of Suez, the refinery where Ambani worked became the centre of political activism, and the streets of homeless migrants evolved into vast political recruiting grounds. New slogans began to appear in graffiti across Aden's working-class areas such as 'Foreigners, Quit Our Country' and 'Boycott and Prepare for Jihad'.[83] But who was a foreigner? For someone like Luqman the word meant somebody who had not resided in Aden for several generations, as his family had.[84] For others, the vast population of Yemeni migrants were the foreigners. But for the Yemeni-majority Aden Trade Union, it meant any non-Arab. One pamphlet read:

> We must achieve, by force if necessary, the halt of immigration to Aden. Aden is an Arab city and there is today, out of a population of 150,000, over 80,000 non-Arabs. We must therefore create a hostile and dangerous environment for non-Arabs. Immigrants must be reminded often and with force that this is and always will be an Arab city. It was created for us and despite British imperialism, it is still ours.[85]

This sort of sentiment was reflected by the president of the South Arabian League, who told the *Sunday Times* correspondent and MI6 operative John Slade-Baker, 'The average Indian is politically indifferent. Aden is not their homeland.'

'Suppose we left the colony,' said Slade-Baker in response. 'What would happen to the Indian and all the other racial elements of the population?'

To this, the president responded that there were three types of people who lived in Aden: Arabs, those who had been Arabised and 'those who retain their nationalities and touch with home'. This last category, he told Slade-Baker, 'will be given full protection of the law but will have no political rights'.[86]

Arab nationalism was now firmly in vogue. Whereas Luqman's generation of Arabs had sought education in Bombay and in Aligarh, the new generation were often educated in Arab cities like Beirut and Cairo. By the end of 1957, the governor of Aden proudly reported that it was soon to surpass New York as the world's busiest refuelling port.[87] But just as in Rangoon thirty years earlier, booming business masked seething racial discontent. 'The political climate in Aden had changed,' reflected Kokilaben Ambani. 'Indians were no longer welcome there.'[88]

Kokilaben gave birth to her firstborn, Mukesh, a year after Suez in April 1957. She and Dhirubhai were overjoyed and sent large tins of dried fruit back to family in India to celebrate. But becoming parents also meant they had to re-evaluate their future, and Dhirubhai decided his family was no longer safe in Aden. They stayed until he was eligible for permanent residency – a back-up option if India didn't work out – and that December they boarded a ship with eight-month-old Mukesh and sailed back to India.

Kokilaben's memoirs note how sudden the decision had been. 'Our immediate task was to convince our worried families we had made the right decision,' she writes.[89] In the event, their doubts were vindicated. Four months after their departure, a series of bomb blasts targeting 'foreigners' rocked Aden. By 1959 Adeni musicians were deriding Indian musical influence because of 'Indian colonization'.[90] As the city slipped into extremism, Dhirubhai's brother and sister-in-law left as well. Gradually, the trickle of people out of Aden turned into a torrent.

The Indian subcontinent and the Arabian Peninsula were drifting ever further away from each other. The Partition of Arabia from the Indian subcontinent had begun in the 1930s with the Aden Separation and continued with the 1947 Gulf Transfer and the expulsion of Hyderabadi Arabs during Operation Polo. Yet it was not until 1957, when Arab nationalism was at its height, that the last land border between the subcontinent and an Arabian state finally disappeared.

Although largely forgotten today, the strategic deep-sea port of Gwadar on the Pakistani coastline was still under the rule of the Sultan of Muscat and Oman well into the mid-1950s. A sandy isthmus shaped like a hammerhead shark, Gwadar had been granted to an Omani prince in 1783 by the Baluchi Khan of Kalat, and it had remained under Omani rule even after the Khanate of Kalat itself was dissolved.[91] In the 1950s Gwadar had developed into a major smuggling base, where cheap goods and even slaves could be slipped across the undefined border into Pakistan, and 'Indian secret agents' were constantly spotted among the town's decaying forts and wooden balconies. Rumours even circulated that India intended to lease the port from Oman.[92] Pakistan made frantic attempts to try and claim Gwadar, but whenever a resolution seemed close its ruler backtracked and the British interlocutors pleaded that 'the Sultan is the head of an independent state, and there are limits beyond which we cannot press'.[93]

Sultan Said bin Taimur, the ruler of Oman, was himself a relic of the Raj, so Indian-ised that the British consul general affectionately nicknamed him 'Babu'.[94] When journalist David Holden travelled to meet him, he encountered a ruler more comfortable in the world of princely India than among his own subjects. Said had been educated at Mayo Princes College, in Ajmer in Rajputana, becoming 'one of the best-educated of all Arabia's traditional rulers' in Holden's estimate, yet was 'loth to let even his immediate family enjoy the same advantages'.[95] A few years before the dissolution of British India, Bin Taimur had been named Hon. Knight Grand Commander of the Order of the Indian Empire, and Omani Army titles were still given in Urdu, a language he had learned at school in Rajputana but one little understood by Oman's population. Much of his business was conducted through the Cutchi date exporter Gokaldas Khimji, and he went as far as deliberately denying Arabs education and positions of power.[96] 'That is why you lost India,' Sultan Said bin Taimur told one of his British colonels. 'Because you educated the people.'[97]

It took Firoz Khan Noon, a wealthy and outspoken Pakistani lawyer turned politician, to bring the Gwadar dispute to international prominence. The stylish and sardonic Noon came from a large landholding family that owned the second largest citrus orchard in Pakistani Punjab, and he was obsessed with the latest developments in 'mechanical farming'.[98] He read widely and his library in Lahore was filled with books on history, politics and the odd John Buchan novel. An avid writer himself, he had penned a novel called *Scented Dust*, a study of the Canadian administrative system and a book on Kashmir.[99] Now foreign minister, Noon dived into the Kalat state archives and by late 1957 he believed he had found proof the Khan of Kalat had given Gwadar to the Sultan of Oman as a 'jagirdar', or landowner, not a transfer of national sovereignty, which would mean Pakistan was entitled to resume its possession of Gwadar at any time.[100]

In the middle of his research, Noon was unexpectedly invited to become the seventh prime minister of Pakistan. Though Nehru was still in power in India, not a single prime minister before Noon had managed to complete a term: 'Pakistan had six prime ministers and one commander-in-chief in eight years (1950–58) whereas in the same period India had one prime minister and six commanders-in-chief.'[101] Pakistan still hadn't agreed on a constitution, and throughout Noon's rule his government would be in a state of near total political turmoil. He didn't know yet that he would be Pakistan's last civilian leader for over a decade.

Nonetheless, his patient realpolitik made him one of the unsung heroes of Pakistani diplomacy. From the start, the British were concerned he 'seemed to be taking an even stronger line about the matter [of Gwadar] than his predecessor'.[102]

Noon made it known that he was considering military action over the issue, and cleverly extracted assurances that British officers would not be used in the state's armed forces against Pakistan, and that the UK would not sign a new defence treaty with the Sultan of Oman until the Gwadar border was resolved. The assurances were a coup. The Omani Army was tiny, and war in the Omani interior meant the Sultan of Oman desperately needed a new defence treaty with the British. Soon after, Noon expressed his intention to cordon off the neck of land to the north of Gwadar with a border fence, two aeroplanes, four motor boats and five new customs posts 'of the fortress type'.[103] To up the pressure, in early 1958 a group of Pakistanis drove through the heat of the Makran desert towards Gwadar and knocked down a small rocky cairn, which was, in the eyes of the Omani authorities, the border post dividing Pakistan and Oman.[104]

The situation was tense when, on the morning of 22 May, violence in Gwadar's fish market almost sent Pakistan and Oman to war. A guard went berserk, pulling out a gun and shooting at three passers-by, two of whom died on the spot. He then unsheathed his *khanjar* blade, stabbing an old woman and four others. The khanjar broke off at the handle as he stabbed his fifth victim, leaving the blade inside and enabling him to be arrested.

Rumours were rife as to what had triggered the massacre. Some suggested the man was mad and had burst into a fit of rage after a dispute over the price of fish. Others argued he was not mad at all but was taking revenge on the Baluchi sepoys who had helped suppress a recent rebellion in the Omani interior.[105] The only thing anyone knew for certain was that nine people had been killed and that three of them were Pakistanis.[106]

Events moved fast. As the outraged Gwadar public carried the deceased through the bazaar in a large procession, a group of young Pakistani nationalists proclaimed a strike against the Sultan of Oman. Furious about the death of Pakistani citizens, Noon issued orders for the Pakistani Navy to take up positions around the Gwadar isthmus. War seemed imminent.[107] But at the last minute Noon pulled the troops back. He raised the matter of Gwadar with the British one last time, threatening to take military action if they didn't force the Sultan into discussions.[108] Two villages in Gwadar – Pishkan and Garok – declared they were now part of Pakistan, and finally, on 11 July, the Sultan of Oman laid out his demands for a peaceful transfer of the territory: $3 million plus 10 per cent of any oil revenues found in the area in the next twenty-five years,[109] as well as allowing Pakistanis to serve in all roles in the Sultanate's armed forces. Gwadar's citizens would have a choice to stay as Sultanate subjects or become Pakistani citizens.[110] Five days later Pakistan accepted the terms and the words 'Pak Flag Flies Over Gwadar' appeared as headlines in the *Civil & Military Gazette*.[111] Noon's voice sounded over Radio Pakistan:

> I welcome the residents of Gwadar into the Republic of Pakistan ... These negotiations, and the return of Gwadar to Pakistan, should help to illustrate that international disputes can be resolved in a peaceful and satisfactory manner, provided that the parties to a dispute are prepared to approach the problem in a spirit of fairness and justice ... Gwadar is the first fruit of this policy of goodwill and cooperation. I fervently hope and pray that it will be possible to resolve our other international disputes in an equally peaceful and reasonable manner. Pakistan Zindabad.[112]

The sale of Gwadar marked a turning point in the relationship between Arabia and South Asia. The final land border between the Indian and Arabian subcontinents had disappeared. Only Qu'aiti State – Hyderabad's former Arab vassal – still linked the Arab and Indian worlds.

Qu'aiti State is relatively obscure today, yet for most of the twentieth century the old Hyderabadi vassal was considered one of the most important regions in the Arabian Peninsula. This was in sharp comparison with Dubai, which had long been one of the most obscure states in all the Indian Empire. Dubai was one of the least populated regions, and at the start of the twentieth century it consisted of a collection of mud forts and a few thousand mostly nomadic residents. As late as 1911, when Qu'aiti nobles had been invited to the Delhi Durbar to mark the coronation of King Edward VII as emperor of India, Dubai's Sheikh had been denied an invitation.

But the fate of these two regions would undergo a dramatic reversal.

Through a random shake of the dice, the initially minor Sheikhs of the Gulf have ended up extraordinarily wealthy, whereas the rulers of the much richer and more prestigious states of southwestern Arabia – which were far grander from their proximity to Aden and Hyderabad – have ended up refugees. This happened through the most casual negligence of their British patrons.

In the coming years, two new countries would be forged from the former princely states of the Indian Empire – the United Arab Emirates and the People's Democratic Republic of Yemen. One through federation and the other through revolution. The change that overcame the Arabian Peninsula in these years is not well known, but it should be, for it laid many of the foundations of the Gulf War, the Yemeni civil war and the rise of Dubai. Fuelled by Arab nationalism and sparked by Britain's abandonment of her allies, the political separation and the cultural rupture between the Arabian and Indian subcontinents that began in 1937 was about to culminate here on the sandy shores of Arabia.

12

The Last Days of the Raj

The decade and a half following the Gwadar transfer would see Britain's position in the Arabian Raj collapse like a pack of cards. As Arab nationalism clashed with British imperialism, rebel groups would force Britain out of Aden, and by 1971 even tiny states like Dubai and Bahrain would gain independence.

In the aftermath of Suez, the British government at first initiated a new 'forward policy' to try to consolidate their influence in the region. But their refusal to embrace decolonisation would only further radicalise its inhabitants, and a few years later British policymakers made the first of many U-turns, arguing that it would be better to hand over power to friendly governments in the region.

Kuwait was the first of the Arabian states to be granted independence in 1961, but things went awry immediately. The Iraqi government began referring to Kuwait as a 'lost province of Iraq', arguing that its independence was an artificial creation of Britain's Viceroys, and forcing Britain to send in troops to defend it. Kuwait's independence held, but on such shaky ground that Saddam Hussein would use the episode to justify his invasion of Kuwait three decades later.[1] The irony of the situation was not lost on journalist David Holden. 'For 62 years,' he wrote,

> while Kuwait was one of Britain's dependent sheikhdoms, no significant British land force had ever been summoned to its defence. Now, in the first month of its independence, nearly 6,000 British troops poured into the country.[2]

Uncertain that any of their other Arabian states would be able to survive alone, Britain tried to federate the smaller states of the Arabian Raj. A 'South Arabian Federation' was formed and in 1962 Aden itself was merged into this fledgling state.³

The new federation caused more problems than solutions, however. Adeni liberals vehemently opposed the power of feudal princes in the federation, while the princes themselves protested the dilution of their authority. To make matters worse, the very same day that Aden was forced into the South Arabian Federation, a Nasserite revolution occurred in the neighbouring country of Yemen. Overnight Nasser's radical Arab nationalism was brought 'to Britain's Arabian doorstep and the proxy war between Egypt and Britain was transformed into a direct conflict'.⁴ Through its proxies in Yemen, Nasser sponsored the creation of a new militant organisation called the National Liberation Front (NLF), which started sponsoring rebellions against the Sultans and their British overlords.

The British response, codenamed 'Operation Nutcracker', was as brutal as it was ineffective. The RAF firebombed villages and poisoned crops 'in the hope of terrorising the rebels into submission'. But in the words of one official, 'It was a pretty nasty policy, a real throwback to colonial times, and it didn't work.'⁵

Punitive measures by British troops only helped increase support for the NLF. The British would drop leaflets telling entire villages to clear out and then bomb their villages to smithereens. In the following months tens of thousands of penniless peasants fled over the border to Yemen as refugees, and many of them later joined the NLF to regain their dignity.

All the while the British remained clueless as to who exactly they were fighting, christening their mysterious new enemies 'the Red Wolves of Radfan'.⁶ By the time they banned the NLF in June 1965, two whole years after the revolution had been launched, the organisation had already penetrated the federal army, the Aden police, the oil refinery and even the Coca-Cola factory. That September high commissioner Richard Turnbull dismissed the newly created constitution of the South Arabian Federation and imposed direct colonial rule over South Arabia.

British officials recorded 286 acts of 'terrorism' that year, but as one army officer recalled, 'It was by now virtually impossible to find any

Adeni who was prepared to testify in court as a witness of any act of terrorism … he saw little advantage in dying for "the departing Raj".'[7] In desperation some British soldiers turned to interrogating civilians for information. George Lennox, a corporal in the Royal Army Ordnance Corps, worked in the communications office at Fort Morbut, where the interrogations were held, and was one of several whistle-blowers who tried to expose the torture of Adeni civilians to the British public in a letter to the *Sunday Times*:

> Nearly every night after the state of emergency was declared and after a lot of suspects were being taken in, we used to hear, sitting in our Corporals' Club drinking, a lot of screaming and shouting … from the Interrogation Centre and it was a common thing for us to just laugh and joke about it. 'There's another cunt getting fucking done in … we thumped this wog last night and he's really screaming.'[8]

How frequent these human rights abuses were is unknown. A recent analysis of Fort Morbut's medical records suggests the torture of civilians was not carried out as systematically as some commentators have claimed in the past.[9] But it is also clear that significant human rights abuses did take place, and they only helped the revolution spread rapidly across the princely states of the Arabian Raj.

The rebels themselves were far from unified, however. The NLF soon split into a pro-Egyptian faction called FLOSY (Front for the Liberation of Occupied South Yemen) and an increasingly anti-Egyptian rump of Marxists who retained the name NLF. Aden descended into a battle between the two so that by 1966 all-out civil war had ensued.[10]

That same year Amir Ghalib Al-Qu'aiti was preparing for his admission to Oxford University when he received news that he was about to become Sultan of Qu'aiti State, the third largest in the Arabian Peninsula. His kingdom would stretch from the seaside capital of Mukalla across a beautiful terrain of desert canyons and fortress villages to the Wadi Hadhramaut, where enormous canyons carved their way through a sparse plateau. The Soviet Union had just landed the first unmanned spacecraft on the moon and the Arabian Raj was in turmoil. Ghalib was eighteen years old.

Ghalib was heir to a rather extraordinary heritage, as for almost two hundred years his family had exercised increasing sway over this stretch of the Arabian Peninsula, often ruling from the outskirts of Hyderabad. As a result this Arabian outpost of the British Raj had transformed into a forgotten centre of Deccani Indian culture, and perhaps the most notable result of this cultural mingling was *haleem*, Hyderabad's famous take on the Arabian dish *harees*. His father was an Arab Sultan and his mother was the Nizam of Hyderabad's niece. Indeed it was on a visit to his mother in Hyderabad that he first learned news of his father's deteriorating health.

Sultan Awadh bin Saleh, Ghalib's diabetic father, had been in decline for years, and his habit of lavishly spreading Du'ani honey on his toast each morning only aggravated his health condition. Now he was gravely ill. Ghalib travelled immediately to Qu'aiti State but by the time he reached the azure shores of Mukalla, he was too late. Ghalib bent to kiss his father's forehead, and with a shock realised his father was in a state of delirium and unable to speak.[11] But after senior Arab and British officials were summoned for the final rites, the frail man regained his senses momentarily and grabbed his son's hand, saying, 'Farewell in Allah's care.' Then he slumped back into a coma.

The next morning, 11 October 1966, the Sultan's coffin was carried through the main street of Mukalla to be laid to rest. Ghalib followed in a black mourning tunic. 'We buried poor old Sultan Awadh today,' wrote Mukalla's British resident, Jim Ellis, in a letter to his father-in-law:

> We gave him a slap-up funeral, but I think the astounding crowds who turned out were in sympathy with his son rather than in sorrow for Dad ... Ghalib is 18 and he is going to have a hard row to hoe. May God look after him.[12]

The resident's wife Joanna was equally concerned: 'Now his father has died, I do not know how he will manage to continue his studies,' she wrote. 'He took his A levels in England last summer and did very well. He would have liked to go to university ... He is a charming, gentle, kind, and extremely intelligent young man but has not had time to mature. His new responsibilities will undoubtedly hasten this process, but he is in for a very difficult time.'[13]

Ghalib's great-uncle, the Nizam, had once warned him against taking the Qu'aiti throne. Now aged eighty, Nizam Osman Ali Khan had largely retired from public view, and was rarely seen outside the walls of his moss-covered palaces. But throughout Ghalib's childhood he had remained a distant yet towering presence. The Nizam had never forgotten how his British allies had abandoned him, and he warned Ghalib the British would soon forsake the princes of Arabia, just as they had abandoned him in Hyderabad.

'Alas,' wrote Ghalib many years later, 'events were to prove the Nizam right.'[14] Within a year the British would desert Ghalib and render him a stateless refugee. The Qu'aiti State would vanish from the map, along with nineteen other princely states in the Arabian Raj. In its place, a new country called South Yemen would form. The large Indian and Pakistani population would be exiled from Arabia, or forced to hide their origins, in a mirror image of events in Hyderabad almost twenty years earlier.

In November 1966 an Aden Airways Dakota landed in Mukalla's dusty RAF station and a delegation of Hyderabadi family members walked out onto the runway. 'We had to come down in "burkha",' complained Ghalib's seventeen-year-old sister Saleha in a letter to her aunt and uncle back in Hyderabad. But any discomfort was dispelled by the warm smile of her elder brother who was waiting on the tarmac. Two months had passed since Sultan Awadh's death, and after forty days of mourning the time had come for Ghalib's coronation.

The journey from Hyderabad to Mukalla had been long and dangerous, passing through Aden, which had descended into a three-way battle between the British, the NLF and FLOSY. 'The situation in Aden is very explosive,' Saleha wrote to her uncle and aunt:

> Every day a few bombs and anti-personnel mines explode and then the British patrol men start shooting blindly at everything and everybody ... The buildings of Aden are like those of Bombay [but] many have been vacated ... [and] the merchants are trying to sell off all they have.

The day after they flew into Mukalla, an Aden Airways flight was blown up in mid-air and all regular plane services to the city were cancelled.[15] 'Some idiot placed a bomb in a plane flying between some other state and Aden,' wrote a shaken Saleha, and '32 passengers including the pilot were killed'.

In contrast to the chaos in Aden, which had recorded 480 terror attacks that year, life in Mukalla went on as normal.[16] The city itself was buzzing with activity. The roads, houses and even boats were decorated with flags and fairy lights. Everyone was getting ready for Ghalib's coronation. The cool weather and the sound of the waves lapping against the palace walls enchanted Saleha. 'Mukalla looks as though it has just stepped out of a fairy tale,' she wrote:

> We have many geese here [and] they speak Arabic ... when they cackle, they produce a sound that is considerably different from our [Hyderabadi] geese ... Mummy is teaching the cook to make some Hyderabad dishes so that Ghalib bhai can have a change of food.

The celebrations began with military timing at 7.33 in the cool of Thursday morning.[17] RAF planes flew over Mukalla's harbour in formation, dipping above the palace, and the now moustachioed Ghalib emerged from his compound of lime-washed palaces exuding the confidence of an English public schoolboy.[18] Crowds came out in their thousands to catch a glimpse of their new Sultan as Royal Navy vessels and the state military fired the eleven-gun salute granted by the Indian Viceroy decades earlier.[19] Water schemes were inaugurated, three white pigeons were symbolically set free, and the customs department set off a series of blindfolded boat races. 'This was great fun,' writes Saleha. 'All the canoes were dashing into each other and one canoe went on and on into the deep and then a motor boat had to go and fetch the man.'

At lunch Ghalib changed into an embroidered Hyderabadi sherwani and welcomed guests into his Durbar Hall.[20] Saleha's status as a woman meant that she was kept apart from some of these celebrations, and instead spent her time learning about the women of the city. 'The girls and modern women of Mukalla are very fashionable even though they observe "purdah",' she wrote to her aunt and uncle.

They wear sleeveless frocks up to their knees and their 'burkhas' too are short, say, a few inches below the knees. They do full make-up and all kinds of hair-do's as in India ... The custom of greeting here is to kiss each other's hands and so women practically soak their hands in perfumes.

The coronation was filled with pomp, a demonstration of princely power and popularity. A small controversy ensued when the Hadhrami Bedouin Legion accidentally pledged an oath of loyalty to the young Sultan rather than to the British Queen Elizabeth, but except for this one hiccup things went off without a hitch. Celebrations culminated on Saturday evening at the municipal football stadium, with the much-awaited final between the teams of Qu'aiti Sultanate's two port cities: Mukalla and Shihr. 'The coronation celebrations all went extremely well,' wrote Joanna Ellis a week later:

> In fact, the Palace with the Residency are still bedecked with bunting and fairy lights ... In the afternoon we had a parade in the Palace and Sultan Ghalib made a speech from the throne which was excellent. In the evening, the Residency put on a firework display and the minesweepers (which were flood-lit) fired off rockets ... Not to be outdone, I had the Begum and the Amira [Saleha] plus further wives making up a total of 578 for dinner here [at the Residency]. Then all went to an enormous feast at the palace.[21]

Ghalib took a rather romantic view of his new role, imitating his great-grandfather, the sixth Nizam of Hyderabad, in disguising himself as a poor man at night to listen to his subjects' thoughts.* Unfortunately, Ghalib found it didn't work as well as he had hoped and on one occasion when he left disguised with a sooty face and plain dress, the police recognised him and saluted him the moment they saw him. Changing tactics, Ghalib got into a habit of working with manual labourers thrice a week to teach his subjects 'the true meaning of socialism in conformity with the teachings of Islam'.[22]

---

* This was done after the fashion of the Abbasid caliph Harun al-Radhid, who famously attempted something similar in *The Arabian Nights*.

For much of the previous decade Nasser's radio programme had been labelling the princes of the Arabian Raj as imperial pawns who needed to be overthrown, but Ghalib was greeted as a reformist, and enthusiastically welcomed.[23] Nonetheless, Ghalib was bewildered by Britain's confusing policy changes. Months before his coronation, the British had announced they would abandon their military base after all and support their princely allies from Bahrain. Then, on 28 December 1966, he received a letter from the high commissioner stating that Britain would be ending its treaty relations with Qu'aiti State and pulling out of South Arabia altogether. Ghalib's protests proved futile.

To make matters worse, Ghalib's great uncle, the Nizam of Hyderabad, died soon after his nineteenth birthday.

The great question that faced him now was what Qu'aiti State would look like after the British left. Ghalib thus organised a Grand Tribal Assembly to understand his people's views, and between 5 and 7 April 1967, chiefs representing about 60 per cent of the population gathered under one roof. The chiefs rejected the idea of joining the South Arabian Federation, and instead agreed to work towards a merger with the neighbouring princely states of Al-Kathiri and Al-Mahra. But over cups of watermelon juice, British officials continued to try and convince him to join the collapsing South Arabian Federation.

In 1967 the British government appointed a new high commissioner to get Britain out of Aden with minimal British casualties. The job fell to Humphrey Trevelyan, a diplomat from an old East India Company family who had served in Hyderabad, negotiated India's standstill agreement with Sikkim and been ambassador to Egypt during the Suez crisis. 'Poor man,' remarked Harold Macmillan when Trevelyan got the job. 'The situation was [now] so dangerous … that his wife was not allowed to accompany him.'[24] His task, like Mountbatten's two decades earlier, was to wind up the British presence in the region with as little fuss as possible. Just as with Mountbatten, many of Britain's princely allies would be betrayed in the process, including Ghalib.

Within a month of Trevelyan's arrival, Britain was accused of siding with Israel in the 1967 Six-Day War, ending with the defeat of a coalition of Arab states and Nasser's resignation as president of Egypt. The Suez Canal closed and overnight the Egyptian and South Arabian economies simultaneously crumbled. In Aden the slogan 'A bullet against Britain is a bullet against Israel'[25] began to resound through the streets and days later the South Arabian Army and the Aden police both mutinied. Crater, the district of Aden where Ambani had recently lived, was occupied by rebel forces and the British Army withdrew. All-out war between the NLF and FLOSY followed.

The British would be unable to enter Crater for almost two weeks until a Scott called Colin 'Mad Mitch' Mitchell decided to take matters into his own hands. Mitch was a 'surreal relic of Britain's colonial past; a crazed fusion of the Celtic madman, belligerent imperialist and cantankerous military commander' who berated 'the 'squeamish politicians', 'prowling journalists' and 'white Arabs' (liberal English) who got in his way.[26] He ordered the pipe major to play 'Monymusk', the regimental charge, on the bagpipes as the troops marched single file into Crater.[27] On 4 July 1967, at 6 a.m., Ken Robson stood on the Aden Commercial Institute in the city, belting out the Crimean Long Reveille. This was the first time that most of its residents realised the British were back.[28]

For Ghalib, sitting in Mukalla, events were proceeding at an alarming pace. While newspapers raved about the newly released Beatles album *Sgt. Pepper's Lonely Hearts Club Band*, he learned the South Arabian Federation had crumbled. Shortly afterwards the NLF began its mission to topple the princely states of the southwestern Arabian Raj. Small NLF militias fanned out across the western states, taking advantage of sapped morale. The same day as the mutiny in Aden, they seized the capital of a princely state called Dali, quickly followed by another called Shu'ayb. Next came Muflahi State, whose ruler was arrested by the NLF on 13 August. By the end of the month no fewer than twelve of the federated princely states were in the hands of the NLF, who swiftly established people's committees to govern and maintain order in their new territories.[29] The British did nothing to help their allies.

Nonetheless, except for the murders of two British officers due to personal grudges, Ghalib's state had remained largely free from violence. Trevelyan himself admitted that there were 'only few [NLF] adherents in the Eastern Aden Protectorate',[30] yet covert discussions still took place between the British and the NLF with the aim of thwarting the Egyptian-backed FLOSY. What happened next is still heavily contested, but many Arab scholars, including Ghalib himself, believe that Trevelyan subsequently set in motion the victory of the NLF and the downfall of Britain's princely allies.

Ghalib and the Sultans of Al-Kathiri were drawing up plans for a UN plebiscite to decide the future of their states when Trevelyan arrived in his capital and advised them to travel to Geneva to put their demands for independence before the UN. They set off on 19 August, but little did they know they were heading into a trap. Britain wanted to get out of South Arabia at any cost, and Trevelyan had already secretly contacted the NLF to discuss a future for South Arabia without them.[31] Only a few days after Ghalib's departure, acting British resident adviser Michael Crouch was woken up by an SAS signaller and handed a coded message: 'You should evacuate Mukalla and close down the British presence.' Crouch's memoirs vividly portray the sense of betrayal:

> What a way to go, it was not as if we were even under attack ... I decided we should make it look as if some of us were going to Riyan to meet an aircraft and others could pretend they were on the way to the beach (with towels round their necks) ... To add verisimilitude, I summoned Ahmad al-Sameen and gave him instructions for an entirely fictitious dinner that night to entertain someone from Aden. I sent two shirts to the laundry just to add that extra touch ... And then, with minimum fuss, we drove out of the compound ... I was the last. The British never went back ... Her Majesty's Government, and I as its agent, had behaved with a mixture of incompetence and immorality.[32]

In Geneva, Ghalib had spent a day defending the British presence to the UN. But when he returned to his hotel, he found a panicked message from his state administrative secretary scrawled in Arabic: 'Is it possible for you to return? Advise us of your instructions.'[33] The British had used his absence as an opportunity to abandon his state.

Ghalib hastened to Beirut with the Kathiri Sultan, where they hoped to be conducted on to Mukalla. 'If the NLF wanted a fight they could have one,' Ghalib declared during a meeting at the British Embassy.[34] In response, however, he was told that the British could no longer conduct them onward. In desperation, therefore, the two Sultans requisitioned a cattle ship named *Fawziah* to drop them in Mukalla on the way to picking up some camels and cows from Somalia.³⁵

That was the last anyone saw of the three for some days. Back in Hyderabad, Ghalib's mother was frantically trying to find out his whereabouts. She managed to contact Trevelyan through the Nizam's chief secretary, who reassured her that Ghalib was safe on a ship on the high seas. She only learned what had actually happened days later.

When Ghalib had sent word to Mukalla of his imminent arrival, it had caused extreme trepidation in Mukalla, as the state's armed forces had been led to believe that the Sultan would not be returning, and as the armed forces and the British force the Hadhrami Bedouin Legion (HBL) in the federation had opted to support the NLF, it would be in their best interests in order to avoid bloodshed to do the same. Upon the arrival of Ghalib's message, an urgent meeting lasting all night was to take place, with the senior officers of the HBL and the state's forces in a total quandary. Finally it was decided to stop him from landing at all cost. The deputy commander of the HBL declared a curfew in the city and neutralised Ghalib's palace guards by stationing armoured cars opposite the building.³⁶

The cattle ship bearing the Sultans drifted into Mukalla's harbour before dawn on 17 September 1967, the nineteenth anniversary of the fall of Hyderabad. The sky was still dark, the air quiet. Soldiers of the Hadhrami Bedouin Legion were waiting for them at the harbour with two armoured cars, but something wasn't quite right. Then a uniformed HBL platoon of around fifty men boarded the Sultans' vessel. Four men with grenades and pistols in hand approached Ghalib on the upper deck and revealed themselves to be representatives of the NLF. One walked up to negotiate with Ghalib. He recalls:

> Good looking and fair skinned, his name was Salim Al-Dayyini and his family had fled from Osmanabad [in Hyderabad State] during the Police Action. On board the ship, he presented me with leaflets to let me know that the armed forces had taken over ... The four men were shivering, even though I was unarmed. People were so nervous that if I landed, there would be great bloodshed between the state forces and the Bedouin Legion.³⁷

Dayyini and the NLF representatives offered Ghalib the chance to abdicate, but Ghalib protested that he had already agreed for the UN to hold a referendum in Qu'aiti State and decide its political future. Dayyini then made him an offer: if he abdicated now, they would try and help him settle in the South of France, but he had to 'sign the abdication within half an hour, or else'.[38]

Ghalib wanted to keep the NLF on board as long as possible, in the hope that someone in the town might come to his aid. But another thirty HBL soldiers came on board and the Sultans were persuaded to turn their boat around and save Mukalla from bloodshed. And so the three sailed off into exile, via Berbera to pick up the cattle.[39]

Ghalib subsequently inferred that Britain had ordered the HBL to support the NLF takeover of Hadhramaut and avoid further bloodshed. Support for the NLF had been tiny in the region, and it seemed impossible that the coup could have taken place without British orders. Years later, the historian Jonathan Walker uncovered a secret British report that supports Ghalib's theory. In a telegram dated two weeks after the coup, the resident adviser Jim Ellis explained why 'the Sultan must not be allowed to land' in Mukalla because 'violence would surely break out' as Ghalib would potentially become a 'popular leader' and opposition to the NLF.[40] To save the region from a potential civil war, Ghalib had to go.[41]

There is a striking symmetry between the fall of the Qu'aiti Sultanate and the fall of its parent state of Hyderabad. Both took place on 17 September, nineteen years apart, during missions for international recognition at the United Nations, when the British abandoned their allies in defiance of their treaty commitments and unceremoniously pulled out. Nationalist forces occupied both states as they descended into virtual civil wars and revolutionary fervour. 'They played exactly the same game,' says Ghalib, 'the same dose of medicine, you know. Politicians tend to follow patterns, especially if they have been successful – that's what the Sanskrit philosopher Kautilya said. Of course, Trevelyan was an old-India hand.'[42]

On 18 October 1967 the NLF newspaper *al-Thawriyy* announced that every prince between Aden and Muscat and Oman had fled or been arrested. Alongside was a table, detailing those princely states that had been taken over in the previous two months:

District	Date of Power Takeover	Results
Maflahi	12 August	The Shaykh has been arrested
Lahej	13 August	The ruling family has fled
Dathinah	13 August	The Shaykh has fled
'Awadhil	27 August	The ruling family has fled
Zinjibar	28 August	The ruling family has fled
Lower Yafi'	28 August	The Sultan and members of his family have been arrested
Upper Yafi'	2 September	The Shaykhs have been arrested
The Shaykhdom of 'Aqrabi	2 September	The Shaykh and members of his family have been arrested
Lower Al-'Awaliq	9 September	The ruler (Na'ib) and others have been arrested
Al-Qu'aiti	16 September	The Sultan has been expelled
Bayhan	18 September	The Sharif and his son have fled to Saudi Arabia
Harib (in the YAR)	19 September	The monarchists have been expelled
Al-Kathiri	2 October	The Sultan and his henchmen have been expelled
Mahrah	14 October	The Sultan and his henchmen have been arrested[43]

The future of South Arabia was now set. On a dark and overcast November afternoon Trevelyan presided over the last cocktail party in Aden's Government House, as guests chatted with 'that especial, glassy frenzy found only on such occasions'.[44] A few days later he boarded his plane for England, as a military band struck up a rendition of 'Fings Ain't Wot They Used to Be'. 'It was hardly traditional,' noted Julian Paget, 'but not perhaps inappropriate, and the point was not lost on those present.'[45] All British troops were evacuated from Aden by 29 November, and at the stroke of the midnight hour a new country called the People's Republic of South Yemen awoke to an uncertain future.

The NLF victory had taken everyone by surprise – including the NLF themselves. The basic questions of South Yemen's future had never been decided. Would the new government be capitalist or communist? How would the NLF victors fix the crumbling economy? In an interview with an Egyptian journalist, the Marxist NLF leader 'Abd al-Fattah

Ismail admitted, 'The accession of power came as quite the surprise to us, for which we had not yet prepared ourselves. This is a truth that cannot be denied.'[46]

After a brief internal power struggle, the NLF declared South Yemen the first Marxist country in the Arab world. The new state was beset with problems on all fronts. The closure of the Suez Canal had already caused the collapse of the port economy, and the takeover triggered a largely forgotten refugee crisis: eighty thousand people fled Aden in the first year alone.[47]

For the first two first years of its existence, the new state would go out of its way to assure foreigners they were safe and welcome to stay in Aden. In 1969, however, the new government would encourage peasants to seize land from landowners and the South Asian merchant families who had risen under the Raj. Of all the partitions of the Indian Empire, the separation of Arabia had produced the fewest casualties, but now as their property was seized, people fled to India, Pakistan and the port of Dubai, which after the fall of Aden had been transformed into the premier Arabian port to do business.

Treatment of refugees largely depended on their passport privilege and the 'race' recorded on their identity cards. The last of Aden's once thriving Jewish population had already been evacuated to Israel, while Somalis set out across the Red Sea to the young nation of Somalia. Those with Indian, Indonesian or Singaporean passports moved with ease, and those with British passports even had the right to move to the UK. Khozem Merchant's experience was typical. Born into a family of Bohra opticians from Surat and Bombay, he spoke both Arabic and Gujarati at home. Yet he remembers wistfully: 'We didn't feel Gujarati or Arab, to be honest, we felt Adeni.' When he was nine, his parents made the decision to abandon Aden and move to London. The switch from upper-middle-class glass traders to a working-class factory life was one they never really recovered from. It was emblematic of the cultural rupture in the former Indian Empire that the young Indian-origin Adeni was derided as a 'Paki' in London. Nonetheless, Merchant's enterprising parents encouraged him to complete his education, and years later he would become the first British Asian editor on the *Financial Times*.[48]

For those without passports, life as a refugee would be altogether more challenging. The ex-British resident Michael Crouch described the plight of the Indian families flying out of Aden to Kenya, 'all desperate to leave before they too were ravaged in the final holocaust'. Their 'presence was anathema to petty Kenyan officialdom. Did they have visas, entry permits, relatives? All negotiations were conducted in basic English, minimal Swahili and with much hand waving and shouting.'[49]

For some the fall of Aden marked an opportunity. Dhirubhai Ambani found himself perfectly placed to hire his dispossessed Adeni colleagues. He had just ended a business partnership with his cousin and gone solo, forming a new company called the Reliance Commercial Corporation. When the NLF nationalised his old company Besse & Co., Ambani found use of 'a ready-made source of educated managers, accountants and salesmen, drilled to European standards'.[50] Some employees, such as Liladhar Gokaldas Sheth, had worked in Burma before Aden, and this was the second time they had lost everything to anti-Indian nationalists. Dhirubhai made it known that he would find his old friends jobs and a dozen accepted. 'All of us were new,' recalled one Adeni who joined Reliance. 'It was very small ... and after fifteen years in Aden I was not knowing anything about India.'[51] Reliance ballooned in the years after the fall of Aden, underpinned by a generation of Indian-origin Adenis versed in free market capitalism rather than Nehruvian socialism. Reliance would grow to be the first Indian company to exceed US $200 billion in market capitalisation, and Ambani's son Mukesh would become the richest man in Asia.[52]

For others the fall of Aden meant the loss of a home and the erasure of a legacy. Muhammad Ali Luqman had passed away a year earlier, and branding him a 'collaborator' with the British, the NLF banned his works. His daughter Huda recalls: 'There was a lot of looting and violence around our house on the island of Sira and we were receiving messages saying, "If you don't leave, you will be killed."'[53] One day in 1968 the revolutionaries went to the family office, demanded the keys and burned the *Fatat al-Jazira* newspaper archives to the ground. 'The NLF were going around burning anything published during the British time,' says Huda, 'but one particular bookshop managed to bury some books underground and keep them from destruction. My mother was afraid. One day she locked up our house, left somebody to look after it, and just ran away.'[54] Taking a flight out of Aden was a privilege few could afford, and so like thousands of others the Luqmans drove north to escape across the border. The family lived the rest of their lives in exile, scattered between the Gulf, Saudi Arabia and the United Kingdom.

The destruction of the Luqman archives was only one example of the way the intense connections that once existed between South Yemen and the Indian Empire were purged from the record. The Qu'aiti dynasty were caricatured as 'feudals' and their legacy surgically removed. Faysal Al-Attas, the NLF cadre who took power in Mukalla, quickly began demolishing heritage structures across the city, from old gateways to shrines and tombs, a process replicated across the region. The NLF tried and executed most of the Sheikhs and Sultans who remained in South Arabia, and those who had escaped were tried and condemned in absentia.[55]

After losing his wealth and status overnight, Ghalib settled in Jeddah as a refugee to start his life anew. His riches-to-rags fate was typical of those Sultans and Amirs who escaped. Today the idea of a Hyderabad-born Sultan ruling over Eastern Yemen seems completely bizarre, but this is only because of the deliberate erasure of these histories. Even in the British records the connections are difficult to see. South Arabian records are divided between the Colonial Office library in Kew and the India Office records in the British Library. In Hyderabad, the Qu'aiti Sultan's main residence has been converted into a military officers' mess. Since it is off limits to the general public, there is little awareness in the city that the ruler of what is now Eastern Yemen once resided there, nor that the building kickstarted an entire architectural tradition in the Arabian Peninsula.

Saudi refugee documents enabled Ghalib to attend both Oxford and Cambridge, and find employment with his former subjects the Bin Ladens, who he had befriended at Millfield boarding school in Somerset. Ghalib left the company to join the booming oil industry in 1980, the same year as his boss's meek and orthodox half-brother Osama joined the Mujahideen resistance in Afghanistan. In the ensuing decades Ghalib partially supported his family as a private collector of Arabic and Islamic art, publishing ten history books and funding some of the earliest research on the fall of Hyderabad and South Arabia. At the time of writing, he continues to find himself stateless. 'I can't travel,' he explains. 'I don't have a job or a bank account. I'm really stuck, you know. I'm hoping for a solution.'[56]

★ ★ ★

'The dilemma of Britain in the Persian Gulf today,' mused David Holden as British rule collapsed in South Arabia

> is rather like that of a man trapped on the sixth floor of a blazing building. If he runs down the stairs he will certainly be burned to death, and if he jumps from the window, he may dash himself to death. It seems easier, therefore, for him to stay where he is and hope the fire brigade arrives before he slowly suffocates.[57]

As the victorious revolutionaries gathered in Aden, the surviving princely rulers of the Gulf were so anxious that Britain would abandon them as well that British minister of state Goronwy Roberts personally flew out to reiterate Britain's commitment to the Gulf states. Two months later, however, a meek Goronwy was sent back to notify the same Sheikhs that Britain had changed its mind and would indeed be withdrawing from the entire region. The British pound had been devalued by 14.3 per cent and Britain could no longer afford the annual £12 million that it spent on keeping its forces in the region.[58] British prime minister Harold Wilson decided to end the British Empire east of Suez, abandoning the Gulf – along with places like Malaysia and the Maldives – by 1971.[59]

The Gulf rulers tried to convince the British to stay but British secretary of defence Denis Healey went live on the BBC to say, 'I don't very much like the idea of being a sort of white slaver for the Arab sheikhs ... It would be a very great mistake if we allowed ourselves to become mercenaries for people who like to have a few British troops around.'[60] The Sheikhs were shocked.

Soon after seizing Aden, the NLF contacted would-be revolutionaries from elsewhere in the Gulf and pledged to spread their revolution 'from Aden to Kuwait'.[61] The fear of revolution would drive the Sheikhs of the Gulf to cooperate with each other and their British interlocutors, and merge their emirates into the United Arab Emirates – the modern UAE. Through careful negotiations these states would end up being the only princely states of the Indian Empire other than Bhutan and Nepal that remain independent today.

'The latest episode in colonialist policy is the so-called Emirates federation,' raged the revolutionary paper *Al-Hurriya*, 'The base deformity and impotent colonial excretion will not last ... the feudalist

Sultanates, Emirates and Imamates will be removed by conscious revolutionary violence.' In their eyes, the United Arab Emirates would be nothing but a 'replica of the federation of the Southern Emirates which had been rejected and brought down by our heroic people in the Yemeni south with the force of arms.'[62]

An assassination attempt on the ruler of the Sharjah Sheikhdom 'led to the first coordinated operation by the Gulf States security organisations'.[63] It proved that if the Emirates worked together, they might just be able to survive the revolution.

If the Sheikhdoms of the Gulf proved remarkably effective at stopping the spread of the revolution to their states, the same could not be said of Oman's ruler. In the decade and a half since his sale of Gwadar, Sultan Said bin Taimur – the ruler once known as Babu – had become increasingly paranoid, 'averse to trousers and sunglasses, both of which he [had] banned', and reportedly owned five hundred slaves.[64] Rumours circulated about their mistreatment, and according to one, he used to make them

> swim in the water underneath his balcony and then amuse himself by shooting at the fish around them ... When slaves began to evade control, he passed a law under which all people of African descent were classed as slaves.[65]

Under such an unpopular figurehead, Omani rebels allied with the NLF in South Yemen and started a revolution of their own. This new set of rebels used the monsoon rains for cover, hiding in the thick 'cloud forest' and darting out in extraordinary offensives. They took the town of Rakhyut in 1969 and soon they had control of almost all of the Dhofar region.[66] So, in 1970, the British decided Sultan Said bin Taimur was a liability. In the words of one dispatch to the Gulf Residency, 'If there is a general feeling in the country now, it is that the Sultan's rule cannot go on.'[67]

Senior British officers began to plan the overthrow of their closest ally in the region and on 23 July 1970, a group of twelve British soldiers and four Omanis walked unopposed into the royal palace. Contract officer Ray Kane would later describe his role in the coup:

We rounded blind corners to the right and left ... Double doors led into a windowless, carpeted majlis room lit by chandeliers. On its floor, as though ready for a monopoly session – piles of stacked banknotes, and some, tipped in the same direction, suggested a hurried departure ... I ordered the Sultan to surrender, adding that otherwise all inside would be burnt to death by the phosphorous grenade I threatened to throw into his room ... [Then] in perfect English, calm and unflustered, the Sultan offered his surrender.[68]

The Sultan was replaced by his son, Qaboos, who immediately set out major reforms for the country. Qaboos spurned the exclusive Arab nationalism elsewhere in the region, and would declare many communities from across the Indian Ocean as indigenous tribes. The Gujarati merchant Kanak Khimji, for example, was subsequently declared Sheikh of the new 'Bania' tribe. A 'royal decree came printed in its own book and in the newspapers,' remembers Kanak.[69] Henceforth he would be responsible for the upkeep of Oman's Hindu temples, resolve local disputes and act as the patriarch of the two hundred thousand-strong Hindu community in Oman.

He was the first Hindu Sheikh in the history of the Arab world, and his family remains a lasting symbol of the ties that once unified these disparate parts of Southern Asia.

By late 1971 the British were ready to pull out of the Gulf altogether. 'In a few months now,' wrote David Holden, in July,

> for the first time since the heyday of Britain's East India Company, all the territories around the Gulf will be at liberty to seek their own salvation without the threat of British intervention, or the comfort of British protection. This final remnant of the British Raj – for that, in effect, is what it is – has been for some years now an obvious, if in some ways charming, anachronism ... But its day is over, and we must be prepared now for some fairly bracing years of readjustment, if not of revolution, in its wake.[70]

Arabia had changed in unimaginable ways since his arrival as a correspondent two decades earlier and these changes were the subject of Holden's recently published book *Farewell to Arabia*. Revolution had swallowed up the south of the peninsula, and new oil wealth transformed the east. Writing for *Foreign Affairs*, Holden judged the prospects of the Gulf states' survival. He felt hopeful about Bahrain, Qatar and Dubai. Abu Dhabi was now 'per capita, the richest state bar none – although only ten years ago it was sunk in the traditional penury of desert isolation'.[71] Sheikh Zayed of Abu Dhabi's 'forefathers ruled the desert from the back of a camel,' noted Holden. Zayed 'rides it in a limousine'.[72] Yet he felt uncertain of the future of those smaller Sheikhdoms like Sharjah which were little more than a collection of fishing villages. 'Their chief pastime,' wrote Holden, 'is dreaming of the day when they, too, may strike it rich.'[73]

There remained two threats to the stability of their future, he felt. One was the interference of Saudi Arabia, Iraq and Iran, who might have expansionist designs on the Sheikhdoms – as demonstrated in Kuwait a decade earlier. The other threat was the revolutionary movements, which were still potent.[74] Yet slowly the states had begun to cooperate with one another and gain the upper hand. In December the Trucial Oman Scouts had been sent out to crush a rebel uprising on the Musandam Peninsula in the deceptively named 'Operation Breakfast'. Then, in July, a secret agreement between Abu Dhabi and Dubai 'unlocked the door' to unifying their codes of law and foreign policy. It would be too difficult to get Bahrain and Qatar to join, but on 18 July 1971 a new union called the United Arab Emirates was announced, formed out of Abu Dhabi, Dubai, Ajman, Fujairah, Kalba and Umm Al-Quwain. A seventh, Ras al-Khaimah, joined soon after.[75]

Two months later Nasser had a heart attack and died. With him, Arab nationalism started to disappear as a political force. Meanwhile, newly discovered oilfields flooded the Gulf with wealth. More than counterinsurgency tactics, it was the wealth generated by oil that gradually subdued the revolution. Oman, the United Arab Emirates, Qatar and Bahrain each proved capable of coordinating an offensive against the rebels. After coming to power, Qaboos offered an amnesty if the rebels would stop the fighting and help him rebuild the region. In a major blow to the organisation, some of the less Marxist members accepted, and over the next six years Oman succeeded in entirely pacifying Dhofar. At the same time the British India Line, connecting India with the Gulf ports, was finally absorbed into the P&O Group, symbolically marking the end of British India's final outposts.[76]

That December the last British ships left the Gulf. The day was uneventful and in contrast to Mountbatten's flamboyant ceremonies two and a half decades earlier, without fanfare. Yet the transfer of power was also the most peaceful of all of them. Sir Geoffrey Arthur described the day in a dispatch from Bahrain:

> At about half past two in the afternoon of 19 December 1971, HMS *Intrepid*, 12,000 tons, moved slowly through the tortuous channel that leads from Mina Sulman, the port of Bahrain, out to the open sea. There was no ceremony as the last British fighting unit withdrew from the Persian Gulf: a British merchant vessel in the opposite berth blew her siren, and *Intrepid*'s lone piper, scarcely audible above the bustle of the port, played what sounded like some Gaelic lament. That was all.[77]

Having lost most of its empire, Britain now looked to Europe for her future. A month later Britain joined a new 'European Economic Community' – the future European Union.

13

Proxy Wars

The 1960s saw the ties that had once linked Arabia to South Asia largely disappear. But in India, Pakistan and Burma, where the new borders crossed land rather than sea, it was not so easy to forget the links that previously united the region.

Throughout their first decade of independence, all three countries had taken much closer trajectories than is often appreciated. Each aspired to democratic socialism, each economy was dominated by military spending and each faced the challenge of rehabilitating the millions displaced in the violent 1940s. All three countries were also keen to avoid being pulled into the global Cold War, receiving arms from the US to battle revolutionary communism, while also preaching socialism and establishing close relations with the USSR and China. In 1955 India, Pakistan and Burma collaborated with Indonesia and Ceylon to organise the Bandung Conference – a grand meeting of Asian and African countries – and promote anti-colonialism and non-alignment on a global scale.*

As the 1960s progressed, however, the threat of communist overthrow waned and the tentative alliance between India, Pakistan and Burma started to fall apart.[1] Three ethnic communities – the Nagas, the Mizos and the East Bengalis – had been seeking independence from their respective nations for over a decade, and in their attempts to shift the borders of the Radcliffe Line,

---

* The South Asian blurring of lines between the eastern and western bloc was never clearer than when the ostensibly capitalist Republic of India voted in a communist federal government in the South Indian province of Kerala.

each would become embroiled in a proxy war between India and Pakistan.

In 1971 the Bengalis of East Pakistan would succeed in forging a new nation state called Bangladesh. But at the start of the 1960s it was the Naga liberation struggle, spearheaded by the half-paralysed former insurance salesman Angami Zapu Phizo, which looked most likely to succeed.

By the 1960s Angami Zapu Phizo was a bitter man, horrified at the way Nagaland had become part of the Indian Union yet nearby Sikkim and Bhutan had escaped merely through their respective monarchs signing protectorate treaties with India after independence.[2] 'Had Nagaland been a Kingdom,' he later said, 'her personality would have been recognised internationally, as happened in case of the tiny Kingdoms of Bhutan and Sikkim, in the further northeast of India. But Nagaland has always been a land of tribal democracies without the leadership of a single person like a King or a Prince.'[3] Phizo opposed the moderate line of other Naga politicians, who sought regional autonomy within the Indian Union, and instead lobbied on both sides of the Indo-Burmese border for outright Naga independence.[4] Rustomji, adviser to the governor of Assam, recorded that

> what struck me about Phizo was his extraordinary thoroughness and pertinacity. He was around with neatly typed, systematically serialised copies of all documents relevant to the Naga problem and he gave the impression of carrying, single-handed, in his little briefcase, the destinies of the Naga people.[5]

In 1951 Phizo set about collecting a range of 'thumbprints and signatures',[6] and then publicly announced that 99.99 per cent of Nagas had voted for independence. It remains unclear how this 'plebiscite' was carried out and who had taken part, but when Nehru heard the news he considered Phizo's demands to be an 'absurd ... fairy tale'.[7] Rebuffed by Nehru, Phizo announced the Nagas would perform a Gandhian 'satyagraha' and 'face bullets without retaliation', if that was what it took to reunite them with the '400,000 [Nagas] ... on the Burmese side' of the Patkai Hills.[8] Indian official Jaipal Singh met the Naga leader afterwards and tried to persuade him against 'any further fragmentation of India in the form of a new Pakistan'. But Phizo was unmoved, and a journalist who observed the meeting noted 'the fires of [his] dedicated eyes'.[9]

In 1953 Phizo had crossed into Burma, from where he planned to take his proposals to the United Nations, but a Burmese border police patrol discovered him and detained him in Monywa.[10] Indian authorities pressured the Burmese to extend his detention, and Nehru used the opportunity to visit the Naga Hills with U Nu, his Burmese counterpart. The two prime ministers found themselves rebuffed, however, and when they arrived to give a public address, the public simply walked away and 'bared their bottoms as they went'.[11]

From this point on it was a gradual slide into open Naga rebellion. Upon his release, Phizo formed a parallel government and, in the words of one Indian official, 'began planning for armed resistance'.[12] By 1954 murders were being reported across the region, targeting both the Indian Army and Naga politicians. This culminated on 22 March 1956, when Phizo formally declared Nagaland an independent state. Moderate Naga leaders who opposed Phizo's use of violence were found dead in mysterious circumstances.[13]

Most explanations of the Naga revolt view Phizo's movement through the lens of secessionism but it is perhaps more useful to see it as an attempt to undo the partition of India and Burma and reunite the Nagas on both sides. As his own family members claimed at the time, 'The Naga revolt against India was due to this accident of geography whereby an ethnic community was slashed into various bits by artificial frontier lines.'[14]

As the administration in the Naga Hills collapsed, an Indian general requested permission to 'machine-gun hostiles using aircraft' in the same way the British had during the Quit India protests. Nehru refused, and his army instead took to creating irregular militias of Naga volunteers to suppress Phizo's movement.[15] Nonetheless, it was a watershed: 'Nowhere else in the country, not even in Kashmir, had the army been sent in to quell a rebellion launched by those who were formally citizens of the state.'[16] India, people would soon learn, could be much harsher in crushing rebellions than even her colonial predecessor.

On 16 December 1957 Phizo was smuggled to the East Pakistani border, hidden inside a human coffin with one hundred thousand

rupees in cash.[17] 'I remember looking down to the plain covered by a layer of winter mist,' he later told his biographer.

> The sun was not yet above the horizon, but I looked on the promise of safety. We waited until cowdust-time, as the people of the plains call dusk, to make the final crossing of the border. Praise God we have survived, I told those with me as we gathered in prayer.[18]

Safely across the border, Phizo and his companions set out for Dacca to meet Pakistan's defence minister Ayub Khan. With a waxed moustache not unlike the surrealist artist Salvador Dalí's, Ayub Khan had commanded a battalion in the Assam Regiment before Partition and had worked closely with the Nagas during the Second World War. If anyone in Pakistan was likely to be sympathetic, thought Phizo, it was him. But the Naga leader was in for a 'great shock' when Ayub detained him inside a Dacca police compound and sent 'astonishingly unreliable intelligence officers' to interrogate him.[19] Phizo probably assumed he was going to be deported back to India or handed to the Indian authorities but instead the intelligence officers tried to persuade him that Assam – including the Naga Hills – rightfully belonged to Pakistan. Pakistan, it seems, was convinced that Indian subterfuge lay behind the political restlessness in East Pakistan and decided to keep hold of Phizo, as a threat. The peace established by Liaquat and Nehru still held, but cooperation was giving way on both sides. Phizo had become a pawn in a much larger struggle. A South Asian cold war was afoot.

In 1958, a decade after the departure of the British, the dreams of an independent and democratic South Asia were ebbing away.

India would be the first to curtail its citizen's rights. On 11 September, Nehru placed the Naga Hills under martial law in the form of the AFSPA (Armed Forces Special Powers Act), a regulation directly based on those Britain had used during the Quit India movement. The act allowed soldiers to kill civilians on mere suspicion in 'disturbed areas', and protected them from the law. Democracy would continue in most of India, but it would not return for several years in the Northeast. The AFSPA remains in place to this day.

Pakistan followed suit three weeks later when the man holding Phizo in captivity – Ayub Khan – staged a coup, becoming Pakistan's first military president. The end of Pakistani democracy had been set in motion when, on 23 September, the nation's Provincial Assembly descended into a brawl that ended with deputy speaker Shahed Ali dead.[20] Until this point, Firoz Khan Noon's premiership had been a success and since resolving the Gwadar dispute he had gone on to settle numerous other disputes between East Pakistan and India, and West Pakistan with Iran. Although today he is often derided as a 'feudal lightweight', Noon is the only Pakistani leader other than Jinnah to have achieved the geographic expansion of Pakistan. With the brawl in the assembly, things started to fall apart. A few days later the Khan of Kalat announced he would be pulling out of the Pakistani union and on 7 October Pakistan's Bengali governor general Iskander Mirza declared martial law and suspended democracy. He informed Prime Minister Noon of the coup with a letter:

My Dear Sir Firoz
After very careful searching of the heart, I have come to the conclusion that the country cannot be sound unless I take full responsibility and take over the administration … My only regret is that this drastic revolutionary action I have to take while you were Prime Minister. By the time you get this letter Martial Law will come into operation and General Ayub whom I have appointed as the Chief Martial Law Administrator will be in position. For you personally I have great regard and will do all that is necessary for your personal happiness and well-being.
    Yours sincerely
    Sd. Iskander Mirza[21]

Mirza's rule lasted twenty days, until Ayub Khan overthrew him in a military coup and abrogated the constitution. At almost exactly the same time Burma's democratic experiment was also abrogated. A split within the leading AFPFL party threatened to bring about a coup there too, and Shan groups threatened to secede. Worried about the Burmese Union falling apart, U Nu asked the military leader Ne Win to step in and form a caretaker government until political order had been restored. So it was that in little over a month in 1958, 'democratic politics and civilian authority' were collectively dissolved across 'East Pakistan, Burma, and India's northeast'.[22]

In January 1960, days after her daughter's wedding, Edwina Mountbatten flew out from England to join Nehru at India's tenth Republic Day parade.

It was a bitterly cold morning but nonetheless a vast crowd swathed in shawls and mufflers had gathered along New Delhi's central vista. Much had changed since Edwina's first visit to the city: the old

Kingsway had been renamed 'Rajpath' and the Indian Mutiny was now referred to as the First War of Independence. Delhi's parliament building was 'gradually being adorned by the portraits of the great men of independent India' and old British haunts like the Roshanara Club were 'now strangely lacking in activity'.[23] But other things hadn't changed, and that morning a stream of soldiers, folk dancers and elephants with 'intricately painted' ears paraded up and down the Rajpath, just as they had in the great pageants of the Raj. Later that evening Nehru's house guest Marie Seaton spotted Edwina chatting away to Nehru's guests on white wicker chairs.[24] 'Some people believed that she exerted a great influence upon Jawaharlal,' Seaton wrote, 'but at least one of his friends was of the opinion that it was she who hung on every word he said.'[25]

Every year for the last decade, Edwina had visited Nehru in the Indian capital, and he returned the favour, visiting Edwina in England.[26] Indeed, in the early 1950s Edwina had once handed her husband a bundle of her and Nehru's 'love letters' and admitted to

> the strange relationship – most of it spiritual – which exists between us. J[awaharlal] has obviously meant a great deal in my life, in these last years, and I think I in his too. Our meetings have been rare and always fleeting, but I think I understand him, and perhaps he me, as well as any human beings *can* ever understand each other.[27]

Through her visits, Edwina had seen the country change in unimaginable ways. She had also witnessed the new dynamics of Nehru's family, particularly the rise of his daughter Indira Gandhi, who was gaining increasing prominence in New Delhi's political inner circle.

Indira Gandhi was a shy woman, occasionally vindictive, but warm to those she loved. Schooled in Bengal under Rabindranath Tagore, then Oxford, she had married the handsome bachelor Feroze Gandhi (no relation of the Mahatma), who provided her with the only Indian surname more famous than Nehru's. Over time, however, the marriage evolved into a deeply unhappy one, and on one occasion she wrote to her father, 'I have felt like a bird in a very small cage.'[28] Feroze didn't get on particularly well with the Nehrus, and rumours soon abounded about his extramarital affairs. Then, in the late 1950s rumours had begun to spread of Mrs Gandhi's own love affair with her father's secretary M. O. Mathai. The alleged affair remains both fascinating and elusive, particularly in the wake of claims he was a CIA plant in Nehru's cabinet. 'Mathai did a lot of damage to Nehru,' Congress politician Natwar Singh told Mrs Gandhi's biographer. 'He was close to the CIA ... [and] between 1946 and 1959 every single paper that passed Nehru's desk went to the CIA.'[29]

The whole affair seems to have ended in humiliation for Indira.* Mathai was later forced out of Nehru's office due to a financial scandal. Indira, meanwhile, reached her lowest point. But a year before Edwina's visit to Delhi, Indira had finally started to take control of her life. That February she got herself elected Congress president and although she was initially regarded as little more than 'a delicate lamb',[30] she soon displayed the uncanny ability to outmanoeuvre her opponents. Protests had erupted against the recently elected communist government of Kerala, and Indira now demonstrated for the first time the authoritarian streak that would mark her out so strongly from her father, and ultimately provide her with more power than he ever held. According to her husband's biographer: 'She orchestrated the unrest from New Delhi through her loyal [All India Congress Committee] workers in the state ... hand in hand with the communal Hindus in the state and with the Muslim League ... she showed that she could be a stiff and authoritarian leader and it paid off.'[31] By the time Edwina arrived in Delhi, Kerala's government had been dismissed 'to vociferous outrage, notably from Feroze himself',[32] and Indira had started building her own political platform.

---

* A scandalous chapter widely available online, allegedly an unpublished part of Mathai's autobiography, purports that she got pregnant with Mathai's child. 'She has Cleopatra's nose, Pauline Bonaparte's eyes and breasts of Venus,' reads the alleged chapter, and 'in the sex act she has all the artfulness of French women and Kerala Nair women combined'. There is no doubt that a chapter of Mathai's autobiography was redacted before publication. Indeed the book itself refers to a 'chapter on an intensely personal experience of the author's, written without inhibition' which was 'withdrawn by the author at the last moment'. The director of India's Intelligence Bureau T. V. Rajeswar would later admit handing Mrs Gandhi 'a copy of a chapter written by M. O. Mathai' which pertained to their relationship. The question is, of course, whether the widely circulated chapter available online is the same chapter that was redacted. Certainly, the Gandhi family continue to deny the affair, as they deny Nehru's relationship with Edwina Mountbatten, and Natwar Singh would claim that Mathai spread all these tales for his own reasons.

A few days after Republic Day, Edwina sat on the grass with Nehru, Indira and Marie Seaton to watch a performance by some Naga dancers. The Naga conflict had recently escalated and the Indian Army had taken to 'grouping' civilians in new settlements to flush out insurgents. This had only alienated more Nagas, and Isak Chishi Swu recalls being driven to join the Naga underground after seeing locusts dropped 'from helicopters to destroy our crops'.[33] Paradoxically, the government was also working hard to integrate the region and the troupe of Naga dancers had been specially invited to Republic Day to show India's 'Unity in Diversity'.

'Don't they have beautiful bottoms,' Edwina remarked to Marie Seaton.

'Very beautiful,' Seaton agreed.[34]

Little did they know that this was to be Edwina's last visit. After a tearful farewell, she flew on to Borneo where she developed a headache, and on 21 February was found dead in her room, surrounded by Nehru's letters. When her husband was notified, he scrawled the word 'TRAGEDY' atop his diary entry for the day.[35] 'Shocked and stunned to learn of Edwina's passing,' Nehru wrote to Mountbatten that afternoon. 'She was so well when she was here a fortnight ago.'[36]

Nehru appeared emotionless for days, and an Australian diplomat noted that he 'must have had strong feelings about the utterly sudden death of Lady Mountbatten but he showed no sign of it'.[37] Privately, however, he was a wreck. 'It is difficult to realise that Edwina has gone,' he wrote in early March. 'I have to remind myself often that she is not coming back.'[38] A short while later he wrote to his sister asking what he should do with all the things 'left by Edwina' at Teen Murti House such as her pressure cooker.[39] Ironically, while Delhi's British High Commission held no memorial service that day, the Indian parliament observed a two-minute silence for its last vicereine.[40]

Four days after her death, Edwina's coffin was cast into the sea, and an Indian frigate called the *Trishul* was personally dispatched by Nehru to throw a wreath of marigolds after her. The suddenness of her death at the age of fifty-eight generated numerous rumours, and one of her relatives even privately claims she was murdered by the wife of a Malay lover. The reason she was buried so quickly and in such an unusual manner, so the story goes, was to prevent the public from seeing the body.[41] But Edwina had been ill for years, and the cause of her death was more likely to have been medical. She had recently had surgery, and before her trip she had been warned that if she didn't take more rest, she would only have months to live.[42]

In the wake of Edwina's death, Nehru appeared to age and India's political situation weighed more heavily upon him. Tensions were growing with China, and Marie Seaton writes that

> I did not notice how Nehru had changed ... until one evening in the summer of 1960 when Indira suggested I stay for a meal ... That afternoon he had been dealing with the difficult situation of the Naga Hills ... [and] throughout the entire meal, Nehru sat with his head bowed, not uttering a single word. It was almost as if he was not there.[43]

Later that year another death shook Nehru's family. Feroze Gandhi, Indira's husband, had a heart attack and died. Indira receded into herself while Nehru was diagnosed with a kidney infection and put on a strict diet. It was obvious to everyone around him that he was in decline.

Two weeks after Edwina's death, the half-paralysed Phizo arrived at Zurich Airport, Switzerland, under the fake name of Prudencio Llach and armed with a forged El Salvadorean passport. A man in a white uniform was waiting for him on the tarmac, and without revealing his name, he waved 'Prudencio' through Swiss customs and immigration. That evening he checked into the Hotel Sonnenburg and linked up with Michael Scott, a rogue Anglican priest from Sussex who had served in Bombay and Calcutta before becoming the first white man to be arrested for protesting South African apartheid. The two men remained in Zurich for some time. Then, one 'blustery, cold night' in late Spring, they were detained by rather confused immigration officials in London, who refused to accept 'Prudencio's documentation. Scott, 'in full clerical garb', argued with the tired and irritable officials, but to no avail. Eventually 'Prudencio' himself raised his voice. 'When the British came to my country,' Phizo declared, revealing his identity, 'they did not bring any passport with them.'[44]

Phizo's journey to London had not been easy. After his daring escape from India inside a coffin, he had spent two years detained in

East Pakistan. In Dacca, his facial paralysis had worsened, but there were still 'times when humour touched his one good eye even if it did not reach his lips'.[45] Phizo was never sure who handed him the passport that had helped him fly to London, nor who the man in the white uniform was. Perhaps it was Pakistani intelligence, or perhaps someone from the US. But from London he would finally resume his mission of seeking international support for the Naga struggle.

On 26 July 1960, the Naga leader gave a dramatic press conference from the British capital, crying out that 'Kali, the Hindu goddess of destruction, could not have conceived of more barbarity than that which has overtaken my country since Britain relinquished power'.[46] The very next day Nehru publicly announced his plans to carve out a separate state of Nagaland *within* the Indian Union, splitting the Naga movement down the middle between those who were happy with some form of autonomy and those who weren't. 'They are traitors, every one of them,' Phizo scowled when told that a faction of Nagas was now working with the Indian government. 'They have betrayed us and dishonoured the martyrs who died for our cause.'[47]

Phizo would not find the support he had hoped for in Britain, but ironically in London he at last started to make an impression on the man who had earlier arrested him: Pakistan's new military ruler Ayub Khan. The tall and imposing Ayub had settled happily into his presidency, with one US diplomat describing how he 'liked to relax with the young army officers, indulging in such horseplay as being carried around the garden in a chair or participating in wild dances from the Northwest Frontier'.[48] Ayub obsessed over 'modernisation' initiatives and, unusually for the ruler of an Islamic republic, berated Islamic scholars as 'idiots or rascals'.[49] Pakistan would thrive economically under his rule, becoming one of Asia's fastest-growing economies.

Khan had surprised everyone with his willingness to engage with India and even proposed a military alliance between India and Pakistan.[50] After a 1960 treaty resolved the two countries' water disputes along the Indus, cries of 'Nehru Zindabad' echoed through the streets of Pakistan's capital: unimaginable a decade earlier.[51] But when, on the same trip, Ayub attempted to reopen the Kashmir dispute with Nehru, their relationship had begun to sour. 'Mr Nehru looks down on me with such contempt,' he bitterly told an Indian diplomat afterwards.[52]

The biggest wedge between Ayub and the Indian leadership, however, came a few months later, when India used military force to seize the Portuguese colony of Goa, the last European enclave left in the subcontinent. It was in some ways a repeat of Pakistan's seizure of Gwadar from Oman, and the event features little in much of the scholarship on the Indo-Pakistani relationship. Yet by seizing territory that it considered part of some greater Indian nation, India only convinced Ayub of its expansionist and irredentist aims. Henceforth, the India–Pakistan relationship would be one of pure hostility.

In the wake of Goa's annexation, Khan re-established contact with Phizo, still imprisoned in Dacca, to offer military and financial assistance against India. It was a turning point, and one that is not fully appreciated. In the following months Naga training camps were established in Sylhet, Dacca and the Chittagong Hill Tracts, and the Naga Home Guards was reorganised into a Naga Army. 'When our boys went to Pakistan for training ... they were treated very well,' recalled Phizo's foreign secretary.[53] 'There were former instructors from the Assam Rifles and from the Assam regiment who trained our people. They taught our people discipline.'[54]

India and Pakistan were not technically at war but ten years of remarkable cooperation between them had now come to an end. Henceforth the two nations would be enveloped in a decade-long proxy war that continues to this day. Each funded secessionist movements within the other's territories, culminating in the partition of Pakistan and the independence of Bangladesh.

The Nagas would be the first of many groups from India's Northeast to seek military aid in East Pakistan. In July 1962, another dissident Indian group contacted Pakistan – the Mizo National Front – seeking aid in the wake of a massive famine, the second to hit the Bengal delta and its surrounding regions since independence. With the hills' economy already eviscerated by Partition,* the first signs of famine arrived in 1958, but the Indian government 'scoffed at the idea' of such 'tribals' being able to predict a famine. When the famine hit, therefore, the Indian authorities were completely unprepared. An astonishing 5 per

---

* Until 1947 the Mizo economy was closely tied to the Bengali port city of Chittagong, which was just a hundred kilometres away. After 1947, however, the nearest usable port was some 1,700 kilometres distant – in Calcutta.

cent of the entire Mizo population died of starvation in the following months.⁵⁵

The Mizo National Front that now contacted Pakistan had begun as a local relief organisation, but in 1961 it started calling for independence from India. The group had actually attempted to court US support but the States 'was not interested since communism was not a threat', so a delegation approached Pakistan instead.⁵⁶ This time they struck lucky and by the end of the year Mizos too were being armed by Pakistan as part of a programme called Operation JIM.⁵⁷

Around this time India also began to 'provide political and material (primarily financial) support to Pakhtoon dissidents on Pakistan's northwest frontier'.⁵⁸ Far more consequentially, at precisely the same moment as Ayub Khan was offering support to Naga and Mizo rebels, discontented rebels from East Pakistan were attempting to contact India.

The onset of military rule in Pakistan had been disastrous for Bengalis, who had constituted a meagre 1 per cent of Pakistan's armed forces at independence, as the colonial pseudoscience of 'martial races' continued to deny them entry into the Punjabi-dominated military. By the 1960s this 55 per cent of Pakistan's population were essentially excluded from having a say in the country's governance, and many Bengali politicians mused that colonial rule had not ended in 1947. Some Bengalis took out their frustration by targeting all Urdu-speakers – regardless of their proximity to the government – and there was a visible decline in Bengali and non-Bengali romances.⁵⁹ One US diplomat noted how 'a favourite quip in East Pakistan was that three things held Pakistan together': Islam, the English Language and Pakistan International Airlines.⁶⁰

Former prime minister Suhrawardy and his pipe-smoking acolyte Mujibur Rahman (better known as Mujib) were among those to become disillusioned, turning their political party, the Awami League, into a mouthpiece for Bengali frustrations with the state. With his bushy moustache and thick horn-rimmed glasses, Mujib cut a particularly striking figure. His politics were populist, his attitude uncompromising, and in the run-up to the 1954 elections he had 'threatened to peel off the skin of the Chief Minister, Nurul Amin, and turn it into a pair of slippers'. The home secretary subsequently ordered his arrest and one civil servant remembers: 'When Sheikh Mujib was brought to my office, he denounced Punjabi bureaucrats and threatened to bring down the government. But why did he want to peel off the Chief Minister's skin? "Because it was so thick" was his spontaneous response.'[61] This brash uncompromising attitude would ultimately transform Mujib into the founding father of Bangladesh, and already he was beginning to consider outright independence from Pakistan. A young university student remembers that during one meeting between Mujib and Suhrawardy:

> Mujib said that the secession of the East wing was not a difficult job. He required only a canful of kerosene and a matchbox. When all of us questioned how he would do it, Mujib nonchalantly said he would go to Kurmitola Airport, splash kerosene on the runway and ignite fire with a matchstick. That would end the bondage between the two wings.[62]

Precisely how much support the idea of secession had at this point is controversial, but in 1961 Mujib founded a group called the Swadhin Bangla Biplobi Parishad (Free Bengali Revolutionary Council).* In February 1962 Mujib crossed from East Pakistan into India seeking military training for his new organisation. 'Only my mother, I and other siblings knew about it,' recalled his daughter Hasina when she became prime minister of Bangladesh. 'Pakistani intelligence agents ... tried to trace him by quizzing us repeatedly.' In the Indian city of Agartala, Mujib met with a senior Congressman and 'sought Nehru's support for an armed insurgency against the military regime aimed at liberation from Pakistan',[63] but Mujib ended up back in the hands of Pakistani border guards for reasons that remain unclear. 'It is unfortunate that Mujibur Rahman was handed over to the Pakistan authorities,' wrote Nehru in a secret telegram shortly afterwards. 'If anyone from East Pakistan comes to India and seeks refuge, we should certainly give it.'[64]

Mujib was released from Pakistani prison five months later, but he had lost none of his conviction. In the early hours of Christmas Day, he

---

* The following section on Mujib's early contacts is deeply indebted to the work of Avinash Paliwal, whose brilliant work on the subject has illuminated a whole new side to this well-trodden history. See Paliwal, A., *India's Near East: A New History* (London: Hurst, 2024).

made another attempt to gain Indian support. The plot unfolded in rather cinematic fashion, according to the memoir of Indian diplomat S. S. Banerjee, who writes how, after returning from a Christmas Eve party, a mysterious fourteen-year-old boy knocked on his door and told him to come to the office of the Bangla-language *Daily Ittefaq*. Puzzled, Banerjee duly went, to find the editor Manik Mia sitting in a chair. Mia explained he wanted to introduce Banerjee to a certain friend of his, and Banerjee was surprised to find himself face to face with Mujib.

Mujib 'gave me a firm and vigorous handshake,' writes Banerjee, 'and looked straight into my eyes as if he was itching to say something important to me.'[65] He engaged in small talk for almost two hours, before producing a small letter and explaining why he had summoned the diplomat. The letter, Mujib explained, contained a plan to carve out 'a sovereign independent homeland of the Bengali-speaking people of East Pakistan'.[66] All he needed was Nehru's support.

Banerjee claims to have written to Nehru straightaway to inform him of Mujib's letter. But when Nehru responded, his offer was unexpected. India's prime minister was convinced that a Pakistan run by pro-India Bengalis would be more beneficial to India than a Pakistan riven by civil war. Mujib, he believed, had the capacity to be a secular mass leader of Pakistan as a whole, a Pakistani Atatürk, who could unshackle the country from religious nationalism and lead it into a new era. If Banerjee's memoir is to be believed, Nehru urged Mujib to build a mass political base in the Bengali countryside rather than seek secession, and to begin organising a non-violent Gandhian campaign against the Pakistani military.

Mujib was flummoxed. He didn't particularly agree with Gandhian non-violence, finding greater inspiration from Subhas Chandra Bose's more violent methods of liberation. Moreover, there was 'a heaven and hell difference,' he told Banerjee, 'between the Pakistani military dictatorship, a brutal force of evil … and British imperialism, certainly an engine of exploitation, but under popular pressure open to persuasion and reason'.[67] Nonetheless, according to Banerjee, the Indian government drew up a 'memorandum of understanding' with Mujib, promising to extend 'moral, political and material support' to his movement so long as they refrained from immediately seceding from

Pakistan.* A covert channel was established between Mujib and Indian intelligence, and India started preparing for a more hostile relationship with its neighbour. By 1963, therefore, across the east of the subcontinent, rebel groups seeking to change Partition's borders had become pawns in a South Asian cold war. Pakistan was funding Mizo and Naga rebels in India, and India was funding Bengali rebels in Pakistan.

Four events in quick succession from 1962 to 1964 shifted the balance of power in the subcontinent. The first came on 2 March 1962, when General Ne Win toppled the Burmese government in a coup d'état. The coup galvanised support for ethnic rebel groups and government control of the Patkai slipped away. Crucially, the Burmese administration had lost control of the northern Kachin region bordering China. That October, therefore, when China and India went to war, Chinese troops were able to surprise the Indians by crossing into India through Burma's Kachin rather than over their mutual border.[68] The war ended with India's military humiliation. When Ne Win set about the mass eviction of Burma's remaining Indian population, therefore, Nehru issued little more than a stern warning. Four hundred thousand Indians were forced out of the country in a matter of months in what was arguably the largest refugee crisis India had seen since Partition.[69]

The third event took place on 27 December 1963 when a sacred relic of the Prophet Muhammad went missing in Kashmir. In Dacca protests turned into a massacre of Hindus and within days an astonishing 693,000 Hindus and Christians had crossed into India – around 7 per cent of all non-Muslims remaining in Pakistan.[70] Anti-Muslim pogroms in India's West Bengal broke out in retaliation and although they rarely feature in the nation's history books, they remain the 'most violent Hindu-Muslim conflagration of post-colonial India'.[71] One in fifty Indian Muslims – some eight hundred thousand individuals – fled across the border into East Pakistan.

The fourth event to change South Asia was Nehru's decline. When Mountbatten visited the Indian prime minister in 1964, he found Nehru 'shockingly weak and uncomprehending' and told him not to work

---

* Crucially, this memorandum has never been published; Banerjee's memoir is the only evidence that such a document exists.

himself into an early grave, noting: 'That is what Edwina did, to the great distress of all who loved her whom she left behind.'[72] But Nehru refused to follow Mountbatten's advice. In May he organised a temporary ceasefire in Nagaland and three days later he suffered a stroke. The next morning, Jawaharlal Nehru, India's first prime minister was declared dead. Over the following days an endless stream of dignitaries arrived to pay their respects. The British prime minister flew in personally, as did Pakistani foreign minister Zulfikar Ali Bhutto and, as noted by Marie Seaton:

> The face most contorted by emotion was ... that of the once blithe Louis Mountbatten. He appeared to sag at the sight of the alabaster head of Jawaharlal, the friend with whom it had been possible to forge a chapter unparalleled in history ... Theirs had been a harmony of difference, cemented by their mutual admiration of the Mahatma, on the one hand, and the very human Edwina, on the other.[73]

For Pakistan's leadership, Nehru's death and India's weakened position in the wake of its defeat to China presented a rare opportunity to resolve the Kashmir dispute. After flying back to Pakistan from the funeral, Ayub Khan assigned Zulfikar Ali Bhutto as chair of a new 'Kashmir Cell'. The son of Junagadh's old prime minister and a Hindu nautch girl, Bhutto was a socialist aristocrat who made much of his Oxford education and Savile Row suits. He reminded many people of a young Muhammad Ali Jinnah, if Jinnah had been a habitual womaniser.[74] It was only after he married his second wife that he told her about the existence of a first wife; later Bhutto fell for a married woman called Husna Sheikh in Dacca and their affair evolved into a national scandal. Nonetheless, Bhutto brushed off such accusations with characteristic charm by saying that

> yes, he was fond of women: as men were supposed to be. And as regards drinking, well, he may drink alcohol but at least he did not drink the blood of the poor.[75]

In decades to come, Bhutto would be seen as one of Pakistan's most influential prime ministers, strengthening ties with China, initiating the country's nuclear programme and enacting the biggest land reforms in its history. 'No individual in the history of Pakistan achieved greater popular power or suffered so ignominious a death as Zulfikar Ali Bhutto,' writes his biographer.[76] Indeed he would become so anti-military that the military hanged him for it, yet in the late 1960s all this was still to come. At the time he was close to Ayub Khan and reportedly even referred to the general as 'Daddy'.[77] Bhutto had only renounced Indian citizenship in 1958 to become Pakistani, but by 1963 he was the country's foreign minister and the same year he signed a deal recognising China's sovereignty over parts of Jammu and Kashmir in exchange for its backing in the dispute. Despite his tilt towards China, however, Bhutto also managed to charm US officials. 'Mr Bhutto, if you were an American you would be in my cabinet,' US president John Kennedy told him on his first visit to the country. 'Mr Kennedy,' Bhutto responded, 'if I were an American, you would be in mine.'[78]

Now in charge of the Kashmir Cell, Bhutto urged Ayub Khan to seize the region once and for all. In April 1965 Ayub ordered Pakistani troops to occupy the Rann of Cutch, the disputed swathe of flamingo-populated salt flats that separated the old princely state of Cutch from Sindh. India responded with barely a whimper and so, egged on by Bhutto, Ayub decided to send troops into Kashmir. On 6 September Pakistan's president announced on the radio, 'We are at war.'[79]

Despite the proxy war already playing out in the east, this was the first time India and Pakistan had been in open conflict in fifteen years. Telephone lines were cut off, flights were suspended, cross-border travel was banned and foreign diplomats were rounded up by their respective authorities. One Indian diplomat would give birth to a baby under this curious form of house arrest without access to a doctor.[80]

When war started, Pakistan's leadership had expected the 'fullest co-operation' from Kashmiri Muslims,[81] but such support never materialised. Ironically, one group that *did* provide cooperation were the Buddhists of East Pakistan and a Bengali magazine printed during the war shows the Bohmong Raja of the Chittagong Hill Tracts leading the community prayers for Pakistan's swift victory.[82] On 6 September India ordered its army to wage war in Punjab and as its tanks rolled towards Lahore, 'startled Pakistani soldiers rushed to the front line still wearing their pyjamas'.[83] But before the clash could develop, the United States and USSR negotiated a settlement.

Open hostilities ended on 23 September and a new agreement was signed the following January in the USSR between Ayub Khan and Nehru's successor, Lal Bahadur Shastri, in the historic city of Tashkent to try and get Indian and Pakistani armies to retreat to a pre-1965 cease-fire line. Just a day after the agreement was signed, however, Shastri died under mysterious circumstances.*

Nehru's daughter Indira Gandhi was hastily appointed his successor. 'She was at sea at the beginning,' BBC journalist Mark Tully observed years later. 'At a press conference in 1966 she just sat there looking shell shocked while being attacked by journalists from all sides.' But over the next five years, she would evolve into a dominating presence. When Tully met her again five years later, he couldn't believe the difference. 'She had become a completely different person,' he recalls, 'very determined, someone you couldn't break in an interview.'[84]

The 1965 war achieved little for either nation, its main legacy instead the complete shattering of remaining Indo-Pakistan ties and the enactment of draconian laws allowing the seizure of 'enemy' property. India defined an 'enemy' as any Muslim who migrated to Pakistan, and Pakistan defined it as any Hindu or Sikh who had migrated to India. The legislation thus had a profound impact on cross-border relationships, disrupting lives and complicating ties with the other side. The flow of migrants had persisted since Partition, but now it became difficult for refugees to claim property on the other side of the border.

The war did not even bring lasting peace. Indeed, with the signing of the Tashkent Agreement, the conflict only changed from a 'hot' war back to a 'cold' proxy war. Within a month of Tashkent in 1966, the Mizo National Front finally rebelled against Indian rule. The Indian Army's response would be on a completely different scale to anything felt in the Naga insurgency further north: under orders from Indira Gandhi, the Indian Air Force started bombing the rebels into submission, 'the only time that the Government of India resorted to air strikes

---

* His death remains one of the great unsolved mysteries in South Asian history and India's government continues to block access to files associated with his death, claiming that it would harm foreign relations.

in its own territory'.[85] Rumours circulated that Mizo leader Laldenga was on his way to London to meet Phizo[86] and the AFSPA, the same emergency ordinance used in the Naga Hills, swiftly applied to the Mizo.

In the coming months, the Indian Army forcibly resettled 82 per cent of all Mizos into 'voluntary grouping centres'. Cowboy hats, flared jeans and platform shoes became a symbol of support for the rebels and Mizo musicians started spurning the influence of Hindi songs, instead choosing to rekindle pre-independence connections with Burmese musicians.[87] The indifference of Indians elsewhere only heightened the Mizos' sense of alienation, triggering a dramatic migration of Mizos to Burma and East Pakistan, in the latter to take up arms.

The Mizos who crossed into East Pakistan found a country only marginally less divided than their own. Ayub Khan's reputation had taken a bashing after the 1965 war. West Pakistanis resented his failure to seize Kashmir, but the anger was on another level in East Pakistan, which Pakistan's military had left virtually undefended during the war. 'Just as we noticed that there was no one to protect us,' remembers one Bengali professor, 'we also noticed that India didn't attack us.'[88] A *National Geographic* article entitled 'Problems in a Two-Part Land' noted how East Pakistani mobs had begun to 'smash government-building windows and overturn official vehicles to work off their frustration'.[89]

It was Mujibur Rahman, the pipe-smoking Bengali activist who had contacted Nehru in 1962, who gave voice to Bengali frustrations. That year he had been elected president of the Awami League, the leading Bengali nationalist party, and Archer Blood, the US consul general in Dacca, remembers how, 'Mujib's very appearance suggested raw power, a power drawn from the masses ... He was taller and broader than most Bengalis, with ruggedly handsome features and intense eyes.'[90] On 5 February 1966, Mujib proclaimed a six-point demand which would rapidly become the central issue in Pakistani politics, summarised as follows:

> There should be a Federation of Pakistan on the basis of the Lahore Resolution.
> Federal government should be limited to Defence and Foreign Affairs.

There should be two separate currencies for the two wings or measures to stop capital flight from East to West.

The centre should have no tax-raising powers.

Foreign exchange earnings of each wing should remain with each wing.

A militia or paramilitary force for East Pakistan should be set up.[91]

Although Mujib may have desired secession three years earlier, his actions suggest that in 1966 he was seeking to be prime minister of all Pakistan. Whatever the case, Ayub Khan had recently learned of Mujib's trip to India in 1962, as well as of his links to Indian Intelligence, and was now convinced Mujib was making a bid for independence. Banerjee, the Indian diplomat who Mujib had contacted in Dacca, was thus ordered to leave Dacca immediately and in April 1967 Mujib, Manik Mia and much of the Awami League leadership were arrested by the Pakistani government.[92]

Ayub's government made Mujib's trial – dubbed the 'Agartala Conspiracy Case' – public in the hope it would destroy Mujib's reputation. Instead Ayub's government was unable to produce any evidence that Mujib had intended to break Pakistan and many Bengalis started to wonder if the trial had just been staged to further undermine Bengali politics.[93] 'We felt it was a conspiracy to tarnish Mujib, to suppress our demands,' remembers one Bengali professor. 'Mujib had been very cautious in his demands, but ... students became very vocal, they wanted separation.'[94] Rather than destroying Mujib's reputation, Ayub Khan had accidentally turned him into a martyr.

East and West Pakistan were growing ever further apart. Karachi-based journalist and critic Muneeza Shamsie recalls her friend Naz arriving off a plane from East Pakistan:

She would comment on how surreal Karachi seemed to be, with all of us carrying on as normal and going off to the movies and a Chinese meal afterwards, whilst Dacca was so palpably tense. She was astonished to find that instead of being concerned about the political crisis, there was much excitement in Karachi because a local cinema was showing *My Fair Lady!*[95]

For Urdu-speaking families in East Pakistan, remembers Asif Ali, 'the Agartala Conspiracy Case was the turning point'.[96] Asif's family had migrated to Pakistan as Urdu-speaking 'Muhajirs' not because of riots, but because his parents were 'madly in love with the idea of Pakistan'.[97] Asif's family moved around different parts of the country for jobs, but it was only when they moved from West to East Pakistan in his teens that Asif found his own place in the world. Living in East Pakistan 'was the best part of my life,' he recalls,[98] and he had quickly learned the Bengali language and made a host of Bengali friends. He had been shocked, however, by the discrimination they faced and found that even among his own family, 'Bengalis were considered culturally and racially inferior'. No one else in his family was ever interested in learning Bengali.

Until Agartala, however, Asif himself had never felt out of place as a non-Bengali. It was only afterwards that he began to notice subtle changes in the way he was treated. His Bengali friends started to refer to anyone from West Pakistan derisively as 'Shaala Punjabi', regardless of whether they were Punjabi or not, and soon they 'shut up about politics whenever I walked into the canteen,' he recalls. 'Friends would begin to get quiet around me. I could see the change in their eyes.'[99]

The divide widened when Asif started working in his family's company as an army contractor. The firm imported its unskilled labour from the West, and one day when he confronted his uncle about this, the man merely replied, 'These Bengalis are useless, they have no idea how to work.'[100] Asif also found that West Pakistanis were convinced 'that all the teachers in East Pakistan were Hindu'.

> These people would keep insisting, even though they had never been to East Pakistan ... that these Hindu teachers had turned our children against Islam, against Pakistan ... They even went so far as to say that Hindus in East Pakistan were R&AW [Indian Secret Service] agents ... I would say, 'For God's sake, nothing of this sort is happening, yaar. These people are not spies ... these are just people fighting for their political rights.'[101]

As tensions between the two wings of Pakistan reached a climax in 1968, an interconnected web of protest swept across the world, linked by the rise of TV news. The US civil rights movement was galvanised in the wake of Martin Luther King Jr's assassination and student demonstrations seeking social justice tore across Yugoslavia. Demonstrators in Moscow took to the streets, student protests very nearly overthrew the government in Paris and the NLF seized power from the British in South Arabia.

Rock and roll played an unlikely and important role in bringing ideas of cultural, sexual and political revolution to the subcontinent. Western musicians from the Beatles to the Byrds were incorporating classical Indian *ragas* into their music, and the Rolling Stones released a new 'lips and tongue' logo based on a Bengali image of the goddess Kali's tongue. The cultural exchange went two ways, and the bestselling Indian song 'Dum Maro Dum' depicted the decadence of Hippie culture. The Bengali musicians Luxman and Purna Das Baul would eventually make it to the cover of Bob Dylan's album *John Wesley Harding*, with the latter going on to play with Mick Jagger and even exorcise spirits from his house in Chelsea.[102]

Indeed, the countercultural movement produced many brands and institutions that continue to play an important role in South Asia today. Rajput motorbike-enthusiast Jatinder 'John' Singh was amazed when he met Faith Hardy, the rebellious daughter of colonial missionaries who had ridden the 'hippie trail' to Jaipur, and the two fell in love, an unconventional pairing that couldn't have happened two decades earlier. Together the couple leased out the basement of Rambagh Palace from Jaipur's royal family and set up a nightclub called the Fertile Egg, which they touted as 'India's first psychedelic disco'. When the business failed, they turned their efforts to reviving crafts endangered by the collapse of princely patronage, and the result was a block-printing clothing company called Anokhi, which remains popular to this day.[103]

International students helped link diverse student protest groups across borders. Tariq Ali, a Pakistani student agitator who organised pro-democracy protests against Ayub Khan's government, was subsequently elected head of the Oxford Union, befriending the likes of Malcolm X and John Lennon, becoming one of Britain's leading agitators against the Vietnam War.[104] Salahdin Imam, later a guerrilla soldier for the Bengali Mukti Bahini paramilitary, started his revolutionary journey as the rock and roll correspondent for the *Harvard Crimson*.[105] 'Youthful dissidence ... is a worldwide phenomenon,' noted the CIA that year. 'Student power is no longer a chimera.'[106]

Most importantly for South Asia, a communist-inspired peasant revolt broke out in West Bengal's Naxalbari, on the 'chicken's neck' connecting Northeast India to the rest of the country.[107] A new vocabulary of liberation swept across the Bengal delta.

As protest rocked the world, a paper by the chief economist of Pakistan's Planning Commission revealed that just twenty-two Pakistani families owned 87 per cent of the country's banking and 66 per cent of its industries.[108] The paper galvanised opposition to Ayub's rule and on 7 November 1968 protests against police brutality in Gordon College Rawalpindi snowballed. Within days other universities in West Pakistan went on strike and by 6 December students in East Pakistan had joined the picket line. Over time it evolved into a mass movement against Ayub Khan's rule, and in both wings the urban middle class took to the streets.

Zulfikar Ali Bhutto would emerge as one of the major leaders of the movement. The future British high commissioner to Pakistan, Nicholas Barrington, met with Bhutto at his house around this time and noticed that his 'magnificently stocked and decorated library' was lined with books on Napoleon. Bhutto was 'elegant' and 'remarkably fit,' he wrote back to the British Foreign Office, and when questioned on the infiltration of Kashmir that had kicked off the 1965 war, he 'smiled and did not deny that he had instigated the affair'. Bhutto was sympathetic to East Pakistan's frustrations, wrote Barrington, and felt that West Pakistanis needed to spend more time there. Bhutto, Barrington felt, was aiming to be Ayub Khan's successor as leader of Pakistan. Ayub himself was aware of this, and months after the meeting Bhutto was taken into custody and, just as Mujib had been, transformed into a political martyr.[109]

On 15 February a Pakistani prison guard marched up to the cell of one of those accused in the Agartala Conspiracy Case, pulled out a gun and shot the Bengali in the belief he was saving the Pakistani nation. Instead he galvanised a new wave of protests, involving marches and even attacks on police stations and non-Bengali businesses. The firebrand 'Red Maulana' Abdul Hamid Bhashani even told a crowd in Dacca, 'Oh my children, why have you come here. Have you come here to see my beard? Go out to the countryside and spread fire.'[110]

'Dacca came under the virtual control of the students,' wrote US diplomat Archer Blood, and 'there were frequent strikes and "gheraos" in which strikers locked managers inside their offices until they met their workers' demands'.[111] When several West Pakistani leaders refused to work with Ayub Khan unless Mujib was released from prison, Ayub realised the game was up. The Agartala case was withdrawn and Mujib emerged from incarceration a national hero, granted the title 'Bangabandhu' or 'Friend of Bengal'.[112] Within a month, a humiliated Ayub Khan stepped down from office altogether, appointing General Yahya Khan to take his place.

The British government had already begun to assume that Mujib would emerge as Pakistan's next leader, however. Indeed, when Mujib arrived in London that October to raise funds for his party, he was given covert support by the British government. 'We are offering him limited and discreet assistance on the assumption that he might emerge ultimately as the Prime Minister of Pakistan,' reads one secret British government communiqué. 'Our interest in him is, however, being maintained in a low key to avoid offending the Martial law regime [in Pakistan].'[113]

Soon afterwards Mujib added a seventh demand to his six points: 'The eastern province of Pakistan will be called "Bangla Desh" [land of Bengalis].'[114]

By the late 1960s Bengalis faced an enormous amount of discrimination from West Pakistan, not least in the attempts to stifle their language. Only 10 per cent of the military and 15 per cent of federal government offices were occupied by East Pakistanis, despite them constituting most of the population. Only 5 per cent of officers in the Pakistani military were Bengali because of the belief that Bengalis were not 'martial' enough. As a result East Pakistan rarely benefited from the country's vast defence budget and from 1950 to 1970 government spending in the East was less than half of that in the West.[115]

Nonetheless, many Bengalis believed fervently in the dream of a united Pakistan. A survey in 1963 found that 48 per cent of factory workers interviewed saw themselves as Pakistani first and foremost, and only 11 per cent considered their primary identity as Bengali.[116] 'There was no issue with my Bengali identity and my Pakistani one,' remembers Salahdin Imam, a Bengali student whose family had migrated from Calcutta to Dacca in 1947. Instead Sal conceived of Pakistan as a 'noble experiment' to see if Islam could help its varied peoples 'overcome their cultural differences'.[117]

Slim and long-haired, Sal was the son of Bengali diplomats who had worked their way to the top of the country's foreign service. Some of his first memories were of living in the old Japanese HQ in Burma's Akyab, where his father was Pakistan's first consul general, and of his mother's sobs at learning of Liaquat Ali Khan's assassination in 1951. Brought up on Mozart, Beethoven and Elvis Presley, Sal attended boarding school in West Pakistan, where, he noticed, his favourite sport hockey was 'considered the preserve of the Punjabi boys, and certainly beyond the capabilities of a mere Bengali'.

Despite such moments, however, Sal felt the discrimination was not systematic, and his two best friends at the school – Javed and Sikander – were themselves West Pakistanis. 'We were so close in our attitudes to life and our interests,' he smiles, 'that we were universally referred to as the Three Musketeers.'[118] He continued to hope that 'truly national institutions could gradually be built ... despite the huge physical distance between the two Wings'.[119] When he got into Harvard University, therefore, he felt like 'the only Pakistani on the East Coast and certainly the only Bengali'.[120]

Remarkably, the political divide between East and West plays a less prominent role in Sal's early memories than the countercultural movement that was then sweeping the world. No event would show off this unlikely new cultural exchange more than the Woodstock festival, which Sal himself set out to cover as rock and roll correspondent for the *Harvard Crimson* on the twenty-second anniversary of Indian and Pakistani independence.[121] The festival was opened by a saffron-clad Swami called Satchidananda Saraswati, and amid performances by Jimi Hendrix and Jefferson Airplane was a set of tabla, tambura and sitar performed by Alla Rakha, Maya Kulkarni and Ravi Shankar. 'There was an extended family present, from grandparents to squabbling kids,' recalls Sal, and 'I came across ... a tall man turned out in a large maroon cloak and wearing a cowboy hat with a feather stuck in its band.' Three girls from 'the city' chatted away about sexual liberation and a young couple offered Sal a place to sleep that night in their tent 'without a second thought'. Only a single haunted-looking man didn't seem to be enjoying himself. 'You think this is all there is in the world? All this bullshit jumping up and down?' the man asked, before offering Sal some crisps and explaining that he had just returned from Vietnam. 'In war, man, there are no heroes,' the veteran whispered, 'only terrified junkies.'[122]

Over the next two days Sal 'grooved' to Janis Joplin and Joe Cocker, and became convinced he had spotted Jesus in the crowd. When the festival eventually drew to a close, he snatched 'some sleep on a narrow bunk bed in the medical hall, sharing it with a stranger'.[123] Nonetheless, it would be the veteran whose words were most predictive of where Sal's life was headed. He could never have imagined it then, dancing in the muddy fields of Yasgur's Farm, but within a year Sal would be a guerrilla fighter, taking up arms against the government his parents worked for.[124]

After Woodstock Sal spent his last months at Harvard joining political marches, reviewing rock concerts and experimenting with LSD. In his last semester another Pakistani student called Benazir Bhutto walked into his study group. The daughter of Pakistan's opposition leader, she was 'a young lady of striking looks and flinty, energetic demeanour' but with some rather shocking attitudes, Sal remembers. 'Her version of Pakistan's history was erratic,' he writes:

> She was particularly terrified of the 'Bengalis', whose rebellious militancy had shaken up the country more than once. We argued frequently because, as a Bengali myself, I stood up for the interests of East Pakistan. Our poor Professor had a hard time mediating.[125]

As Sal at last confronted the political divide that gripped his country, his father passed away unexpectedly. Having recently graduated, Sal reluctantly returned home to care for his mother. Upon arriving in Dacca in May 1970, he committed a cultural faux pas by smoking a cigarette in front of his elders. He spent his days lounging around, meeting half-forgotten relatives, and moved into his uncle's house where mongooses and cobras meandered around the garden. Politics, he quickly learned, was all anyone talked about. Just two days before he arrived, a bomb had gone off at Pakistan's Council for National Integration, and bomb blasts targeting the Pakistani government would occur with ever greater frequency in the following months.[126]

Ayub Khan's replacement, Yahya Khan, was a short soldier with a clipped British accent who had escaped a German PoW camp during the war, and soon after taking power he had acknowledged that East Pakistanis were 'fully justified in being dissatisfied' with the present state of affairs.¹²⁷ A diplomat described him as a 'heavy built [man] ... verging on fatness with thick, black eyebrows and a small, pinched mouth'. A white patch parted Yahya's hair and he was apparently 'known to claim, like Samson', that his hair was the origin of his strength.¹²⁸ Yahya frequented Karachi's myriad nightclubs, drank heavily, and rumours abounded of his slew of affairs with Bengali mistresses. 'Outside of the military and women,' noted the diplomat, 'Yahya's only known interest was birds. He kept Australian parrots around President's House in Islamabad, as well as a number of cranes and swans in a specially built pool.'¹²⁹

Yahya would later be derided in both Pakistan and Bangladesh as the man who initiated the bloodletting of 1971, but at the time his appointment was regarded with much hope. In an announcement that surprised everyone, he revealed he would be scrapping the previous policy of 'parity' between the country's two wings, and that East Pakistan's greater population would be reflected in its number of seats. Even more astonishing, Yahya declared that two and a half decades after independence, general elections would finally be coming to Pakistan.

The 'frenzy of anticipation' about the upcoming elections was wild, remembers Sal.¹³⁰ Numerous parties stood for election, including the 'Red Maulana' Bhashani, who, in September 1970, publicly supported the idea of East Pakistan's secession if regional disparities were not resolved.¹³¹ Mostly, however, the elections were a clear race between Mujibur Rahman's Awami League and Zulfikar Ali Bhuttos' 'Pakistan People's Party'.

It was 'at this moment of nervous public excitement,' recalls Sal, that 'the Elements themselves swooped in to deal a decisive blow.'¹³² On 12 November 1970, a full moon night, one of the deadliest tropical cyclones ever recorded hit the Bengal coastline. Winds reached 150 miles an hour, whole buildings vanished, and trees were uprooted and hurled out of sight. Entire districts were flooded with seawater, not only destroying crops but salifying the ground. Officer Zahir Alam Khan, the son of a Burma veteran from Bangalore, was appointed to the flood-affected areas around Comilla and recalls that 'the whole area was one mass of water ... From one bank of a river, you could not see the other bank.'¹³³ When the cyclone subsided, three hundred thousand people were estimated to have been killed.

The Pakistani Army's response to the disaster was sluggish, pushing the fracturing relationship between Pakistan's two wings to breaking point. Mujib spoke to the foreign press of how, through neglect, the Pakistani government was 'guilty of almost cold-blooded murder' and that if the elections were delayed again there would be civil war.[134] Having previously considered himself apolitical, Sal became convinced that Mujib's six points were the way out. 'It was as if our whole society was given a slap,' he recalls.[135]

As a result West Pakistanis increasingly found their reception in the East hostile. Zahir Alam Khan, remarks that:

> While walking through a village or in a 'haat' the feeling was that you were in a foreign country, you could understand nobody, and nobody understood you ... We discovered we were not liked ... At places like the railway station, the staff would speak only in Bengali leading to quarrels. Language was the great divide.[136]

It took days for Yahya Khan to visit his benighted eastern province. 'There were still bodies floating in inland rivers, mass graves being dug with backhoes, everyone wearing masks because of the smell,' observed *New York Times* correspondent Sydney Schanberg, whose life later became the subject of the award-winning film *The Killing Fields*, and Yahya 'was walking through with polished boots and a walking stick with a gold knob ... We asked a few questions, and he brushed us off with blah-blah, then went home.'[137]

Despite Yahya Khan's sluggish response to the cyclone, the president pressed ahead with the general election on 7 December. 'The polling places were well guarded by soldiers and police, and there was no intimidation of voters, either by security forces or by any of the political parties,' writes diplomat Archer Blood. 'Everyone agreed the polling was fair and free. Of the 56 million people on the electoral rolls throughout Pakistan, 57.7 per cent voted. Women, who were allowed to vote for the first time, turned out in large numbers.'[138]

Zulfikar Bhutto's party swept Punjab and Sindh, the National Awami Party swept Baluchistan, and a coalition government emerged in NWFP. But in East Pakistan the Awami League under Mujib captured 160 directly elected seats out of 162 and so, despite not having received a single seat in West Pakistan, he emerged with a majority and the chance to write Pakistan's new constitution.

It could have been the start of a new era for Pakistan. In a speech on 3 January, Mujib welcomed West Pakistani politicians to join him in making a constitution based on the six points and Awami League processions released 'dozens of pigeons and hundreds of balloons' into the air in celebration.[139] Yahya called upon Bhutto and Mujib to put their differences aside and start preparing for the future, and even referred to Mujib as the next Pakistani prime minister.

There was just one problem. When Yahya visited Bhutto for a duck shoot at his family estate in Sindh, Bhutto berated the president for having 'made Mujib prime minister' when no one in the west had voted for him. Yahya replied that he 'had not made Mujib prime minister; Mujib's majority had.' But Bhutto worried Mujib's six points would inevitably lead to Bengali secession. Mujib was 'a clever bastard,' he told Yahya, and could not be trusted. Had he not recently been on trial for having tried to break up Pakistan? Bhutto told Yahya to test if Mujib was 'a true Pakistani' by postponing the National Assembly and seeing Mujib's reaction.[140]

A few days later Bhutto flew to Dacca to try and hammer out a power-sharing deal with Mujib. But Mujib, having won the election, did not understand why he was being asked to negotiate with his defeated opponent. Many Awami Leaguers began to suspect there was a plot to deny Bengalis power yet again.

The gulf between Mujib and Bhutto opened up the following January after two young Kashmiris hijacked an Air India flight and forced it to land in the Pakistani city of Lahore. Bhutto publicly applauded the hijackers as heroes, while an outraged Mujib demanded the government act against them. The Pakistan Army had long worried the Bengalis were not committed enough to the war against India, so sided with Bhutto. India subsequently banned Pakistani flights from passing over its territory, tripling the flight time between East and West Pakistan.[141] The divide between East and West was widening.

Soon after, Bhutto upped the ante, saying he would raise all of West Pakistan 'from the Khyber to Karachi' in violent protest unless Mujib offered him a role in the government. If any of his party members went to Dacca, he promised to 'break their legs' and ensure they were never welcome in the West again.[142] When US ambassador Joseph Farland met Mujib the same day, he found him cordial but a bit nervous. Mujib lamented that a consensus with Bhutto – who he called a 'callous cowboy' – was becoming impossible. Mujib's sole aim was now to follow his six-point mandate even at the expense of Pakistani unity. He still hoped to maintain some form of Pakistani confederation but if Bhutto refused to play fair he promised that 'the life struggle of Bangla Desh would begin'.[143]

With Pakistan facing the 'gravest political crisis' in its history, Yahya took twenty-four hours to decide what to do.[144] According to recently released Indian intelligence files, Yahya's hand was eventually 'forced by Army hardliners ... on 28 February. Hardliners like Gen. Tikka Khan and Attique Rahman insisted that the Awami League leadership should be given shock treatment.'[145]

So, on 1 March, Yahya made his decision, and postponed the assembly.

Sal Imam was in the Motijheel area of Dacca, in the sixth-floor office of his friend Obaid, when he heard the news. 'He's done it!' someone shouted out 'in tones of mixed anger and tearfulness'. For many in East Pakistan, Yahya's speech confirmed the theory that West Pakistan could simply not tolerate being ruled from the East. Crowds gathered on the streets, and Sal remembers:

> The whole of Motijheel was full of people chanting slogans, waving fists, some just screaming, mounting hysteria everywhere. Shopkeepers brought down their shopfronts and rushed to participate. An international Cricket Test Match between Pakistan and a Commonwealth XI which had been taking place in the nearby stadium was abandoned as spectators started setting fire to the stands. More and more people joined in from every direction. Obaid ... kept me close as we shuffled carefully through the wild, excited, crowds ... stopping occasionally for a snack or a swig of fresh pineapple juice.[146]

In Dacca's New Market, just fifteen minutes away, life initially continued as normal. But when rumours spread that Dacca would be placed under curfew, people rushed to the markets to stock up on supplies. 'Shopkeepers were having a difficult time handling the customers,' wrote Jahanara Imam in her diary, but 'somehow I managed to buy biscuits, match boxes, candles, milk powder ... [and] torch cells'. At Dacca University students gathered under a vast banyan tree to protest the postponement, and 'there was a bonfire of Pakistan flags and Jinnah portraits'.[147] Government House's water supply was cut off,[148] and pro-Awami Leaguers wearing green and white hats marched around the streets with lathi sticks and iron rods, enforcing a general strike. 'In that charged atmosphere,' noted Sal, 'it wouldn't have taken much to turn normal people into a murderous mob.'[149]

Life would be more difficult for non-Bengali communities living in East Pakistan after that day. Awami Leaguers charged through Dacca's Intercontinental Hotel ripping down non-Bengali signs and Dacca's British Council was set on fire. Vendors of food, drink and petrol all refused to sell their wares to the army.[150] Even non-Bengalis indigenous to the region began to worry.

Raja Tridiv Roy was an indigenous rights activist and astrology enthusiast who worried his community – the Chakmas – would lose their status within an independent Bangladesh. He had been one of two non-Awami League candidates to win in the East Pakistan elections and his constituency, a Buddhist-majority district bordering Burma, had only 2 per cent Bengali population. He had thus been alienated by Mujib's Bengali nationalism and disappointed when Mujib refused any safeguards for the indigenous communities in the districts.[151] He was sipping a beer at the Dacca Club when he learned that Yahya Khan had postponed the National Assembly. 'Two of the bearers, in hushed tones, informed me there would be trouble,' he writes. As predicted:

> Trouble started within the hour – processions, slogans, arson. The Naz Cinema that exclusively showed English films belonged to a non-Bengali named Dossani. He also owned the popular Gulistan Cinema and the Chu Chin Chow Chinese restaurant in the same building in the heart of Dhaka city. All of them were burned down ... As a result of various clashes between Bengalis and non-Bengalis, about 150 people were taken to hospital.[152]

That afternoon US consul Archer Blood witnessed the events from the rooftop of the US consulate building in Adamjee Court and later recalled that 'hundreds of Bengalis were running from their shops and offices, shouting and screaming ... They were like a swarm of bees that had been disturbed in their hive.' Returning downstairs to his office, Blood typed out a message to the US State Department that would prove to be prophetic: 'I believe I have just seen the end of a unified Pakistan.'[153]

Dacca changed forever that March. The Pakistani government announced new curfews over old WW2-era air-raid sirens, while the Awami League organised strikes and tried to bring the province to a standstill. Two rival forms of authority emerged, with much of the population following Mujib, rather than the governor's orders. In response the Martial Law administration banned the publication of any news that was 'against the integrity and sovereignty of Pakistan'. On 3 March the Pakistani Army opened fire on curfew-breakers. The same day three hundred non-Bengalis were reported to have been killed in mob violence and many people stopped venturing outside. 'Didn't see a car, rickshaw, scooter or even a bicycle,' wrote Jahanara Imam in her diary. 'Even the fish and vegetable market was closed.'[154]

Bengali civilians grew more wary of their non-Bengali neighbours, and vice versa. Mujib condemned attacks on non-Bengalis, but he was no longer entirely in control of events and student agitators across the province set out intimidating their rivals. Waliul Islam, the vice president of the Chittagong Students Union, later told one oral historian how he took to robbing firearms shops across Dacca and stashing weapons in a college hostel. One day he pulled a knife on the driver of a parked government vehicle and told him: 'There is only one government in the country now, that of the Awami League, and today is the last day of your life.' Islam dragged the driver to a teak tree 'and told him to start praying', only letting him go when the man was convinced he was headed to an early grave.[155] Such violence pushed many otherwise sympathetic observers – including tens of thousands of Bengalis – into siding with the government rather than the Awami League. 'Mujib's "non-violent non-cooperation movement",' writes the Chakma Raja Tridiv Roy, was one that 'Mahatma Gandhi would have found difficulty in recognizing'.[156]

Yahya responded with several concessions, including a date for opening the National Assembly: 25 March.[157] But around this time high-ranking soldiers in Pakistan's armed forces also started to recommend military action against the Awami League. There were several conscientious objectors to such an action, including the soft-spoken governor of East Pakistan, Admiral Ahsan Khan, and the chief commander of Pakistan's Eastern wing Sahabzada Yaqub Khan, both of whom resigned in protest. But their absence meant the military command was even more cut off from the actual realities of life in the East. On 7 March Yahya installed the feared Tikka Khan – later known as the 'Butcher of Bengal' – as East Pakistan's new governor.

That same day Mujib prepared to address hundreds of thousands of people at Ramna Race Course. Helicopters flew overhead, and women, children and even a 'procession of blind boys' were among the crowd. The sun was 'blinding hot' that day but Sal recalls he 'cared not a whit for the hazards and only felt more defiant'.[158] Finally Mujib himself took to the stage. Everyone expected him to declare independence, but he stopped short and instead called for a 'peaceful satyagraha' and 'emancipation'.[159] People on all sides of the political spectrum were divided over how to respond, and Jahanara Imam wrote in her diary that even within her own household, 'Some people want Sheikh [Mujib] to declare independence while others oppose it.'[160] Rumi, her seventeen-year-old son, was obsessed with the idea of revolution and nine days later Jahanara wrote:

> I am really worried about Rumi ... After spending a few days at home consuming huge quantities of Moghlai parathas along with his friends ... he has now gone back to the streets ... Today, while cleaning his dressing room, I discovered a huge mortar and pestle pair in his wardrobe behind the pair of shoes ... Jami reluctantly informed me that this sort of mortar is needed to make explosive ... [and] showed me two polythene bags behind the clothes rack, fat bags tied with strings.[161]

Rumi was far from the only one doing this, with students everywhere making 'homemade explosives and Molotov cocktails to face the guns of government troops'.[162]

Tension was not limited to the cities, and soon permeated the countryside too. After the 'complete stress and anxiety' of Dacca, Sal found work at the Duncan Bros Tea Company outside Sylhet, one of the only Bengalis working in a managerial job on the plantation; his two main colleagues were both Punjabis: Abdus Sattar and Iftekhar Ahmed Randhawa. 'They feared that the Pakistan Army was out of its depth and had no idea of the difficulties they would face in the hostile terrain of this land,' writes Sal. 'We would hold long, anxious discussions about such issues which kept bubbling to the surface however much we tried to ignore them.'[163]

News started fracturing along community lines so that just like in 1947 rival groups heard the same events differently. At Joydebpur the Pakistani Army fired on a crowd of civilians. Four eyewitnesses – Bengali and non-Bengali – all agree that a West Pakistani Brigadier Arbab had visited the 2nd East Bengal Regiment and that many locals had become convinced he was going to disarm the Bengali soldiers there. In the event nothing of the sort happened. Arbab had a sit-down lunch with his officers and no one was disarmed. Upon trying to leave, however, he and his men found an armed crowd of Bengalis barricading the road, led by a local Awami Leaguer. The troops eventually convinced the Awami Leaguer that no Bengalis had been disarmed, but others in the crowd refused to believe them. After an argument someone opened fire and soon both army and crowd were shooting at one another. Two civilians were killed.

Later accounts by Bengali and non-Bengali officers disagree over Arbab's intentions. Had he ordered his soldiers to shoot directly at the crowd? The reports are contradictory, but they all agree the crowd had been armed and two people died.[164] Within hours of the incident, however, the story had morphed completely. Diplomat Archer Blood recalled how 'Army sources claimed one person was killed after troops fired in self-defence ... [while] a pro-Awami League newspaper claimed that twenty were killed in the firing.' Mujib himself 'condemned the Pakistani army for firing on an "unarmed" crowd'.[165] Misinformation thrived and people on all sides were left scared, wondering what they would do to protect their loved ones.

★ ★ ★

On 15 March 1971, Yahya Khan flew into Dacca for a last-ditch round of negotiations with Mujib for the transfer of power. The airport was quiet when he arrived, and steel-helmeted guards stood to attention in the otherwise empty terminal. 'It was a strange, eerie atmosphere,' recalls one observer, and 'charged with a deadly stillness'.[166] Outside, trucks fitted with machine guns waited to take him to Governor's House, a whitewashed modernist structure, faintly reminiscent of the old Viceroy's House in New Delhi. It was built in the old grounds of the Nawab of Dacca, and a fifteenth-century Sufi saint was said to have been buried somewhere in the complex. An older thatched building had been destroyed in a storm a decade earlier, and the new building was meant to symbolise the hopes, dreams and aspirations of a modern and united Pakistan.

Mujib joined Yahya there the next morning, driving in 'a white car flying a black flag'.[167] He welcomed Yahya as 'a guest of Bangla Desh', after which Yahya (ignoring the slight) invited Mujib into the drawing room. Mujib 'strongly objected', however, and said he wanted to discuss matters somewhere more private. So it was that Yahya ordered two chairs to be placed in the presidential bathroom, and 'it was there that the final negotiations to save Pakistan began'.[168]

The meeting in the president's bathroom lasted more than two and a half hours, and when the two men walked out both refused to tell anyone what they had discussed. Students gathered outside the presidential mansion, crying out 'Enemy troops, go home!' and 'Independent Bangla Desh!', and speculation everywhere was rife.[169] Later the next day five aides were invited to join in the negotiations, and on 19 March Yahya sent a message urging Bhutto to hurry over to Dacca as soon as he could. A form of resolution, he told Bhutto, was in sight.

Bhutto set out two days later, but almost immediately things started to go awry. His plane had to make an emergency landing when two of its engines failed in mid-flight. Emerging from the aircraft, Bhutto was horrified to find Dacca Airport filled with non-Bengali 'refugees' who had been forced out of their homes by angry Bengali nationalists.[170] Awami League protesters lined up outside the terminal, shouting curses at him, and even the police escort that arrived to meet him waved Bangladesh flags. Bhutto's delegation refused to go anywhere with them, and ended up being driven to the Intercontinental Hotel by soldiers of the Pakistani military.[171] Archer Blood was sitting in the hotel lobby as Bhutto entered, and he writes:

> I thought I was watching a re-run of a 1930s gangster film. Bhutto strode into the hotel flanked by two machine-gun toting bodyguards. The hatred of the Bengalis in the lobby was palpable; they blamed Bhutto much more than Yahya for the crisis. For his part Bhutto stared ahead, his reptilian eyes fixed on the wall. He was in the enemy's camp and he knew it.[172]

The next day, at 11 a.m., Yahya attempted to mediate a meeting between the two but Bhutto and Mujib sat looking away from one another and refused to speak. Yahya joked they were acting like 'bashful newly-weds' rather than statesmen, and it was only when he 'took them by the hand' and pleaded with them to cooperate that they finally began to talk.[173] After finishing coffee, Yahya and his aides then left the room, leaving Mujib and Bhutto to speak to one another alone for the first time. According to Awami League leaders, Bhutto tried to persuade Mujib not to trust the military, but Bhutto himself claimed the opposite:

> [Mujib] grasped me by the hand and made me sit next to him. He told me that the situation was very grave and that he needed my help to overcome it ... Thinking the room might be bugged, we walked out to the verandah towards the back of the house and sat in the portico behind the President's salon. Sheikh Mujibur Rahman ... went on to say that things had now gone too far and there was no turning back ... He suggested that I should become the Prime Minister of West Pakistan and he would look after East Pakistan ... He cautioned me against the military and told me not to trust them: if they destroyed him first, they would also destroy me.[174]

Despite the high passions that week, the negotiations proved a remarkable success and a formula was worked out that essentially granted Bangladesh within a united Pakistan, much as the cabinet mission had offered Pakistan within the scheme of a united India twenty-five years earlier. By the evening of 22 March only a few minor issues were left unresolved. 'PAKISTAN'S LEADERS REPORTED IN ACCORD' was the headline in the *New York Times*.[175]

Then everything fell apart. The 23rd of March was the anniversary of the Lahore Resolution, which had first put forward the idea of independent Muslim states, and the Awami League celebrated it as 'Resistance Day'. As houses across the city flew a newly designed red, green and yellow flag featuring the map of 'Bangla Desh', Dacca Television refused to play the national anthem, and it seems that on this day the army had at last decided that the Awami League was irredeemably separatist. During the tense negotiations that day, an Awami Leaguer mentioned that the name of the country should be changed from the 'Federation of Pakistan' to the 'Confederation of Pakistan' and immediately a 'distinguished member of the government team' lost his cool, jumped up from his seat and shouted that this was out of the question.[176]

Precisely why things fell apart so quickly is the subject of numerous tomes of scholarship. Some argue Bhutto never intended to share power with Mujib, others that Mujib was already dead-set on an independent Bangladesh. Given how carefully planned the subsequent slaughter was, it is highly possible Yahya Khan had already set his mind on a military solution. Equally likely, however, is that talks simply collapsed through mistrust, misunderstandings and miscommunication.

Whatever the case, negotiations soured rapidly. Army leaders announced their refusal to work with Mujib, while a previously conciliatory Mujib now opposed including Bhutto in his cabinet, calling him a 'Trojan horse'.[177] At 'teatime' Yahya finally lost it. That evening he gave the go-ahead for a plan called 'Operation Searchlight'. This plan had been drawn up five days earlier as an emergency measure and not only entailed a crackdown on the Awami League, but also disarming – and if needed suppressing – all Bengali regiments in the Pakistani Army.

It was nothing less than a declaration of war on the East.

14

Liberation

On the evening of 25 March 1971, exactly two years after Yahya Khan had been appointed president of Pakistan, he flew out of Dacca along with most of the politicians from West Pakistan. At the same time thousands of plainclothes soldiers started to arrive at Dacca Airport and 'shiploads of weapons' were sighted being offloaded from the port at Chittagong.[1]

The American diplomat Archer Blood was hosting a dinner party that night with his wife Meg. Their guests included American visitors, two Bengali High Court judges and even the Yugoslav consul, and they were watching 'an old, downbeat Spencer Tracy movie' when the phone rang. From the other end of the line, Blood was warned that Bengali students were 'barricading the streets against Pakistan Army vehicles' and that a confrontation was expected to begin quite soon. When the diplomat told his dinner party the news, the two High Court Judges ran off into the darkness to be with their families. An American couple followed but returned shaken a few minutes later after finding a dead body lying in the neighbouring street.

The remaining guests, including the Yugoslav consul, ended up camping out at the Bloods' house that night and 'Meg rushed about accumulating sleeping gear' as Blood himself tried to get more information about what was going on. Then 'the more ominous clatter of machine guns and the heavy clump of tank guns' started up. Blood and his guests went onto the roof and there they were shocked to see the city aflame, lit up by a 'flash of tracer bullets' streaking 'across the dark sky'.[2]

Across East Pakistan, the army swept into motion, disarming their Bengali soldiers, police and border force units. As a post-war Pakistan government report admitted, in the Comilla Cantonment, '17 Bengali Officers and 915 men were just slain by a flick of one officer's fingers.'[3] Awami League politicians and supporters were also rounded up, and one of the first targets was Mujib himself. At 1 a.m. Pakistani soldiers arrived at his house in Dhanmondi, armed with rocket launchers. One team jumped over the wall and opened fire, killing Mujib's watchman, and officer Alam Khan found 'a very shaken Sheikh Mujib'.

Mujib 'kissed his weeping wife' and walked with the soldiers down the lane towards the army jeep. When they reached the car, the politician hesitated. 'I have forgotten my pipe and tobacco!' he called out. So Alam Khan accompanied him to find them, before formally arresting him. 'I was given a chair,' recalled Mujib later, and 'they offered me tea'.[4]

The army did not want to turn Mujib into a martyr, and orders had been given to capture him alive. But other suspected Awami Leaguers were 'sent to Bangladesh', a code for execution.[5] 'The army killed people indiscriminately,' recalls Mr Anupam Sen. 'They couldn't speak Bengali, and they couldn't tell who was a friend and who was their enemy, so everyone became their enemy.'[6] One Bengali student, Nazrul Islam, witnessed a group of soldiers set fire to the slum below his home and shoot at people as they ran out of their homes. Moments later soldiers burst through his door, shot him and his friends, and looted their room for valuables. He survived only thanks to a different Pakistani soldier who found him sometime later and saved his life.[7]

Another of the army's main targets that evening was Dacca University, which was considered the hub of Bengali nationalism. With student politics so closely intertwined with the Bangladesh movement, the Pakistan Army had ordered a detachment to round up the university's leaders. The provost of Jagannath Hall, Jyotirmoy Guhathakurta, was grading exam papers when he heard a group of young men were barricading the roads. A few hours later three soldiers burst through the door shouting, 'Where is the professor?' They dragged Jyotirmoy from the room. He was found outside a few minutes later, paralysed and bloodied.

Footage recorded by Professor Ula shows soldiers rounding up unarmed students and executing them at point-blank range. Students were made to bury the corpses of their class fellows while 'soldiers smoked and abused them for demanding Bangladesh'.[8] Asif Ali was one of the only non-Bengalis at Dacca University that day, and he remembers how the army broke down the university gates. 'Bengali girls and boys formed a human chain to prevent the soldiers from proceeding,' he recalls, 'but the soldiers began to fire upon them.' One of those killed was Asif's best friend Moin. '[Moin's] girlfriend and he were both there,' he told oral historian Anam Zakaria, 'but she survived, and he was shot. Right in front of me. I saw his body ... I still have nightmares.'[9]

The army also targeted the press that evening. Army tanks fired unannounced at the offices of pro-Awami League newspapers, including Manik Mia's *Daily Ittefaq*, and the buildings were found to 'still be burning two days later, with a charred corpse lying outside'.[10] Both foreign and Pakistani correspondents were rounded up in the Intercontinental Hotel and 'told that they would be shot if they tried to step out of the building'. *New York Times* bureau chief Sydney Schanberg was among the journalists trapped there, and his writing from his room remains one of the most vivid testimonies to survive from that terrible day. 'From the hotel,' he writes:

> huge fires could be seen in various parts of the city, including the university area and the barracks of the East Pakistan Rifles ... 'My God, my God,' said a Pakistani student watching from a hotel window. 'They're killing them. They're slaughtering them.'[11]

Together journalists watched in horror as a Pakistani Army jeep mounted with a machine gun started spraying a shopping centre opposite full of bullets and fired a rocket into one of the shops. The reporters heard the soldiers shouting 'Pakistan Zindabad' [Long Live Pakistan], and one of the hotel clerks in the lobby burst into tears. When a group of newsmen protested to the army captain guarding the front door, the soldier simply shouted, 'If I can kill my own people, I can kill you!'[12]

Zulfikar Ali Bhutto was staying at the same hotel, and Schanberg writes that shortly after 8 a.m. a 'black 1959 chevrolet' pulled up outside. Moments later Bhutto appeared in the lobby, flanked by armed guards. 'He looked frightened,' thought Schanberg, 'and brushed off all newsmen's questions with, "I have no comment to make."'[13] At 6.15 p.m., the army men ordered the journalists themselves to pack up their belongings and leave for the airport. Hotel officials protested, terrified the crackdown would get infinitely worse once the press had left, but to no avail. The reporters, including Schanberg, were deported and their film reels confiscated. Only a few escaped the crackdown, such as *Daily Telegraph* reporter Simon Dring, who had been hiding on the hotel rooftop. Once the army had gone, he broke out of the hotel without being spotted, successfully interviewed a few people in the city and then smuggled his notes out of the country in his socks.[14]

The army nonetheless failed to catch those like Jahanara Imam's son Rumi who *had* been stockpiling weapons. That evening Jahanara's family was woken by the echo of machine-gun fire and the 'heartrending cries' coming from the student hostels.[15] Rumi was pulling down the Bangladesh flags flying on their roof, and 'nobody uttered a word'. Remembering Rumi's stockpiled explosives, the family got to work:

> Rumi and Jami opened up the polythene packets and unloaded the contents into the commode, a little at a time lest it get blocked, and then pulled the flush. Jami washed the mortars and pestles very carefully with dish-washing powder to remove the smell of chemicals. After that Rumi packed all his books on Marx, Engels as well as Mao Tse Tung's military writings into a polythene bag ... I remembered a gap between Barek's room and the boundary wall ... [and] we threw the pack of books in there ... [Then] Rumi covered the packet with a few dried fronds of palm.[16]

As the dawn sun rose across a smoky sky, 'I could still hear the whistle of bullets,' wrote Jahanara Imam in her diary. 'I could hear dogs barking and people screaming ... [but] all the birds ... [had] disappeared. I could not even hear a crow.'[17]

When Bhutto arrived back in Karachi that afternoon, he announced to the press, 'Thank God, Pakistan has been saved.'[18] But in reality the heavy-handed actions of the Pakistani military had pushed events in the East past the point of no return. Although younger Bengalis had been protesting against the Pakistani government for years, the older generation had continued to cling to the dream that Jinnah had preached to them two decades earlier. 'My father didn't want independence,' remembers Mr Tariq Ali, a bespectacled Bengali man. 'He had faced discrimination in India and thought Pakistan would help Muslims develop ... he was adamant against separation. But that night, as he stood on the veranda and saw the killings, he said there was no turning back.' For millions of people in East Pakistan, Operation Searchlight had not saved Pakistan. Instead it had finally shattered 'the Pakistan dream'.[19]

'Jinnah's Pakistan died on March 26, 1971,' recalled Tariq Ali years later, 'with East Pakistan drowned in blood.'[20]

The year 1971 remains the most significant in the history of post-colonial South Asia. The nine months following Operation Searchlight would see people from all classes and backgrounds dragged into multiple conflicts, risk nuclear war between the USA and the Soviet Union, and ultimately change the entire map of South Asia. The precise order of events is heavily controversial, and even the basic vocabulary is disputed. Bangladeshis speak of a 'Liberation War', Pakistanis talk of a 'Civil War',* and India of the 'Third Indo-Pakistan War'. Statistics are equally contested, with the Bengali death toll varying wildly from three hundred thousand to three million. What is more certain is that in a matter of months, some ten million refugees crossed into India, and that by the end of the year hundreds of thousands of people had been rendered stateless. Pakistan would be cut in half, and the fifth partition of the former Indian Empire would carve its way through the subcontinent. The war of 1971 was a conflict that – just as much as 1947 – made South Asia what it is today.

With most journalists deported, news of what had happened in Dacca was slow to leak. When Sal Imam woke on 26 March, he found Sylhet blanketed by 'an eerie silence'. Telephone lines were dead and information of the events in the city only trickled out in bits and pieces:

---

* Antara Datta writes: 'There are those who vehemently disagree that a "civil war" took place in Bangladesh. It implies that what took place was an "internal" struggle that could have been resolved peacefully, but instead devolved, somewhat unfortunately, into a bloody war. Most Bangladeshis who oppose the term suggest that it minimises the violence and rupture that 1971 signifies. To many Bangladeshis, the more appropriate term is the "Liberation War" or the "Muktijuddho". In Dhaka, there is a Liberation War Museum and a Liberation War ministry. The term signifies the momentousness of the events of 1971 and suggests that it not only marked freedom from tyrannical oppression, but that the acquisition of this freedom was legitimate.' Datta, A., *Refugees and Borders in South Asia: The Great Exodus of 1971* (Abingdon: Routledge, 2013) p2.

'A leak from the district administration, a railway station manager's anguished report to his family members, followed by some confused and incomplete foreign radio broadcasts.'[21] In the afternoon the tea garden manager received a telex from London, informing them that a 'bloody massacre' had taken place.[22] It was only when a plantation radio crackled with the voice of a Bengali soldier called Major Zia-ur-Rahman that they began to understand the scale of what was happening:

> This is Swadhin Bangla Betar Kendra [Independent Bengal Radio Station]. I, Major Zia-ur-Rahman, on behalf of Bangabandhu Sheikh Mujib-ur-Rahman, hereby declare that the independent People's Republic of Bangladesh has been established. I call upon all Bengalis to rise against the attack by the West Pakistani Army. We shall fight to the last to free our motherland. By the grace of Allah, victory is ours. Joy Bangla [Victory to Bengal].[23]

It soon emerged that many Awami League leaders had escaped the crackdown, slipping into the countryside 'dressed in the garb of peasants'.[24] Mujib's right-hand men – Tajuddin Ahmad and Syed Nazrul Islam – had even managed to get to India. At the same time five battalions of the East Bengal Regiment had mutinied, including that of Major Zia-ur-Rahman, who had killed his West Pakistani commanding officer and briefly seized control of Bengal's largest port, Chittagong. Of course, there were many people in the army whose loyalties were divided like Ikram Sehgal, a second lieutenant in the 2nd East Bengal Regiment whose father was Punjabi and whose mother was Bengali. Under suspicion from both sides, Sehgal was eventually released from duty.[25]

Like millions of others, Sal lay awake that night after Operation Searchlight in 'mental agony',[26] worried about his mother and brothers, who were scattered between Dacca and Murree in West Pakistan. As rumours spread, so too did a pervasive anxiety and paranoia. Neighbours looked at each other with suspicion, and Sal remembers how the West Pakistanis on his tea estate were suddenly blamed for all the Pakistani Army's wrongdoings. His two Punjabi friends – Sattar and Randhawa – were particularly terrified, and whispered to him that everyone was looking at them 'with an evil eye'. Rumours were even circulating that Bengalis were massacring Urdu-speaking Biharis around Comilla. The Biharis had mostly arrived as refugees in the 1947 Partition and had initially been welcomed in East Pakistan. But their use of the Urdu language now marked them as potential collaborators with the Pakistani Army in the eyes of many Bengalis.

Sattar and Randhawa now asked Sal for help getting them both to the Indian border. 'They knew they would be arrested by the Indians,' Sal remembers, 'but they thought it would be safer than being caught by a Bengali mob in Sylhet. Thanks to the actions of the Pakistani Army, the population had descended into tribal aggression – it was sad to watch.' So at dawn the next morning, the trio set off towards the border in a white Toyota, clad in their tea plantation's khaki uniforms. 'I left them at the border,' recalls Sal, 'waved at them, and watched them flee into enemy territory ... I think I saved their lives.'[27]

Moments like this would repeat themselves over and over as the year progressed. The year 1971, like 1947, was characterised not only by mindless killing but by numerous friends helping each other out across ethnic, linguistic and religious lines. The conflict that played out that year would rarely be as simple as national narratives of 'Pakistanis versus Bangladeshis' tend to suggest. Instead people everywhere were caught with conflicting loyalties. The massacres of 1971 may have been much more one-sided than those of 1947, but in the following weeks, the line between victim and perpetrator would often be a blurred one.

On the morning of 27 March, two days after Operation Searchlight had been launched, Radio Pakistan announced an end to the daytime curfew in Dacca and called for people to return to work. Fires still burned across the city, army jeeps patrolled the streets and the birds seemed to have fled, but with the rattle of machine guns dying down, and the whole city back under the control of the Pakistani military, the denizens of Dacca began to confront the events of the previous two days. 'People started peeping out of their doors,' wrote Jahanara Imam.

> Rumi and I went out in a car ... [and] we found the entire market burnt to ashes. Coils of smoke were still rising from the glowing embers ... [and] the entire city was on the move in search of safety. People barely had time to exchange a few words ... Rumi

impatiently dropped me home and rushed out to find the fate of his friends.[28]

As Jahanara quickly discovered, Dacca had fundamentally changed. The Pakistani Army had demolished the Shaheed Minar monument dedicated to the 'language martyrs' of 1952, along with the Hindu temple on Ramna Race Course and Dacca University's cafeteria. Meanwhile, the government issued edicts in either Urdu or strangely garbled Bengali, leaving many people unable to decipher what they were being ordered to do. 'Among the things that people had to surrender to the Pakistanis,' recalls one man, was 'a bicycle-making machine. Did one exist? Perhaps the metal pipes in the frames could be used as gun barrels. Or maybe they wanted a monopoly in the bicycle market. Did they want to restrict our movement?'[29] Later he learned the order had meant to read 'cyclostyle machine' – used to print handwritten letters. But with a lack of Bengali speakers in the new regime, the orders had been distorted.

Not everyone emerged from hiding so quickly, and three days later a Hindu friend of Jahanara's arrived on her doorstep with bloodshot eyes and filthy crumpled clothes. He revealed he had spent five days hidden in a nearby cowshed and was fearful that as a Hindu, he would be targeted. He was right to be afraid. As even the post-war Pakistani Hamoodur Rahman Commission has admitted, several Pakistani Army generals actively encouraged the killing of Hindus, asking their units how many they had killed. In May there would even be 'an order in writing to kill Hindus ... from Brigadier Abdullah Malik of 23 Brigade'.[30]

Around this time a team of US diplomats and aid workers working under Archer Blood began touring Dacca and collecting evidence of what had transpired over the previous days. They interviewed priests, soldiers, shopkeepers and students, and in the absence of journalists, Blood's situation reports have become some of the most valuable sources on what was going on in the capital. The first, sent off to Washington the very evening the curfew was lifted, noted 'thousands of Bengalis streaming through the city, carrying personal belongings and obviously trying to get out to villages'. The military crackdown on the Awami League seemed to have been carried out 'swiftly, efficiently ... and often with ruthless brutality'. For the time being, things had returned to relative normality. Far more worrying, however, was the situation for Dacca's Hindu residents. Blood's team learned that the Hindu-majority Tanti Bazar and Sankhari Bazar Mohallas neighbourhoods had 'been surrounded by the military and houses have been burnt and people butchered. Large numbers of casualties [were] feared. Residents fleeing from this area were not spared.'[31]

In the following days Blood's missives grew ever more alarmed. One day a torrent of rain exposed two mass graves in Dacca University. On 28 March he captioned a telegram 'Selective Genocide'. 'We are mute and horrified witnesses to a reign of terror,' he wrote, estimating that 4,000–6,000 people had been killed in Dacca alone since the military action started. He reflected that although

> the term 'genocide' was not appropriate to characterize all killings of Muslim Bengalis ... the term 'genocide' struck us as applying fully to the naked, calculated and widespread selection of Hindus for special treatment ... The evidence seemed to suggest that the Pakistani military were unable to make a distinction between Indians and East Pakistani Hindus ... [and] had been indoctrinated with the line that Hindus (who compromise 13% of the East Pakistan population) were responsible for secessionist currents in East Pakistan.[32]

To Blood's dismay, however, neither the embassy in Islamabad nor the US State Department would respond to his reports. The US government had already taken its side in the conflict. The Cold War was at its height and President Nixon was hoping that Pakistan's leadership would help the USA open diplomatic dialogue with the Chinese and help end the Vietnam War. Moreover Pakistan's military was reliably anti-communist, while India under Mrs Gandhi was increasingly pro-Soviet. Nixon's racist distaste for Indians in general – and for Mrs Gandhi in particular – only strengthened his fondness for Pakistan, and he thus chose to ignore Blood's pleas. 'It's better not to have it [Pakistan] come apart,' Nixon told his national security adviser Henry Kissinger after receiving Blood's telegram. 'That's right,' Kissinger responded, 'and of course the Bengalis have been extremely difficult to govern throughout their history.' A short while later, when conversation turned back to Blood's reports, Kissinger said: 'That Consul in Dacca doesn't have the strongest nerves.'[33]

Despite silence from the White House, however, Blood continued to collect information. Armed Bengali groups were retaliating against the Pakistani Army, and one US aid worker on Blood's team noted that Bengali rebels were doing 'some pretty atrocious things to Urdu speakers'. Of course, most people just wanted the conflict to be over and the same aid worker observed a rather bewildered group one evening:

> Bengalis and Pakistanis were mixed together, all wailing with grief over what essentially was another Partition. They couldn't understand. They had brothers in Islamabad, they had studied in Lahore. They were bemoaning this war among one family.[34]

On 6 April, convinced the army's crackdown was to blame for what was increasingly becoming a fratricidal civil war, Blood's team issued what remains arguably the strongest expression of dissent in US diplomatic history. Known today as 'the Blood Telegram', the cable was signed by twenty members of the Dacca diplomatic staff, and read:

> Our government has failed to denounce the suppression of democracy. Our government has failed to denounce atrocities. Our government has failed to take forceful measures to protect its citizens while at the same time bending over backwards to placate the West Pak[istan] dominated government and to lessen likely and deservedly negative international public relations impact against them. Our government has evidenced what many will consider moral bankruptcy ... [W]e have chosen not to intervene, even morally, on the grounds that the Awami conflict, in which unfortunately the overworked term genocide is applicable, is purely [an] internal matter of a sovereign state. Private Americans have expressed disgust. We, as professional public servants, express our dissent with current policy.[35]

The telegram did not go down well in Washington. A few weeks later, Blood was transferred out of Dacca.

Yahya Khan had intended Operation Searchlight to save Pakistan from fragmentation, but instead it triggered a whole new conflict, with one side fighting for Bangladeshi independence and another fighting to preserve the Pakistani union. Resistance to the Pakistan Army's crackdown was initially scattered and uncoordinated, but over time defected Bengali military personnel and police started to link up with one another, and a more cohesive military response began to take shape.

The first reports of an organised Bangladeshi 'Liberation Army', known initially as the 'Mukti Fauj' and later as the 'Mukti Bahini', came in early April from the small town of Kushtia, the great centre of Baul mysticism and former home of poet Rabindranath Tagore.[36] Pakistani forces had moved into the small town within hours of Searchlight and had successfully disarmed five hundred Bengali policemen. However, when the curfew was lifted, fifty-three of the policemen managed to break into a weapons locker, and fled into the countryside with a stash of rifles. On 31 March they returned to the city, accompanied by five thousand other policemen, soldiers, students and farmers, and tried to 'liberate' the city.[37]

The Kushtia rebellion would be short-lived, but the Mukti Bahini 'Liberation Army' proved longer lasting. In its early days there was no obvious chain of command and it was left to defected Bengali commanders 'to organize logistics, including creating safe houses in East Pakistan, and assess which villages would have hospitable homes where the guerrillas could hide, recuperate, get food and shelter'.[38] Soon, however, a command structure emerged under the thickly moustachioed Muhammad Osmani, a retired Sylheti colonel from the Pakistani Army known fondly as 'Papa Tiger'. Under Osmani, the Mukti Bahini started to train, feed and shelter the many thousands flocking to their banner, civilians with no previous military experience and often little more than students, journalists and musicians.

One such unlikely recruit of the Mukti Bahini was Sal Imam who had decided to follow Sattar and Randhawa into India. 'Thanks to my West-Pakistani education in Murree I probably could have stayed put,' he recalls, 'but I had long associated with the Awami League, and I didn't like the idea of sitting passively as these men came in with their guns and artillery ... I didn't plan to join the resistance, I just wanted to get out.' Sal scouted out another man who wanted to flee, 'a tea planter with a reputation for being a scoundrel', and on 11 April they snuck out of the tea garden in the dead of night. They had barely driven thirty minutes, however, when their car broke down in the middle of another tea estate called Teliapara. Nearby they could see a large bungalow on a hill and so walked over and discovered, to their surprise, it was the headquarters of the defected soldiers of the 3rd East Bengal Regiment. 'I decided to join their ranks,' Sal remembers, and 'Shishu, the number 2, handed me a submachine gun the day I joined.'[39]

The Teliapara camp was divided between ex-military personnel and young civilians like Sal.[40] As a result of his bad Bengali, he was advised by the Mukti Bahini not to speak too much lest he be confused for a Bihari, and he recalls that most of his time was spent doing mundane tasks like patrolling or oiling his gun. 'We walked on the ridges between paddy fields at night as rebels fighting a covert operation,' he recalls, and after about three weeks he experienced his first battle. 'I was just the mortar guy,' he says:

> sitting back far away from the front line ... I fired again and again, readjusting the mortar. Then we did a charge, with a great scream overcome with fear ... The Pakistanis were firing back, and then they stopped firing. I'm not sure if there were many dead – it's a blur.[41]

The former rock and roll correspondent of the *Harvard Crimson* was now a guerrilla fighter. 'I kept thinking of my Harvard hippie friends,' remembers Sal. 'What would they think of me now.'[42]

When Operation Searchlight was launched in March 1971, both Indian and Pakistani publics liked to think of their territories as watertight and well-defined entities. But looking at borders on a map could often be a misleading enterprise. Twenty-four years after Radcliffe's line had sliced Bengal in half, much of this eastern border was still unfenced. The border was porous and the two countries were forced to maintain a symbiotic relationship – never fully detached from the other. As a result, Pakistan's conflict with the Mukti Bahini quickly spilled into India. In the five days after Searchlight around three hundred refugees were reported crossing into Indian territory. Two weeks later, the number had increased to 119,566[43] and by the end of the month it hovered around 1.5 million, with sixty thousand new arrivals recorded every day.

Muneeza Shamsie, a journalist and literary critic based in Karachi, remembers learning that her friend's brother-in-law, the economist

LIBERATION

Rahman Sobhan, had gone on the run. 'He was close to the Awami League but was not a politician,' she recalls.

> No one imagined that he would have to go into hiding. Salma came home one morning to find her house filled with soldiers. Her nine-year-old son had got out of the bath to let them in. A Bengal-based 'West Pakistani' friend persuaded the authorities to allow her to leave for Karachi. I will never forget the harrowing story of her fear and terror. She had no idea where her husband was.[44]

In fact, Sobhan had slipped across the border into India, and was now staying with his old university friend Amartya Sen. Sobhan writes that Amartya was

> surprised and much relieved to hear from us, fearing we were both dead. He and his wife Nabaneeta immediately ... took us to their residence near the Delhi university campus located in Old Delhi. That night we had our first hot bath and a relaxed meal in three days. Nabaneeta prescribed us sleeping pills, which ensured a good night's sleep.[45]

The flight of East Bengali refugees across the border into India had an enormous impact on Indian society. Initially there was a groundswell of support for the refugees, and in India's West Bengal it led to a reappraisal of pan-Bengali unity. Within a month, however, India's border states were reporting that they were running low on sugar, salt and kerosene. By May water too was in short supply. Slowly the groundswell of support for refugees began to give way – anxieties grew 'over rising prices, competition for scarce resources, and the physical occupation of space by the refugees'.[46] This proved particularly damaging in the non-Bengali provinces neighbouring East Pakistan – Assam and Tripura – where thousands of people who spoke a different language streamed over the border. Here there was increasingly a sense of a Bengali takeover, giving added weight to virulent anti-immigration lobbies in the area.

With so many extra people to feed, the economy of Northeast India started to fall apart. From June the Indian government tried to move refugees away from the tense borderlands to camps further inland, but most refugees refused to board the government trains that were made available. Black markets arose around unruly refugee camps, and criminal gangs were reported to be 'siphoning off government rations and foreign aid'. By September armed clashes would be reported in the Khasi Hills (modern Meghalaya) between refugees and local communities, and by the end of the year the Indian narrative surrounding refugees had transformed from one of 'homecoming' to one of 'infiltration'. Indeed the destabilisation of Assam society that resulted from the crisis would play an important role in the proliferation of insurgency there throughout the last quarter of the twentieth century.[47]

'It was as if we were reliving the Partition,' recalled Indian politician Jaswant Singh.[48] The Indian government deliberately obfuscated the religious demographics of the refugees, but in May 1971 an estimated 80 per cent of the refugees entering West Bengal were Hindus.[49] This triggered mass protests across India against 'Hindu Genocide', and helped revive the Hindu nationalist movement, which had been somewhat dormant since Gandhi's assassination. Twenty-one-year-old Narendra Modi was one of those to join these rallies, and according to his biographer it was these protests that gave the future Indian prime minister his 'first real brush with national politics' and convinced him that politics was his 'true calling'. Modi subsequently decided to dedicate his life to the Hindu nation, and months later – horrified by Pakistan's targeting of Hindus – he formally became a *pracharak* of the RSS.[50]

With refugees streaming over the border, the Indian government was soon considering a population exchange of Hindus and Muslims between the two Bengals, just like the one organised in Punjab in 1947.[51] The plan never gained much traction, however, and India's response to the 1971 refugee crisis would prove quite different from the crisis of 1947. This time refugees were treated as foreigners with no right to remain in India, and the Indian government started to enact laws to stop the refugees claiming Indian citizenship. Moreover not all were treated equally. The supposedly secular Indian officials were more suspicious of letting Muslims remain in West Bengal than Hindus, lest they change the region's demographics, and Bihari Muslims were frequently arrested on the suspicion of supporting Pakistan.[52]

West Bengal was also facing a communist 'Naxalite' revolution at the time, and India worried that if left unattended Bengali nationalists from Pakistan could link up with those in India and form a joint front. India thus wanted to stop the refugees entering the country from thinking of India as a permanent home and to foster a hope of a return home.[53] Indira Gandhi's top adviser, P. N. Haksar, felt that 'the dangers of a link-up between the extremists in the two Bengals are real' and that the refugee crisis 'constitutes a grave security risk which no responsible government can allow to develop'.[54] A week after Operation Searchlight, Mrs Gandhi's advisers received a dossier from K. Subrahmanyam,* director of the Institute for Defence Studies and Analyses, arguing they should use 'the Bangla Desh genocide' to isolate Pakistan from its Chinese and American allies, and then escalate the conflict into a two-front all-out war. This was the perfect opportunity, Subrahmanyam argued, for India to break Pakistan and emerge as the major power in South Asia.[55]

How soon India actually began offering support to the Mukti Bahini [Liberation Army] remains a matter of dispute, but Major Chandrakant Singh insists the first decisions to help the Mukti Bahini were made by men on the spot rather than Indian high command. 'For the first few months, we had no idea what our government's intentions were,' he laughs. When Searchlight was launched, Chandrakant had been on a reconnaissance mission in East Pakistan's Chittagong Hill Tracts, spying on rebel Mizo camps, yet he maintains he had no orders about what to do when Bengali soldiers from the Pakistani Army started crossing into India. This question became particularly pressing on 7 April 1971 when Zia-ur-Rahman – the man responsible for the Bangladesh independence broadcast – ferried a car across the river border and started demanding military assistance.[56] 'Zia was a lightly built man,' remembers Chandrakant, 'a bit of a recluse, and although he had declared Bangladesh as an Islamic Republic, he had no hesitancy in sharing our whiskey ... He appeared serious and later I realised that he had left his wife behind when he had come over. That was bugging him.' For the next three months, Zia would spend much of his time living in Chandrakant's tent, preparing for battles against the Pakistan Army.

---

* Subrahmanyam is also the father of India's current minister of external affairs S. Jaishankar.

One of the most intriguing comments comes from Jacob-Farj-Raphael Jacob, the chief of staff of India's Eastern Command, a distinguished Sephardic Jewish soldier who had first joined the Indian Army during the Second World War after hearing reports of the Holocaust in Europe. According to his memoir, Army chief Sam Manekshaw called him within a week of Operation Searchlight, asking him 'to move immediately into East Pakistan'. India and Pakistan could have gone to war there and then, but Jacob resisted. Any movement of Indian troops, he argued, would be impractical until after the monsoon rains and Eastern Command was already fighting both communist and ethnic insurgencies in the Bangladesh-India borderlands. Jacob estimated that his men would only be able to wage war in Pakistan from 15 November onwards.[57]

Whatever the case, the Indian intelligence service was soon deeply invested in the Mukti Bahini. The initial aim, it seems, was to counter Pakistan's sponsorship of Naga and Mizo proxies in Northeast India and the former head of counter-terrorism later wrote: 'It was partly to put an end to the activities of the ISI in India's Northeast from East Pakistan that Mrs Gandhi decided to assist the Bengali people of East Pakistan in their efforts to separate from Pakistan.' India soon began to open training camps and even a Bangladeshi embassy in Calcutta, and started organising for a 'psychological warfare ... campaign against the Pakistani rulers by disseminating reports about the massacres of Bengalis in East Pakistan'.[58]

On 17 April a small detachment of soldiers from India's Border Security Force accompanied senior leaders of the Awami League across the border into a mango grove in the East Pakistani village of Baidyanathala. The location had been carefully selected by the Indian secret service, in collaboration with several defected officers in the East Pakistan Rifles, and here the Awami League leaders read out a proclamation, declaring themselves the 'elected representatives of the people of Bangladesh'.[59] By the end of the day Mujib's former right-hand men – Tajuddin Ahmad and Syed Nazrul Islam – had become the prime minister and acting president of a Bangladeshi government-in-exile. The town of Baidyanathala, meanwhile, was renamed Mujibnagar.

Direct orders for the Indian Army to help the Mukti Bahini would eventually be given on 29 April 1971, over a month after the conflict erupted and by early May Mrs Gandhi was backing what Haksar termed a 'total struggle for national liberation'.⁶⁰ Indian intelligence had been working with East Bengali nationalists for a decade at this point, something that belies its argument that the war of 1971 was purely the result of Pakistani aggression.

Rebel bases in India became strange liminal spaces where families divided by Partition could meet again. Sal, for example, was eventually sent to Calcutta to help the Mukti Bahini's propaganda wing and he managed to get in touch with his father's brother who had remained Indian after Partition. 'Calcutta felt like another world,' he remembers, exciting and full of life. 'I imagined my uncle living with a dog and two kids in the suburbs but as it turned out he had never married ... Anyway, finally after months of warfare I was with family – Indian family! What a moment that was. Of all the situations to reconnect a family divided by Partition, it was as a rebel in the Mukti Bahini!'⁶¹

Settling into Calcutta society was difficult. 'I'd been away for just three months,' he recalls, and 'for the first time there was no danger of being shot. It felt like an alien spaceship ... I couldn't process it. Where was I?'⁶² Sal's mind turned to the Vietnam veteran he had met at Woodstock, who, he suddenly realised, 'must have been suffering from exactly this form of cognitive dissonance'.⁶³ Sal would remain in Calcutta for the rest of the war, working to share pro-Bangladesh propaganda in a newsletter.⁶⁴

It was not just men who joined the Mukti Bahini. Laila Ahmed was a twenty-year-old student at medical college in Rajshahi and had been looking forward to graduating when the conflict broke out. On 14 April, when Pakistani forces entered her town, Laila had assumed her family would be safe – after all her father was a Pakistani intelligence officer. But that afternoon her father was lined up with a group of other Bengali men and shot. 'The death of my father was the turning point in my life,' she later recalled.⁶⁵

With her father dead, Laila knew her options were few. She and her family fled for their ancestral village, perched along the India border, but soon the Pakistani Army arrived there as well. 'I saw them rape many girls,' she later told historian Yasmin Saikia, '[and] the Indian Army started firing towards where we were.' Laila decided to take matters into her own hands and in May 1971 she crossed into India and set off for Calcutta. 'I wanted to join the medical wing of the Mukti Bahini, since I was a medical student,' she recalls. '[I] had to sell everything I owned, like my gold chain, to generate money to pay for my expenses.'[66] Towards the end of June, however, she made it to Gobra camp, a women's training camp based in the heart of Calcutta. It was a large sprawling place, in the garden of an old palace, a short walk from South Park Street Cemetery. Here young women were trained in first aid and taught how to shoot guns.

Not everyone was so impressed by the camp, however. Mumtaz Begum, secretary of the Jessore Students' League and already proficient in rifle-shooting, was keen to get to the front line as soon as she could. Like Laila, Mumtaz later found her way to Calcutta to join the resistance, but when she was offered a place in Gobra camp, she turned it down. 'The general training in Gobra was nursing,' she later recalled. 'I told them I have come here to learn how to fight, not to do bloody stitching.' Mumtaz was subsequently rejected and turned away. 'I was discriminated against because of my gender,' she maintains.[67]

India's collusion with the Mukti Bahini only further convinced Pakistani authorities that they were right to have suppressed the rebellion, and that the Bangladesh movement had been an Indian plot all along. Indeed Yahya's inner circle never grasped that Bengali nationalism was a real force – a crucial error based on their stereotyped views of Bengalis as weak, effeminate and non-martial. 'It is unfortunate,' announced Yahya Khan one day, 'that our neighbour, which has never missed an opportunity to weaken or cripple our country, rushed to help the secessionists with men and material to inflame the situation further. This was all pre-planned.'[68]

In response, the Pakistani Army took to recruiting their own paramilitary groups. They recruited civilians into the East Pakistan Civil Affairs Force to help provide security, and created an 'auxiliary force of loyalist Bengalis' called the Razakars to help with local intelligence, divided into two groups called Al-Shams and Al-Badr.[69] Many of the young recruits were sourced from religious institutions in West Pakistan and so arrived in the eastern province with a warped sense of what was going on. As one West Pakistani based in Dacca recalled:

> I was sitting with a friend of mine on my lawn ... [when] three or four bearded men came to my gate and asked for water ... I asked them who they were and they said ... ['We are Al-Badr']. 'What

do you do here?' I asked. 'We do jihad.' 'Against whom? This is Pakistan,' I said perplexed ... The men retorted saying that they were doing jihad against the Bengalis as they were Hindus. I insisted, 'Look, I live here, I study here. These are Muslims, they aren't Hindus. Whom are you calling Hindus?' But the men were adamant. They told me, 'This is your perception. These are Hindus posing as Muslims. Deep down, they are Hindus and we have come to set them right. And until they become right, we will not leave.'[70]

Despite situations like this, decisions of which side to join in the conflict were never simple, and just as in 1947, family members frequently ended up on opposite sides.[71] Moreover, rebel groups from both India and Pakistan soon found themselves pulled into the vortex of war, including the Mizo rebels from India who now joined forces with the Pakistani military. For all intents and purposes, the Mizos and Bangladeshis should have allied with one another – both struggles were rooted in having become second-class citizens in the wake of Partition and a sense that one foreign rule had been replaced with another.[72] But by 1971 Mizo rebels were dependent on the Pakistani Army for support, so as Bengali soldiers linked up with India, Indian Mizo dissidents joined up with the Pakistani Army. The proxy wars of the last decade were coming to a head.

'The Mizo Army consisted of three battalions of six hundred men each,' writes Zahir Alam Khan, the Pakistani officer who had arrested Mujib. 'I agreed to supply them with about one ton of rice per day [and] ... In return their army would be under my command.'[73] The Mizos were given a liaison office in Rangamati ... and were sporadically deployed in a conflict which they had no stake in.[74] As Indian intelligence documents reveal, 'The Mizos also rendered active help to the Pakistani troops in suppressing the Mukti Fauj [Bahini] of Bangla Desh ... A cash allowance of Rs, 1.43 per head per day and a pocket allowance of Rs 15 per month was paid to the Mizo hostiles.'[75]

The Pakistani Army also managed to recruit Chakma fighters in the Chittagong Hill Tracts, the district of East Pakistan straggling the Patkai Hills where most of the population was neither Bengali nor Muslim. More than any other community in the subcontinent, the Chakma embodied the false promises of the subcontinent's many partitions. A community of five hundred thousand, they had ended up in India after Burma's separation despite being Buddhist and speaking a language closely related to Burmese. Then, in 1947, their land had been given to Pakistan, making their district the only Buddhist-majority one in the Islamic Republic. When the Bangladesh war first broke out, the Chakmas initially helped Bengali rebels like Zia-ur-Rahman escape to India. But after a massacre of non-Bengalis, the Chakma Raja Tridiv Roy sued for a peaceful takeover by the Pakistani military.[76] Pakistani officer Zahir Alam Khan began inviting Roy around for drinks in the evening and helping him secure economic opportunities for the Chakma community in Pakistan. He writes:

> One of the problems of the Chakmas, he told me, was they had almost no government jobs. I arranged for the recruitment of about two hundred Chakmas in the East Pakistan Rifles. After receiving about a month's training they were given uniforms of khaki shirts, shorts and a side cap which made them look very smart. When they came back after their training, I gave them the task of guarding bridges; there were no rifles available so they were given shotguns. These probably became the nucleus of the 'Shanti Bahini', the Chakma guerrilla organization which has been fighting the Bangladesh government.[77]

Communities divided between India and Burma like the Mizos and Chakma thus found themselves pulled into the war over Pakistan. Later India would send a battalion of Tibetan refugees against them, so that on the eastern front the battle over the future of the Islamic Republic of Pakistan ironically involved two rival Buddhist militias – neither of them Bengali.

By May 1971, with the help of their new paramilitary groups, the Pakistani Army had managed to re-establish control over almost all the cities in East Pakistan. Schools reopened, curfews relaxed, and Tikka Khan, the feared 'Butcher of Baluchistan', announced that 'organized armed resistance has been liquidated all over the Province'. Yahya Khan offered an amnesty to all refugees who returned home and sent a relieved cable to King Hussein of Jordan with the words 'Ordeal now over'.[78]

Yet a political settlement to the crisis remained a distant dream. Bhutto was still calling for the army to hand over power to his party which, after the banning of the Awami League, was now the largest in the country. Yahya, however, continued to delay. In response Bhutto hinted his party 'might begin military armed resistance' to Yahya's government. 'We are preparing for every possibility,' he told the *New York Times* in September. 'Governments could be changed in parliamentary ways or by revolution or coup d'etat.'[79]

In the absence of a political solution, the Pakistani Army would be drawn into a months-long conflict against increasingly confident rebel groups. The Mukti Bahini staged attacks from Indian territory and life was still a daze for everyone living in East Pakistan. 'People are avoiding fish these days,' wrote Jahanara Imam. 'I stopped eating fish since late March when dead bodies were floating in the river. We all need to take the cholera vaccine.'[80]

As all this was happening in the East, life in West Pakistan remained eerily normal. Muneeza Shamsie would later write vividly about life in Karachi during the war:

Today, most Pakistanis confess that 'we didn't know what was happening [in 1971]'. The point is: I knew and many others knew. But most people preferred to believe a censored press, a systematic machinery of rumour and disinformation, and that age old maxim: 'it's all a foreign plot.'[81]

Part of the issue was the influx of non-Bengali refugees from East into West Pakistan, which helped turn public opinion further against the Bengali cause. Shamsie remembers how her cousin Tasneem arrived destitute in Karachi with her daughter who was now blind in one eye. Tasneem's husband had worked at the Ispahani factory in Chittagong, and one day the Mukti Bahini had rounded up all the non-Bengalis there and shot or bayoneted them. Tasneem's husband and son had been killed in the attack, but she and her daughter 'survived miraculously, though a bayonet had destroyed her daughter's eye'. As a result of stories like these, Shamsie writes, most people in Karachi 'were incensed only at the suffering of West Pakistanis and Urdu-speaking people in East Pakistan. Cruelties committed by the army on Bengalis were glossed over with the words, "Well, you can't really blame them when you see what the Bengalis have done.""[82] She and her husband protested that the army was meant to follow better standards than the mob, but anti-Bengali sentiment had reached a fever pitch.

> I was scandalized at the fascist arguments I heard from people I considered friends. Bengalis were all branded traitors, virtual Hindus and Indians; they were described as an unreliable black-skinned, shifty, racially inferior people ... I even heard someone say that Bengali women were immoral and therefore fair game, because they didn't wear blouses with their sarees ... [Over time], we went out less and less, even to visit close friends – because all it meant was argument and anger.[83]

Nonetheless, it would be wrong to characterise all West Pakistanis as simply standing by as Bengalis were massacred. Indeed it was a West Pakistani man who finally placed the war in the global spotlight.

Anthony 'Tony' Mascarenhas, was a Goan Catholic from Karachi. He was a 'well dressed man in his early forties,' wrote his editor, and 'had the bearing of a military man, square set and mustached, with appealing, almost soulful eyes'.[84] In late April Mascarenhas and seven other Pakistani journalists had been invited by the Ministry of Information to report on the 'return to normalcy' in East Pakistan. Mascarenhas was horrified by what he saw and on 18 May 1971 he walked into the *Sunday Times* office in London and offered up one of the most explosive stories the paper would ever publish. Mascarenhas' family was swiftly arranged passage to the UK, and on 13 June his article was published with the headline 'GENOCIDE'.[85] It opened with the lines:

> Abdul Bari had run out of luck.
>   Like thousands of other people in East Bengal, he had made the mistake, the fatal mistake of running within sight of a Pakistani army patrol. He was 24 years old, a slight man surrounded by soldiers. He was trembling, because he was about to be shot.
>   'Normally we would have killed him as he ran,' I was informed chattily by Major Rathore, the G-2 Ops. of the 9th Division, as we

Pakistan's first Bengali prime minister, Khawaja Nazimuddin

1960s Pakistan coin featuring both Urdu and Bengali

Indira Gandhi at a Congress session, Delhi, 1967

Over the course of the 1960s, the secessionist movements of Angami Zapu Phizo (above left) and Mujibur Rahman (above right) would draw India and Pakistan into a long-drawn-out proxy war

Poster for Bangladeshi independence, inspired by the art of Jamini Roy

A young man singing during the 1971 Bangladesh Liberation War. Bengali music and poetry played a central role in mobiliing public sentiment for an independent Bangladesh

The Bangladesh crisis would see India tilt towards the Soviet Union

A political poster of Zulfikar Ali Bhutto and his daughter Benazir

On 7 March 1971, Sheikh Mujibur Rahman announces to a crowd in Dacca, 'The struggle this time is a struggle for our independence.' Eighteen days later, the Pakistani Army launched Operation Searchlight

US president Nixon and Pakistani president Yahya Khan

Mukti Bahini fighters on the cover of *Newsweek*

Salahdin Imam, rock and roll correspondent for the *Harvard Crimson*, shortly before joining the Mukti Bahini

The Bengali sitar player Ravi Shankar would help bring international attention to the Bangladeshi cause with the help of Beatles member George Harrison

The Concert for Bangladesh was the first major charity rock concert ever performed, a precursor to Live Aid, and would bring the term 'Bangladesh' into common parlance outside of South Asia for the first time

Pro-Pakistan residents of Dacca protesting against 'Indian aggression' in December 1971

Mukti Bahini fighters capture pro-Pakistan 'Razakars' in December 1971

Niazi, Jacob and Gavin Young at the 'Surrender Lunch' shortly before Pakistan's surrender in 1971

At the Dacca Race Course, Gen. Aurora (left) of the Indian Army, and Gen. Niazi (right) of the Pakistani Army sign the Pakistani Instrument of Surrender, ending the Great South Asian War of 1971. Despite this, Pakistan would refuse to recognise Bangladeshi sovereignty until February 1974

Indian Army officers examine a pile of rifles taken from Pakistani troops after Pakistan's surrender in 1971

Ishar Das Arora – the grandfather of Sparsh Ahuja – who fled his home

Sparsh crosses into Pakistan to meet the family that saved his grandfather's life, 2021

stood on the outskirts of a tiny village near Mudafarganj, about 20 miles south of Comilla. 'But we are checking him out for your sake. You are new here and I see you have a squeamish stomach.'

'Why kill him?' I asked with mounting concern. 'Because he might be a Hindu or he might be a rebel, perhaps a student or an Awami Leaguer. They know we are sorting them out and they betray themselves by running.'

'But why are you killing them? And why pick on the Hindus?' I persisted. 'Must I remind you,' Rathore said severely, 'how they have tried to destroy Pakistan? Now under the cover of the fighting we have an excellent opportunity of finishing them off.'[86]

Mascarenhas' article is widely regarded as 'one of the most influential pieces of South Asian journalism' ever written.[87] It successfully put the Bangladesh war in the global spotlight and years later Indira Gandhi told the *Sunday Times* editor Harold Evans the report had so deeply shocked her she set out 'on a campaign of personal diplomacy in the European capitals and Moscow to prepare the ground for India's armed intervention'.[88] Mascarenhas' accusation of genocide has lingered over the events of 1971 ever since.

Whether or not Pakistan's crackdown can truly be labelled a genocide is still hotly disputed today. Pakistanis have argued the military crackdown was no different to the Indian Army's own actions in Northeast India. Others have argued, however, that there is a crucial difference in the way violence was meted out to women. That October *Time* magazine revealed that 563 young Bengali women – many just students – had been forced into sex camps at the Pakistani Army cantonment in Dacca and that 'Bengali gynaecologists' had been hired to facilitate regular abortions.[89] In the coming months, more and more evidence would emerge of rape being weaponised by members of the Pakistani Army. This evidence was even recognised by an inquiry sponsored by the Pakistani government, although the inquiry denied any charge of genocide, pointing out that it was still unclear who had ordered the creation of rape camps.[90]

The use of rape remains the most vile and contemptible aspect of the Bangladesh war of 1971. Yet the Pakistani Army was not the only one weaponising the use of rape during the conflict. Sal Imam recalls how one Bengali sergeant of the Mukti Bahini once asked him whether his mother would forgive him for raping a young Bihari woman whose family he had killed.[91] As another woman told Yasmin Saikia:

> Don't ask me who killed whom, who raped whom, what was the religion, ethnic or linguistic background of the people who died in the war. The victims in the war were the women of this country – mothers who lost their children, sisters who lost their brothers, wives who lost their husbands, women who lost everything, their honour and dignity. In the war, men victimized women.[92]

Some scholars have recently begun to assert that two genocides took place in 1971, one against Bengalis and the other against the Urdu-speaking Biharis who had migrated to East Pakistan after Partition.[93] Even Mascarenhas himself noted that 'West Pakistani soldiers are not the only ones who have been killing in East Bengal', and that 'thousands of non-Bengalis have vanished without a trace'.[94] This argument has proved deeply controversial to many Bangladeshis, however.* On an individual level, Bengali soldiers may have committed atrocities, just like their West Pakistani counterparts, but a distinction needs to be drawn between the well-organised state-sponsored violence of the Pakistani Army and the violent actions of disorganised Bengali militias.

★ ★ ★

---

* One of the best appraisals comes from Yasmin Saikia, a scholar of the conflict, who writes: In East Pakistan death was not produced in a factory-like environment nor was there one group of perpetrators. Violence was a passionate outburst staged in intervals as a reaction to previous episodes. The violence happened between and within communities of people who knew each other and lived alongside each other, as neighbours, as teachers and students, as colleagues and co-workers, as strangers and friends. These people were driven by the passion of their group interest, politics, personal vendettas, and even material greed. Violence was also carried out by outsiders – the Pakistan Army and the Indian Army. No single group had a monopoly on committing violence, nor did one single group control the production of death in East Pakistan. Pakistani Punjabi soldiers, nationalist Bengali militias, Bengali supporters of West Pakistan, Bihari civil armed guards, and Indian Army men, along with other less identifiable groups, killed, tortured, and destroyed those who opposed them and their politics. It is true that the West Pakistani soldiers and their supporters killed large numbers and that they were supported by the institution of the army, a state apparatus, to carry out violence against the people of East Pakistan. What motivated the Pakistani soldiers to kill nationalist Bengalis who were until then a part of Pakistan and were citizens of the same country?

By the summer of 1971 the Bangladesh conflict was playing out on a global scale. Defections of Bengali officials from Pakistani missions were reported worldwide, while Yahya Khan, anxious about the changing tide of world opinion, 'personally sent messages to Heads of State and Governments explaining his point of view'.[95] The Soviet Union condemned Pakistan, while China – increasingly Pakistan's closest ally – declared the chaos an internal matter for Pakistan. Burma, meanwhile, stopped all sale of aviation fuel to the Pakistani Army, so as not to involve itself in the growing war. Intriguingly, the government of South Yemen, whose own revolutionary state had been created out of the Raj just a few years earlier, offered to help the Bangladeshi forces 'in organizing the supply of arms and other material'.[96]

The relief of refugees in India – who by August numbered around eight million – had become an international endeavour. U Thant, the Burmese secretary general of the UN, lobbied globally for aid donations. Perhaps the most famous face of the relief mission, however, would be an Albania-born Indian nun based in Calcutta called Mother Teresa. Born in 1910 in the Ottoman Empire, Teresa had opened a hospice in Calcutta in the wake of the 1943 Bengal famine and gained recognition caring for refugees in the wake of 1947. Her white and blue outfit would become a famous icon of the conflict.

Meanwhile, Pakistan itself was increasingly in dire straits. With the massive bulge in military spending, the economy had begun to tank and the power supply in East Pakistan was starting to break down due to incessant attacks by the Mukti Bahini. India too was changing thanks to the war. With the Indian Army now massed along the borderlands, Indira Gandhi used the opportunity to drive the Naxal communist rebels from West Bengal. The Indian armed forces launched Operation Steeplechase that summer and imprisoned twenty thousand West Bengali communists in a matter of months.[97] By the end of the summer the phrase 'police encounter' had been added to the Indian lexicon to refer to extrajudicial killings carried out by Indian police.

At the same time, the monsoon rains had arrived and the conflict became mired in mud. The Mukti Bahini controversially took to recruiting child soldiers, many of whom were trained in combat under the supervision of the Indian Army. Indira Gandhi even publicly praised the 'young boys of even 12 years of age who joined the Mukti Bahini'. But distrust was growing between Indian and Bangladeshi forces.

Indian troops turned increasingly resentful of the absurd demands of the Bangladesh government-in-exile, such as that the Indian government provide them with 'Lasser beams'.[98] All the while the Bangladesh government-in-exile resented India's refusal to intervene in the war, increasingly fearful that after a Pakistani defeat, India might try to annex East Pakistan herself. 'By now there was much more that separated them from India than most Indians realised. Undoing Pakistan was one thing, but undoing Partition was no option for Bangladeshis at all: the first flags of Bangladesh showed the outline of the new country, lying comfortably within the embrace of Radcliffe's line.'[99]

In fact Mrs Gandhi and her cabinet were consciously avoiding reuniting the two Bengals under Indian sovereignty. But outside the Indian cabinet, calls to reunite the two Bengals were common. At one Calcutta coffee house, Sal's friend Abhijit – a high-level Indian Administrative Service member in Calcutta – suggested to him the Mukti Bahini should seek 'to repair the human and economic damages of the Partition' and make East Bengal 'an integral and honoured part of the whole Indian system'. When he heard this, Sal was horrified. Bengali Muslims had fought for years to escape Hindu domination. Just because they were now being dominated by Punjabi Muslims, that didn't mean they would choose to be dominated by the Hindus once again. Sal spent the next hour explaining to Abhijit that 'it would be a big mistake for the Indian authorities to put forward any formal or informal proposals for political union, as it would enflame a wide range of sensitivities on our side'.[100]

When Operation Searchlight was launched, East Pakistan was still suffering from the aftermath of the Bhola cyclone four months earlier. By midsummer, therefore, the threat of famine loomed once again over the Bengal delta and the chairman of Pakistan's Planning and Development Board privately admitted it might be 'worse than 1942'.[101] In a strange reversal of the previous Bengal famine, British officials jumped to offer aid, but were initially rejected by the Pakistani government, who diverted East Pakistan-bound aid to Karachi.[102] Indeed aid only began to be accepted a few weeks later, when the scale of the crisis became clearer.

Calls for aid grew louder in the coming months, however, and one of the most unlikely allies of the Bangladeshi cause would come in the form of rock and roll, a movement made possible by Ravi Shankar, the Bengali sitar player who had moved to Bombay after the decline of princely patronage. Shankar had become a close collaborator with the Beatles over the course of the 1960s, and that summer he was working with ex-Beatle George Harrison on a soundtrack to *Raga*, 'their first musical collaboration'. During a recital, Shankar suggested to Harrison that they organise an aid concert for Bangladeshi refugees. 'After half an hour he talked me into being on the show,' recalled Harrison. 'The war had been going on for a bit, and I had hardly even heard of it, so he fed me a lot of newspaper articles about it.'[103]

Together the duo hastily organised a Concert for Bangladesh in New York's Madison Square Garden, and formed a supergroup for the occasion, including Ringo Starr, Bob Dylan, Billy Preston and Eric Clapton. They started writing songs about the conflict. The Concert for Bangladesh was the first major charity rock concert ever performed, a precursor to Live Aid. Tickets sold out within hours, and by explicitly using the word 'Bangladesh' rather than 'East Pakistan' or 'East Bengal', the duo brought the word into common parlance in the West for the first time.

The concert itself got off to a rough start, and when Clapton arrived he was suffering severe heroin withdrawals. 'He's pretty messed up,' noted George Harrison. 'Somebody is finding some heroin to give him.'[104] But at 2.30 p.m. on 1 August 1971, Ravi Shankar opened the show with Alla Rakha and Ali Akbar Khan, speaking about the plight of the Bengali refugees in India, and with footage from the camps playing in the background. Later that afternoon, Harrison played his new hit single 'Bangla Desh':

Bangla Desh, Bangla Desh
Where so many people are dying fast
And it sure looks like a mess
I've never seen such distress
Now won't you lend your hand, try to understand
Relieve the people of Bangla Desh

Never before had rockstars called so convincingly for the establishment of a new country. '[The Concert for Bangladesh] was very important for me,' remembers Sal, then still living in Calcutta. 'I realised that my friends in the US HAD noticed what was happening to us in Bangladesh. To see my heroes – Clapton, Dylan, Harrison and Shankar – fighting for us was incredible.'[105] By the end of the day, $243,000 had been raised for UNICEF's refugee fund, and reviews of their newly released songs were glowing. 'Concise, direct, and with a killer saxophone solo, "Bangla Desh" makes a convincing argument,' read one:

> Yes, the '60s were done. The Manson murders terrified a nation, Altamont crashed and burned, Joplin and Hendrix were dead, and the Vietnam War raged on. Fear and doubt had poisoned the well of idealism. But right here, right now, Harrison suggests, you can honor some of the decade's lost promises by lending a hand to help a fellow man.[106]

The concert, and the bestselling album that followed, successfully placed the Bangladesh cause at the heart of the western countercultural movement. Their message was explicitly political, and the album sleeve lambasted the actions of the Pakistani Army as 'undoubtedly the greatest atrocity since Hitler's extermination of the Jews'.[107] Other rockstars took up the cause for themselves, with Joan Baez writing the hit single 'Song of Bangladesh', and the Who staging their own relief concert in London. 'It was a miracle,' Ravi Shankar recalled later.[108] Even Hippie-trail guidebooks seemed to turn on the Pakistani leadership, and one such called *Overland to India* wrote of West Pakistan: 'There's lots there to keep you happy and stoned ... [but only] if you can keep thoughts of the slaughter in East Pakistan out of your head.'[109]

That September the American Beat poet Allen Ginsberg showed up to Sal's office in Calcutta, 'dressed in a plain kurta pajama', hoping to learn more about the conflict.[110] Ginsberg had long been enchanted by India and on his previous visit had befriended several Bengali radicals.[111] 'He was taller than I expected,' writes Sal, 'of medium build and his best-known feature, a big curly beard, had been clipped short.'[112] Sal was appointed Ginsberg's tour guide, to take him and several others around the teeming refugee encampments along Calcutta's Jessore Road. Ginsberg recorded his impressions:

Heavy rain, cholera epidemic. A man standing on the road with a many pronged spear. Tensions between poor residents and refugees. 'You are behaving like a lord' the refugees complain to the poor villagers. 'The refugees are shitting on our lawns', the residents complain.[113]

Months later Ginsberg published a poem about the experience entitled 'September on Jessore Road', which was put to music by Bob Dylan. 'Ginsberg's poem, like the songs of Harrison and Baez, strummed the conscience of global opinion, particularly in the Western world, by braiding Bangladesh with the causes espoused by young protesters around the world,' writes historian Srinath Raghavan. 'For a few months in 1971, Bangladesh seemed to distil all the hopes and fears of the Swinging Sixties.'[114]

In late July the Pakistani high commissioner in Tanzania, Dr M. Osman Ghani, formally defected from his post and announced his allegiance with the Bangla Desh government. Then came Mohiuddin Ahmed, the third secretary of the Pakistani High Commission in London, who explained his hand had been forced by the Pakistani High Commission continuing to deny the 'genocide in East Bengal'.[115] Ahmed then told the press his intention to keep working in London, but for a new Bangla Desh mission rather than a Pakistani one, sparking a fierce controversy over whether he should be allowed to stay. The row culminated in a sheepish message to the Pakistani authorities that as Ahmed had entered the UK on a diplomatic passport, they could not legally deport him.

But the defections were only the beginning. Bengali diplomatic workers defected en masse from Pakistani missions in the US, Nigeria and Argentina, and on 23 August it emerged that the Pakistani ambassador in Baghdad, Mr A. Fateh, had defected along with £30,000 from the High Commission's treasury, driven across the Kuwait border and flown from there to London. He declared to the press that 'London has become the nerve centre of Bangla Desh rebels', an announcement that put the British Foreign Office in a supremely awkward position.[116]

By late September the British Foreign Office had opened an entire file on defected Pakistani diplomats, simply to keep track of them all. And then, as the trickle of defections turned into a tidal wave, the increasingly confident Bangla Deshi government announced on 3 October that Bengali diplomats still working for Pakistan had only fifteen more days to declare their allegiance. Otherwise they would be 'deemed enemies' and suitable action would be taken against them.[117]

As the Bangladesh war went global, the subcontinent was pulled into the cold war. Between 9 and 11 July, Henry Kissinger made a secret trip to Beijing, via Islamabad, resulting in an opening between the US and China. In response India signed a friendship treaty with the Soviet Union a few weeks later, promising to come to the other's military aid. On 27 September Indira Gandhi flew to Moscow to seek both military and diplomatic support from the Soviets. Then she flew to Europe to lobby leaders from Brussels to Vienna to support the Bangladesh cause.[118] Yahya Khan, meanwhile, set out on a similar diplomatic trip, and the opportunity to lobby on his country's behalf presented itself in mid-October, when the Shah of Iran organised 'the largest meeting of monarchs and heads of state in modern history' in order to commemorate the 2,500th anniversary of the Persian Empire.[119] Indira Gandhi declined to attend but almost every other notable leader in the world – including Yahya – was there.

It was one of the most extravagant parties ever recorded, and still holds the Guinness world record for longest and most lavish official banquet: 'Air-conditioned tents, roasted peacock, and gallons of champagne were all on offer within a specially made artificial oasis ... [and] 15,000 trees and 15,000 flowers were imported from across Europe, some from the gardens of Versailles ... To save the distinguished guests from being bitten or stung, all the thousands of scorpions and snakes within a 30km area were exterminated with pesticides.' A tent city specially erected for guests included an '18-hole golf course ... sixteen hair salons and four beauty parlours (staffed by Parisian stylists) ... a social club with a bar, cabaret suite, and even a secret gambling room'.[120] In hindsight, the Persepolis Festival's lavish expense would contribute to the growth of revolutionary sentiment in the country and the overthrow of the Iranian monarchy.

Behind the festivities, the celebrations were a den of political intrigue. The event was in some ways a 'coming out' for the Gulf monarchs whose independence had only recently been conceded. With no Indian or Pakistani princes invited, the gathering also displayed the extraordinary reversal of fortunes for the Gulf states since 1931, when they had been seen as so irrelevant that they warranted no gun salute. Now the Sheikhs and Sultans of the Gulf stood on equal footing with the rulers of India and Pakistan, in great contrast to states like Hyderabad, Travancore and Kashmir. Meetings between the Sultan of Oman and the Shah opened the gateway to a mutual security agreement, which would help Oman fight off the remaining revolutionary groups in its territory,[121] while Yahya Khan successfully persuaded the Shah of Iran to declare 'that his government supports Pakistan, one hundred per cent'. According to officials at the Afghan embassy, Yahya was able to secure some foreign exchange, which he needed to keep the Pakistani economy afloat.[122]

Of more consequence, however, was a secret meeting arranged between Yahya Khan and the Soviet president Nikolai Podgorny at the festival. Yahya explained his plans to resolve the political crisis after the Awami League had been suppressed, but Podgorny simply asked, 'Why don't you begin the process by starting talks with Sheikh Mujib? He is an essential factor in any peace process. If you can release him and secure his agreement to future plans, everything will fall into its proper place.' Yahya only growled that he would never negotiate with 'that traitor'. 'Please Mr President,' responded Podgorny. 'You do not have unlimited time.'[123]

By the time Yahya returned to Pakistan, Indian troops were preparing for war. Sydney Schanberg, the *New York Times* correspondent who had earlier been forced out of Dacca, was surprised at the cavalier attitude of many Indian border officials. 'We're doing things we just can't let you see,' one told him. 'The border is hot. All around.'[124]

According to official Indian accounts of 1971, the war that erupted between India and Pakistan began on 3 December when the Pakistani Army launched a massive pre-emptive air strike on India. Yet Pakistan claims with some justification that the war started many weeks earlier, when Indian troops had begun making excursions into East Pakistani territory. As early as 8 November, the *New York Times* had reported on Indian troops firing on Pakistani troops on their own soil 'to silence Pakistani guns that had been shelling Indian territory'.[125]

India and Pakistan lurched towards all-out war. A full-scale air battle took place between the Indian and Pakistani Air Forces in late November, and three days later Mrs Gandhi admitted India had shot down three Pakistani Sabre jets. Meanwhile, the Indian Army began to encroach upon Pakistani territory. 'Chaugacha was firmly in our hands by 29 November, thanks to the Mukti Bahini,' wrote Major-General Jacob in his memoir.[126] Remarkably, the Indian Army was already in control of parts of East Pakistan long before the two countries were officially at war.

By the first week of December, an estimated ten million refugees were living in India, an astonishing one in twelve Pakistani citizens.[127] That week witnessed a flurry of diplomatic manoeuvres, with both countries attempting to garner further international support for their respective causes. In the corridors of power, whispers of war hung heavy in the air, and all the while events escalated. Pakistan too was on a war footing and 'Crush India' posters appeared across the country.[128] The Islamic Republic declared a national emergency and 'Yahya drunkenly told a *New Yorker* reporter that he expected to be at war within ten days'.[129] Pakistani intelligence got word India was planning to attack in early December, and so on the third of the month Pakistani troops launched their strike on Indian airfields.

That night the sky was ablaze with the fiery dance of fighter jets and Indira Gandhi announced to the Indian public: 'Today the war in Bangla Desh has become a war on India.'[130] Of course, India had been preparing to do exactly that just a day later. 'We were going to attack on December 4,' admitted the country's director of naval intelligence years later. 'They guessed it, I suppose.'[131]

Indian blamed Pakistan, and Pakistan blamed India. Whatever the case, the Great South Asian War of 1971 had, officially, begun.

15

The Partition of Pakistan

The war of 1971 would be the first total war the subcontinent had seen since the Second World War.[1] Public emotions were deeply jingoistic, and unlike in previous conflicts, many of the younger generation had never known the pre-Partition world where Indians and Pakistanis had been one people. It would thus be the first major conflict in which young men and women from India, Pakistan and the nascent nation of Bangladesh treated each other as completely alien. Anglo-Bengali historian Joya Chatterji was seven years old at the time, and later wrote about the simplistic image she had of the war:

> Over our early supper before lights-out, Ini and I discussed the 'heroic' deeds of Indira Gandhi and the 'evil' Yahya Khan of Pakistan ... [Our cook] Diwan Singh, a condescending Hindu Rajput with a hennaed handlebar moustache, convinced us that just as Hindus and Muslims were polar opposites, so Pakistan was the obverse of India. Yahya Khan, he told us, ate with his elbows instead of his hands. In Pakistan ... the rain flowed heavenwards instead of falling to the ground.[2]

Even advertisements took on an unusually jingoistic tone. 'Exterminate the enemy once and for all,' read an advert by the Pakistani parcel delivery service PAKTRACK. 'Ladies! Rush To Join Jehad,' urged one Karachi-based clothing brand alongside a message about their slashed prices for woollen jerseys.[3] 'Advance and strike at the enemy with the rallying call of Allah-o-Akbar,' read a particularly unusual advert for soap.

For the first two days, the Great South Asian War was a battle of the skies. Joya Chatterji recalls, 'the blackened-out windows of our home in Delhi, the wailing air-raid sirens, [and] the darkened tops of cars' headlamps that made them look like Noddy-cars gazing coyly downwards'.[4] Each night after curfew, Joya would play Monopoly with her brother, while their mother worried anxiously about their house being bombed. The Pakistani Air Force dropped bombs over Amritsar and Agra, and the Taj Mahal was only protected thanks to being 'camouflaged with a forest of twigs and leaves and draped with burlap'.[5]

The Indian Air Force, meanwhile, responded by decimating Pakistani airfields in the east. Civilians of both countries cowered in fear as bomber planes darted over their cities, and even Dacca's Intercontinental Hotel – officially a 'neutral zone' thanks to a demand from the Red Cross – would regularly see dogfights play out overhead. The hotel itself began to resemble 'a railway station' as civilians, Red Cross observers – and even a poodle – tried to cram themselves within the safety of its walls, and each morning the staff had to use 'magnet fishing poles to remove shrapnel from the swimming pool'.[6]

Finally the battle over Bangladesh came to the people of West Pakistan. *Time* magazine's correspondent Louis Kraar reported how the streets of Rawalpindi, the centre of Pakistan's military establishment, had taken on an almost absurd veneer.

> Pakistanis have taken to caking mud all over their autos in the belief that it camouflages them from Indian planes. In nightly blackouts, the road traffic moves along with absolutely no lights, and fear has prevailed so completely over common sense that there has probably been more bloodshed in traffic accidents than in the air raids. The government has begun urging motorists only to shield their lights, but peasants throw stones at any car that keeps them on.[7]

Further south in Karachi, India's aerial bombing was even more persistent. 'We heard air raid sirens,' recalls Muneeza Shamsie, 'saw aeroplanes flying low overhead, and listened to television bulletins on blackouts and civil defence in the evenings.' A friend in the air force suggested Muneeza move her baby Saman's cot into the better-protected dining room, just in case a bomb landed on the house, and a day later exactly that happened. 'There was a jolt, a flash of lighting, the tinkling of shattered glass,' she writes, but miraculously baby Saman was unharmed.

The following night was long, as the young family waited for the dawn that seemed to never come. Only later did they realise the sun had risen long before, and that the sky remained dark only because of a thick black smoke that stretched across the horizon. The Indian Navy and Air Force had mounted a joint attack on Karachi's oil installations, which held four-fifths of Pakistan's oil supply, and the city would burn for seven days. 'All I can recollect of those days of the war … is the chill of fear each time I heard an air raid siren,' she writes. 'We watched censored television broadcasts which reported great victories, though it was quite obvious the reverse was true. We were all adept at "reading between the lines".'[8]

Within three days, India had successfully established its supremacy over skies and seas, obliterating the airfields of East Pakistan and blockading the Chittagong and Chalna ports. Gavin Young, East Pakistani correspondent for the *Observer*, reported how in the early days of the war the Pakistani pilots he met were still cocky about their victory, appearing 'in flowery shirts and silk cravats, all cock-a-hoop'. Just three days later, however, the same pilots 'admitted sadly into their whisky that they could not take off any more since the runway was cut up by bombing'.[9]

On the western front, an Indian victory looked less certain. Pakistani tanks burst across the desert borders of Rajasthan, while Pakistani artillery fired upon Indian positions in Kashmir. Each morning General Manekshaw updated Indira Gandhi over breakfast with increasingly good news from the eastern front, but increasingly depressing news of the western front. 'But Sam, you can't win every day,' Mrs Gandhi told him.[10]

For many Indian and Pakistani troops experiencing combat for the first time, the outbreak of war was terrifying. 'The smell of human blood mixed with that of cordite from bullets and art[iller]y shells cannot be described in words,' writes one soldier. 'The memory of bodies torn apart and shredded to smithereens even after almost fifty years is still fresh.'[11] Nonetheless, for many Bangladeshi troops, it was a relief. 'For the first time since the 25th of March 1971 I felt that there was no more for me personally to do,' recalls Sal. Feeling that the fate of his country was now in safe hands, he would spend the latter half of December exploring the cultural life of Bengal's erstwhile capital: attending classical dance performances and even dancing at Calcutta's nightclubs. 'I sneaked over to the DJ,' he recalls, and 'asked him to play "Monkey Man" by the Stones.'[12]

On 6 December Indira Gandhi formally recognised the nation of Bangladesh. Mukti Bahini soldiers would subsequently play a key role in the Indian advance, and one commander proudly claimed: 'Once again we demonstrated to the world that the Bengalis are a fighting martial race.'[13]

Within a day of this announcement, Indian and Bangladeshi troops took their first city from the Pakistani Army. 'Jessore, India's first strategic prize, fell as easily as a mango ripened by a long Bengal summer,' read *Time* magazine. 'The Pakistani 9th Division headquarters had quit Jessore days before the Indian advance, and only four battalions were left to face the onslaught.' After months of keeping journalists away from their activities, the Indian Army was now only too happy to let foreign correspondents rush to the scene of its victory. 'The closer you get to the front,' one journalist noted with pleasure, 'the more tea and cookies you get.'[14]

The same day as the fall of Jessore, Yahya Khan announced he would be handing over power to a new prime minister of Pakistan, and to everyone's surprise his new candidate was a Bengali. Nurul Amin remains one of the most controversial figures in Bangladeshi history, derided by most as Yahya's lightweight puppet and a traitor to the nation. In Pakistani history, he is mostly forgotten, but his importance can be understood by the fact that he was later buried in Jinnah's tomb, beside the founder of Pakistan.

A squat man with a large double chin, Amin was born to a Bengali Muslim family near the border of Tripura. Like many Muslims in rural Bengal, he had become enamoured by the Muslim League during the Second World War, and by the late 1940s was one of Muhammad Ali Jinnah's most trusted lieutenants. Amin was later appointed chief minister of East Bengal, but during the language protests of 1952, he became convinced the Language Movement was just a conspiracy by Pakistan's Communist Party.[15] When the Muslim League were roundly defeated in the provincial elections, Amin lost his seat.

Despite his opposition to the Bengali Language Movement, however, Amin would remain a central force in Bengali politics for decades to come. In the 1960s he marched alongside the National Democratic Front as a leading campaigner against Ayub Khan's military rule and according to veteran politician Sherbaz Khan Mazhari, the drafters of Mujib's six points had originally asked Nurul Amin to be their spokesman before they approached Mujib.[16] Amin had rejected the offer but by March 1969 he had apparently 'come round to Mujib's point of view' regarding Punjab's hegemony over the Pakistani state.[17]

Why then did he choose to side with Pakistan over Bangladesh?

In 1971 seventy-four-year-old Nurul Amin had become the 'oldest of the old guard'[18] and one of only two non-Awami Leaguers to win the elections, along with Tridiv Roy. He opposed the Awami League's aggression and subsequently devoted his energies to re-establishing communication between Pakistan's two wings and helping curb the military's excesses from within the establishment. In June Amin visited Rawalpindi 'somewhat reluctantly' to meet with Yahya Khan and to try to persuade him to visit Dacca.[19] Like many other Bengalis, Nurul Amin clung dearly to the Pakistani dream. Bangladeshi nationalist literature tends to reduce a complex range of decisions to a simple binary between 'collaborators' and 'freedom fighters', but in the words of Willem van Schendel:

> Many Bengalis (no one knows how many) took sides only when it was safe to do so, at the very end of the war. Other Bengalis (again, no one knows how many) actively supported the Pakistan side, and among them were armed militias. It is misleading to portray the war as 'the Bengalis' confronting the Pakistani enemy.[20]

So it was that united Pakistan's eighth and final prime minister was a Bengali.

For the first week of the war, Indian troops actively avoided marching on Dacca and focused on securing the border areas. India's military aim was to capture enough territory to establish a viable Bangladeshi state, not necessarily to take Dacca.[21] But on 9 December Lt-Gen. Sagat

Singh announced his troops would attempt to cross the furious, miles-wide Meghna river, separating his troops from Dacca. He enlisted the help of Captain Chandan Singh's helicopter pilots, and together they managed to ferry 650 Indian troops onto the other bank, just thirty miles from Dacca.[22] Ironically, as noted by K. S. Nair, 'much of the Bangladesh victory was, in fact, due to imaginative officers on the ground, up to and including Lieutenant-General Sagat Singh, exceeding their brief'.[23]

At the same time the Indian Army moved against the Naga and Mizo bases in East Pakistan. Pakistan's sponsorship of these insurgents a decade earlier had inspired India's own sponsorship of Mujib and Bengali separatists in the first place. Now it was time to put an end to their decade-long proxy war. Most Mizo and Naga rebels managed to escape, but Indian troops managed to seize a treasure trove of documents from the Mizo rebel headquarters, offering important information about their connections with Pakistani and Chinese intelligence.[24]

In the White House, it was beginning to dawn on US president Richard Nixon that he was backing the losing side. 'The Partition of Pakistan is a fact!' he cried to Kissinger. The two saw the war in simplified Cold War terms, with India aligned with the Soviets and Pakistan with the US. Moreover US intelligence suspected India's aim was not only to free Bangladesh but to shatter Pakistan as a whole. Kissinger thus proposed a three-part solution: to persuade Iran and Jordan to illegally send US aircraft to Pakistan, to ask China to mass troops near India, and most importantly to threaten India with the US Navy. This might risk a wider war between superpowers, but it might just make Pakistan win. Nixon signed off the order. 'I would tell the people in the State Department not a goddamn thing,' he told Kissinger. 'They don't need to know.'[25]

The hare-brained plan would send the Cold War to its hottest point since the Cuban Missile Crisis. Mention the USS *Enterprise* in South Asia today and most people assume you are talking about the space ship from *Star Trek*. Far fewer people know, however, that Captain James T. Kirk's famous starship was based on a very real US aircraft carrier that almost brought nuclear war to South Asia.

The *Enterprise* had been built in 1961 as the world's first nuclear-powered aircraft carrier, and it was almost as long as the Empire State Building was tall. US president John F. Kennedy had dispatched the ship to blockade Cuba as part of the Cuban Missile Crisis and in 1970 it was sent back to America to be fitted with a brand-new set of state-of-the-art nuclear reactor cores. Now, in the wake of Nixon's decision, the *Enterprise* was deployed to the Bay of Bengal. The mission was simple: intimidate India into ending its naval blockade of East Pakistan.

The deployment triggered mixed responses. One Indian official called it 'a nuclear-studded armada including the most powerful ship in the world'. Another author has called the charade 'an atomic-powered bluff'. General Jacob thought there was no way America would risk getting embroiled in the war, while Vice Admiral N. Krishnan warned that if they did it could cause 'the end of the world' or mire the Americans in 'a Vietnam to end all Vietnams'. Indira Gandhi would later brush the incident off with a characteristic nonchalance:

> If the Americans had fired a shot … yes, the Third World War would have exploded. But in all honesty, not even the fear occurred to me.[26]

As the USS *Enterprise* set off towards the Bay of Bengal, news arrived that it was being tailed by a Soviet nuclear submarine. The Chinese leadership requested to meet Nixon and Kissinger, and both men knew that if China entered the war on Pakistan's side, the Soviet Union would be forced to come in on India's side. The record shows clearly that, in actual fact, China had no intention of doing so. Nonetheless, today Bangladesh is often treated as if it is peripheral to global affairs, but that December in 1971 it could have led to the end of the world.

'What do we do if the Soviets move against them? Start lobbing nuclear weapons in?' Nixon asked Kissinger.

'Well,' replied Kissinger, 'if the Soviets move against them in these conditions and succeed, that will be the final showdown.'[27]

Luckily for both South Asia and the world, however, Chinese premier Zhou Enlai thought that 'East Pakistan was already unable to be saved'.[28] China was at the height of the chaos of the Cultural Revolution, and it was not keen to get into another foreign conflict.

This meant that China never intervened, something that prevented the Great South Asian War turning into a global one.*

The approach of the USS *Enterprise* towards the Bay of Bengal made India's race to Dacca a race against time. Sam Manekshaw, the chief of the Indian Army, ordered that troops quickly take as many cities as they could so that if a ceasefire was forced through, India would have control over as many cities as possible. However, the soldiers on the ground ignored Manekshaw's orders and kept pushing towards Dacca.[29] An end to the war was in sight.

In Dacca, the morale of the Pakistani leadership was waning. On the morning of 13 December, the Indian Air Force bombed Government House and in the aftermath most of the government of East Pakistan resigned.

The following night a fleet of microbuses driven by members of the pro-Pakistan Al-Badr militia set off around Dacca, abducting pro-liberation artists, journalists, professors and doctors. The Bengali accountant Dilawar Hossain was picked up and blindfolded and had his hands tied. The captors, he recalled later, all seemed to speak Bengali, and at one point one of his fellow prisoners cried out, 'You are Bengalis and you are killing us!' That evening the prisoners were all marched to a field and their captors began to execute them with killing squads and bayonets. Hossain would have died too, but managed to untangle his loosely tied hands and made a run for it across the field. After a terrifying couple of minutes, he hid in the undergrowth by the banks of a nearby river. Dilawar Hossain is today recognised as the sole survivor of what would come to be known as the massacre of the intellectuals.[30]

Many Bangladeshis today believe these executions were a deliberate attempt to stunt the viability of an independent Bangladeshi nation. It

---

* It is questionable, of course, whether anyone in 1971 actually intended to let all hell loose. As the brilliant scholar of 1971, Gary Bass, wrote to me in an email: 'There was quite a scary moment on Dec 12 1971, yet in the end cooler heads prevailed. First, Mao's China was not about to move troops to threaten India, even if asked to do so by Kissinger; second, the Soviets were quite content with India's victory & not about to escalate ... There was some risk in Kissinger's request for Chinese troop movements, but China did no such thing. Nuclear deterrence is very strong and it held in this case. The Cuban missile crisis was quite a bit scarier, real risk of escalation all the way to nuclear war ... I think there was little danger from the Enterprise carrier group.'

remains disputed who gave the order, and Pakistan maintains the Al-Badr militia, and not the Pakistani Army, was behind the executions.[31] A page in the diary of Pakistani major-general Rao Farman Ali contains the names of many of those executed, suggesting that he may have been in some way involved.

It was to be the closing act in the bloody conflict. On 14 December Yahya Khan wrote to General Niazi, the commander of Dacca, telling him: 'You have now reached a stage where further resistance is no longer humanly possible nor will it serve any useful purpose ... You should now take all necessary measures to stop fighting.'[32] The very next day a message from Niazi was relayed through Washington to New Delhi, announcing his willingness to accept a ceasefire. That afternoon India's General Jacob flew a helicopter towards Dacca, carrying with him an instrument of surrender. He changed helicopters in Jessore, and was met at a Dacca helipad by the Pakistani chief of staff's car, which drove him to Eastern Command HQ. The Mukti Bahini had by this point entered the capital and were firing upon Pakistani troops in the streets. 'We had barely proceeded a few hundred yards,' writes Jacob, 'when a group of freedom fighters blocking the road fired at the car. I jumped out exclaiming "Indian army" ... They stopped firing but wanted to kill the Pakistani chief of staff. I reasoned with them, trying to persuade them to allow us to proceed.'[33]

Jacob arrived at Dacca Army Headquarters a short while later, and organised for a table and two chairs to be placed at the race course, so the instrument of surrender could be signed publicly. General Niazi was furious. 'Who said I am surrendering?' he cried out. 'You have only come to discuss a ceasefire and withdrawal as proposed by me!' Jacob threatened Niazi that unless he signed now the Indian Army would start bombing Dacca once more and would 'not take responsibility for the safety of their families and ethnic minorities'. Jacob himself later admitted his threat was an empty bluff. 'Niazi had 26,400 troops in Dacca, we had about 3,000 some 30 miles out,' he writes. 'I was in a quandary as what to do in the event of his refusing.' Over the next half an hour Jacob paced up and down the headquarters, anxiously puffing at his pipe. Then he walked back inside, and confidently grasping at the surrender document, told a tearful Niazi, 'I take it as accepted.'[34]

Jacob describes the next three hours, as he and Niazi waited for Indian troops to arrive, as feeling 'unreal'. Niazi invited him to join him for lunch, and on their way over to the mess he bumped into Gavin Young of the *Observer*, who subsequently found himself invited to the historic 'Surrender Lunch' of curried chicken legs and bananas.[35] 'The whole scene looked unreal to me,' wrote Jacob later, 'with mess silver on display and Pakistani officers lunching and chatting away as if it were a normal peace time function ... I stood at one corner with little desire to fraternize or eat.'[36]

After lunch Jacob had to get Niazi to the race course to sign the surrender. At 4 p.m. a truck rolled up at the airport, full of soldiers of the Kaderia Bahini, a pro-independence militia similar to the Mukti Bahini but answerable only to its leader Kader Siddiqui. Jacob worried they would kill Niazi. 'I had to ensure that Niazi lived to sign the Instrument of Surrender,' he writes. 'I politely asked Siddiqui to leave the airport ... [but] he did not respond. I repeated the request. He still did not respond. I then shouted to him to get his truckload of fighters off the airfield, and heaved a sigh of relief when they left.' India's heavy-handed attitude towards the Bangladeshi freedom fighters would eventually grow into a major political issue in years to come.[37]

Half an hour later Jagjit Singh Aurora, the commanding general of India's Eastern Command, arrived at Dacca's airfield and the generals of India and Pakistan set off together for the race course. Jacob later recalled the surrender ceremony:

> Niazi removed his epaulette, took out his revolver and handed it to Aurora; tears rolled down his cheeks. It was getting dark. The crowd at the Race Course began shouting and there were threats to lynch Niazi; anti-Pakistani slogans and abuses resounded. Then they moved towards Niazi. The senior officers present formed a cordon around him and whisked him off in one of our jeeps.[38]

The fifth and final Partition of the former Indian Empire had now taken place.

'What the defeated Pakistani Army leaves behind it is a legacy of bitterness and hatred,' reported BBC correspondent Alan Hart from Dacca that afternoon.

After all that's happened, it is natural I suppose for the people of Bangladesh to bay for blood. Their soil is soaked with it. But the lust for revenge is a bad foundation for nationhood ... In 1947, we the British carved up the subcontinent and created two separate states. Today, twenty-four years later, after a war that lasted only thirteen days, there are now three states.[39]

That same day the USS *Enterprise* at last entered the Bay of Bengal. But the war was already over. Bangladesh was now a fact, and with Pakistan halved in size, India became South Asia's only major power. Strangest of all, the remainder of Pakistan, a country once billed as a homeland for South Asia's Muslims, now had a smaller Muslim population than either India or Bangladesh.[40] 'Today we have sunk Jinnah's two-nation theory in the Bay of Bengal,' announced a triumphant Indira Gandhi.[41]

Yahya held power for four more days. But in the streets of what remained of Pakistan, 'crowds screamed for Yahya and his cronies to be put on trial as traitors. Infuriated by Yahya's drinking, mobs in Karachi burned liquor stores.'[42] Then, on 20 December, news rattled in over the radio that Yahya Khan had resigned and handed the remaining half of Pakistan to a civilian government with Zulfikar Ali Bhutto as president and the Bengali prime minister Nurul Amin as the truncated country's first vice-president.

For many of the people who had now officially become Bangladeshis, the Pakistani surrender on 16 December 1971 was a moment of joy. Massive pots of food were hastily arranged in celebration and Bangladeshi flags were hoisted across the country, often made from cut-up saris. Millions of people streamed across the border, mostly refugees, but many Indians too – eager to see what life was like on the other side of the Radcliffe Line. Mukti Bahini fighters were openly garlanded in streets, showered in petals and given sweets.[43] 'We went out and fired in the air in jubilation,' remembers one member of the Mukti Bahini. 'Then we went fishing with grenades. It must have been hard on the fish. All kinds of things floated up.'[44]

But Gavin Young, the reporter who had joined the Surrender Lunch, noted that this joy was not shared among the soldiers. 'That first morning of the ceasefire, when victors and vanquished met at last at Army headquarters in north Dacca, I saw the officers of both sides looking at one another bleakly but without rancour. There was no Indian jubilation, simply a drained sense of sad futility.' As a result, Young was left thinking about the impact of the subcontinent's many partitions. 'Officers who had been comrades at the same staff colleges, who wear the same North Africa or Burma Stars on their chests ... stood looking at one another wondering who to blame.' Young asked Indian Major-General Gandharv Nagra if he had met the surrendered Pakistani General Niazi yet. 'Oh, Yes,' Nagra responded. 'He said he was very happy to see me. We knew each other in college.'[45]

Bangladesh was not fully independent yet, though. Despite the Bangladeshi flags flying across the city, Niazi had surrendered to India, not to the Bangladeshi government-in-exile. The lieutenant-general who had forded the Meghna, Sagat Singh, was placed in charge of Bangladesh, and the country would remain under Indian military occupation for almost two weeks, as it hurriedly attempted to install a provisional government

With the old order swept away, it quickly became evident that there was a complete administrative void. Pockets of Pakistani troops still dotted the countryside, and in several places they declined to give up their arms. Within a day of the surrender, a group of Pakistani soldiers who refused to believe their army had surrendered took Mujibur Rahman's wife and children hostage. It was only after a tense hostage negotiation that Mujib's family was released and the rogue soldiers arrested.[46] Even more worrisome was the way that some Bengali civilians began 'hunting down and killing "collaborators"' of the Pakistani army.[47] Urdu-speaking Biharis were massacred in their thousands regardless of whether or not they were collaborators. 'We saw TV coverage of ... a guerrilla leader and his men bayoneting tied up prisoners,' recalls one man, which 'didn't exactly endear the locals towards the freedom fighters'.[48]

In the following days India set out to round up both the Pakistani Army and Indian rebels still scattered across Bangladesh. Pakistani soldiers were marched in single file towards the capital, and one witness to the great march noted an anxious 'young woman, very pretty and very pregnant ... [who] was walking with a Pakistani, her hand in his'.[49]

Meanwhile, Thenoselie Keyho, general of the Naga Army, was at the Dacca cantonment under the supervision of Indian intelligence when the Indian Army began arriving. 'There were quite a few of us Nagas [in Dacca],' he recalls, and he and his compatriots were forced to give themselves up to the Indian Army.[50] An Indian Ministry of External Affairs document records that: 'When Bangla Desh was liberated, a large number of Naga and Mizo hostiles along with some of their important leaders who were in Bangla Desh surrendered to the Indian Security Forces.'[51] Of the rebels being sponsored by Pakistan, only a handful of Mizos led by the firebrand Laldenga managed to escape into Burma.[52]

The experience of Mr Shamsuddoha, manager of the Central Bank of Pakistan's Dacca branch, is informative of the chaos of those first few days. Shamsuddoha had long sympathised with the Liberation movement, and indeed his house had been a hub for rebels throughout the year. Shortly before Pakistan's surrender, Pakistani troops had taken him to the bank and ordered he break open the main safe. 'The army wanted to burn all the bank notes to cripple the economy of Bangladesh,' explains his granddaughter. But the crafty Mr Shamsuddoha took them to a dummy safe filled with demonetised banknotes, essentially saving the fledgling country's cash reserves. News of his act quickly got around and a day after the surrender he was picked up again, this time by members of the Mukti Bahini. Knowing he had access to the bank vault, they wanted the money for themselves and so, once again, Mr Shamsuddoha had a gun pointed at his head and was made to open the vault. Unlike the Pakistani Army, however, the rebels knew about the dummy vault. This time he was forced to open the real one and the men stuffed their bags full of as much money as they could. According to Mr Shamsuddoha's family, several later became 'big names' in Dacca society.[53]

Indian troops and Mukti Bahini soldiers gradually managed to get the country under a semblance of control. Yet they increasingly found themselves coming into conflict with each other. Many Indian soldiers didn't give due respect to Bangladeshi commanders, sowing the seeds of future conflict. As the commander who had broadcast the Bangladeshi declaration of independence, future Bangladeshi president Zia-ur-Rahman would never forget the slight when he was told he could not sit on stage alongside an Indian major-general during a speech.[54] Years later his tenure as president would see relations with India, initially so warm, turn sour.

The Bangladeshi government-in-exile arrived in Dacca only on Christmas Day, and when it assumed control many of the Liberation Army soldiers regarded it as a 'do-nothing group living in luxury in Calcutta' while others had done the fighting.[55]

A few days later Bhutto released Mujib from prison and arranged for him to fly to London. He was then flown back to Dacca on an RAF plane, smoking Erinomore tobacco in his favourite pipe all the way home.[56] He arrived back to a rapturous crowd, who quickly broke through the security cordon protecting him. After being garlanded, he climbed into an open truck and was taken to the Ramna Race Course. Soon after he began to form a new government, and on 12 March 1972, almost three months after the Pakistani surrender, Indian troops finally started to leave Dacca.

Unlike the previous divisions in the subcontinent, the Partition of Pakistan came about through war and surrender, not through the paperwork of bureaucrats. The result, however, was much the same: a mass transfer of populations. The first to move were the ten million refugees living in India, and within just a few months over nine million made their way to the new nation of Bangladesh.[57] Sal returned a week after Mujib and recalls the atmosphere.

'When I landed in Dacca in mid-January the wreckage of destroyed fighter planes still lined the runway,' he remembers.

> The airport was functioning, but its systems were operating in a spirit of goodwill for all ... I went out of the airport in a daze and spotted my mother, beaming like a beautiful flower. I ran headlong into her arms ... It was strange but it took me several hours before I could adjust enough to feel sure that ... [she] would not disappear like a mirage.

It was a shock coming home and finding his house completely looted, the only remaining object being an old Quran. But for Sal's family, it was time for celebration. 'A major party took place,' he recalls, and everyone still alive 'dropped in, uncles and aunts, first cousins and distant cousins, special friends and neighbours'.[58]

There were other people clamouring to move too. Niazi's surrender saw the largest capture of PoWs since the Second World War, and the

Indian military now held some ninety-three thousand 'Pakistanis' – including more than thirteen thousand civilians – under arrest. In Pakistan, meanwhile, tens of thousands of Bengalis were fired from jobs, denied healthcare and even detained on random suspicions. Two hundred thousand Bengali civilians living in what remained of Pakistan thus called to be 'repatriated' to Bangladesh.

Most controversial of all was the fate of the seven hundred thousand non-Bengalis who had been in Bangladesh at the moment of surrender and were now collectively branded 'collaborators' and 'traitors' regardless of which side they had fought on during the war. The government of Bangladesh denied them citizenship and by mid-1972 most Biharis and West Pakistanis were confined to the squalor of refugee camps, awaiting 'repatriation' to Pakistan. Bhutto announced he had 'no interest' in receiving refugees who had never even been to West Pakistan. They might speak Urdu, he argued, but they were Bangladesh's problem rather than Pakistan's.[59]

Partly to try and resolve the deadlock, Indira Gandhi and Zulfikar Ali Bhutto met face to face in June 1972 in the old Raj summer capital of Simla. Mrs Gandhi was in a conciliatory mood, spending hours before Bhutto's arrival obsessing over the upholstery at his accommodation. Her biographer writes:

> When she arrived at Himachal Bhawan, where Bhutto would be staying, she found the arrangements were shoddy, the colours of the upholstery did not match, the furniture had been clumsily placed and the curtains ended a foot above the floor. So she took it upon herself to decorate and arrange Bhutto's living quarters ... A marathon session of rearrangement followed ... [and Mrs Gandhi] mentioned her desire to be an interior designer.[60]

Bhutto arrived in Simla accompanied by his daughter Benazir and several members of his entourage. Negotiations were fraught, but a subsequent agreement focused on the return of prisoners of war, the withdrawal of forces, and changing the Kashmir ceasefire line into the Line of Control. Mrs Gandhi probably could have insisted Pakistan recognise Jammu and Kashmir as an integral part of India during the conference, but she did not. 'My assessment is that she wanted to be generous to Pakistan at the hour of its greatest humiliation,' writes

B. Raman, the head of counterterrorism at India's foreign intelligence service, 'to strengthen the political leadership of Pakistan and enable it to stand up to the army.'[61]

Nonetheless, the Kashmir dispute was subsequently enshrined as a bilateral issue, removing UN oversight and bypassing any demands for Kashmiri independence. India also gave back more than thirteen thousand square kilometres of land, withdrawing to its pre-war borders in the west, with a few small exceptions like the Balti village of Turtuk. The citizens of these villages were suddenly forced to change nationalities overnight, often cutting them off from their loved ones. According to resident of Turtuk Mohammad Kacho Yagbo:

> In our Turtuk, I feel there is not a single household that doesn't have relatives in Pakistan. And this separation from relatives almost paralyzes you. For the first 2–3 years we weren't even allowed outside of Turtuk. After that we were associated with Ladakh, but ... their language, their living style, everything was very different ... Eventually, though, we did get adjusted. The Indian Army was really good to us. They took care of us, arranged for our food-groceries, ration etc.[62]

By the end of the year Pakistan's leadership still refused to recognise Bangladesh as an independent nation. Meanwhile, families were torn between the hostile nations. When the UN sat down to discuss Bangladesh's application for membership, Pakistan sent an envoy to oppose this: the Buddhist king from Eastern Bangladesh who had given up his throne for Pakistan. Scared of the rise of Bengali nationalism, the Chakma Raja Tridiv Roy had sided with Pakistan during the Liberation War and afterwards Tridiv had been forced to move to Islamabad.[63] He started working on potential tourism opportunities for Pakistan to explore – perhaps Swat should open up some tourist resorts – and partying at Karachi's Playboy Club, 'a nightclub minus the bunnies, where you could drink, dance and occasionally see a floor show'.[64]

On 6 August 1972, Tridiv Roy learned from his private secretary that President Bhutto had called him several times the previous evening and wanted him to represent Pakistan at the UN General Assembly in New York. He eagerly accepted. But as Pakistan sent Tridiv Roy to oppose Bangladesh's entry into the United Nations, Bangladesh's nascent government responded by sending in his mother. He writes how on the anniversary of his father's death,

> Mother came to my hotel. She looked more tired and harassed since I had seen her about a year ago, but her voice was the same and her spirit was unbroken. My uncle came with her as her escort. They brought letters from the family ... Sheikh Mujib and Foreign Minister Samad had sent my mother and asked her to get me back.[65]

Tridiv refused, incensed by the new Bangladeshi government's demand that all ethnic minorities 'become Bengali'. He writes:

> I knew I could not return, not in these circumstances, not in a manner that smacks of betrayal ... Once I was under Mujib's authority, I would be forced to serve his government and his policies, and these went directly against my people's just demand for autonomy.[66]

Tridiv Roy remained a Pakistani national and represented the country at the UN days later. He would never return to his home, or indeed Bangladesh. His son Devashish was twelve years old when his father disappeared from his life, and remembers a feeling of great abandonment. 'I was absolutely lost as to what was happening,' remembers Devashish. 'I myself had been caught up in Bangladeshi nationalism ... then suddenly my father was gone.'[67]

For many of the people now changing their nationalities, it was their second or third nationality change in as many decades. For Mohammad Zaul Hassan it was his fourth.

He had been born in Delhi four years before Partition, the son of a Bihari driver, and in 1947 his family had migrated to Pakistan after their street was attacked in a riot. Pakistan, however, had failed to live up to their expectations. Struggling with a refugee crisis, its amenities had seemed very rudimentary, and in 1948 the family had set off back to Bihar in India, where their ancestors had initially come from. Communal animosity towards Muslims had yet to die down, however, and a year later another round of riots forced them to migrate again,

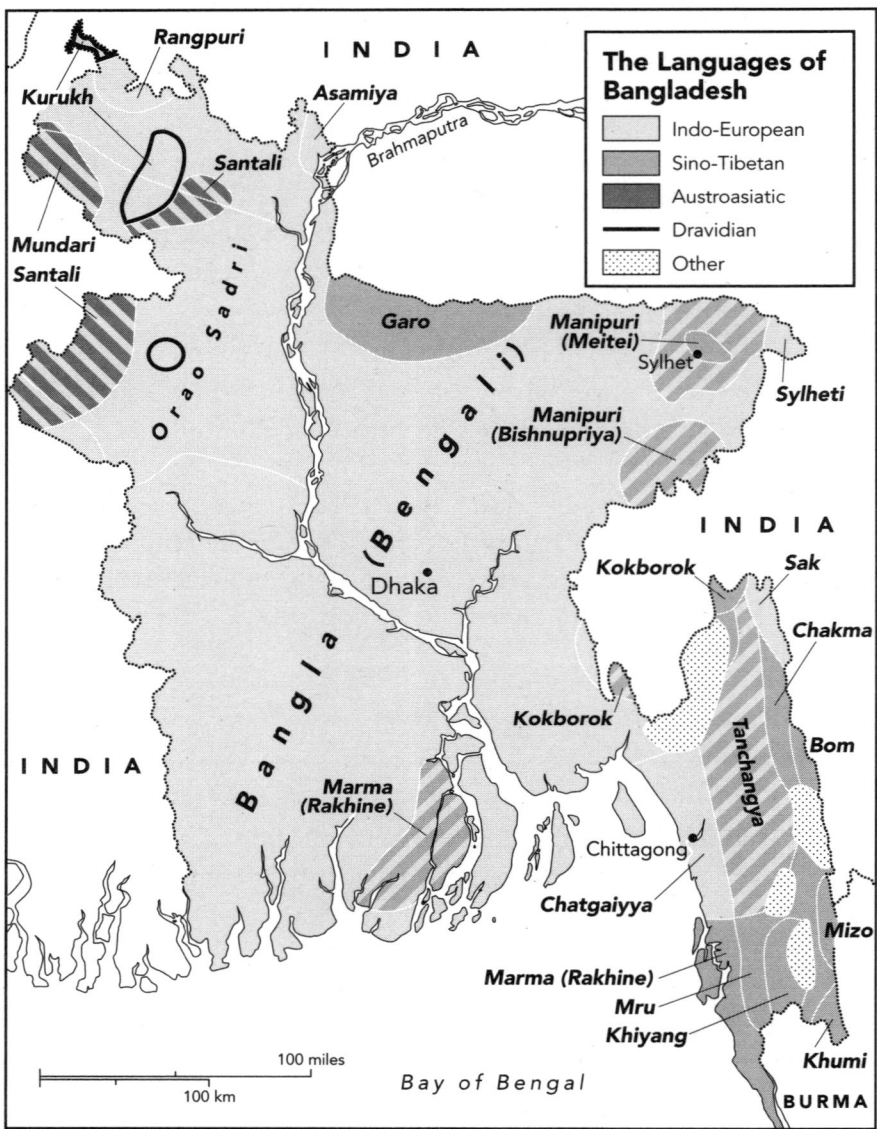

this time to Dacca. Hassan thus grew up in East Pakistan, and here his brother eventually made enough money to put him through Dacca University. 'We were all Pakistanis,' he recalls. 'There wasn't any difference between Bengalis and Biharis, but it fermented very fast. My flatmate was a Bengali called Fazlul Kareem and we were very close. He told me I was very naïve. Things were very dangerous. But I didn't believe him. I didn't believe it would be that fast.'[68]

Shortly before the events of 1971, Hassan had left Dacca to do a master's in urban planning in Turkey. He had thus been forced to watch helplessly via the television as the turmoil gripped the country. Soon his family stopped replying to letters, and it was only weeks later that a friend back in Dacca informed him in a letter that his family had fled to the West. His accountant brother had managed to buy plane tickets and flew to Karachi with one suitcase each. 'I cried so much in Ankara,' Hassan recalls. 'I lost a country and a family. Not knowing what was happening was the worst. It was emotional of course. My family had uprooted itself in 1947 ... Now it was happening again.'[69]

After his master's was finished in 1972, Hassan joined his family in Karachi. But he would never be able to persuade himself the city was home and would spend the remainder of his life working in different countries across the Middle East. Finally, years later, he managed to find work in Britain where for the first time he was able to settle down properly. Today his daughter is a consultant, his son an endocrinologist, and he himself runs an elderly singing group consisting of Indian, Pakistani and Bangladeshi Alzheimer patients called Singing for the Brain. 'It's difficult to answer where I am from,' he laughs.

> I was born in India, grew up in Bangladesh, became a citizen of Pakistan, now I'm British. But I'm grateful that time has given me this perspective ... The one thing that makes me sad is that I can't go back to India. It is quite hurtful actually. I tried but didn't get the visa.[70]

In 1973, two whole years after the Pakistani surrender, the ninety-three thousand West Pakistanis – including more than thirteen thousand civilians – remained in Indian detention.[71] India did not want to keep these camps open indefinitely, but refused to release them until Bangladesh approved their release. Bangladesh, however, refused to do so until Pakistan recognised Bangladeshi independence and allowed certain officers to be placed on trial for war crimes. Prisoners whiled away the time playing cards, chess and ludo, and some tried to call out the double standards of the Indian Army in looking down on them while not hesitating to crush its own separatist movements. 'They asked what would India do if any of her states wanted to secede,' writes Indian Colonel S. P. Salunke. 'Would it be allowed to happen? What action had been taken against the Nagas and Mizos who wanted to declare themselves independent?'[72]

As the months turned into years, life in the PoW camps turned more desperate. Several prisoners carried out daring prison breaks, and Colonel Salunke notes that a 'spree of tunnelling seemed to spread like wildfire'. Some of these escape attempts worked, but most didn't and soon some of the prisoners began to go mad. In the male-only camps, notes Salunke, 'the main cause of serious quarrels was homosexual activities'. In more mixed camps, there were other controversies. In one, 'an educated internee's daughter fell in love with one of the sentries ... and eventually they both decided to marry'.[73]

Some of the more intriguing interactions at the PoW camps revolved around families divided in 1947. One day a group of Sikhs approached the guards and tried to get one of the prisoners released. 'During partition the family of the PoW had helped them to come out of Pakistan safely,' writes Salunke. 'In return they wanted to reciprocate the goodwill by obtaining the release of the PoW ... They were disappointed when they were told their mission was futile.' Another Sikh gentleman contacted the camp authorities and demanded to meet his interned cousins. It turned out his aunt had been kidnapped in 1947, forcibly converted to Islam and had become Pakistani. Her son had eventually wound up as one of the PoWs kept at the camp and the Sikh gentleman had come to meet his estranged cousin from across the border.[74]

The mass internment of Pakistani PoWs continued for almost two years until, on 28 August 1973, the New Delhi Agreement was signed by India and Pakistan – setting into motion the largest repatriation in human history. The agreement provided for the repatriation of all Bengalis in Pakistan to Bangladesh, and all the PoWs in India to Pakistan, other than 195 wanted for war crimes. West Pakistanis in Bangladesh would also be repatriated. It was the culmination of the last Partition of the former Indian Empire.[75]

A subsequent appraisal reads:

> On a sunny day in Karachi, several hundred people waited for three buses at the Karachi International Airport that would take them to a gleaming Boeing 707 waiting on the tarmac. Before boarding, they were inspected by International Red Cross officials wearing red and white armbands ... Flight DI 055 from Pakistan

to Bangladesh, carrying 214 Bengalis ... [was just] one of many flights, chartered by the United Nations High Commission for Refugees, criss-crossing its way across the subcontinent between 1973 and 1974, moving huge swathes of humanity in the largest planned, simultaneous, and controlled mass migration in history. Bengalis from Pakistan to Bangladesh, non-Bengalis from Bangladesh to Pakistan ... and, by train, nearly 90,000 Pakistani PoWs from India to the Wagah border were all part of this human exchange.[76]

Of all the great migrations and population exchanges the subcontinent had seen over the last four decades, this was the most orderly. No one was killed along the way, and the trains criss-crossing the subcontinent travelled without issue. Bhutto eventually announced Pakistan's recognition of Bangladesh on 22 February 1974, and released civilians 'received a welcoming shower of marigold petals from Pakistani officers' as they crossed the border into Pakistan.[77] Many people noticed, however, that such marigold petals were not reserved for the surrendered soldiers. The very last PoW to be repatriated, on 30 April that year, was Lt-General Niazi. 'He looked demoralized and tired as he stepped over the whitewash line dividing the two neighbouring nations,' noted Salunke, and 'there was no live television coverage. Only official photographers were allowed to take pictures and a limited number of people lined the route.'[78]

There remained a major sticking point between the three new governments, however: the Biharis, many of whom had never been to West Pakistan. Bhutto saw no reason why he should be responsible for them even though Bangladesh now regarded them as traitors. The Biharis of Bangladesh would thus be transformed into one of the largest stateless populations in the world, a situation that prevailed until 2008 when many were at last granted Bangladeshi citizenship.

The dispute revealed a bitter truth: Pakistan was no longer a homeland for South Asian Muslims. Indeed, the Pakistan that emerged after the fifth partition of the former Indian Empire proved a very different country to the one created by Jinnah. Ethnic identity would become increasingly important in Pakistan, and the refugee 'Muhajir' families who moved to Pakistan in 1947 were increasingly sidelined.

★ ★ ★

As the last great migration came to an end in 1974, there was an opportunity for a new start in the subcontinent. India, Pakistan and Bangladesh were now all run by democratically elected populist leaders. But the wave of democratic populism that spread over the subcontinent would be remarkably short-lived. The first to go was Mujib.

Mujib's job was always going to be an uphill task. In the first three months of 1972, a rehabilitation centre aided by the World Health Organization in Dacca reported 170,000 aborted pregnancies caused by rape, and the births of 30,000 'war babies'. Meanwhile, armed militias still roamed the countryside. His first job was to try and make the several hundred thousand armed civilians give up their weapons. Bangladesh was a traumatised and broken nation.

In the months after coming to power, Mujib launched a major rehabilitation effort for refugees and declared women who had been raped to be war heroines, or 'Birongonas'. Yet under his rule, Bangladesh also saw major industrial and economic decline. Mujib struggled to govern and in the face of growing opposition, he showed an increasingly dictatorial face. There were reports of widespread corruption among his party, and within months of his arrival a communist insurgency broke out in the country. Mujib's government responded by forming the Jatiya Rakkhi Bahini, a paramilitary group filled with freedom fighters from the war, and they were soon being accused of large-scale human rights abuses and sending out death squads.

By 1974, the same year that the great migrations of the fifth Partition drew to a close, Mujib's government's mismanagement led to another Bengal famine. It was the third and final major post-colonial famine to break out in the Bengal delta and its surroundings, and in the following year, 'One and a half million people are thought to have died of starvation and hunger-related illnesses ... a demographic catastrophe no less shocking than the war itself.'[79] Just as the wartime Bengal famine of 1943 had destroyed all remaining support for British rule in Bengal, and the smaller 1954 Khulna famine had eviscerated support for Pakistan in the region, so would the 1974 Bengal famine destroy the reputation of Mujib and the Awami League. A group of officers in the new Bangladeshi Army began to plot, and on 15 August 1975, exactly twenty-eight years after the end of British rule, they assassinated Mujib and his family.

A chaotic power struggle ensued, and within two years General Zia-ur-Rahman, the very man who had once declared Bangladeshi independence in Mujib's name, assumed office. Zia changed Bangladesh's constitution from a secular republic to an Islamic one and with Mujib gone, its relationship with India fell apart. Bangladesh fell into the same cycle of authoritarianism that it had fought to escape. Moreover the new nation proved no kinder to its minorities than its predecessor and the new constitution did not recognise ethnic groups other than Bengalis. As a result, in 1977, the 'Shanti Bahini' or 'Peace Force', an armed Buddhist insurgent group made up of mostly Chakmas, launched its own armed independence struggle.

Back in India, Indira Gandhi's new popularity in India would also not last.

She became 'very arrogant' after the war, recalled her secretary years later, and 'she loved being called Durga. The Bangladesh victory was a turning point.'[80] With her newfound popularity, in March 1972 Mrs Gandhi announced new elections for thirteen of India's states. She won in all thirteen.

With her massive majority, she turned to reshape India in her image. Her first target was India's troubled Northeast. Mrs Gandhi swiftly enacted the North-Eastern Areas (Reorganisation) Act, dividing it into a map that remains today, with regions called Meghalaya, Mizoram, Nagaland Tripura, Arunachal Pradesh and Assam. Border stones were swiftly established between Indian and Burmese Nagaland and 'Naga affairs were transferred from Foreign to the Home Ministry'.[81] After the loss of Naga bases and the arrest of major leaders in Dacca, the Naga underground splintered, and several leading rebels surrendered to the Indian government. Four years later an agreement would be signed in Shillong between the government of India and representatives of the Naga federal government – including Phizo's brother Kevi Yallay – who 'accepted the Constitution of India of their own volition'.[82] The remaining Naga leadership retreated across the border to Burma, where the rump was taken over by a new generation of Marxists and Phizo's remaining hold on the movement vanished.

Phizo's dream of resisting the partition of erstwhile British India and uniting the Naga peoples on both sides had died. The author Bertil

Lintner met Phizo sometime after and described him as 'a very tragic figure'.

> There was some interest in the Naga cause when he arrived in the UK, but by then he was forgotten ... We actually had some trouble finding his house, and had to ask some neighbours who said, 'yes, there's an Asian-looking man living down the street. Not sure who he is, though.'[83]

In 1990 Phizo passed away in London. The Indian government permitted his funeral in Kohima and he was received as a hero, but his dream for Naga unity and the repudiation of the partition of his people were more distant a reality than ever before.

If 1971 marked the end of any chance that India and Pakistan, or indeed India and Bangladesh, would ever reunite, it also marked the hardening of the Indian border with Burma. Peace would therefore not arrive in the Northeast for several more decades. The Mizos continued their struggle. Meanwhile, the same anti-immigration lobbyists who had opposed the arrival of Bengali refugees from East Pakistan began calling for all-out war against the state as ever more Bengali refugees sought refuge in India's Northeast. The term 'infiltrators', first used by parliamentarians in Tripura to identify Bengali immigrants, would gain currency across the region.[84] In 1985 the 'Assam Accords' were signed to stop Bangladeshi migration to Assam State and prevent it from 'turning into another Tripura'. To do so, a National Register of Citizens was established in the state. In 2019 Indian home minister Amit Shah announced that the National Register of Citizens would be extended to the entire country.* Attached to the register was a controversial new Citizenship Amendment Act, which made it easier for non-Muslims to enter India, while encouraging the deportation of Muslim immigrants from post-1971. As protests broke out across the country, the European Parliament warned that the legislation is 'set to create the largest statelessness crisis in the world'.[85]

★ ★ ★

---

* While Shah made this announcement in 2019, the NRC has not yet been implemented nationwide at the time of writing.

If Mrs Gandhi used her newfound popularity to reshape Northeast India, she also took the opportunity to demolish the ruins of the old princely order.

India's princely aristocracy were increasingly emerging as a major political powerhouse in Indian democracy. Indeed, by 1971, almost a third of privy purse-endowed princes were in politics, armed with a vendetta against the Congress Party and an election rate of 80 per cent. They had proved crucial to cementing India's opposition and were a force to be reckoned with at the ballot box.[86] Mrs Gandhi had been trying to remove their privileges from the day she came to power, but her bill had failed to pass thanks to opposition in the Upper House of Parliament and an untimely intervention by the Supreme Court. She had also faced political pressure from Lord Mountbatten, who tried to impress on her that forging the Indian Union had only been possible because the princes had given up their kingdoms. 'I honestly cannot give any further advice as I am quite and utterly powerless,' he wrote. 'The whole thing is shaming, inexcusable and disgraceful.'[87]

In the wake of the 1971 victory, however, she now had the power to bend Indian politics to her will. That winter Mrs Gandhi wielded 'her parliamentary sword' and 'deftly and definitively consigned the princely order to the history books'.[88] The last of the promises given by Sardar Patel and V. P. Menon to the princes was ripped up, as the entirety of princely India had their status derecognised. Henceforth the princes would be normal Indian civilians. Pakistan would follow suit a few months later when Zulfikar Ali Bhutto passed a similar order removing princes' 'rights' to their privy purses, although tentatively continuing to provide them for the time being.[89]

The changes of fortune that accompanied this revolution were nothing short of extraordinary. Since the fall of the Ottoman Caliphate decades earlier, the Nizam of Hyderabad had been arguably the world's foremost Muslim ruler and his capital the most prominent city of Muslim learning outside Arabia. Now, within a few short decades of the princely revolution, the Nizam's heir was forced to sack his army of fourteen thousand servants and flee to the Australian outback where he became a sheep farmer. His son, the heir to both Hyderabad and the Ottoman thrones, became a cameraman for *Indiana Jones and the Last Crusade*.[90]

As the fallen aristocracy tried to raise money for their elections, they started selling off the vast art collections built up over centuries, resulting in an extraordinary, unparalleled exodus of Indian art overseas. Although it is difficult to quantify, it is likely more Indian art left India between the 1950s and 1970s than during the whole of colonial rule. Few maharajas knew the true value of their masterpieces, and on one occasion a single Frenchwoman – Ariane Dandois – managed to buy the Maharaja of Bikaner's entire marble furniture collection for a meagre twenty-five thousand dollars.[91] Bill Archer's collection of miniature paintings, which today forms much of the V&A's Indian collection, was likewise collected from maharajas eager to sell off their antiquities in order to sustain their lifestyles after the end of colonialism.

The scattering of Hyderabad's art is representative of what happened in many of the five hundred-odd kingdoms that were abolished. With Hyderabad State gone, the last Nizam's son, Mukarram Jah, left his collections with a lot of dodgy custodians and much of the art in the great Chowmahalla and Falaknuma palaces subsequently vanished under mysterious circumstances. Other Hyderabadi artwork moved with the Hyderabadi diaspora to the Gulf and to Pakistan, and much of the Qatari Al-Thani collection originated in princely India. It was only in 1972 – a whole year after the princely order was consigned to the history books – that India ultimately banned the export of antiques from the country.[92]

Not all princely art went abroad of course. An art schoolteacher called Jagdish Mittal also began buying sacks of paintings at this time and despite his meagre salary, he gradually acquired one of the great miniature painting collections in the world, simply by having a keen eye. Miniatures were considered almost worthless at the time, with British ideas of their inferiority to western art still in vogue even in India. Mittal was thus able to build up what is now regarded as one of India's greatest private collections of miniatures, and the former schoolteacher eventually established his own private museum.[93]

Years later Jacqueline Kennedy described her visit to Hyderabad, where she witnessed the last breaths of a now vanished world.

We had an evening with the old noblemen of the old Nizam's court, men with long white hands transparent like alabaster ... There were three ancient classical musicians playing in the moonlight and they, the noblemen, were speaking of how all that was disappearing, that the youth didn't appreciate the ways of the old culture, the great chefs were being taken by the Emirates – etc. This over civilized, rarified world – you could feel it – but you knew it was too rarified to survive – you felt so fortunate to be able to sense for those hours what it had been ... That evening was profoundly sad. My son John told me the next day that the sons of the house had taken him to their rooms, because they couldn't stand the classical music – and had offered him a tall glass filled with whisky and had put a pornographic cassette in the Betamax and the Rolling Stones on the tape deck. They wore tight Italian pants and open shirts, and all the while, their fathers ... were speaking of how sad they made them.[94]

By 1975, as Bangladesh fell into military rule, democracy waned in India too. Surrounding herself with sycophants, Indira Gandhi had started to marginalise her brilliant adviser Haksar in favour of her son Sanjay. 'There are those who can't cope with success,' recalls Mrs Gandhi's foreign policy and environmental adviser Moni Malhoutra. 'The mass adulation, the sweeping victory – coping with that kind of success was a problem and resulted in hubris. Her success became overwhelming and she went off the rails a bit. The darker side of her character began to surface.'[95] In 1975 Allahabad High Court indicted her for alleged electoral malpractice. Days later, on 26 June that year, people across the world learned that Indira Gandhi had suspended the world's largest democracy and imposed 'Emergency' rule.

'In the name of democracy,' she announced on All-India Radio, 'it has been sought to negate the very functioning of democracy.' In the course of the next year and a half, 110,000 Indians would be imprisoned, including a fifth of opposition MPs, and another eleven million Indians were sterilised. Fourteen per cent of Delhi's population would be displaced in beautification drives. For a strange twelve months, Pakistan was the only democracy in the former Indian Empire.[96]

Then, in 1977, Indira Gandhi abruptly ended her 'Emergency' and announced new elections. That spring the Congress Party was finally voted out of power and replaced by a loose coalition of Hindu nationalists and disillusioned Congressmen known as the Janata Party. When this party split, the nationalist faction formed the Bharatiya Janata Party, or BJP, which would tower over Indian politics for decades to come. Intriguingly, one of its most important early funders was the billionaire Bombay-based businessman Nusli Wadia, the only grandson of Muhammad Ali Jinnah. The Jinnah dynasty would not only help create the Islamic Republic of Pakistan, but also help lay the foundations for the rise of the BJP in India as well.[97]

The loss of Bangladesh should have been a moment of self-reflection for what remained of Pakistan. Six days after coming to power, Bhutto had ordered chief justice Hamoodur Rahman to stage a judicial inquiry into what had gone wrong in East Pakistan. But like the Sunderlal Report after India's annexation of Hyderabad, the Hamoodur Rahman report was so damning towards the country's military that its revelations were suppressed. Indeed, the report only came into the public eye in 2000, after being published in an Indian magazine.

Rather than learning from its heavy-handed actions, Pakistan's military would only grow more fearful of the country's Balkanisation at the hands of India. After all, in 1971 India's foreign minister 'had secretly told his diplomats about other ways to crack up West Pakistan itself, by stirring up rebellion in restive areas such as Baluchistan and the North-West Frontier Province – hoping to get these places to follow Bangladesh's lead'.[98]

The nuclearisation of India and Pakistan's proxy war was another direct result of 1971. On 20 January 1972, just a month after Niazi's surrender, Bhutto 'called a historic meeting of the country's senior nuclear scientists in Multan to solicit their views on the possibility of building a bomb'.[99] At the very same time India was accelerating its own nuclear programme.[100] The first South Asian nuclear bomb was detonated by India in May 1974, with Pakistan following in May 1998.

Moreover, Pakistan would become even less forgiving to its separatist movements. In 1973 Bhutto once again dispatched the country's military against its own population, this time in Baluchistan. Then, in 1977, a few months after the end of Mrs Gandhi's dictatorship, Zulfikar Ali Bhutto was overthrown in a military coup by General Zia-ul-Haq, who would begin Islamising the country like never before. 'The long struggle for democracy was overcome by a long night of suppression across India, Pakistan and Bangladesh.'[101]

India and Pakistan's proxy war continues to this day, with ever more dangerous consequences for the world. Pakistan would increase its own sponsorship of Indian separatists. After 1971 these included the Kashmiri separatists in the course of the 1990s, as well as the Khalistani movement for a Sikh homeland. Recently declassified Intelligence reveals that during November 1971, shortly before the Great South Asian War erupted, the Pakistani government made contact with the former finance minister of Indian East Punjab Dr Jagjit Singh Chauhan who started to speak on Pakistan Radio about setting up a Liberation Army for 'Khalistan', a proposed Sikh homeland. At the time the Indian ambassador in Islamabad considered it 'a desperate bid to develop a parallel in India to the Bangla Desh situation' within Indian territory.[102] Chauhan's contact with Pakistan would prove a turning point in the demand for Khalistan, which would grow into one of India's most fraught separatist movements and culminate in Mrs Gandhi's storming of the Golden Temple in 1984 and her subsequent assassination by her own Sikh bodyguards shortly afterwards.

Perhaps most catastrophically for the world, the Pakistani Army began to sponsor the Taliban and Lashkar-e-Taiba in order to undermine Indian influence in the region. When Osama bin Laden was finally killed by US Navy SEALs in 2011, it was in Abbottabad, in the heart of the Pakistani military establishment. The psychological ruptures and suspicions of multiple partitions continue to undermine any peaceful solution to the Kashmir conflict, which is today one of the most militarised regions and dangerous nuclear flashpoints on the planet.

In the wake of 1971, it was no longer possible to make the journey that Gandhi had made four decades earlier, in 1931. The links that tied together a quarter of the world's population had been shattered. Aden was an Arab city, Dacca a Bengali city, while Rangoon was a Burmese one. Karachi and Lahore were now Muslim cities, while Hyderabad, Delhi and Agra had become Hindu cities, their erstwhile status as Muslim capitals forgotten.

The Chakma Raja Tridiv Roy would not be alone in pondering 'the value and significance of labels like 'citizenship' and 'nationality', and the concept of the nation. He writes in his autobiography:

Someone who is Bangladeshi today was a Pakistani before December 1971, and before August 1947 he or she was an Indian citizen. A man and his place of birth may undergo transformations of their nationality and citizenship without his being consulted, international borders being changed any number of times.

He is just a bit of flotsam in the whirlwind of politics.[103]

EPILOGUE

Over just forty years, between 1931 and 1971, Five Partitions divided the Indian Empire into twelve separate nation states. Today these lines have become so embedded in our subconscious that it is easy to forget there were other possibilities for a post-colonial South Asia.

Several prominent nationalist figures including Indian prime minister Nehru and Burma's founding father Aung San had once spoken of an 'Asiatic federation' in the 'not very, very distant future', a 'United Nations of South Asia' encompassing India, Pakistan, Ceylon and Burma.[1] Long after the British departed, many still hoped the new borders might prove temporary. But Five Partitions tore that hope apart, and Asia's new states were born resentful of one another and suspicious of their minorities.

In every single one of these countries, governments have made sure to paper over the shared cross-border heritage of their peoples. After all, if the insurgencies of the post-colonial decades signified anything, it was that anyone with cross-border sympathies should be treated as suspect in the eyes of the state. Yet bizarrely, virtually none of these new hegemonic national identities existed before the 1930s. 'The next time you are told about the timeless unity of the Indian nation,' writes scholar Partha Chatterji, 'ask yourself why Nagaland is a part of India, but not Myanmar, why Sikkim is a part of India but not Nepal or Bhutan ... [Then] you will begin to distinguish between the truths and lies of nationalism.'[2]

In Burma the hundred years of being a part of India are today treated as an anomaly, a break in over a thousand years of Burmese nationhood. It's not that its shared history doesn't feature in the national imagination, but rather that the national narrative privileges the idea of a 'natural' border with India having always been waiting to come into existence. Burma is poorer for it. In the 1930s more people sought the Burmese Dream than the American one, and Rangoon rivalled New York in its sophisticated and cosmopolitan crowd. Partition shattered that world. 'By the 1970s,' writes Thant Myint-U, 'Burma had become a much simpler place, without luxury, stripped of its once cosmopolitan crown, without landlords and fat cats – only farmers, soldiers, marauding bands, and the decaying buildings of empire, perhaps like Britain under the early Anglo-Saxons.'[3]

In India and Pakistan meanwhile, 'Partition' is usually synonymous with the division of the Punjab and nothing else. Growing up in New Delhi, as I did, Pakistan always loomed large in the imagination. Virtually everyone I went to school with had some sort of family heritage from 'that side' of the border. Yet the fact that it had even affected India's Northeast, let alone that this region was among the places most affected by it, was sidelined.

In Bangladesh the 'Liberation War' is now venerated as the foundational moment in its history. Mujib's daughter Sheikh Hasina was the prime minister of Bangladesh for twenty years between 1991 and 2024, and Zia's wife Khaleda Zia was prime minister for most of the time that she wasn't. Much of their politics revolves around varying understandings of their families' role in the Liberation War, yet the region's earlier partitions from India and Burma have been virtually erased from public memory. When Anglo-Bengali historian Joya Chatterji visited Bangladesh in the 1980s, she was shocked by the historical amnesia.

> A young boy, aged about fifteen, sold me a cold drink. We got chatting in Bangla, and ... He asked me where I was from. India, I said. Then how come you speak Bangla, he asked mystified. I said that I was a Bengali, from West Bengal in India. He shook his head in wonder. He did not know that there had been a partition of Bengal in 1947. He did not know that there had been a partition at all in 1947. As a scholar researching that partition, I was dumbstruck.[4]

Of all the national narratives produced in the wake of the Indian Empire's demise, it is the surviving princely states that have proved most successful in eradicating the memory of their relationship with the Indian Empire. From Bahrain to Bhutan, the relationship with Britain is highlighted, while the fact that they were governed as part of the Indian Empire is omitted in textbooks. The myth of an ancient sovereignty is crucial to keeping the monarchies alive. Yet on an individual level, memories of the old ways persist, particularly of the unimaginable class reversal that the Gulf has seen. In 2009 Gulf scholar Paul Rich recorded an elderly Qatari gentleman who

> still got angry when he related to me the beating he received when as a young boy of seven or eight he stole an orange, a fruit which he had never seen before, from an Indian employee of the British agent. The Indians, he said, were a privileged caste during his youth, and it gave him immense pleasure that the tables had turned and they now came to the Gulf as servants.[5]

Perhaps the country for whom the historical amnesia about the Indian Empire is most accentuated is Britain itself. Between 1931 and 1971, Britain went from being the largest Muslim power in the world to having a tiny Muslim minority.[6] Today most Brits seem convinced that immigration is a relatively new phenomenon that started with the HMT *Empire Windrush* docking outside London in 1948. But of course, Bengal was annexed by the British East India Company in 1757, just fifty years after the Act of Union with Scotland and nearly fifty years *before* the Act of Union with Ireland. The region of modern Bangladesh was once crucial to the very formation of Great Britain.

It is perhaps inevitable that I am not detached from the conflicts that appear within the pages of this book. My own grandfather witnessed the Great Partition and in forty years of my family living in Delhi he always refused to visit us on account of what he saw in 1947. Many of the friends I grew up with in Delhi, or friends I later made living in Lahore, have similar family stories.

For most of my life, however, Partition seemed peripheral to the present – something that happened in the past. It was only when I started to research it myself that I realised that Partition is not over.

Questions about citizenship and belonging, about who is an 'outsider' still plague much of the region today. No truth and reconciliation mission has ever tried to address any of the deep-seated traumas of the fifth of the world's population whose lives are daily informed by these great tragedies.

One of the great ironies is that in the twenty-first century it is easier for Indians, Pakistanis and Bangladeshis to meet in England, their former colonial power, than to meet in the subcontinent itself. My own journey with Partition began in 2017, the seventieth anniversary of the British departure, over a conversation with friends in Oxford.

Two of my friends, one Indian and one Pakistani, were chatting about their grandparents' journeys in 1947 and how their grandparents longed to see their ancestral homes across the border again. Seventy-five years after their birth, India and Pakistan still have no tourist agreement, and the millions of people displaced in the largest forced migrations in history are unable to go home. And so we came up with an idea: to use virtual reality to allow the elder generation to return home. We excitedly made a small Instagram post to share our plans with friends and families, not knowing how many people would reach out in the coming weeks, volunteering their own family stories – of lost lovers and childhood friends, temples and mosques, and school playgrounds left behind three-quarters of a century before. The result was Project Dastaan, which reconnected Partition survivors with their ancestral villages through virtual reality.

We would interview Partition survivors in one country and then send out a team in the other to track down their ancestral homes, communities, mosques, mandirs and gurudwaras. As a Scot raised in Delhi, I was able to be the go-between for the countries. We managed to do this for about thirty people.

Speak to those who lived through these great ruptures and they paint a complex picture of loss, not only of a home, but language, deep friendships, divided families, land. A whole generation still feel strong ties to the place they left. After seventy-five years there is still no shared understanding of the profound collective loss for them and subsequent generations in the Indian subcontinent and diaspora. Many families we interviewed were shocked to realise that 'the other side' experienced exactly the same as their own families.

EPILOGUE

My co-founder Sparsh had wanted to save his grandfather's story for a time when he managed to cross into Pakistan himself. Sparsh had an Australian passport and so it was easier for him to get a Pakistani visa than his grandfather. In 2021 he was granted one, and together we set out to find whatever remained of his ancestral village of Bela.

Sparsh's grandfather Ishar – whose story appeared in Chapter 5 – didn't have any photos from the time, but before we set off from India, Sparsh's grandfather taught him how to tie a turban in the Bela style. The fashion turned out to be very out of date, like arriving in central London today dressed in a top hat and carrying a walking stick and hoping to blend in.

On the day we set out together, initially it was a beautiful big flat road completely tarmacked, but gradually it grew more bumpy. The Punjabi plains turned into hills. Eventually we arrived in a small valley with mud huts and cows roaming around old fruit trees. It was bright green with a big blue river flowing in between. We tracked down the village headman, a short man sporting a blue shalwar kameez and a large bushy moustache, and explained that seventy-five years earlier a man called Sher Khan had saved Sparsh's grandfather's life. Might any surviving relatives still live in the village?

The man went quiet, before whispering, 'You are talking about my father.'

Sher Khan's son tearily invited us inside, offered us a cup of tea and began to narrate his own version of the very story that had brought Sparsh and me to Pakistan, of how his father Sher Khan had saved a Hindu family from a mob during the chaos of 1947. Afterwards Sher Khan's family took Sparsh by the hands, and led us through the village of Bela. We walked through fields of chickens and partridges, until we reached a small courtyard surrounded by mudbrick walls. Sher Khan's son revealed that this had been where Sparsh's family had lived seventy-five years ago.

Sparsh fell to the ground in tears and kissed the earth beneath his feet. He rose only after what seemed like an eternity, and hugged Sher Khan's family, all of whom were also in tears. He grasped a handful of pebbles from the ground and slipped them in his pocket, to turn into jewellery for his family. 'It was just the weight of that moment,' he later told our friend Kavita. 'I felt like I had finally made it there. It's not something I ever expected would be possible in my lifetime, given the way these countries are.'[7]

Today the divides across South Asia grow ever wider. Politicians still stoke the embers for their own ends with the now nuclear-armed nations of India and Pakistan continuing to teeter on the brink of all-out war. In Burma the military maintains its assault on the Rohingya minority and at the time of writing the Indian government was planning to fence the Indo-Burmese border, one of the last unfenced borders in the region. The last decade has witnessed the decline of globalisation, the strengthening of borders and the resurgence of nationalism across the world. India's Partitions are a dire warning for what such a future might hold.

Appendix
Princely States

From 1865, a book called the *Alqabnamah* functioned as the standard list of princely states subordinate to the Indian Empire. It contained information on how each prince should be addressed and how many gun salutes they should be given. The first page of the 1935 edition, seen overleaf, opens alphabetically with Abu Dhabi and also features Bhutan, Bahrain and Ajman. The Aga Khan also appears, but as a prince without any land. Nepal is listed later in the book, but as an 'Independent State', while Bhutan and the Arabian States are titled 'Protectorates' of the Viceroy – a title that is also extended to Chitral, Hunza and Nagar in modern-day Pakistan.

INDEX.

A

	Pages
Abu Dhabi	16
Aga Khan	110
Ajaigarh	22
Ajman	16
Akalkot	42
Al Hauta (Lahej)	12
Alipura	22
Al Qara	12
Ali Rajpur	22
Alwar	74
Aroot	112
Athgarh	46
Athmallik	46
Aundh	42

B

	Pages
Baghal	102
Baghat	102
Bahawalpur	62
Bahrain (Euler)	14
Balasinor	52
Balsan	102
Bamra	46
Banganapalle	58
Banka Pahari	22
Bansda	52
Banswara	74
Baoni	22
Baramba	46
Baraundha	24
Baria	52
Baroda	52
Barwani	24
Bashahr	102
Bastar	46
Baud	46
Baria	52
Baroda	52
Barwani	24
Bashahr	102
Bastar	46
Baud	46
Bija	102
Benares	98
Beri	24
Bhaisaunda	24
Bhajji	102
Bharatpur	76
Bhavnagar	94
Bhopal	24
Bhor	42
Bhutan	8
Bihat	26
Bijawar	26
Bijna	26
Bikaner	76
Bilaspur	62
Bombay, Aga Khan	110
Bonai	46
Bundi	78

C

	Pages
Cambay	52
Chamba	62
Changbhakar	46
Charkhari	26
Chhatarpur	26
Chhota Udepur (Mohan)	52
Chhuikhadan	46
Chitral	8
Cochin	58
Cooch Behar	100
Cutch	94

D

	Pages
Danta	78
Darkoti	102
Daspalla	46
Datia	28
Dewas (Senior)	28
Dewas (Junior)	28
Dhala	12
Dhami	102
Dhar	28
Dharampur	52
Dhenkanal	46
Dholpur	78
Dhrangadhra	94
Dhrol	94
Dhurwai	28
Dibai	12
Dujana	102
Dungarpur	80

F

	Pages
Fadhli (Shuqra)	12
Faridkot	64

F

	Pages
Fadhli (Shuqra)	12
Faridkot	64

G

	Pages
Gangpur	46
Garauli	28
Garhwal (see Tehri)	100
Gaurihar	28
Gondal	94
Gwalior	54

H

	Pages
Hindol	46
Hindur (Nalagarh)	104

NOTES

Archives
Colonial Office Records at the National Archives, Kew (CO)
Foreign Office Records at the National Archives, Kew (FO)
Dominion Office Records at the National Archives, Kew (DO)
War Office Records at National Archives, Kew (WO)
India Office Records at the British Library, London (IOR)
Hopetoun House Archives (HHA)
Imperial War Museum Archives (IWM)
Mountbatten Papers, Southampton University (MP)
Middle East Centre Archive, St Antony's College, Oxford (MECA)
National Archives of India, New Delhi (NAI)
Junagadh Archives, Junagadh (JA)
Qatar Digital Library, Online (QDA)
Arabian Gulf Digital Archive, Online (AGDA)
1947 Partition Archive, Online (1947PA)
Digital South Asia Library, Online
British Newspaper Archive, Online
Gandhi Heritage Portal, Online
The Anglo-Burmese Library, Online
Project Dastaan Digital Archive, Online
Andrew Whitehead Digital Archive, Online
Adnan Noon Private Collection
Avtar Singh Hoonjan Private Collection
Sultan Al Qu'aiti Private Collection
Pablo Bartholomew Private Collection
Brigid Keenan Private Collection

Introduction
1. Saddiki, S., *World of Walls: The Structure, Roles and Effectiveness of Separation Barriers* (Cambridge: Open Book Publishers, 2017) p51
2. Marshall, T., *Divided: Why We're Living in an Age of Walls* (London: Elliot & Thompson, 2018) Chapter 5; Saddiki, S., 'Fencing the Desert: Contexts and Politics of the Gulf Border Walls', *Journal of Borderlands Studies*. 2023
3. Everyone in British India was entitled to an Indian passport – including in Aden and British Burma – and the rupee was used across the territory. Things were a bit more complicated in the patchwork of princely states, where people were treated as 'British Protected Persons' rather than 'British Subjects'. The British accepted certain state passports and other certificates of identity, such as those issued from Bahrain or Muscat, but these would only be valid when stamped by a Government of India Political Agent. See QDL IOR/L/PS/12/1461 'Aden Protectorate Boundaries: Inclusion of the Hadhramaut': pp69–76; IOR/R/20/A/3397: *National Status of Natives of the Hadhramaut*; Onley, J., *The Arabian Frontier of the British Raj: Merchants, Rulers, and the British* (Oxford: Oxford University Press, 2007); Blythe, R., *The Empire of the Raj: India, Eastern Africa and the Middle East, 1858–1947* (Basingstoke: Palgrave Macmillan UK, 2003)
4. *Civil & Military Gazette* (Lahore), 4 January 1928
5. *Weekly Dispatch* (London), 1 January 1928
6. *Civil & Military Gazette* (Lahore), 4 January 1928; *Taunton Courier and Western Advertiser*, 4 January 1928; *Western Daily Press*, 2 January 1928
7. *Civil & Military Gazette* (Lahore), 4 January 1928

8. The modern Republic of India has an area of approximately 3,287,000 km². By contrast, the Raj was closer to 4,900,000 km². See Onley, J., 'The Raj Reconsidered: British India's Informal Empire and Spheres of Influence in Asia and Africa', *Asian Affairs*, 40:1, p54
9. QDL IOR/L/PS/20/C91/1 'Gazetteer of the Persian Gulf'. Lorimer's *Gazetteer of Arabia* used the same 32-miles-to-the-inch scale as the *Imperial Gazetteer of India*, so that the Arabian map could be 'fitted alongside the map of India, thus giving, at a glance, a map of that portion of the world between Burma and Egypt'. Yet while the *Gazetteers of India* were publicly available, the Arabian ones were top secret and only made available a decade after Indian independence. See Lowe, D. A., 'Colonial Knowledge: Lorimer's Gazetteer of the Persian Gulf, Oman and Central Arabia' in Qatar Digital Library (https://www.qdl.qa/en/colonial-knowledge-lorimer's-gazetteer-persian-gulf-oman-and-central-arabia)
10. Onley, *The Arabian Frontier of the British Raj* pp24–6
11. The Indian Civil and Political Services had a larger presence in the Persian Gulf than in today's Arunachal Pradesh, Nagaland and Mizoram. See Onley, 'The Raj Reconsidered: British India's Informal Empire and Spheres of Influence in Asia and Africa', p54
12. Rich, P., *Creating the Arabian Gulf: The British Raj and the Invasions of the Gulf* (Lexington Books: Plymouth, 2009) p84
13. There were various legal distinctions between different types of suzerainty that the Viceroy exercised over states. Some states were labelled 'protectorates' and some were labelled 'protected states'. Some states such as Nepal and the Sultanate of Muscat and Oman never signed an exclusivity agreement and also had treaties confirming their legal independence. Nonetheless, they were completely dependent on India and indirectly ruled by the Viceroy through a 'residency' in precisely the same way as the other states. James Onley has shown that there was virtually no practical difference between the two on the ground. The very title 'Sultan' was actually given to the Sultans of Oman by the government of India and they were subsequently schooled at Mayo College in Rajasthan, along with the other Maharajas, and even appeared at the Delhi Durbars. Oman adopted the rupee and, when threatened, it was the Indian Army that would come to the Sultanate's protection. Contrary to popular perception, the Viceroy's indirect rule over states like Kashmir or Jaipur was more or less identical to the rule exerted over states like Oman and Dubai, and the terms 'princely state' and 'native state' were frequently applied to both. See Onley, *The Arabian Frontier of the British Raj*
14. Copland, I., *The Princes of India in the Endgame of Empire 1917–1947* (Cambridge University Press: 1997) p8
15. Pillai, M. S., *The Ivory Throne* (HarperCollins India, 2015) p461
16. https://www.theguardian.com/travel/2008/jun/28/india
17. Das, S., *India, Empire, and First World War Culture: Writings, Images and Songs* (Cambridge, Cambridge University Press, 2018) p11; https://www.india1914.com/Price_of_war.aspx#:~:text=India's%20Financial%20Contribution,to%20around%20%C2%A314%20billion
18. *Taunton Courier and Western Advertiser*, 4 January 1928
19. Kozicki, R., *India and Burma 1937–1957: A Study in International Relations* (PhD Thesis, University of Pennsylvania, 1959) p90
20. This term comes from Yasmin Khan's eponymous book, and here I will be using it more specifically for the 1947 Partition of British India
21. Dalrymple, W., 'The Great Divide: The Violent Legacy of Indian Partition', *New Yorker*, 22 June 2015, newyorker.com/magazine/2015/06/29/the-great-divide-books-dalrymple
22. Myint-U, T., *Where China Meets India: Burma and the New Crossroads of Asia* (New York: Farrar, Straus and Giroux, 2018) p246

Chapter 1: The Great Uprising

1. Bodleian, Ms. Eng. D. 3254: John Simon to his father, 5 March 1915, and Simon to his mother, 20 January 1928, Additional Papers of John Allsebrook Simon, 1st Viscount Simon 1915–34
2. Bodleian, Ms. Eng. C. 4792 fols 1–25: Attlee to his brother John, 28 January

1928, Letters of Clement Attlee, 1st Earl Attlee (1883–1967) to his brother Tom
3. Bodleian, Ms. Eng. D. 3254: Simon to his mother, 20 January 1928
4. Ibid. 24 January 1928
5. Waugh, E., *Remote People* (London: Penguin Books, 2019) pp153–76. Waugh's interlocutors only protested the Bank of India's policy of giving Indians larger advances than Arabs, and do not specifically suggest a transfer. Indeed there is dispute over just *how many* Adeni Arabs cared about Indian rule. As scholar Itamar Toussia Cohen wrote to me in an email: 'In my reading on the sources, I do not get the sense that the Adeni Arabs were particularly bothered about Indian rule. [Bernard] Reilly certainly pushes this agenda, but … the record simply does not back up his claims. As late as 1931, the Arabs are described as being either indifferent to – or vaguely in favour of a transfer, while the Arab commercial elite are depicted as toiling under some sort of Indian-induced false consciousness – i.e., being anti-separationists.'
6. Cadogan, E., *The India We Saw* (London: John Murray, 1933) p19
7. Bew, J., *Citizen Clem: A Biography of Attlee* (London: Riverrun, 2017) pp141–2
8. Cadogan, *The India We Saw* p8
9. Ibid. p21
10. Ibid. p23
11. Attlee, C. R., *As It Happened* (London: William Heineman Ltd, 1954) p64
12. Cadogan, *The India We Saw* pp23–6
13. Ibid. p14
14. Von Tunzelmann, A., *Indian Summer: The Secret History of the End of an Empire* (London: Simon & Schuster, 2007) p91
15. Hoodbhoy, P., *Pakistan: Origins, Identity and Future* (New York: Routledge, 2023) p153
16. This section on Jinnah is deeply indebted to Sheela Reddy's masterpiece *Mr and Mrs Jinnah*, by far the best work on Jinnah as a young man. Reddy, S., *Mr and Mrs Jinnah: The Marriage That Shook India* (Gurgaon: Viking Penguin Random House, 2017) p1
17. Jalal, A., *The Sole Spokesman: Jinnah, the Muslim League and the Demand for Pakistan* (Cambridge: Cambridge University Press, 1994) p9
18. Hajari, N., *Midnight's Furies: The Deadly Legacy of India's Partition* (Stroud: Amberley Publishing, 2015) p9
19. Reddy, *Mr and Mrs Jinnah* p17
20. Ibid. p137
21. Ibid. pp120–5
22. Ibid. p99
23. Ibid. p131
24. Ibid. pp121, 142
25. Wolpert, S., *Jinnah of Pakistan* (Oxford: Oxford University Press, 1984) p74
26. Lelyveld, J., *Great Soul: Mahatma Gandhi and His Struggle with India* (New York: Knopf, 2011) p147
27. Singh, J., *Jinnah: India – Partition – Independence* (New Delhi: Rupa Publications, 2009) p79
28. Von Tunzelmann, *Indian Summer* p91
29. Reddy, *Mr and Mrs Jinnah* p318
30. Ibid. pp247, 285
31. Ibid. p324
32. Ibid. p326
33. Singh, *Jinnah* p168
34. Reddy, *Mr and Mrs Jinnah* p331
35. Cadogan, *The India We Saw* p32
36. Amrith, S., *Crossing the Bay of Bengal: The Furies of Nature and the Fortunes of Migrants* (Harvard: Harvard University Press, 2013) pp160–4; and Khan, Y., *The Great Partition: The Making of India and Pakistan* (London: Yale University Press, 2007) pp14–17; Brendon, P., *The Decline and Fall of the British Empire: 1781–1997* (London: Jonathan Cape, 2007) p385
37. Bodleian, Ms. Eng. D. 3254: John Simon to his mother, 31 October 1928
38. Ibid. 14 November 1928
39. Collis, M., *Trials in Burma* (London: Faber and Faber, 1945) p55
40. Bodleian, Ms. Eng. C. 4792 fols 1–25: Clement Attlee to Tom Attlee, 4 February 1929
41. Lunt, J., *A Hell of a Licking* (Collins, 1986) p23, quoted in Keane, F., *Road of Bones: The Epic Siege of Kohima 1944* (London: HarperCollins, 2011) p1
42. Amrith, *Crossing the Bay of Bengal* p148
43. Myint-U, T., *The River of Lost Footsteps: A Personal History of Burma* (London: Faber and Faber, 2008) p194
44. Bhaumik, P., *Burma in Bangla Literature (1886–1948): Representations, Appropriations and Fictionalization of Burmese Cultures in Bangla Literary Discourses* (Doctor of Philosophy: Jadavpur University, Kolkata, 2016) pp19, 201
45. Bhattacharya, S., 'A Close View of Encounter between British Burma and British Bengal', unpublished paper

presented at 18th European Conference on Modern South Asian Studies, Lund, Sweden, 6–9 July 2004 p1. The history of Indian imperialism within the British Empire is a fascinating and neglected topic. The best book on the subject is Blythe, *The Empire of the Raj: India, Eastern Africa and the Middle East, 1858–1947*. Also see Mccleery, A., 'Creation and Collapse: The British Indian Empire In Mesopotamia Before and After World War I' (Undergraduate Honors Thesis: University of Colorado Boulder, 2018) pp28–35. For the young Gandhi as an Indian imperialist see Metcalf, T. R., *Imperial Connections: India in the Indian Ocean Arena, 1860–1920* (Berkeley: University of California Press, 2007). Matthew Bowser argues that these same Indian elites acted in a 'co-colonial' manner in Burma, successfully alienating the province. See Bowser, M. J. 'Partners in Empire? Co-colonialism and the Rise of Anti-Indian Nationalism in Burma, 1930–1938', *Journal of Imperial and Commonwealth History*. 2021. 49(1): 118–47

46. For Ottama, I draw heavily from the spectacular work of Sana Aiyar, especially Aiyar, S., 'Revolutionaries, Maulvis, Swamis, and Monks: Burma's Khilafat Moment' in Bose, S., and Jalal, A. (eds), *Oceanic Islam: Muslim Universalism and European Imperialism* (London: Bloomsbury, 2020); Moscotti, A. D., *British Policy in Burma, 1917–1937* (Political Science PhD Thesis, Yale University, 1950) p29

47. Guyot-Réchard, B. 'Tangled Lands: Burma and India's Unfinished Separation, 1937–1948', *Journal of Asian Studies*. 2020, 4

48. Bodleian, Ms. Eng. C. 4792 fols 1–25: Clement Attlee to Tom Attlee, 4 February 1929

49. Collis, *Trials in Burma* p58

50. Attlee, *As It Happened* p65

51. 'Burma and India: The Separation Demand', *Scotsman*, 7 August 1929, p10. For details on the controversy, see Proceedings of the Burma Legislative Council, 18 February 1929, quoted in British Library: *All About the Separation of Burma: A Symposium* (Rangoon: Major & Co., 1930)

52. For Gandhi's trip to Burma, primary sources include Desai, M. and Pyralal., 'With Gandhiji in Burma' in Gandhi, M. K. (ed.), *Young India*. 28 March 1929. 11(13): 97–103 and Gandhi, M. K., *The Collected Works of Mahatma Gandhi (1927–9)* (New Delhi: Publications Division, Ministry of Information and Broadcasting, Govt of India, 1970) pp122–5. For a unique Burmese perspective of the trip, see Edwards, P., 'Gandhiji in Burma, and Burma in Gandhiji' in Ganguly, D., and Docker, J., *Rethinking Gandhi and Nonviolent Relationality: Global Perspectives* (London: Routledge, 2007). This work includes translations of an account of Gandhi's visit by the Burmese author Baragu. Good secondary accounts can be found in Mitra, K., 'Relations during the Late Colonial Period: Role of Mahatma Gandhi' in *Proceedings of the Indian History Congress*. 2015, 76: 637–47; Shekhar, R., *Myanmar's Nationalist Movement (1906–1948) and India* (New Delhi: South Asian Publishers, 2006); Tendulkar, D. G., *Mahatma: Life of Mohandas Karamchand Gandhi* (Bombay: Vithalbhai K. Javeri, 1951) pp465–6

53. Brendon, *The Decline and Fall of the British Empire* p228

54. Metcalf, T. R., *Imperial Connections: India in the Indian Ocean Arena, 1860–1920* (Berkeley: University of California Press, 2007)

55. French, P., *Liberty or Death: India's Journey to Independence and Division* (London: Flamingo, 1998) Chapter 2

56. Guha, R. *Gandhi: The Years that Changed the World, 1914–1948* (London: Allen Lane, 2018) pxi

57. Guha, R., *Rebels Against the Raj: Western Fighters for India's Freedom* (London: William Collins, 2022)

58. Desai, M. and Pyralal., 'With Gandhiji in Burma' in Gandhi (ed.), *Young India* 97–103

59. Baragu, *Mahatma Gandhi and Burma* (Rangoon), quoted in Edwards, 'Gandhiji in Burma, and Burma in Gandhiji' pp164–9

60. Desai and Pyralal., 'With Gandhiji in Burma' 97–103

61. Gandhi, M. K. 'Burma and Ceylon' in Gandhi (ed.), *Young India*. 10 March 1927. (11)13: 97–103

62. See Gandhi, M. K., *The Collected Works of Mahatma Gandhi XXXIV (June–September 1927)* (New Delhi: Publications Division, Ministry of Information and Broadcasting, Govt of India, 1970) pp185–6, and Gandhi,

M. K., *The Collected Works of Mahatma Gandhi XXXVI (February–June 1928)* (New Delhi: Publications Division, Ministry of Information and Broadcasting, Govt of India, 1970) p173

63. See Gandhi, *The Collected Works of Mahatma Gandhi XXXIV (June–September 1927)* pp185–6, and Gandhi, *The Collected Works of Mahatma Gandhi XXXVI (February–June 1928)* p173
64. *Civil & Military Gazette*, 9 March 1929
65. Shekhar, *Myanmar's Nationalist Movement (1906–1948) and India* p123
66. Gandhi, *The Collected Works of Mahatma Gandhi XXXX (February–May 1929)* (New Delhi: Publications Division, Ministry of Information and Broadcasting, Govt of India, 1970) pp122–5
67. Tendulkar, *Mahatma* pp465–6
68. Gandhi, *The Collected Works of Mahatma Gandhi XXXX (February–May 1929)* p183
69. Lelyveld, *Great Soul* p200
70. Wolpert, *Jinnah of Pakistan* p100
71. Reddy, *Mr and Mrs Jinnah* p355
72. Ibid. p358
73. Ibid. p350
74. Ibid. p367
75. Hajari, *Midnight's Furies* p29
76. QDL IOR/L/PS/12/1485 'Aden. Administration and control: changes consequent on Indian constitutional reforms; transfer to HMG' pp730–2. Interestingly, around half of India's salt was provided by salt manufacturers in Aden at this point. Aden exported 275,000 tons annually
77. Gandhi, M., *Selected Political Writings. Edited, with Introduction by Dennis Dalton* (Cambridge: Hackett Publishing Company Inc., 1996) p72
78. Hardiman, D., *Gandhi in His Time and Ours: The Global Legacy of His Ideas* (New York: Columbia University Press, 2003) p113
79. In Rangoon, the salt protest was experienced through the trial of 'Gandhi's lieutenant' Jatindra Mohan Sengupta, who had been on his way to join the Mahatma when he was arrested for sedition. There is 'no Hindu-Muslim quarrel,' he had proclaimed a street away from the British Secretariat, and 'no Indo-Burman disunion. The Indians and Burmans are faced with only one problem ... and that problem has been created by the British.' When he was subsequently arrested, he announced to the press, 'I am to be the first casualty in Gandhi's campaign.' For more see Collis, *Trials in Burma*; Khan, W., 'Deshpriya Jatindra Mohan & Nellie Sengupta', *Daily Star*, 1 February 2021; Chappell, P., 'How a Small Society of Indian Cambridge Students Helped Destroy the British Raj', *Varsity*, 16 September 2018. Thanks to Waqar Khan for organising an interview with Nellie's descendants, notably Jai Sengupta; private interview: Jai Sengupta, Zoom, English, September 2021; see also Bowser, M. J., *Misdirected Rage: The Fascist Response to Co-Colonialism and Capitalism in Burma and the Origins of Burmese Islamophobia, 1929–1942* (History PhD: Northeastern University, Boston, Massachusetts, 2020)
80. The armaments man of the group had been Nirmal Chandra Sen, a member of the Rangoon Jugantar Party, whose ties with both the Bengal and Burmese undergrounds allowed him to smuggle arms through Upper Burma to Chittagong. See Mukherjee, S., 'The Bengali Revolutionaries in Burma, 1923–1933', *Proceedings of the Indian History Congress*. 2000–1, 61(2): 1108, and NAI/Home Political/1931/F-13-24 'Legislation Department Proceedings Regarding the Burma Criminal Law Amendment Ordinance 1931 (Ordinance No 1 of 1931)' p35
81. Ghosh, D., *Gentlemanly Terrorists: Political Violence and the Colonial State in India, 1919–1947* (Critical Perspectives on Empire) (Cambridge: Cambridge University Press, 2017); Chatterjee, M., *Do & Die: The Chittagong Uprising 1930–34* (New Delhi: Picador, 2010); Bhattacharya, 'A Close View of Encounter between British Burma and British Bengal'
82. Singer, N. F., *Old Rangoon: City of the Shwedagon* (Stirling: Paul Strachan-Kiscadale, 1995) p194
83. Turnell, S. and Vicary, A., 'Parching the Land: The Chettiars in Burma', *Australian Economic History Review*. 2008, 48(1): 1
84. Edwards, 'Gandhiji in Burma, and Burma in Gandhiji' p172
85. Singer, *Old Rangoon* p198
86. Collis, *Trials in Burma* pp159–60
87. Simon Commission Report on India (Indian Statutory Commission) Volume 2 (Delhi, Swati Publications, 1988) p16

88. NAI/Home Political/1931/F-50-I 'Publication of a Report by the Burma Govt on the Burma Rebellion' p7
89. NAI/Home Political/1931/F-13-24 'Legislation Department Proceedings Regarding the Burma Criminal Law Amendment Ordinance 1931 (Ordinance No 1 of 1931)' p82
90. NAI/Home Political/1931/F 5-33 'Rebellions Out-Break in Certain Villages Close to Tharrawaddy in Burma' p115; Kwarteng, *Ghosts of Empire* p191
91. Foucar, E. C. V., *I Lived in Burma* (London: D. Dobson, 1956) p71
92. Kwarteng, *Ghosts of Empire* p191
93. NAI/Home Political/1931/F-50-I 'Publication of a Report by the Burma Govt on the Burma Rebellion' p8
94. Although never proven, Ottama and some Bengali revolutionaries from Chittagong were also accused of instigating the rebellion. Ottama had never wholeheartedly approved of Gandhi's non-violent tactics for ending British rule, and had once been recorded telling a Japanese journalist that 'though a priest, he would not mind killing an Englishman'. Secret files considered him 'the most dangerous and irreconcilable enemy of British rule in Burma'. Ottama had remained close to the Indian National Congress and a few months after Gandhi's visit to Rangoon he represented the Congress at Sun Yat-sen's funeral in Nanking. Upon his return to Burma, he was approached by members of the Congress Party to 'help to embarrass the Government and so prevent separation from Burma'. Ottama agreed to tour the districts of Shwebo, Moulmein and Tharrawaddy with them, and the rebellion began in precisely these districts shortly after. As far as the governor of Burma was concerned, Ottama was the inspiration for the rebellion. A warrant was placed for his arrest and his passport cancelled. Soon after, he was detained in Calcutta where he would remain in exile for five years. See NAI/Home Political/NA/1932/NA/F-30-103/32 'Question in the Leg Assembly by Rai Bahadur Sukhraj Rai Regarding the Refusal of a Passport to the Ottama'; NAI/Home Political/NA/1931/NA/F-31-5/K.W 'Detention of U Oktama Under Bengal Regulation lii of 1818 and Cancellation of his Passport', pp43, 51, 52, 67–9; NAI/Home Political/1931/F-13-24 'Legislation Department Proceedings Regarding the Burma Criminal Law Amendment Ordinance 1931 (Ordinance No 1 of 1931)' p11
95. Myasein Taungyo Pagoda. Today the nearest town is Phar Shwe Kyaw village, twenty minutes outside Tharrawaddy
96. See Collis, *Trials in Burma* Chapter 7. See also Kwarteng, K., *Ghosts of Empire* (London: Bloomsbury, 2011) pp191–3, and Solomon, R. L., 'Saya San and the Burmese Rebellion'. Collis' account is based on information gathered at Saya San's trial. It demonstrates how imperial officials understood events to have occurred, but its accuracy in describing Saya San's coronation itself may be dubious, as persuasively argued by Maitrii Aung-Thwin in *The Return of the Galon King: History, Law, and Rebellion in Colonial Burma* (Athens: Ohio University Press, 2010)
97. NAI/Home Political/1931/F-50-I 'Publication of a Report by the Burma Govt on the Burma Rebellion' p8
98. *New York Times*, 28 December 1930; *The Times*, 6 January 1931
99. *Daily Herald*, 29 December 1931
100. The Saya San rebellion was closely linked with the Naga rebellions of Jadonang and Rani Gaidinliu. For more, see Haksar, N., and Hongray, S. M., *Kuknalim: Naga Armed Resistance – Testimonies of Leaders, Pastors, Healers and Soldiers* (New Delhi: Speaking Tiger, 2019) pp17–19; Aung-Thwin, *The Return of the Galon King*; Ghosh, P., *Brave Men of the Hills: Resistance and Rebellion in Burma 1825–1932* (London: Hurst & Company, 2000); Saha, J. 'Communal Geographies and Peasant Insurgencies in Colonial Myanmar', *South Asia: Journal of South Asian Studies*. 2024; Saha, J. 'Is It In India? Colonial Burma as a "Problem in South Asian History"', *South Asian History and Culture*. 2015, 7(1): 23–9
101. Amrith, *Crossing the Bay of Bengal* p185
102. Cady, J. F., *A History of Modern Burma* (Ithaca: Cornell University Press, 1958) pp312–13
103. NAI/Home Political/1931/F-177/31 'Exposure at Prome of the Heads of 15 Rebels in an Engagement with the Govt Forces'; for the best discussion on this incident see Saha, J., 'Racial Capitalism

and Peasant Insurgency in Colonial Myanmar', *History Workshop Journal*. 2022, 94: 42–60
104. Ba U., *My Burma: The Autobiography of a President* (Kindle Edition: Eschenburg Press, 2017) pp108, 162
105. Bowser, *Misdirected Rage* p147
106. Burma Round Table Conference, *Proceedings* (London: His Majesty's Stationery Office, 1932) pp80, 94
107. Emanuel Sarkisyanz quoted in Shekhar, *Myanmar's Nationalist Movement (1906–1948) and India* p138
108. NAI/Home Political/1931/F-22-142/31KW 'Attacks by Burmans on Indians'. The army also had many Karen and Kachin troops, contributing to the alienation of those communities from the Burman majority
109. Gandhi, M. K., *The Collected Works of Mahatma Gandhi XXXXVII (June–September 1931)* (New Delhi: Publications Division, Ministry of Information and Broadcasting, Govt of India, 1970) p28
110. NAI/Home Political/1931/F-22-142/31KW 'Attacks by Burmans on Indians'; Bowser, *Misdirected Rage* p96
111. Saha, 'Racial Capitalism and Peasant Insurgency in Colonial Myanmar' 42–60

Chapter 2: The First Partitions of India
1. Grant Irving, R., *Indian Summer: Lutyens, Baker and Imperial Delhi* (London: Yale University Press, 1984) p341
2. NAI II/149/2, 1931 President Secretariat, 'Inauguration of New Delhi – February 1931. Sound Films of the Ceremonies' p4
3. NAI 1/VIII, 1931, President Secretariat, 'Garden Party at Delhi on 10th February, 1931 during the inauguration week'; NAI II/149/2, 1931, President Secretariat, 'Inauguration of New Delhi – February 1931. Sound Films of the Ceremonies'; *Civil & Military Gazette* (Lahore), 10 February 1931; Grant Irving, *Indian Summer* Chapter 10
4. Brendon, *The Decline and Fall of the British Empire* pp246–7
5. Letter from Byron to his mother, 30 December 1929, in Butler, L. (ed.), *Robert Byron: Letters Home* (London: John Murray, 1991) p151
6. Grant Irving, *Indian Summer* p90
7. Huxley, A., *Jesting Pilate: The Diary of a Journey* (London: Paladin Books, 1985) pp104–6

8. *Stones of Empire*, Channel 4 documentary. Part 6
9. Quoted in Grant Irving, *Indian Summer* p351
10. Grant Irving, *Indian Summer* p350
11. Singh, S. P., 'Indian Nationalism and Burma', *Proceedings of the Indian History Congress*. 1998, 59: 895–6; Government of India, Indian Round Table Conference, 12th November, 1930–19th January 1931: Proceedings
12. *Western Mail*, 19 January 1931
13. Gopal, S., *The Viceroyalty of Lord Irwin 1926–1931* (Oxford: Clarendon Press, 1957)
14. Ibid. p353
15. Ibid.
16. During WW1 it was briefly suggested that the Arab states be made into a separate colony. The idea was shot down by a coalition of Bombay merchants – Parsis, Shias, Hindus and Jains – who feared the division of their home and ancestral lands, but Pandora's box had been opened. The reaction of the liberal Indian politician Tej Bahadur Sapru was typical: 'I am myself very strongly opposed to our losing Aden,' he announced, and 'am not much a believer in any guarantees given by the Colonial Office in regard to the status and treatment of Indians'. See Blythe, *The Empire of the Raj* p184
17. Sarojini Naidu to Padmaja and Leilamani Naidu, 6 September 1931 in ed. Paranjape, M., *Sarojini Naidu: Selected Letters 1890s to 1940s* (Delhi: Kali for Women, 1996)
18. For Gandhi's trip to Aden, see Gandhi, *The Collected Works of Mahatma Gandhi XXXXVII (June–September 1931)* pp388–92; Lokman, M. A., *Men, Matters and Memories: Compilation and Introduction by Professor Ahmed Ali Al-Hamdani* (Aden: No Publisher, 2009) pp118–19, and 'Mahatma Gandhi's Historic Sojourn in Aden', *The Free Library*. 2011 Al Bawaba (Middle East) Ltd. 24 Sep 2022
19. Gavin, R. J., *Aden under British Rule, 1839–1967* (London: Hurst, 1975) p425; Reese, S. S., *Imperial Muslims: Islam, Community and Authority in the Indian Ocean, 1839–1937* (Edinburgh: Edinburgh University Press, 2018) p37; Nagi, S., 'The Genesis of the Call for Yemeni Unity' in Pridham, B. R. (ed.), *Contemporary Yemen: Politics and Historical Background* (London: Croom Helm and Centre for Arab-Gulf Studies, University of Exeter, 1984)

20. QDL IOR/L/PS/12/1444 'Administrative policy: arrangements for achievement of Imperial purposes at Aden; transfer of administration to Government of India (from Government of Bombay)' p127; Hickinbotham, T., *Aden* (London: Constable & Company Ltd, 1958) pp20–4; Blythe, R., *The Empire of the Raj*; Bhattacharya, T., *Ocean Bombay: Space, Itinerancy and Community in an Imperial Port City, 1839–1937* (PhD Thesis, Columbia University, 2019)
21. Here I am indebted to Scott Reese's invaluable scholarship: Reese, *Imperial Muslims: Islam, Community and Authority in the Indian Ocean, 1839–1937*. I am also thankful to Luqman's daughter Huda for providing me with a copy of Luqman's autobiography Lokman, *Men, Matters and Memories*
22. Lokman, *Men, Matters and Memories* pp99, 121
23. For Gandhi's trip to Aden, see Gandhi, *The Collected Works of Mahatma Gandhi XXXXVII (June–September 1931)* pp388–92; Lokman, *Men, Matters and Memories* pp118–19; Ali, A., *The Image of Mahatma Gandhi in Modern Arabic Literature* (New Delhi: Educreation Publishing, 2018) p56; and 'Mahatma Gandhi's historic sojourn in Aden', *The Free Library*
24. QDL IOR/L/PS/12/1444 'Administrative policy: arrangements for achievement of Imperial purposes at Aden; transfer of administration to Government of India (from Government of Bombay)' p770
25. Sarojini Naidu to Padmaja and Leilamani Naidu, 23 September 1931 in Paranjape (ed.), *Sarojini Naidu*
26. Aga Khan, *The Memoirs of the Aga Khan: World Enough and Time* (London: Cassell and Company Ltd, 1954) p227
27. Ibid. p227
28. Sarojini Naidu to Padmaja and Leilamani Naidu, 23 September 1931 in Paranjape (ed.), *Sarojini Naidu*
29. Sarojini Naidu to Padmaja and Leilamani Naidu, 27 November 1931 in ibid.
30. NAI/Home Political/1934/F22/XI/34 'Questions in the Legislative Assembly Regarding the Refusal of a Passport to Reverend Bikkhu Ottama'; Bhaumik, *Burma in Bangla Literature (1886–1948)*
31. Ottama., *The Case against the Separation of Burma from India: A Statement by Ottama Bhikkhu of Burma* (Calcutta: Carmichael Medical College Hospital, 1931)
32. Bodleian, Ms. Eng. Hist. d. 352/8. D. 14.xii 71: Government of the United Kingdom, Burma Round Table Conference, *Proceedings* (London: His Majesty's Stationery Office, 1932) p74
33. Ba Maw, *Break Through in Burma: Memoirs of a Revolution* (London: Yale University Press, 1968) p18
34. Ibid. p14
35. QDL IOR/L/PS/12/1444 'Administrative policy: arrangements for achievement of Imperial purposes at Aden; transfer of administration to Government of India (from Government of Bombay)' p274. At this point, all that was announced was Aden's transfer from Bombay administration and its reformation as an independent chief commissionship under Delhi. At that time, while there was certainly scheming going on behind the scenes, the British flat-out denied that any further transfer was on the cards. It wasn't until 1933 that talks (and protest) began in earnest about making Aden into an entirely separate colony, which was indeed confirmed in the Government of India Act 1935.
36. IOR/Mss Eur E240/12a 'Teleg Willingdom to Hoare, 4 March 1933', quoted in Blythe, *The Empire of the Raj* p192; Christian, J. L., 'Burma Divorces India', *Current History*. 1937, 46(1): 85
37. NAI/Home Political/1934/F22/XI/34 'Questions in the Legislative Assembly Regarding the Refusal of a Passport to Reverend Bikkhu Ottama'
38. *Civil & Military Gazette* (Lahore), 22 April 1935
39. NAI/Home Political/1935/F-18-11 'Fortnightly reports from Local Governments and Administrations on the Political Situation in India, for the Month of November 1935' pp22, 60. Ottama's response to Jinnah is recorded in the *Civil & Military Gazette* (Lahore), 3 May 1935. Ottama himself didn't help the situation by vocally attacking Burma's Muslim community, and several leading Muslims like Jinnah accused Ottama and the Mahasabha of Hindu supremacy. 'The Mahasabha does not stand for Hindu Raj,' Ottama told the press in Delhi, 'it only wishes to make it clear that Muslim Raj is an idle dream. Let Mr Jinnah and

his followers pledge themselves to work against Muslim communalism and I will be the first and foremost in seeing that Muslims do not lose a bit by trusting their Hindu brethren.'
40. Maung, U Maung, *Nationalist Movements in Burma, 1920–40: Changing Patterns of Leadership, from Sangha to Laity* (Master of Arts, ANU, 1976) p283
41. NAI/Home Political/NA/F-18-8 35/1935 'Fortnightly Report from Local Government and Administrations on the Political Situation in India, for the Month of August 1935' p20
42. For Ramnath Biswas I am indebted to the work of Parthasarathi Bhaumik, who first brought this figure to my attention through his two monographs; Bhaumik, P., *Bengalis in Burma: A Colonial Encounter (1886–1948)* (Abingdon: Routledge, 2022) and Bhaumik, *Burma in Bangla Literature (1886–1948)*. As I am unfamiliar with the Bengali language, I use Anindita Roy's translations of Biswas' book 'Brahmadeshe Chhoy Mās' as my primary source. See Biswas, R., 'Brahmadeshe Chhoy Mās'. Translated by Roy, A. in Bhaumik. O. and Nayak, J. K. (eds), *Memory, Images, Imagination: An Anthology of Bangla and Oriya Writings on Colonial Burma (1886–1948)* (Calcutta: Jadavpur University, 2010). For some parts of Biswas' biography, I have relied upon Basu, A. 'Performing Other-Wise: "Death-Defying" China as Seen by Ramnath Biswas', *China Report*. 2007, 43(4): 485–99
43. Biswas, 'Brahmadeshe Chhoy Mās' p73
44. Ibid. pp66–9
45. Ibid.
46. Ibid.
47. Bhaumik, *Burma in Bangla Literature (1886–1948)* pp182–4
48. Hopetoun House Archives: Newspaper Cuttings: *Sunday Express*, 9 April 1936
49. Hopetoun House Archives: Newspaper Cuttings: 'Making Delhi Healthier'
50. Taylor, D. D., *Indian Politics and the Elections of 1937* (PhD Thesis, University of London, 1971)
51. Guyot-Réchard, 'Tangled Lands: Burma and India's Unfinished Separation, 1937–1948' 5
52. IOR/Mss Eur E252/21 'Printed Official Reports on Expeditions to the Naga Hills' p67
53. Konyak, P., and Bos, P., *The Konyaks: Last of the Tattooed Headhunters* (New Delhi: Lustre Press, 2017) p9
54. Steyn, P. *Zapuphizo: Voice of the Nagas* (London: Kegan Paul, 2002) p38
55. Ibid.
56. Some confusion surrounds the transfer of the protectorates. Many sources claim the protectorate was transferred earlier than Aden Colony but in fact both were transferred in 1937. The protectorates remained governed by the Indian (Foreign Jurisdiction) Order in Council of 1902 – the same ordinance that governed other princely states – until the passing of the Aden Protectorate Order of 1937. See Robbins, R. R., 'The Legal Status of Aden Colony and the Aden Protectorate', *American Journal of International Law*. 1939, 33(4): 705; QDL IOR/L/PS/12/1461 'Aden Protectorate Boundaries: Inclusion of the Hadhramaut'
57. 'Sword for Pen', *Time*, 12 April 1937
58. QDL IOR/L/PS/12/1485 'Aden. Administration and control: changes consequent on Indian constitutional reforms; transfer to HMG' pp16–20; CO 725/47/2, T 8161/37, No 63 Confidential, 16/3/37: 'Telegram from the Secretary of State for the Colonies on behalf of His Majesty the King of England to the Resident at Aden'
59. 'The King's Messages to India and Burma', *Northern Whig*, 1 April 1937; 'Separation of Burma', *Yorkshire Evening Post*, 1 April 1937
60. Zwillinger, S., *A Catalogue of Burmese Cachets 1937–1948* (Silver Spring Maryland: Self published, 2005)
61. Christian, 'Burma Divorces India' 86
62. Amrith, *Crossing the Bay of Bengal* p191
63. Numerous other communities were also left divided. For example, the Mizo community ended up in India, separated from their Chin and Kuki kinsmen, as well as the sacred Rih lake where many Mizos believed the souls of their ancestors resided. For more see Nag, S., *The Multiple Partitions* (Unpublished)
64. Nibedon, N., *Nagaland: The Night of the Guerrillas* (New Delhi: Lancer, 2022)
65. Jha, D. K., *Gandhi's Assassin: The Making of Nathuram Godse and His Idea of India* (Gurugram: Penguin Random House, 2021)

66. *Civil & Military Gazette* (Lahore), 15 April 1935; 29 April 1935; 3 May 1935; 9 May 1935; 21 June 1935; 28 July 1935; 13 October 1935
67. Maung Maung, *Nationalist Movements in Burma, 1920–40* p536. Smith, D. E., *Religion and Politics in Burma* (Princeton: Princeton Legacy Press, 1965) p121; Charney, M. W. A., *History of Modern Burma* (Cambridge: Cambridge University Press, 2009) p33

Chapter 3: The Drums of War

1. Foucar, *I Lived in Burma* p84; IOR/M/3/1113 'Visit of Premier U Saw to UK: invitation and biographical notes; Reports of death of U Saw, and denial 8 Aug–1 Sep 1942' p29; Min, U. Kyaw, *The Burma We Love* (Calcutta: Bharati Bhavan, 1945) p29
2. Amrith, *Crossing the Bay of Bengal* p183
3. For U Saw's experiences in Japan see Ei Thandar Aung., 'Study of Galon U Saw's Experiences in Japan in 1935', *Journal of Humanities and Social Sciences Okayama University*. 2019, 47(3): 2019–230
4. Saaler, S., 'The Kokuryu Kai (Black Dragon Society) and the Rise of Nationalism, Pan-Asianism, and Militarism in Japan, 1901–1925', *International Journal of Asian Studies*. 2014, 11(2): 125–60; for the growing Japanese presence see Bayly, C. and Harper, T., *Forgotten Armies: Britain's Asian Empire & War with Japan* (London: Penguin Books, 2005) Prologue Part 1. For focus on Burma see Cockett, R., *Blood, Dreams and Gold: The Changing Face of Burma* (Padstow, Cornwall: Yale University Press, 2015) pp23–4; Myint-U, *The River of Lost Footsteps* Chapter 9; for the impact of Japan on the Gulf states see Morton, M. Q., *Masters of Pearl: A History of Qatar* (London: Reaktion Books, 2020) pp88–9
5. Bayly and Harper, *Forgotten Armies* p97
6. IOR/M/3/1113 'Visit of Premier U Saw to UK: invitation and biographical notes; Reports of death of U Saw, and denial 8 Aug–1 Sep 1942' p30
7. See Markovits, C., *India and the World: A History of Connections, c. 1750–2000* (Cambridge: Cambridge University Press, 2021) p144, and Khan, Y., *The Raj at War* (London: Penguin Random House UK, 2015) p9; for more on paramilitary militias in 1930s Burma, see Callahan, M. P., 'State Formation in the Shadow of the Raj: Violence, Warfare and Politics in Colonial Burma', *Southeast Asian Studies*. 2002, 39(4): 513–36
8. Bowser, *Misdirected Rage* p17
9. U Ba Pe's rival 'Five Flowers Alliance' had actually secured more votes in the election, but had splintered almost immediately, so Ba Maw was brought in as Burma's first premier
10. U Myint, 'Foreword by U Myint, Former Justice of the Burma Supreme Court' in Ba Maw, *Break Through in Burma* pxiii
11. Ba Maw, *Break Through in Burma* p52
12. Raven-Hart, R. *Canoe to Mandalay* (London: F. Muller, 1939)
13. Bowser, *Misdirected Rage* p198
14. Angelene Naw, *Aung San and the Struggle for Burmese Independence* (Denmark: NIAS, 2001) p21
15. Bo Let Ya, 'Snapshots of Aung San' in Maung Maung, *Aung San of Burma* (The Hague: Published for Yale U, Southeast Asia Studies by M. Nijhoff, 1962) p10
16. For Aung San, see Naw, *Aung San and the Struggle for Burmese Independence*; Aung San Suu Kyi, *Aung San of Burma: A Biographical Portrait by His Daughter* (Edinburgh: Kiscadel, 1991); Maung Maung, *Aung San of Burma*; Myint-U, *The River of Lost Footsteps*; Bayly and Harper, *Forgotten Armies*; Bayly, C. and Harper, T., *Forgotten Wars: The End of Britain's Asian Empire* (London: Penguin Books, 2008); Bowser, *Misdirected Rage*
17. Bowser, *Misdirected Rage*
18. Ibid. p130
19. Ibid. p183
20. Bowser, 'Partners in Empire? Co-colonialism and the Rise of Anti-Indian Nationalism in Burma, 1930–1938' 118–19
21. *Civil & Military Gazette* (Lahore), 29 July 1938
22. *Halifax Evening Courier*, 28 July 1938; *Torbay Express and South Devon Echo*, 29 July 1938
23. Pandian, A. and Mariappan M. P., *Ayya's Accounts: A Ledger of Hope in Modern India* (Bloomington: Indiana University Press, 2014) p52
24. Ibid. pp3, 36, 183
25. Ibid. p53
26. Bowser, *Misdirected Rage* p210
27. Khan, L. A., *Resolutions of the All-India Muslim League from October 1937 to*

December 1938 (1938). The following resolution was passed: 'The All-India Muslim League expresses its deep sympathy with the Indians in general and the Muslims in particular in Burma who have suffered great losses during riots, and asks the Government of India to press the Government of Burma for adequate compensation to the Muslims who have in any way suffered during the riots. Further this Session requests the All-Burma Muslim League to keep the Muslims of India in touch with the general and political affairs of the Burma Muslims'; Singh, *Jinnah* p257
28. Bowser, *Misdirected Rage* p254
29. Amrith, *Crossing the Bay of Bengal* p181
30. Ibid. p228
31. Sen, A., *Home in the World: A Memoir* (London: Allen Lane, 2021) pxiii
32. Von Tunzelmann, *Indian Summer* p95
33. IOR/R/1/1/2444 'Interception of Correspondence from Mrs. Sarojini Naidu and Devadas Gandhi to Miss Padmaja and Leilamani Naidu, Hyderabad, under Sec. 26 of the Indian Post Offices Act'
34. Frank, K., *Indira: The Life of Indira Nehru Gandhi* (London: HarperCollins, 2001) p7
35. Nehru, J., *Towards Freedom: The Autobiography of Jawaharlal Nehru* (New York: Cornwall Press, 1941) p39
36. A wonderful narrative of this scene, utilising a number of newer sources, can be found in Harper, T. N., *Underground Asia: Global Revolutionaries and the Assault on Empire* (London: Allen Lane, 2020) p340
37. Von Tunzelmann, *Indian Summer* p79
38. Hajari, *Midnight's Furies* pp30–3
39. Von Tunzelmann, *Indian Summer* p92
40. Ibid. pp91–3
41. Jalal, *The Sole Spokesman* p22
42. This would be Nehru's first trip to Burma, and after some concern that he might not make it due to fever, father and daughter sailed to Rangoon on 7 May, just a month after separation. 'Burma and India must carry on together' was Nehru's message to the press, 'although now they have been geographically separated by England.' The trip was brief, with Nehru and Indira travelling north to Mandalay then east to Moulmein, meeting both political and student leaders. They attended the All-Burma Students Conference at Mandalay, at which Aung San was president, implying that Nehru and Aung San encountered each other earlier than the Ramgarh Session in 1940, when they are commonly understood to have met. Reports certainly confirm that Nehru met with members of the Tharrawaddy Do Bama, and Khin Nyo recalls seeing both Nehru and Aung San at the meeting. On his penultimate night, Nehru discussed the future of the Congress Party in separated Burma, and attended a tea party. Anti-separationists hoped that India and Burma could maintain their close relationship, but when Nehru visited Ba Maw during the trip, an 'unfortunate personal misunderstanding' put a strain on their relationship, as well as that between the colonies they represented. It was a foreboding start to the new relationship. *Civil & Military Gazette* (Lahore), 09 May 1937; Kozicki, R., *India and Burma 1937–1957* p121; Khin Nyo, 'Our Selfless Sayagyi' in (ed.) *U Razak: A Teacher, A Leader, A Martyr* (Bangkok: OS Printing House, 2007) p32; *Liverpool Echo*, 22 April 1937; *Civil & Military Gazette* (Lahore), 06 April 1937; 25 April 1937; 2 May 1937; 19 May 1937; 20 May 1937
43. Moon, P., *Divide and Quit* (London: Chatto and Windus, 1961) p15
44. Copland, *The Princes of India in the Endgame of Empire 1917–1947* pp73, 181, 279; Basu, N., *V. P. Menon: The Unsung Architect of Modern India* (New Delhi: Simon & Schuster, 2020) p132
45. Karnad, R., *Farthest Field: An Indian Story of the Second World War* (London: William Collins, 2015) p3
46. Khan, *The Raj at War* p1
47. Bayly and Harper, *Forgotten Wars* p7
48. Sen, *Home in the World* p143
49. Raghavan, S., *India's War: The Making of Modern South Asia, 1939–1945* (London: Allen Lane, 2016) p48
50. Khan, *The Raj at War* p5
51. Raghavan, *India's War* p1; Bhaumik, *Burma in Bangla Literature (1886–1948)* p228
52. Khan, *The Raj at War* pxiii
53. Allen, C., and Dwivedi, S., *Lives of the Indian Princes* (London: Century Publishing, 1984) p158
54. Martial race thinking played a role in the Burman-Karen-Kachin tensions, the militarisation of Punjab (rather than

Bengal) after WW2, and finally the Punjabi racism towards Bengal and the Bengali sense of wanting to be a martial race. In 1941, there were only 1,893 'Burmans' in Burma's armed forces. There were almost double the number of 'Indians'. In addition, there were 2,797 Karens in Burma's armed forces, despite this ethnic group making up only 9 per cent of the colony's population. For statistics see Callahan, 'State Formation in the Shadow of the Raj: Violence, Warfare and Politics in Colonial Burma' 513–36; see also Siddiqa, A., *Military Inc: Inside Pakistan's Military Economy* (London: Pluto Press, 2007) pp59–61. For the ways martial race theory was applied in Yemen and Burma, see Willis, J. M., *Unmaking North and South: Cartographies of the Yemeni Past* (London: Hurst, 2013) pp47–50, and Myint-U, T., *The Hidden History of Burma* (New Delhi: Juggernaut, 2019) pp20–7; Jha, S., and Wilkinson, S., 'Veterans and Ethnic Cleansing in the Partition of India' (2010)
55. Guyot-Réchard, 'Tangled Lands: Burma and India's Unfinished Separation, 1937–1948' 6
56. Steyn, *Zapuphizo* p54
57. Indian troops had been sent to Aden in April 1939 after Hitler's seizure of Czechoslovakia to prepare in case of war. Congress immediately condemned 'their employment for British imperialist purposes'; Moon, P., *The British Conquest and Dominion of India* (London: Duckworth, 1990) p1086; Esdaile, M. J., *Aden and the End of Empire 1937–1960* (PhD, Harvard University, 2011) pp94–5
58. Brendon, *The Decline and Fall of the British Empire* p330
59. Ba Maw, *Break Through in Burma* p24
60. Ibid. p36
61. Pau, P. K., *Indo-Burma Frontier and the Making of the Chin Hills: Empire and Resistance* (Abingdon: Routledge India, 2020) p212
62. Hajari, *Midnight's Furies* p37
63. Moon, *The British Conquest and Dominion of India* p1091
64. Basu, *V. P. Menon* p140
65. Ayesha Jalal has argued that the Pakistan demand was merely a bargaining chip to Jinnah, although recently Ishtiaq Ahmed has pushed back against this thesis. See Jalal, *The Sole Spokesman* and Ahmed, I., *Jinnah: His Successes, Failures and Role in History* (Gurgaon: Viking, 2020)
66. Moon, P., *The British Conquest and Dominion of India* (London: Duckworth, 1990) p1092
67. Ambedkar, B. R., *Thoughts on Pakistan* (Bombay: Thacker and Company Limited, 1941) p60
68. Habib, S. I., *Maulana Azad: A Life* (New Delhi: Aleph Books, 2023) ppix, 7
69. Ibid. p8
70. Bayly and Harper, *Forgotten Armies* p103; Myint-U, *The River of Lost Footsteps* p223
71. Suzuki, K., 'Aung San and the Burma Independence Army' in Maung Maung, *Aung San of Burma* p55
72. IOR/M/3/1113 'Visit of Premier U Saw to UK: invitation and biographical notes; Reports of death of U Saw, and denial 8 Aug–1 Sep 1942' p21
73. Ibid. p16
74. Bowser, *Misdirected Rage* pp252–64
75. Gandhi, M. K., *The Collected Works of Mahatma Gandhi LXXIV (April–October 1941)* (New Delhi: Publications Division, Ministry of Information and Broadcasting, Govt of India, 1970) p190
76. Ibid. pp255–9
77. Myint-U, *The Hidden History of Burma* pp9–10
78. Bowser, *Misdirected Rage* p271
79. IOR/M/3/1113 'Visit of Premier U Saw to UK: invitation and biographical notes; Reports of death of U Saw, and denial 8 Aug–1 Sep 1942' p12; also quoted in Bowser, M. J., '"Buddhism Has Been Insulted. Take Immediate Steps": Burmese Fascism and the Origins of Burmese Islamophobia 1936–38', *Modern Asian Studies*. 2020: 1–39
80. Hopetoun House Archives: Bundle 3514 – *Diary of Captain P. G. Carter, Derbyshire Yeomanry, Aide-De-Camp to the Viceroy of India 1941–3, Vol. I* p75
81. Raghavan, S., *India's War: The Making of Modern South Asia, 1939–1945* (London: Allen Lane, 2016) p78
82. Bayly and Harper, *Forgotten Armies* pp96–102
83. Stockwell, A. J. 'Southeast Asia in War and Peace: The End of European Colonial Empires' in Tarling, N. (ed.), *The Cambridge History of Southeast Asia: Volume Four: From World War II to the Present* (Cambridge: Cambridge University Press, 2007) p14

84. Karnad, *Farthest Field* p54
85. Bayly and Harper, *Forgotten Armies* p103
86. IOR/M/3/1113 'Visit of Premier U Saw to UK: invitation and biographical notes; Reports of death of U Saw, and denial 8 Aug–1 Sep 1942' p10
87. IOR/L/I/1/895 'Visit to UK by U Saw, Premier of Burma, 1941' p23
88. IOR/M/3/1111 'Visit of Premier U Saw to USA'
89. Charney, *History of Modern Burma* p49; Myint-U, *The River of Lost Footsteps* p218; Bowser, *Misdirected Rage* pp290–3; Bayly and Harper, *Forgotten Armies* p104
90. IOR/M/5/101 'Return of U Saw to Burma after his detention in Uganda during war; his political views as leader of Myochit Party' p39
91. IOR/L/I/1/895 'Visit to UK by U Saw, Premier of Burma, 1941' p5
92. Leigh, M. D., *The Evacuation of Civilians from Burma: Analysing the 1942 Colonial Disaster* (London: Bloomsbury, 2014) p77
93. Keane, *Road of Bones* p9
94. See Headrick., LCDR A. C., *Bicycle Blitzkrieg: The Malayan Campaign and the Fall of Singapore* (Ebook: Verdun Press, 2014)
95. Keane, *Road of Bones* p77
96. Cockett, *Blood, Dreams and Gold* p51

Chapter 4: The Long March
1. Myint-U, *The River of Lost Footsteps* p223
2. Vaz Ezdani, Y., *New Songs of the Survivors: The Exodus of Indians from Burma* (New Delhi: Speaking Tiger, 2016) pp40–1
3. Ibid. p39
4. Ibid. p42
5. Ibid. p43
6. Ibid. p51
7. Ibid. p49
8. Ibid. p55
9. Leigh, *The Evacuation of Civilians from Burma* p81
10. Vaz Ezdani, *New Songs of the Survivors* p49
11. Leigh, *The Evacuation of Civilians from Burma* p83
12. Vaz Ezdani, *New Songs of the Survivors* p57
13. Amrith, *Crossing the Bay of Bengal* p203
14. Vaz Ezdani, *New Songs of the Survivors* p61
15. Brendon, *The Decline and Fall of the British Empire* p432. Ba Maw's autobiography suggests this oft-quoted statement that Aung San's head cost as much as a chicken may have occurred at an earlier of Aung San's arrests. See Ba Maw, *Break Through in Burma* p65
16. Naw, *Aung San and the Struggle for Burmese Independence* p63
17. Tinsa Maw-Naing and Han, Y. M. V., *A Burmese Heart* (Self-published, 2015) p61
18. Aung San, 'Blue Print for Burma' in Silverstein, J. (ed.), *The Political Legacy of Aung San: Revised Edition* (SEAP, 1993) p20. This document remains controversial. Dr Maung Maung has argued that it is the most authentic description of Aung San's vision for independent Burma, while Silverstein has asserted that 'When it is read in conjunction with other documents its importance fades.' More recently, Gustaaf Houtman has brought Aung San's authorship of the document itself into question. See Houtman, G., 'Aung San's lan-zin, the Blue Print and the Japanese occupation of Burma' in Nemoto, Kei (ed.), *Reconsidering the Japanese Military Occupation in Burma (1942–45)* (Tokyo: Tokyo University of Foreign Studies, 2007)
19. Bayly and Harper, *Forgotten Armies*
20. The story of the Thirty Comrades has been much mythologised in Burmese nationalist rhetoric. This account is based on Bayly and Harper, *Forgotten Armies* pp9–14 and Myint-U, *The River of Lost Footsteps* pp228–31
21. Ba Maw, *Break Through in Burma* p139
22. Bayly and Harper, *Forgotten Armies* p169
23. Leigh, *The Evacuation of Civilians from Burma* p125
24. Amrith, *Crossing the Bay of Bengal* p203
25. Tinker, H., 'A Forgotten Long March: The Indian Exodus from Burma, 1942', *Journal of Southeast Asian Studies*. 1975, 6(1): 2
26. Leigh, *The Evacuation of Civilians from Burma* pp94–5
27. Bayly and Harper, *Forgotten Armies* p162
28. Keane, *Road of Bones* p13
29. Khan, *The Raj at War* p95
30. Keane, *Road of Bones* p18; Bayly and Harper, *Forgotten Armies* p171
31. Raghavan, *India's War* p211
32. Tinker, 'A Forgotten Long March: The Indian Exodus from Burma, 1942' 1–15
33. Until recently Amitav Ghosh's book *The Glass Palace* was one of the few books to address the Long March
34. Bhaumik, *Burma in Bangla Literature (1886–1948)* pp253–4

35. Statistics from Bayly and Harper, *Forgotten Armies*. Harper and Bayly arrived at this number as a mean between the higher figures quoted by Indian nationalists and the lower numbers cited in Tinker, 'A Forgotten Long March: The Indian Exodus from Burma, 1942'. Leigh argues convincingly that while the official evacuation numbers are likely to be somewhere close to the mark, the death toll was consistently underestimated. Leigh, *The Evacuation of Civilians from Burma* Chapter 1. In *The Evacuation of Civilians* and *Misdirected Rage*, both Leigh and Bowser wrongly argue that no Indian accounts survive. In fact, many survive. A good survey of Bengali literature can be found in Bhaumik, *Burma in Bangla Literature (1886–1948)*
36. Sharpe, E. K., Register of Evacuees from Burma: Volume 1, European, Anglo-Burman, Anglo-Indian and Other Non-Indian Evacuees; Volume 2: Indians, A–L; Volume 3, Indians, M–Z (Calcutta: Evacuee Enquiry Bureau GOI, 1943)
37. Leigh, *The Evacuation of Civilians from Burma* p53. For a full account of Helen's journey, see Vaz Ezdani, *New Songs of the Survivors* pp165–70; Bowser, *Misdirected Rage* p294
38. Pandian and Mariappan, *Ayya's Accounts* p47
39. Min, *The Burma We Love* p4
40. Pandian and Mariappan, *Ayya's Accounts* p57
41. Ibid. p58
42. Keane, *Road of Bones* p14
43. Pandian and Mariappan, *Ayya's Accounts* p58
44. Ibid. p59
45. Leigh, *The Evacuation of Civilians from Burma* p120
46. Pandian and Mariappan, *Ayya's Accounts* p59
47. Leigh, *The Evacuation of Civilians from Burma* p122
48. IOR/Mss Eur 390, 'Memoir, dated 1980, by Peter Murray (b 1915), Burma Civil Service 1938–49, on "North Arakan 1942", detailing the collapse of British Administration in the area, with a brief historical introduction and a short account of subsequent events; also office stamp British Military Administration, Burma, and epaulette of officer of Civil Affairs Service (Burma)'. For a greater discussion on this, see Matthew Bowser's *Misdirected Rage* p311: 'Kyaw Khine has since been held up as one of the first martyrs of "Bengali Muslim" violence by Rakhine ultranationalists, and the anti-Rohingya social media campaign of 2012 used his martyrdom as one of its main propaganda pieces to spark the anti-Muslim riots in Rakhine state that year. This narrative ignores the fact that Kyaw Khine was not an innocent third-party simply trying to maintain order, but had erased the Rohingya from the census to benefit Rakhine nationalists just a year before'
49. This anecdote comes from an interview with acclaimed Swedish journalist Bertil Lintner. 'I interviewed one of the last surviving members of the 30 Comrades, back in the 1980s. I asked him: "You were 30 young guys in Tokyo, and three didn't even make it back to Burma, and you came back to Bangkok, set up the army and entered Burma. Suddenly you are invading with an army; where did the army come from?" He replied: "We set up in Thailand, we mixed our blood and drank it and so on. At that time there were quite a few Burmese in Thai prisons; those convicts were given the choice to stay in jail or go and fight. That way we raised a force of around 1,000 soldiers." Official Burmese histories never want to point out that the original independence army was actually made up of convicts.' See fivebooks.com/best-books/bertil-lintner-on-burma/
50. A British attempt to re-enter Arakan that winter ended in dismal failure, and secret British documents later revealed that Baluch troops in the Indian Army had taken 'revenge on the Arakanese' for earlier attacks on the Muslims of Arakan. See IOR/Mss Eur 390: 'Memoir, dated 1980, by Peter Murray (b 1915), Burma Civil Service 1938–49, on "North Arakan 1942", detailing the collapse of British Administration in the area, with a brief historical introduction and a short account of subsequent events; also office stamp British Military Administration, Burma, and epaulette of officer of Civil Affairs Service (Burma)' p8; Bayly and Harper, *Forgotten Armies* p276
51. Keane, *Road of Bones* p132
52. Bowser, *Misdirected Rage* p311

53. This section is taken from the groundbreaking article Sarkar, J. 'Battlefields to Borderlands: Rohingyas Between Global War and Decolonisation' in Guyot-Réchard, B., and Leake, E. (eds.), *South Asia Unbound: New International Histories of the Subcontinent* (epub: Leiden University Press, 2023) pp11–17
54. Bayly and Harper, *Forgotten Armies* p183
55. Simms, S. S., *Great Lords of the Sky: Burma's Shan Aristocracy* (Cambridge: Asian Highlands Perspectives 48, 2017) p177
56. The following section is drawn from Uttam Singh's Punjabi-language diary as well as an interview with his son Avtar, who still remembers the long walk back to India. Avtar Singh Hoonjan Private Collection: Singh, U., *Uttam Singh's Diary 1942* (Unpublished, translation from Punjabi by Harleen Singh Sandhu); Private Interview, Avtar, Sanvir and Raminder Singh Hoonjan, London, English, September 2021
57. Avtar Singh Hoonjan Private Collection: Singh, U., *Uttam Singh's Diary 1942* loose pages
58. Ibid. p8
59. Ibid. p10
60. Ibid. p12
61. Ibid. p14
62. Private Interview, Avtar, Sanvir and Raminder Singh Hoonjan, London, English, September 2021
63. Avtar Singh Hoonjan Private Collection: Singh, U., *Uttam Singh's Diary 1942* p29
64. Bayly and Harper, *Forgotten Armies* p252
65. Keane, *Road of Bones* p30
66. Avtar Singh Hoonjan Private Collection: Uttam Singh letter for claiming a lorry, 1 March 1943
67. Leigh, *The Evacuation of Civilians from Burma* p2
68. Ibid. p173; Myint-U, *The River of Lost Footsteps* p227
69. Orwell, G., '970. Newsletter, 10' in Orwell, G., and Davidson, P. (ed.), *George Orwell: The Collected Non-Fiction* (Ebook: Penguin Books, 2017)
70. Hopetoun House Archives: Bundle 3515 – *Diary of Captain P.G. Carter, Derbyshire Yeomanry, Aide-De-Camp to the Viceroy of India 1941–3, Vol. II* p26
71. See Raghavan, *India's War* p258, and Khan, *The Raj at War* p106
72. Amrith, *Crossing the Bay of Bengal* p205
73. Myint-U, *The River of Lost Footsteps* p184
74. Bhaumik, S. *Insurgent Crossfire: North-East India* (New Delhi: South Godstone, 1996) p68
75. Maroof Culmen interview with Asad Javed of Burma Biscuits. Available at instagram.com/reel/CnR9plnqKU4/?igshid=YmMyMTA2M2Y=
76. Raghavan, *India's War* p269
77. Azad, Maulana A. K., *India Wins Freedom* (New Delhi: Orient Longman, 1988) p40, quoted in Khan, *The Raj at War* p98
78. Copland, *The Princes of India in the Endgame of Empire 1917–1947* p186
79. Keane, *Road of Bones* p26
80. Slim, W. J., *Defeat into Victory* (London: Pan, 2009) p150
81. Bhaumik, *Burma in Bangla Literature (1886–1948)* 236–9
82. Sen, *Home in the World* p59
83. Ibid. p17
84. Moon, *The British Conquest and Dominion of India* p1105
85. Leigh, *The Evacuation of Civilians from Burma* p66
86. Khan, *The Raj at War* p119
87. Von Tunzelmann, *Indian Summer* p122
88. Khan, *The Raj at War* p107
89. Gandhi, M. K., *The Collected Works of Mahatma Gandhi LXXVI (April–December 1942)* (New Delhi: Publications Division, Ministry of Information and Broadcasting, Govt of India, 1970) p392
90. Asaf Ali's memoirs, quoted in Khan, *The Raj at War* p179
91. Raghavan, *India's War* p271
92. Von Tunzelmann, *Indian Summer* p127
93. Khan, *The Raj at War* Chapter 14
94. Hopetoun House Archives: Bundle 3514 – *Diary of Captain P. G. Carter, Derbyshire Yeomanry, Aide-De-Camp to the Viceroy of India 1941–3, Vol. II* p41
95. French, *Liberty or Death* p159
96. Karnad, *Farthest Field* p76
97. Bayly and Harper, *Forgotten Armies* p248
98. Leigh, *The Evacuation of Civilians from Burma* p72
99. Khan, *The Raj at War* p186
100. Bayly and Harper, *Forgotten Armies* pp240–6
101. Bapu, P., *Hindu Mahasabha in Colonial North India, 1915–1930* (Ebook: Routledge, 2013) p103
102. Guha, *Rebels Against the Raj* p185
103. Nichols, B., *Verdict on India* (London: Jonathan Cape, 1944) p180

104. Manto, S. H., 'Bombay in the Riots' in Patel, A. (ed.), *Why I Write: Essays by Saadat Hasan Manto* (Chennai: Tranquebar Press, 2014)
105. Jalal, A., *The Pity of Partition: Manto's Life, Times, and Work across the India-Pakistan Divide* (Princeton: Princeton University Press, 2013) p126

Chapter 5: War in the Borderlands

1. Scheidel, W., Fibiger Bang, P., and Bayly, C. A., *The Oxford World History of Empire: Volume One. The Imperial Experience* (Oxford: Oxford University Press, 2020) p103
2. Bayly and Harper, *Forgotten Armies* p269
3. Ba Maw, *Break Through in Burma* pp223–33; Tinsa Maw-Naing and Han, *A Burmese Heart* pp10, 85
4. Tinsa Maw-Naing and Han, *A Burmese Heart* p83
5. Ibid. p86
6. Ba Maw, *Break Through in Burma* pp239–40
7. Tinsa Maw-Naing & Han, Y. M. V., *A Burmese Heart* (Self published: 2015) p86
8. Ba Maw, *Break Through in Burma* pp239–40
9. Ibid. pp242–52
10. Ibid. p254
11. Ibid. p210
12. Tinsa Maw-Naing and Han, *A Burmese Heart* p54
13. Charney, *History of Modern Burma* p50
14. Ba Maw, *Break Through in Burma* p182
15. Ibid. p177
16. Ibid. p178
17. Keane, *Road of Bones* p105; Bayly and Harper, *Forgotten Armies* p233. There were never very many Indian or Burmese victims at UNIT 731 – most prisoners were Korean, Chinese or Russian
18. Naw, *Aung San and the Struggle for Burmese Independence* p83; for Suzuki's transfer, see Lebra, J., *Japanese-Trained Armies in Southeast Asia* (Singapore: ISEAS Publishing, 2010) Chapter 3
19. Naw, *Aung San and the Struggle for Burmese Independence* p91
20. Ba Maw, *Break Through in Burma* p266
21. After the BIA was dissolved, the new army was briefly called the Burma Defence Army. It was renamed the BNA only after Burma was granted 'independence' in 1943. For the sake of clarity, I will refer to it as the BNA throughout
22. Bhaumik, *Burma in Bangla Literature (1886–1948)* p72; Singh, B., *Independence and Democracy in Burma, 1945–1952: The Turbulent Years* (Ann Arbor: University of Michigan CSSEAS Publications, 1993) p3
23. For Abid Hasan's eyewitness account, see Bose, K., and Bose, S., *Netaji: Subhas Chandra Bose's Life, Politics and Struggle* (New Delhi: Picador India, 2022) pp120–32
24. Hayes, R., *Subhas Chandra Bose in Nazi Germany: Politics, Intelligence and Propaganda* (London: C Hurst & Co., 2011) p67
25. Raghavan, *India's War* p246
26. Macintyre, B., *Colditz: Prisoners of the Castle* (London: Penguin Books, 2022) pp117–19
27. See Bose and Bose, *Netaji*
28. Bose's INA was actually the second attempt at creating a pro-Japan Indian Army. Back in February 1942, 85,000 British Empire soldiers had surrendered in Singapore to a mere 30,000 Japanese troops. The Indian soldiers were divided, with half going to concentration camps and half marching off to fight alongside Japan. Mohan Singh was put in charge, but when he began to openly question why Japan refused to recognise India as independent, he was arrested. By December the same year, the first INA had been disbanded, the soldiers becoming Japanese prisoners of war
29. Sahay Choudhry, B., *The War Diary of Asha-san: From Tokyo to Netaji's Indian National Army* (Translated by Tanvi Srivastava) (Gurugram: HarperCollins, 2022) pp3–6
30. NAI, INA Records FN. 92, Private Papers 2998090: 'Interrogation Report (Azad Hind Dal)' p74
31. See Amrith, *Crossing the Bay of Bengal* p205, and Vijayan, S., *Midnight's Borders: A People's History of Modern India* (Chennai: Context, 2021) p91
32. Sahay Choudhry, *The War Diary of Asha-san* p93
33. Ibid. p101
34. Amrith, *Crossing the Bay of Bengal* pp199–201
35. Ba Maw, *Break Through in Burma* pp350–1
36. Jackson, A., *Persian Gulf Command: A History of the Second World War in Iran and Iraq* (Llandysul: Yale University Press, 2018) p251
37. Bayly and Harper, *Forgotten Armies* p196

38. Khan, *The Raj at War* pp86, 139, 170
39. A mosque built by Gedu Mian still stands in central Agartala. See Dalrymple, S., 'Gedu Mian and the Partition of Tripura', *Partition Studies Quarterly*. 2002, 5
40. Guyot-Réchard, 'Tangled Lands: Burma and India's Unfinished Separation, 1937–1948' 8–9
41. Reid had toured the Indian side of the hills in December 1940, when members of the Mizo community had told him they could not 'tolerate the idea of being swamped by the Indian' and that they 'might be better off if attached to the hill areas of Burma'. A year later, Reid had written down his thoughts. The 'boundary between our [Indian] hills and the Burma hills is as artificial as it is imperceptible,' he observed. The hill people 'are not Indians in any sense of the word, neither in origin, nor in language, nor in appearance, not in habits, nor in outlooks, and it is by historical accident that they have been tacked on to our Indian province'. It was the same argument that had previously been used to separate Aden and Burma, and as in those debates, the terms 'India' and 'Indian' remained curiously undefined. Intriguingly, Reid refers to the hill peoples as 'Mongolian' and 'Mongoloid', a racial description that colonial officials had also applied to the people of Burma. See Reid, R. N., 'A Note on the Future of the Present Excluded, Partially Excluded and Tribal Areas of Assam', reprinted in Syiemlieh, D. R., *On the Edge of Empire: Four British Plans for North East India, 1941–1947* (New Delhi: SAGE Publications, 2014); Syiemlieh, D. R., 'Burma: Flirting with Reid's Plan', in Sangma, M. S. (ed.), *Essays on North-East India* (New Delhi: Indus Publishing Co., 1994)
42. Reid, 'A Note on the Future of the Present Excluded, Partially Excluded and Tribal Areas of Assam' p68
43. The great scholar on the Reid plan is David Syiemlieh. Suggested areas to compose this 'North Eastern Frontier Province' included 'the hill tracts of Arakan, Pakokku and Chittagong, the Chin Hills, the Lushai Hills, the North Cachar Hills, the Naga Hills, the parts of the Upper Chindwin District and the hills administered on the west bank of the Chindwin from the upper Chindwin District, and the Hukong valley, together with the Sadiya and Balipara Frontier Tracts, the Lakhimpur Frontier Tract, the states of Manipur and Tripura, and the Shan state of Thangdut'. Instead of forming them into a unified province, the 1935 Act of India and Burma left the region divided between Assam, Bengal and Burma. The proposed districts were redesignated 'Excluded' or 'partially-excluded' areas to account for their difference. See Syiemlieh, 'Burma: Flirting with Reid's Plan'; Syiemlieh, *On the Edge of Empire*
44. It is unclear how many inhabitants of the Patkai were aware of these debates. Certainly, several Mizo chiefs agreed to fight the Japanese on the explicit understanding that their land would be kept separate from both India and Burma, but besides odd groups like this, the debating was mostly done by the British. Van Schendel, W., and Pachauu, J. L. K., *The Camera as Witness: A Social History of Mizoram, Northeast India* (Cambridge: Cambridge University Press, 2015) p200
45. Syiemlieh, 'Burma: Flirting with Reid's Plan' p232
46. Guyot-Réchard, 'Tangled Lands: Burma and India's Unfinished Separation, 1937–1948' 9
47. Rice accounted for 40 per cent of Burma's exports to India in 1941. See Kozicki, *India and Burma 1937–1957*
48. Raghavan, *India's War* p355
49. Charney, *History of Modern Burma* p56; Esdaile, *Aden and the End of Empire* pp96–8; Tripodi, C., '"A Bed of Procrustes": The Aden Protectorate and the Forward Policy 1934–44', *Journal of Imperial and Commonwealth History*. 2016, 44(1): 95–120
50. There is a varied literature on the Bengal famine. See Mukherjee, J., *Hungry Bengal: War, Famine and the End of Empire* (Oxford, Oxford University Press, 2015); Sen, A., *Poverty and Famines: An Essay on Entitlement and Deprivation* (New York: Oxford University Press, 1981); Sen, *Home in the World* Chapters 7 and 25; Bayly and Harper, T., *Forgotten Armies* Chapter 5; Khan, *The Raj at War* Chapter 15; for the Bengal famine as the result of the India-Burma Partition, see Amrith, *Crossing the Bay of Bengal* Chapter 6
51. Sen, *Home in the World* pp114–15
52. Ibid.

53. Bayly and Harper, *Forgotten Armies* p288
54. Karnad, *Farthest Field* p167
55. Winston Churchill to the Peel Commission of Inquiry, 1937, quoted in Prasad, A., and Prasad, P., 'The Postcolonial Imagination' in Prasad, A. (ed.), *Postcolonial Theory and Organizational Analysis: A Critical Engagement* (New York: Palgrave Macmillan, 2003)
56. Mukerjee, M., *Churchill's Secret War: The British Empire and the Ravaging of India during World War II* (New York: Basic Books, 2010) pp232–4
57. French, *Liberty or Death* p179
58. Moon, *The British Conquest and Dominion of India* p1130
59. Mukerjee, *Churchill's Secret War* pp232–4
60. Sen, *Home in the World* p116
61. Ibid. p119
62. The famine's final death toll would be almost double, and around half of all deaths would occur after the year 1943. See Mukherjee, *Hungry Bengal*. For three Million, see Puri, K., *Three Million* (William Collins, forthcoming). For Vietnam War statistics, see 'Statistics of Democide', Charlottesville, Virginia: Center for National Security Law, School of Law, University of Virginia, 1997
63. Irani, A. A., *The Muhammad Avatara: Salvation History, Translation, and the Making of Bengali Islam* (New York: Oxford University Press, 2021)
64. Van Schendel, W., *A History of Bangladesh* 2nd edn (Cambridge: Cambridge University Press, 2020) pp36–9
65. Mukherjee, *Hungry Bengal* pp177, 192
66. Keane, *Road of Bones* p88
67. Raghavan, *India's War* p383
68. Ibid. pp208, 379
69. Keane, *Road of Bones* p93
70. Ibid. pp85–7
71. Karnad, *Farthest Field* p241
72. Middle East Command was initially solely concerned with the Mediterranean world of Egypt, Sudan and Cyprus, and only later had its remit extended to Aden, the protectorate and the Gulf states which until then were still under India's remit. This would have important consequences, as for the first time cities like Dubai and Aden would be considered part of the 'Middle East' rather than 'South Asia'. See Jackson, *Persian Gulf Command* p362; Raghavan, *India's War* pp8–9; Satia, P., *Spies in Arabia: The Great War and the Cultural Foundations of Britain's Covert Empire in the Middle East* (Oxford: Oxford University Press, 2008) p14
73. Lownie, A., *The Mountbattens: Their Lives and Loves* (London: Blink Publishing, 2020) p14
74. Von Tunzelmann, *Indian Summer* p70
75. Lownie, *The Mountbattens* p89
76. Ibid. p2
77. Von Tunzelmann, *Indian Summer* p76
78. Ibid.
79. Lownie, *The Mountbattens* p98
80. In 1987, Mountbatten's former chauffeur Norman Nield claimed to the New Zealand tabloid *Truth* that during this time he was paid to drive young boys aged eight to twelve to Mountbatten's residence. FBI files reveal that, in 1944, one Baroness Decies accused Mountbatten of 'being a homosexual with a perversion for young boys'. Similar accusations have been made by a number of others, notably the former residents of Kincora Boys Home in Belfast. A number of files on Mountbatten in both the FBI and the British National Archives currently remain closed to the public. For more on these allegations, see Lownie, *The Mountbattens* Chapter 28
81. Von Tunzelmann, *Indian Summer* p129
82. Bayly and Harper, *Forgotten Armies* p271
83. Bayly and Harper, *Forgotten Wars* p12
84. Von Tunzelmann, *Indian Summer* p129
85. The wonderful story of Rikki Tikki the mongoose has been taken from Keane, *Road of Bones* pp123–4
86. Radio SEAC would remain operational until 1949, two years after the British themselves finally left India. See Fernandes, N., *Taj Mahal Foxtrot: The Story of Bombay's Jazz Age* (New Delhi: Roli Books, 2012) p89
87. Charney, *History of Modern Burma* p54
88. Ba Maw, *Break Through in Burma* p325
89. Myint-U, *The River of Lost Footsteps* p233. A more accurate translation would be 'he who stands at the front'
90. Rajshekhar, *Myanmar's Nationalist Movement (1906–1948) and India* (New Delhi: South Asian Publishers, 2006) p189
91. Sahay Choudhry, *The War Diary of Ashasan* p23
92. Bayly and Harper, *Forgotten Wars* p89

93. Aung San Suu Kyi, *Aung San of Burma* p28
94. Sahay Choudhry, *The War Diary of Ahasan* p101
95. The Japanese had not initially thought it could wage open warfare in the Patkai. Until this point, invading India had not been their aim. But the success of the Chindits convinced Japanese general Mutaguchi Renya that a Japanese army could invade India through the Patkai, rather than through the coastal Arakan. Now it seemed like Mutaguchi could help topple the British Empire. For more on the reasoning of Mutaguchi and Japanese high command behind the invasion of India, see Keane, *Road of Bones*
96. Keane, *Road of Bones* pp46–52
97. Steyn, *Zapuphizo* p58
98. Phizo, A. Z., *An Appeal to the World* (London: 1960)
99. Nibedon, N., *Nagaland: The Night of the Guerrillas* (New Delhi: Lancer, 2022) p30
100. NAI, Home, NEFA, NII/102(42)/70, 'Background note on Angami Zapu Phizo and Rev. Michael Scott prepared by U. S(Naga) in April 1970' p5
101. Steyn, *Zapuphizo* p60
102. As an admirer of Ottama and the last Congressman to lead a rally in Aden before the separation, Bose seems to have been against the 1937 separations in the first place. For Ottama and Bose, see Bhattacharya, 'A Close View of Encounter between British Burma and British Bengal' p21. For Bose in Aden see 'Mahatma Gandhi's historic sojourn in Aden' The Free Library. Unfortunately, few records exist of the relationship between Bose and Phizo. This summary is largely drawn from Steyn, *Zapuphizo*, and Nibedon, *Nagaland*
103. Bayly and Harper, *Forgotten Armies* p382
104. Katoch, H. S. *The Battlefields of Imphal: The Second World War and Northeast India* (New Delhi: Routledge India, 2016) p167
105. Slim, *Defeat into Victory* p330, quoted in Katoch, *The Battlefields of Imphal* p8
106. Meetei Kangjam, Y., *Forgotten Voices of the Japan Laan: The Battle of Imphal and the Second World War in Manipur* (New Delhi: INTACH Aryan Books Int, 2019) p112
107. Bose, S. 'Sarmila Bose on events of 1971', *The Times of Bombay*. 15 November 2010
108. Lownie, *The Mountbattens* p158
109. Bose and Bose, *Netaji* pxxvi
110. The following account of the battle of Kohima is taken from Fergal Keane's masterful *Road of Bones* pp221–5
111. Keane, *Road of Bones* p228
112. Ibid. p229
113. Ibid. p231
114. Ibid. pp266–87
115. Ibid. p298
116. Ibid. pp299–303
117. Ibid. pp310–18
118. 1947PA: Kh Nasii, Oral History Interview by Schulu Duo 10395
119. Katoch, *The Battlefields of Imphal*
120. Ba Maw, *Break Through in Burma* p365
121. Naw, *Aung San and the Struggle for Burmese Independence* p108
122. Von Tunzelmann, *Indian Summer* pp133–6
123. Naw, *Aung San and the Struggle for Burmese Independence* p125
124. Aung San, 'Aung San's Letter' in Maung Maung., *Aung San of Burma*
125. Slim, *Defeat into Victory* pp517–19
126. When Bose's elder brother Sarat visited Rangoon in July 1946, Aung San would claim: 'We did have an understanding in those days that, in any event, and whatever happened, the INA and the BNA should never fight each other. I am glad to tell you that both sides did observe the understanding scrupulously on the whole.' The validity of this is unknown. See Aung San, 'Burma's Challenge, 1946', printed in Silverstein (ed.), *The Political Legacy of Aung San* p141
127. Ba Maw, *Break Through in Burma* p359
128. Hersey, J., *Hiroshima* (St Ives: Penguin Modern Classics, 2001) p25
129. Bayly and Harper, *Forgotten Wars* p4
130. For a discussion on the speech and Oppenheimer's grounding in Hindu philosophy, see Hijiya, J. A., 'The "Gita" of J. Robert Oppenheimer', *Proceedings of the American Philosophical Society*. 2000, 144(2): 123–67

Chapter 6: Direct Action Day

1. *Civil & Military Gazette* (Lahore), 15 August 1945
2. Ibid. 30 August 1945
3. QDL IOR/R/15/2/323 'File 8/22 Eastern Aden Protectorate Intelligence Summaries' p564; *Civil & Military Gazette* (Lahore), 21 August 1945; 25 August 1945;

30 August 1945; and IOR/R/15/6/367 'File 11/14 Gwadur General: Diary Notes etc.' p388; see also Khan, *The Raj at War* Chapters 22–3
4. Khan, *The Raj at War* p302
5. Ibid. p299
6. Singh, *Independence and Democracy in Burma, 1945–1952* p18
7. Khan, *The Raj at War* p135
8. *Mr Jinnah: The Making of Pakistan.* Documentary directed by Christopher Mitchell, Akbar Ahmed, 1997
9. Brendon, *The Decline and Fall of the British Empire* p401
10. Khan, *The Great Partition* p30
11. French, *Liberty or Death* pxx
12. Von Tunzelmann, *Indian Summer* p145
13. Wolpert, *Jinnah of Pakistan* p243
14. nobelprize.org/prizes/economic-sciences/1998/sen/biographical/
15. Sen, *Home in the World* p76
16. Ibid. p150
17. Vaz Ezdani, *New Songs of the Survivors* p140
18. Pandian and Mariappan, *Ayya's Accounts* p78
19. Singh, *Independence and Democracy in Burma, 1945–1952* pp20–4
20. Specifically, 'the Andamans, the Nicobars, Burma, Thailand (Siam), French Indochina south of 16 degrees north latitude, Malaya, Borneo, the Netherlands Indies, New Guinea, the Bismarcks and the Solomon Islands'. See Connor, S. B., *Mountbatten's Samurai: Imperial Japanese Forces under British Control, 1945–1948* (UK: Seventh Citadel, 2015) p6
21. The French had been eager to move in earlier, but Mountbatten had resisted entering Indochina until Japan's formal surrender. See Smith, T. O., *Vietnam and the Unravelling of Empire: General Gracey in Asia 1942–51* (New York: Palgrave Macmillan, 2014) pp40–2; Bayly and Harper, *Forgotten Wars* p147
22. Smith, *Vietnam and the Unravelling of Empire* p4
23. Bayly and Harper, *Forgotten Wars* p147
24. For the British involvement in the Vietnam War, see Bayly and Harper, *Forgotten Wars*; Stockwell, A. J. 'Southeast Asia in War and Peace: The End of European Colonial Empires'. For a more sympathetic view of Gracey in Vietnam, and a more damning picture of Mountbatten, see Smith, *Vietnam and the Unravelling of Empire*; for Edwina Mountbatten in Saigon, see Morgan, J., *Edwina Mountbatten: A Life of Her Own* (London: HarperCollins, 1991)
25. The use of Indian soldiers against Southeast Asian nationalists also provoked anger against the Indian diaspora there. Indian trading communities such as the Chettiars of Saigon were hounded out of the country. See Bayly and Harper, *Forgotten Wars* pp155–6
26. Bayly and Harper, *Forgotten Wars* p172
27. Smith, *Vietnam and the Unravelling of Empire* p53
28. Connor, *Mountbatten's Samurai* p80
29. Driberg, T., *Ruling Passions* (New York: Setin and Day Publishers, 1978) p214
30. Bayly and Harper, *Forgotten Wars* p27
31. Driberg, *Ruling Passions* p215
32. Ramnath, K., *Boats in a Storm: Law, Migration, and Decolonization in South and Southeast Asia, 1942–1962* (Epub, Stanford University Press, 2023); Charney, *History of Modern Burma* p59
33. Lownie, *The Mountbattens* p169
34. Driberg, *Ruling Passions* pp223–6
35. Ibid. p217
36. In Driberg's memoir, this encounter happens upon his arrival in Rangoon in September. However, Dorman-Smith himself only arrived in Rangoon in October. Cady's *History of Modern Burma* notes that this meeting took place after the Japanese surrender in Singapore
37. Driberg, *Ruling Passions* p215
38. Maung Maung, *Burmese Nationalist Movements 1940–1948*
39. Driberg, *Ruling Passions* p216
40. Ibid. p215
41. scroll.in/article/723440/forged-in-the-chaos-of-world-war-ii-a-pakistani-burmese-love-affair
42. Khan, *The Raj at War* p310
43. Ibid. p314
44. Bayly and Harper, *Forgotten Wars* p89
45. Khan, *The Great Partition* p39
46. Basu, *V. P. Menon* p126
47. Khan, *The Great Partition* p45
48. Hussain, S. *Kashmir in the Aftermath of Partition* (New Delhi: Cambridge University Press, 2021) p63
49. Private interview, Santosh Anand, New Delhi, English, September 2021

50. Khan, *The Great Partition* p49
51. Many Nagas were still animist, but it is generally assumed a majority had converted to Christianity by the end of the war
52. Lintner, *Great Game East* p66
53. Steyn, *Zapuphizo* p72
54. Private interview, Niketu Iralu, Kohima, English, October 2021
55. Throughout the war, the British had been planning to change the Indo-Burmese border, but the sudden race to independence meant that by 1946, redrawing the border was no longer a political priority. People living in the Patkai Hills, however, continued to contest the border. Some Mizo politicians, along with a friend of Aung San named U Nu, wanted the Lushai Hills to become part of Burma, as they shared similar ethnicity and language with the Chin Hills in Burma. See Guyot-Réchard, 'Tangled Lands: Burma and India's Unfinished Separation, 1937–1948' p12, and Zochungnunga, 'Integration or Independence: The Debate in Mizoram on the Eve of Indian Independence' in Nag, S., Gurung T., and Choudhury, A. (eds), *Making of the Indian Union: Merger of the Princely States and Excluded Areas* (New Delhi: Akansha Publishing House, 2007) p208; Sangkima 'The Process of Merger of Mizo Hills with India' in Nag, Gurung and Choudhury (eds), *Making of the Indian Union* p220
56. Nibedon, *Nagaland* p34; For Phizo's return to Nagaland, see Steyn, *Zapuphizo*; Phizo, A., *A Portrait of A.Z. Phizo on his Birth Centenary (1904–2004)* (Urra, Nagaland: The Naga National Council, 2004)
57. Gurung, T., 'Ethnicity and Political Development in Darjeeling on the Eve of Indian Independence' in Nag, Gurung and Choudhury (eds), *Making of the Indian Union* p94; Butalia, U., *The Other Side of Silence: Voices from the Partition of India* (Duke University Press, 2000) pp318–19; Shani, G., *Sikh Nationalism and Identity in a Global Age* (London: Taylor & Francis, 2007) pp51–2
58. Copland, *The Princes of India in the Endgame of Empire 1917–1947* p226
59. Khan, *The Great Partition* p68
60. Childs, D., *Britain since 1945: A Political History* (London: Routledge, 2001) p22
61. Kapoor, P., *1946 Royal Indian Navy Mutiny: Last War of Independence* (Delhi: Lotus Collection Roli Books, 2022) p4
62. Ibid. p15
63. Chaudhuri, N. C., *Thy Hand, Great Anarch!: India 1921–1952* (New Delhi: Times Books Int., 1987) p795
64. Bawa, V. K., *The Last Nizam: The Life and Times of Mir Osman Ali Khan* (New Delhi: Penguin Books India, 1992) p204
65. See Sundarayya, P., *Telangana People's Struggle and Its Lessons* (Hyderabad: Cambridge University Press, 2014)
66. *The Hindu*, 21 March 1946
67. Lownie, *The Mountbattens* p179
68. After Dorman-Smith had refused Aung San's demand for an AFPFL majority in Burma's Executive Council, Aung San had begun to engage in a game of brinkmanship – attacking the British but stopping short of a call for full-blown revolution. Dorman-Smith felt Nehru's presence in Burma would only rile things up further
69. Bayly and Harper, *Forgotten Wars* p225; Kozicki, *India and Burma 1937–1957* p203
70. IOR/M/5/101 'Return of U Saw to Burma after his detention in Uganda during war; his political views as leader of Myochit Party'
71. Kozicki, *India and Burma 1937–1957* p205
72. Bayly and Harper, *Forgotten Wars* p71
73. Foucar, *I Lived in Burma* p197
74. IOR/M/5/101 'Return of U Saw to Burma after his detention in Uganda during war; his political views as leader of Myochit Party' p15
75. IOR/M/4/2638 'Political organizations: Myochit Party (Leader U Saw) 1946–7' p5
76. Bayly and Harper, *Forgotten Wars* p227
77. Collis, *First and Last in Burma*, quoted in Myint-U, *The River of Lost Footsteps* p248
78. Bayly and Harper, *Forgotten Wars* p 257
79. Maung Maung, *Aung San of Burma* p116
80. IOR/M/4/2638 'Political organizations: Myochit Party (Leader U Saw) 1946–7' p18
81. IOR/Mss Eur D1108 'Papers of Col Claude Hugh Morley Toye (b 1917), British Army 1939, as acting chief intelligence officer, Burma Command, relating chiefly to political affairs in Burma; also note by Toye, dated 1985, entitled "Arms in the Lake" on certain of the events surrounding the murder of Aung San.'

82. Tinsa Maw-Naing and Han, *A Burmese Heart* p178
83. In fact, most Sikkimese were probably Hindu at this point
84. Chawla, S., 'How Bhutan Came to Not Be a Part of India' in The Wire, 8 February 2019; Chawla, S., '"Nothing in Common with 'Indian' Indian": Bhutan and the Cabinet Mission Plan' in Guyot-Réchard, B. and Leake, E. (ed) *South Asia Unbound: New International Histories of the Subcontinent* (epub: Leiden University Press, 2023) p62; Chawla, S., 'Fashioning a "Buddhist" Himalayan Cartography: Sikkim Darbar and the Cabinet Mission Plan', *Indian Quarterly*. 2023, 79 (1); Duff, A., *Sikkim: Requiem for a Himalayan Kingdom* (Edinburgh: Birlinn) p30
85. *Mr Jinnah: The Making of Pakistan*. Documentary directed by Christopher Mitchell, Akbar Ahmed, 1997
86. Von Tunzelmann, *Indian Summer* p143
87. Hajari, *Midnight's Furies* pp19–20
88. *Civil & Military Gazette* (Lahore), 13 August 1946
89. Samaddar, R., 'Policing a Riot-Torn City: Kolkata, 16–18 August 1946', *Policies and Practices 69* (Calcutta: Mahanirban Calcutta Research Group, 2015) p1
90. Mukherjee, *Hungry Bengal* p206
91. Hajari, *Midnight's Furies* p12
92. See Chatterji, *Bengal Divided*
93. For more on the growth of paramilitary groups, see Legg, S., 'A Pre-Partitioned City? Anti-Colonial and Communal Mohallas in Inter-War Delhi', *South Asia: Journal of South Asian Studies*. 2019, 42(1): 170–87
94. Choudhary, A., *Vajpayee: The Ascent of the Hindu Right 1924–1977* (New Delhi: Picador India, 2023) p37
95. Chatterji, *Bengal Divided* p230
96. Ibid. pp84–5
97. National Archives: Calcutta riots: report from CGS India, 24 August 1946 (WO 216/662)
98. Hajari, *Midnight's Furies* p13
99. Mukherjee, *Hungry Bengal* p205
100. Flasinski, T., 'Dr Jekyll, Mr Hyde or Bengali Hamlet? Hussein Shaheed Suhrawardy as the last Prime Minister of Undivided Bengal', *Rocznik Orientalistyczny*. 2020, 73(2): 48–9
101. Rahman, Sheikh M., and Alam, F., *The Unfinished Memoirs* (Dhaka: The University Press Limited, 2012) p68
102. National Archives: Calcutta riots: report from CGS India, 24 August 1946 (WO 216/662)
103. Rahman and Alam, *The Unfinished Memoirs* p68
104. No transcript of the speech survives. A reporter present summarised it with the words: 'He had seen to Police and Military arrangements who would not interfere. The audience should move in groups and defend their co-religionists.' Many have argued that Suhrawardy bears responsibility for the violence that followed. Recently, an article by Tomasz Flasinski has challenged this interpretation, arguing that although biased against Hindus, Suhrawardy did not actively incite the Great Calcutta Killings, and indeed attempted to calm them. See Flasinski, 'Dr Jekyll, Mr Hyde or Bengali Hamlet? Hussein Shaheed Suhrawardy as the last Prime Minister of Undivided Bengal' 38–110
105. See Mukherjee, *Hungry Bengal* pp209–27
106. WO 216/6: Calcutta riots: report from CGS India, 24 August 1946 (62)
107. Mukherjee, *Hungry Bengal* p247
108. Chaudhuri, *Thy Hand, Great Anarch!* p811
109. Rahman and Alam, *The Unfinished Memoirs* p70
110. Malhotra, A., *In the Language of Remembering: The Inheritance of Partition* (Gurugram: HarperCollins India, 2022) p137
111. Rahman and Alam, *The Unfinished Memoirs* p71
112. Von Tunzelmann, *Indian Summer* p143
113. Hajari, *Midnight's Furies* pp21–2
114. Ibid. pp19–20
115. Mukherjee, *Hungry Bengal* p221; Bayly and Harper, *Forgotten Wars* p250; Khan, *The Great Partition* p71; Sherman, T., *Muslim Belonging in Secular India: Negotiating Citizenship in Postcolonial Hyderabad* (Cambridge: Cambridge University Press, 2015) p20
116. Khan, *The Great Partition* p72
117. Jha, D. K., *Golwalkar: The Myth Behind the Man, the Man Behind the Machine* (Delhi: Simon & Schuster, 2024) p143
118. Hajari, *Midnight's Furies* p63
119. Guha, R., *India after Gandhi: The History of the World's Largest Democracy* (London: Pan Macmillan India, 2017) p11
120. Von Tunzelmann, *Indian Summer* p144

121. Brendon, *The Decline and Fall of the British Empire* p404
122. Sen, D., *The Decline of the Caste Question: Jogendranath Mandal and the Defeat of Dalit Politics in Bengal* (New Delhi: Cambridge University Press, 2018) p157
123. French, *Liberty or Death* pp256–9
124. Choudhary, *Vajpayee* pp53–4
125. *Civil & Military Gazette* (Lahore), 29 September 1946
126. Kozicki, *India and Burma 1937–1957* p210
127. Naw, *Aung San and the Struggle for Burmese Independence* p188
128. Bayly and Harper, *Forgotten Wars* p302
129. Driberg, *Ruling Passions* p217
130. *East Special: Who Really Killed Aung San*. Presented by Fergal Keane, BBC, 1997
131. U Tin Tut, 'It Was a Historic Moment' in Maung Maung, *Aung San of Burma* p110
132. Charney, *History of Modern Burma* p64
133. Silverstein (ed.), *The Political Legacy of Aung San: Revised Edition* p10
134. Simms, *Great Lords of the Sky* p77
135. Sao Sanda Simms, *Moon Princess: Memories of the Shan States* (Amazon Kindle: River Books, 2018) Chapter 7
136. In fact, like the Naga 'excluded areas', they were never completely 'outside' the Burmese Union. Nonetheless, Shan nationalists today argue that 'Japanese recognition, following the British precedent, of the traditional Shan Sawbwas as the rightful rulers of the hills and a prohibition on armed Burman units from entering their territory, are further proof of the historic independence of the Shan peoples'. Smith, M., *Burma: Insurgency and the Politics of Ethnicity* (London: Zed Books, 1991) p64
137. Aung San, 'Let Us Unite' in Maung Maung, *Aung San of Burma* p123
138. Smith, *Burma: Insurgency and the Politics of Ethnicity* pp78–80
139. Steyn, *Zapuphizo* p65
140. Bayly and Harper, *Forgotten Wars* p308
141. Phillips Talbot to Walter S. Rogers, 16 February 1947, published in Rediff, 'The Gandhi March is an Astonishing Sight', 2 October 2020. Available at: rediff.com/news/special/phillips-talbot-the-gandhi-march-is-an-astonishing-sight/20201002.htm
142. Rahman and Alam, *The Unfinished Memoirs* p86
143. French, *Liberty or Death* p344
144. Bayly and Harper, *Forgotten Armies* p306
145. Karnad, *Farthest Field* p236
146. Butalia, *The Other Side of Silence* p45
147. Ibid.
148. Private interview, Ishar Das Arora, Hindu and Urdu, September 2019

Chapter 7: Dividing an Empire

1. Holden and Johns, *The House of Saud* p141
2. Khan, *The Great Partition* p83
3. Von Tunzelmann, *Indian Summer* p157
4. Ibid. p162
5. Lownie, *The Mountbattens* p193
6. Campbell-Johnson, A., *Mission with Mountbatten* (Bungay, Suffolk: Richard Clay and Company Ltd, 1951) p39
7. Shahid Hamid, S., *Disastrous Twilight: A Personal Record of the Partition of India* (London: Leo Cooper, 1993) p155
8. Campbell-Johnson, *Mission with Mountbatten* p40
9. French, *Liberty or Death* p279
10. Zubrzycki, J., *Dethroned: Patel, Menon and the Integration of Princely India* (New Delhi: Juggernaut Books, 2023) p76
11. Mosley, L., *The Last Days of the British Raj* (London: Weidenfeld and Nicolson, 1961) p158
12. In *Indian Summer*, Von Tunzelmann points out that although Mountbatten mentions this much-quoted anecdote on several occasions, such a document does not seem to exist in either British or Indian archives. Whether this is just another story made up by Mountbatten (of which there were many) is uncertain. What *does* exist is a 'breakdown plan'. Wavell was firmly against India's partition, viewing the unity of India as Britain's greatest contribution to the subcontinent. Whitehall had rejected the plan already, but America was leaning on Britain to quit India. Von Tunzelmann, *Indian Summer* p163
13. *Civil & Military Gazette* (Lahore), 25 March 1947
14. Von Tunzelmann, *Indian Summer* p167
15. Campbell-Johnson, *Mission with Mountbatten* p40
16. Ibid. p42
17. *Belfast Telegraph*, 24 March 1947
18. Zubrzycki, J., *Dethroned* p15
19. Shahid Hamid, *Disastrous Twilight* p152; *Civil & Military Gazette* (Lahore), 25 March 1947
20. *Daily Herald*, 24 March 1947
21. Lownie, *The Mountbattens* p195

22. Campbell-Johnson, *Mission with Mountbatten* p43
23. Shankar, R., *My Music, My Life* (San Rafael: Mandala Publishing, 2007) p87
24. 'Delegates from Kirghizia and Turkmenistan did not arrive until a day after the conference had ended': Stolte, C., 'The Asiatic Hour: New Perspectives on the Asian Relations Conference, New Delhi 1947', in Miskovic, N., Fischer-Tiné, H., and Boskovska, N., *The Non-Aligned Movement and the Cold War: Delhi – Bandung – Belgrade* (London: Taylor & Francis Group, 2014) p57
25. Shahid Hamid, *Disastrous Twilight* p148
26. Amrith, *Crossing the Bay of Bengal* p222. To this day, dual citizenship is not allowed in almost all countries in Asia (notable exceptions are Pakistan and Bangladesh). A direct consequence of this is that almost all countries in the region have serious issues with politics over who is indigenous or not
27. Campbell-Johnson, *Mission with Mountbatten* p43
28. Baroda had already joined in February 1947
29. Bhopal believed that if the princes stayed out of the Constituent Assembly until independence, they would automatically become independent and have thus mastered delaying tactics to perfection. One exasperated secretary noted that 'His Highness, the Nawab of Bhopal, required a special type of coffee and a special type of paan … He would not agree to sit for more than an hour at a time, and then the meetings had to adjourn to enable him to partake of his refreshments.' See Basu, V. P. Menon p285; Zubrzycki, *Dethroned* p115
30. Akins, H., *Conquering the Maharajas: India's Princely States and the End of Empire, 1930–50* (Manchester: Manchester University Press, 2023) p103
31. Ibid. p92
32. Gandhi, R., *Patel: A Life* (Ahmedabad: Navajivan Publishing House, 2020) p343
33. Zubrzycki, *Dethroned* p10
34. Campbell-Johnson, *Mission with Mountbatten* p43
35. QDL IOR/L/PS/12/1444 'Administrative policy: arrangements for achievement of Imperial purposes at Aden; transfer of administration to Government of India (from Government of Bombay)' p274
36. Balfour-Paul, G., *The End of Empire in the Middle East: Britain's Relinquishment of Power in Her Last Three Arab Dependencies* (Cambridge: Cambridge University Press, 1991) p220
37. Darwin, J., *Unfinished Empire: The Global Expansion of Britain* (Bloomsbury Press, New York: 2012) p353
38. Hay, quoted in Al-Baharna, H. M., *The Legal Status of the Arabian Gulf States: A Study of Their Treaty Relations and Their International Problems* (Manchester: Manchester University Press, 1968) p9
39. Rich, *Creating the Arabian Gulf* p247
40. Thanks to administrative wrangling, however, it remained under the authority of the India Office in London for another year until on 1 April 1948 it was fully transferred to the Foreign Office. See Blythe, *The Empire of the Raj* p211; Rich, *Creating the Arabian Gulf* p245
41. Darwin, J., *Unfinished Empire: The Global Expansion of Britain* (Bloomsbury Press, New York: 2012) p353
42. Campbell-Johnson, *Mission with Mountbatten* p45
43. Von Tunzelmann, *Indian Summer* p171
44. Shahid Hamid, *Disastrous Twilight* p153
45. French, *Liberty or Death* p291
46. Ibid. p293
47. Campbell-Johnson, *Mission with Mountbatten* p46
48. See French, *Liberty or Death* p280
49. Von Tunzelmann, *Indian Summer* p178
50. Campbell-Johnson, *Mission with Mountbatten* p56
51. Jalal, *The Sole Spokesman* p179
52. Campbell-Johnson, *Mission with Mountbatten* p56
53. Lownie, *The Mountbattens* p199
54. Von Tunzelmann, *Indian Summer* p175
55. Ibid. p178
56. French, *Liberty or Death* p277
57. Campbell-Johnson, *Mission with Mountbatten* p70
58. IOR/Mss Eur E 341/46: Telegram from Govsecben to P. S. V., 26 April 1947
59. IOR/Mss Eur E 341/46: Telegram from Viceroy to Governor of Bengal, 28 April 1947
60. scroll.in/article/907754/why-did-british-prime-minister-attlee-think-bengal-was-going-to-be-an-independent-country-in-1947
61. Shahid Hamid, *Disastrous Twilight* p151
62. Von Tunzelmann, *Indian Summer* p177

63. Campbell-Johnson, *Mission with Mountbatten* p84
64. Brendon, *The Decline and Fall of the British Empire* p241
65. MP MS62/MB32/24/EM/Edwina Mountbatten's Diary Jan-Jun 1947, 6 May 1947
66. Ibid. 8 May 1947
67. Campbell-Johnson, *Mission with Mountbatten* p88
68. Von Tunzelmann, *Indian Summer* p189
69. Ibid. p191
70. Campbell-Johnson, *Mission with Mountbatten* p90
71. Basu, *V. P. Menon* inside jacket
72. Ibid. p217
73. Zubrzycki, *Dethroned* p63
74. Ismay, H. L., *The Memoirs of General Lord Ismay* (New York: Viking, 1960) p424
75. Anil, P., *Another India: The Making of the World's Largest Muslim Minority* (London: Hurst & Company, 2023) p69
76. MP MS62/MB1/D126/4: Telegram from Secretary of State to Viceroy, 2 June 1947
77. Khan, *The Great Partition* p85
78. Campbell-Johnson, *Mission with Mountbatten* p106
79. *Birmingham Daily Gazette*, 4 June 1947
80. *Civil & Military Gazette* (Lahore), 3 June 1947
81. *Indian Express*, 3 June 1947; *Civil & Military Gazette* (Lahore), 3 June 1947
82. Khan, *The Great Partition* p4
83. All-India Radio, 3 June announcement
84. Ibid.
85. Campbell-Johnson, *Mission with Mountbatten* p107
86. Ibid. p108
87. Albinia, A., *Empires of the Indus: The Story of a River* (London: John Murray, 2009) p10
88. Shahid Hamid, *Disastrous Twilight* pp178–9
89. Lownie, *The Mountbattens* p208
90. *Civil & Military Gazette* (Lahore), 4 June 1947
91. IOR/L/P&J/7/12391 Enquiries about nationality of a British descent
92. IOR/Mss Eur F226/10 Memoir of the Career of Sir Reginald Michael Hadow p7
93. Khan, *The Great Partition* p4
94. French, *Liberty or Death* p306
95. Ibid. p307
96. Naim, C. M., 'The Maulana Who Loved Krishna', *Economic and Political Weekly*. 2013, 48(17): 37–44
97. *Indian Express*, 7 June 1947
98. When Khaksars mobbed Jinnah's meeting at the Imperial Hotel, there was an Intelligence Bureau agent present, feeding information back to Patel. French, *Liberty or Death* p307
99. Campbell-Johnson, *Mission with Mountbatten* p115
100. Shahid Hamid, *Disastrous Twilight* p182
101. Chopra, P. S., *1947: A Soldier's Story from the Records of Maj. Gen. Mohinder Singh Chopra* (New Delhi: Military Studies Convention, 1997), quoted in partitionstudiesquarterly.org/article/1947-a-soldiers-story-from-the-records-of-maj-gen-mohinder-singh-chopra/
102. Dutta, B. 'Muslims against Pakistan: The Jamiat-ul-Ulama-i-Hind against Partition in Colonial Assam, 1947', *Partition Studies Quarterly*. 2021, 4
103. Basu, *V. P. Menon* p268
104. Campbell-Johnson, *Mission with Mountbatten* p130
105. Malhotra, *In the Language of Remembering* p372
106. Butalia, *The Other Side of Silence* p82; Campbell-Johnson, *Mission with Mountbatten* p124
107. Van Schendel, W., *The Bengal Borderland: Beyond State and Nation in South Asia* (London: Anthem Press, 2005) p39
108. Lownie, *The Mountbattens* p215
109. Hussain, I., 'Resistance, Pacification and Exclusion: The Hill People and the Nationalist Upsurge', in Bhuyan, A. (ed.), *Nationalist Upsurge in Assam* (Guwahati: Government of Assam, 2000) p294
110. Lownie, *The Mountbattens* p268
111. Shahid Hamid, *Disastrous Twilight* p172
112. Ahmed, A. S., *Jinnah, Pakistan and Islamic Identity: The Search for Saladin* (London: Routledge, 1997) p162
113. The official Mountbatten line is that if their relationship ever turned sexual, this was only after the Mountbattens had left India. Yet with access to Nehru and Edwina's letters still off limits to the public on the grounds of national security at the time of writing, it is difficult not to question this line
114. IWM 19975 Reel 3: Massey, Patrick (Oral History), available on Imperial War Museum Digital Archive
115. The border with West Pakistan was largely determined by the rulers of

Kutch, Jodhpur, Jaisalmer, Bikaner, Kashmir, Bahawalpur and Khairpur. The border with East Pakistan, meanwhile, was determined by the rulers of Cooch Behar, Tripura, and the Khasi states of Nongstoin, Langrin, Maharam, Dwara, Shella, Mawlong, Cherra and Khyrim

116. Von Tunzelmann, *Indian Summer* p219
117. Chawla, '"Nothing in Common with 'Indian' Indian": Bhutan and the Cabinet Mission Plan' p72
118. Ibid. p74
119. Bangash, Y. K., *A Princely Affair: The Accession and Integration of the Princely States of Pakistan, 1947–1955* (Karachi: Oxford University Press, 2015) p85; Hodson, H. V., *The Great Divide: Britain – India – Pakistan* (London: Hutchinson, 1969) p367
120. Zubrzycki, *Dethroned* p67
121. Corfield, C., *The Princely India I Knew: From Reading to Mountbatten* (Madras: Indo-British Historical Society, 1975) p158
122. IOR/Mss Eur F226/10 Memoir of the Career of Sir Reginald Michael Hadow p7
123. Zubrzycki, *Dethroned* p5
124. Guha, *India after Gandhi* p41
125. Menon, V. P., *The Story of the Integration of the Indian States* (Bangalore: Longmans Green and Co., 1955) p98
126. Hodson, *The Great Divide* p368
127. Campbell-Johnson, *Mission with Mountbatten* p140
128. spectator.co.uk/article/a-hindu-cromwell-courteously-decapitates-hundreds-of-maharajas/
129. Zubrzycki, *Dethroned* p9
130. Morrow, A., *Highness: The Maharajahs of India* (London: Grafton, 1987) p3
131. Campbell-Johnson, *Mission with Mountbatten* p142
132. Basu, *V. P. Menon* p78
133. spectator.co.uk/article/a-hindu-cromwell-courteously-decapitates-hundreds-of-maharajas/
134. Akins, *Conquering the Maharajas* p97
135. Mountbatten's response was that men like Patel were 'as frightened of communism as you yourself are. If only they had support from all other stable influences such as that of the Princely Order, it might be possible for them to ward off the communist danger' Guha, *India after Gandhi* p47
136. Guha, *India after Gandhi* p45
137. Zubrzycki, *Dethroned* p85
138. Ibid. p12
139. Ibid. pp88–90
140. That summer a report had begun to circulate claiming that Aung San had been invited to the state capital of Imphal to discuss its integration with Burma. Until the eighteenth century, Manipur had been culturally and linguistically closer to Burma than to Bengal or Assam, and it had been under the rule of the Burmese Empire until the East India Company had annexed it. Aung San's cabinet claimed that if Nehru permitted, they would not 'discourage the State from joining Burma'. But Congress was shaken and immediately emphasised to the Maharaja that 'The future of Manipur State obviously lies with the Union of India.' In early August, the Maharaja finally signed India's Instrument of Accession. *Hindustan Standard*, 12 May 1947; Nehru Memorial Museum and Library, Krishna Menon Papers, Nehru to the Maharaja of Manipur, 22 May 1947, quoted in Basu, *V. P. Menon* p288; for more on this often-forgotten episode see Chishti, S. M. A. W., *Political Development in Manipur 1919–1949* (DPhil in Political Science: Aligarh Muslim University, 1979) Chapter IX, and Sudhirkumar Singh, H., *Socio-Religious and Political Movements in Modern Manipur (1934–51)* (PhD Thesis, Jawaharlal Nehru University) Chapter 6; Bangash, *A Princely Affair*
141. Sen, A., 'The Integration of Cooch Behar State' in Nag, Gurung and Choudhury (eds), *Making of the Indian Union* p75
142. Copland, *The Princes of India in the Endgame of Empire 1917–1947* p260
142. Krishna, B., *Sardar Vallabhbhai Patel: India's Iron Man* (New Delhi: Indus, 1995) p313
144. NAI, MoHA, Instrument of Accession, R-1/10/47, 1947 'Bikaner State – Instrument of Accession and Standstill Agreement signed between Maharaja Sadul Singh, Ruler of Bikaner State and the Dominion of India'
145. Krishna, *Sardar Vallabhbhai Patel* p313
146. Menon, *The Story of the Integration of the Indian States* p113
157. Krishna, *Sardar Vallabhbhai Patel* p313
148. John Zubrzycki has recently shown that Menon's account may be a case of self-aggrandisement. The event may have been intended as a practical joke that

'backfired'. The 'revolver' was concealed in a pen and had been crafted as a magic prop. It was later gifted to Lord Mountbatten and was recently sold at auction. Zubrzycki, *Dethroned* p114
149. Menon, *The Story of the Integration of the Indian States* p113
150. For Kutch, see NAI, MoHA, Instrument of Accession, B-III/46/47, 1947 'Kutch State – Instrument of Accession and Standstill Agreement signed between Lt. Col. H. H. Maharajadhiraj Mirza Maharao Shri Sir Vikjayarajji Savai Bahadur, Ruler of Kutch State and the Dominion of India'; For Jaisalmer, see NAI, MoHA, Instrument of Accession, R-I/16/47 'Jaisalmer State – Instrument of Accession and Standstill Agreement signed between Jawahir Singh, Ruler of Jaisalmer State and the Dominion of India'
151. Bikaner signed the Instrument of Accession on 7 August 1947. Of the other states that would form the India–Pakistan boundary, Cooch Behar would sign on 9 August, followed by Jodhpur and Kutch on 11 August. Jaisalmer signed on 12 August, and Tripura on 13 August. Bahawalpur and Khairpur acceded to Pakistan on 3 October. It remains disputed whether the Maharaja of Kashmir acceded to India before Indian troops landed on 26 October, or after on 27 October. On 15 December, twenty Khasi states acceded to India, including the states of Langrin, Maharam, Dwara, Shella, Mawlong, Cherra and Khyrim which all bordered Sylhet District of East Pakistan. Mawlong state acceded to India on 10 March 1948, and nine days later, on 19 March, the final border state – Nongstoin – acceded to India as well.
152. Bayly and Harper, *Forgotten Wars* p312
153. Ibid. p314
154. *Frontier Areas Committee of Enquiry* 1947, quoted in Simms, *Great Lords of the Sky* p80
155. IOR/Mss Eur D1108 'Papers of Col Claude Hugh Morley Toye (b 1917), British Army 1939, as acting chief intelligence officer, Burma Command, relating chiefly to political affairs in Burma; also note by Toye, dated 1985, entitled "Arms in the Lake" on certain of the events surrounding the murder of Aung San' p8
156. Ibid. p10
157. Charney, *History of Modern Burma* pp68–70
158. MP MS62/MB1/D126/5/10 Telegram from Viceroy of India to Governor of Burma, 19 July 1947
159. Gandhi, M. K., *The Collected Works of Mahatma Gandhi LXXXVIII (May–July 1947)* (New Delhi: Publications Division, Ministry of Information and Broadcasting, Govt of India, 1970) pp380–2
160. *East Special: Who Really Killed Aung San.* Documentary presented by Fergal Keane, BBC, 1997
161. IOR/M/4/2721 Law and Order: U Saw's Trial
162. Maung Maung, *Aung San of Burma* p65
163. Myint-U, *The River of Lost Footsteps* p266
164. IOR/Mss Eur D1108 'Papers of Col Claude Hugh Morley Toye (b 1917), British Army 1939, as acting chief intelligence officer, Burma Command, relating chiefly to political affairs in Burma; also note by Toye, dated 1985, entitled "Arms in the Lake" on certain of the events surrounding the murder of Aung San' p43
165. IOR/M/4/2721 Law and Order: U Saw's Trial p5
166. Smith, *Burma*

Chapter 8: A Red Dawn

1. Taunsvi, F., *The Sixth River: A Journal from the Partition of India*, translated by Maaz Bin Bilal (New Delhi: Speaking Tiger, 2019) p42
2. Ibid. p27
3. Fikr Taunsvi, quoted in Khan, *The Great Partition* p112
4. Taunsvi, *The Sixth River* pp46–7
5. Ibid. p50
6. Hajari, *Midnight's Furies* p114
7. Butalia, *The Other Side of Silence* p73
8. French, *Liberty or Death* p346
9. Brigid Keenan Private Collection: Letters to Maisie, 13 August 1947
10. spectator.co.uk/article/passage-from-india/
11. Brigid Keenan Private Collection: Letters to Maisie, 13 August 1947
12. MB1/D76/1 Record of interviews with Lord Mountbatten Jan 1948–Feb 1948
13. French, *Liberty or Death* p338
14. Brigid Keenan Private Collection: Letters to Maisie, 16 October 1947
15. *Civil & Military Gazette* (Lahore), 13 August 1947

16. Butalia, *The Other Side of Silence* p86
17. Hodson, *The Great Divide* p351
18. Campbell-Johnson, *Mission with Mountbatten* p154
19. Jinnah's speech was later suppressed by General Zia-ul-Haq for its supposedly secular leanings. For a discussion on its various interpretations and legacies, see Hoodbhoy, P., *Pakistan: Origins, Identity and Future* (New York: Routledge, 2023) Chapter 5 and particularly Ahmed, *Jinnah* Chapter 16
20. Campbell-Johnson, *Mission with Mountbatten* p155
21. Contrary to popular belief, Jinnah did not cut off ties with Dina after her marriage to Neville Wadia. They remained in touch for years afterwards, and Dina later told the journalist Hamid Mir that their last meeting was in late 1946. See hilal.gov.pk/view-article.php?i=8033
22. hilal.gov.pk/view-article.php?i=8033
23. Bangash, *A Princely Affair* p7
24. Campbell-Johnson, *Mission with Mountbatten* p156
25. Fernandes, *Taj Mahal Foxtrot* p16
26. Campbell-Johnson, *Mission with Mountbatten* p156
27. Von Tunzelmann, *Indian Summer* p4
28. Jawaharlal Nehru's 'Tryst with Destiny' speech, 14 August 1947
29. Campbell-Johnson, *Mission with Mountbatten* p161
30. Sen, *Home in the World: A Memoir* p46
31. Quoted in Guha, *India after Gandhi* p7
32. IOR/Mss Eur F226/28 'Thim Days Is Gone' by Patrick Tandy p121; IOR/Mss Eur F226/23 A Grandfather's Tale: Memoirs being mainly concerned with service in the Indian Army and the Indian Political Service in India and the Persian Gulf from 1932–1947 p97; youtube.com/watch?v=E22GVIHndlE
33. Steyn, *Zapuphizo* p77
34. Quoted in Guha, *India after Gandhi* p8
35. Samal, J. K., 'Integration of the Princely States of Orissa: 1947–49' in Nag, Gurung and Choudhury (eds), *Making of the Indian Union* p272
36. IOR/L/I/1/770/462/21F (M) 'Partition of Bengal and the Punjab: Appointment of the Boundary Commission' p17
37. Pandian and Mariappan, *Ayya's Accounts* p85
38. Taunsvi, *The Sixth River* p56
39. Jalal, *The Pity of Partition*
40. Taunsvi, *The Sixth River* p65
41. Ibid. p71
42. Private Interview, Seyyed Muhammad Abbas Ali Meerza and Seyyed Muhammad Raza Ali Meerza, Murshidabad, English and Urdu, November 2021
43. Van Schendel, *A History of Bangladesh* p118; Van Schendel, *The Bengal Borderland* p49
44. See Eaton, R. M., *The Rise of Islam and the Bengal Frontier* (Berkeley: University of California Press, 1993)
45. Quoted in Raghavan, S., *1971: A Global History of the Creation of Bangladesh* (Cambridge, Massachusetts: Harvard University Press, 2013) p6
46. Hajari, *Midnight's Furies* p150
47. IWM 19975 Reel 3: Massey, Patrick (Oral History), available on Imperial War Museum Digital Archive
48. Keenan, B., *Full Marks for Trying* (London: Bloomsbury Publishing, 2016) pp55–6
49. Butalia, *The Other Side of Silence* p3; Fazila-Yacoobali Zamindar, V., *The Long Partition and the Making of Modern South Asia: Refugees, Boundaries, Histories* (New York: Columbia University Press, 2007) p6
50. Malhotra, *In the Language of Remembering* p54
51. Butalia, *The Other Side of Silence* p81; Fazila-Yacoobali Zamindar, *The Long Partition and the Making of Modern South Asia* p34
52. newyorker.com/magazine/2015/06/29/the-great-divide-books-dalrymple
53. Private Interview: Avtar and Raminder Singh Hoonjan, London, English, September 2021
54. Project Dastaan Digital Archive, Online, Mussarat Abrar
55. Butalia, *The Other Side of Silence* p73
56. Fazila-Yacoobali Zamindar, *The Long Partition and the Making of Modern South Asia* p43
57. Van Schendel, *A History of Bangladesh* p13; Bayly and Harper, *Forgotten Wars* p300
58. Keenan, *Full Marks for Trying* p56
59. Jalal, *The Pity of Partition* pp1–2
60. Ibid. p38
61. Manto: The Unsentimentalist Sunil Khilnani Incarnations
62. newyorker.com/magazine/2015/06/29/the-great-divide-books-dalrymple

63. theguardian.com/books/2016/jun/11/saadat-hasan-manto-short-stories-partition-pakistan
64. Jalal, *The Pity of Partition* p131
65. Taunsvi, *The Sixth River* pp81, 94
66. Ibid. p117
67. Ibid. p121
68. Ibid. p73
69. scroll.in/article/938301/this-journal-by-a-hindu-writer-from-lahore-is-a-rare-non-fiction-account-of-the-partition
70. Taunsvi, *The Sixth River* pp108–12
71. Butalia, *The Other Side of Silence* p3
72. Von Tunzelmann, *Indian Summer* p266
73. For Jaipur, Private Interview, Abid Saghir, Jaipur, English and Urdu, January 2023; for Bahawalpur State, see Moon, *Divide and Quit*. For Malerkotla, see thewire.in/history/malerkotla-india-history-tolerance-communalism
74. Choudhary, *Vajpayee* p41
75. Private Interview: Khalid Bashir Khan Rai, London, English, July 2018, available in the Project Dastaan Archive
76. Hajari, *Midnight's Furies* p120
77. Keenan, *Full Marks for Trying* p58. A version of this story appears in James's letter to Maisie on 27 September: 'I saw H.H. about it [the massacre] and he confirmed he could do nothing. He said his Sikhs want to kill their Muslims just because they are Muslim and he had been so good to them that his subjects were calling his state "Chota Pakistan". Anyway he would do nothing to force them to give up what had been stolen, the SWINE'
78. Copland, I., 'The Further Shores of Partition: Ethnic Cleansing in Rajasthan 1947', *Past & Present*. 1998, 160(1): 203–39
79. Heaney, G. F., *The Winding Trail*, quoted in Hajari, *Midnight's Furies* p149
80. Quoted in Copland, 'The Further Shores of Partition: Ethnic Cleansing in Rajasthan 1947' 203–39
81. Brendon, *The Decline and Fall of the British Empire* p406
82. Anil, *Another India* p117
83. Jha, *Golwalkar* p168; Choudhary, *Vajpayee* p54
84. Jha, *Golwalkar* pp189–92; Six, C., *Secularism, Decolonisation, and the Cold War in South and Southeast Asia* (Abingdon, Routledge, 2018) p106
85. French, *Liberty or Death* p360
86. Von Tunzelmann, *Indian Summer* p280
87. Six, *Secularism, Decolonisation, and the Cold War in South and Southeast Asia* p105
88. Jha, *Golwalkar* p213
89. Taunsvi, *The Sixth River* pp140–1, 161
90. Ibid. p141
91. Ibid. p172

Chapter 9: Into the Abyss

1. Private Interview, Khushi Ram, Ragbir Singh and Manish Sharma, Dujana, Hindi, January 2022
2. Bangash, *A Princely Affair* p144. The secretary said: 'He however continued to make representations for a maintenance allowance ... the nawab would have been well advised to stay on in India, where he would have received a substantial privy purse. We could not possibly accept the accession of a state next door to the capital of India. So, we can only consider him a displaced person, however much we sympathise with him.' Locals in Dujana maintain the Nawab didn't seriously consider a merger with Pakistan but wanted to pressure the government of India into giving Dujana a better deal
3. NAI: *States General 1948–1950*, NAI, Digitised Private Papers of Sardar Patel, 1948, PP_000000005920; NAI: *List of States who has signed Instruments of Accession and Stand Still Agreement*, NAI, Home, Treaty/Agreement, 1/Poll/Mics, 1950. In Dujana today it is commonly believed the Nawab didn't receive a proper salary from Pakistan, fell into poverty, and began working at a dhaba. In 2022, when I visited and conducted a number of interviews in Dujana, most of the mosques were in ruins, used for drying cow dung. Apparently only a hundred Muslim families remain in the city – notably Fazal Hussein who chose to stay and care for the Qasi Sahib Mosque when his community left the town. Many of the abandoned mosques were taken over by Hindu and Sikh groups after Partition, and their 'reclamation' in recent years by the Waqf board has caused much controversy
4. Gandhi's old translator in Aden, Muhammad Ali Luqman, was at that very moment penning a novel called *Kamala Devi* based on his family in Junagadh
5. For years writing on the Junagadh crisis has largely relied on a single source: Menon, *The Story of the Integration of the Indian States*. However, a new generation

of scholars have recently challenged decades of nationalist mythmaking and orientalist stereotypes – most notably, Rakesh Ankit and Praduman Khachar. In Ankit's own words, 'The Junagadh affair was neither a "fantasy" nor a "farce" and certainly not a "comedy" as it has been variously called.' Ankit, R., 'The Accession of Junagadh, 1947–48: Colonial Sovereignty, State Violence and Post-Independence India', *Indian Economic and Social History Review*. 2016, 53(3): 402

6. Hajari, *Midnight's Furies* p162; a similar description is given by Guha, *India after Gandhi* p49, among other books
7. 'On History, Foolishness and Vietnam', *New York Times*, 12 July 1975, nytimes.com/1975/07/12/archives/on-history-foolishness-and-vietnam.html
8. Agarwal M. K., *From Bharata to India: Volume 2: The Rape of Chrysee* (iUniverse: Bloomington, 2012)
9. Sheikh, G. A., *The Mahabat Album (With Short Biographical Sketches of the Babi Family and the Nawab Sahebs of the Junagadh State)* (Surat: Muslim-Gujarat Press, 1936) pp16–22; Divyabhanusinh, 'Junagadh State and its Lions: Conservation in Princely India, 1879–1947', *Conservation & Society*. 2006, 4(4), and Divyabhanusinh, *The Story of Asia's Lions* (Navi Mumbai: Marg Publications, 2008)
10. Mosley, *The Last Days of the British Raj*, quoted in Bangash, *A Princely Affair* p108
11. Bennett-Jones, O., *The Bhutto Dynasty: The Struggle for Power in Pakistan* (London: Yale University Press, 2020) p25
12. Hajari, *Midnight's Furies* p162
13. Bangash, *A Princely Affair* p110; for Shahnawaz Bhutto, see Bennett-Jones, *The Bhutto Dynasty* Chapter 1
14. Akins, *Conquering the Maharajas* p184
15. Menon, *The Story of the Integration of the Indian States* p134
16. Ibid. p130
17. Ankit, R., 'Junagadh, India and the Logic of Occupation and Appropriation, 1947–49', *Studies in History*. 2018, 34(2): 115
18. Quoted in Hajari, *Midnight's Furies* p162; Ankit, 'The Accession of Junagadh, 1947–48: Colonial Sovereignty, State Violence and Post-Independence India' p377
19. Menon, *The Story of the Integration of the Indian States* p131
20. Ibid. p131
21. Hajari, *Midnight's Furies* p170
22. Bangash, *A Princely Affair* p113
23. Hajari, *Midnight's Furies* p173
24. McDonald, H., *Ambani & Sons* (New Delhi: Roli Books, 2010) Chapter 1
25. The Junagadh Archives contain a list of signatures compiled by Bhutto after going to hundreds of towns across Junagadh, getting village heads to sign that they would not object whatever the decision of the Nawab might be. The list is inches thick, showing the number of people who Bhutto was able to pressure to join Pakistan. See Junagadh Archives: Reform Daftar, file no. 24, 7 October 1947; it is interesting to compare this to the plebiscite later held in Junagadh, where the population overwhelmingly voted to join India
26. Ankit, 'Junagadh, India and the Logic of Occupation and Appropriation, 1947–49' p121
27. Ibid. p120
28. Khachar, P., *Tasviro Ma Junagadh* (Rajkot, Pravin Publication, 2011) p39
29. Divyabhanusinh, *The Story of Asia's Lions*, and Divyabhanusinh, 'Junagadh State and its Lions: Conservation in Princely India, 1879–1947'
30. Private Interview, Nawabzada Muhammad Jahangir Khanji, Zoom, English, October 2022
31. McDonald, *Ambani & Sons* Chapter 1
32. Parekh, R., 'Of Gujarat, Wali Dakani and Qazi Ahmed Mian Akhter Junagarhi', *Dawn*, 5 August 2008. dawn.com/news/1071428
33. Private Interview, Shakira Afzal and Gulnaz Ahteshamuddin Ghausi, Zoom, English and Urdu, October 2022
34. Private Interview, Nawabzada Muhammad Jahangir Khanji, Zoom, English, October 2022
35. Private Interview, Shakira Afzal and Gulnaz Ahteshamuddin Ghausi, Zoom, English and Urdu, October 2022
36. Divyabhanusinh, *The Story of Asia's Lions* p169
37. Bangash, *A Princely Affair* p117
38. Menon, *The Story of the Integration of the Indian States* p141
39. Private Interview, Nawab Salauddin Khan Babi and Sultana Aaliya Babi, Balasinor, English, October 2022
40. For this section I am indebted to the fantastic work of Rakesh Ankit, whose

monographs on the aftermath of Junagadh's annexation are the finest work done on the state to date
41. Ankit, 'Junagadh, India and the Logic of Occupation and Appropriation, 1947–49' p125
42. Ibid. p127
43. See Bennett-Jones, *The Bhutto Dynasty*
44. forbes.com/sites/ranisingh/2016/07/12/kashmir-in-the-worlds-most-militarized-zone-violence-after-years-of-comparative-calm/; theguardian.com/commentisfree/2019/feb/25/the-guardian-view-on-kashmir-the-worlds-most-dangerous-place
45. My description of Hari Singh is based on Singh, H., *Maharaja Hari Singh: The Troubled Years* (New Delhi: Brahaspati Publications, 2011), as well as Kwarteng, *Ghosts of Empire* Chapter 6; Zubrzycki, *Dethroned* p95
46. My narrative of events in Kashmir draws particularly heavily from the work of Andrew Whitehead, especially his masterful *A Mission in Kashmir*, but also the extensive collection of oral history interviews that he has digitised on his blog. Whitehead, A., 'The People's Militia: Communists and Kashmiri Nationalism in the 1940s' in Butalia, U. (ed.), *Partition: The Long Shadow* (Delhi: Zubaan, 2015) pp128–38
47. Snedden, C., *Kashmir: The Unwritten History* (Noida: HarperCollins, 2012) p15
48. Rai, M., *Hindu Rulers, Muslim Subjects: Islam, Rights and the History of Kashmir* (Ranikhet: Permanent Black, 2004); Hussain, S., *Kashmir in the Aftermath of Partition* (New Delhi: Cambridge University Press, 2021) p57; Whitehead, A., *A Mission in Kashmir* (New Delhi: Viking, 2007) p23
49. French, *Liberty or Death* p373
50. Snedden, *Kashmir* p15
51. Christopher Beaumont, Radcliffe's private secretary, later revealed that Mountbatten interfered on Nehru's behalf with regard to some parts of the border. He nonetheless maintained that no changes were made to the Gurdaspur line. See Bennett-Jones, O., *Pakistan: Eye of the Storm* (London: Yale University Press, 2000) p60; Whitehead, *A Mission in Kashmir* p28
52. Whitehead, *A Mission in Kashmir* p32
53. In his memoir, Karan Singh merely blames Swami Sant Dev, a religious guru in the Maharaja's court, for the Maharaja's dreams of independence. Nonetheless, it is difficult to ignore the influence on the Maharaja of Nehru's acquiescence in allowing Bhutan, Sikkim and Nepal to remain independent on the basis that they were Himalayan states
54. Singh, K., *Heir Apparent: An Autobiography* (Delhi: Oxford University Press, 1984) p53
55. For the best treatment of the Poonch Uprising, which forms the basis for much of this section, see Snedden, *Kashmir*. See also FO 371/63570 *Transfer of power in India: relations of India with the United Kingdom, September–November 1947 (Folder 6)* p115
56. Hajari, *Midnight's Furies* p182
57. See Prasad, S. N., and Pal, D., *Operations in Jammu & Kashmir 1947–8* (History Division, MoD Government of India, 1987)
58. Snedden, *Kashmir* p60
59. Khan, A., *Raiders in Kashmir* (Delhi: Arya Offset Press, 1975) p11
60. Quoted in Hussain, *Kashmir in the Aftermath of Partition* p242
61. Akbar Khan's was not the only plan. Another suggested that former INA officers lead raids over the Jammu border and another led by Khurshid Anwar would enter the state further north. Khan, *Raiders in Kashmir* pp10–18
62. Hyat Khan, S., *The Nation That Lost its Soul* (Lahore: Jang Publishers, 1995) p215
63. For the accession of princely states to Pakistan, see Bangash, *A Princely Affair*; Loyd, A., *Bahawalpur: The Kingdom That Vanished* (Gurgaon: Penguin Random House, 2020); Ayres Wilcox, W., *Pakistan: The Consolidation of a Nation* (London: Columbia University Press, 1963), and Zubrzycki, *Dethroned* Chapter 13
64. Campbell-Johnson, *Mission with Mountbatten* p217
65. Snedden, *Kashmir* p59
66. It's impossible to know precisely when Jinnah first learned of his government's plans to intervene in the uprising in Poonch, but on 26 October George Cunningham wrote in his diary, 'Apparently Jinnah himself first heard of what was going on about 15 days ago.' This would indicate around 11 October 1947. See Whitehead, *A Mission in Kashmir* p58
67. Quoted in Basu, *V. P. Menon* p367

68. Partition Voices: Frank Leeson on the invasion of Kashmir by Frontier tribesmen from Waziristan in October 1947 and evacuating those trapped at the Catholic mission at Baramulla – talking to Andrew Whitehead, Worthing, June 2001. Original Recording in the SOAS Archive, London. Also available at andrewwhitehead.net/partition-voices-frank-leeson.html
69. Leeson, F., *Frontier Legion: With the Khassadars of North Waziristan* (Ferring: Leeson Archive, 2003) p205
70. Quoted in Hajari, *Midnight's Furies* p185
71. Hajari, *Midnight's Furies* p187
72. Schofield, V., *Kashmir in the Crossfire* (London: I. B. Tauris & Co Ltd, 1996) p143
73. Khan, *Raiders in Kashmir* p35
74. andrewwhitehead.net/for-the-conversion-of-kashmir.html
75. DO 133/39 Political situation: Kashmir, November–December 1947 (Folder 2) p13
76. Whitehead, *A Mission in Kashmir* p61
77. Literally *Hindu ka Zar, Sikh ka Sar*. Translation from Singh, A., *Lost Heritage: The Sikh Legacy in Pakistan* (New Delhi: Aegean Offset Printers, 2019) p245
78. Zakaria, A., *Between the Great Divide: A Journey into Pakistan-Administered Kashmir* (Noida: HarperCollins, 2018) p34
79. Inder's other two sons had been captured alive by the raiders, to 'dance around the fire as they cooked their food'. Several months later the young boys would escape and reunite with their mother. Zakaria, *Between the Great Divide* pp33–5; Singh, *Lost Heritage* p4
80. Mehta, K., *Chaos in Kashmir* (Calcutta: Signet Press, 1954) p35
81. Guha, *India after Gandhi* p66
82. See Whitehead, *A Mission in Kashmir*; Father Shanks' diary, available at andrewwhitehead.net/father-shankss-kashmir-diary.html
83. Singh, *Heir Apparent* p57
84. Partition Voices: Karan Singh talking in Delhi in April 2003 to Andrew Whitehead about the start of the Kashmir conflict. Original recording in the SOAS Archive, London. Also available at andrewwhitehead.net/partition-voices-karan-singh.html
85. Father Shanks' diary, available at andrewwhitehead.net/father-shankss-kashmir-diary.html
86. Whitehead, *A Mission in Kashmir* p70
87. Ibid. p78
88. Father Shanks' diary, available at andrewwhitehead.net/father-shankss-kashmir-diary.html, and Whitehead, *A Mission in Kashmir* p70
89. andrewwhitehead.net/for-the-conversion-of-kashmir.html
90. Whitehead, *A Mission in Kashmir* p88
91. Ibid. p125
92. Khan, *Raiders in Kashmir* p38
93. DO 133/39 Political situation: Kashmir, November-December 1947 (Folder 2) p14
94. Singh, *Heir Apparent* p58
95. Ibid. pp58, 76
96. Menon, *The Story of the Integration of the Indian States* p399
97. Mahajan, M. C., *Looking Back: The Autobiography of Mehr Chand Mahajan* (London, Asia Publishing, 1963) p154
98. Ibid. p155
99. Manekshaw, interviewed by Prem Shankar Jha in 1994. Full transcription printed in Jha, P.S., *Kashmir: Rival Versions of History* (Delhi: Oxford University Press, 1996) Appendix I
100. Alastair Lamb was the first to prove that Menon could not have flown to Jammu on the evening of the 26th. Prem Shankar Jha later argued that the Maharaja signed the accession on 25 October, before the emergency meeting. More recently, Andrew Whitehead has argued that the accession was signed on 27 October, but that the Maharaja had given permission to his deputy prime minister four days earlier to sign the instrument of accession 'subject to the condition that the terms of accession will be the same as would be settled with H.E.H. The Nizam of Hyderabad'. See Lamb, A., *Birth of a Tragedy: Kashmir 1947* (Karachi: Oxford University Press, 2001); Jha, *Kashmir*; Whitehead, *A Mission in Kashmir*
101. bbc.com/news/world-south-asia-11693674
102. Raghavan, S., *War and Peace in Modern India: A Strategic History of the Nehru Years* (Ranikhet: Permanent Black, 2010) p108
103. For the best analysis of the available evidence, see Andrew Whitehead's 'I accede to the Dominion of India: When and how the Maharaja of Kashmir signed the Instrument of Accession'
104. Snedden, *Kashmir*

105. Hussain, *Kashmir in the Aftermath of Partition* p79
106. Whitehead, *A Mission in Kashmir* pp147–150
107. Partition Voices: Usha Khanna talking in August 2008 by phone from Mumbai to Andrew Whitehead about being a member of the left-wing women's militia in Kashmir and the Cultural Front in 1947–8
108. FO 371/63570 *Transfer of power in India: relations of India with the United Kingdom, September–November 1947 (Folder 6)* p154
109. Bangash, *A Princely Affair* pp134–8
110. The accounts of Captain Mirza Hassan of the Jammu and Kashmir 6th infantry and Subehdar Major Babar Khan of the Gilgit Scouts both deny that William Brown ever played a major role in the Gilgit Rebellion, with Mirza Hassan going so far as to claim that Brown was arrested before the revolution even took place. For a summary of these arguments, see Bangash, Y. K., 'Three Forgotten Accessions: Gilgit, Hunza and Nagar', *Journal of Imperial and Commonwealth History*. 2010, 38(1): 117–43
111. Brown, W., *Gilgit Rebellion: The Major Who Mutinied Over Partition of India* (Epub: Pen & Sword Military, 2014) Chapters 2–3
112. Ibid.
113. Bangash, 'Three Forgotten Accessions: Gilgit, Hunza and Nagar' pp117–43
114. Brown, *Gilgit Rebellion* Chapter 4
115. It remains disputed whether it was actually Brown giving commands, and several other actors have taken credit for the subsequent coup. The best analysis of the varying accounts can be found in Bangash, 'Three Forgotten Accessions: Gilgit, Hunza and Nagar' pp117–43
116. Bangash, 'Three Forgotten Accessions: Gilgit, Hunza and Nagar' p131
117. Schofield, *Kashmir in the Crossfire* p155
118. Bangash, 'Three Forgotten Accessions: Gilgit, Hunza and Nagar' p139
119. Schofield, *Kashmir in the Crossfire* p155
120. Bangash, 'Three Forgotten Accessions: Gilgit, Hunza and Nagar' p133
121. 'Proposals Offered to Quaid-e-Azam Mohammed Ali Jinnah Governor-General of Pakistan, by Lord Louis Mountbatten, Governor-General of India, on 1 November 1947, at Government House, Lahore', quoted in Noorani, A. G., *The Destruction of Hyderabad* (Delhi: Tulika Books, 2013) Appendix 10
122. Noorani, *The Destruction of Hyderabad* p168
123. Zubrzycki, *Dethroned* p170
124. Hajari, *Midnight's Furies* p196
125. Khan, *Raiders in Kashmir* p1
126. Ibid. p40
127. Ibid. p44
128. Quoted in Kwarteng, *Ghosts of Empire* p129
129. Malhotra, *In the Language of Remembering* p304
130. DO 133/39 *Political situation: Kashmir, November–December 1947 (Folder 2)* p68
131. FO 371/63570 *Transfer of power in India: relations of India with the United Kingdom, September–November 1947 (Folder 6)* p199
132. DO 133/39 *Political situation: Kashmir, November–December 1947 (Folder 2)* p21
133. Campbell-Johnson, *Mission with Mountbatten* p244
134. Ibid. p250
135. Choudhary, *Vajpayee* pp57–9
136. One Indian cabinet member wrote with distress that 'tactics similar to those employed in the case of Kashmir are being resorted to by Pakistan for creating trouble in Tripura state', and the maharani had to fly to New Delhi to persuade Patel to help to 'abort a possible Kashmir-type operation'. Chakravarti, M., 'Documentation of the Process of Integration of Princely Tripura with the Indian Union' in Nag, Gurung and Choudhury (eds), *Making of the Indian Union* p320; Bhaumik, *Insurgent Crossfire* p70
137. Hajari, *Midnight's Furies* p221
138. Ankit, R., 'To Issue "Stand Down" or Not …: Britain and Kashmir, 1947–49', *Britain and the World*. 2014, 7(2): 238–60
139. French, *Liberty or Death* p363
140. Quoted in Kwarteng, *Ghosts of Empire* p130
141. Singh, *Independence and Democracy in Burma, 1945–1952* p68
142. Campbell-Johnson, *Mission with Mountbatten* p261
143. *New Times of Burma*, 11 January 1948
144. Kozicki, *India and Burma 1937–1957* pp264–5
145. Bayly and Harper, *Forgotten Wars* p374
146. Sarkar, S., *Modern India: 1885–1947* (Delhi: Pearson Education, 2014) p375

147. Hajari, *Midnight's Furies* p225
148. Gandhi, M., *Last Glimpses of Bapu* (Agra, Shiva Lal Agarwala & Co. Ltd., 1962) pp119–74
149. Hajari, *Midnight's Furies* p179
150. Campbell-Johnson, *Mission with Mountbatten* p271
151. Gandhi, *Last Glimpses of Bapu* p300
152. Ibid. p307
153. Jha, *Gandhi's Assassin* p5
154. nationalheraldindia.com/india/nehrus-iconic-speech-on-january-30-1948-the-light-has-gone-out
155. *Civil & Military Gazette* (Lahore), 31 January 1948
156. Edwards, 'Gandhiji in Burma, and Burma in Gandhiji' p173
157. Keenan, *Full Marks for Trying* p61
158. Malgonkar, M., *The Men Who Killed Gandhi* (New Delhi: Lotus Collection, 2008) p152
159. Guha, *India after Gandhi* p23
160. French, *Liberty or Death* p361
161. Campbell-Johnson, *Mission with Mountbatten* p279
162. British Library: India Office Records and Private Papers, 'File 8/16 Bahrain Intelligence Summary' IOR/R/15/2/319 (p.37/206); Allen, C. H., *Khimji Ramdas: Biography of an Indo-Omani Company* (Unpublished) Chapter 3; Bayly and Harper, *Forgotten Wars* p402

Chapter 10: The Fall of Hyderabad

1. Brigid Keenan Private Collection: Farewell to British Troops, Bombay, 28 February 1948
2. Keenan, *Full Marks for Trying* p62
3. Brigid Keenan Private Collection: Letters to Maisie, 14 October 1947
4. Bayly and Harper, *Forgotten Wars* p402
5. Private Interview, Brigid Keenan, London, English, January 2021
6. spectator.co.uk/article/passage-from-india/
7. Ibid.
8. Ibid.
9. Lintner, *The Rise and Fall of the Communist Party of Burma* p12
10. Whitehead, *A Mission in Kashmir* p201
11. See Lintner, *The Rise and Fall of the Communist Party of Burma*; Bayly and Harper, *Forgotten Wars* pp13, 385–8; Lintner, *Great Game East*; Ali, K. A., *Communism in Pakistan: Politics and Class Activism, 1947–1972* (London: I. B. Tauris, 2015)
12. Communist Voices: Amina Dasgupta on being a Communist in Calcutta in the late 1940s including a snatch of a song – talking to Andrew Whitehead, London, June 1992. Original recording in the SOAS Archive, London. Also available at andrewwhitehead.net/communist-voices-anima-dasgupta.html; Singh, M., 'Establishing the Communist Party of Pakistan' in Guhathakurta, M., and Van Schendel, W. (eds), *The Bangladesh Reader: History, Culture, Politics* (London: Duke University Press, 2013) p171
13. Singh, 'Establishing the Communist Party of Pakistan' p172
14. See Lintner, *The Rise and Fall of the Communist Party of Burma* pp13–16; Bayly and Harper, *Forgotten Wars* pp385–8; Roose, J., 'Passive Revolution meets Peasant Revolution: Indian Nationalism and the Telangana Revolt', *Journal of Peasant Studies*. 2001, 28(4): p74; Radhakrishnan, P., *Peasant Struggles, Land Reforms and Social Change: Malabar, 1836–1982* (Delhi: Cooperjal Limited, 2007); Singh, 'Establishing the Communist Party of Pakistan'
15. Campbell-Johnson, *Mission with Mountbatten* pp300–1
16. *Hindustan Times*, 13 March 1948
17. Campbell-Johnson, *Mission with Mountbatten* p304
18. For the Khasi states' attempts to join Pakistan, see Syiemlieh, D. R., 'The Integration of the Khasi States into the Indian Union' in Nag, Gurung and Choudhury (eds), *Making of the Indian Union*; Bangash, *A Princely Affair* p156
19. *Civil & Military Gazette* (Lahore), 30 March 1948; 31 March 1948
20. Laloo, T. S., 'Wahlong: Colonial Demarcations Forged in Blood and Tears', *Partition Studies Quarterly*, 2020, 3. partitionstudiesquarterly.org/article/wahlong-colonial-demarcations-forged-in-blood-and-tears/ Accessed October 2023
21. Akins, *Conquering the Maharajas* p217
22. Bangash, *A Princely Affair* p177
23. Ibid p186
24. Ibid. pp188–9
25. Akins, *Conquering the Maharajas* pp234–5
26. Luther, N., 'And Still I Long for Hyderabad' in Akbar, M. (ed.), *Hyderabad:*

The Power of Glory (Hyderabad: Deccan Books, 1998) p1
27. Mackenzie Shah, A., 'Hyderabad under the Asaf Jahis (1724–1950)' in Philon, H. (ed.), *Silent Splendours: Palaces of the Deccan 14th–19th Centuries* (Mumbai: Marg Publications, 2010)
28. Gala, D., 'Hunters' Tales' in Akbar (ed.), *Hyderabad* p17
29. Cooper, quoted in Zubrzycki, J., *The Last Nizam: The Rise and Fall of India's Greatest Princely State* (Sydney: Picador, 2006) p108
30. Private Interview, Sultan Ghalib Al-Quaiti, Zoom, February 2021
31. Bawa, *The Last Nizam* pp64–6
32. Zubrzycki, *The Last Nizam* p114
33. Sherman, *Muslim Belonging in Secular India* p77
34. CO 935/19/78018/37/No 53 'Correspondence regarding Aden Colony and Aden Protectorate' p25; El Edroos, S. A., and Naik, L. R., *Hyderabad of 'The Seven Loaves': A historical account of the Asaf Jahi dynasty with an autobiographical sketch of the Author, covering the events of Hyderabad's merger with the Indian Union* (M/s. Laser Prints (P) Ltd., 1994) p91
35. Noorani, *The Destruction of Hyderabad* p1
36. Luther, 'And Still I Long For Hyderabad' p1
37. These were Gadwal, Wanaparthi, Jatprole, Amarchinta, Paloncha, Gopalpet, Anagundi, Gurgunta, Narayanpet, Domakonda, Rajapet, Dubbak, Papanapet and Sirnapalli. Many of them had ruled their lands since the time of the Kaktiya or Vijayangara kings. For a discussion of these understudied rulers, see Cohen, B. B., *Kingship and Colonialism in India's Deccan: 1850–1948* (New York: Palgrave Macmillan, 2007)
38. Bawa, *The Last Nizam* p164
39. Chapalgaonkar, N., *The Last Nizam and His People: Profiles and Sketches from Hyderabad*, Translated by Sharadchandra Panse (Abdingdon: Routledge, 2022) pix
40. Dalrymple, W., *The Age of Kali: Indian Travels and Encounters* (London: Bloomsbury, 2004) p197
41. Purushotham, S., 'Internal Violence: The "Police Action" in Hyderabad', *Comparative Studies in Society and History*. 2015, 57(2): 439
42. 1947PA/2930, Nusratullah Shah interviewed by Fakhra Hassan
43. Zubrzycki, *The Last Nizam* p180
44. Bawa, *The Last Nizam* p249
45. Akins, *Conquering the Maharajas* p155
46. Guha, R., *India after Gandhi* p53
47. Bawa, *The Last Nizam* p201
48. Ibid. pp232–3
49. 1947PA/9591, Shashikant Ratilal interviewed by Jaya Murthy
50. Akins, *Conquering the Maharajas* p152
51. Sherman, T., 'The Integration of the Princely State of Hyderabad and the Making of the Postcolonial State in India, 1948–56', *Indian Economic & Social History Review*. 2007, 44(4): 5; Akins, *Conquering the Maharajas* p153
52. Roose, 'Passive Revolution meets Peasant Revolution: Indian Nationalism and the Telangana Revolt' 74
53. El Edroos and Naik, *Hyderabad of 'The Seven Loaves'* p124
54. Ibid. p128
55. *SWJN*. Series 2, Volume 7, p196; see also Munshi, K. M., *The End of an Era* (Bombay: Bharatiya Vidya Bhavan, 1957) pp150, 180
56. NAI, External Affairs, Passport & Visa – I, 3(7)-PV I, 1948, 'Refusal of landing at Bombay to certain Arab nationals coming from Mukalla to Join Hyderabad. State Forces objection raised by the Political resident Bahrain regarding the alleged grant of visa for Muscat'
57. El Edroos and Naik, *Hyderabad of 'The Seven Loaves'* p132
58. Cotton, S., and Baker, R., *Aviator Extraordinaire: The Sydney Cotton Story* (London: Chatto & Windus, 1969) p226
59. Ibid. p227
60. Hajari, *Midnight's Furies* p237; Cotton and Baker, *Aviator Extraordinaire* p227
61. Van Schendel, *A History of Bangladesh* p134
62. Rahman and Alam, *The Unfinished Memoirs* p104
63. Hajari, *Midnight's Furies* p237
64. This section draws heavily for the incredible work of Nisid Hajari, to whom I am much indebted
65. Choudhary, *Vajpayee* p69
66. Basu, *V. P. Menon* p399
67. Choudhary, *Vajpayee* p67
68. Mohammad, A., *Remaking History: 1948 Police Action and the Muslims of Hyderabad* (Cambridge: Cambridge University Press, 2023) p28

69. Purushotham, 'Internal Violence: The "Police Action" in Hyderabad' p445
70. Choudhary, *Vajpayee* p68
71. Purushotham, 'Internal Violence: The 'Police Action' in Hyderabad' pp445–9; Roose, 'Passive Revolution meets Peasant Revolution: Indian Nationalism and the Telangana Revolt' p75
72. Hyder, M., *October Coup: A Memoir of the Struggle for Hyderabad* (New Delhi: Lotus Collection | Roli Books, 2012) p24
73. Ibid. pp25–6
74. Ibid. pp11–15
75. Mohammad, *Remaking History* p241
76. Akins, *Conquering the Maharajas* pp155–9
77. Purushotham, 'Internal Violence: The "Police Action" in Hyderabad' pp436–9; Sherman, T., Muslim Belonging in Secular India p24
78. 'Confidential Notes Attached to the Sunderlal Committee Report', quoted in Noorani, *The Destruction of Hyderabad* Appendix 15
79. 1947PA/4352, Champabai Dattambhat Purohit interviewed by Padmashree Balasubramanian
80. Bawa, *The Last Nizam* p264
81. Hyder, *October Coup* p50
82. 1947PA/8115, Awadh Rani Bawa interviewed by Titas Biswas
83. Mohammad, *Remaking History* p11
84. 1947PA/4258, Yezdyar Kaoosji interviewed by Arshad Mirza
85. See Al-Qu'aiti, Sultan G., *Arabian and Other Essays* (Jeddah: Self-published, 1998) and Al-Qu'aiti, Sultan G., *'Fair Play' or Poisoned Chalice: The Last Years of Britain's Presence and Policy in Southern Arabia* (London: Darf Publishers, 2021). Freitag, U., *Indian Ocean Migrants and State Formation in Hadhramaut: Reforming the Homeland* (Leiden: Brill, 2003)
86. El Edroos and Naik, Hyderabad of 'The Seven Loaves' p115
87. Noorani, *The Destruction of Hyderabad* p179
88. Purushotham, 'Internal Violence: The "Police Action" in Hyderabad' pp442–3
89. Omvedt, G., *Dalits and the Democratic Revolution: Dr Ambedkar and the Dalit Movement in Colonial India* (New Delhi: SAGE, 1994) pp296–307
90. Zubrzycki, *Dethroned* pp183–5; Raghavan, S., *War and Peace in Modern India* p80
91. Lownie, *The Mountbattens* p237
92. Ibid. p238
93. MP, MS62/MB1/D178/9 Relations with Hyderabad after the Transfer of Power: report By Mr A. Campbell Johnson's Visit to Hyderabad from the 15th–18th May, 1948
94. Ibid.
95. Ibid.
96. Campbell-Johnson, *Mission with Mountbatten* p355
97. Ibid. p229
98. Quoted in Noorani, *The Destruction of Hyderabad* p15
99. See Cotton and Baker, *Aviator Extraordinaire* p239; Bawa, *The Last Nizam* pp269–73
100. Bawa, *The Last Nizam* pp269–73
101. Raghavan, *War and Peace in Modern India* p136
102. Lownie, *The Mountbattens* p240
103. Mountbatten, P., *India Remembered: A Personal Account of the Mountbattens During the Transfer of Power* (London: Pavillion Books, 2007) p221
104. Lownie, *The Mountbattens* p241
105. Ibid. p241
106. Ibid. p242
107. Nehru to Mountbatten on 1 August 194 *SWJN*. Series 2, Volume 7, p203
108. See firstpost.com/india/partition-and-ladakh-silent-mountains-bear-testimony-to-ethnic-linguistic-and-cultural-fragmentation-3937377.html
109. Sen, L. P., *Slender Was the Thread: Kashmir Confrontation 1947–48* (New Delhi: Orient Longman, 1994) p173
110. MacDonald, Myra, *White as the Shroud: India, Pakistan and War on the Frontiers of Kashmir* (Hurst, 2020) p67
111. Whitehead, *A Mission in Kashmir* p206
112. Malhotra, A., *Remnants of a Separation* (Noida: HarperCollins, 2017) pp268–82
113. Hyder, *October Coup* p57
114. Nehru to Krishna Menon, 24 August 1948 *SWJN*. Series 2, Volume 7, p215
115. Omvedt, *Dalits and the Democratic Revolution* p309
116. Radhakrishnan, *Peasant Struggles, Land reforms and Social Change* p64
117. Roose, 'Passive Revolution meets Peasant Revolution: Indian Nationalism and the Telangana Revolt' 80
118. Ali, L., *The Tragedy of Hyderabad* (Lahore: Pakistan Co-operative Book Society, 1962)
119. Cotton and Baker, *Aviator Extraordinaire* p254

120. Sherman, 'The Integration of the Princely State of Hyderabad and the Making of the Postcolonial State in India, 1948–56' p10
121. Singh, *Jinnah* pp472–5; Wolpert, *Jinnah of Pakistan* pp369–70; French, *Liberty or Death* p27
122. *Mr Jinnah: The Making of Pakistan*. Directed by Christopher Mitchell, Akbar Ahmed, 1997; available: youtube.com/watch?v=r4EbiHKjn64
123. Lownie, *The Mountbattens* p245
124. Quoted in Singh, *Jinnah* p476
125. Wolpert, *Jinnah of Pakistan* pvii
126. Hajari, *Midnight's Furies* p250
127. Hyder, *October Coup* p71
128. El Edroos and Naik, Hyderabad of 'The Seven Loaves' p138
129. Hyder, *October Coup* pp74–5
130. Mohammad, *Remaking History* p70
131. *Civil & Military Gazette* (Lahore), 14 September 1948
132. Ali, L., 'The Five Day War' in Khalidi, O. (ed.), *Hyderabad: After the Fall* (Wichita, Kansas USA: Hyderabad Historical Society, 1988) pp46–7
133. Eagleton, C., 'The Case of Hyderabad Before the Security Council' in Khalidi (ed.), *Hyderabad*
134. Dalrymple, *The Age of Kali* p208
135. Akins, *Conquering the Maharajas* p170
136. 1947PA/2110, Syed Moazzam Ali Taufeeq interviewed by Fakhra Hassan
137. 1947PA/5198, Waheed Un-Nisa Rehman interviewed by Hira Rasool
138. 1947PA/2218, Khalid Aziz interviewed by Fakhra Hassan
139. 1947PA/9475, Arun Kumar Chatterjee interviewed by Rohit Dutta Roy
140. Sherman, *Muslim Belonging in Secular India* p31; Sherman, 'The Integration of the Princely State of Hyderabad and the Making of the Postcolonial State in India, 1948–56' p12
141. See Hyder, *October Coup*
142. Sherman, *Muslim Belonging in Secular India* p42
143. Ibid. p64
144. Ibid. p42
145. Ibid. p65
146. Ibid. p62
147. Ibid. p71
148. Manger, L., 'Hadramis in Hyderabad: From Winners to Losers', *Asian Journal of Social Science* SPECIAL FOCUS: Arabs in Asia. 2007, 35(4/5): pp424–31
149. Al-Qu'aiti, *Arabian and Other Essays* p109
150. Zubrzycki, *The Last Nizam* p198
151. McGarr, P. M., *The Cold War in South Asia: Britain, the United States and the Indian Subcontinent, 1945–1965* (Cambridge: Cambridge University Press, 2013) p21
152. *Time* magazine, 20 September 1948
153. Cotton and Baker, *Aviator Extraordinaire* p258
154. 'The consequences lasted well into the post-independence decades in Maharashtra where Marathwada became a scene for anti-Dalit rioting and in the context of the Dalit struggle for common lands, provided the main rural base for caste tension and a growing Shiv Sena influence in the late 1980s'; See Omvedt, *Dalits and the Democratic Revolution* pp316–19
155. Omvedt, *Dalits and the Democratic Revolution* p298
156. Noorani, *The Destruction of Hyderabad* p226
157. Nehru to Ministry of States, 14 November 1948, *SWJN*. Vol 8. p106
158. 'Confidential Notes Attached to the Sunderlal Committee Report', quoted in Noorani, *The Destruction of Hyderabad* Appendix 15
159. Akins, *Conquering the Maharajas* p172
160. 'The Sunderlal Committee Report on the Massacre of Muslims', quoted in Noorani, *The Destruction of Hyderabad* Appendix 14
161. Ibid.
162. frontline.thehindu.com/other/article30159646.ece
163. Purushotham, 'Internal Violence: The "Police Action" in Hyderabad' 455
164. Ibid. 458
165. Sherman, *Muslim Belonging in Secular India* p38
166. Noorani, *The Destruction of Hyderabad* p246
167. Akins, *Conquering the Maharajas* p257
168. Zubrzycki, *Dethroned* p4

Chapter 11: Mother Tongues

1. Raghavan, *War and Peace in Modern India* p150
2. MP MS62/MB1/F8 Relations Between India, Pakistan & Burma: Jawaharlal Nehru to Lord Mountbatten, 5 March 1950
3. Khan, *The Great Partition* p193; Raghavan, *War and Peace in Modern India* p154
4. Choudhary, *Vajpayee* p87
5. Raghavan, P., *Animosity at Bay: An Alternative History of the India-Pakistan*

Relationship, 1947–1952 (Gurugram: HarperCollins India, 2020) Chapter 4
6. *Civil & Military Gazette* (Lahore), 12 April 1950
7. Raghavan, *Animosity at Bay* p85 and Chapter 2
8. Khan, *The Great Partition* p193
9. Talbot, I., *Divided Cities: Partition and its Aftermath in Lahore and Amritsar 1947–1957* (Oxford: Oxford University Press, 2007) p158; Khan, *The Great Partition* p172
10. Private Interview: Pablo Bartholomew, New Delhi, English, July 2022; Roy, A., 'To "Barty", With Love', *The Wire*, 3 October 2021; Sharma, T., 'Remembering Rati Bartholomew: Teacher, Friend and Mentor to Generations of Theatre Practitioners', *The Wire*, 13 October 2021
11. *Indian Express*, 1 January 1950
12. Markovits, *India and the World* p172; web.archive.org/web/20120325203429/; http://gulfnews.com/news/world/india/awaara-most-successful-film-of-all-times-1.258697
13. The exception here, of course, is Bangladeshi literature that prioritises the year of 1971 over 1947
14. Rich, *Creating the Arabian Gulf* p245
15. Morton, M. Q., *A Fateful Intrusion: The British India Line in the Arabian Gulf, 1862–1982* (Abu Dhabi: National Archives, 2018); Parsons, A., *They Say the Lion: Britain's Legacy to the Arabs – A Personal Memoir* (London: Jonathan Cape, 1986) p112
16. Holden, D., *Farewell to Arabia* (London: Faber and Faber, 1966) pp141, 176. Occasionally a British official would suggest changing the titles of British officials in the Gulf: 'an unfortunate survival of the British Raj in India because of their obviously imperial connotations'. See Bradshaw, T., *The End of Empire in the Gulf: From Trucial States to United Arab Emirates* (London: I. B. Tauris, 2019) p66
17. Al-Qu'aiti, *'Fair Play' or Poisoned Chalice*
18. Johnston, C. H., *The View from Steamers Point: Being an Account of Three Years in Aden* (London: Collins, 1964) p91
19. Van Schendel, W., and Pachuau, J. L. K., *The Camera as Witness: A Social History of Mizoram, Northeast India* (Cambridge: Cambridge University Press, 2015) p273
20. Hazarika, S., *Strangers of the Mist: Tales of War and Peace from India's Northeast* (New Delhi: Penguin India, 2011) p102
21. In fact, thanks to Laisaizawk's cowboy-themed comic book series 'Sudden Muanga', cowboy outfits were far more popular at home, and cowboy hats were ubiquitous across the hills at the time. Van Schendel and Pachuau, *The Camera as Witness* Chapter 16
22. The same happened in the Chittagong Hill tracts of East Pakistan. See Van Schendel and Pachuau, *The Camera as Witness* Chapter 14; Van Schendel, W., Mey, W., and Dewan, A. K., *The Chittagong Hill Tracts: Living in a Borderland* (Dhaka: University Press Ltd., 2001) Chapter 9
23. Sarkar, J., 'Battlefields to Borderlands: Rohingyas Between Global War and Decolonisation' in Guyot-Réchard and Leake (eds), *South Asia Unbound* pp19–21
24. NAI, External Affairs, Overseas II, Progs., Nos. 3(1)-OSII, 1949, 'Burma-Communists activities in Burma and on the Indo-Burma Border-Intelligence reports regarding'. This was not entirely true, and officers along East Pakistan's frontier with Arakan did provide some Arakanese Muslims with weapons and medical treatment in exchange for smuggled rice
25. Van Schendel, *The Bengal Borderland* p100
26. NAI External Affairs, Overseas II, Progs., Nos. 3(1)-OSII, 1949, 'Burma-Communists activities in Burma and on the Indo-Burma Border-Intelligence reports regarding'; NAI External Affairs, N.E.F. Progs., Nos. 143-NEF, 1949, 'Reports on Communist Activities on Assam-Burma Frontiers and in the tribal Areas of Assam' p15; see also Paliwal, A., *India's Near East: A New History* (London: Hurst, 2024) p80; according to a 1970 report, Phizo was arrested inside a 'communist den' in Calcutta. See NAI, Home, NEFA, NII/102(42)/70, 'Background note on Angami Zapu Phizo and Rev. Michael Scott prepared by U. S(Naga) in April 1970'
27. Paliwal, *India's Near East* pp84–8; Raghavan, *Animosity at Bay*
28. Myint-U, *The River of Lost Footsteps* pp294–6; Lewis, N., *Golden Earth: Travels in Burma* (London: Eland Publishing Ltd., 2003)
29. Owen, N. G. 'Economic and Social Change' in Tarling (ed.), *The Cambridge History of Southeast Asia* p162

30. Chatterji, J., *Shadows at Noon: The South Asian Twentieth Century* (Gurugram: Penguin Random House, 2023) p115
31. Ibid. p122
32. Dryland, E., 'Faiz Ahmed Faiz and the Rawalpindi Conspiracy Case', *Journal of South Asian Literature*. 1992, 27(2): 175–85
33. Chatterji, *Shadows at Noon* p124
34. Another Bengali famine in 1975 would decimate the Awami League's popularity in the aftermath of Bangladeshi independence
35. NAI, External Affairs, Bengal, Progs., Nos. 1321(202)-BL, 1952, 'Fortnightly reports from the Deputy High Commissioner for India in Pakistan Dacca'; See also Alam, A., United Front Election of 1954: The Struggle for Democracy (Unpublished Dissertation, 2023)
36. Ibid. p10
37. NAI, External Affairs, Bengal, Progs., Nos. 1321(202)-BL, 1952, 'Fortnightly reports from the Deputy High Commissioner for India in Pakistan Dacca'. pp3–10
38. Rahman and Alam, *The Unfinished Memoirs* p134
39. IOR/L/P&S, 5/250, 3/79 'Fortnightly Report (February 1947)'
40. *Vogue*, 1 November 1947
41. NAI, External Affairs, Bengal, Progs., Nos. 1321(202)-BL, 1952, 'Fortnightly reports from the Deputy High Commissioner for India in Pakistan Dacca' pp12–13
42. Ibid. pp30–3
43. Rahman and Alam, *The Unfinished Memoirs* pp208, 263
44. Keay, J., *Midnight's Descendants: South Asia from Partition to the Present Day* (London: William Collins, 2014) p98
45. Zakaria, *1971* p60
46. Chatterji, *Shadows at Noon* p144
47. Zakaria, *1971* p72
48. Chatterji, *Shadows at Noon* p127
49. Guha, *India after Gandhi* p196
50. Ibid.
51. *Civil & Military Gazette* (Lahore), 20 April 1954
52. Bennett-Jones, O., *Pakistan* p154
53. *Manchester Evening News*, 31 May 1954
54. bengalgazette.org/2022/02/18/the-last-bengali-prime-minister-of-pakistan/
55. Paliwal, *India's Near East* p111
56. Rahman and Alam, *The Unfinished Memoirs* p208
57. Jalal, *The Sole Spokesman* p179
58. Brendon, *The Decline and Fall of the British Empire* p486
59. *Civil & Military Gazette* (Lahore), 20 April 1954
60. Balfour-Paul, *The End of Empire in the Middle East* p148
61. The Anglo-Iranian Oil Company – later known as BP – was Britain's most important overseas investment for a time, and in the early twentieth century Britain had threatened to annex the town where it was located – Abadan – to its Indian Empire. The local Sheikh began appearing in official lists of Indian princes, and a new 'Mosque of the People of Rangoon' was erected near the refinery, its lotus finials symbolising the empire that tied Burma to the Persian Gulf. During WW2, the Indian Army had even occupied Southern Iran just to maintain Britain's hold over this one refinery. To Iranian nationalists it was a symbol of national humiliation. When, in 1951, the pyjama-clad Muhammad Mossadegh was elected prime minister of Iran, he nationalised the Oil Company, expelling the British from Abadan. See Corley, T. A. B., *A History of the Burmah Oil Company 1886–1924* (London: Heinemann, 1983) p283; see QDL IOR/R/15/1/734: 'Alqabnamah: A List Showing the Names, Titles and Modes of Address of the More Important Sovereigns, Ruling Princes, Chiefs, Nobles etc., Having Relations with the Indian Government'; blogs.bl.uk/asian-and-african/2014/12/curzons-durbars-and-the-alqabnamah-the-persian-gulf-as-part-of-the-indian-empire.html
62. Rogan, E. *The Arabs: A History* (London: Penguin, 2012) p474
63. Morton, *Masters of Pearl* p142
64. Brendon, *The Decline and Fall of the British Empire* p499
65. See Naumkin, V., *Red Wolves of Yemen: The Struggle for Independence* (Cambridge: Orleander Press, 2004) p14, and Halliday, F., *Arabia Without Sultans: A Survey of Political Instability in the Arab World* (New York: Vintage Books, 1975) p172
66. Esdaile, *Aden and the End of Empire 1937–1960* pp59, 183
67. CO PRO 859/1197: Aden Labor Department Report 1957: Commentary by Foggon of the Colonial Office, Quoted

in Esdaile, *Aden and the End of Empire 1937–1960* p269
68. Reese, *Imperial Muslims* p34
69. An intense mythology has been woven around Dhirubhai Ambani, a rags-to-riches story about the son of a Gujarati schoolteacher who created one of Asia's largest business empires. A British journalist who comes from a similar Adeni-Gujarati family (born in the same Adeni hospital as Ambani's son Mukesh) put it succinctly: 'You won't find Mukesh Ambani speaking about his Adeni lineage like the rest of us. It's part of the rich folklore of his father – the young man who went to seek fortune abroad, didn't make it abroad but came back with something bigger – which was an idea. That mythology cannot entertain a segment that is not Indian.' The best primary source on Dhirubhai's early life is his wife's exceptional memoir, a virtual archive of Ambani's life, filled with scans of Ambani's first passport, his Adeni resident card etc., all of which is useful to scholars of the Indian presence in the Arabian Peninsula. The latter half of the book is filled with essays on Ambani by those who knew him (Kokilaben, *Dhirubhai Ambani: The Man I Knew* (Mumbai: Reliance Industries Ltd, 2007)). Critical secondary sources are altogether rarer. Although there are whole shelves full of 'biographies' of Dhirubhai Ambani, most are hagiographical texts, written as self-help guides for businessmen. By far the best biography is by McDonald, *Ambani & Sons*, which was previously published as *The Polyester Prince* before the Indian publisher was served with a legal notice not to distribute it. Sunil Khilnani has also written an interesting essay on Dhirubhai Ambani as the bookend to Khilnani, S., *Incarnations: India in 50 Lives* (London: Allen Lane, 2016). Johan Mathew has utilised the Indian Office Files to illuminate some aspects of Dhirubhai's life in Aden (Mathew, J., 'Gilding the Waves: Gold Smuggling and Monetary Policies Around the Arabian Sea, 1939–1967' in Serels, S., and Campbell G. (eds), *Currencies of the Indian Ocean World* (Cham: Palgrave Macmillan, 2019)
70. Kokilaben, *Dhirubhai Ambani: The Man I Knew* (Mumbai: Reliance Industries Ltd., 2007) p48
71. Esdaile, *Aden and the End of Empire 1937–1960* p109
72. Sherman, *Muslim Belonging in Secular India* p87
73. Dahlgren, S., *Contesting Realities: The Public Sphere and Morality in Southern Yemen* (United States: Syracuse University Press, 2010) p143
74. Quotes are taken from Evans, H., *My Paper Chase: True Stories of Vanished Times* (London: Little Brown & Company, 2009) Chapter 17. Holden's editor at the *Sunday Times*, Harold Evans, spent years researching Holden's mysterious assassination and a chapter of his autobiography is devoted to Holden's life. Much of the chapter is reprinted in Evans, H., 'Harold Evans: Murder, CIA and the Sunday Times' in *The Times* (London, England), 6 September 2009, thetimes.co.uk/article/harold-evans-murder-cia-and-the-sunday-times-5jjz98b3sfn. Holden's own writings are also naturally valuable sources on his life, particularly Holden, D., *Farewell to Arabia* (London: Faber and Faber, 1966)
75. Holden, D., 'Britain's Arabian Oil Empire: Its Rise and Fall' in *The British Empire Magazine* 83 britishempire.co.uk/maproom/britainsarabianoilempire.htm
76. Holden, *Farewell to Arabia* p21
77. Ibid. p55
78. Ibid. pp20, 55
79. Ibid. p21
80. Ibid. p24
81. Al-Nakib, F., 'Inside a Gulf Port: The Dynamics of Urban Life in Pre-Oil Kuwait' in Potter, L. G. (ed.), *Persian Gulf in Modern Times: People, Ports and History* (New York: Palgrave Macmillan, 2014) p221
82. On the new citizenship laws of the 1950s, see Al-Baharna, *The Legal Status of the Arabian Gulf States* pp124–30, and Kinninmont, J., 'Citizenship in the Gulf' in *The Gulf States and the Arab Uprisings* (Spain: Gulf Research Centre, 2013) p51. For a valuable case study of Kuwait, see Halliday, *Arabia Without Sultans* p449, and Al-Nakib, F., *Kuwait Transformed: A History of Oil and Urban Life* (Stanford California: Stanford University Press, 2016). For Bahrain, see Gardner, A. M., *City of Strangers: Gulf Migration and the Indian Community in Bahrain* (New York: Cornell University Press, 2010). For the

best general overview of the impact of these new laws on the Gulf's South Asian communities, see Onley, J., 'Indian Communities in the Persian Gulf c.1500–1947' in Potter (ed.), *Persian Gulf in Modern Times*
83. Esdaile, *Aden and the End of Empire 1937–1960* pp213, 266
84. Luqman defined an Adeni as 'the person born in Aden, whose parents were born in Aden and lived in Aden without abandoning it. Also, a person born in Aden to be his permanent domicile. Aden is Arab and the Arabs have prior rights and privileges in it and are entitled before all others to enjoy its benefits and manage its high posts and administer the land.' See Lokman, M. A., *Men, Matters and Memories: Compilation and Introduction by Professor Ahmed Ali Al-Hamdani* (Aden: No Publisher, 2009)
85. Esdaile, *Aden and the End of Empire 1937–1960* p225
86. MECA, GB165-0263/5/1: Slade-Baker Middle East Diary May–Dec 1956 p1367
87. Esdaile, *Aden and the End of Empire 1937–1960* p220
88. Kokilaben, *Dhirubhai Ambani* p59
89. Ibid. pp64–5
90. Lavin, G. W., 'Music in Colonial Aden: Globalization, Cultural Politics, and the Record Industry in an Indian Ocean Port City c1937–1960', *British Yemeni Society Journal*. 2021, 29
91. Ahmad, A., 'Gwadar: A Historical Kaleidoscope', *Policy Perspectives*. 2016, 13(2): 155–6
92. It is hard to ascertain how involved the Indian government actually was. Certainly two hundred Hindu Sindhi businessmen had migrated to the port after Partition, and after taking Indian citizenship, and the Pakistanis were worried these nationals would become a nuisance. The prominence of Gokaldas Khimji in the Sultan's inner circle likely triggered some of these thoughts. Arabian Gulf Digital Archive (AGDA) FO 371/126929 (1957): Negotiations between Sultan of Muscat and Pakistan Concerning Gwadur Oil Rights pp74–6. There were 'instances of Pakistanis having been kidnapped from Karachi, Baluchistan and the North Western regions of West Pakistan from time to time at these markets'. See AGDA FO 371/126929 (1957): Negotiations between Sultan of Muscat and Pakistan Concerning Gwadur Oil Rights p77
93. AGDA FO 371/126929 (1957): Negotiations between Sultan of Muscat and Pakistan Concerning Gwadur Oil Rights p54
94. Takriti, A. R., *Monsoon Revolution: Republicans, Sultans, and Empires in Oman 1965–1976* (Oxford: Oxford University Press, 2013) p148
95. Holden, *Farewell to Arabia* p20
96. He had managed to maintain ties with Gujarat – helping the Maharao of Cutch to convert his summer palace into a school. Allen, *Khimji Ramdas* Chapter 3
97. Barr, J., *Lords of the Desert: Britain's Struggle with America to Dominate the Middle East* (Simon & Schuster: London, 2018) p279
98. Adnan Noon Private Collection: 'Sir Firoz Khan Noon: Knight Bachelor Knight'
99. The narrative around the Transfer of Gwadar has been frequently credited to Firoz Khan Noon's second wife Viqar-un-nissa Noon. See 'Who Do We Thank for Gwadar?', *Daily Times*, 23 May 2018, and 'Gwadar ki Shaan, Begum Waqar un Nissa Noon', *Daily Urdu* columns, 17 January 2019. However, I have found no documentary evidence for her involvement, and Noon's grandson Adnan is convinced she was not involved. The narrative has been pieced together using the following primary sources: Noon, F. K., *From Memory* (Islamabad: National Book Foundation, 1993); Adnan Noon Private Collection: Noon, S. U., and Noon T. H., Life of the Seventh Prime Minister of Pakistan, Malik Firoz Khan Noon, The Man Behind Gwadar: A Collection of Private Historical Documents Compiled by the Great Grandsons of Malik Firoz Khan Noon (Unpublished); AGDA FO 371/126929 (1957) and FO 132790, FO 132791, FO 132792, FO 132793 (1958): Negotiations between Sultan of Muscat and Pakistan Concerning Gwadur Oil Rights
100. AGDA FO 371/126929 (1957): Negotiations between Sultan of Muscat and Pakistan Concerning Gwadur Oil Rights
101. Malik, I, *State and Civil Society in Pakistan: Politics of Authority, Ideology and Ethnicity* (London: Macmillan Press Ltd., 1997) p27

102. The anxiety about Noon's renewed pressure comes across clearly in official documents which show that colonial officials were worried 'Pakistan or India could no doubt claim to be successor states' to the Indian Empire, whose treaty with the Sultanate still underwrote Britain's relationship with the Gulf states. If either country put forward such a claim, they could potentially displace Britain in the region. AGDA FO 371/126929 (1957): Negotiations between Sultan of Muscat and Pakistan Concerning Gwadur Oil Rights p207
103. AGDA FO 371/132790 (1958): Negotiations between Sultan of Muscat and Pakistan Concerning Gwadur Oil Rights p66
104. Ibid. pp105–20
105. AGDA FO 371/132791 (1958): Negotiations between Sultan of Muscat and Pakistan Concerning Gwadur Oil Rights pp35–9
106. AGDA FO 371/126931 (1958): Negotiations between Sultan of Muscat and Pakistan Concerning Gwadur Oil Rights p33
107. AGDA FO 371/132791 (1958): Negotiations between Sultan of Muscat and Pakistan Concerning Gwadur Oil Rights p5
108. See Adnan Noon Private Collection: Noon and Noon Life of the Seventh Prime Minister of Pakistan, Malik Firoz Khan Noon, The Man Behind Gwadar p61
109. One of the Sultan's main reasons for keeping hold of Gwadar was the potential for discovering oil. By the mid-1950s the Sultan of Muscat had only a nominal sway over the interior Imamate, where oil *had* been discovered. The Sultan needed cash to conquer the Omani interior, and selling Gwadar could provide just that, as long as he did not lose the oil rights there. It was the perfect bargaining chip
110. AGDA FO 371/132791 (1958): Negotiations between Sultan of Muscat and Pakistan Concerning Gwadur Oil Rights p124
111. Ibid. p166; *Civil & Military Gazette* (Lahore), 10 September 1958
112. Adnan Noon Private Collection: Recording 'Radio Address by PM Malik Firoz Khan Noon Announcing the Transfer of Gwadar to Pakistan from Oman'

Chapter 12: The Last Days of the Raj

1. See Onley, J., *Britain and the Gulf Sheikhdoms, 1820–1971: The Politics of Protection* (Doha: CIRS Occasional Papers, 2009)
2. Holden, *Farewell to Arabia* p155
3. MECA, GB165-0263/5, 13/6: Slade Baker Collection: The East Aden protectorate and the Federation of South Arabia p61
4. Mawby, S. *British Policy in Aden and the Protectorates 1955–67: Last Outpost of a Middle East Empire* (London: Routledge, 2015) p77
5. Brendon, *The Decline and Fall of the British Empire* p504
6. Naumkin, *Red Wolves of Yemen* pvi
7. Paget, J., *Last Post: Aden, 1964–67* (London: Faber and Faber, 1969) p151
8. Halliday, *Arabia Without Sultans* pp216–17
9. Walker, J., *Aden Insurgency: The Savage War in Yemen 1962–67* (Barnsley: Pen & Sword Military, 2014) p187
10. Halliday, *Arabia Without Sultans*
11. Sultan Al Qu'aiti Private Collection: *Manuscript from Unpublished Memoir of Ghalib Al-Qu'aiti*, 1969 Chapter VI 'In Mukalla'
12. These excerpts from Jim and Joanna Ellis' letters have been published in Al-Qu'aiti, *'Fair Play' or Poisoned Chalice* p311
13. Ibid.
14. Ghalib writes extensively on his relationship with the Nizam in the unpublished manuscript, Sultan Al Qu'aiti Private Collection: *Manuscript from Unpublished Memoir of Ghalib Al-Qu'aiti*, 1969 Chapter VI 'In Mukalla'
15. Ledger, D., *Shifting Sands: The British in South Arabia* (London: Peninsular Publishing, 1983) p84
16. Statistics taken from Paget, *Last Post* p264. Mukalla had seen only a single attack. Ghalib writes how 'a grenade was thrown into an outside lavatory of the official residence of the State's Minister, Saiyyid Ahmad Muhammad al-'Attas as the head of the administration. Its most probable aim was to frighten him against dealing too harshly with the SAL prisoners then detained for trial. Of course, there had been no injuries.' Al-Qu'aiti, *'Fair Play' or Poisoned Chalice* p107
17. The following account of the coronation is based on private interviews with both Ghalib Al-Qu'aiti (in Jeddah) and

his half-brother Obaid Ur Rehman (in Hyderabad). Several accounts of the day have been published, along with photographs in Al-Qu'aiti, *'Fair Play' or Poisoned Chalice* Appendices. The unpublished letters of Saleha Al-Qu'aiti have also proven to be a useful source: Sultan Al Qu'aiti Private Collection: *Saleha Al-Qu'aiti letters to Mamu and Mumani about Coronation of Ghalib Bhai*, 1966, and Sultan Al Qu'aiti Private Collection: *Programme of the Celebration of the Coronation of His Highness Sultan Ghalib bin Awadh Al-Qu'aiti*, 1966. Footage of the coronation can be found in the BBC documentary *Faces of Islam: Till the Raven's Wings Turn White*, directed by Ovidio Salazar, BBC One, 2000. Ghalib Al-Qu'aiti's Private Archive contains many photographs of the day, some of which are available on his website alquaiti.com/home/
18. Joanna Ellis' letter, published in Al-Qu'aiti, *'Fair Play' or Poisoned Chalice* Appendices
19. The Arabian Raj largely continued the system of gun salutes that it had inherited from the Indian Empire. However, a few modifications were made. By 1949 the gun salutes were given as follows: Muscat 21 dynastic; Lahej 9 dynastic, 11 personal; Shihr and Mukalla 9 dynastic, 11 personal; Fadhli 9 dynastic; Qishn and Socotra 9 dynastic; Dhala 9 dynastic; Bahrain 7 dynastic, 11 personal; Kuwait 7 dynastic, 11 personal; Trucial Sheikhdoms: average 3 dynastic, 5 personal; Lower Yafai 9 personal; other states were not entitled to gun salutes. See Qatar Digital Library: 'Resident and Chief Commissioner: Salutes and Table of Precedence'. IOR/L/PS/12/1451Coll 1/13
20. The very concept of a durbar was an Indo-Persian state practice that had been transplanted into South Arabia during the Raj. See Willis, 'Making Yemen Indian: Rewriting the Boundaries of Imperial Arabia' 23–38
21. Joanna Ellis' memories of the day have been published in Al-Qu'aiti, *'Fair Play' or Poisoned Chalice* Appendices
22. Al-Qu'aiti, *'Fair Play' or Poisoned Chalice* p320
23. Freitag, *Indian Ocean Migrants and State Formation in Hadhramaut* p523
24. britishempire.co.uk/maproom/aden/sirhumphreytrevelyan.htm#:~:text=In%20May%201967%20the%20foreign,government%20which%20could%20ensure%20stability
25. Brendon, *The Decline and Fall of the British Empire* p506
26. Halliday, *Arabia Without Sultans* p238
27. Edwards, A., *Mad Mitch's Tribal Law: Aden and the End of Empire* (London: Mainstream Publishing, 2015) p203
28. Ibid. p208
29. Accounts of the fall of the federal states can be found in Mawby, *British Policy in Aden and the Protectorates 1955–67*; Brehony, N., *Yemen Divided: The Story of a Failed State in South Arabia* (London: I. B. Tauris, 2013); Ledger, *Shifting Sands*; Paget, *Last Post*; Halliday, *Arabia Without Sultans* p230; Naumkin, *Red Wolves of Yemen* pp250–70
30. Trevelyan, H., *The Middle East in Revolution* (Kindle, Lume Books, 2019) p218
31. Mawby, *British Policy in Aden and the Protectorates 1955–67* p173
32. Crouch, M., *An Element of Luck: To South Arabia and Return* (London: Rawlhouse Pub, 2001) pp220–1
33. 'Message received from Aden for Sultan Ghalib Al Qa'titi', published in Al-Qu'aiti, *'Fair Play' or Poisoned Chalice* Appendix Nine
34. Mawby, *British Policy in Aden and the Protectorates 1955–67* p172
35. Al-Qu'aiti, *'Fair Play' or Poisoned Chalice* p229
36. Freitag, *Indian Ocean Migrants and State Formation in Hadhramaut* p526
37. Private Interview, Sultan Ghalib Al-Quaiti, Jeddah, English, March 2022
38. Al-Qu'aiti, Sultan G., *'Fair Play' or Poisoned Chalice: The Last Years of Britain's Presence and Policy in Southern Arabia* (London: Darf Publishers, 2021) p231
39. Private Interview, Sultan Ghalib Al-Qu'aiti, Jeddah, English, March 2022
40. FCO 8/252 NA: Ellis, J, to High Commission, 5/10/1967. Ghalib's interpretation can be found in Al-Qu'aiti, *'Fair Play' or Poisoned Chalice: The Last Years of Britain's Presence and Policy in Southern Arabia* pp194–5
41. Britain still denies having supported the NLF takeover of Hadhramaut and Ulrike Freitag writes how British documents presented to the UN 'claimed that the

Sultans, notably the Kathiri, prevaricated in Jeddah and did not return as quickly as would have been possible. British support for the Beduin Legion was, they protested, merely in compliance with their duty to reinforce law and order. The Legion was the only legitimate force and was fighting against an unruly tribe. According to this version, the bombardment therefore did not constitute active support for the NLF.' However, many Hadhrami scholars disagree: 'For al-Bakri, it seems quite clear that the British followed a plan to hand Hadhramaut over to the NLF, in spite of the fact that the NLF had only some sixty supporters in all of Hadhramaut. This view is shared by Sultan Ghalib, according to whom the last Resident Adviser later confessed that the British followed the above-described course of action in Hadhramaut because of their concern that the Sultan would not leave the country on his own account. They feared that his resistance might cause great loss of life, including possibly his own. Al-Jabiri adds that the Qu'ayti armed forces had no alternative but to negotiate with the NLF. According to his version, the Kathiri tribes decided to oppose the changes, although their resolve was weakened by the Sultan's return to Jeddah. By early October, the badly armed tribes lost the war of nerves against the better armed NLF and the Sultan's deputy handed power to the NLF on October 3.' Freitag, U., *Indian Ocean Migrants and State Formation in Hadhramaut: Reforming the Homeland* (Leiden, Netherlands: Brill, 2003) p526
42. Private Interview, Sultan Ghalib Al-Quaiti, Zoom, February 2021
43. Brendon, *The Decline and Fall of the British Empire* p507
44. The translation of this table is taken from Namukin, Red Wolves of Yemen p257
45. Paget, *Last Post* p255
46. Naumkin, *Red Wolves of Yemen* p292
47. Halliday, *Arabia Without Sultans*
48. Private Interview: Khozem Merchant, New Delhi, English, April 2021
49. Crouch, *An Element of Luck* pp234–5
50. McDonald, *Ambani & Sons* p44
51. Ibid. Chapter 4
52. news18.com/news/business/reliance-first-indian-firm-to-reach-usd-200-billion-m-cap-becomes-worlds-40th-most-valuable-company-2866731.html
53. Private Interview, Huda Luqman, Zoom, English, February 2021
54. Private Interview, Huda Luqman, Zoom, English, February 2021. Also see Al-Hamdani, A. A., 'Preface' in Lokman, *Men, Matters and Memories* p2
55. Petouris, T., 'Faysal al-'Attas: The Maoist Sayyid', *British-Yemeni Society Journal*. 2014, 22: 32–40. This did not include Ghalib and his Kathiri colleague, who were viewed as constitutional Sultans
56. Private Interview, Sultan Ghalib Al-Quaiti, Zoom, February 2021
57. Holden, *Farewell to Arabia* p151
58. This was a lie. As Onley writes: 'The Government could afford to keep its forces in the Gulf, especially given the importance of Gulf oil to the British economy: nearly half the oil used in Britain came from there and £12 million was a small price to pay for the protection of Gulf oil exports worth £2 billion a year. The reason for [Harold] Wilson's decision to withdraw was the fear that keeping British forces in the Gulf would undermine Labour's attempts to justify to the British electorate the deep cuts it was about to make to the civil budget, particularly social programs such as the National Health Service.' See Onley, *Britain and the Gulf Sheikhdoms, 1820–1971* p21
59. Balfour-Paul, *The End of Empire in the Middle East* Chapter 4
60. Onley, *Britain and the Gulf Sheikhdoms, 1820–1971* p22
61. Takriti, *Monsoon Revolution* p99
62. Ibid. p102
63. Bradshaw, *The End of Empire in the Gulf* p129
64. Barr, *Lords of the Desert* p279
65. Halliday, *Arabia Without Sultans* p290
66. Ibid. pp336–7
67. Takriti, *Monsoon Revolution* pp171–2
68. Kane, R., *Coup D'état Oman* (Smashwords Edition, 2012) pp93–5
69. Marfatia, M., *The Khimji Memoirs* (Unpublished) Chapter 4
70. Holden, D., 'The Persian Gulf: After the British Raj', *Foreign Affairs*. 1971, 49(4): 721–35
71. Ibid.
72. *Farewell Arabia*. Directed by Randal Beattie, written and narrated by David

Holden, NET, 1968; available: youtube.com/watch?v=KnPrI2fc_vo&ab_channel=NuclearVault
73. Holden, 'The Persian Gulf: After the British Raj' 721–35
74. Ibid.
75. Bradshaw, *The End of Empire in the Gulf*
76. Morton, *A Fateful Intrusion* p236
77. Bradshaw, *The End of Empire in the Gulf* pp149–50

Chapter 13: Proxy Wars
1. Paliwal, *India's Near East*
2. Singh, A. K. J., *Himalayan Triangle: A Historical Survey of British India's Relations with Tibet, Sikkim and Bhutan 1765–1950* (London: British Library, 1988) p264
3. Phizo, An Appeal to the World
4. 'Questions remain about the extent to which the vote represented the popular will of all Naga communities. Suggestions that the plebiscite was an overwhelmingly Angami dominated affair have been put forward. Similarly, the extent of the electorate's knowledge about the NNC's political obstinence and the reliability of the 99.9% approval figure remain open to interpretation. A lack of source material surrounding the plebiscite makes definitive conclusions difficult.' Holt, B. M., *The Long Decolonization of the Assam Highlands, 1942–72* (PhD: University of Leeds, 2021) p111
5. Hazarika, *Strangers of the Mist* p89
6. Guha, *India after Gandhi* p265
7. *The Times of India*, 1 January 1952
8. Ibid., 12 March 1952
9. Guha, *India after Gandhi* p266
10. Phizo's daughter Adino claims Indian officials 'hoodwinked' the Burmese border guards, while Phizo's biographer Pieter Steyn suggests their discovery had been 'entirely fortuitous'. Phizo, A., *A Portrait of A. Z. Phizo on his Birth Centenary* p5; Steyn, *Zapuphizo* p87
11. Guha, *India after Gandhi* p268
12. Paliwal, *India's Near East* p125
13. NAI, Home, NEFA, NII/102(42)/70, 'Background note on Angami Zapu Phizo and Rev. Michael Scott prepared by U. S(Naga) in April 1970' p6
14. Nibedon, *Nagaland* p59
15. Paliwal, *India's Near East* pp130–1
16. Guha, *India after Gandhi* p274
17. NAI, Home, NEFA, NII/102(42)/70, 'Background note on Angami Zapu Phizo and Rev. Michael Scott prepared by U. S(Naga) in April 1970' p7; Nibedon, *Nagaland* p89
18. Phizo, quoted in Steyn, *Zapuphizo* p101
19. Paliwal, *India's Near East*
20. Kux, D., *The United States and Pakistan, 1947–2000: Disenchanted Allies* (Oxford: Oxford University Press, 2003) p99
21. The reply was equally polite: 'My Dear Iskander, I have received your letter of 7th evening. Now that you have undertaken this great responsibility, I wish you all success and pray for peace in Pakistan and the happiness of its people. Thank you for all your friendliness, cordiality and cooperation I received from you during my tenure in office. Your sinc. Firoz Khan Noon', Adnan Noon Private Collection: Coup Letters, 7 October 1958
22. Paliwal, *India's Near East*
23. Higgins, D., *In the Wake of the Raj: Travels in 1950s India* (Ely: Melrose Books, 2009) p5
24. Seaton, M., *Panditji: A Portrait of Jawaharlal Nehru* (New York: Taplinger, 1967) p280; Hough, R., *Edwina, Countess Mountbatten of Burma* (New York: W. Morrow, 1984) p3
25. Seaton, *Panditji* p281
26. According to Zareer Masani, Nehru 'used to spend the night with her ... much to the chagrin of his Foreign Service minders, one of whom was my uncle'. See Lownie, *The Mountbattens* pp265–8
27. Quoted in Lownie, *The Mountbattens* p265
28. Ghose, S., *Indira: India's Most Powerful Prime Minister* (New Delhi: Juggernaut Books, 2017) p71
29. Ibid. p63
30. Ibid. p68
31. Quoted in ibid. p69
32. Ibid.
33. Quoted in Haksar and Hongray, *Kuknalim* p59
34. Hough, *Edwina, Countess Mountbatten of Burma* p4
35. MP MS62/MB31/40/LM/Louis Mountbatten's Diary Jan–Jun 1960; 21 Feb 1960
36. *SWJN*. Series 2, Volume 57, '252: To Louis Mountbatten: Condolences' p451
37. Guha, R., 'The Day Edwina Died' in *The Hindu*. Available at ramachandraguha.in/archives/the-day-edwina-died-the-hindu.html

38. *SWJN*. Series 2, Volume 58, '253: To Barbara Cartland: Remembering Edwina' p368
39. *SWJN*. Series 2, Volume 57, '253: To Vijaya Lakshmi Pandit: Edwina Mountbatten's Pressure Cooker' p451
40. Seaton, *Panditji: A Portrait of Jawaharlal Nehru* p285
41. This account was detailed to me in September 2023 by a relative of the Mountbattens who wishes to remain anonymous
42. Morgan, *Edwina Mountbatten* p479
43. Seaton, *Panditji* p286
44. Steyn, *Zapuphizo* p106; Also see Pillai, M., '"I'm a Naga first, a Naga second, and a Naga last"' in Mint Lounge lifestyle. livemint.com/news/talking-point/im-a-naga-first-a-naga-second-and-a-naga-last-111646984189904.html
45. Steyn, *Zapuphizo* pxiv
46. Ibid. p115
47. Ibid. p118
48. Blood, A. K., *The Cruel Birth of Bangladesh: Memoirs of an American Diplomat* (Dhaka: University Press Limited, 2005) p16
49. McGarr, *The Cold War in South Asia* p83
50. Ibid. p85
51. Ibid. p77
52. Quoted in Raghavan, T. C. A., *The People Next Door: The Curious History of India's Relations with Pakistan* (London: C. Hurst & Co., 2019) p70
53. Haksar and Hongray, *Kuknalim* p60
54. Ibid.
55. Van Schendel and Pachuau, *The Camera as Witness* pp299–300
56. Ibid. p304
57. NAI: Home Affairs, NE, File No. NII/102(33)/72, 1971: 'Foreign involvement in insurgency in North Eastern India – Preparation of white paper on the subject by the Ministry of Defence' p30
58. Sisson, R., and Rose, L. E., *War and Secession: Pakistan, India, and the Creation of Bangladesh* (Oakland: University of California Press, 1990) p43
59. Mohua, M., and Mowtushi, M., 'Bangladesh', *Journal of Commonwealth Literature*. 2023, 58(4): 788–98
60. Blood, *The Cruel Birth of Bangladesh* p2
61. Gauhar, A., *Ayub Khan: Pakistan's First Military Ruler* (Lahore: Sang-e-Meel Publications, 1993) p29
62. Tripathi, S., *The Colonel Who Would Not Repent: The Bangladesh War and Its Unquiet Legacy* (New Delhi: Aleph Book Company, 2014) p61
63. Paliwal, *India's Near East* p228
64. *SWJN*. Series 2, Volume 76, '465: To Y. D. Gundevia: Mujibur Rahman' p509
65. Banerjee, S. S., *India, Mujibur Rahman, Bangladesh Liberation & Pakistan* (Self-published, 2011) available songramernotebook.com/archives/371870
66. Ibid.
67. Banerjee, *India, Mujibur Rahman, Bangladesh Liberation & Pakistan*
68. Raman, B., *The Kaoboys of R&AW: Down Memory Lane* (Epub: Lancer Publications LLC, 2013) Chapter 2
69. Paliwal, *India's Near East* p174
70. See Bal, E., 'The Garo Exodus of 1964' in Guhathakurta and Van Schendel (eds), *The Bangladesh Reader*
71. Anil, *Another India* p8
72. Von Tunzelmann, *Indian Summer* p356
73. Seaton, *Panditji* p474
74. Blood, *The Cruel Birth of Bangladesh* p46
75. Bennett-Jones, *The Bhutto Dynasty* p59
76. Wolpert, S., *Zulfi Bhutto of Pakistan* (Oxford: Oxford University Press, 1993)
77. Bennett-Jones, *The Bhutto Dynasty* p46
78. Ibid. p49
79. NAI: Ministry of External Affairs, Historical Division (Research & Intelligence Section), 1966, HI/1011(10)/66-II 'Annual Reports from Dacca for 1965' p3
80. Ibid. pp4–5
81. Hussain, *Kashmir in the Aftermath of Partition* p203
82. Van Schendel, Mey and Dewan, *The Chittagong Hill Tracts* p79
83. McGarr, *The Cold War in South Asia* p317
84. Ghose, *Indira* p93
85. Van Schendel and Pachuau, *The Camera as Witness* p305
86. Holt, *The Long Decolonization of the Assam Highlands, 1942–72* p185
87. Ibid. Chapter 21
88. Zakaria, *1971* p83
89. *National Geographic*, January 1967
90. Blood, *The Cruel Birth of Bangladesh* p47
91. This summarised version of the Six Points is taken from Bennett-Jones, *Pakistan* p157
92. NAI, Ministry of External Affairs, Historical Division (Research and Intelligence Section), 1969,

HI/1011(10)/69-II 'Annual Report, Dy. High Commissioner of India, Dacca (East Pakistan), 1968' p8; for identification of Ojha with Banerjee, see Paliwal, *India's Near East* p5
93. Tripathi, *The Colonel Who Would Not Repent* p57
94. Zakaria, *1971* p80
95. Ibid. p115
96. Private interview, Asif Ali, English, WhatsApp, December 2023
97. Zakaria, *1971* p117
98. Private interview, Asif Ali, English, WhatsApp, December 2023
99. Ibid.
100. Zakaria, *1971* p122
101. Ibid. p126
102. Private Interview, Mick Jagger, Calcutta, English, November 2023
103. Private Interview, Faith Singh, Jaipur, English, November 2022; also see mumbaimirror.indiatimes.com/mumbai/other/let-your-juniors-enjoy-the-reward/articleshow/15986311.cms
104. Raghavan, *1971* p18
105. Private Interview, Salahdin Imam, Dhaka, English, July 2022
106. Quoted in Raghavan, *1971* p15
107. Van Schendel, *The Bengal Borderland* p270
108. dawn.com/news/279413/people-who-own-greatest-amount-of-wealth
109. FCO 37/185/7: Political Activities of Mr Z A Bhutto p2
110. Blood, *The Cruel Birth of Bangladesh* p60
111. Ibid. p32
112. Tripathi, *The Colonel Who Would Not Repent* p57
113. 'Note for Secretary of State for Cabinet Meeting on 30 October: Sheikh Mujibur Rahman' in FCO 37/467: Political Activities of Sheikh Mujibur Rahman
114. Zakaria, *1971* p89
115. Reports of the Advisory Panels for the Fourth Five Year Plan 1970–75, Vol. I, published by the planning commission of Pakistan
116. Ibid
117. Private Interview, Salahdin Imam, Dhaka, English, July 2022
118. Imam, S. I., *My Five Year Hyperlife: Magical Realism, from Harvard Yard to Woodstock to the Bangladesh Liberation War* (Unpublished, 2023) p24
119. Ibid. Appendix 1
120. Private Interview, Salahdin Imam, Dhaka, English, July 2022
121. Imam, *My Five Year Hyperlife* p151
122. Ibid. p156
123. Ibid. pp156–60
124. Ibid. p5
125. Ibid. p224
126. Salik, S., *Witness to Surrender* (Karachi: OUP, 1997) p23
127. Blood, *The Cruel Birth of Bangladesh* p33
128. Ibid. p42
129. Ibid. p43
130. Imam, *My Five Year Hyperlife* p253
131. Blood, *The Cruel Birth of Bangladesh* pp59–60
132. Imam, *My Five Year Hyperlife* p276
133. Khan, Z. A., *The Way It Was* (Karachi: Ahbab Printers, 1998) p251
134. Blood, *The Cruel Birth of Bangladesh* p116
135. Private Interview, Salahdin Imam, Dhaka, English, July 2022
136. Khan, *The Way It Was* p249
137. Schanberg quoted in Bass, G. J., *The Blood Telegram: India's Secret War in Pakistan* (Gurgaon: Random House India, 2014) p24
138. Blood, A. K., *The Cruel Birth of Bangladesh: Memoirs of an American Diplomat* (Dhaka: University Press Limited, 2005) p128
139. Ibid. p137
140. Sisson, R., and Rose, L. E., *War and Secession: Pakistan, India, and the Creation of Bangladesh* (Oxford: University of California Press, 1990) p66
141. Ibid. pp70, 76
142. Ibid. p89. Dr. Maryam S. Khan has since argued that this is a mistranslation of Bhutto's speech and that he had intended to say something more like 'No leg to stand on'.
143. Blood, A. K., The Cruel Birth of Bangladesh: Memoirs of an American Diplomat (Dhaka: University Press Limited, 2005) p151
144. Bass G. J., *The Blood Telegram: India's Secret War in Pakistan* (Gurgaon: Random House India, 2014) p28
145. NAI: Ministry of External Affairs, Historical Division (Research & Intelligence Section), HI/1012(30)/71, 'Political Reports etc. (other than annual reports) from Islamabad (W. Pakistan)' p17
146. Imam, *My Five Year Hyperlife* pp290–2
147. Imam, J., *Of Blood and Fire: The Untold Story of Bangladesh's War of Independence* (Translated by Mustafizur Rahman)

(Dhaka: Charulipi Prokashon, 2022) pp12–13
148. Sisson and Rose, *War and Secession* p102
149. Imam, *My Five Year Hyperlife* pp290–2
150. Blood, *The Cruel Birth of Bangladesh* p158; Khan, *The Way It Was* p261
151. In his autobiography, Roy writes, 'We were aware that the Awami League wanted to make the Hill Tracts an ordinary district. The hillmen would become like tea garden labourers – the lands would belong to the wealthy Bengalis.' Roy, T., *The Departed Melody (Memoirs)* (Islamabad: PPA Publications, 2003) p196
152. Roy, *The Departed Melody* p210
153. Blood, *The Cruel Birth of Bangladesh* p155. As far as I am aware, we do not actually have this cable, with this line only appearing in Blood's memoirs. It is possible therefore that this line is post-hoc
154. Imam, *Of Blood and Fire* pp14, 17
155. Firdousi, I., *The Year That Was* (Dhaka: Bastu Prakashan, 1996) p17
156. Roy, *The Departed Melody* p211
157. It is of course possible that he was just playing for time until the start of the shooting on 25 March
158. Imam, *My Five Year Hyperlife* p294
159. Sisson and Rose, *War and Secession* p93, and Zakaria, *1971* p145
160. Imam, *Of Blood and Fire* p26
161. Ibid. p33
162. Ibid.
163. Ibid. pp293–6
164. This comparison draws on the work of Bose, S., *Dead Reckoning: Memories of the 1971 Bangladesh War* (London: Hurst & Company, 2011) Chapter 2. This controversial work received a slew of criticism for its sympathy with the Pakistani side. While I disagree with some of Bose's conclusions, she raises numerous important questions and her comparisons of eyewitness accounts, particularly in the early chapters, are invaluable to scholars
165. Blood, *The Cruel Birth of Bangladesh* p182, quoted in Bose, *Dead Reckoning* p35
166. Salik, *Witness to Surrender* p59
167. Sisson and Rose, *War and Secession* p113
168. Ibid.; also see Bhutto, Z. A., *The Great Tragedy* (Reproduced by Sani H. Parwar, Self-published) p33
169. *New York Times*, 17 March 1971
170. Bhutto, *The Great Tragedy* p35
171. Sisson and Rose, *War and Secession* p120
172. Blood, *The Cruel Birth of Bangladesh* p191
173. Sisson and Rose, *War and Secession* p122
174. Bhutto, *The Great Tragedy* p38
175. *New York Times*, 25 March 1971
176. Sisson and Rose, *War and Secession* p127
177. Ibid. p130

Chapter 14: Liberation
1. Imam, J., *Of Blood and Fire* p43
2. Blood, *The Cruel Birth of Bangladesh* pp195–6
3. Hamoodur Rahman Commission Report
4. For Khan's account see Khan, *The Way It Was* p269. For Mujib's own account, see nytimes.com/1972/01/18/archives/he-tells-full-story-of-arrest-and-detention-sheik-mujib-describes.html
5. Hamoodur Rahman Commission Report p26
6. Tripathi, *The Colonel Who Would Not Repent* p92
7. Bose, *Dead Reckoning* p70
8. Ibid. pp59–64
9. Zakaria, *1971* pp119, 134
10. Bass, *The Blood Telegram* p51
11. *New York Times*, 28 March 1971
12. Ibid.
13. Ibid.
14. Tripathi, *The Colonel Who Would Not Repent* p84
15. Imam, *Of Blood and Fire* p45
16. Ibid. p46
17. Ibid. p49
18. tbsnews.net/supplement/26-march-1971-it-was-391366
19. Zakaria, *1971* p99
20. Shamsie, M., '1971: Reassessing a Forgotten National Narrative' in *The Routledge Companion to Pakistani Anglophone Writing* (Abingdon: Routledge, 2019) p22
21. Imam, *My Five Year Hyperlife* p357
22. Private Interview, Salahdin Imam, Dhaka, English, July 2022; Imam, *My Five Year Hyperlife* p300
23. The precise wording of this speech would later become highly contentious when members of the Bangladesh Nationalist Party, under Zia's wife Khaleda Zia, started claiming Zia made the announcement in his own name rather than Mujib's. Journalist Salil Tripathi writes: 'At root is not only

the conflict over who was the greater freedom fighter and greater patriot – Zia or Mujib – but also, who played a bigger role in winning Bangladesh's freedom: civilian Awami politicians or East Pakistani soldiers who rebelled under the command of various sector commanders. But it is a puerile controversy. In *Muktir Gaan* (Freedom Song), the documentary of film-makers Tareque and Catherine Masud, there is a recording of Zia's announcement, which clearly states that he was speaking on behalf of Sheikh Mujib. And yet, the issue has become so divisive in Bangladesh now, that it is impossible for anyone to express a view about what may really have happened, for fear of being accused of partisanship.' Tripathi, *The Colonel Who Would Not Repent* p362

24. Sisson and Rose, *War and Secession* p159
25. Saikia, Y., *Women, War and the Making of Bangladesh: Remembering 1971* (New Delhi: Women Unlimited, 2011) p128
26. Imam, *My Five Year Hyperlife* p360
27. Private Interview, Salahdin Imam, Dhaka, English, July 2022
28. Imam, *Of Blood and Fire* p51
29. Firdousi, *The Year That Was* p35
30. Hamoodur Rahman Commission Report p21. For more evidence of the targeting of Hindus, see Bass, *The Blood Telegram*
31. Blood, *The Cruel Birth of Bangladesh* p198
32. Ibid. pp207–16
33. Bass, *The Blood Telegram* p65
34. Ibid. p86
35. Ibid. p78
36. Tripathi, *The Colonel Who Would Not Repent* p128
37. Coggins, D., 'Pakistan: The Battle of Kushtia' in *Time* magazine, 19 April 1971
38. Tripathi, *The Colonel Who Would Not Repent* p154
39. Private Interview, Salahdin Imam, Dhaka, English, July 2022
40. Imam, *My Five Year Hyperlife* p310
41. Private Interview, Salahdin Imam, Dhaka, English, July 2022
42. Ibid.
43. Saikia, *Women, War and the Making of Bangladesh* p53
44. Shamsie, M., '1971: Reassessing a Forgotten National Narrative' p11
45. Sobhan, R., *Untranquil Recollections: The Years of Fulfilment* (New Delhi: Sage Publications, 2016) p361
46. Datta, A., *Refugees and Borders in South Asia: The Great Exodus of 1971* (Abingdon: Routledge, 2013) p56
47. Ibid. pp109, 129, 143–4
48. Bass, *The Blood Telegram* p119
49. Datta, *Refugees and Borders in South Asia* p133
50. Mukhopadhyay, N., *Narendra Modi: The Man, The Times* (New Delhi: Westland, 2013) p111
51. Bass, *The Blood Telegram* p125
52. Datta, *Refugees and Borders in South Asia* p72
53. Ibid. p28
54. Raghavan, *1971* p77
55. Bass, *The Blood Telegram* p93
56. Private Interview, Chandrakant Singh, Jaipur, English, November 2023; Singh, Maj. C., *Meghna: River of Victory* (New Delhi: Sabre and Quill Publishers, 2021)
57. Jacob, Lt-Gen. J. F. R., *Surrender at Dacca: Birth of a Nation* (New Delhi: Manohar, 2006) p36
58. Raman, *The Kaoboys of R&AW* Chapter 2
59. 'Mujibnagar: Proclaiming a New Country (17 April 1971) in Guhathakurta and Van Schendel (eds), *The Bangladesh Reader*
60. Bass, *The Blood Telegram* pp96–9
61. Private Interview, Salahdin Imam, Dhaka, English, July 2022
62. Ibid.
63. Imam, *My Five Year Hyperlife* p333
64. Private Interview, Salahdin Imam, Dhaka, English, July 2022
65. For this section on women in the Mukti Bahini, I am indebted to the work of Yasmin Saikia: Saikia, *Women, War and the Making of Bangladesh* p237
66. Saikia, *Women, War and the Making of Bangladesh* pp235–9
67. Ibid. pp246–55
68. Sisson and Rose, *War and Secession* p170
69. Bose, *Dead Reckoning* p99
70. Zakaria, *1971* p128
71. Bose, *Dead Reckoning* p92
72. Van Schendel, W., 'A War Within a War: Mizo Rebels and the Bangladesh Liberation Struggle', *Modern Asian Studies*. 2016, 50 (1): 75–117
73. Khan, *The Way It Was* p304
74. Van Schendel, 'A War Within a War: Mizo rebels and the Bangladesh Liberation Struggle' 75–117
75. NAI: Home Affairs, NE, File No. NII/102(33)/72, 1971: 'Foreign involvement in insurgency in North

Eastern India – Preparation of white paper on the subject by the Ministry of Defence' p31
76. Khan, *The Way It Was* p298
77. Ibid. p308
78. NAI: Ministry of External Affairs, Historical Division (Research & Intelligence Section), HI/1012(30)/71, 'Political Reports etc. (other than annual reports) from Islamabad (W. Pakistan)' p27; Datta, *Refugees and Borders in South Asia* pp31–3
79. FCO 37/896/1: Government of Bangla Desh in East Pakistan; *New York Times*, 23 September 1971
80. Imam, *Of Blood and Fire* p125
81. Shamsie, '1971: Reassessing a Forgotten National Narrative' p11
82. Ibid. p1
83. Ibid. p12
84. Evans, *My Paper Chase* Chapter 16
85. 'Obituary of Mr Anthony Mascarenhas', *The Times* (London, England), 8 December 1986; Mascarenhas, A., *The Rape of Bangladesh* (New Delhi: Vikas Publications, 1971) pv
86. *Sunday Times*, 13 June 1971
87. bbc.com/news/world-asia-16207201
88. Evans, *My Paper Chase* Chapter 16
89. *Time* magazine, 25 October 1971
90. Hamoodur Rahman Commission Report p15
91. Imam, *My Five Year Hyperlife* p374
92. Zakaria, *1971* p218
93. Chatterji, *Shadows at Noon* p160
94. *Sunday Times*, 13 June 1971
95. NAI: MEA, Historical Division (Research & Intelligence Section), HI/1012(30)/71, 'Political Reports etc. (other than annual reports) from Islamabad (W. Pakistan)' p2–32
96. NAI, MEA, AMS, File No.WII/105/16/71, Chronology of principal events in Bangladesh, p35; Raghavan, *1971* p215
97. Lawoti, M., Pahari, A. K. (eds), *The Maoist Insurgency in Nepal: Revolution in the Twenty-first Century* (London: Routledge, 2009) p208
98. Bass, *The Blood Telegram* pp182–4
99. Van Schendel, *The Bengal Borderland* p268
100. Imam, *My Five Year Hyperlife* p350
101. FCO 37/945: Famine Relief to East Pakistan; *Yorkshire Post*, 20 April 1971 p21
102. *Yorkshire Post*, 20 April 1971
103. Craske, O., *Indian Sun: The Life and Music of Ravi Shankar* (London: Faber and Faber, 2020) pp392–3
104. Raghavan, *1971* p143
105. Private Interview, Salahdin Imam, Dhaka, English, July 2022
106. pitchfork.com/reviews/albums/george-harrison-ravi-shankar-the-concert-for-bangladesh/
107. Raghavan, *1971* p145
108. Craske, *Indian Sun* p396
109. Brown, D., *Overland to India* (New York, Outerbridge & Dienstfrey; distributed by E. P. Dutton 1971)
110. Imam, *My Five Year Hyperlife* p427
111. Raghavan, *1971* p146
112. Imam, *My Five Year Hyperlife* p428
113. Raghavan, *1971* p146
114. Ibid. p147
115. FCO 37/945: Declaration for Bangla Desh by members of diplomatic service of Pakistan p39
116. Ibid. p19
117. *Janomot Bengali Newsweekly*, 3 October, 1971
118. Raghavan, *1971* pp224–6
119. joshwest63.medium.com/the-billion-dollar-party-that-ended-a-2500-year-old-monarchy-8567c0d46080
120. Ibid.
121. Jones, J., and Ridout, N. P., *A History of Modern Oman* (New York: Cambridge University Press, 2015) p156
122. NAI: MEA, Historical Division (Research & Intelligence Section), HI/1012(30)/71, 'Political Reports etc. (other than annual reports) from Islamabad (W. Pakistan)' p70
123. Raghavan, *1971* p226
124. *New York Times*, 21 November 1971
125. Ibid. 8 November 1971
126. Jacob, *Surrender at Dacca* pp71–2
127. Bass, *The Blood Telegram* p190
128. NAI: MEA, Historical Division (Research & Intelligence Section), HI/1012(30)/71, 'Political Reports etc. (other than annual reports) from Islamabad (W. Pakistan)' p88
129. Bass, *The Blood Telegram* p263
130. Zakaria, *1971* p183
131. Bass, *The Blood Telegram* p268

Chapter 15: The Partition of Pakistan
1. Chatterji, *Shadows at Noon* p159
2. Ibid. p84
3. dawn.com/news/1151200

4. Chatterji, *Shadows at Noon* p84
5. *Time* magazine, 20 December 1971
6. Singh, *Meghna* p51; *Observer*, 19 December 1971
7. *Time* magazine, 20 December 1971
8. Shamsie, M., 'When We Were Young: Karachi, 1963–1971', *Postcolonial cities – South Asia*. 2013, 13(2): 13
9. *Observer*, 19 December 1971
10. Bass, *The Blood Telegram* p281
11. Singh, *Meghna* 93
12. Imam, *My Five Year Hyperlife* p385
13. Bass, *The Blood Telegram* p276
14. *Time* magazine, 20 December 1971
15. Rahman and Alam, *The Unfinished Memoirs* p128
16. Mazari, S. K., *A Journey to Disillusionment* (Oxford: Oxford University Press, 1999) p149
17. Gauhar, *Ayub Khan* p462
18. Raghavan, *1971* p29
19. Khan, R. F. A., *How Pakistan Got Divided* (Karachi: Oxford University Press, 2017) p121
20. Van Schendel, 'A War Within a War: Mizo rebels and the Bangladesh Liberation Struggle' 75–117
21. Raghavan, *1971* p236
22. The decision to go for Dacca is traditionally credited to Jacob, but more recent writings from within the Indian Army give the credit to Sagat
23. Nair, K. S., *Surrender in Dacca: The Indian Armed Forces and the 1971 Bangladesh Liberation War* (Delhi: Harper Collins, 2022) p283
24. Raman, *The Kaoboys of R&AW* Chapter 2
25. Bass, *The Blood Telegram* pp289–99
26. Ibid. pp311–15
27. Raghavan, *1971* p256
28. Ibid. p257
29. Ibid. p255
30. Bose, *Dead Reckoning* pp155–6
31. Hamoodur Rahman Report: 'Although there was some talks of arresting persons known to be leaders of the Awami League or Mukti Bahini so as to prevent chances of a general uprising in Dacca during the closing phases of the war with India, yet no practical action was taken in view of the circumstances then prevailing, namely the precarious position of the Pakistan Army and the impending surrender. We consider, therefore, that unless the Bangladesh authorities can produce some convincing evidence, it is not possible to record a finding that any intellectuals or professionals were indeed arrested and killed by the Pakistan Army during December 1971'
32. The precise meaning of this message has since become controversial. In the words of Salil Tripathi: 'What did the letter mean? Was Yahya instructing Niazi to surrender? Or was he letting him decide the next steps? Was it an opinion or an instruction? An interpretation or a command ... A few hundred, if not a few thousand, lives were lost amidst this indecisiveness.' See Tripathi, *The Colonel Who Would Not Repent* p172
33. Jacob, *Surrender at Dacca* p123
34. Ibid. p124
35. *Observer*, 19 December 1971
36. Jacob, *Surrender at Dacca* p145
37. Ibid. p125
38. Ibid. p126
39. *50 years of Bangladesh*: BBC's exclusive documentary from 1971 – BBC URDU. Available at youtu.be/KWEP7XbO6H8?si=7ByzYPI_WVDqVL6G
40. Jalal, *The Pity of Partition* p4
41. Zakaria, *1971* p53
42. Bass, *The Blood Telegram* p327
43. Khan, *The Way It Was* pp89, 95
44. Ibid. p102
45. *Observer*, 19 December 1971
46. Nair, *Surrender in Dacca* pp294–5
47. Chatterji, *Shadows at Noon* p161
48. Khan, *The Way It Was* p95
49. Ibid. p62
50. Haksar and Hongray, *Kuknalim* pp224–6
51. These included Phillip Lalthangliana, Major-General Thangzuala, Zamawala, Lalmunmuwia, Thinoselie and Nidilie. See NAI: Home Affairs, NE, File No. NII/102(33)/72, 1971: 'Foreign involvement in insurgency in North Eastern India – Preparation of white paper on the subject by the Ministry of Defence' p30
52. Van Schendel and Pachuau, *The Camera as Witness* p341
53. Private Interview, Shahana Siddiqui, Zoom, English, February 2024
54. Sinh, R., *A Talent for War: The Military Biography of Lt Gen Sagat Singh* (Delhi: Vij Books, 2013)
55. Van Schendel, *A History of Bangladesh* p200

56. en.prothomalo.com/bangladesh/13-historic-hours-in-air
57. Salunke, Col S. P., *Pakistani POWs in India* (New Delhi: Vikas Publishing House, 1977) p9
58. Imam, *My Five Year Hyperlife* p386
59. Datta, *Refugees and Borders in South Asia* pp158–65
60. Ghose, *Indira* p126
61. Raman, *The Kaoboys of R&AW*
62. Private Interview by Sarah Shah, Mohammad Kacho Yabgo, Turtuk, March 2021
63. For Roy's short stories see Roy, T., *They Simply Belong* (Rawalpindi: National Publishing House, 1972)
64. Roy, *The Departed Melody* p247
65. Ibid. p252
66. Ibid. p253
67. Private Interview, Raja Devashish Roy, Dhaka, English, July 2022
68. Private Interview, Mohammad Zaul Hassan, WhatsApp, English, September 2022
69. Ibid.
70. Ibid.
71. For the secret negotiations about them, see Bass, G. 'Bargaining Away Justice: India, Pakistan, and the International Politics of Impunity for the Bangladesh Genocide', *International Security*. 41, 2 (fall 2016): 140–87
72. Salunke, *Pakistani POWs in India* pp33, 81
73. Ibid. pp37, 48–9
74. Ibid. pp68–9
75. Datta, *Refugees and Borders in South Asia* p15
76. Ibid. p155
77. Salunke, *Pakistani POWs in India* p94
78. Ibid. p106
79. Chatterji, *Shadows at Noon* p163
80. Ghose, *Indira* p132
81. Private Interview: Penchun Konyak, Longwa, Konyak, October 2021; Imchen, C. L., 'Integration vs. Independence: The Debate in the Naga Hills' in Nag, Gurung and Choudhury (eds), *Making of the Indian Union* p237; Nibedon, *Nagaland* p319
82. Lintner, *Great Game East* p91
83. Private Interview, Bertil Lintner, English, Zoom, July 2023
84. Van Schendel, *The Bengal Borderland* p195
85. indianexpress.com/article/world/set-to-create-largest-statelessness-crisis-in-the-world-european-parliament-to-debate-caa-next-week-6236738/
86. spectator.co.uk/article/a-hindu-cromwell-courteously-decapitates-hundreds-of-maharajas/
87. Ashton, S. R., 'Mountbatten, the Royal Family, and British Influence in Post-Independence India and Burma', *Journal of Imperial and Commonwealth History*. 2005, 33(1): 79
88. Zubrzycki, *Dethroned*
89. Bangash, *A Princely Affair* p2
90. spectator.co.uk/article/a-hindu-cromwell-courteously-decapitates-hundreds-of-maharajas/
91. newyorker.com/magazine/2007/05/07/the-idol-thief
92. *Arts of Asia* magazine records how between 1970 and 1995 when the government of India resolved to acquire some of these antiques, 'a vast number of pieces were sold' and 'today, these items are scattered in museums and private collections around the world'. Balakrishnan, U. R., 'The Nizam of Hyderabad Sarpech (Turban Ornament)', *Arts of Asia*. Autumn 2023; newyorker.com/magazine/2007/05/07/the-idol-thief
93. Speech by Jagdish Mittal at conference in his honour, Hyderabad, January 2018
94. Letter from Jacqueline Kennedy, Quoted in Dalrymple, W., 'Hyderabad under the Asaf Jahi Nizams' in Haider, N. N., and Sardar, M. (eds), *Sultans of Deccan India: 1500–1700 Opulence and Fantasy* (New York, Metropolitan Museum of Art, 2015)
95. Ghose, *Indira* p133
96. Jaffrelot, C., and Anil, P., *India's First Dictatorship: The Emergency, 1975–77* (London: HarperCollins, 2020) pp17–23
97. Sitapati, V., *Jugalbandi: The BJP before Modi* (Delhi: Penguin, 2020)
98. Bass, *The Blood Telegram* p328
99. Jalal, A., *The Struggle for Pakistan: A Muslim Homeland and Global Politics* (Cambridge, Massachusetts: The Belknap Press of Harvard University Press, 2014) p180
100. Bass, *The Blood Telegram* p336
101. Zakaria, *1971* p190
102. NAI: MEA, Historical Division (Research & Intelligence Section), HI/1012(30)/71, 'Political Reports etc. (other than annual reports) from Islamabad (W. Pakistan)' p84
103. Roy, *The Departed Melody* p250

Epilogue

1. Amrith, *Crossing the Bay of Bengal*
2. Chawla, '"Nothing in Common with 'Indian' Indian": Bhutan and the Cabinet Mission Plan' p61
3. Myint-U, *The Hidden History of Burma* p31
4. Chatterji, *Shadows at Noon* p161
5. Rich, *Creating the Arabian Gulf* p.xiv
6. Low, M. C., *Imperial Mecca: Ottoman Arabia and the Indian Ocean Hajj* (New York: Columbia University Press, 2020) p305
7. bbc.com/news/world-asia-62347457

ACKNOWLEDGEMENTS

This book emerged out of an organisation called *Project Dastaan*. Formed after a 2017 conversation between Indian and Pakistani friends in Oxford about their grandparents' 1947 journeys, Dastaan aimed at reconnecting Partition survivors with their childhood friends and communities using virtual reality.

This book would not exist without my co-founders at Dastaan. Sparsh Ahuja not only kickstarted my career with his unstoppable energy but has been a constant companion through its many twists and turns, whale jokes and wild schemes. Inspirational and infuriating in equal measure, Sparsh has the rare gift of dreaming impossibly big and somehow dragging the rest of us along for the ride. Without Saadia Gardezi, meanwhile, Dastaan might have collapsed under the weight of its own ridiculousness. Wise, unflappable, and endlessly kind, she was our anchor in moments of chaos and brought clarity to every debate we would have. Without either Sparsh or Saadia, this book would never have come to fruition.

My thanks also to the rest of the Dastaan team. To Ollie Cameron – the illustrator and artist whose extraordinary work is featured on this cover – I promise you, one day we'll meet a yak in the Himalayas together; Tanya Sujan and Jayosmita Ganguly, our unofficial counsellors and tarot readers, who listened and held space for the emotional undercurrents of our work; Ludo Fraser-Taliente, who worked tirelessly behind the scenes, always with thoughtfulness and resolve; Umar Javed, whose quiet dedication steadied the team through more hurdles than I can count; and to baby Leila – Dastaan's youngest and most joyful addition.

Both Dastaan and this book were deeply shaped by my oral history mentors Aanchal Malhotra and Kavita Puri, who taught me how to hold these stories with care. For help in the archive, my thanks to Akshat Tiwari, whose research into the Aden Transfer brought depth and dimension to a chapter I struggled with for months; and for help with travel research, to Shah Umair Ansari, my trusted companion across so many journeys – from Agartala to Aligarh, Dujana to Hyderabad. To Lucy Davidson and the ever-reliable team at Banyan Tours, thank you for making so many of those journeys possible.

This book would never have come into being without the faith and early encouragement of David Godwin and Aparna Kumar, who believed in it long before it had found its true shape. I've been extraordinarily fortunate to work with Arabella Pike at William Collins, Udayan Mitra and Anant Padmanabhan at HarperCollins India, and Huneeya Siddiqui at Norton. Thank you for your thoughtful readings, and for guiding this book into the world with such care.

For help with translation and language sources, my thanks to Sanjana Anand for her brilliant work across Hindi, Urdu, Punjabi and Bengali, and to Juhi Mendiratta, my exceptional Hindi teacher. For the Konyak language, I am grateful to Phejin Konyak, and for Burmese, to Ko Sai Kenneth. Particular thanks also to Harleen Singh Sandhu for his beautiful Gurmukhi translation of Uttam Singh's diary.

Thanks also to those who read early drafts, offered critique, challenged my assumptions, and shaped this book through conversation: Gary Bass, Andrew Whitehead, Alistair Trueger, Vijay Rajkotia, Harisson Akins, Narayani Basu, Sana Aiyar, Ian Trueger, Matthew Bowser, Aniruddh Kanisetti, Etta Bouzoucous, Tash Parker, Tara Day, Imran Mulla, Itamar Toussia Cohen, Tommy Wide, Abhishek Choudhury, Avinash Paliwal, Kavita Puri, Will Gould, Caspar Bigham, Shahbano Farid and Chris Tylee. Your insights made this a far more nuanced and thoughtful book. Particular thanks go to Sultan Ghalib al-Qu'aiti, whose support for this project proved crucial to both the Arabian and Hyderabad sections of this book. At every stage, Sultan Ghalib was happy to give me his understanding of events, highlighting the often largely forgotten connections between Hyderabad and Hadhramaut.

I am also profoundly grateful to the scholars, archivists and historians whose work laid the foundation for this book, and to the many individuals who shared their stories, memories and insights with me along the way. In particular: Aanchal Malhotra, Basharat Peer, Peter Frankopan, Kavita Puri, James Onley, Sunil Amrith, Owen Bennet-Jones, Michael Christopher Low, Thant Myint-U, Yasmin Khan, Khozem Merchant, Faisal Devji, Willem van Schendel, Sana Aiyar, Penny Edwards, Jonathan Saha, Matthew Bowser, Bertil Lintner, Parthasarathi Bhaumik, Rana Safvi, Abdul Razzaq Takriti. Particular thanks to Antonia Moon in the British Library; Guneeta Singh Bhalla and Emily Pester at the 1947 Partition Archive; and all the teams at the National Archives; the Hopetoun House Archives; Imperial War Museum Archives; Southampton University archives; the Middle East Centre Archive, St Antony's College, Oxford; the Bodleian Archives and Manuscripts, Oxford; the National Archives of India, New Delhi; the Junagadh Archives; the Qatar Digital Library; the Arabian Gulf Digital Archive; Digital South Asia Library; British Newspaper Archive; Gandhi Heritage Portal; the Anglo-Burmese Library; Project Dastaan Digital Archive; Andrew Whitehead Digital Archive. Also thanks to those who opened up their private archives to me: Adnan and Tahia Noon, Avtar Singh Hoonjan, Sultan Al Qu'aiti, Pablo Bartholomew and Brigid Keenan.

Several friends have been a rock throughout this book. To Sam Murphy and Omi Zola Gupta who taught me the joys of travel; Aymaan Zaheer – I wish you were here to read this; Rory Fraser with whom I have endlessly fretted about writer's block; the Lego master Anirudh Kanisetti, who so often managed to shift my way of perceiving history; Karuna Parikh who made me love Calcutta; and to Gurmehar Kaur, whose generosity, clarity and care carried me through much of this journey. Her presence and support during the early years of this book meant more than she knows.

Many others have given their support. In the UK: Sasha Reviakin, Kavita Puri, Malala Yousafzai, Shreya Lakhani, Brigid Keenan, Alan Waddams, Hester Waddams, Sanvir Chana, Somnath Batabyal, Huda Luqman, Phillip Marsden, Jordan Quill, Katy Hessel, Haroon Zaman, Rory Fraser, Yashaswini Chandra and the late Bruce Wannell.

In India: Janice Pariat, Samrat Chaudhary, Suhas Chakma, Anthony Debbarma, Tarun Bhartiya, Sajal Nag, Nathaniel Majaw, David Symlieh, Maharaja Pradyot Manikya Debbarma, Shashi Lalloo, Babloo Loitongbam, Pyu, Elizabeth Ao Imti, Phejin Konyak, Subir Bhaumik,

Professor Pradumankumar Khachar, Aaliya and Salauddin Babi of Balasinor, Amitesh Ray, Yunus Lasania, Abinaya Sivagnanam, Moses Tulasi, Serish Nanisetti, Chandrakant Singh, Unni Karta, Abu'l Faiz Khan, Obaid Ur Rehman, Ali Khusru Jung, Sarah Shah, Seema Alavi, Akram Bagai, Jai Singh, Saba Rajkotia, Pranavesh Subramaniam and Malavika Madgulkar.

In Pakistan: Anam Zakaria, Daniyal Muennudin, Mohsin Hamid, Zainab Omar, Faiysal Ali Khan, Fakhir Uddin, Zeina Naseer, Umair Hashmi, Muhammad Hassan Miraj, Adnan and Tahia Noon, Saadia Gardezi and Khushal Karim.

In Bangladesh: Waqar A. Khan, the Bangladesh Forum for Heritage Studies, Zeeshan Khan, Sadaf Siddiqui, Zahidur Rahman, Waqar Kazi and of course Salahdin Imam.

In Myanmar: Thant Myint-U, Benny Smalls, Win Ma Ma Aye, Martin Michalon, Ko Sai Kenneth, Mya Yoon, Bertie Alexander, and the whole team from Sampan Travel.

In the Gulf: Meghant Burman, James Onley, Aaditya Khimji, Ramesh Khimji, Hrithik Khimji, Abdullah Al-Qu'aiti, Sultan Ghalib Al-Qu'aiti, Alexis Francis and Bronte Gabriella.

Finally to all those who were interviewed for this book, some of whom have sadly not lived to see its publication: Khalid Bashir Khan Rai, Saida Siddiqui, Trilochan Singh, Bahadur Ali, Muhammad Hussein Azad, Ishar Das Arora, Kamala Devi, Brojesh Chandra Sen, Manjari Dasgupta, Mohan Kahlon, Rabin Sengupta, Sunanda Biswas, Kailiash Nath Tiwari, Tarapada De, Iqballuddin Ahmed, Meenakshi Meyyapam, Hari Krishan Lal Anand, Umarjit Kaur, Brigid Keenan, Maqbool Fatima, Huda Luqman, Mohammad Kacho Yabgo, Adnan Aurangzaib, Khozem Merchant, Avtar and Raminder Singh Hoonjan, Jai Sengupta, Avinder Bindra, Santosh Anand, Pradyot Manikya Debbarma, Babloo Loitongbam, Sana Yaima, Mohan M. Mohan and Kamamkan Naidu, Niketu Iralu, Gingto Konyak, Nyungam Konyak, Penchun Konyak, Teihwang Konyak, Seyyed Muhammad Abbas Ali Meerza, Seyyed Muhammad Raza Ali Meerza, Obaid Ur Rehman, Sandeep Ahlawat, Hassan Ali, Dipti Salgoacar, Khushi Ram, Ragbir Singh, Manish Sharma, Aaditya, Khimji, Ramesh Khimji, Hrithik Khimji, Abdullah Al-Qu'aiti, Sultan Ghalib Al-Qu'aiti, Raja Naser Khan Yabgo, Vijay Gulia, Raja Devashish Roy Chakma, Waqar Kazi, Pablo Bartholemew, Mohammad Zaul Hassan, Nawab Salauddin Khan Babi, Sultana Aaliya

ACKNOWLEDGEMENTS

Babi, Pradumankumar Khachar, Nawabzada Muhammad Jahangir Khanji, Shakira Afzal, Gulnaz Ahteshamuddin Ghausi, Faith Singh, Abid Saghir, Martand Khosla, Ahmad Rafay Alam, Bertil Lintner, Mick Jagger, Chandrakant Singh, Mishaal Akbar Omar, Tariq Aqil, Manjit Singh, Symran Dugal Waseer, Shahana Siddiqui, Ko Sai Kenneth and U Khyaw Soe.

Throughout the last five years of writing, my wonderful family has been an unwavering rock. To Ibby and Adam – my Covid flatmates and source of constant enthusiasm and laughter; to Dad, who first persuaded me to pick up a pen in the first place, and to Mum, my unofficial editor-in-chief, who patiently read through virtually every version of this book and offered her wisdom with every comment. I couldn't have done this without all of you.

ILLUSTRATIONS

FIRST PLATE SECTION
The India–Pakistan border as seen from space (*NASA*)
Indian Empire passport
Indian banknote (*History and Art Collection/Alamy Stock Photo*)
The Ruling Princes of India (*Look and Learn/Elgar Collection/ Bridgeman Images*)
Aden, still India's westernmost city, celebrates (*PA Images/Alamy Stock Photo*)
'The Viceroy's House …' (*World History Archive/Alamy Stock Photo*)
Ruttie Jinnah
A young Muhammad Ali Jinnah
The Simon Commission provoked mass protests (*Keystone/Stringer/ Getty*)
Saya San
Gandhi in Burma
Lacquer Burmese bowl of Gandhi (© *The Trustees of the British Museum*)
Mahatma U Ottama
Sarojini Naidu and Gandhi attend the Round Table Conferences (*Douglas Miller/Getty*)
A Saopha Prince arrives (© *Victoria and Albert Museum, London*)
The Round Table Conferences (*Emery Kelen, Coloured Print 1931. Orphan Works License: OWLS000200-1*)
Stamps
U Saw (*Popperfoto/Getty*)
A new recruit to the Indian Army (*piemags/ww2archive/Alamy Stock Photo*)

Parsi women training for air raids (*piemags/archive/military/Alamy Stock Photo*)

SECOND PLATE SECTION
Indian infantrymen train for war (*Keystone/Stringer/Getty*)
Aung San and two of his Thirty Comrades (*Hum Historical/Alamy Stock Photo*)
The Japanese conquest of Rangoon (*Popperfoto/Getty*)
Uttam Singh and Sikhs of Bawdwin (*Sanvir Chana private archive*)
Indian civilians fled Burma for India (*British Library/Bridgeman Images*)
Ma Baw and Subhas Chandra Bose
Subhas Chandra Bose tries to get support (*Universal History Archive/Getty*)
Muhammad Ali Jinnah
West African troops arriving in India (*IWM/Getty*)
Japanese and British propaganda during WWII
The tennis court of Kohima (*Author's own collection*)
Lahore Fort (*Author's own collection*)
A map of the Bengal Famine (*Maps: A Geographical Analysis of Resource Distribution in West Bengal and Eastern Pakistan by S. P. Chatterjee, published by Orient Blackswan Private Limited*)
Rahmat Ali Chaudhury's Vision of Pakistan (*Image courtesy the Partition Museum (Delhi and Amritsar), The Arts and Cultural Heritage Trust*)
Gandhi and Jinnah (*Universal History Archive/Getty*)
Communist delegates marching in Punjab (*Margaret Bourke-White/The LIFE Picture Collection/Shutterstock*)
The Indian interim government with Nehru
A statue of Sardar Patel (*Sam Panthaky/Getty*)
Louis and Edwina Mountbatten sworn in as Viceregal couple (*Hulton Deutsch/Getty*)

THIRD PLATE SECTION
'How India May Be Split' (*Daily Herald, 4 June 1947*)
Aung San, wearing Nehru's jacket, meets Clement Attlee (*Fox Photos/Stringer/Getty*)
'Nehru's relationship with Lady Mountbatten is sufficiently close' (© *Fondation Henri Cartier-Bresson/Magnum Photos*)

ILLUSTRATIONS

Nehru and Edwina in Simla, May 1947
Direct Action Day in Calcutta (*Keystone-France/Getty*)
An exhausted and defeated Nehru (*Nehru Memorial Museum and Library*)
Nehru and Aung San (*Fox Photos/Getty*)
Jinnah (*AFP/Getty*)
Gandhi leads a peace march (*Dinodia Photos/Alamy Stock Photo*)
Cyril Radcliffe (*Evening Standard/Stringer/Getty*)
The Kotwali gate of Gaur (*Christie's Images/Bridgeman Images*)
The Great Partition in 1947, top (*Margaret Bourke-White/The LIFE Picture Collection/Shutterstock*) and below (*World History Archive/Alamy Stock Photo*)
Map of India published by *The Hindu* on Independence Day (*The Hindu*)
Crowds celebrate Indian independence (*Bettmann/Getty*)
The Wali of Swat (*Courtesy Miangul Aurangzeb Archives, Swat*)
Junagadh (*Photo by Bernard Gagnon, GNU Free Documentation License*)
The Nawab of Junagadh
The Women's Militia of Srinagar (*Artwork by eminent artist Sobha Singh*)
The Nizam of Hyderabad (*Interfoto/Alamy Stock Photo*)
Egyptian president Gamal Abdel Nasser
The Gulf's oil economy skyrocketed (*Courtesy of DeGolyer Library, Southern Methodist University*)
The Sultans of Qu'aiti State
Sultan Ghalib Al-Qu'aiti (*Courtesy of Ghalib al-Qu'aiti*)
The first hoisting of the United Arab Emirates flag
Poster for Pakistan's National Dance Ensemble

FOURTH PLATE SECTION
Pakistan's first Bengali prime minister (*Popperfoto/Getty*)
1960s Pakistan coin (*Sudarshan Bhatla/Shutterstock*)
Indira Gandhi (© *Raghu Rai/Magnum Photos*)
Angami Zapu Phizo (*Leopald Joseph/ANL/Shutterstock*)
Mujibur Rahman
Poster for Bangladeshi independence (*Courtesy of the International Institute of Social History*)
A young man singing (*Film still from Muktir Gaan, by Catherine Masud and Tareque Masud*)

The Bangladesh crisis
A political poster (© *Abbas/Magnum Photos*)
Sheikh Mujibur Rahman addresses a crowd
US president Nixon and Pakistani president Yahya Khan (*Bettmann/Getty*)
Mukti Bahini fighters (© *Newsweek, 1971*)
Salahdin Imam (*Courtesy of Salahdin Imam*)
Ravi Shankar with George Harrison (*PA Images/Alamy Stock Photo*)
The Concert for Bangladesh (*Everett Collection, Inc./Alamy Stock Photo*)
Pro-Pakistan residents of Dacca protesting (*Rolls Press/Popperfoto/Getty*)
Mukti Bahini fighters capture Pro Pakistan 'Razakars' (*Michael Brennan/Getty*)
The 'Surrender Lunch' (© *Abbas/Magnum Photos*)
General Aurora and General Niazi (*Getty/Bettmann*)
Indian Army officers examine a pile of rifles (*Getty/Bettmann*)
Ishar Das Arora (*Courtesy of Sparsh Ahuja*)
Sparsh in Pakistan, 2021 (*Courtesy of Sparsh Ahuja*)

INDEX

Abbottabad, Pakistan, 423
Abdullah, Sheikh Mohammad, 140, 227, 236, 237, 242, 244, 286
Abdulmecid II, Caliph, 255
Abrar, Musarrat, 208
Abu Dhabi, 3, 169, 323
Abu Dhabi, Sheikh Zayed of, 323
Aden: Arab nationalist movement, 295, 296, 297–9; Arab–Indian differences, 37; and Arabs of Hyderabad, 276; Britain–NLF–FLOSY conflict, 308–9; British departure, 311, 316; British torture, 306; on defeat of Japan, 130; Gandhi visit, 36–9; Indian flag unfurled, 202; Italian air raids, 61; Luqman archives destroyed, 318–19; merges into South Arabian Federation, 305; migrants as 'foreigners', 298–9; migrants leave, 317–19; Mitchell's gambit, 312; Mountbatten trip (1921), 116; oil transforms, 294; Partition inauguration ceremony, 47; propaganda against Indians, 295–6; as Raj at its height, 285, 294, 296–7; Round Table Conference decision on, 41; South Yemen's assurances to foreigners, 317; as start of 'India', 10; starts second Partition, 6; Waugh on, 10; as world port, 294–5, 299; WWII refugees in India, 108
Aden Trade Union, 298
Afghanistan, 8, 62, 190, 252, 253, 319
Afzal, Shakira, 223, 224
Afzalpur, India, 264
Aga Khan, 39, 95
Agartala, India, 338
Agartala Conspiracy Case, 346, 348, 349
Agra, India, 57, 396
Ahmad, Tajuddin, 368, 378
Ahmadiyya community, 178
Ahmed, Laila, 379–80

Ahmed, Mohiuddin, 391
Ahmed, Sultan, 154
Ahmednagar fortress, India, 95
Ahuja, Sparsh, 429–30
Ailamma, Chityala, 143
Air India hijack (1971), 354
Akyab, Burma, 81
Al Nahda (newspaper), 276
Ali, Ahmed, 207
Ali, Aruna Asaf, 95, 169–70
Ali, Asif, 346, 364–5
Ali, Laik, 267, 270–1, 273–4, 275
Ali, Maj.-Gen. Rao Farman, 403
Ali, Shahed, 329
Ali, Tariq (activist), 347
Ali, Tariq (Bengali man), 366–7
All-India Radio, 175–6, 253, 273, 283, 421
Alwar, India, 213–14
Alwar, Maharaja of, 213–14
Amb, Pakistan, 285n
Ambani, Dhirubhai, 222, 295, 297, 298, 299, 318
Ambani, Kokilaben, 299
Ambani, Mukesh, 318
Ambedkar, B. R., 37, 56, 63–4, 96
Amery, Leo, 67, 112, 113
Amin, Nurul, 290, 291, 337, 338, 398–9, 405
Amoy, China, 75
Amritsar, India: 'Free Thinkers' circle, 209–10; Golden Temple attack, 423; Keenan on Sikh–Muslim killings, 197, 198; massacre (1919), 5, 57; Pakistani Air Force bombs, 396; refugee camp, 216
Andaman Islands, 92, 120, 180
Anglo-Iranian oil company, 294
Anti-Fascist People's Freedom League (AFPFL), 137

Anwar, Khurshid, 154, 230, 231, 232, 235–6, 240–1
Arabian Raj: and Arab nationalism, 297–8, 305–6; attack on Yemeni NLF, 305–6; Britain abolishes protectorates, 286; Britain pulls out of Gulf, 322–4; Britain's intransigence radicalises, 304; defence of Kuwait, 304; departure from Aden, 311, 316, 317–19; direct colonial rule imposed, 305; map, 284; NLF topples princely states, 312, 315–16, 347; oil, discovery of, 294; Oman sultan replaced, 321–2; princely states vanish from map, 308; Qu'aiti Sultanate falls, 312–16; Raj lingers in, 283–5, 294, 296–7; records, in London, 319; reports to Whitehall, 283; *Sawt Al-Arab* on princes, 311; South Arabian Federation created, 305; treated as single unit, 283n; UAE created, 320–1
Arakan, Burma, 66, 82–4, 111, 156, 158
Arakan Mujahed Party, 287
Arora, Ishar Dar, 160–2, 429
Arunachal Pradesh, India, 417
Assam, India: Bangladesh migration halted, 418; communist 'infiltrators', 287; drawing of Burma border, 45; East Bengali refugees, 375–6; Indira Gandhi reorganises, 417; Nagaland administration, 60; Pakistan claims, 329; Patkai colony proposal, 109–10; WWII flight from Burma, 84, 89
Assam Accords (1985), 418
Assam Rifles, 252, 336
Assam Tea Planters' Association, 89
atomic bombs, 129, 130, 131, 177
Al-Attas, Faysal, 319
Attenborough, Richard, 118
Attlee, Clement: Arabian territories withdrawal rejected, 168; Aung San meeting, 156–7; on Burma, 19, 20; Dorman-Smith concerns, 145; Great Partition green light, 174; offers Mountbatten Viceroyalty, 163; on Rangoon, 18; as Simon Commissioner, 10–11, 16; sympathetic to Pakistan, 243; wins 1945 election, 132
Auchinleck, Sir Claude, 237–8, 241
Aung Hla, U, 31
Aung San: at Asian Relations Conference, 166; on 'Asiatic federation', 425; assassination, 192–4, 251; Attlee meeting, 156–7; Burmese Independence Army, 75–6; as de facto prime minister, 146; Great Partition briefing, 175; Jinnah meeting, 156; leads Burma Oil strikes, 52; as minister of defence, 119; Mountbatten champions, 127, 137–8; Nehru meetings, 144, 156; Slim negotiations post-volte face, 128; supports

Ba Maw in puppet government, 102–3; turns against Japan, 120, 127; U Saw rivalry, 145–6; U Saw's arrests, 67
Aung San Suu Kyi, 128
Aurangzeb, Mughal emperor, 95, 274
Aurora, Jagjit Singh, 404
Australia, 249, 259, 279, 419, 429
Awaara (film), 283
Awami League: Amin opposes, 399; as Bengali mouthpiece, 337; and Bhutto visit to Dacca, 360, 362; forms government-in-exile, 378; general strike, 356; Joydepur misinformation, 359; Lahore Resolution as 'Resistance Day', 362; Mujib as president, 344; 1970 elections, 353–4; 1974 Bengal famine destroys, 416; Operation Searchlight crackdown, 362, 364, 365, 368, 370, 372, 375; organises strikes, 357; Pakistani armed forces resignations, 358; Pakistani hardliners on, 355; Pakistani mass arrests, 345; violence alienates Bengalis, 357
Azad, Abdus Samad, 411
Azad, Maulana Al-Hussaini, 64, 94, 95, 174–5
Azad Hind, *see* Bose, Subhas Chandra
Azad Hind Radio, 105

Ba Maw: admits Axis defeat, 126–7; Bose meeting, 107–8; captured in Japan, 128; criticises Round Table Conference, 41; escape from Mogok jail, 100–2; as first Burmese premier, 51; Japan grants Burma independence, 119; Japan leads puppet Burmese government, 102–4; letter from Aung San, 127–8; Nazism and imperialism as indistinguishable, 61; Saya San trial, 31; U Saw ousts, 55
Ba Pe, U, 677
Babariawad, India, 223, 224
Babi, Aaliya, 225
Babi, Parveen, 225
Babi, Vali Mohammad Khan, 225
Al-Badr (paramilitary group), 380, 402, 403
Baez, Joan, 390, 391
Bahadur Shah Zafar, 119
Bahawalpur, Pakistan, 212, 230, 285n
Bahrain: anti-rebel capability, 323; British support princes from, 311; independence, 304; last British ships leaves, 324; Persian Gulf Residency, 283–4; pre-oil poverty of rulers, 168; in Raj, 2
Baidyanathala, Bangladesh, *see* Mujibnagar
Bakht, Mirza Mohammad Bedar, 91
Baluchistan: Bhutto acts on separatist movement, 422; Gwadar market massacre rumour, 302; Junagadh as first act, 218; Pakistan's move on Kalat, 252, 253;

separatist movement, 286; Simon on, 16; as 'TAN' in Pakistan, 62; vote to join Pakistan, 180
Bandung Conference (1955), 325
Banerjee, S. S., 339, 345
'Bangla Desh' (Harrison), 389, 390
Bangladesh: Bengalis 'repatriated' from Pakistan, 409; Bengalis vs Pakistan as oversimplification, 399; and British history, 427; and Chakma guerrillas, 382; Concert for Bangladesh (1971), 389–90; defensive border, 1; Direct Action Day narrative, 153; economic mismanagement and famine, 416; flag, 360, 362, 366, 388, 405; foundational moment and historical amnesia, 426; government-in-exile, 378, 388, 406, 408; 'India recognises, 398; India supports Mukti Bahini, 377–9, 380; 'inevitability' of creation, 7; Language Movement sows seed, 291; 'Liberation War' term, 367; map of languages, 412; migration to Assam halted, 418; Mujib assassinated, 416; Mujib forms government, 408; name, as Mujib's seventh demand, 349; nationality changes, 411–13, 424; New Delhi Agreement repatriation, 414–15; non-Bengalis denied citizenship, 409; Pakistan recognises, 415; Pakistan refuses to recognise at UN, 410–11; Pakistani diplomats defect to, 391; in Raj, 2; raped women as war heroines, 416; refuses Pakistani PoW release, 413; Zia-ur-Rahman as president, 417; *see also* Indo-Pakistani war (1971); Partitions, Fifth
Bangladeshi Liberation Army, *see* Mukti Bahini
Baramulla, Kashmir, 234–6
Bari, Abdul, 384–5
Baroda, India, 261n
Bartholomew, Richard, 282
Bass, Gary, 402n
Batala, India, 204, 212
Batra, Rati, 282
Baul, Purna Das, 347
Bawa, Awadhi Shirani, 264
Bawdwin, Burma, 85, 208
BBC, 2–3, 5, 264, 320, 343, 404
Beatles, the, 347, 389
Bedi, Freda, 227
Begum, Mumtaz, 380
Bela, Pakistan, 160–2, 429–30
Benegal, Ramesh, 138
Bengal, India: 'Bangalistan' homeland call, 142; boats destroyed pre-Japanese arrival, 78, 111; British annex (1757), 427; Burmese WWII refugees, 91; communist insurrection, 251; community in Burma, 18, 30, 43–4, 55–6; Direct Action Day, 149–55; famine (1943), 79, 100, 110–14, 133, 387, 416; Great Partition vote, 176; internal religious-based migration, 133; irony of Muslim League majority, 140; Jinnah on Partition, 172; Khulna famine, 289, 416; Kissinger on difficulty of governing, 371; Mizo famine, 336–7; Mountbatten independence plan, 172; Muslims flee to East Bengal, 206; partitioning of Gaur, 205; post-Partition calm, 212–13; post-Partition uncertainty, 177; proportion of non-Muslims in Pakistan, 204; Quit India parallel government, 96; revolutionary societies in Burma, 26; and Rohingya people, 66n; 'second famine', 148, 151; vote to Partition, 180; wealthy flee Japanese, 92–3; *see also* Bangladesh; East Bengal; East Pakistan; West Bengal
Bengal Boundary Commission, 205
Bengali (language): Bangladesh languages map, 412; Bengali script rejection proposal, 290, 291; biography of Muhammad, 114; Gandhi learns, 245; Jinnah's gravestone, 293; as national language, 292, 294; Nurul Amin opposes Language Movement, 398–9; perceived as inferior, 346, 349; permission for college use, 290; protest at state language rejection, 260
Besse & Co., 295, 318
Bhagavad Gita, 129
Bharat (ancient Hindu holy land): Burma and Aden partitions facilitate, 6, 7, 22, 48; facilitates creation of Pakistan, 48; Gandhi identifies with India, 22; and Jinnah's 'Pakistan Resolution,' 63; Kashmir as central to, 227; as 'Undivided India', 41–2
Bharatiya Janata Party (BJP), 422
Bharatpur, India, 213
Bhashani, Abdul Hamid 'Red Maulana', 348, 352
Bhopal, Hamidullah Khan, Nawab of, 167, 168, 188
Bhopal, India, 184
Bhutan: demands return of lands, 184–5; Congress recognises independence right, 185; independence rights secured, 147; persistence as princely state, 5, 6, 228, 320, 326; in Raj, 2
Bhutto, Benazir, 351, 409
Bhutto, Shahnawaz, 220, 221, 222, 223, 224
Bhutto, Zulfikar Ali: arrest, 348; character, 341; during Operation Searchlight, 365, 366; elections (1970), 352, 353; as influential politician, 342; leads anti-Ayub Khan

Bhutto, Zulfikar Ali (*cont ...*)
  movement, 348; Mujib meeting in Dacca, 360–2; Mujib power-sharing demand, 354–5; nuclear programme, 422; postwar Indira Gandhi meeting, 409–10; as president, 405; recognises Bangladesh, 415; refuses refugees from Bangladesh, 409; regulates princes' privy purses, 419; releases Mujib, 408; sends Roy to UN, 410; supports Air India hijack, 354; threatens coup d'etat, 383; Zia-ul-Haq coup, 422
Bidar, India, 273
Bihar, India, 154, 155, 207
Biharis of Bangladesh, 207, 369, 374, 386, 406, 411–12
Bikaner, India, 184, 191, 217
Bikaner, Karni Singh, Maharaja of, 420
Bikaner, Sadul Singh, Maharaja of, 167, 168, 190
Bilaspur, India, 184
bin Laden, Osama, 319, 423
Bin Laden family, 319
Biswas, Ramnath, 42–4
Bizinjo, Ghaus Bakhsh, 252
Black Dragon Society, 50–1
Blood, Archer: on Bhutto, 361; on Dacca students, 348; on 'end of unified Pakistan', 357; on Joydebpur shootings, 359; on Mujib, 344; on 1970 Pakistan elections, 352; on Operation Searchlight, 363, 370, 371–2
Blood, Meg, 363
'Blood Telegram', 372
Bogra, Mohammad Ali, 292
Bohmong Raja, 342
Bollywood, 79, 207, 225, 283
Bombay, India: *firangis*' 'transit camps', 249; Gandhi's Quit India call, 94, 95; Manto on 'communal hatreds', 210; migration to, 207; Muslim politicians detained, 271; revolutionary mood, 143; Simon Commissioners arrive, 10
Bombay Province, India, 10, 41, 42
Bose, Satyendra Nath, 133
Bose, Subhas Chandra: Ba Maw meeting, 107–8; blames Bengal famine on British, 112; death, 128; as guest at Burmese independence, 119; at Imphal, 123; as INA leader, 106; inspires Mujib, 339; names government for Azad Hind, 119–20; Nazi collaboration, 104–6; Phizo on, 121; and planned Axis invasion of Raj, 104, 106, 120
Bourke-White, Margaret, 153
Bower, Ursula Graham, 120
Bowser, Matthew, 50n, 79
Britain: Cold War, 188; downplays size of Raj, 3; forgetting Raj, 427; India–Pakistan cooperation against communism, 287–8; joins EEC, 324; postwar financial debt to India, 131; retreat from empire, 163; Suez crisis, 296, 297, 298; supports Mujib, 349; *see also* Arabian Raj; British Raj
British Burma Army, 78
British East India Company, 226, 249, 322, 427
British India Line, 283, 324
British Raj: Aden as 'start', 10; apparent invincibility of, 35; Bose–Japan plan to overthrow, 104–8; British generals on different sides (1948), 242; cost of First World War; 4; 'decay' of (Naidu), 131–2; extent, 2–3; first princely states relinquish sovereignty, 158; and Gandhi's funeral, 247; George VI 'self-government' promises, 132; Gwadar claim, 300; and historical amnesia, 427; last British soldiers leave India, 248; lingers in Arabian Raj, 283–5; Operation Madhouse, 164; partitions, sequence of, 6–7; Patkai colony proposal, 109–10; post-1946 election downsizing, 141; reaction to Quit India movement, 95–7; religious fluidity, 4; Round Table Conferences on, 35–6, 58; Salt Act and protest, 25, 26–7, 35; Saya San rebellion, 28–32, 35; Simon Commission report's conclusions, 27; status of protectorates, 3–4; untold story of collapse, 8; *see also* Arabian Raj; Partitions
Brooke, Gen. Alan, 98
Brown, Maj. William, 238–40
Buddhists, Buddhism: Bodhi tree sapling in Burma, 243; Burmese manufactured outrage vs Muslims, 52–5; Burmese reject as official religion, 192; Chittagong Hill Tracts becomes Pakistan, 204; conflict with Muslims in Arakan, 83–4; Eastern Bangladesh king at UN, 410; militias in Bangladesh, 382, 417; Nizam of Hyderabad's support of, 256; Ottama as head of Hindu Mahasabha, 42; and Partition of Princely India, 6; prayers for Gandhi, 245; support Pakistani invasion of Kashmir, 342; U Saw's policies in Burma, 65–6
Burma: anti-Indian xenophobia, 27, 31–2, 34, 43, 50–5, 78; anti-separatist election win, 42; Aung San assassination, 192–4, 251; Aung San as de facto prime minister 146; Aung San's planned rebellion, 156–7; Aung San–U Saw rivalry, 145–6; Bandung Conference, 325; BIA¬Japan fallout, 102–3; Biswas's bike trip, 42–4; British 'South East Asian Command', 100; Buddhist–Muslim violence in Arakan, 83–4; census, and the Rohingya, 66, 82, 84; Chindits fight in border areas, 115, 120; communist

INDEX 501

insurgencies, 251, 287–8; complacency over Japanese threat, 67–8; differentiating Burmese from Indians, 31–2; Dorman-Smith–Mountbatten rift, 137–8; economy, 288; evacuees return, 133–4, 175; forgotten ties to India, 8; Gandhi visit, 21–3; and Gandhi's funeral, 247; George VI promises 'self-government', 132; Great Depression, 26, 28; immigration to, 18, 43; immigration barriers, 192; independence (1948), 243; Indian border hardens post-1971, 418, 430; Indian condescension, 18, 44; Indian nationalism in, 7; Indian past as anomalous, 425–6; Indians evicted, 340; Indians fear Japanese invasion, 70, 74; Indians forbidden WWII evacuation, 76–7; Indians' WWII 'Long March', 78–90, 81, 136; Indo-Burma Immigration Agreement, 66, 67; IRA opposition to Raj, 26; Japan grants independence, 119; Japanese atrocities, 103; Japanese defeat, 121–8; 'Japanese Government Rupees', 97; Japanese puppet states, 98–9, 102–4; Manipur considers acceding to, 190; Mizo migration, 344; Naga revolt, 327–9; Nagaland administration, 60; Ne Win's military rule, 330, 340; no official religion, 192; Ottama's influence eclipsed, 49; Panglong Conference, 157–8, 192; and Partition of Princely India, 6; Patkai colony proposal, 109–10; in Raj, 2, 3; refugees' ambivalence to Raj, 96; Rohingya armed insurgency, 287; Roosevelt on, 96; rump Naga leadership, 417; Saya San rebellion, 28–31, 35; Simon Commission, 18–20, 27; slide into martial law, 288; suspicion of Junagadhi Muslims, 225; throne returned, 251; U Nu as prime minister-in-waiting, 193–4; U Saw hanged, 194; U Saw as premier, 65; WWII militarisation, 60; WWII scorched earth policy, 78; *see also* Partitions, First
Burma Biscuits Co., 91
Burma Road, 67
Burmese Defence Army, 104, 120
Burmese Independence Army (BIA), 75–6, 83, 102–4
Burmese National Army (BNA), 127, 128, 137; *see also* Patriotic Burmese Forces
Butcher, Gen. Roy, 152–3, 279
Byron, Robert, 34

Cadogan, Edward, 10, 11, 12, 16
Calcutta, India: Bangladeshi embassy opens, 378; Bengal Club, 112; Bengal famine victims, 111–12, 113; Bose arrested, 104; Burmese WWII refugees, 91; 'Calcutta Free City' plan, 172; 'Dhakeshwari' idol moved to, 203; Direct Action Day, 150–4, 155; Gandhi–Suhrawardy protest fast, 202, 212; Ginsberg in, 390–1; Gobra training camp, 380; Grand Hotel, 108; Indian Communist Party congress, 250–1; Japanese bombing, 93; Jinnah on Pakistan without, 171, 293; Mother Teresa in, 387; Sal Imam in, 379; Sen family moves to, 133; 'Week of the Long Knives' ('Great Calcutta Killings'), 153
Calcutta Municipal Gazette, 148
Cambridge, University of: Bose at, 104; Choudhary at, 62; Ghalib at, 319; and Nazimuddin's cabinet, 290; Nehru at, 56
Campbell-Johnson, Alan: on Burmese communism, 251; on Burmese independence, 243; on debt and Kashmir dispute, 242; on Gandhi's funeral, 247; on Jinnah assassination attempt, 179; on Jinnah at independence, 200; on Jinnah and Partition, 172; on Jinnah's paranoia, 230; as Mountbatten's press attaché, 164, 171; on Nehru, 169, 173; on Nizam of Hyderabad, 266–7; on Partition minutiae, 180; on Punjab fires, 201; on signing of Instruments of Accession, 186–7
Ceylon, 166–7, 325
Chakma people, 356, 357, 381–2, 410, 417
Chandra Pal, Narayan, 152–3
Channgoo, Burma, 86
Chaplin, Charlie, 40, 117
Chatterjee, Arun Kumar, 275
Chatterji, Joya, 395, 396, 426
Chatterji, Partha, 425
Chaudhuri, Maj.-Gen. Jayanto Nath, 274, 279
Chaudhuri, Nirad, 143, 152
Chaugacha, Bangladesh, 394
Chauhan, Dr Jagjit Singh, 423
Chettiars, 26, 30, 31, 43, 50, 110
Chettinad region, 110
Chin people, 158
Chindwin river, 86–7, 121
China: and Burmese communist insurgency, 287; communist–nationalist struggle, 188; declines Bangladesh involvement, 401–2; drops Hunza claim, 239n; India war, 340, 341; Kissinger mission, 392; Mizo intelligence documents, 400; Pakistan ties, 342, 371, 377, 387; restaurants in South India, 91
Chitral, Pakistan, 285n
Chittagong, Bangladesh: Buddhist-majority population join Pakistan, 204; East Bengal Regiment seizes, 368; IRA 'Easter Rising', 26; in kingdom of Mrauk U, 66n; Mizo

Chittagong, Bangladesh (*cont ...*)
economic dependence, 336n; Mukti Bahini kill non-Bengalis, 383; Operation Searchlight weapons unloaded, 363; Pakistani blockade (1971), 397; refugee camps, 287; refugees flee Japanese, 80, 82; Students Union firearms stash, 357
Chittagong Hill Tracts, 204, 336, 342, 377, 381–2
Choudhary, Rahmat Ali, 62
Christianity, 4, 141, 234–5
Churchill, Winston: appoints Mountbatten SEAC head, 116, 118; bayonetted effigies, 107; blamed for Bengal famine, 112; division of India plan, 167; on Gandhi, 36, 113; Keenan on Nehru's fears, 199; loses 1945 election, 132; racism, 112–13, 115; U Saw petitions for independence, 68
CIA, 332, 347
Civil & Military Gazette, 148, 175, 246
Clapton, Eric, 389, 390
Cold War: Czech coup, 250; India, Pakistan and Burma avoid, 325; Kissinger China visit, 393; and Pakistan civil war, 285; US anti-communism funding in India and Pakistan, 288n; US tolerance of Operation Searchlight, 371; USS *Enterprise* deployment, 400–2; USSR–India friendship, 371, 392
Colditz prison, 105
Collis, Maurice, 20, 27
Comilla, Bangladesh, 352, 364, 369
communism: in Burma, 287–8; in Hyderabad, 143, 188, 261, 263, 264–5, 270, 275, 287; in Kashmir, 227; princely fears, 188; South Asia inroads, 51; US anti-communism funding in India and Pakistan, 288n, 325; West Bengali 'Naxalite' revolution, 348, 377, 387
Communist Party of India, 139, 142, 178–9, 208, 250
Communist Party of Pakistan, 250–1, 289, 398
Conan Doyle, Dennis, 258
Concert for Bangladesh (1971), 389–90
Congress Party: and Andaman Islands, 180; attacks racist WWII evacuation, 93–4; Aung San's tact, 156; Azad as president, 64; Burmese wing, 21; Direct Action Day, 153; Gandhi as leader, 21; goal of independence, 5; HMS *Talwar* flag, 142; Indira Gandhi as president of, 332; Jinnah on Gandhi's influence, 14; Jinnah leaves, 14; Jinnah's paranoia, 230; leaders freed, 131; Linlithgow arrests leaders, 94–5, 96; loses 1977 elections, 421–2; Mountbatten favours, 171,
178, 183; Nehru leads in 1937 elections, 56, 57–8; Nehru–Patel rift, 215; 1946 election landslide, 139; on overseeing Partition, 178; plea for people to stay put, 206; pre-independence control of intelligence, 170, 176; princes' vendetta against, 419; rejects princely states' independence rights, 185; WWII resignations, 62; Youth Wings, 51
Cooch Behar, Maharaja of, 190
Cooper, Elizabeth, 254
Corbett, Jim, 115
Corfield, Conrad, 185–6
Cotton, Sydney, 259–60, 270, 273, 277
countercultural movement (1960s), 347, 350–1, 374, 389–91
Crater, Aden, 295, 297, 312
Cripps, Isobel, 171
Cripps, Sir Stafford, 93, 243
Crouch, Michael, 313
Cuban Missile Crisis, 400, 401, 402n
Cunningham, George, 231, 241
Curzon, George Nathaniel Curzon, 1st Marquess, 3, 283n
Cutch, India, 187, 190, 191, 217, 223n, 342

Dacca, Bangladesh: assembly postponement protests and curfew, 355–7; Banerjee ordered out, 345; Bengali–Bihari riots, 292; 'Dhakeshwari' idol, 203; Hindu–Muslim violence, 133; Indian Air Force bombs, 402; Indian Army approaches, 399–400; Indian Army departs, 408; Intercontinental Hotel in Indo-Pakistani war, 396; Jinnah promotes Urdu, 260; massacre of the intellectuals, 402–3; Mujib–Bhutto meeting, 360–2; Mujib–Yahya meeting, 360; Operation Searchlight crackdown, 363–6, 369–72; Pakistan Army sex camps, 385; Pakistani surrender, 403–4; Phizo detained, 329, 336; post-Muhammad relic Hindu massacre, 340; and Sen family, 92, 133; student protests, 348–9
Dacca University, 133, 290–1, 356, 364–5, 370, 371, 412
Daily Herald, 165–6, 167
Daily Ittefaq, 339, 365
Dalits ('untouchables'): Communal Award grants electorate, 56; Hyderabad violence against, 277; join Razakars, 265; Luqman's road trip, 37; migration changes status, 207; Muslim League campaigning, 180; as Muslim target in East Bengal, 281; relation to Hinduism, 178; stigma not perceived in Burma, 54, 82; support Nizam of Hyderabad, 257, 259, 265

Dass, Diwan Jermani, 219n
Dawn (Jinnah's paper), 148
Al-Dayyini, Salim, 314–15
Deccan Radio, 263, 273
Delhi, India, 34, 203, 207, 214, 215, 421, 423; *see also* New Delhi
Dera Ghazi Khan, Pakistan, 203
Dhaheru, India, 89
Dhofar, Oman, 321, 324
Dimapur, India, 89
Dir, Khan of, 190
Dir, Pakistan, 285n
Diu, India, 224
Divyabhanusinh (author), 219n
D'Mello, Doris, 134
Dogra dynasty, 226
Dorman-Smith, Lady, 73, 109
Dorman-Smith, Sir Reginald: anxiety over Japan, 67–8; condemns Rangoon evacuation panic, 77; escape to New Delhi, 90–1; evacuates government, 78; final flight from Burma, 90; forbids Aung San–Nehru meeting, 144; Mountbatten rift, 137–8; overruled on Aung San contact 127; Patkai Hills border proposal, 109; resigns as Burma governor, 145; supports U Saw, 64–5, 67, 194; U saw scraps marriage clause, 67
Driberg, Tom, 136–7, 138, 156
Dring, Simon, 366
Dubai: and Gandhi's funeral, 247; Holden on, 323; independence, 304; joins UAE, 323; obscurity of, 303; persistence as princely state, 5; port benefits from Aden's fall, 317; in Raj, 2, 3; separated from India, 169
Dujana, India, 217–18, 285n
'Dum Maro Dum' (Indian song), 347
Durga (Burmese photographer), 30
Durga (Hindu goddess), 48, 417
Durgarpur, India, 223n
Dutch East Indies, 135
Dutt, B. C., 138
Dwarka, India, 220
Dyer, Brig.-Gen. Reginald, 5, 57, 64
Dylan, Bob, 347, 389, 390, 391

Earhart, Amelia, 52
East Bengal (1947–55): administrative paucity, 209; anti-Jinnah protests over Urdu, 260; Bengali language tensions, 290, 291; Bengali as national language, 292, 294; boats burned to deprive Japan, 78, 111; boundary established, 205, 252; 'Calcutta Free City' plan, 172; Dacca University protests, 290–1; International Mother Language Day (1952), 291; Khasi farmers blocked from markets, 252; migration to, 207; and Muslim League, 140n; Muslims forcibly convert Hindus, 154; Muslims migrate to, 207; Nurul Amin as chief minister, 398; Pakistani crackdown in Khulna, 281; post-Direct Action Day, 154; reaction to Mujib's trial, 345; representation in Pakistani government, 288, 290, 291, 293; and Rohingya armed insurgency, 287; Urdu-speakers' status, 289–90; *see also* East Pakistan
East Pakistan (1955–71): administrative void post-1971 war, 406–7; Awami League violence, 357; Benazir Bhutto on, 351; Bengali employment disadvantages, 337, 349; Bengali–Punjabi differentiation, 337, 346, 350; Bihari genocide, 386; created by Bogra, 292; cyclone (1970), 352–3, 388; election and protests (1970–71), 352–7; famine and aid (1971), 388–9; hostility to West Pakistanis, 353; India aids Mukti Bahini, 377–9; and India–Pakistan proxy war, 325–6, 381; Joydebpur incident, 359; Mascarenhas on genocide, 384–5; military rule disadvantages, 337, 349; Mizo migration, 344; Mizo support for Pakistan Army, 381; Mujib seeks Indian support, 338–40; Mujib–Bhutto meeting, 360–2'; Mujib's six-point demand, 344–5, 349, 353, 354, 355, 399; and Muslim League, 140n; Pakistani Army's Operation Searchlight, 362–7, 369–74; Pakistani identity as primary, 349, 399; Phizo smuggled to and detained, 327–9; refugees flee to India, 375–6; sexual violence, 385–6, 416; student protests (1968), 348–9; surrender to Indian Army, 123; Tikka Khan as governor, 358; and West Pakistan prejudice, 380–1, 383–4; *see also* Bangladesh; Bengali (language); Partitions, Fifth
East Pakistan Civil Affairs Force, 380
Edward, Prince of Wales, 41
Edward VII, King, 303
Egypt, 293–4, 296, 311–12
El Alamein, Second Battle of, 98
El Edroos, Gen. Syed Ahmed, 258–9, 265, 273, 274, 276
Elizabeth II, Queen, 163, 258, 310
Ellis, Jim, 307, 315
Ellis, Joanna, 307, 310
Empire Windrush, HMT, 427
Encyclopaedia Britannica, 180
Enterprise, USS, 400–1, 402, 405
European Economic Community, 324
European Parliament, 418
Evans, Harold, 385
Ezdani, Yvonne Vaz, 73

Faiz, Faiz Ahmed, 231, 289
Faridkot, Maharaja of, 213
Farland, Joseph, 354–5
Farouk I, King of Egypt, 273, 293
fascism, 51, 55, 61, 105, 112
Fatat al-Jazira (newspaper), 318
Ferozepore, Pakistan, 198
Fields-Clarke, V. H. T., 29
Financial Times, 317
First World War, 4, 11, 124, 259
Foreign Affairs, 323
Fort Morbut, Aden, 306
France, 184, 256, 257, 296, 315, 347
French, Patrick, 132
Front for the Liberation of Occupied South Yemen (FLOSY), 306, 308–9, 312
Fujairah, 323
Furnival, John, 243

Galon Tat (paramilitary group), 51
Gandhi, Abha, 132
Gandhi, Devdas, 95
Gandhi, Feroze, 331, 332, 334
Gandhi, Indira: assassination, 423; attacks West Bengal communists, 387; authoritarian streak, 332; avoids reuniting both Bengals, 388; dismantles princely status, 419; Golden Temple attack, 423; imposes 'Emergency' rule, 421; as Indian prime minister, 343; and Indo-Pakistani war (1971), 394, 397; on Jinnah's two-nation theory, 405; marriage and affair, 331–2; and Mascarenhas's article, 385; orders bombing of Mizo rebels, 343–4; post-1972 reshaping of India, 417; postwar Bhutto meeting, 409–10; praises child soldiers, 387; as pro-Soviet, 371, 392; recognises Bangladesh, 398; supports East Pakistan separatists, 378–9; on USS *Enterprise* deployment, 401
Gandhi, Kasturba, 20, 95
Gandhi, Mahatma: accidental Jinnah meeting, 172–3; Aden visit, 36–9; agrees to Great Partition, 174; alienates Muslims, 39, 40; arrest (1942), 95; assassination, 245–7, 251, 261; attacks racist WWII evacuation, 94; and Aung San assassination, 193; backs 'Nehru Report', 23; 'brahmacharya' experiments, 132; Burma visit, 21–3; collapses Cabinet Mission plan, 147; early career, 20–1; fanaticism, 56; as Indian National Congress leader, 21; on Indo-Burma Immigration Agreement, 65; influence in Burma and Yemen, 7; Jinnah power-sharing approach, 132; Jinnah relationship, 14; Jinnah's paranoia, 230;
Junagadh as local, 218; Kashmir war fast, 244–5; on Kashmiri self-determination, 228; map of travels (1929–31), 38; Mountbatten relationship, 170; Mountbatten on wooing princely states, 188; Nagas brief on independence, 181–2; Nehru relationship, 57; Ottama as follower, 19; Partition-bloodshed fast, 202, 212; post-Direct Action Day fury, 153; Quit India call, 94; rejects Cripps's WWII offer, 93; at Round Table Conferences, 35–6, 39–40; Salt Act protest, 25, 26–7, 35; and Saya San rebellion, 31; sole leader opposing Partition, 172; supports Burmese separation, 21–2; trans-India walk for calm, 159, 423; WWII pessimism, 92
Gandhi, Manu, 245
Gandhi, Sanjay, 421
Gandhi, Shyamaldas, 222
Garauli, prince of, 58–9
Garhmukteshwar, India, 154, 155
Gaur, India/Pakistan/Bangladesh, 205
George V, King, 3
George VI, King, 47, 132
Germany, 55, 59, 61, 77, 98, 104–6, 120
Gilgit, Kashmir, 238, 239–40
Ginsberg, Allen, 390–1
Girnar, India (volcano), 218, 222
Goa, India, 336
Godavari river, 142
Godse, Nathuram, 246
Gracey, Maj.-Gen. Douglas, 135, 237–8, 279
Granth Sahib, Guru, 160n
Great Depression (1929), 26, 28
Great South Asian War, see Indo-Pakistani war (1971)
Greece, 108, 163
Guha, Ramachandra, 292
Guhathakurta, Jyotirmoy, 364
Gujarat: integrating princely states sorrow, 261n; migrants in Aden, 295; Muslims leave for Sindh, 207; Muslims shelter in Junagadh, 220–1, 222; Salt Act protest, 25; Telugu language, 292
Gulf states, *see individual states*
Gurgaon, India, 217
Gwadar, Pakistan, 299–303

Hadhrami Bedouin Legion (HBL), 310, 314, 315
Hafiz, Begum Khurshid Abdul, 275
Hajari, Nisid, 153–4
Haksar, P. N., 377, 378–9, 421
Hamid, Shahid, 166, 176; on Edwina–Nehru relationship, 182–3; on speed of Partition, 180

INDEX

Hardy, Faith, 347
Harrison, George, 389, 390, 391
Hart, Alan, 404–5
Harvard University, 350, 351, 374
Hasan, Abid, 104, 105, 107
Hasan, Mehdi, 283
Hasina, Sheikh, 426
Hassan, Mohammad Zaul, 411–13
Hayllar, Lt, 123, 124–5
Healey, Denis, 320
Himalayan states, 3, 228, 285; *see also* Bhutan; Nepal; Sikkim
Hindu Mahasabha: call for Bengal partition, 148; Gandhi assassination plot, 246; Jinnah's paranoia, 230; Ottama alliance, 42; Savarkar's rise, 49; WWII allegiance, 96
Hindus, Hinduism: aggravation of Bengali famine, 114; and boundaries of Bharat, 6, 7, 22, 42, 48, 227; and Christianity, 4; condemnation of 'Pakistan Resolution,' 63; as Congress Party 'instrument', 14; Delhi as legendary, 34; on Direct Action Day, 151–4; East Pakistan perceived as, 346; flee Hyderabad, 263–4; and 'Great Partition', 6; Hindu–Muslim riots, 133; Junagadh as sacred, 220; Kashmir as centre of learning, 227; leave Pakistan post-Partition, 204; massacre Jammu Muslims, 228–9; Meo Muslim ethnic cleansing, 213–14; migration from Lahore, 196; Muslim holy sites become temples, 279; Nehru's anti-theocracy, 215; Nizam of Hyderabad's support of, 256; in Oman, 322; Pakistan Army kills in East Pakistan, 370, 371, 384–5; Pakistani definition of 'enemy', 343; Partition as dismemberment of goddess, 178; Partition of Princely India, 6; post-Partition Punjab violence, 195, 196–8; prayers for Gandhi, 245; Punjabi reverence towards Sikh gurus, 160n; rebirth of Hindu nationalism, 376; relation to Dalits, 178; removing idols from Pakistan, 203; role of RSS, 148–9; Savarkar's 'Hindutva', 49; and Sikhism, 4; syncretism, 114
Hindustan, 160, 195, 198, 209
Hiroshima, 129, 131
Hitler, Adolf, 59, 60, 61, 69, 105, 113, 129, 390; *Mein Kampf*, 51, 65
Ho Chi Minh, 135
Holden, David, 284, 296–7, 300, 304, 320, 322–3
Hunza, Pakistan, 238, 285n
Huq, Fazlul, 292
Al-Hurriya (newspaper), 320–1
Hussein, Saddam, 304
Huxley, Aldous, 34

Hyder, Mohammad, 261–2, 264, 269, 272–3, 275–6
Hyderabad, annexation of (1948; Operation Polo): Arab deportations, 276, 299, 308, 314; Hyderabad's surrender, 274; Hyderabad's under-equipped army, 272–3; Indian Army marches on Hyderabad, 272; Junagadh as first act, 218; Mountbatten learns of Polo plan, 265–6; Muslim arrests and deportations, 275–6; Muslims replaced by Hindus in administration, 279; Nehru approves, 272; Nizam's mood, 273–4; terrifies Pakistan, 277; violence against Muslims and Dalits, 277–9
Hyderabad, India: bluff maintains law and order, 259; border raids from India, 261–2; British–Mughal opulence, 253–4, 267; Campbell-Johnson buffet dinner, 267; communists, 143, 188, 261, 263, 264–5, 269–70, 275, 287; comparison to pre-Revolution France, 256, 257; Corfield arms Nizam, 185; Cotton airlift offer, 259–60; as 'country in its own right', 255; Dalits support Nizam, 257, 259, 265; disappearance of old ways, 421; displaced people, 263, 265; dissolution of state, 5; export of princely art, 420; fate of left to Nizam, 184; as feudal state, 256; *haleem* (dish), 307; independence vote offer withdrawn, 267; India blockades, 258, 259; India captures Nanaj, 269; Laik Ali's Pakistan mission, 270–1; Muslim Nizam in Hindu state, 220; Patel readies troops on border, 261; place in Islamic world, 4, 255; post-Partition plans and wishes, 142, 184, 257; post-Partition strike, 175; post-Partition violence, 213, 263–5, 270; Qu'aiti forces in, 255, 259; Razvi's Islamic hate speech, 262–3; Telugu-language movement 291; *see also* Qu'aiti State
Hyderabad, Mahboob Ali Khan, 6th Nizam of, 310
Hyderabad, Osman Ali Khan, 7th Nizam of: Campbell-Johnson audience, 266–7; Corfield arms, 185; death, 311; fate of heirs, 419; frosty Jinnah relationship, 257–8; lofty independence plans, 142; Mountbatten on effect of Diwan's death on, 190; offers 'treaty of association', 257; orchestra disbanded, 279; palace lights out, 275; plans for Islamic Caliphate, 4, 255; political agility, 254–5; remains figurehead post-annexation, 276–7; responsibility for state's fate, 184; title, character and appearance, 254, 256; uses Razvi's Razakars, 213, 262, 263; warns Ghalib of taking Qu'aiti throne, 308

Hyderabad Radio, 273

Imam, Jahanara, 356, 357, 358, 366, 369–70, 383
Imam, Rumi, 358, 366, 369–70
Imam, Salahdin: in Calcutta, 379, 397–8; on Concert for Bangladesh, 389–90; as Ginsberg's tour guide, 390–1; as *Harvard Crimson* hack, 347; as hippie, 351; joins Mukti Bahini, 373–4, 379; on Mujib's Dacca address, 358; on Mukti Bahini rape, 385–6; opposes union with India, 388; on Pakistan as 'noble experiment', 349; post-Operation Searchlight, 367–9; on postwar Dacca, 408; at Woodstock, 350–1; on Yahya's postponement, 355, 356
Imphal, Battle of, 122–3, 125
India: annexes Goa, 336; Bengal famine (1943), 79, 100, 110–14, 387, 416; Bose–Japan plan to overthrow Raj, 104–8; Britain–Pakistan cooperation against communism, 287–8; British departures, 248–50; Burmese border hardens post-1971, 418, 430; China war, 340, 341; Communist Party repression, 251; defensive border, 1; definition during Raj, 3n; Direct Action Day violence, 149–55; East Bengali refugees, 375–6; election (1937), 56, 57–8; election (1946), 139–41; export of princely art, 420; fascism in, 51; Gandhi assassination and funeral, 245–7; 245–7, 261; George VI promises 'self-government', 132; Goa annexation, 336; independence celebrations, 202; Indira Gandhi reshapes, 417, 419; Indira Gandhi's 'Emergency' rule, 421; international condemnation of Bangladesh conflict, 387; linguistic reorganisation strengthens, 292; Mountbatten as governor general, 202; Mujib seeks support, 338–40, 345; Mukti Bahini support, 377–9, 380; Naga Hills martial law, 329; Naga revolt, 327–9; National Register of Citizens, 418; Nehru on independence, 201; Nehru–Liaquat Pact, 281–2, 329; Nehru's inaugural government, 155; New Delhi Agreement repatriation, 414–15; no consultation over WWII, 59–60; non-Muslims flee Pakistan, 340; nuclear programme, 422; Operation Madhouse, 164; Pakistan invades Kashmir (1965), 342–3, 348; Patkai colony proposal, 109–10; proxy Naga and Mizo wars against Pakistan, 336–7, 340, 343–4, 378, 400; Quit India movement, 95–7; recognises Bangladesh, 398; reuniting both Bengals, 388; signs USSR friendship treaty, 392; Telugu-language movement 291–2; two million British graves in, 249; 'Undivided', 7, 42; US anti-communism funding, 288n; and Western counterculture, 347; Whitehall announces British withdrawal, 163; withholds fuel from Pakistan, 387; WWII economy, 108; WWII militarisation, 60; WWII refugees in, 108; *see also* Indo-Pakistani wars; Partitions

Indian Air Force, 273, 274, 343–4, 393–4, 396–7, 402
Indian Army (to 1947): battles of Imphal and Kohima, 122, 123, 124–6, 141; British troops scaled down, 172; Burma left almost defenceless, 78; Burma Corps retreat, 92; Chindits, 115, 120; demobilisation, 138–9; handing Southeast Asia back to colonial masters, 134–8; marches into Burma, 133–4; Partition anxieties, 206; Saya San rebellion, 29; Slim's innovations, 115; Singapore surrender, 76; suppresses Viet Minh, 135; WWII size, 60, 116; *see also* India Command; Middle East Command; Punjab Boundary Force; South East Asia Command
Indian Army (post-Partition): Abdullah's key role in Kashmir, 237; annexes Hyderabad, 272–5; blockades Hyderabad, 258, 259; bombs lashkar near Srinagar, 241; complicity in Hyderabad violence, 278; forcible Mizo resettlement, 344; Ladakh clash with Pakistan, 269; last British unit leaves, 248; Naga volunteers against Phizo, 327; Operation Steeplechase, 387; share Pakistani Army background, 406; supports Mukti Bahini, 377–9; *see also* Indo-Pakistani wars
Indian Civil Service, 104, 209
Indian Empire, *see* British Raj
Indian Express, 282
Indian National Army (INA): aids Pakistani forces in Kashmir, 233; Anwar in, 232; consequence of not joining, 106; on Direct Action Day, 152; diversity and inclusion, 106–7; few Indian recruits, 115–16; at Imphal, 123–4; Phizo in, 121, 141; surrenders to British in Rangoon, 128; war-crimes trial, 139
Indian Political Service: and Arabian Raj residents, 283; Persian Gulf administration disappears, 168; post-Partition colour bar, 177; and protectorates, 3
Indian Republic Army (IRA), 25–6
Indiana Jones and the Last Crusade (film), 419
Indonesia, 135, 142, 325
Indo-Pakistani war (1947–48): Baramulla convent attacked, 234–5; 'ceasefire line'

agreed, 279; contested date of Pakistan intervention, 229, 230; Gandhi's fast, 244–5 'jehad' starts in Muzaffarabad, 232–3; Jinnah orders army into Kashmir, 238, 260; Jinnah stations permanent Kashmir force, 240; Junagadh as first act, 218; Khurshid Anwar's key role, 232; Ladakh clash, 269; lashkar driven from Srinagar, 241; maharaja's signature date contested, 236–7; Mountbatten Partition plan rejected, 268; Operation Datta Khel (Gilgit Scouts), 239–40; RSS troops sent, 242; UN debates, 242, 244; winter lull, 242

Indo-Pakistani war (1971): air battle, 393–4, 396; Hamoodur Rahman Report, 422; India bombs West Pakistan 396–7; India captures Jessore, 398; India holds Pakistani PoWs, 408–9, 413–15; India's air and sea supremacy, 397; Indian Army approaches Dacca, 399–400; Indian Army departs Dacca, 408; jingoism in, 395; massacre of the intellectuals, 402–3; Mizo and Naga surrender, 406–7; Pakistani pre-emptive air strikes, 393, 394; Pakistani surrender in Dacca, 403–4; post-war transition and massacres, 406–7

Indus river, 180, 247, 335
Iqbal, Allama, 62
Iralu, Niketu, 141
Iran, 252, 294, 323, 329, 400
Iran, Shah of, 392, 393
Iraq, 304, 323
Ireland, 120, 197
Irrawaddy river, 52, 85, 247
Irwin, Lord (Edward Wood, 1st Earl of Halifax), 33, 35–6
Islam, *see* Muslims, Islam
Islam, Syed Nazrul, 364, 368, 378
Islamabad, Pakistan, 410
Ismail, 'Abd al-Fattah, 316–17
Ismay, Lionel Ismay, 1st Baron, 174
Israel, 296, 311
Italy, 61, 104

Jacob, Maj.-Gen. Jacob-Farj-Raphael, 378, 394, 401, 403–4
Jagger, Mick, 347
Jah, Mukarram, 420
Jainism, 204, 218
Jaipur, India, 108, 212, 347
Jaisalmer, Maharajah of, 190
Jamat-i-Islami, 208
Jameet-ul-Musalmeen, 223–4
Jamiat-ul Ulama-i-Hind, 180
Jammu and Kashmir, *see* Kashmir

Jammu and Kashmir, Hari Singh, Maharaja of: on anti-Muslim violence, 229; falling popularity of 226–7; flees after Baramulla attack, 236; as Hindu ruler of Muslim state, 220, 226; ignores Mountbatten's advice, 227–8; legitimacy after fleeing, 237; offers accession to India, 233, 236–7; prefers independence to plebiscite, 228; protests against, 143, 227, 229; states' fate determined by, 184

Janata Party, 422
Janjira, India, 280
Japan: atomic bombs, 129, 131; Ba Maw leads puppet Burmese government, 102–4; battles of Imphal and Kohima, 122, 123, 124–6; BIA fights Indians in Arakan, 83–4; BIA supports, 75–6; Black Dragon Society influence, 50–1; bombs Calcutta, 93; Bose, INA and overthrow of Raj, 104–8; Burma granted independence, 119; captures Burma, 90; Chindits terrify, 115; defeat in WWII, 130–1; Dorman-Smith's anxiety in Burma, 67–8; extent of empire (1942), 100; fall of Singapore, 76; flight from Rangoon, 128; Greater East Asia Co-Prosperity Sphere, 120; idolised in liberal India, 61; India invasion postponed, 98; and Indian/Aden famines, 110; Indian opposition to, 96; 'Japanese Government Rupees', 97; 'Mountbatten's Samurai' as peacekeepers, 136; Pearl Harbor, 68, 69, 71; puppet states in Burma, 98–9; Rangoon bombing, 71–4; start of war with British Empire, 69; surrender in Singapore, 136, 137; U-Go offensive, 121–6; U Saw's overtures to, 65, 69

Jatiya Rakkhi Bahini (paramilitary group), 416
Jehan, Begum Akbar, 227
Jessore, Bangladesh, 398, 403
Jews, 50, 295, 317, 390
Jhelum, Pakistan, 165
Jhelum river, 232, 234, 241
Jinnah, Dina, *see* Wadia, Dina
Jinnah, Fatima, 171, 199, 201, 270
Jinnah, Muhammad Ali: accepts accession of Junagadh, 218, 220, 221; accepts princely states' independence rights, 185; approves Cotton's Hyderabad airlift, 260; agrees to Great Partition, 174; agrees to united India, 147; announces Great Partition, 176; anti-Simon Commission boycott, 15; assassination attempt, 179; Aung San meeting, 156; Burma as precedent for Pakistan, 97; on Calcutta, 171, 293; calls Azad 'sellout', 64; character and career, 12–13; complex relationship to Hyderabad,

Jinnah, Muhammad Ali (*cont ...*)
257–8; Dacca portraits bonfire, 356; death, 271–2; defends Corfield, 185; delays Hunza and Nagar recognition, 239; 'Direct Action Day' call, 148; dream of Pakistan dies, 366–7; dynasty, 422; expands Muslim League National Guards, 154; failure as 1937 elections leader, 58; first Mountbatten meeting, 170–1; as founder of Pakistan, 12, 16, 415; Gandhi power-sharing approach, 132; Gandhi relationship, 14, 40, 172–3; Indira Gandhi on, 405; influence in Burma and Yemen, 7; Junagadh as local, 218; on Kashmir intervention, 229; Kashmiri self-determination, 228; Laik Ali's futile Hyderabad meeting, 270–1; leaves Congress Party for Muslim League, 14–15; Linlithgow's 'all Indians' request, 62, 63; loss of faith in Mountbatten, 183; marriage to Ruttie, 13–15, 16, 23; Menon friendship, 174; Mountbatten plebiscite pledge, 240; Mountbatten's independent Bengal plan, 172; with Mountbattens at birth of Pakistan, 199–201; 'Muslim States' as typo, 149; 'Muslims in Hindu provinces' error, 140; Naga Hills claim, 141; neglected daughter, 15; and Nurul Amin, 398; opposes 'Nehru Report', 23; orders army into Kashmir, 238, 260; 'Pakistan Resolution,' 63, 131, 139–40; as Pakistan's first governor general, 202; paranoia over Indian politicians, 230; Partition of Punjab and Bengal, 171–2; pressures Kalat, 252–3; promotes Urdu in Dacca, 260; protests India–Bharat identity, 48; as 'Quaid-i-Azam' ('Great Leader'), 132; rejects Cripps's WWII offer, 93; rejects Nehru as joint governor-general, 182; religious tolerance, 199–200; rivalry with Nehru, 58; at Round Table Conferences, 39, 40, 58, 174; Ruttie's suicide, 24; Simon Commission meeting, 12, 16; supports Travancore, 189; tempts Maharajas of Jodhpur and Jaisalmer, 191; tomb, 293, 398; unaware of rebellion in Kashmir, 230, 231
Jodhpur, India, 6, 191, 217
Jodhpur, Maharajah of, 191
Joydebpur, Bangladesh, 359
Junagadh, India: attempted accession to Pakistan, 218, 219–20, 285n; Kathiawar Defence Force blockades, 220, 230; links to Gandhi, Jinnah and Nehru, 218; Menon's plan, 221–2; Muslims' property sold, 225; Muslims massacred, 223; Shyamaldas' provisional government, 222; votes to join India, 224–5

Junagadh, Mahabat Khanji III, Nawab of, 218–20, 221, 222–3, 224–5
Junagadhi, Qazi, 223–4
Jung, Salar, 254

Kachin people, 43, 158, 287, 340
Kaderia Bahini (paramilitary group), 404
Kak, Ram Chandra, 227
Kalat: accedes to Pakistan, 285n; Gwadar given to Oman, 300, 301; Indian accession conflict, 253; Jinnah pressure to accede, 252–3; leaves Pakistani union, 330; seeks independence, 184
Kalat, Khan of, 253, 301, 330
Kalewa, Burma, 86, 87
Kali (goddess), 335, 347
Kandy, Ceylon, 119
Kane, Ray, 321–2
Kannada (language), 256
Kaoosji, Yezdyar, 265
Kapoor, Motia Devi, 235
Karachi, Pakistan: anti-Yahya protests, 405; Aung San–Jinnah meeting, 156; Bengali repatriation, 414–15; birth of Pakistan, 199–201; Cotton's Hyderabad airlift, 260; Hyderabad Colony established, 275n; in Indo-Pakistani war (1971), 396–7; Jinnah's death and funeral, 271; knowledge of East Pakistan war, 383–4; as Pakistan's new capital, 199; Playboy Club, 410; post-Partition excitement, 175
Karen people: absent from Panglong Conference, 158; BIA attacks, 83; Campbell-Johnson on, 251; independence movement inspires Phizo, 141; mutiny in Burmese Army, 287; rebellions, 288; return to Rangoon, 104; state Burmese Union conditions, 193; support Aung San, 127, 158
Kashmir: Abdullah installed as leader, 237; Abdullah jailed, 227, 286; Air India hijack, 354; anti-Maharaja protests, 143, 227, 229; and Ayub Khan–Nehru relationship, 335; Chinese sovereignty, 342; communists in National Conference Party, 188; economy, 226; fate determined by Maharaja, 184; Hindu Maharaja in Muslim state, 220, 226; Hindus massacre Muslims, 228–9; independence preferred to plebiscite, 228; in Indo-Pakistani war (1971), 397; Jinnah rejects plebiscite pledge, 240; Jinnah's Mountbatten's advice, 227–8; as 'K' in Pakistan, 62; Line of Control established, 409; Muhammad relic disappears, 340; Nehru–Liaquat Ali Khan talks, 241–2; and nuclear proliferation, 226; Pakistan invades (1965), 342–3, 348; Pakistan-administered

area, 285n; Pakistani government first involved, 230, 231; Pakistan-sponsored separatists, 423; seeks independence, 184; spread of communism anxiety, 250; UN oversight removed, 410; *see also* Indo-Pakistani war (1947–48)
Kashmir, Maharajah of, 184
Kashmir War, First, *see* Indo-Pakistani war (1947–48)
Kathiawar, India, 221, 224
Al-Kathiri, South Arabia, 311, 313–15
Kaur, Basant, 159–60
Keenan, Brigid, 209, 248, 249–50
Keenan, John, 197–9, 206, 213, 246, 248–9, 250
Kennedy, Jacqueline, 420–1
Kennedy, John F., 342, 401
Kennedy, John F. Jr, 421
Kenya, 249, 318
Kerala, India, 4, 325n, 332
Keyho, Gen. Thenoselie, 406–7
Khaksar movement, 179
Khalistani movement, 423
Khan, Brig. Akbar, 229, 230, 231–2, 235, 241, 289
Khan, Ali Akbar, 389
Khan, Ayub: detains Phizo, 329; Goa annexation, 336; at Imphal, 123; military coup, 329, 330; moves against Mujib, 345; Phizo's assistance against India, 335, 336; in Punjab Boundary Force, 197–8; releases Mujib, 349; resigns, 349; sends troops to Kashmir, 342, 343; student protests against, 348–9; Tariq Ali organises protests, 347; and Zulfikar Ali Bhutto, 342
Khan, Sardar Ibrahim, 229–30, 231, 241
Khan, Liaquat Ali: assassination, 289, 350; Corfield meeting, 185; as finance minister, 155, 165; instals Bengalis in government, 288; on military budget, 277; as minister of finance, 155; minority-rights pact, 281; at Mountbatten's swearing-in ceremony, 165; Nehru pact, 281–2, 329; Nehru talks on Kashmir, 241–2; on Pakistan lacking space for refugees, 208; sends troops to Kashmir, 242; shrugs off Messervy, 231; stalls on Hunza and Nagar, 239; support for rebellion in Kashmir, 230
Khan, Mohammad Abdul Barik (Gedu Mian), 108–9
Khan, Muhammad, 160, 161, 162
Khan, Sahabzada Yaqub, 358
Khan, Shah Rukh, 207
Khan, Sher, 161–2, 429
Khan, Brig. Sher, 241
Khan, Shoebullah, 269

Khan, Sir Sikander Hyat, 63
Khan, Gen. Tikka, 355, 358, 382
Khan, Gen. Yahya: Bhutto's coup threat, 383; character, 352; cyclone response, 353; on East Pakistan, 351–2; East Pakistan amnesty, 382; hands power to Nurul Amin, 398; instructs Niazi on ceasefire, 403; introduces elections (1970), 352, 354; launches Operation Searchlight, 362, 372; misunderstands Bengali nationalism, 380; Mujib meeting in Dacca, 360; Persepolis Festival lobbying, 392, 393; Podgorny advice on Mujib, 393; postpones assembly, 355, 356; replaces Ayub Khan as leader, 349; resigns, 405; sends Tikka Khan to East Pakistan, 358
Khan, Zahir Alam, 352, 353, 381, 382
Khanji, Dilawar, 223
Khanji, Mahabat, 223
Kharan, Pakistan, 253, 285n
Khasi Hills, 376
Khasi states, 190, 252, 253, 285n
Khimji, Gokaldas, 300
Khimji, Kanak, 322
Khonoma, Nagaland, 48–9
Khrushchev, Nikita, 280
Khuldabad, India, 255
Khulna, Bangladesh, 281, 289, 416
King, Martin Luther, 346
Kinmama, Daw, 100–2
Kissinger, Henry, 371, 392, 400, 401, 402n
Ko Chet Pon, 79, 134
Kohima, Battle of, 122, 123, 124–6
Kohima, Nagaland, 45, 182n, 418
Krishna (god), 179, 213
Kushtia, Bangladesh, 373
Kuwait: independence, 304; Indian and Pakistan flags raised, 202; as 'lost province of Iraq', 298, 323; pre-oil poverty of rulers, 168; in Raj, 2; separated from India, 169; and Suez crisis, 298; use of term 'Kuwaiti', 298

Ladakh, 241, 269, 410
Lahore, Pakistan: Air India hijack, 354; Confectioners Federation protest, 165; on defeat of Japan, 130; India's Punjab war, 342–3; Jinnah delivers 'Pakistan Resolution,' 63; monsoon flood rumours, 211; post-Partition uncertainty, 203; post-Partition violence, 195–6, 198; Punjab Boundary Force in, 198; RSS armaments training, 154; Taunsvi leaves, 215–16
Lahore Resolution (1940), 178n, 292, 344, 362
Laldenga (Mizo leader), 344, 407
Las Bela, Pakistan, 253, 285n

Lashkar-e-Taiba (jihadist group), 423
Linlithgow, Victor 'Hopie' Hope, 2nd Marquess of: admits retreat from India, 94; arrests Congress leaders, 94–5; asks Jinnah for 'all Indians' proposal, 62, 63; demands release of Bengal rice, 112; fails to consult over WWII, 60; as implementor of Partition, 44; negotiates with princes, 58–9; Patkai colony proposal, 109; prayers after Gandhi assassination, 246; rebuffs Nehru's WWII demand, 62; response to Quit India, 96; U Saw perturbs, 67
Lintner, Bertil, 417–18
London: Attlee–Aung San meeting, 156–7; British Library, 319; Gandhi's taste for East End, 39; Merchants move to, 317; Mujib supported, 349; Pakistani diplomatic defections, 391; Phizo's flight to, 334–5; Ritz Hotel, 39; U Saw visit, 68; V&A Indian collection, 420; *see also* Round Table Conferences
Lu Gyi, 31–2
Ludhianvi, Sahir, 215
Luqman, Huda, 318
Luqman, Muhammad Ali, 36–8, 295, 296, 298, 299, 318–19
Lutyens, Sir Edwin, 33, 34

Mac, Ken, 201
Mackawwi, Muhammad, 37
Macmillan, Harold, 311
Madras, India: avoiding famine, 112, 113; integrating princely states protests, 261n; Muslim politicians detained, 271; post-Partition strike, 175; Quit India sabotage, 96; Telugu-language movement 291–2
Mahabharata (Hindu epic), 22, 256
Mahajan, Mehr Chand, 236
Al-Mahra, South Arabia, 311
Majumdar, M. I., 287
Makran, Pakistan, 253, 285n, 301
Malaya, 69, 107, 143
Malaysia, 320
Maldives, 320
Malerkotla, India, 212
Malhoutra, Moni, 421
Malik, Brig. Abdullah, 370
Mamdot, Khan of, 197
Manavadar, India, 222, 285n
Mandal, Jogendra Nath, 155, 172, 180
Mandalay, Burma, 19, 55, 85, 119, 287
Manekshaw, Sam, 123, 236, 378, 397, 402
Mangrol, India, 218, 221
Manipur, India, 122–3, 188, 190, 224
Manki Sharif, Pir of, 232
Manto, Saadat Hasan, 97, 209–11

Mao Zedong, 283, 287
Margui, Burma, 43
Mariappan, M. P., 53–4, 77, 79–82, 134, 203
Mascarenhas, Anthony 'Tony', 384
Massey, Paddy, 183
Mathai, M. O., 332
Mathieson, Capt. Jock, 238–9
Maung Gyi, Sir J. A., 28
Maung Maung, 49
Maymyo, Burma, 103
Mazhari, Sherbaz Khan, 399
Meghalaya, India, 417
Meghna river, 400, 406
Mehta, Pranjivan, 50
Meikhel monolith, Nagaland, 5
Menezes, Donald, 72, 73–4
Menezes, Eric, 71, 73, 74, 76
Menon, V. K. Krishna, 182, 269–70
Menon, V. P.: creates Great Partition plan, 173–4; on Hyderabad's communists, 270; on Hyderabad's future, 257, 267; Indira Gandhi overturns princely pledge, 419; integrates princely states, 186, 187, 190; Jodhpur drama, 191; Junagadh plan, 221–2; on Nawab of Junagadh's dogs, 225; on Partition, 280; and start of Kashmir crisis, 236, 237
Meo Muslims, 213–14
Merchant, Khozem, 317
Messervy, Frank, 231
Mia, Kader, 133
Mia, Manik, 339, 345, 365
Middle East Command, 116
Midway, Battle of, 98
Mina Sulman, Bahrain, 324
Miraben (Gandhi disciple), 95
Mirpur, Azad Kashmir, 241
Mirza, Iskander, 292, 330
Mishra, Krishna, 227
Mitchell, Colin 'Mad Mitch', 312
Mittal, Jagdish, 420
Miyazaki (Japanese soldier), 126
Mizo National Front, 336–7, 343
Mizo people: at Indian independence parade, 286–7; and India–Pakistan proxy war, 325–6, 340, 343–4, 378, 381, 400; Indians seize intelligence documents, 400; post-1971 struggle, 418; support for Pakistan Army, 381; surrender in Bangladesh, 407
Mizoram, India, 417
Moazam, Mir, 274
Modi, Narendra, 376
Mogok, Burma, 100–1
Mohammad, Khair, 106
Mohani, Hasrat, 178–9
Mohenjo Daro necklace, 181

INDEX 511

Monywa, Burma, 86, 327
Moon, Sir Penderel, 58, 139–40, 163
Morning News (Dacca), 291
Moulmein, Burma, 76, 103
Mountbatten, Edwina: death, 333–4; Driberg on, 136–7; India tour (1921–2), 116–17; on Jinnah, 171; marriage and affairs, 117, 118, 127; Nehru relationship, 169, 173, 182–3, 228, 266, 268, 330–1, 333, 341; on Patel, 170; PoW visits, 136–7; in Saigon, 135; on Simla, 173; Singapore rescue, 143–4; as Vicereine, 163
Mountbatten, Lord Louis: advice to Indira Gandhi on princes, 419; advice on Kashmir post-Partition, 227–8; announces Great Partition, 175; appointed SEAC head, 116, 118; on Aung San assassination, 193; on Bengal–Punjab contrast, 212–13; and Burmese independence, 243; Burmese throne ceremony, 251; champions Aung San, 127, 137–8; Dorman-Smith rift, 137–8; Edwina admits to Nehru relationship, 331; on Edwina's death, 333; El Edroos meeting in London, 258; final act as Viceroy, 201; first Jinnah meeting, 170–1; first Nehru meeting, 143–4; forms Punjab Boundary Force, 197; Gandhi relationship, 170; Imphal absence, 123; independent Bengal plan, 172; on Indian princes, 164; as India's first governor general, 202; Japanese surrender in Singapore, 136, 137; with Jinnah at birth of Pakistan, 199–201; Jinnah rejects plebiscite pledge, 240; Jinnah's Hyderabad warning, 257; on Jinnah's illness, 271; Jinnah's Junagadh warning, 221; Jodhpur accedes to India, 191; Kandy HQ, 119; Kashmir and Hyderabad failures, 268; Keenan unimpressed with, 198–9; marriage and affairs, 117, 127; Menon's princely states plan, 186; 'Mountbatten's Samurai', 136; moves Partition date forward, 176–7, 181; Nehru farewell speech, 268; Nehru relationship, 169, 340–1; and Operation Polo, 265–6; and Patel, 170; PoW visits, 136–7; on precedent of Travancore, 189; presents Plan Balkan to Nehru, 173; princely India meetings, 167, 168; as pro-Congress, 171, 178, 183; on question of local independence movements, 135–6; raises West Kents morale, 118; in reconquered Rangoon, 128; as reluctant new Viceroy, 163; revolver prop, 191n; sends Campbell-Johnson to Hyderabad, 266, 267; signing of Instruments of Accession, 187–8; suggests Nehru as joint governor-general, 182;

swearing-in ceremony, 165; undermines Corfield, 185
Mountbatten, Pamela, 173, 330
Mountbatten, Patricia, 117, 181
Mountbatten, Philip, 163, 258
Mudafarganj, Bangladesh, 385
Muflahi State, South Arabia, 312
Mughal Empire, 56, 64, 91, 226, 253, 274
Muhammad, Prophet, 114, 340
Mujib (Mujibur Rahman): arrest and trial ('Agartala Conspiracy Case'), 345–6; assassination, 416; attempts to gain Indian support, 338–40, 345; Bhutto power-sharing offer, 354; British support, 349; Direct Action Day, 150, 152, 153; disillusionment with Pakistan, 290; elections (1970), 352, 353–4; family taken hostage, 406; forms Bangladesh government, 408; on Gandhi, 159; Jinnah Urdu protest in Dacca, 260; on Joydebpur incident, 359; Nehru on, 338; 1974 Bengal famine destroys, 416; Operation Searchlight arrest, 364; as Pakistani nationalist, 293; Podgorny's advice to Yahya, 393; Ramna Race Course speech, 358; Roy's mother's UN mission, 411; six-point demand, 344–5, 349, 353, 354, 355, 399; threat against Amin, 337–8; Yahya and Bhutto meetings in Dacca, 360–2
Mujibnagar, Bangladesh, 378
Mukalla, Qu'aiti State / South Yemen, 306, 307, 308–10, 312, 313, 314–15, 319
Mukti Bahini (Bangladeshi Liberation Army): captures Chaugacha, 394; child soldiers, 387; conflict spills into India, 374–5, 383; Dacca bank robbery, 407; enters Dacca, 403; formed in Kushtia, 373; garlanded, 405; Indian support for, 377–9, 380; Indian Army disrespect, 407; kills Chittagong non-Bengalis, 383; Laila Ahmed in, 379–80; Mizo attacks on, 381; power supply attacks, 387; Sal Imam in, 347, 373–4, 379; scorns government-in-exile, 408; sexual violence, 385–6
Mukti Fauj, *see* Mukti Bahini
Multan, Pakistan, 203
Mumtaz (Batala Muslim), 203, 204, 211–12
Murshidabad, India, 204
Muscat and Oman: anti-rebel capability, 323–4; British replace sultan, 321–2; Curzon on, 3; Dhofar pacified, 324; and Gandhi's funeral, 247; Gwadar dispute with Pakistan, 299–303; Hyderabad Qu'aitis stranded, 259; in Raj, 2, 3
Muscat and Oman, Said bin Taimur, Sultan of, 300, 301, 302, 321–2

Muslim Conference (Kashmir), 227, 230
Muslim League: and Andaman Islands, 180; anti-Sikh pogroms in Rawalpindi, 159–60; attacks racist WWII evacuation, 94; Aung San's tact, 156; centrality of Bengal in, 140; condemns Burma riots, 55; Direct Action Day, 148–53; East Bengal Assembly rout, 292; HMS *Talwar* flag, 142; horror at Partition, 178–9; Jinnah builds base, 148, 149, 150, 152, 153; Khasi states attempt to join Pakistan, 190; Mountbatten quizzes Jinnah, 171; Mujib as activist, 150–1; National Guards, 51; 1937 election failure, 58; 1946 election success, 139–41; and Nurul Amin, 398; on overseeing Partition, 178; plea for people to stay put, 206; schism over 'Pakistan', 149–50; WWII popularity, 97, 131
Muslim League National Guards: commonplace nature of, 51; and Jinnah assassination attempt, 17; Jinnah's hundredfold expansion, 154; Partition voting intimidation, 180; Patel bans, 246; pogroms, 156; post-Partition Punjab violence, 197, 198; support rebellion in Kashmir, 230; youth self-defence training, 148
Muslims, Islam: and Ahmadiyya community, 178; Al-Badr misunderstanding in East Pakistan, 380–1; arrests, deportations and violence against, 275–9; Aub Khan berates scholars, 335; Bangladesh's Islamic constitution, 417; Bengali syncretism, 114; conflict with Buddhists in Arakan, 83–4; Delhi as sacred, 34; ethnic cleansing of, in Burma, 52–5; Gandhi alienates in London conference, 39–40; Gandhi's son converts, 56; and 'Great Partition', 6; Hindu policy worsens Bengali famine, 114; Hindu–Muslim riots, 133; Hindus massacre in Jammu, 228–9; Hyderabad holy sites become temples, 279; Indian definition of 'enemy', 343; Indian's Citizenship Amendment Act, 418; 'jehad' in Kashmir, 231–2; Jinnah assassination attempt, 179; Jinnah on Muslim war effort, 63; Jinnah's 'Pakistan Resolution,' 63, 139–40; migration to Hyderabad, 263; migration from India, 196, 207; migration to secular states, 207; Muslim-majority provinces vote on Pakistan, 180; 'Nehru Report', 23; Nizam of Hyderabad's 'caliphate', 4, 255, 419; opposition to India–Bharat identity, 48; Pakistan no longer South Asia homeland, 415; Pakistan as 'noble experiment', 349; and Partition of Princely India, 6; as political pariahs, in India, 204; populations in India, 150; post-Partition Punjab violence, 195–8; prayers for Gandhi, 245; Punjabi modernisation, 16; Razvi's hate speeches, 262–3; Rohingya–Bengali distinction, 66n; Ruttie's conversion, 13; variety in Kashmir, 226; Zia-ul-Haq Islamises Pakistan, 422
Mussolini, Benito, 61, 69
Mutharasu (Nadar Tamil), 77, 79–82
Muzaffarabad, Azad Kashmir, 232–3
My Favourite Brunette (film), 201
Myochit party, 51, 55
Mysore, India, 4, 292

Naga Army, 336
Naga Hills: Nehru imposes martial law, 329; Nehru and Jinnah claim, 141; Nehru–U Nu visit, 327; Pakistan claims, 329; Uttam in, 89
Nagaland Tripura, India, 417
Nagar, Pakistan, 238, 239, 285n
Nagas, Nagaland: British and Japanese vie for influence, 120–1; dancers in New Delhi, 333; and India–Pakistan proxy war, 325–6, 378, 400; Indira Gandhi reorganises, 417; mainly in India post-Partition, 48–9; map, 328; Nehru division plans, 335; opposition to India–Burma Partition, 45–7; Pakistan assistance against India, 335, 336; Phizo declares independence, 327; Phizo promotes independence, 141–2, 181–2, 202, 326–7; post-1946 sense of betrayal, 141; revolution peters out, 324, 417–18; sketchy central administration, 60; surrender in Bangladesh, 406–7; uninvited at Panglong, 158; WWII recruitment problems, 60–1
Nagasaki, 129, 131
Nagra, Maj.-Gen. Gandharv, 406
Nai Zindagi (journal), 282
Naidu, Padmaja, 15, 24, 57, 182, 277
Naidu, Sarojini: as Congress president, 15; on decay of Raj, 131–2; disillusioned with Gandhi, 39, 56; on Gandhi, 25, 36; on Jinnah 'as Lucifer', 153; on Jinnah's character, 12–13; at Round Table Conferences, 40; on Ruttie's suicide, 24
Nankana Sahib, Pakistan, 204
Nasser, Gamal Abdel, 293, 296, 297, 311, 323
National Conference Party (Kashmir), 227
National Geographic, 344
National Liberation Front (NLF): Britain–NLF–FLOSY conflict in Aden, 308, 312; British support, 313–14, 315; controls South Yemen, 316–17, 347; destroys Luqman archives, 318–19; Ghalib negotiations, 314–15; Hadhramaut takeover, 315; Marxist

NLF–FLOSY split, 306; Nasser sponsors, 305; nationalises companies, 318; rebellions against South Arabia sultans, 305, 312–13, 315–16
Nawanagar, Maharaja Jam Sahib of, 186–7
Nazimuddin, Khawaja, 290, 291
Ne Win, 75, 288, 330, 340
Nehru, Jawaharlal: agrees to Great Partition, 174, 175; announces Great Partition, 176; anti-RSS theocracy, 215; approves Operation Polo, 272; arranges Asian Relations Conference, 166; arrest (1942), 94, 95; on 'Asiatic federation', 425; attacks Corfield, 185; Aung San meetings, 144, 156; background, 56; on Bhutan and Sikkim, 147; Britain as 'second-class power', 78; and CIA plant, 332; claims Naga Hills, 141; collapses Cabinet Mission plan, 147; condemns Burma's immigration bill, 192; decline and death, 334, 340–1; demands halt to SEAC involvement, 136; on Direct Action Day, 155; on East Bengal as 'colony', 292; Edwina Mountbatten relationship, 169, 173, 182–3, 266, 268, 330–1, 333, 341; farewell speech to Mountbattens, 268; first Mountbatten meeting, 143–4; on Gandhi assassination, 245; Gandhi relationship, 57, 341; on Hindus in East Bengal, 281; on Hyderabad, 267, 269–70, 277; Hyderabad ultimatum, 271; ideological awakening, 56–7; inaugural government, 155; on independence, 201; on Indian Political Service, 177; Jinnah assassination attempt, 179; Jinnah rejects as joint governor-general, 182; on Jinnah's death, 271–2; Jinnah's paranoia, 230; on Kashmir, 228; Keenan on, 198–9; leads Congress in 1937 elections, 56, 57–8; Liaquat Ali Khan talks on Kashmir, 241–2; Liaquat pact, 281–2, 329; Linlithgow rebuffs WWII demand, 62; makes Mountbatten governor general, 202; minority-rights pact, 281; on Mountbatten's charm, 169; at Mountbatten's swearing-in ceremony, 165; on Mujib, 338; Naga Hills visit, 327; Nagaland plans, 335; 'Nehru Report' proposes independence, 5; on New Delhi celebrations, 35; on Operation Polo, 266; Patel olive branch, 246; Patkai Hills ignorance, 286; on Phizo's 'absurd' demands, 326; Plan Balkan reaction, 173; rejects Cripps's WWII offer, 93; rejects UN Hyderabad mediation, 270; rivalry with Jinnah, 58; sends troops to Kashmir, 236–7; threatens Travancore, 189; underestimates Muslim League, 131; views on USSR and Japan, 61; Wavell's gift of poems, 113

Nehru, Kamala, 57
Nehru, Motilal, 12, 35
Nepal: Congress recognises independence right, 185; Gurkhas, 206; independence rights secured, 147; nationalist downplaying of Raj, 7; persistence as princely state, 6, 228, 320; in Raj, 2, 3
New Delhi, India: Asian Relations Conference, 166–7, 282; author's childhood, 426, 427, 428; beautification drive displacement, 421; communal riot, 164, 165; construction of, 34; Dorman-Smith in, 90–1; Gandhi assassination and funeral, 245–7; inauguration as capital, 33, 35; independence celebrations, 202; Persian prophecy, 35; post-Partition protest, 175; Purana Qila, 166; Simon Commissioners in, 11–12, 16; tenth Republic Day parade, 330–1; Viceroy's House, 33–4, 36, 90, 164–5, 175, 268
New Delhi Agreement (1973), 414–15
New York, 18, 299, 389–90, 410–11, 426
Niazi, Gen. A. A. K., 123, 403–4, 406, 408, 415, 422
Nixon, Richard M., 371, 400, 401
Noakhali, India, 154, 155
Noon, Firoz Khan, 300–1, 302, 329–30
North-Eastern Areas (Reorganisation) Act 1971, 417
North-West Frontier, 96, 140, 147, 176, 200n, 231, 232, 422
Nu, U: bombs Rohingya in Patkai Hills, 287; as Burma's new prime minister-in-waiting, 193–4; Mountbatten discussion on communism, 251; Naga Hills visit, 327; requests military rule, 330
Nuruddin (friend of Mujib), 150–1

Oak, P. N., 120n
Oberoi, Mohan Singh, 108
Oman, *see* Muscat and Oman
Oman, Qaboos bin Said Al Said, Sultan of, 322, 323, 393
Operations: Datta Khel, 239–40; JIM, 337; Madhouse 164; Nutcracker, 305–6; Polo, 266, 272–7; Searchlight, 362–7, 369–70, 372–5; Steeplechase, 387
Oppenheimer, J. Robert, 129
Orwell, George, 68, 90, 188
Osmanabad, India, 261–2, 269, 272, 276, 314
Osmani, Muhammad 'Papa Tiger', 373
Ottama, U: as anti-separatist at Round Table Conference, 40; influence in Burma wanes, 49; Gandhi rift over separation, 22; as Gandhian, 19; Hindu Mahasabha alliance, 42

Ottoman Empire, 3, 4, 255, 419
Oxford, University of: Ghalib at, 306, 319; Indira Gandhi at, 331; and Nazimuddin's cabinet, 290; Project Dastaan founded, 428; Tariq Ali at, 347; Zulfikar Ali Bhutto at, 341

Paget, Julian, 316
Pakistan: as acronym, 62, 227; Ayub Khan military coup, 329, 330, 337; Bengal cyclone (1970), 352–3, 388; Bengalis in government, 288, 290, 292, 293, 337, 349; Bengalis 'repatriated' to Bangladesh, 409 Bhutto dynasty created, 220; Britain–India cooperation against communism, 287–8; China ties, 342, 371, 377, 387; Communist Party repression, 251; crackdown on East Bengal Hindus, 281; 'created' by Jinnah–Nehru rivalry, 58; Direct Action Day narrative, 153; East and West Pakistan created, 292; East–West spending difference, 349; economy 335, 387; elections (1970), 352–4; fights East Pakistan rebels, 374–5, 383; Gwadar dispute with Oman, 299–303; idea of Pakistan as novel and fluid, 62, 140; invades Kashmir (1965), 342–3, 348; Jinnah as founder, 12, 16; Jinnah as governor general, 202; Jinnah's death, 271–2; Liaquat assassinated, 289; military budget, 242–3, 277, 349, 387; Mizo intelligence documents, 400; Mujib arrested and tried, 345–6; Mujib seeks Indian support, 338–40; Mujib's six-point demand, 344–5, 349, 353, 354, 355, 399; Muslims flee India, 340; Nawab of Bahawalpur saves economy, 230; Nehru–Liaquat Pact, 281–2, 329; New Delhi Agreement repatriation, 414–15; no longer South Asia Muslim homeland, 415; nuclear programme, 342, 422; Nurul Amin as prime minister, 398–9; and Partition of Princely India, 6–7, 284n; perception of East Pakistan as Hindu, 346; proxy Naga and Mizo wars against India, 336–7, 340, 343–4, 378, 381, 400; its purpose questioned, 211; recognises Bangladesh, 415; refuses to recognise Bangladesh at UN, 410–11; student protests (1968), 348–9; supports Khalistan separatists, 423; surrenders in Dacca, 403–4; US values anti-communism of, 288n, 371; wealth inequity, 348; Yaha Khan replaces Ayub Khan, 349; Zia-ul-Haq coup, 422–3; *see also* Indo-Pakistan wars; Partitions, Third and Fifth
Pakistani Air Force, 292, 393–4, 396, 39

Pakistani Army: administers Hunza and Nagar, 239n; and anti-Bengali sentiment, 383–4; Ayub Khan coup, 329, 330; British ignore Kashmir 'jehad', 231; Burma withholds fuel, 387; and Chakma guerrillas, 382; cyclone response (1970), 353; East Bengal Regiment mutiny, 368, 374; East Pakistan action as genocide, 384–5, 390, 391; East Pakistan paramilitary groups, 380–1; East Pakistan Rifles defectors, 378; forces assembly postponement, 355; Gilgit Scouts, 238–40; Ibrahim Khan introduced to, 229; Jinnah orders into Kashmir, 238, 260; Joydebpur civilian deaths, 359; kill East Pakistan Hindus, 370, 371, 384–5; Ladakh clash with India, 269; Mascarenhas on 'genocide', 384–5; Mizo support for, 381; objectors to Awami League action, 358; Operation Datta Khel, 239–40; Operation Searchlight, 362–7, 369–74; PoWs held by India, 408–9, 413–15; Punjabis preferred to Bengalis, 337, 349; refusal to work with Mujib, 362; sexual violence in East Pakistan, 385, 416; shares Indian Army background, 406; sponsors Taliban and Lashkar-e-Taiba, 423; supports Air India hijack, 354; withheld from Kashmir protest, 230; Zulfikar Ali Bhutto's animus towards, 342; *see also* Indo-Pakistani wars
Pakistani Hamoodur Rahman Commission, 370
PAKTRACK (parcel delivery service), 395
Palestine, 163
Paliwal, Avinash, 338n
P&O Group, 324
Panglong Conference (1947), 157–8, 192
Parsis, 13, 265
PARTITIONS
First (1937, India–Burma): Ba Maw as first premier, 51; Bengal famine as consequence, 100; Burmese opposition to separation, 19, 22–3, 31; ceremony in Rangoon, 47; and Chakmas, 382; commemorative stamp, 47; completion of, 97; date of 1937 set for separation, 41; demarcating India– Burma border, 45–7, 46; Frontier Areas, 137; fulfils Hindu demand for Bharat, 6, 22, 48; Gandhi supports separation, 21–3; Indian exodus, 55–6, 78–83, 81; Nagaland accorded mainly to India, 48–9; Phizo's attempt to undo, 327; as precedent for Pakistan, 97; Round Table Conference, 40–1
Second (1937–57, India–Arabian Peninsula): 'Arab' no longer Indian ethnicity, 276; ceremony in Aden, 47; fewest Partition casualties, 317; fulfils Hindu demand for

INDEX 515

Bharat, 7, 22, 48; Hyderabad Arabs deported, 276, 299; last remnants of princely states, 6, 320; Persian Gulf Residency separated from India, 168–9; pre-oil poverty of rulers, 168; regional reversals, 303; Reilly on, 37; Round Table Conferences decision on, 41; sale of Gwadar, 299–303; South Asian exclusion from Arabia, 298; starts with Aden, 6; *see also* Arabian Raj

Third 'Great' (1947, India–Pakistan): administration, India vs Pakistan, 209; aid distribution, 208; Bharat helps create Pakistan, 48; birth of Pakistan celebrations, 199–201; Burma as precedent, 97; Cabinet Mission nearly averts, 147–8; and Chakmas, 382; Congressman controls intelligence, 170, 176; Direct Action Day as turning point, 153; as dismemberment of Hindu goddess, 178; dividing Punjab, 160, 171–2; families divided, 200; few European deaths, 234; friends set apart, 210–12; Gandhi alone opposes, 172; Gandhi–Suhrawardy protest fast, 202, 212; geographical oddities, 206; gods on the move, 203; greatest migration in history, 207; haphazardly planned, 179–80; independence but no border, 199, 200–1; Indian refugee camps, 216; India's asset debt to Pakistan, 244, 245; Jinnah on Calcutta, 171; Jinnah's 'Pakistan Resolution,' 63, 131, 139–40; Lahore violence, 195–6; Menon creates plan, 173–4; Mountbatten moves date forward, 176–7, 181; Muslim League schism over 'Pakistan', 149–50; Muslim-majority provinces vote on Pakistan, 180; and 1971 PoW camps, 414; Pakistan lacking space for refugees, 208–9; 'Pakistan' most popular in Hindu provinces, 140; Pakistan refugee camps, 216; Pakistan as slippery slope, 142; partitioning police and Indian Army, 206; partitioning rivers, books and necklaces, 180–1; Patel compares to 'diseased limb' amputation, 214; Plan Balkan, 173; post-Partition Punjab violence, 195–8, 208, 211; post-Partition uncertainties, 177–8; princely states' role, 213; Radcliffe flees, 199; Radcliffe Line, 204–6, 211, 289, 325, 388; Radcliffe as unbiased but uninformed, 181; rebellious acts against British, 142–3; refugees' abandoned quilts, 209; religious consequences, 203–4; religious-majority provinces fiasco, 204; Rohingya agenda, 156; role of 1946 election, 140; role in South Asian history, 6, 204; RSS violence, 197, 213, 214–15; sexual violence, 212, 213; strikes and protests at, 175; Third as Partition's sole meaning, 426; violence ceases post-Gandhi assassination, 246

Fourth (1947, Princely India): absent constitutional link to Raj, 167; acceding to other countries, 190; British connection remembered over Indian, 427; Congress rejects independence rights, 185; cultural and employment consequences of, 280, 282–3; independence plans, 142, 146–7, 183–6; India formally abolishes monarchies, 286; infrequent alignment to ruler's religion, 184; integration or independence, 6–7; Junagadh's quandary, 218–26; Kalat conflicted, 252–3; Khasi states accede to India, 252; Khrushchev's question, 280; map of, 187, 203; Mountbatten plebiscite pledge, 240; number of states, 203, 284; Pakistan rejects Dujana, 217–18; Patel merges state administrations with India, 261; princes choose India over Pakistan, 191, 217; princes' misplaced confidence in Mountbatten, 164; princes sign Instruments of Accession, 186–92; States Department administers Partition, 186; as tragedy for residents, 261n; *see also* Hyderabad, annexation of (1948); Indo-Pakistani war (1947–48)

Fifth (1971, Pakistan–Bangladesh): Calcutta Free City' plan, 172; and Cold War powers, 285; cumulative nationality changes, 411–13, 424; death toll, 367; different terms to describe, 367; East Bengali refugees in India, 375–6; effected by Pakistani surrender, 404–5; as final Partition, 7; Gandhi–Bhutto meeting, 409–10; India recognises Bangladesh, 398; India supports Bangladeshi rebels, 377–9, 380; mass transfer of populations, 408; Mountbatten independent Bengal plan, 172; and Muslim League, 140n; New Delhi Agreement, 414–15; *see also* East Pakistan; Indo-Pakistani war (1971)

Pataudi, Nawab of, 261

Patel, Sardar Vallabhbhai: and Alwar ethnic cleansing, 213–14; arrest, 94; blockades Junagadh, 220; calls for war over East Bengal, 281; contiguous Pakistani land worry, 190; controls intelligence, 155, 170, 176; Corfield meeting, 185; criticises Sunderlal Committee, 279; dismissive of Mountbatten, 164; on dividing Punjab, 171; heart attack, 260–1; and Hyderabad post-independence, 257, 258, 267; on Hyderabad as 'ulcer', 267; on Hyderabad–Kashmir trade-off, 240; Indira Gandhi overturns

Patel, Sardar Vallabhbhai (*cont* ...)
  princely pledge, 419; integrates princely states, 186; Jinnah's paranoia, 230; Junagadh as local, 218; Junagadh plebiscite, 224–5; Mountbatten relationship, 170; Nehru and troops to Kashmir, 236; Operation Polo date, 266; readies troops on Hyderabad border, 261; reconciled with Nehru, 246; RSS protection, 214–15; 'sends' RSS to Kashmir, 242; on separating religious groups, 198; threatens Travancore, 189; use of RSS, 156; withholds debt to Pakistan, 244, 245
Pathans, 269, 276, 292
Patiala, Maharaja of, 92, 213
Patkai Hills: absence of railways, 19; battles of Imphal and Kohima, 122, 123, 124–6, 141; Burmese lose control, 340; Chakma struggle, 381–2; on defeat of Japan, 130; Indo-Burmese border, 60, 109–10; Indian 'Long March' over, 78–9, 80, 87, 91; investment in, 108–9; Japanese and INA copy Chindits, 120; Japan's U-Go offensive, 121–6; no British rule, 45; Phizo's pledge, 326; separatist movement, 286–7; Slim fights troops' malaria, 115
Patriotic Burmese Forces, 128
Paukkaung, Burma, 30
Pawsey, Charles, 125–6
Pearl Harbor attack, 68, 69, 71
Persepolis Festival (1971), 392–3
Persia, 108, 168, 392
Persian Gulf states, *see* Arabian Raj; Partitions, Second; *and individual states*
Peshawar, Pakistan, 140, 232
Petit, Ruttie, 13–15, 16, 23
Phillips, Bunny, 118, 127
Phizo, Angami Zapu: arrested as 'communist', 287; deal with Japanese, 121; declares Nagaland independence, 327; dream of uniting Nagas dies, 417–18; escape to Zurich and London, 334–5; Khonoma in 'excluded area', 48; promotes Naga independence, 45–7, 141–2, 181–2, 202, 326–7; smuggled to and detained in Dacca, 327–9, 336; tries to join Royal Artillery, 60–1
Pirzada, S. S., 183
Podgorny, Nikolai, 393
Poona, 95, 138
Poonch, India/Pakistan, 229, 241
Portal, Iris, 35, 256, 257
Portugal, 66, 69, 142, 336
Prasad, Dr Rajendra, 202, 243
Project Dastaan, 428–30
Prome, Burma, 30, 74, 80

Pu, U, 55, 65
Pudukkottai, India, 261n
Punjab: Baisakhi festival, 87; Bengali differentiation, 337, 346, 350; Campbell-Johnson on fires, 201; Congress call for religion-based division, 160, 171; domination of Pakistan military, 337; Great Partition vote, 176; hegemony over Pakistan, 399; India wages war, 342–3; length of refugee caravans (*kafilas*), 207, 213; militarised in WWII, 60; modernisation in, 16; Mountbatten on dividing, 171; Muslim anti-Sikh pogroms, 159–60; Muslim League election failure (1937), 58; as 'P' in Pakistan, 62; post-Partition uncertainty, 177; post-Partition violence, 195–8, 208, 211–12, 213, 217–18, 228–9; professions disappear, 208; RSS refugee rehabilitation, 215; vote to partition, 180
Punjab Boundary Force, 197–8, 206
Purohit, Champabai Dattambhat, 264

Qatar: Al-Thani collection, 420; anti-rebel capability, 323; pre-oil poverty of rulers, 168; in Raj, 2; separated from India, 169; tables turned on Indians, 427
Qu'aiti, Amir Ghalib Al-Qu'aiti, Sultan of: accedes as sultan, 306–7; coronation, 308, 309–10; Mukalla landing prevented, 314–15; Nizam's warning, 308; organises Grand Tribal Assembly, 311; poor-man disguise, 310; stateless, 319; Trevelyan's UN plan, 313, 315
Qu'aiti, Awadh bin Saleh, Sultan of, 265, 307
Al-Qu'aiti, Saleha, 308, 309–10
Qu'aiti State: British departure, 313; death of Sultan Awadh, 307; end of Hyderabad association, 276, 319; and Hyderabadi uniforms, 285; importance in Arabian Peninsula, 303; Nizam of Hyderabad's forces, 255, 259; NLF removes legacy, 319; Sultan's family stuck in Hyderabad, 265; vanishes from map, 308; women in, 309–10

racism: anti-Indian, in Burma, 27, 31–2, 34, 43, 50–5, 78; Attlee's stereotyping in Burma, 19; British institutional, in Raj, 61; Churchill's towards Indians, 112–13; Gandhi in South Africa, 20–1; Mountbatten, and black men, 117; Nixon's distaste for Indians, 371; in WWII evacuation, 76–7, 89, 92, 93–4; WWII racial pseudoscience, 60
Radcliffe, Cyril, 181, 184, 199, 204, 228, 388
Radio Pakistan, 283, 369
Rahman, Hamoodur, 422

Rahman, Hasina, 338
Rahman, Mujibur, *see* Mujib
Rai, Lajpat, 16
Rajasthan, 397
Rajshahi, Bangladesh, 379
Rajastan, 167
Rajkot, India, 222
Rajkot Hindu Sabha (political group), 222
Rakha, Alla, 350, 389
Ralli, Sydney, 59
Raman, B., 410
Rambrai, India, 252
Rampur, Nawab of, 4
Rance, Sir Hubert, 145–6, 193
Randhawa, Iftekhar Ahmed, 359, 368, 369, 373
Rangoon, Burma: anti-Indian pogrom, 27, 44, 53; anti-state militias, 287; Aung San–Nehru meeting, 144; and Burmese dream, 18, 426; Burmese independence, 243; earthquake (1929), 26–7; famine advice, 110; Gandhi visit, 21–3; Governor's Horse Racing Cup, 69; INA surrender, 128; Indians killed on British departure, 78; Japanese bombing and destruction, 71–4, 102, 136; Japanese flee, 128; Partition inauguration ceremony, 47; planned communist insurrection, 251; Saya San rebellion, 31; Simon Commission visit, 18; WWII evacuation, 76–7
Rangoon Gazette, 55
Rann of Cutch, 342
Ras al-Khaimah, 323
Rashtriya Swayamsevak Sangh (RSS; paramilitary group): Delhi massacres, 214; distributes aid, 208; enters Kashmir, 242; Partition voting intimidation, 180; Patel bans, 246; Patel leans on, 156; Patel readies for Hyderabad, 261; Patel–Nehru rift, 215; post-Partition violence, 197, 213, 214–15; purpose, 149; Vajpayee in, 148–9
Rathore, Maj., 384–5
Rauf, M. A., 225
Rawalpindi, Pakistan: Amin–Yahya meeting, 399; anti-Ottama nationalist protest, 42; anti-Sikh pogroms, 159–60; Gordon College protests, 348; in Indo-Pakistani war (1971), 396; Liaquat assassination, 289
Razakars (Hyderabadi paramilitary group): casualties in annexation, 274; Dalits join, 265; fall of Nanaj, 269; Indian Army bans, 275; murder Shoebullah Khan, 269; Nehru on, 270; Nizam of Hyderabad relies on, 213, 262, 263; Operation Polo justification, 266; Razvi's planned Hindu massacre, 273; revenge killings against, 277, 278; size of force, 264; Telangana attacks, 263–4

Razakars (Pakistani paramilitary group), 380–1
Razvi, Kasim, 262–3, 264, 265, 266, 273, 275, 278
Red Cross, 396, 414
Reddi, Krishna, 287
Reddy, G. K., 227
Rees, Maj.-Gen. T. W., 197
Reid, Robert, 109
Reilly, Bernard, 37, 47
Reliance Commercial Corporation, 318
Rich, Paul, 283, 427
Richardson, Helen, 79
Roberts, Goronwy, 320
Robson, Ken, 312
rock and roll, 347, 350–1, 389–90, 391
Rohingya people: caught between three countries, 84; continued Burmese assault on, 430; demand to merge with Pakistan, 156, 158; Patkai Hills armed insurgency, 287; Saw classifies as Indian foreigners, 66, 82; uninvited at Panglong, 158
Rolland, Romain, 21
Rolling Stones, the, 347, 421
Roosevelt, Franklin D., 68, 69–70, 107, 118
Round Table Conferences, London (1931): on Burma, 40–1; Gandhi alienates Muslims, 39–40; Gandhi's participation, 35–6; Jinnah walks out, 58
Roy, Devashish, 411
Roy, Raja Tridiv, 356, 357, 382, 399, 410–11, 423–4
Royal Air Force, 96, 142, 305, 309
Royal Geographical Society, 45
Royal Navy, 180, 309, 310
Rushdie, Salman, 206

Sahay, Asha, 106–7, 178
Saigon, 135
Saikia, Yasmin, 386
Salunke, Col. S. P., 413–14
Samasthans (Hindu vassals), 256, 257
al-Sameen, Ahmad, 313
Sample, Major, 60–1
Sao Sanda, 157–8
Sao Shwe Thaike, 157, 158
Sattar, Abdus, 359, 368, 369, 373
Saudi Arabia, 323
Savarkar, Vinayak, 49, 96, 114, 189, 246
Saw, U: acquitted of causing riots, 54; assassination attempt, 146; and Aung San assassination, 192, 193–4; Aung San rivalry, 145–6; census, 66; defends San, 30–1; Dorman-Smith's support, 64–5; engineers anti-Indian pogrom, 53–5; execution, 194; imprisoned in Uganda, 69; Indo-Burma

Saw, U (*cont* ...)
  Immigration Agreement, 65–6, 67;
  marshals anti-Indian hatred, 50, 51;
  overtures to Japan, 65, 69; petitions
  Churchill for independence, 68; return to
  Burma, 134, 144; Roosevelt on, 69; spurns
  Aung San–Attlee agreement, 157
Sawt Al-Arab (Voice of the Arabs), 294, 311
Saya San, 29–31, 35
Schanberg, Sydney, 353, 365–6, 393
Schendel, Willem van, 399
Schenkl, Emilie, 105
Seaton, Marie, 331, 333, 334, 341
Second World War: atomic bombs, 129, 130, 131; Axis reversals, 98; Ba Maw leads Burma against British, 51; battles of Imphal and Kohima, 122, 123, 124–6, 141; Burmese support for Japan, 75–6; casualties in Asia, 59; evacuee literature, 92; fall of Singapore, 76; Indian ambivalence over war, 93, 96; Indian and Burmese militarisation, 60; Indians flee Burma, 78–90, 81; Japan's defeat, 130–1; Japan's invasion of India postponed, 98; Jinnah's proposal for Muslim war effort, 63; Pearl Harbor, 68, 69, 71; Slim's Chindits, 115, 120; start of Japan–British Empire war, 69
Secunderabad, India, 258
Sehgal, Ikram, 368
Sen, Amartya: on Bengal famine, 110, 111, 113, 114; on flight from Bengal, 92–3; harbours Rahman Sobhan, 375; on Hindu–Muslim violence, 133; on India in WWII, 5; Mandalay childhood, 55–6
Shah, Amit, 418
Shah, Nusratullah, 257
Shakoor, Yunus Hajee, 225
Shamsie, Muneeza, 345, 374–5, 383–4, 396–7
Shamsie, Saman, 396–7
Shamsuddoha, Mr (bank manager), 407
Shan Hills, 119, 243
Shan states, 158, 192
Shankar, Ravi, 166, 282–3, 350, 389, 390
Shanks, Father George, 234–5
Shanti Bahini (Chakma guerrillas), 382, 417
Shantiniketan, India, 92–3, 110–11
Sharjah, 321, 323
Shastri, Lal Bahadur, 343
Sheth, Liladhar Gokaldas, 318
Shihr, Qu'aiti State / South Yemen, 310
Shillong, India, 207, 252, 417
Sholapur, India, 262, 278
Shu Maung, *see* Ne Win
Shu'ayb, South Arabia, 312
Shwedagon Pagoda, Burma, 53, 68
Siddiqui, Kader, 404

Sikhs, Sikhism: agree to Great Partition, 174; anti-Sikh pogroms in Rawalpindi, 159–60; Batala mob killings, 212; community in Burma, 85, 86, 87; Delhi as martyrs' site, 34; and Hinduism, 4; and Indian PoW camps, 414; Indira Gandhi assassination, 423; Khalistani movement, 423; leave Pakistan post-Partition, 204; migration post-Partition Punjab violence, 195, 196, 197–8; Muzaffarabad massacre, 233; Nankana Sahib in Pakistan, 204; prayers for Gandhi, 245; Punjabi syncretism, 160n; 'Sikhistan' / 'Khalistan' homeland call, 142
Sikkim, 147, 185, 228, 326
Sikkim, Maharaja of, 146–7
Simla, 109, 138, 173, 183, 409–10
Simon, Lord John, 9, 16, 19, 40
Simon Commission: in Burma, 18–20; discovers India's size and diversity, 16; fails to meet Gandhi, 20; ignorance of India, 5, 10; Indian boycott, 11–12, 15; Jinnah meeting, 12, 16; map of journey, 17; Nagas petition for colony, 45; report released, 27; Ottama opposes report, 40; trip to India, 9–12
Sindh: accedes to Pakistan, 180; migration to, 207; no Partition violence, 199; and Rann of Cutch, 342; as 'S' in Pakistan, 62
Singapore: Ba Maw–Mose meeting, 107–8; fall of, 76; Japanese surrender, 136, 137
Singh, Amarinder, 233
Singh, Avtar, 87, 88, 89
Singh, Balwant, 131, 134, 176, 243
Singh, Capt. Chandan, 400
Singh, Maj. Chandrakant, 377
Singh, Gian, 116
Singh, Halvidar, 217
Singh, Jaipal, 326–7
Singh, Jaswant, 376
Singh, Jatinder 'John', 347
Singh, Karan, 228, 233–4, 236
Singh, Maj.-Gen. Kartar, 130
Singh, Moni, 251
Singh, Narayan, 84–5
Singh, Lt-Gen. Sagat, 399–400, 406
Singh, Master Tara, 159, 160n
Singh, Col. Thakur Kesari, 191
Singh, Uttam, 84–90, 122, 208
Slade-Baker, John, 298–9
Slim, Gen. Sir Bill, 92, 115, 122, 123, 128
Sobhan, Rahman, 375
Sodha, Jaisukhal, 219n
Somalia, 108, 297, 314, 317
'Song of Bangladesh' (Baez), 390, 391
South Africa, 20, 334
South Arabian Federation, 305, 311–12

INDEX

South Arabian League, 298–9
South Asia: Ayesha as militarised zone, 1; and creation of Bharat, 48; eastern–western bloc blurring, 325; ebbing of democratic dream, 329; fascism and communism in, 51; 'Great Partition' as central event, 6, 204; 1950s as beginning of modernity, 283; other possible futures, 425; Pakistan no longer Muslim homeland, 415
South East Asia Command (SEAC): and local independence movements, 135–6; Mountbatten appointed head, 116, 118; pacifying surrendered Japanese, 134
South Yemen: creation of, 308, 316; as first Marxist Arab country, 317; Indians and Pakistanis exiled, 308; NLF on UAE as replica, 321; offers Bangladeshi forces help, 387; Operation Nutcracker against NLF, 305–6; peasants seize landowners' land, 317; purged of Raj connection, 318–19
Srinagar, Kashmir: Abdullah's militia formed, 237; Indians drive off lashkar, 240–1; literacy (1901), 226; Menon flies in, 236; Muslim lashkar approaches, 233, 234, 235
Sriramulu, Potti, 291
Statesman, 148, 149, 229
Stephens, Ian, 113–14, 228–9
Suez Canal, 311–12, 317
Suez Crisis, 296, 297, 298, 304, 311
Suhrawardy, Huseyn: blanks Maharaja of Cooch Behar, 190; character, 149; criticises Pakistani leadership, 289, 290, 337; Direct Action Day, 149–50; Mountbatten's independent Bengal plan, 172; Partition-bloodshed fast, 202
Sukarno, 135
Sunday Times, 296, 298, 306, 384–5
Sunder, Shyam, 265
Sunderlal Committee, 277–9, 422
Suzuki, Keiji, 65, 75–6, 103
Swadhin Bangla Biplobi Parishad, 338
Swat, Pakistan, 285n, 410
Swu, Isak Chishi, 333
Sylhet, Bangladesh, 176, 180, 207, 336, 359, 367–9

Tagore, Rabindranath, 18, 331, 373
Taliban, 423
Tamil Nadu, India, 292
Tamils: in Burma, 53–4; in Ceylon, 166–7; murdered for spurning INA, 106; separatism, 62; *see also* Chettiars
Tamluk, India, 96
Tamu, Burma, 88, 89
Tashkent Agreement (1966), 343
Taunsa, India, 212

Taunsvi, Fikr, 195–6, 203, 204, 211, 212, 215–16
Taunsvi, Kailash, 212
Taunsvi, Rali, 212
Tavoy, Burma, 75
Tawngpeng, Burma, 84
Telangana, India, 263–4, 270
Teliapara tea estate, Bangladesh, 373–4
Telugu (language), 256
Teresa, Mother, 387
Teresalina, Mother, 235
Thailand, 42, 68, 106, 120
Thakins (Burmese nationalist group), 67, 75, 83
Than Tun, 251
Thant, U, 193, 387
Thant Myint-U, 8, 426
Tharrawaddy plains, 28
Thaton, Burma, 134
al-Thawriyy (newspaper), 315–16
Thein Pe, 96, 100
Thimayya, Maj.-Gen. K. S., 242
Thoa Khalsa, India, 159–60
Thuriya (U Saw's newspaper), 44, 50, 51, 53
Tiger Legion militia, 105, 106
Time magazine, 277, 385, 398
Tin Tut, 157
Tipu Sultan, 105
Travancore, India, 189, 251
Trevelyan, Humphrey, 311, 312–13, 314, 315–16
Tripura, India, 108, 188, 207, 242, 251, 375, 418
Tully, Mark, 343
Turnbull, Richard, 305
Turtuk, Ladakh, 410
Tyabji, Nadir, 108–9

Ula, Prof. (Dacca academic), 364
Umm Al-Quwain, 323
United Arab Emirates: anti-rebel capability, 323; British negligence fuels rise, 303; formed from fear of revolution, 320–1; Hyderabadi chefs, 421; members of, 323; nationalist downplaying of Raj, 7; pre-oil poverty of rulers, 168; in Raj, 2; react to Sharjah attempted assassination, 321
United Nations: Bangladesh aid lobbying, 387; debates Hyderabad annexation, 274; debates Kashmir conflict, 242, 244; delegation in Kashmir, 250; and Kashmir plebiscite, 240, 242; Kashmir oversight removed, 410; Nongstoin's appeal to, 252; Pakistan denies Bangladesh recognition, 410–11; proposed South Arabia plebiscite, 313, 315
United Provinces, India, 154, 214

United States: Battle of Midway, 98; Bengali diplomatic defections, 391; Blood's Operation Searchlight reports, 370–2; civil rights movement, 346–7; Cold War, 188; Gulf oil rivals, 294; and Hyderabadi independence, 184; India and Pakistan anti-communism funding, 288n; Kissinger mission to China, 392; Pearl Harbor, 68; and Suez crisis, 296, 297; uninterested in Mizo cause, 337; USS *Enterprise* nears Bay of Bengal, 400–2

Urdu (language): anti-Urdu protests in East Bengal, 260, 290–1; Bihari genocide in East Pakistan, 386, 406; as Hyderabad state language, 256; Jinnah's gravestone, 293; Omani Army titles in, 300; speakers targeted in East Pakistan, 337, 369, 372; status of, in Bengal, 289–90; as symbol of Pakistani colonialism, 291

USSR: Bose in, 105; condemns Pakistan in Bangladesh war, 387; Czech coup, 250; India signs friendship treaty, 392; Indira Gandhi as friend, 371, 392; inspires Sheikh Abdullah, 227; mediates Kashmir conflict, 343; Mohani's Pakistan modelling, 179; Nehru idolises, 61; Podgorny–Yahya meeting, 393; and Suez crisis, 296; in WWII, 8, 105

Vajpayee, Atal Bihari, 148–9
'Vande Mataram' (national song of India), 48
Varanasi (Kashi), India, 220, 246
Vaz, Isabelle, 71, 73, 74, 76
Viet Minh, 135
Vietnam, 142; Democratic Republic of, 135
Vietnam War, 135, 347, 350, 379
Vivian, Capt. David, 194
Vogue magazine, 290
Völkischer Beobachter (Nazi newspaper), 55
Vrindavan, India, 203

Wa states, 192
Wadi Hadhramaut, 306, 315
Wadia, Dina, 24, 199, 200
Wadia, Nusli, 422

Wagah border, 1, 415
Walker, Jonathan, 315
Wana, Pir of, 232
Waugh, Evelyn, 10
Wavell, Field Marshal Archibald: addresses Bengal famine, 113; Churchill deprecates arming Indians, 115; failed post-Direct Action Day reconciliation, 153; on Gandhi and Jinnah, 133; knights Slim, 123; INA war-crimes blunder, 139; Mountbatten replaces as Viceroy, 163, 164; Nehru intercession request, 143

West Bengal, India: anti-Muslim pogroms, 340; and Calcutta's role, 172; and cause of Khulna famine, 289; communist-inspired 'Naxalite' revolution, 348, 377, 387; Nehru's prognosis, 281; and pan-Bengali unity, 375; suspicion of East Bengali refugees, 376

Who, the, 390
Wilson, Harold, 320
Wilson, Sir Leslie Orme, 11
Wolpert, Stanley, 272
Woodstock festival (1969), 350–1, 379
World Health Organization, 416

Yagbo, Mohammad Kacho, 410
Yallay, Kevi, 417
Yamuna river, 247
Yeats-Brown, Francis: *The Lives of a Bengal Lancer*, 61
Yamagami, Lt, 124
Yemen: civil war, 303, 306, 312; 'Greater Yemen', 296; Indian nationalism in, 7; in Raj, 2, 3; *see also* Aden; South Yemen
Young, Gavin, 397, 404, 405–6
Young, Maj. Henry, 194
Yugoslavia, 347

Zakaria, Anam, 140n, 291, 365
Zhou Enlai, 401
Zia, Khaleda, 426
Zia-ul-Haq, 422–3
Zia-ur-Rahman, Maj., 368, 377, 382, 417
Zoji-La Pass, 269
Zoroastrians, Zoroastrianism, 2, 245